MASTER THE GRE®

23rd Edition

PETERSON'S®

Sustainability—Its Importance to Peterson's

What does sustainability mean to Peterson's? As a leading publisher, we are aware that our business has a direct impact on vital resources—most importantly the raw material used to make our books. Peterson's is proud that its products are printed at SFI Chain-of-Custody certified facilities and that all of its books are printed on SFI certified paper with 10 percent post-consumer waste using vegetable-based ink.

Supporting the Sustainable Forestry Initiative® (SFI®) means that we only use vendors—from paper suppliers to printers—who have undergone rigorous certification audits by independent parties to demonstrate that they meet the standards.

Peterson's continuously strives to find new ways to incorporate responsible sourcing throughout all aspects of its business.

ANOTHER RECOMMENDED TITLE

Peterson's GRE®/GMAT® Math Review

Contents

PART III: ANALYTICAL WRITING

PART IV: VERBAL REASONING

APPENDIXES

Before You Begin

Master the GRE® 23rd Edition is your guidebook for navigating the GRE® revised General Test. In 2011, the test changed dramatically from the previous version. The current version of the GRE® is designed to better predict test-takers' overall performance in graduate school. The emphasis is on the test-takers' ability to think. You'll see that in the design of questions.

You'll find reading comprehension questions that ask you to critique the validity of an author's argument or ask you to identify information that supports an author's argument. Other questions in the Verbal Reasoning section ask you to select the best word choice based on analyzing the context of a sentence or passage. In the Analytical Writing section, you'll be asked to evaluate someone else's argument and to develop an argument of your own. To de-emphasize computation and emphasize the thought processes used to arrive at answers in the Quantitative Reasoning section, you will find an on-screen calculator for the computer-based version. If you are taking the paper-and-pencil version, you will be given a calculator.

You needn't begin to hyperventilate at this information. *Master the GRE® 23rd Edition* will

- walk you through the parts of the test.
- give you strategies to use for each type of question.
- explain how to avoid some common writing problems.
- review basic arithmetic, algebra, geometry, and data analysis.
- help you develop your vocabulary for word-choice questions.
- provide simulated practice with four practice tests.

HOW THIS BOOK IS ORGANIZED

Master the GRE® 23rd Edition is divided into six parts to facilitate your study:

- **Part I** explains basic information about the GRE® revised General Test and provides an overview with examples of the different question types you'll find on the test.
- **Part II** offers a diagnostic test to help you identify your areas of strength and those areas where you will need to spend more time in your review sessions.
- **Part III** explores the Analytical Writing section of the test and offers strategies for developing well-supported and coherent responses to the types of tasks that you will be required to answer.
- **Part IV** goes into detail about the different question formats that you will find in the Verbal Reasoning section and offers strategies for answering each type.
- **Part V** describes the different question formats in the Quantitative Reasoning section of the test and offers strategies to help you figure out answers to the math questions.

- **Part VI** has three more tests that provide you with simulated practice in taking the GRE® exam under timed conditions.

- The **Appendixes** offer two additional chapters to help you improve your writing. "Appendix A: Common Errors in Grammar and Mechanics," can help you avoid such mistakes as sentence faults, misplaced modifiers, subject-verb agreement, and pronoun problems. If misspelled words are a problem for you, check out "Appendix B: Often Confused and Confusing Words." Here you'll find a list of commonly misspelled words—words that sound somewhat similar but have completely different meanings and when used incorrectly could lower your score.

Each chapter in Parts IV and V contains practice sections to help you review what you have just learned.

SPECIAL STUDY FEATURES

Master the GRE® 23rd Edition has several features that will help you get the most from your study time.

Overview

Each chapter begins with a listing of the major topics in that chapter followed by an introduction that explains what you will be reviewing.

Summing It Up

Each chapter ends with a point-by-point summary of the main points of the chapter. It can be a handy last-minute guide to review before the test.

Bonus Information

You will find three types of notes in the margin of the *Master the GRE® 23rd Edition* to alert you to important information.

Note

Margin notes marked "Note" highlight information about the test structure itself.

Tip

A note marked "Tip" points out valuable advice for taking the GRE® revised General Test.

Alert

An "Alert" identifies pitfalls in the testing format or question types that can cause mistakes in selecting answers.

USING THIS BOOK TO PREPARE FOR THE COMPUTER-BASED GRE® REVISED GENERAL TEST

Important things to remember as you work through this book: When taking the computer-based version of the GRE® revised General Test, you'll be entering answers by typing on a keyboard or using a mouse. The Analytical Writing section requires that you compose short essays by typing in words, sentences, and paragraphs. The numeric entry questions from the Quantitative Reasoning section require that you type numbers into boxes. Other sections require that you pick choices by clicking on them with your mouse. Since you can't answer in this fashion in a book, you'll have to fill in your answers by hand when taking the tests and completing the exercises. Also, bear in mind that some questions may appear in a slightly different fashion due to the limitations of print. For instance, answer options will appear as letters with parentheses around them [(A), (B), (C), etc.] in this guide. On the actual exam, the answer options may appear as ovals or squares. But rest assured that all of the question content is similar to that found on the GRE® revised General Test.

ACCESS THREE GRE® TESTS ONLINE

Peterson's is providing you with access to three additional GRE® practice tests. The testing content on these three practice tests was created by the test-prep experts at Peterson's. The Peterson's online testing experience resembles the testing experience you will find on the actual GRE® exam. You can access these three practice tests at http://www.petersonspublishing.com/gre. You will be asked to enter your e-mail address, and Peterson's will e-mail you an activation code and the link needed to access the GRE® online practice tests.

YOU ARE WELL ON YOUR WAY TO SUCCESS

You have made the decision to apply to graduate school and have taken a very important step in that process. *Master the GRE® 23rd Edition* will help you score high on the exam and prepare you for everything you'll need to know on the day of your exam. Good luck!

GIVE US YOUR FEEDBACK

Peterson's publishes a full line of books— test prep, career preparation, education exploration, and financial aid. Peterson's publications can be found at high school guidance offices, college libraries and career centers, your local bookstore and library, and at www.petersonsbooks.com. Peterson's books are also available as ebooks.

We welcome any comments or suggestions you may have about this publication. Your feedback will help us make educational dreams possible for you—and others like you.

STRATEGIES FOR ANSWERING DIFFERENT QUESTION TYPES ON THE GRE® REVISED GENERAL TEST

The GRE® revised General Test has three areas of assessment: Analytical Writing, Verbal Comprehension, and Quantitative Reasoning. This section lists in one convenient place the various test-taking strategies that are discussed in this book and that will help you master the GRE®. As you read through the list, put a star next to items that you already know. Draw lines to connect those that are the same between test areas. Pay particular attention to them. The strategies for the two writing tasks are just good writing strategies; there is no mystery about them.

As you work your way through the chapters, practice exercises, and practice tests, be sure to practice the following strategies, so that on test day, the right strategy for the question type will come naturally to you.

Analytical Writing

The writing section is divided into two tasks: an issue that you must agree or disagree with and an argument that you must analyze.

The Issue Task

- State a thesis, and state it early.
- Use a standard pattern of organization.
- Order paragraphs effectively.
- Use a standard pattern of organization.
- Develop each paragraph fully.
- Take with tone and person.
- As time permits, add extras
  - Interest-grabbing opening
  - Apt word choice
  - Varied sentence structure
- Create your writing plan:
  - Prewriting
  - Drafting
  - Consider style
  - Proofreading

The Argument Task

- Look for:
  - Unreliable opinion polls, surveys, questionnaires
  - Faulty cause-and-effect relationships

- o False generalizations
- o False analogies
- o Either-or thinking
- o Assumptions
- Create your writing plan:
  - o Prewriting
  - o Drafting
  - o Proofreading

Verbal Reasoning

The Verbal Reasoning section is made up of three areas: Reading Comprehension, Text Completion, and Sentence Equivalence.

Strategies for Reading Comprehension Questions

Before you begin answering questions, use active reading to:

- Identify the topic, main idea, thesis, or proposition of the passage.
- Clarify your understanding of the content.
- Summarize the passage.

Then, you can apply the following general strategies for:

Multiple-Choice Questions

- Try answering the questions before you read the answer choices.
- Read all the answers before you choose.
- Compare answer choices to each other and the question.
- Avoid selecting an answer you don't fully understand.
- Choose the *BEST* answer.
- Pay attention to structure and structural clues.
- Don't select an answer just because it's true.
- Substitute answer choices in word meaning questions.
- Choose the answer that doesn't fit the EXCEPT questions.
- Choose an answer that answers the question on its own.

Select-in-Passage Questions

- Match the sentence to the information.

Strategies for Text Completion Questions

- Try answering the questions before you read the answer choices.
- Focus on only one blank at a time.
- If there is more than one blank, complete the blanks in the order that makes sense to you.
- Check your answer(s) in place.
- Use structural clues:
  o Restatement
  o Cause and effect
  o Comparison or similarity
  o Main idea and details
  o Tone and style
  o Grammar and usage
- Avoid selecting the word or phrase you don't fully understand if it's unfamiliar.

Strategies for Sentence Equivalence Questions

- Read the stem first.
- Come up with your own answer.
- Check your answers in place.
- Use signal words and structural clues.
- Avoid leaping at the first pair of synonyms.
- Examine connotations.
- Consider grammar and usage.

Quantitative Reasoning

Quantitative Reasoning has three different types of questions: Multiple-Choice (includes Data Interpretation Sets), Numeric Entry, and Quantitative Comparison.

Multiple-Choice Questions

- Pick and plug numbers.
- Work backwards from answer choices.
- Turn verbose or abstract language into concise and concrete wording.
- Calculate the least and greatest possible values.
- Make sure you're answering the correct question.
- Think through data sufficiency questions.

Special Strategies for Data Interpretation Sets

- Quickly scan the data.
- Make sure you're answering the correct question.
- Estimate.

Numeric Entry Questions

- Turn verbose or abstract language into concise and concrete wording.
- Make sure you're answering the correct question.
- Round correctly.

Quantitative Comparison Questions

- Pick and plug numbers.
- Consider when to use pick and plug numbers and when not.
- Simplify the quantities.
- Eliminating terms when simplifying quantities.
- Avoid unnecessary calculations.
- Estimate.
- Redraw the figure.
- Recognize when an answer cannot be (D).

PART I

ABOUT THE GRE® REVISED GENERAL TEST

The Basics of the GRE® revised General Test

chapter 1

OVERVIEW

- Test organization
- Test time limits
- Test tools
- Scoring the test
- Test day
- General test-taking strategies to remember
- International test-takers: paper-and-pencil version
- Summing it up

Can a standardized test be "test-taker friendly?" The Educational Testing Service (ETS), the makers of the GRE® revised General Test, thinks so. As proof, ETS points to the maneuverability and functionality of the computer-based version of the GRE® that was introduced in 2011. Test-takers can edit and change their work and even skip questions within a section to return to before timing-out of that section, which is more like a paper-and-pencil test than a computer-adaptive test. However, the Quantitative Reasoning and Verbal Reasoning sections are also computer-adaptive to a degree. The questions for the second Quantitative Reasoning and Verbal Reasoning sections are based on how well you perform on the first sections of questions. Two other test-friendly functions are the on-screen calculator for doing computation and a word processing program for completing the two Analytical Writing tasks.

According to ETS, the question types introduced in 2011 better mirror the types of reasoning skills that test-takers are called on to use in graduate and business school. The topics in the Analytical Writing section, the problems in the Quantitative Reasoning sections, and the passages used as the basis for questions in the Verbal Reasoning sections simulate the real-world issues and situations that students encounter in their course work for advanced degrees. The scores that result from the revised GRE® are considered by ETS to be "more reliable" than the previous test.

TEST ORGANIZATION

The GRE® revised General Test is divided into three areas of assessment: Analytical Writing, Verbal Reasoning, and Quantitative Reasoning. The first section will always be Analytical Writing. The other sections may appear in any order.

Analytical Writing

Analytical Writing assesses your ability to think critically and transfer your ideas into well-developed, well-reasoned, and well-supported writing. There are two tasks for this section of the test: an Argument Task and an Issue Task. The first requires that you analyze someone else's argument and the second that you build your own argument either in support of or in disagreement with an opinion, policy, recommendation, or claim. Thus, the GRE® assesses your ability to develop and support your own ideas and your ability to analyze another's argument and his or her supporting evidence. In addition, you will also be expected to sustain well-focused and coherent writing and control the elements of Standard Written English.

In addition, the tasks are specific but do not require prior knowledge of the subject. Completing them successfully relies only on your ability to think critically and write analytically.

Verbal Reasoning

NOTE

According to ETS, several thousand business and graduate schools and divisions and departments within these schools now accept the revised GRE®. A number of fellowship programs also accept GRE® scores as part of a candidate's application.

The Verbal Reasoning sections of the GRE® revised General Test assess your ability to understand, analyze, and apply information found in the types of reading you'll be doing in graduate school. According to ETS, the questions "better measure your ability to understand what you read and how you apply your reasoning skills." Among the questions you'll find are ones that ask you to reason from incomplete data; analyze and draw conclusions; identify authors' assumptions and perspectives; distinguish major and minor points; understand the structure of a text; understand the meaning of words, sentences, and passages; and understand multiple levels of meaning.

Three types of questions appear in the Verbal Reasoning section:

1. Reading comprehension
2. Text completion
3. Sentence equivalence

The reading comprehension questions are further divided into multiple-choice questions, text completion questions, and sentence equivalence questions. The multiple-choice questions may require you to select just one answer choice or to pick one or more correct choices. There are also select-in-passage questions that require you to highlight a section of the passage.

Quantitative Reasoning

According to the GRE®, Quantitative Reasoning sections measure your ability to understand, interpret, and analyze quantitative information; use mathematical models to solve problems; and apply basic mathematical knowledge and skills. The Quantitative Reasoning section requires basic knowledge in arithmetic, algebra, geometry, and data analysis. On the GRE® revised General Test, the subject matter of the questions will emphasize real-world scenarios and data interpretation.

The purpose of the on-screen calculator is to de-emphasize computation and emphasize the thought processes used to determine what the question is asking and how to go about finding the answer. While you'll find that the traditional multiple-choice question is the format used for the majority of questions, some multiple-choice questions will ask you to select one or more answers and the numeric entry questions provide no answer options from which to choose.

The Quantitative Reasoning section consists of four types of questions:

1 Multiple-choice questions—select one answer choice

2 Multiple-choice questions—select one or more answer choices

3 Quantitative comparison questions

4 Numeric entry questions

With the exception of quantitative comparison questions, the questions in the Quantitative Reasoning sections may also appear as part of a data interpretation set: a group of questions that refer to the same tables, graphs, or other data presentation.

Number of Questions

The computer version of the GRE® revised General Test is divided into five scored sections and one additional section that may be an unidentified unscored section or an identified research section. The unidentified unscored section may be either a Verbal Reasoning or a Quantitative Reasoning section and may come in any order after the Analytical Writing section, which always comes first. The research section is always the last section and may be either Verbal Reasoning or Quantitative Reasoning. You won't have both unscored sections in any given test.

The breakdown of scored sections by question is:

Section	Number of Sections	Number of Questions
Analytical Writing	One	Two writing tasks
Verbal Reasoning	Two	Approximately 20 questions
Quantitative Reasoning	Two	Approximately 20 questions

Within the Verbal Reasoning and Quantitative Reasoning sections, you will find the different types of question formats mixed together. For example, you may find a sequence of three reading comprehension passages (with several different question formats), a sentence equivalence question, two text completion questions, two reading comprehension passages, and so on. The same is true of Quantitative Reasoning sections, which will mix the two types of multiple-choice questions, numeric entry, and quantitative comparison questions.

TEST TIME LIMITS

The GRE® revised General Test will take approximately 3 hours and 45 minutes. You will also have time for several short breaks, which are not included in the actual testing time. There will be a 10-minute break after you finish the third section. Between the other test sections, you'll be allotted breaks of 1 minute each.

The breakdown of time allotments for each section is as follows:

Section	Number of Sections	Number of Questions	Time Per Section
Analytical Writing	One	Two writing tasks	30 minutes for each writing task
Verbal Reasoning	Two	Approximately 20 questions	30 minutes per section
Quantitative Reasoning	Two	Approximately 20 questions	35 minutes per section

The unscored sections will have the same number of questions and the same time allotments as the scored sections.

TEST TOOLS

Test-takers at computer testing sites will find two on-screen tools as well as increased maneuverability and functionality. For the Quantitative Reasoning sections, you'll find an on-screen calculator with the four basic functions—addition, subtraction, multiplication, division—and a square root. You'll also be able to enter some of the answers directly from the calculator into the answer boxes using a transfer function. According to ETS, a calculator was added to place more emphasis on test-takers' reasoning skills than on their computational skills.

For the Analytical Writing tasks, you'll be working in an ETS-designed word processing program that will allow you to write, insert and delete text, cut and paste, and undo actions. However, the program doesn't have a spell checker or a grammar checker.

The increased functionality of the revised GRE® enables you to move back and forth within a section so you can

- preview and review a section.
- mark questions within a section to return to later.
- change and edit answers within a section.

The testing experience mirrors much of the paper-and-pencil testing process that you've been familiar with since taking your first standardized test. As a result, many of the same strategies such as "skip and return" that you've honed through years of testing can be used with the computerized GRE®.

SCORING THE TEST

For the Verbal Reasoning and Quantitative Reasoning sections of the GRE® revised General Test, the scoring has changed. Instead of the familiar 200 to 800 range with a 10-point increment, the scales for both sections changed to a 130 to 170 range. Perhaps the biggest change is the use of 1-point increments in reporting scores. No longer will scores be reported in jumps of 10 points, but in small increments of 1 point. (So, the score scale has moved from a 61-point scale to a 41-point scale.)

ETS states that the reason for the change in increments is "to produce scores that don't exaggerate small performance differences between examinees." A 2-point difference looks a great deal smaller than a 20-point difference.

Analytical Writing hasn't substantially changed, so it continues to be reported in half-point increments using a 0-to-6 range. Each writing task is evaluated separately, and an average is taken and used as the reported score based on the 0–6 scale.

TEST DAY

There are several rules and restrictions to be aware of on test day. The following bulleted lists are from the ETS website (http://www.ets.org/gre/revised_general/test_day/). You should check the website for more updates as test day approaches.

Test Center Procedures and Regulations for Both Computer-Based and Paper-Based Tests

- Dress so that you can adapt to any room temperature.

- Visitors are not permitted in the testing room while testing is in progress.

- ID verification at the test center may include thumbprinting, photographing, videotaping, or some other form of electronic ID confirmation. If you refuse to participate, you will not be permitted to test and you will forfeit your registration and test fees. This is in addition to the requirement that you must present acceptable and valid identification.

- Food, drinks, and tobacco are not allowed in the testing room.

- If you have health-related needs that require you to bring equipment, beverages, or snacks into the testing room or to take extra or extended breaks, you need to follow the accommodations request procedures described in the *Bulletin Supplement for Test Takers with Disabilities or Health-related Needs* available at http://www.ets.org/s/disabilities/pdf/bulletin_supplement_test_takers_with_disabilities_health_needs.pdf.

- Do not bring cell phones, smartphones (e.g., BlackBerry® devices, iPhones), PDAs, and other electronic or photographic devices into the test center.

- Personal items other than identification documents are not allowed in the testing room. Neither ETS nor the test centers assume any responsibility whatsoever for personal items or devices that you choose to bring into the test center.

- The test administrator will assign you a seat.

- On occasion, weather conditions or other circumstances beyond the test administrator or ETS's control may require a delayed start or the rescheduling of your test appointment. In the event that a technical problem at the test center makes it necessary to cancel your test session, or if it is later determined that your scores could not be reported, you will be offered the opportunity to schedule another test appointment free of charge or receive a full refund of the original test fee.

- You will be asked to designate your score recipients at the test center on test day. If an institution is not listed, ask the test center administrator for the appropriate form to indicate unlisted institutions. Complete the form and turn it in before you leave the test center. The form will not be accepted after you leave the test center.

- If you do not select score recipients on the test day, or you would like to send your scores to more than four score recipients, you will need to submit an Additional Score Report request for a fee of $25 per score recipient.

For Computer-Based Tests Only

The following procedures and regulations apply during the entire test session, which begins at sign-in, ends at sign-out, and includes breaks.

- If you requested and received an authorization voucher from ETS, you must take it with you to the test center.

- You will be required to write (not print) and sign a confidentiality statement at the test center. If you do not complete and sign the statement, you cannot test and your test fees will not be refunded.

- You may be required to sign the test center log before and after the test session and any time you leave or enter the testing room.

- You may be asked to remove your watch and to store it during the test administration.

- The test administrator will provide you with scratch paper that may be replenished after you have used all pages of the scratch paper initially given to you. You may not take your own scratch paper to the test, nor may you remove scratch paper from the testing room at any time.

- If at any time during the test you have a problem with your computer, or for any reason need the administrator, raise your hand.

- Testing premises are subject to videotaping.

- The GRE® revised General Test includes an optional 10-minute break after the third section and 1-minute breaks between the remaining sections of the test. These break times cannot be exceeded. You are required to remain in the test center building or in the immediate area.

- If you need to leave your seat at any time other than the break, raise your hand; timing of the section will not stop.

- You will have access to an on-screen calculator during the Quantitative Reasoning sections.

- Personal calculators are not permitted in the testing room.

- Because of the essay scoring process, you will not be able to view your Analytical Writing scores at the time you test.

- Test centers cannot provide printed copies of unofficial score reports.

For Paper-Based Tests Only

The following procedures and regulations apply during the entire test session, which begins when you are admitted to the test center, ends when you leave the test center, and includes breaks.

- Test administrators will not honor requests for schedule changes.

- Take your admission ticket and identification document(s) to the test center.

- Take three or four sharpened soft-lead (No. 2 or HB) pencils and a good eraser. Pencils and erasers will not be supplied at the center. Mechanical pencils and pens are not permitted.

- No test-taker will be admitted after test materials have been distributed.

- With the exception of your admission ticket, paper of any kind is not permitted in the testing room.

- You must have the test administrator's permission to leave the room during the test. Any time lost cannot be made up. You are required to remain in the test center building or in the immediate area.

- You may wish to pace yourself with your own watch, but the test administrator is the official timekeeper. *Watch alarms are not permitted to track time.*

- You may work only on the test section designated by the test center supervisor and only for the time allowed. You will not be permitted to continue the test or any part of it beyond the established time limit.

- You will write your essay responses and enter your answers to test questions in the test book, rather than on a separate answer sheet.

- You will be provided with an ETS calculator to use during the Quantitative Reasoning sections.

- You may not use your own personal calculator.

- At the end of the test you will be required to return your test book to the test administrator. This material is the property of ETS.

- The GRE® revised General Test includes a 10-minute break after the second Analytical Writing section. This break time cannot be exceeded.

- At the end of the test, you will be given the option to cancel your scores.

GENERAL TEST-TAKING STRATEGIES TO REMEMBER

Not all strategies will work for all questions. But there are some strategies that will work for most, if not all, questions:

- Anticipate and use the clock.
- Skip and return to questions.
- Eliminate answer choices that you know are incorrect.
- Use educated guessing.

The more you practice these and the strategies described for particular kinds of question formats described in this book, the easier the strategies will be to remember, to figure out which are appropriate to use with which questions, and to apply on test day.

Anticipate and Use the Clock

When you take the GRE® revised General Test, a clock icon will appear on your screen to show elapsing time. That is, at all moments, you will know exactly how much time you have remaining. To take full advantage of this on-screen device, time yourself using the practice tests in this book and figure out how much time you have per question.

Suppose you typically do the easier text completion and sentence equivalence items at the rate of 30 seconds per item, whereas the harder ones take you about a minute. Given that approximately

ALERT!

Test-takers can sign up for additional information from ETS about GRE® revised General Test notifications, registration reminders, and webinars at http://www.takethegre.com/gre-news-and-reminders.

half the questions on the Verbal Reasoning sections consist of those two types, and the total number of questions on a Verbal Reasoning section is 20 questions, you might budget about 10 minutes for those two types of questions, adding in a minute or so for review, extra-hard questions, or other issues. For the 30-minute test, that leaves approximately 20 minutes for the reading comprehension questions, or about 2 minutes a question.

If you find at the halfway point for time that you're working significantly faster than is necessary, you may want to slow down and take more time with each question. If, on the other hand, you find at the halfway point you're working slower than you need to be, you may want to speed up and take less time with each question. Keep in mind, however, that you cannot speed-read passages and questions, so speed up only a bit.

Skip and Return to Questions

If at first you don't see how to answer a certain question in a reasonable amount of time, don't hesitate to skip it. If you do skip a question, make sure you click the "Mark" button so that you can find that question quickly on the "Review" screen at a later point. After you've answered all the other questions—and before your time for the section has run out—go back to any question you've left unanswered and try to solve it. Remember: There's no wrong-answer penalty, so don't leave any questions unanswered!

Eliminate Answer Choices You Know Are Incorrect

Don't overlook this time-honored strategy! It will not only help you arrive at the answer, but it can also help calm test jitters as you come closer and closer to the correct answer.

Educated Guessing

Educated guessing builds on the strategy of eliminating answer choices that you know are incorrect, but you have to know something about the question for educated guessing to be effective. The process works this way:

- Eliminate answer choices you know are incorrect.
- Discard any choices in which part of the answer is incorrect.
- Reread the remaining answer choices against each other and against the question again.
- Choose the answer that seems correct to you. More often than not, you'll be right.

INTERNATIONAL TEST-TAKERS: PAPER-AND-PENCIL VERSION

Test-takers outside the United States without access to a computer testing site will have a slightly different paper-and-pencil GRE® test from the paper-and-pencil test given to test-takers in the United States. The test will not have an unidentified unscored or identified unscored research section. The test will be composed of the following sections, number of questions, and time per section:

Section	Number of Sections	Number of Questions	Time Per Section
Analytical Writing	One	Two writing tasks	30 minutes for each writing task
Verbal Reasoning	Two	25 questions	35 minutes per section
Quantitative Reasoning	Two	25 questions	40 minutes per section

The test will take about 3 hours and 30 minutes.

You'll be given a calculator to use for the Quantitative Reasoning sections of the GRE®.

The test will be given up to three times a year, in October, November, and February, and scores will be reported six weeks after the test date.

ALERT!

The paper-and-pencil version has a multiple-choice adaptation of the select-in-passage question. All other question formats are the same.

SUMMING IT UP

- The GRE® revised General Test launched in 2011 is considered by ETS to be a better measure of a test-taker's success in graduate or business school than the previous test.

- The GRE® revised General Test is not computer-adaptive. It allows test-takers to move back and forth within sections to return to skipped questions and to change and edit answers. An on-screen calculator and word processing program are included.

- The GRE® has three sections: Analytical Writing, Quantitative Reasoning, and Verbal Reasoning. Analytical Writing is always first.

- Quantitative Reasoning and Verbal Reasoning have two scored sections each, which may come in any order. The computer version of the test may have an unidentified, unscored Quantitative Reasoning or Verbal Reasoning section or an identified, unscored research section of either type.

- The Analytical Writing section has two tasks: an Argument Task and an Issue Task. You'll be given one prompt for each task and will not have a choice from which to select.

- Verbal Reasoning sections have a mix of reading comprehension, text completion, and sentence equivalence questions. Each has its own question format. Questions based on reading passages may be multiple-choice—select one answer; multiple-choice—select one or more answers; or select-in-passage questions. Text completion questions may require one, two, or three responses selected from lists of multiple-choice answers. Sentence equivalence questions require two answers selected from a single list of multiple-choice options.

- Quantitative Reasoning sections have multiple-choice, quantitative comparisons, and numeric entry question formats. The last does not offer a list of potential answers from which to choose.

- The test takes 3 hours and 45 minutes and has the following time limits and questions:

Section	Number of Sections	Number of Questions	Time Per Section
Analytical Writing	One	Two writing tasks	30 minutes for each writing task
Verbal Reasoning	Two	Approximately 20 questions	30 minutes per section
Quantitative Reasoning	Two	Approximately 20 questions	35 minutes per section

- The scores for the Quantitative and Verbal Reasoning sections are reported on a score scale of 130 to 170 with 1-point increments. The Analytical Writing score is reported on a scale of 0 to 6 with half-point increments.

- Four general test-taking strategies will help in most situations: (1) anticipate and use the clock, (2) skip and return to questions, (3) eliminate answer choices that you know are incorrect, and (4) use educated guessing.

- In some places outside the United States, test-takers will take a paper-and-pencil version of the General Test incorporating the new philosophy of the test items and the new question formats. The number of questions and time allotments per section are slightly different.

A Quick Look at GRE® Question Formats

chapter 2

OVERVIEW

- Analytical Writing
- Answer Option Differences
- Verbal Reasoning
- Quantitative Reasoning
- Summing it up

The GRE® revised General Test assesses three areas: (1) Analytical Writing, (2) Verbal Reasoning, and (3) Quantitative Reasoning. You'll have to write two types of essays for the Analytical Writing section: an essay to support an argument and an essay discussing an issue. While you'll find that the majority of test items are in the multiple-choice format you're familiar with from other standardized tests, the GRE® presents several additional test-item format in both the Verbal Reasoning and the Quantitative Reasoning sections. This chapter introduces each test-item format with examples and also discusses the differences between the two types of writing tasks and their requirements.

ANALYTICAL WRITING

The Analytical Writing section of the GRE® tests both your ability to think critically and your ability to write analytically. The section has two writing tasks: one is called the argument task and the other is the issue task. You'll be given a prompt and a set of directions for each task; you won't have a choice of tasks from which to select.

The argument task prompt will ask you to evaluate an argument and the evidence to support it, not to give your opinion about it. The issue task essay is your opportunity to opine about an issue. In this way, the GRE® assesses both your ability to state a position and to support it as well as your ability to assess another person's position and the evidence supporting it. As you will see below, both types of essay prompts are accompanied by specific instructions about how to respond to the prompt.

Time Limits

If you're taking the computer version, you'll have 30 minutes to read each prompt, gather your ideas, and write your response. In allotting your 30 minutes, take about 5 minutes to read the prompt, decide on your point of view, and marshal your ideas; take about 20 minutes to write your essay; and leave about 5 minutes to reread and edit your essay. Points are not deducted for spelling and grammar mistakes, but as ETS points out: "severe and persistent errors will detract from the overall effectiveness of your writing and lower your score accordingly."

Software

The computer you'll be taking your test on will be equipped with a word processing program developed by ETS. According to ETS, you'll be able to insert and delete text, cut and paste, and undo actions. However, the program doesn't include either a spell checker or a grammar checker, so using a few minutes at the end of the writing period to edit for grammar, usage, and spelling errors can be helpful in ensuring that your essay is clearly expressed.

The Scoring Rubric

Your argument task and issue task essays will be scored on a 6-point scale by two readers. These readers are your audience, and your purpose in writing this essay is to earn the best score that you can. Six is the maximum score your response can earn. The scale ranges in 1-point increments from 6 to 0.

Rubric for the Issue Task

6 Points

To earn 6 points, your response should exhibit these characteristics:

- A clear, focused position on the issue and an overall response to the specific writing task that is thorough, cogent, and sophisticated.
- Fully developed, persuasive support for the position, including, but not limited to, particularly apt or well-chosen examples, facts, and other illustrations, as well as an explanation that clearly and effectively links the support to the specific requirements of the writing task.
- A rhetorically effective method of organization, such as one that organizes support by order of importance and saves the most effective reasons for last. Connections between and among ideas are logical and may also be as subtle as they are effective.
- A formal grace that is a product primarily of well-constructed, varied sentences and exact and rhetorically effective word choices.
- Adherence to almost all the conventions of Standard Written English, including grammar, usage, and mechanics. If there are any errors, they are minor.

5 Points

To earn 5 points, your response will likely have these characteristics, though it may exceed one or more of them yet fall short on another:

- A clear, focused position on the issue and a thoughtful, complete response to the specific writing task.
- Persuasive support for the position, including, but not limited to, examples, facts, and other illustrations, as well as an explanation that clearly links the support to the specific requirements of the writing task.
- An effective method of organization with logical connections between and among all ideas.
- Well-constructed, varied sentences and appropriate word choices that help create clarity as well as interest.

- Adherence to almost all the conventions of Standard Written English, including grammar, usage, and mechanics. If there are any errors, they should be minor.

4 Points

To earn 4 points, a response will have these characteristics:

- A clear position on the issue and a generally complete response to the specific writing task.
- Support for the position, as well as an explanation that links the support to the specific requirements of the writing task.
- A logical method of organization.
- Sentences and word choices that generally create clarity.
- General adherence to the conventions of Standard Written English. Some errors may occur.

3 Points

Your response will earn only 3 points if it has *one or more* of the following characteristics:

- A generally clear position and a response to the specific writing task that may be limited in scope or marred by occasional vagueness, extraneous detail, repetition, or other flaws.
- Limited or inadequate support for the position or a limited or inadequate explanation that links the support to the specific requirements of the writing task.
- Lapses in organization or confusing organization, and/or lack or misuse of transitional words and phrases.
- Sentences and word choices that occasionally interfere with clarity.
- One or more errors in the conventions of Standard Written English that are so significant that they obstruct meaning.

2 Points

Your response will earn only 2 points if it has *one or more* of the following characteristics:

- A wandering, unclear, or limited response characterized by an unclear or not fully articulated position and a response to the specific writing task that is limited or inadequate in scope or marred by vagueness, extraneous detail, repetition, or other flaws.
- Inadequate support and explanation.
- Confusing organization, and/or general lack or misuse of transitional words and phrases.
- Sentences and word choices that interfere with clarity.
- Repeated errors in the conventions of Standard Written English that are so significant that they obstruct meaning.

1 Point

Your response will earn only 1 point if it has *one or more* of the following characteristics:

- An unclear position and almost no response to, or minimal understanding of, the specific task.
- A total lack of support or only illogical or flawed support for the main point or points; a total lack of explanation or only an illogical or flawed explanation of the main points of your argument in relation to the specific details of the task.

- No pattern of organization or confusing organization.
- Sentences and word choices that interfere with clarity.
- So many errors in the conventions of Standard Written English that they obstruct meaning throughout the response.

0 Points

This score is possible under the following circumstances:

- The response does not answer the task in any way.
- The response is written in a foreign language.
- The response simply copies the argument.
- The response is not legible.
- The response is nonverbal.

Rubric for the Argument Task

6 Points

To earn 6 points, your response should exhibit these characteristics:

- A logically sound, well-focused answer to the specific task that is particularly insightful, thoughtful, deep, or sophisticated.
- Fully developed, persuasive support for the main point or points of your response. At this high level of response, examples and other illustrations are particularly apt or well chosen, and their relationship to the focus of your analysis is extremely clear and/or well articulated.
- A method of organization that complements the main ideas of the analysis by effectively creating a flow of well-organized paragraphs and easing the reader's progress through the paper from first word to last. Connections between and among ideas are logical and may also be as subtle as they are effective.
- A formal grace that is a product primarily of well-constructed, varied sentences and exact and rhetorically effective word choices.
- Adherence to almost all the conventions of Standard Written English, including grammar, usage, and mechanics. If there are any errors, they are minor.

5 Points

To earn 5 points, your response will likely have these characteristics, though it may exceed one or more of them yet fall short on another:

- A logically sound, focused answer to the specific task that reflects insight and evidences some deep thought.
- Well-developed, persuasive support for the main point or points of your response. Examples and other illustrations are well chosen, and their relationship to your argument is clear.
- A method of organization that complements main ideas and connects ideas clearly and in a logical order.

- Well-constructed, varied sentences and appropriate word choices that help create clarity as well as interest.
- Adherence to almost all the conventions of Standard Written English, including grammar, usage, and mechanics. If there are any errors, they are minor.

4 Points

To earn 4 points, a response will have these characteristics:

- A generally focused answer to the specific task.
- Varying degrees of adequate and inadequate support.
- A logical method of organization, although some linkages may be missing or unclear.
- Sentences and word choices that generally create clarity, though some problems may exist with structure or usage.
- General adherence to the conventions of Standard Written English. Some errors may occur.

3 Points

Your response will earn only 3 points if it has *one or more* of the following characteristics:

- An inadequate answer to the specific task. It may not quite respond to the task or all aspects of it; it may be limited in its scope or number of points, or it may be vague or confusing in places.
- Inadequate support for the main point or points of your response or support that is illogical.
- A pattern of organization that does not complement the main ideas or causes confusion for the reader.
- Sentences and word choices that occasionally interfere with clarity.
- One or more errors in the conventions of Standard Written English that are so significant that they obstruct meaning, or very frequent minor errors.

2 Points

Your response will earn only 2 points if it has *one or more* of the following characteristics:

- An inadequate or unclear answer to the specific task. It may not quite respond to the task or all aspects of it, or it may be too vague or confusing to answer the task adequately.
- Little, if any, support, or support that is illogical.
- Confusing or inadequate organization.
- Sentences and word choices that interfere with clarity.
- Repeated errors in the conventions of Standard Written English that are so significant that they obstruct meaning.

1 Point

Your response will earn only 1 point if it has *one or more* of the following characteristics:

- Almost no response to, or minimal understanding of, the specific task.
- A total lack of support or only illogical or flawed support.
- No pattern of organization or confusing organization.
- Many sentences and word choices that interfere with clarity.

- So many errors in the conventions of Standard Written English that they obstruct meaning throughout the response.

0 Points

This score is possible under the following circumstances:

- The response does not answer the task in any way.
- The response is written in a foreign language.
- The response simply copies the argument.
- The response is not legible.
- The response is nonverbal.

Understanding Scoring

ALERT!

You will find the pool of all possible issue and argument tasks that could appear on the GRE® on the ETS website at http://www.ets.org/gre/revised_general/prepare/analytical_writing/issue/pool and http://www.ets.org/gre/revised_general/prepare/analytical_writing/argument/pool.

Both the issue task and the argument task have their own scoring rubrics. As you can see from the previous rubrics, the emphasis in evaluating your response will be placed on your ability to put together a cogent and coherent piece of writing. The position that you take is not important. What is important is that you state your position effectively and demonstrate in your response an ability to state, develop, and support your position clearly and with pertinent evidence.

Note also that the rubrics include an assessment of writing style. Varying your sentence structure and using a precise, appropriate, and effective vocabulary can make your response clearer and more interesting and forceful. Lack of sentence variety and vague, imprecise language can pull down your score. While adherence to Standard Written English conventions is part of each rubric, it's less important (according to the test-makers) than your ability to craft a well-developed, well-reasoned, and well-supported piece of writing. However, remember that sloppy and incorrect grammar and spelling can get in the way of coherence.

Each essay is evaluated and scored separately, but a single combined score is reported for Analytical Writing. The combined, or reported, score is an average of the scores for the two essays. The range for the reported score is 0 to 6 with half-point increments, that is, 6 and 5.5, 5 and 4.5, 4 and 3.5, 3 and 2.5, 2 and 1.5, and 1 and 0.5. The evaluation instrument is similar to the rubrics at each level.

The Issue Task

The prompt for the issue task presents you with a very brief statement, recommendation, claim, viewpoint, or policy and asks you to agree or disagree with it. The issue will be of a general nature to which anyone could respond. No special knowledge is required. You can choose to agree or disagree with the issue as long as you follow the set of instructions that accompany the premise that is set up in the prompt. For example, you might find the following prompt and a set of instructions similar to the following wording:

A nation should require all its citizens between the ages of 18 and 30 to serve one year in national service.

Write a response in which you discuss your viewpoint on the proposed policy and the reasons for your point of view. Take into consideration the potential consequences of implementing the policy and the extent to which these consequences influence your viewpoint in developing and supporting your response.

There are six different sets of instructions that the item writers may choose from to state how you should respond to an issue task. These instructions specify the degree or conditions of your agreement or disagreement. For example, you may be asked to respond using instructions similar to the following wording:

1 Discuss how much you agree or disagree with the statement and why, as well as considering how the statement might or might not always be true and how these considerations affect your point of view.

2 Discuss how much you agree or disagree with the recommendation and why. Using specific examples, explain how the circumstances under which the recommendation could be adopted would or would not be advantageous. In developing and supporting your viewpoint, explain how these specific circumstances affect your point of view.

3 Discuss how much you agree or disagree with the claim and include the most compelling reasons and/or examples that someone could use to dispute your point of view.

4 While addressing both viewpoints provided, discuss which more closely aligns with your own. Explain your reasons for holding this position when providing evidence for your response.

5 Discuss how much you agree or disagree with the claim and the reasoning used to support that claim.

6 Discuss your viewpoint on the proposed policy and the reasons for your point of view. Take into consideration the potential consequences of implementing the policy and the extent to which these consequences influence your viewpoint in developing and supporting your response.

The Argument Task

The prompt for the argument task essay presents you with a brief argument and then states your task: to analyze the argument for its logic or reasonableness and express your analysis in a well-developed, well-reasoned, and well-supported response. To do so, you'll have to identify problems in the argument's reasoning, its evidence, the assumptions (stated or implied) on which the argument's claim is based, the conclusions drawn from the argument, or the predictions based on the argument. You may also have to point out a lack of evidence, raise questions, present alternative explanations, and consider other implications. You will not have to—nor should you—agree or disagree with the argument. Save your own views for the issue task essay.

Like the issue task, the argument task provides a prompt and a set of instructions telling you how to craft your response. The prompt—the argument—and instructions might look like the following:

In an effort to save money and be environmentally conscious, Philadelphia replaced all its traffic lights with red, green, and amber LED lights. The move was estimated to save the city $1 million. However, the first heavy snowfall showed a flaw in the plan. The LED lights did not throw off as much heat as the old-style bulb, so the snow did not melt from the traffic lights, causing disruptions at major intersections. A city council member put forward a motion to replace immediately all the LED lights with the older bulbs.

Write a response in which you discuss the questions that need to be asked and answered to determine if the recommendation and the argument on which it is based are reasonable. As part of your response, describe how the answers would help in the evaluation process.

There are eight different sets of instructions for writing your response. For example, you may have wording similar to the following:

1 Discuss the evidence needed to assess the argument. Include specific examples and an explanation of how the evidence might weaken or strengthen the argument.

2 Discuss the stated and/or unstated assumptions and explain how the argument is based on these assumptions and the implications for the argument if the assumptions are shown to be unjustified.

3 Discuss the questions that need to be asked and answered to determine if the recommendation and its argument are reasonable. As part of your response, describe how the answers would help in the evaluation process.

4 Discuss the questions that need to be asked and answered to determine if the advice and its argument are reasonable. As part of your response, explain how the answers would help in the evaluation process.

5 Discuss the questions that need to be asked and answered to determine if the recommendation is likely to result in the outcome that is projected. As part of your response, explain how the answers would help in the evaluation process.

6 Discuss the questions that need to be asked and answered to determine if the prediction and its argument are reasonable. As part of your response, explain how the answers would help in the evaluation process.

7 Presented with an explanation, discuss one or more alternative explanations that could reasonably compete with the proposed explanation. Explain how your explanation(s) account for the facts in the argument that is proposed.

8 Discuss the questions that need to be asked and answered to determine if the conclusion and the argument it is derived from are reasonable. As part of your response, explain how the answers would help in the evaluation process.

A Word About Numbers in Argument Prompts

The GRE® cautions test-takers not to be confused by the purpose of any numbers, percentages, or statistics in the prompts used for the argument task. They are present as evidence and should be evaluated in terms of whether they support the argument that is presented, show flaws in the argument, or are extraneous. Such information may also be evidence that you can use to buttress your own points. The following is an example similar to what you might find on the GRE®:

A recent study showed that fatal crashes were reduced by 24 percent in intersections where traffic safety cameras had been installed. The data was collected between 2006 and 2013 in fourteen large cities that instituted the program during that period. The conclusion was that people were paying more attention to the lights as they got close to them because running a red light meant getting a ticket. The tickets averaged as much as $100. As a result, every major city and medium-sized city should install traffic cameras at busy intersections.

As you think through ideas to write a response, you might turn these pieces of data into questions to ask yourself such as: 24 percent seems like a lot, but is that number cumulative or an average of the fourteen cities? How many fatalities in real numbers does this represent? For how many years was each city actually in the program? Is the percentage skewed downward because the majority of cities were only in it two years, three years, and so on? The data is not meant to provide you with a math problem to solve, but as a source of questions to help you shape your response.

ANSWER OPTION DIFFERENCES

All multiple-choice questions in the computer-based test will have answer options preceded by either blank ovals or blank squares depending on the question type. You will use your mouse to select one or more of these options. The paper-and-pencil test will follow the same format of answer choices, but it will use letters instead of ovals or squares for answer choices.

For your convenience in answering questions and checking answers in this book, we use (A), (B), (C), etc. By using letters with parentheses, you will find it easy to check your answers against the answer key and explanation sections.

Numeric entry questions will have to be typed in, and Analytical Writing essays will need to be composed using a keyboard and mouse in the computer-based test. For this guide and the paper-and-pencil exam, you will have to handwrite all of your answers and essays.

VERBAL REASONING

The Verbal Reasoning section has three components and several question formats. The components are (1) Reading Comprehension, (2) Text Completion, and (3) Sentence Equivalence. While the majority of questions on the Verbal Reasoning sections will be multiple-choice and the majority of those will require choosing a single answer, you will find some nontraditional question formats.

Reading Comprehension Question Formats

The Reading Comprehension questions may be multiple-choice—select one answer choice; multiple-choice—select one or more answer choices; and a select-in-passage format. The multiple-choice questions may refer back to the passage using line or sentence numbers or highlighting text with bold type.

NOTE

For your convenience in answering questions and checking answers, this book uses (A), (B), (C), etc., instead of the blank ovals and squares that appear on the computer-based test.

ALERT!

The computer version will have two Verbal Reasoning sections of approximately 20 questions each to be completed in 30 minutes, and the paper-and-pencil version for test-takers outside the United States will have 25 questions to be completed in 35 minutes.

Multiple-Choice—Select One Answer Choice

You are undoubtedly familiar with this question format from all the other standardized tests you've ever taken. For the GRE®, you'll have a list of five answer choices from which to choose for the majority of reading comprehension questions. On the actual computer-based exam, instead of capital letters in parentheses, you'll see blank ovals. The format will look something like this:

> **FOR THIS QUESTION, CHOOSE ONLY <u>ONE</u> ANSWER CHOICE.**

- ○ The author of the passage would most likely agree with which of the following statements?
- ○ Professor Bates did not take into consideration the number of voters who said they would vote, but didn't.
- ○ Professor Bates did not consider the problems with accuracy inherent in exit polls.
- ● Professor Bates's sample was neither large enough nor random enough.
- ○ Professor Bates should have known that plus or minus 10 points was too large a range to be valid.
- ○ Professor Bates should not have stopped sampling 10 days before the election, considering how volatile the race was.

Multiple-Choice—Select One or More Answer Choices

The list of multiple-choice options for this question format is limited to three. The answer choices for multiple-choice—select one or more answer choices are preceded by blank squares, not ovals. (But again, we use letters in parentheses to indicate answer options in our guide, which allows for easy checking against the answer key and explanation sections.) The question will indicate that you should select all answer choices that apply. You may find that only one of the answers is correct, or you may find that two are, or even all three. The format will look something like this:

> **FOR THIS QUESTION, CONSIDER EACH ANSWER INDIVIDUALLY AND CHOOSE <u>ALL</u> THAT APPLY.**

According to the critic, what qualities were more evident in her later novels than in her earlier ones?

- ■ less social satire
- □ more stereotypically drawn characters
- ■ more dialogue and less description of characters' motivations

A Variation on the Standard Multiple-Choice Question

Within the multiple-choice format—either select one answer choice or select one or more answer choices—you may find questions that use line numbers to refer to a particular line. Questions with line numbers are usually vocabulary questions such as "In line 4, the word 'sterling' most nearly means" followed by a list of possible answers. You're probably familiar with this question type if you have taken the SAT Subject Test on Literature or the AP English Literature and Composition Exam.

A Variation on the Standard Multiple-Choice Passage

You may find a passage with bold type highlighting two parts of the passage and a question that asks you about the two parts. The arrangement might look something like the following:

> . . .**Jones's ultimate mistake in the eyes of historians was his disregard of Turner's thesis on the closing of the frontier.** However, Jones's own theory was found to be no more penetrating nor half as well supported as he claimed Turner's was. For one thing, Jones's argument was considered weak because he had not consulted the territorial records. His articles tended to lack
> 5　statistical support, and his conclusions overly generalized from the spotty data that he had used.
>
> Jones's response centered on the fact that he considered his function in life to be popularizing dull and boring history for a popular audience. This won him no friends in academia, but his books about the colorful frontier made him pots of money—like the pot of gold at the end of a rainbow on a rain-soaked prairie—to satirize Jones's florid prose. **Jones claimed his wealth**
> 10　**evoked jealousy in his peers.**
>
> How does the author of the passage use the two sentences in bold to make his point that Jones was an egotist?

Select-in-Passage Questions

Select-in-passage questions appear on the computer version of the GRE® in one format and on the paper-and-pencil version in another format. On the latter test, select-in-passage questions will be in the form of traditional multiple-choice questions. On the computer version, test-takers will be asked to highlight a sentence within the passage itself.

If the passage is a single paragraph, the entire passage may be the source of the answer. If the passage has several paragraphs, only a certain portion of the passage will be relevant to the question. That portion will be called out between arrows (→). To answer the question, you will need to click on the sentence that is your answer choice. If you try to click on a sentence outside the selected area, the sentence will not be highlighted. The question and directions will be set up similarly to the following arrangement:

> . . . rather than allow for a vote on the bill, the senator chose to begin a filibuster that would last for 24 hours and 18 minutes. ← Senator Thurmond was speaking against the passage of the Civil Rights Act of 1957. Because of the strong emotionalism of the opposition to civil rights for African Americans, the Senate saw another record-breaking filibuster in 1964. Senator
> 5　Robert Byrd and his colleagues held the Senate floor for 75 hours. Senator Byrd who came in time to renounce his opposition to civil rights legislation spoke for 14 hours and 13 minutes. →
>
> Filibusters against civil rights legislation continued during the 1960s as Southern senators fought to keep the status quo in place. However, the Civil Rights Movement had gained momentum and would not be silenced. . . .
>
> Select the sentence that explains the causal relationship between filibusters and proposed civil rights legislation.

Note the arrows within the passage. The portion of the passage that is the subject of the question begins within the paragraph and ends at the end of the same paragraph.

ALERT!

The most important fact to remember about text completion questions is that there is no partial credit given for answers that are partially correct. All blanks must be completed correctly to earn a point.

Text Completion Questions

Text completion questions are based on a single passage. The passage may have from one to three blanks. If the passage has one blank to fill in, there is a list of five answer choices from which to select set up in a column. If the passage has two or three blanks, there will be a list of three answer choices for each blank set up in two to three columns. Once you have decided on your answer, you click on the cell with that answer. In our guide, there will be a letter next to the word choices. The format will look something like the following:

> FOR THIS QUESTION, CHOOSE <u>ONE</u> ANSWER FOR EACH BLANK. SELECT FROM THE APPROPRIATE COLUMN FOR EACH BLANK. CHOOSE THE ANSWER THAT BEST COMPLETES THE SENSE OF THE TEXT.

A major issue that may slow the (i) _____ of electric cars is the difficulty of charging the engines. Until or unless local (ii) _____ legislate the installation of charging stations in new construction, at train stations, and in parking lots, (iii) _____ of electric cars say that the general public will not embrace these environmentally friendly vehicles.

Blank (i)	Blank (ii)	Blank (iii)
(A) manufacturing	(D) municipalities	(G) opponents
(B) proliferation	(E) companies	(H) advocates
(C) building	(F) people	(I) lovers

NOTE

If you're interested, the answers are (B) proliferation, (D) municipalities, and (H) advocates.

Sentence Equivalence Questions

Sentence equivalence questions differ from traditional multiple-choice questions in two significant ways. First, there are six answer choices rather than the usual five. Second, you have to choose two answers from the list to complete the one answer blank. That is, sentence equivalence questions ask you to complete a sentence using two different words that are similar, or equivalent, in meaning. Both completed versions of the sentence must convey a similar meaning. To receive credit for your answer, both answer choices must be correct. The answer choices are preceded by blank squares, not ovals. No partial credit is given if only one of the words is correct.

The direction line for all sentence equivalence questions is the same and is worded something like the following:

> **FOR THIS QUESTION, CHOOSE <u>TWO</u> ANSWERS THAT BEST FIT THE MEANING OF EACH SENTENCE AND THAT RESULT IN COMPLETED SENTENCES WITH THE SAME OR NEARLY THE SAME MEANING.**

The art expert, hired by the potential buyer, was unable to _____ the painting as being from the school of Rembrandt.

- ■ authenticate
- ☐ place
- ☐ authorize
- ■ verify
- ☐ depose
- ☐ approve

Some Advice About Checking Answers

As you work through the practice test, you should get an idea of how long a text completion item takes you. As you increase your proficiency with these items, you may find that a simple text completion, or a text completion with just one blank, takes perhaps twenty to thirty seconds, while the longer two-blank and three-blank text completion items may run 45 seconds to a minute or more to complete.

For this reason, if you come to the end of a Verbal Reasoning section, and you have a minute or two left, your wisest use of time might be to double-check text completion or sentence equivalence items. Every one of them counts just as much as a reading comprehension answer. So, with a remaining 60 seconds, you may be able to skim and, conceivably, correct two text completion items, or 8 percent of the test, whereas 60 seconds spent on a reading comprehension question might not get you through a rereading of a passage and question.

QUANTITATIVE REASONING

The Quantitative Reasoning sections of the test intersperse multiple-choice, quantitative comparison, and numeric entry questions. The multiple-choice questions will be in two formats: the traditional "select one answer choice" and the newer "select one or more answer choices." The majority of questions will be the multiple-choice format, and the majority of those will be the traditional "select one answer choice."

Those taking the computer version of the GRE® will have an on-screen calculator to use. It will allow you to add, subtract, multiply, divide, and find square roots. It will look something like this:

ALERT!
Those taking the computerized version of the Quantitative Reasoning section will have approximately 20 questions to complete in 35 minutes. The paper-and-pencil test for test-takers outside the United States will have 25 questions to be completed in 40 minutes.

Those taking the paper-and-pencil test outside the United States will be given a calculator at the test site. Don't bring your own because you won't be allowed to use it.

Multiple-Choice—Select One Answer Choice

All questions using the multiple-choice—select one answer choice format list five possible answer choices, only one of which is correct. The choices are preceded by an oval to click to select your answer. The question will look something like the following:

FOR THIS QUESTION, CHOOSE <u>ONE</u> ANSWER CHOICE.

NOTE

The last option is the correct answer and the solution $(-3x - 24)^2$ can be rewritten as $(-3(x + 8))^2$, which equals $9(x + 8)^2$. Since $y = (x + 8)^2$, then

$$(-3x - 24)^2 =$$
$$9(x + 8)^2 = 9y$$

If $y = (x + 8)^2$, then $(-3x - 24)^2$ must equal which of the following?

○ $-9y^2$

○ $-3y^2$

○ $-9y$

○ $3y$

● $9y$

Multiple-Choice—Select One or More Answer Choices

This format may have, as the name states, one, two, three, or more correct answers. Unlike reading comprehension test items that use the multiple-choice—select one or more answers format, questions using this format in the Quantitative Reasoning section may have up to eight answer options. However, there will always be at least three answer choices listed and they will all have blank squares in front of them.

In most instances, the direction line with one of these questions will tell you to "indicate all that apply." However, the direction line may specify the number that you should choose. The following example provides a typical direction line for such a question:

> **FOR THIS QUESTION, INDICATE ALL THE ANSWERS THAT APPLY.**

Which two of the following integers give you a product of less than –54?

- ■ –9
- ☐ –5
- ☐ 6
- ■ 9
- ☐ 4
- ☐ –6
- ☐ 5
- ☐ 1

In order to gain credit for multiple-choice—select one or more answer questions, you need to select the correct number of answers and the answers you choose must all be correct. There is no partial credit for partially correct answers.

Quantitative Comparison Questions

Quantitative comparison questions present you with two quantities, A and B. The objective is to compare the two quantities and choose one of the following answers, which always appear in this order:

- ◯ Quantity A is greater.
- ◯ Quantity B is greater.
- ◯ The two quantities are equal.
- ◯ The relationship cannot be determined from the information given.

Some quantitative comparison questions will have additional information centered above the two columns. This information will help you determine the relationship between the two quantities. Any symbol that appears more than once in a question has the same meaning throughout the question; for example, a symbol in the centered information means the same in Quantity A.

NOTE

The correct answers are –9 and 9. You need to look at numbers that when multiplied together result in a negative number. So, –9 × 6 = –54, which is not less than –54. Next, look at –9 × 9 = –81, which is less, so there is no need to do more.

TIP

To save time on the test, memorize the answers so that you don't have to read them each time you come across a quantitative comparison question.

A quantitative comparison question will look like the following:

> **FOR THIS QUESTION, COMPARE QUANTITY A AND QUANTITY B. THIS QUESTION HAS ADDITIONAL INFORMATION ABOVE THE TWO QUANTITIES TO USE IN DETERMINING YOUR ANSWER.**

1 kilo = 2.2 pounds

Quantity A	Quantity B
1 kilo of gold	2.2 pounds of flour

○ Quantity A is greater.

○ Quantity B is greater.

● The two quantities are equal.

○ The relationship cannot be determined from the information given.

Numeric Entry Questions

Unlike the other Quantitative Reasoning question formats, numeric entry questions don't have a list of answer choices from which to choose your answer. Instead, you're given a question and one or two answer boxes. If the answer is an integer or decimal, there will be one answer box. If the answer is a fraction, you'll see two answer boxes, one over the other with a line between them. You'll enter the numerator in the top box and the denominator in the bottom box.

To solve the problem, you'll use the on-screen calculator. If the answer is an integer or decimal, you can use the "Transfer Display" function to enter your answer in the box. If the answer is a fraction, you'll need to type your answer into the two boxes using the keypad.

A numeric entry question will look like the following:

> **FOR THIS QUESTION, ENTER YOUR ANSWER IN THE BOX.**

If x and y are integers, what is the absolute value of y if $y = -6x + 32$ and $x = -4$?

Data Interpretation Sets

In addition to the different types of question formats, you'll probably also find at least one group of questions revolving around the same table, graph, or other data representation. These are known as data interpretation sets. All that means is that to answer the two or three questions related to the data on the graphic, you will need to reference the graphic.

Master the GRE® 23rd Edition

SUMMING IT UP

- The GRE® revised General Test assesses three areas: (1) Analytical Writing, (2) Verbal Reasoning, and (3) Quantitative Reasoning.

- The Analytical Writing section requires two writing assignments: an issue task and an argument task. The issue task asks you to give your opinion about an issue, whereas the argument task asks you to evaluate an argument and the evidence used to support it.

- Each writing prompt is accompanied by a set of instructions indicating how you should respond to the issue or argument. Finished writing tasks are evaluated against a 6-point rubric. The rubrics are different for the two kinds of writing.

- The Verbal Reasoning section has three components: (1) reading comprehension, (2) text completion, and (3) sentence equivalence.

- Reading comprehension questions may be multiple-choice—select one answer choice; multiple-choice—select one or more answer choices; and select-in-passage questions. The last requires test-takers using the computer version to highlight a sentence within the subject passage as the answer. For the paper-and-pencil test, this format has been converted to a multiple-choice—select one answer choice question.

- Reading comprehension questions that use the traditional one-answer multiple-choice format present a list of five answer choices preceded by ovals. The multiple-choice—select one or more answer choices format presents only three possible answers preceded by squares. All three options may be correct, or only one, or only two.

- Text completion questions present a passage with from one to three blanks that must be completed by choosing from a list of possible answers. If the question has only one blank, then five possible choices are provided. If the question has two or three blanks to fill in, there will be a list of only three possible answers for each blank.

- Sentence equivalence questions provide six possible answers, but only one blank to complete. To answer the question, you must use two words from the list that will complete the sentence so that both versions are similar, or equivalent, in meaning.

- Quantitative Reasoning questions may take the form of multiple-choice—select one answer choice; multiple-choice—select one or more answer choices; quantitative comparison; and numeric entry formats.

- Multiple-choice—select one answer choice is the traditional multiple-choice format and lists five possible answer choices preceded by ovals.

- Multiple-choice—select one or more answer choices lists at least three answer choices, but may have as many as eight possible answers. The direction line usually says simply to "indicate all that apply." However, some questions may indicate an exact number to select.

- Quantitative comparison questions are set up as two columns, Quantity A and Quantity B, which you must compare and decide if one is greater than the other, they are equal, or the relationship can't be determined from the information. Some questions may provide additional information above the quantities to help you determine your answer.

- Numeric entry questions don't list answer choices. You must calculate your answer using the on-screen calculator and enter it on-screen. If you're taking the paper-and-pencil test because you're outside the United States, you'll be given a calculator at the test site to use.

- For questions that require more than one answer, credit is given only if all answer choices are correct.

PART II

DIAGNOSING STRENGTHS AND WEAKNESSES

PRACTICE TEST 1: DIAGNOSTIC ANSWER SHEETS

Section 1: Analytical Writing

Analyze an Issue

FOR PLANNING

ANALYZE AN ISSUE RESPONSE

ANALYZE AN ISSUE RESPONSE

_____
_____
_____
_____
_____
_____
_____
_____
_____
_____
_____
_____
_____
_____
_____
_____
_____
_____
_____
_____
_____
_____
_____
_____
_____
_____
_____
_____
_____
_____
_____
_____
_____
_____
_____

answer sheet

ANALYZE AN ISSUE RESPONSE

_____
_____
_____
_____
_____
_____
_____
_____
_____
_____
_____
_____
_____
_____
_____
_____
_____
_____
_____
_____
_____
_____
_____
_____
_____
_____
_____
_____
_____
_____
_____
_____
_____
_____
_____
_____
_____
_____

ANALYZE AN ISSUE RESPONSE

_____
_____
_____
_____
_____
_____
_____
_____
_____
_____
_____
_____
_____
_____
_____
_____
_____
_____
_____
_____
_____
_____
_____
_____
_____
_____
_____
_____
_____
_____
_____
_____
_____
_____
_____

answer sheet

Analyze an Argument

FOR PLANNING

ANALYZE AN ARGUMENT RESPONSE

_____
_____
_____
_____
_____
_____
_____
_____
_____
_____
_____
_____
_____
_____
_____
_____
_____
_____
_____
_____
_____
_____
_____
_____
_____
_____
_____
_____
_____
_____
_____
_____
_____
_____

answer sheet

ANALYZE AN ARGUMENT RESPONSE

ANALYZE AN ARGUMENT RESPONSE

_____

_____

_____

_____

_____

_____

_____

_____

_____

_____

_____

_____

_____

_____

_____

_____

_____

_____

_____

_____

_____

_____

_____

_____

_____

_____

_____

_____

_____

_____

_____

_____

_____

answer sheet

ANALYZE AN ARGUMENT RESPONSE

_____
_____
_____
_____
_____
_____
_____
_____
_____
_____
_____
_____
_____
_____
_____
_____
_____
_____
_____
_____
_____
_____
_____
_____
_____
_____
_____
_____
_____
_____
_____
_____
_____
_____
_____
_____
_____

Section 2: Quantitative Reasoning

1. Ⓐ Ⓑ Ⓒ Ⓓ
2. Ⓐ Ⓑ Ⓒ Ⓓ
3. Ⓐ Ⓑ Ⓒ Ⓓ
4. Ⓐ Ⓑ Ⓒ Ⓓ
5. Ⓐ Ⓑ Ⓒ Ⓓ
6. Ⓐ Ⓑ Ⓒ Ⓓ
7. Ⓐ Ⓑ Ⓒ Ⓓ
8. Ⓐ Ⓑ Ⓒ Ⓓ
9. Ⓐ Ⓑ Ⓒ Ⓓ Ⓔ
10. Ⓐ Ⓑ Ⓒ Ⓓ Ⓔ

11. Ⓐ Ⓑ Ⓒ Ⓓ Ⓔ Ⓕ Ⓖ Ⓗ
12. Ⓐ Ⓑ Ⓒ Ⓓ Ⓔ
13. Ⓐ Ⓑ Ⓒ Ⓓ Ⓔ
14. Ⓐ Ⓑ Ⓒ Ⓓ Ⓔ
15. Ⓐ Ⓑ Ⓒ Ⓓ Ⓔ Ⓕ Ⓖ Ⓗ

16. Ⓐ Ⓑ Ⓒ Ⓓ Ⓔ
17. Ⓐ Ⓑ Ⓒ Ⓓ Ⓔ
18. Ⓐ Ⓑ Ⓒ Ⓓ Ⓔ
19. ☐
20. Ⓐ Ⓑ Ⓒ Ⓓ Ⓔ

Section 3: Verbal Reasoning

1. Ⓐ Ⓑ Ⓒ Ⓓ Ⓔ
2. Ⓐ Ⓑ Ⓒ Ⓓ Ⓔ Ⓕ
3. Ⓐ Ⓑ Ⓒ Ⓓ Ⓔ Ⓕ
4. Ⓐ Ⓑ Ⓒ Ⓓ Ⓔ Ⓕ Ⓖ Ⓗ Ⓘ
5. Ⓐ Ⓑ Ⓒ
6. Ⓐ Ⓑ Ⓒ Ⓓ Ⓔ
7. Ⓐ Ⓑ Ⓒ Ⓓ Ⓔ
8. Ⓐ Ⓑ Ⓒ Ⓓ Ⓔ
9. Ⓐ Ⓑ Ⓒ Ⓓ Ⓔ
10. Ⓐ Ⓑ Ⓒ

11. Ⓐ Ⓑ Ⓒ Ⓓ Ⓔ
12. Ⓐ Ⓑ Ⓒ Ⓓ Ⓔ
13. Ⓐ Ⓑ Ⓒ
14. Ⓐ Ⓑ Ⓒ
15. Ⓐ Ⓑ Ⓒ Ⓓ Ⓔ

16. Ⓐ Ⓑ Ⓒ Ⓓ Ⓔ Ⓕ
17. Ⓐ Ⓑ Ⓒ Ⓓ Ⓔ Ⓕ
18. Ⓐ Ⓑ Ⓒ Ⓓ Ⓔ Ⓕ
19. Ⓐ Ⓑ Ⓒ Ⓓ Ⓔ Ⓕ
20. Ⓐ Ⓑ Ⓒ Ⓓ Ⓔ

Section 4: Verbal Reasoning

1. Ⓐ Ⓑ Ⓒ Ⓓ Ⓔ
2. Ⓐ Ⓑ Ⓒ Ⓓ Ⓔ
3. Ⓐ Ⓑ Ⓒ Ⓓ Ⓔ Ⓕ
4. Ⓐ Ⓑ Ⓒ Ⓓ Ⓔ Ⓕ Ⓖ Ⓗ Ⓘ
5. Ⓐ Ⓑ Ⓒ Ⓓ Ⓔ Ⓕ Ⓖ Ⓗ Ⓘ
6. Ⓐ Ⓑ Ⓒ Ⓓ Ⓔ
7. Ⓐ Ⓑ Ⓒ
8. Ⓐ Ⓑ Ⓒ Ⓓ Ⓔ
9. Ⓐ Ⓑ Ⓒ
10. Ⓐ Ⓑ Ⓒ Ⓓ Ⓔ

11. Ⓐ Ⓑ Ⓒ Ⓓ Ⓔ
12. Ⓐ Ⓑ Ⓒ Ⓓ Ⓔ
13. Ⓐ Ⓑ Ⓒ Ⓓ Ⓔ Ⓕ
14. Ⓐ Ⓑ Ⓒ Ⓓ Ⓔ Ⓕ
15. Ⓐ Ⓑ Ⓒ Ⓓ Ⓔ Ⓕ

16. Ⓐ Ⓑ Ⓒ Ⓓ Ⓔ
17. Ⓐ Ⓑ Ⓒ Ⓓ Ⓔ
18. Ⓐ Ⓑ Ⓒ
19. Ⓐ Ⓑ Ⓒ Ⓓ Ⓔ
20. Ⓐ Ⓑ Ⓒ Ⓓ Ⓔ

answer sheet

Section 5: Quantitative Reasoning

1. Ⓐ Ⓑ Ⓒ Ⓓ
2. Ⓐ Ⓑ Ⓒ Ⓓ
3. Ⓐ Ⓑ Ⓒ Ⓓ
4. Ⓐ Ⓑ Ⓒ Ⓓ
5. Ⓐ Ⓑ Ⓒ Ⓓ
6. Ⓐ Ⓑ Ⓒ Ⓓ
7. Ⓐ Ⓑ Ⓒ Ⓓ
8. Ⓐ Ⓑ Ⓒ Ⓓ
9. Ⓐ Ⓑ Ⓒ Ⓓ Ⓔ
10. Ⓐ Ⓑ Ⓒ Ⓓ Ⓔ

11. Ⓐ Ⓑ Ⓒ Ⓓ Ⓔ
12. Ⓐ Ⓑ Ⓒ Ⓓ Ⓔ
13. ☐
14. Ⓐ Ⓑ Ⓒ Ⓓ Ⓔ
15. Ⓐ Ⓑ Ⓒ Ⓓ Ⓔ

16. Ⓐ Ⓑ Ⓒ Ⓓ Ⓔ
17. Ⓐ Ⓑ Ⓒ Ⓓ Ⓔ
18. Ⓐ Ⓑ Ⓒ Ⓓ Ⓔ Ⓕ Ⓖ Ⓗ
19. Ⓐ Ⓑ Ⓒ Ⓓ Ⓔ Ⓕ
20. ☐
    ☐

Practice Test 1:
Diagnostic

The test begins with general information about the number of sections on the test (six for the computer version, including the unidentified unscored section or an identified research section, and five for the paper-and-pencil version) and the timing of the test (approximately 3 hours and 45 minutes, including one 10-minute break after Section 3, 1-minute breaks after the other sections for the computer version, and 3 hours and 30 minutes for the paper-and-pencil version with similar breaks). The following practice test contains the five scored sections.

Each section has its own time allocation and during that time period, you may work on only that section.

Next, you will read ETS's policy on scoring the Analytical Writing responses. Each essay is read by experienced readers, and ETS may cancel any test scores that show evidence of unacknowledged use of sources, unacknowledged collaboration with others, preparation of the response by another person, and language that is "substantially" similar to the language in one or more other test responses.

Each section has specific instructions for that section.

You will be told when to begin.

chapter 3

SECTION 1: ANALYTICAL WRITING

Analyze an Issue
30 minutes

The time for this task is 30 minutes. You must plan and draft a response that evaluates the issue given below. If you do not respond to the specific issue, your score will be zero. Your response must be based on the accompanying instructions, and you must provide evidence for your position. You may use support from reading, experience, observations, and/or course work.

> To be informed citizens, all students should know the U.S. Constitution. As part of the national social studies standards, all U.S. students should read and learn the U.S. Constitution well enough to be able to pass an exam with specific questions on any or all of the Constitution's articles. Passing such an exam should be a graduation requirement.
>
> Write an essay that expresses the degree to which you agree or disagree with the claim and the reason or reasons that underlie the claim.

Your response will be read by experienced readers who will assess your ability to do the following:

- Follow the set of task instructions.
- Analyze the complexities involved.
- Organize, develop, and explain ideas.
- Use pertinent reasons and/or illustrations to support ideas.
- Adhere to the conventions of Standard Written English.

You will be advised to take some time to plan your response and to leave time to reread it before the time is over. Those taking the paper-and-pencil version of the GRE® will find a blank page in their answer booklet for making notes and then four ruled pages for writing their actual response. Those taking the computer version will be given scrap paper for making notes.

STOP

> If you finish before the time is up, you may check your work in this section only.

Analyze an Argument

30 minutes

The time for this task is 30 minutes. You must plan and draft a response that evaluates the argument given below. If you do not respond to the given argument, your score will be zero. Your response must be based on the accompanying instructions, and you must provide evidence in support of your analysis.

You should not present your views on the subject of the argument, but on the strength or weakness of the argument.

Skybold and Associates has seen a remarkable surge in productivity since it instituted its policy of allowing its creative staff to work from home for as many as two workdays (16 hours) per week. Results of this policy have included employees taking fewer sick and personal days as well as greater employee satisfaction and enhanced employee loyalty. In addition, Skybold envisions in the not so distant future a reduced need for office space as fewer offices and cubicles will be needed to accommodate a smaller in-house staff. This will result in dramatic savings for the company. Skybold's new telecommunicating policy is clearly a win-win situation.

Write an essay that identifies questions to be answered before deciding whether the conclusion and the argument on which it is based are reasonable. Explain how the answers would help you determine whether the argument's conclusion is logical.

Your response will be read by experienced readers who will assess your ability to do the following:

- Follow the set of task instructions.
- Analyze the complexities involved.
- Organize, develop, and explain ideas.
- Use pertinent reasons and/or illustrations to support ideas.
- Adhere to the conventions of Standard Written English.

You will be advised to take some time to plan your response and to leave time to reread it before the time is over. Those taking the paper-and-pencil version of the GRE® will find a blank page in their answer booklet for making notes and then four ruled pages for writing their actual response. Those taking the computer version will be given scrap paper for making notes.

STOP

If you finish before the time is up, you may check your work in this section only.

INSTRUCTIONS FOR THE VERBAL REASONING AND QUANTITATIVE REASONING SECTIONS

You will find information here on the question formats for the Verbal Reasoning and Quantitative Reasoning sections as well as information about how to use the software program, or, if you're taking the paper-and-pencil version, how to mark your answers in the answer booklet.

Perhaps the most important information is a reminder about how these two sections are scored. Every correct answer earns a point, but wrong answers don't subtract any points. The advice from ETS is to guess if you aren't sure of an answer. ETS says that this is better than not answering a question.

All multiple-choice questions in the computer-based test will have answer options preceded by either blank ovals or blank squares depending on the question type. The paper-and-pencil test will follow the same format of answer choices, but it will use letters instead of ovals or squares for answer choices.

For your convenience in answering questions and checking answers in this book, we use (A), (B), (C), etc. By using letters with parentheses, you will find it easy to check your answers against the answer key and explanation sections.

SECTION 2: QUANTITATIVE REASONING

35 minutes • 20 questions

(The paper-and-pencil version will have 25 questions to be completed in 40 minutes.)

For each question, follow the specific directions and choose the best answer.

The test-maker provides the following information that applies to all questions in the Quantitative Reasoning section of the GRE®:

- All numbers used are real numbers.

- All figures are assumed to lie in a plane unless otherwise indicated.

- Geometric figures, such as lines, circles, triangles, and quadrilaterals, *are not necessarily* drawn to scale. That is, you should *not* assume that quantities such as lengths and angle measures are as they appear in a figure. You should assume, however, that lines shown as straight are actually straight, points on a line are in the order shown, and more generally, all geometric objects are in the relative positions shown. For questions with geometric figures, you should base your answers on geometric reasoning, not on estimating or comparing quantities by sight or by measurement.

- Coordinate systems, such as *xy*-planes and number lines, *are* drawn to scale. Therefore, you can read, estimate, or compare quantities in such figures by sight or by measurement.

- Graphical data presentations, such as bar graphs, circle graphs, and line graphs, *are* drawn to scale. Therefore, you can read, estimate, or compare data values by sight or by measurement.

FOR QUESTIONS 1–8, COMPARE QUANTITY A AND QUANTITY B. SOME QUESTIONS WILL HAVE ADDITIONAL INFORMATION ABOVE THE TWO QUANTITIES TO USE IN DETERMINING YOUR ANSWER.

---

1.   Quantity A   Quantity B

$6\dfrac{7}{8}$ 3.42(2)

(A) Quantity A is greater.
(B) Quantity B is greater.
(C) The two quantities are equal.
(D) The relationship cannot be determined from the information given.

QUESTIONS 2–4 REFER TO THE DIAGRAM BELOW.

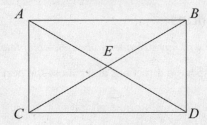

ABCD is a rectangle.

E is the intersection of *AD* and *BC*.

2.   Quantity A   Quantity B
            the area of △*CED*   the area of △*AEC*

(A) Quantity A is greater.

(B) Quantity B is greater.

(C) The two quantities are equal.

(D) The relationship cannot be determined from the information given.

3.   Quantity A   Quantity B
         m∠*ACD* + m∠*CDB*   m∠*AEC* + m∠*CED*

(A) Quantity A is greater.

(B) Quantity B is greater.

(C) The two quantities are equal.

(D) The relationship cannot be determined from the information given.

4.   Quantity A   Quantity B
         $(AB)^2 + (BD)^2$ *AD*

(A) Quantity A is greater.

(B) Quantity B is greater.

(C) The two quantities are equal.

(D) The relationship cannot be determined from the information given.

$$y < x < 0$$

5.   Quantity A   Quantity B
                $|x|$ $|y|$

(A) Quantity A is greater.

(B) Quantity B is greater.

(C) The two quantities are equal.

(D) The relationship cannot be determined from the information given.

$$a > b > 0$$

6.   Quantity A   Quantity B
           $a^2 - b^2$ $(3a + 3b)(-2a + 2b)$

(A) Quantity A is greater.

(B) Quantity B is greater.

(C) The two quantities are equal.

(D) The relationship cannot be determined from the information given.

The area of the triangle is 15.

7.   Quantity A   Quantity B
              n 12

(A) Quantity A is greater.

(B) Quantity B is greater.

(C) The two quantities are equal.

(D) The relationship cannot be determined from the information given.

$$x^2 = 9$$

8.   Quantity A   Quantity B
              x -3

(A) Quantity A is greater.

(B) Quantity B is greater.

(C) The two quantities are equal.

(D) The relationship cannot be determined from the information given.

Questions 9–20 have several formats. Unless the directions state otherwise, choose one answer choice. For the Numeric Entry questions, follow the instructions below.

Numeric Entry Questions

The following items are the same for both the computer-based version of the test and the paper-and-pencil version. However, those taking the computer-based version will have additional information about entering answers in decimal and fraction boxes on the computer screen. Those taking the paper-and-pencil version will have information about entering answers on answer grids.

- Your answer may be an integer, a decimal, or a fraction, and it may be negative.

- If a question asks for a fraction, there will be two boxes. One box will be for the numerator and one will be for the denominator.

- Equivalent forms of the correct answer, such as 2.5 and 2.50, are all correct.

- Enter the exact answer unless the question asks you to round your answers.

9. The local pastry shop sells its doughnuts for $1.90 each, and the shop owner makes an 8% profit on each. How much profit would the owner make if she sold 15 doughnuts?
   (A) $0.15
   (B) $2.28
   (C) $28.50
   (D) $1.12
   (E) $3.45

10. A regular, six-sided die is rolled three times. What is the probability that each of the three rolls will produce an odd number?

   (A) $\dfrac{1}{2}$

   (B) $\dfrac{1}{3}$

   (C) $\dfrac{1}{6}$

   (D) $\dfrac{1}{8}$

   (E) $\dfrac{1}{216}$

> **FOR QUESTION 11, INDICATE <u>ALL</u> THE ANSWERS THAT APPLY.**

11. Find the next 3 numbers in the sequence. 1, 1, 2, 3, 5, 8, ….
    - (A) 12
    - (B) 13
    - (C) 14
    - (D) 21
    - (E) 22
    - (F) 33
    - (G) 34
    - (H) 55

12. Let $f(x) = 2x^3 - x^2 + 7$. Find $f(3)$.
    - (A) 25
    - (B) 19
    - (C) 16
    - (D) 52
    - (E) 54

13. Solve for x: $4(3x - 5) = x + 3$
    - (A) $x = \dfrac{23}{11}$
    - (B) $x = \dfrac{8}{11}$
    - (C) $x = \dfrac{2}{3}$
    - (D) $x = -4$
    - (E) $x = 23$

14. Find the value of x.

    - (A) 55°
    - (B) 35°
    - (C) 90°
    - (D) 145°
    - (E) 125°

FOR QUESTION 15, INDICATE <u>ALL</u> THE ANSWERS THAT APPLY.

---

15. List all the factors of 51.

(A) 1

(B) 2

(C) 3

(D) 7

(E) 16

(F) 17

(G) 48

(H) 51

QUESTIONS 16–18 ARE BASED ON THE FOLLOWING DATA.

Annual State Budgets (in millions of dollars)

	2009	2010	2011	2012	2013	2014, est
State A	53.0	75.9	85.5	101.6	131.2	142.1
State B	14.4	14.5	20.0	19.0	39.2	43.5

16. What is the ratio of the total (State A + State B) estimated budget of 2014 to 2009's budget?

(A) 33.7 : 92.8

(B) 142.1 : 53.0

(C) 43.5 : 14.4

(D) 14.4 : 43.5

(E) 92.8 : 33.7

17. What is the total budget for State A for 2009, 2010, and 2013?

(A) 68.1

(B) 260.1

(C) 268

(D) 276.4

(E) 308.7

18. What year had the biggest percentage increase from the previous year in State B and what was the percentage increase?

(A) 2011, 138%

(B) 2013, 206%

(C) 2011, 37%

(D) 2013, 106%

(E) 2014, 11%

FOR QUESTION 19, ENTER YOUR ANSWER IN THE BOX.

---

19. Mary went to the convenience store with $20. She wanted to buy a newspaper for $1.25, a magazine for $6.50, a soda for $1.75, and then spend the rest of her $20 on dime candy. How many pieces would she get?

20. If p is the greatest prime number that is a factor of 51, and q is the smallest prime number that is a factor of 58, then $p + q =$

    (A) 5
    (B) 17
    (C) 19
    (D) 32
    (E) 46

STOP

> If you finish before the time is up, you may check your work in this section only.

SECTION 3: VERBAL REASONING

30 minutes • 20 questions

(The paper-and-pencil version will have 25 questions to be completed in 35 minutes.)

For each question, follow the specific directions and choose the best answer.

> **FOR QUESTIONS 1–4, CHOOSE <u>ONE</u> ANSWER FOR EACH BLANK. SELECT FROM THE APPROPRIATE COLUMN FOR EACH BLANK. CHOOSE THE ANSWER THAT BEST COMPLETES THE SENSE OF THE TEXT.**

1. The unsophisticated nature of research tools affects the _____ and validity of market research into the potential market for products and programs.

(A) accountability
(B) acceptability
(C) reliability
(D) liability
(E) approval

2. That Jane Austen's satiric wit is lost on some readers is (i) _____ because it is so (ii) _____ as to become caricature; for example, consider the Rev. Collins in *Pride and Prejudice*.

Blank (i)	Blank (ii)
(A) logical	(D) flashy
(B) understandable	(E) showy
(C) inexplicable	(F) overdrawn

3. As a result of overconfidence and a number of (i) _____ errors in judgment to employ a(n) (ii) _____, the majority party in the state legislature became the minority party in the last election.

Blank (i)	Blank (ii)
(A) embarrassing	(D) paradox
(B) inconvenient	(E) aphorism
(C) upsetting	(F) euphemism

4. One consequence of the desire among modern playwrights to bring (i) _____ to the theater has been the diminution of poetry as a dramatic language. On the other hand, realism in language has brought a (ii) _____ end to rant and rhetoric upon the stage. As one critic wrote, modern playwrights have been pushed to develop plays that are (iii) _____ and convincing when they could no longer rely on "verbal pyrotechnics."

Blank (i)	Blank (ii)	Blank (iii)
(A) vibrancy	(D) welcome	(G) more forceful
(B) verisimilitude	(E) final	(H) more cerebral
(C) resemblance	(F) limited	(I) more believable

FOR QUESTIONS 5–20, CHOOSE ONLY <u>ONE</u> ANSWER CHOICE UNLESS OTHERWISE INDICATED.

QUESTIONS 5–7 ARE BASED ON THE FOLLOWING PASSAGE.

The *New York Times* has boldly declared the end of the car culture in the United States. It based its claim on a few salient facts. The number of miles driven dropped steadily between 2005 and 2013. Over an even more extended period, rates of automobile ownership declined. The *Times* also charted changing attitudes toward driving and car ownership by young people,

5   quoting one study that showed a 23-percent decrease in driving among young people. Car sharing, bikes, and public transit were among the reasons cited for this decrease.

But is the automobility of American culture actually over, or is it just in the slow lane? It is true that the era of massive road building projects not only seems to be over, but also actually peaked as long ago as 1980. It is also true that environmental and social factors, as well as

10   the overcrowding of our roads and highways, are shaping new attitudes across all segments of society. During the past two decades, public transportation use has grown at a far faster rate than the population. Another significant factor in the declining number of miles driven has to do with our aging population; over many years, the number of miles driven has been shown to decline by age 45. Vehicle costs as a percentage of income have also been rising

15   since the mid-90s. While all of these data do not prove the end of cars, they may point to the end of the driving boom that characterized twentieth-century America.

FOR QUESTION 5, CONSIDER EACH ANSWER INDIVIDUALLY AND CHOOSE <u>ALL</u> THAT APPLY.

5. The passage suggests that the decline in driving is authenticated by which of the following?
   (A) A 23-percent decline in car ownership among young people
   (B) The end of the era of massive road building projects
   (C) The steady drop in the number of miles driven

6. It can be inferred from the passage that the author most likely thinks that the *Times* writer used the term "the end of car culture" because it

(A) offered the clearest wording to contradict the phrase "automobility of American culture."

(B) generalized the facts about U.S. driving trends in the most succinct and appropriate way.

(C) created a new and appropriate catchphrase for referring to changes in driving.

(D) summarized a number of recent studies and elucidated their results accurately.

(E) reflected some current data and employed enough hyperbole to create interest.

7. In the second paragraph, the author is primarily concerned with

(A) mitigating the *Times*'s assertion that car culture is at an end.

(B) explaining why the number of miles driven has declined recently.

(C) presenting reasons for a changing demographic of car ownership.

(D) disputing the claim that car ownership is in significant decline.

(E) offering further proof for the *Times*'s claim that the car culture is over.

QUESTIONS 8 AND 9 ARE BASED ON THE FOLLOWING PASSAGE.

The connections between the brain, the digestive system, and food behaviors have been subject to increasing scrutiny and the focus of much research over the past few years. It is now understood that the brain is updated via signals from the digestive system's own enteric nervous system (ENS) about both nutrient content and fullness. Influenced by the central
5 nervous system (CNS), the ENS relies on many CNS neurotransmitters to send chemical signals about digestion and to affect ongoing food intake. Different nerve endings transmit varying information to the brain, some of which provide information about stretch or tension, in response to food volume, and some of which provide information about nutrient content. CNS and ENS cross connections ensure not only that the gut informs the CNS, but that signals
10 from outside the nervous system can be relayed back to the gut. In addition, it is known that different peptides may be released in the presence of certain nutrients and play different feedback roles to the brain. **As Abigail Pepin of the National Institute of Health notes, "There are multiple interactions among systems that coordinate overall gastrointestinal (GI) function leading to changing GI states."**

8. This passage suggests that the sensation of fullness is the result of which of the following?

(A) Stretching and tension that result from too much eating

(B) CNS reliance on ENS neurotransmitters

(C) The role of the CNS in monitoring nutrient content

(D) Chemical signals that travel to the brain

(E) Varying ENS nutrient-content signals

9. Which of the following best characterizes the function of the boldfaced sentence in lines 12–14 of the passage?

(A) It provides evidence on which a theory is based.

(B) It presents a specific application of a general concept.

(C) It restates a point made earlier in the passage.

(D) It disproves a commonly accepted theory.

(E) It summarizes general passage information.

QUESTIONS 10–12 ARE BASED ON THE FOLLOWING PASSAGE.

Dutch artist M.C. Escher's work covers a variety of subjects, though he is probably best known for the pieces that he drew from unusual perspectives, which result in enigmatic effects. During the course of his life, Escher adopted a highly mathematical approach, using special notations that he invented himself, including a system for categorizing shapes, colors,

5 and symmetrical properties. Looking at his work, you can see clearly that mathematics played an important role in the development of his distinctive style, yet though he studied and admired various mathematical theories over the years, Escher did not consider himself a mathematician. However, this lack of formal training allowed him to explore mathematics in a unique way, without having to adhere to any set rules or restrictions. In 1958, he wrote:

10 "In mathematical quarters, the regular division of the plane has been considered theoretically . . . . [Mathematicians] have opened the gate leading to an extensive domain, but they have not entered this domain themselves. By their very nature they are more interested in the way in which the gate is opened than in the garden lying behind it."

FOR QUESTION 10, CONSIDER EACH ANSWER INDIVIDUALLY AND CHOOSE <u>ALL</u> THAT APPLY.

---

10. What material would help to support the intersection of art and mathematics in Escher's work?

    (A) Escher's notebooks containing his mathematical notations

    (B) A painting of Escher's demonstrating his use of mathematical principles in his art

    (C) Art criticism of Escher's works

11. From the passage, what is Escher's view of mathematicians?

    (A) They do not grasp how mathematics and art are interconnected.

    (B) They will never have the ability to appreciate Escher's art.

    (C) They cannot translate their theories into their own personalized notations.

    (D) They will never be able to translate their theories into art.

    (E) They cannot see the beauty that is inherent in their theories.

12. In the passage, "enigmatic" (line 2) means

    (A) rational.

    (B) inscrutable.

    (C) comprehensible.

    (D) decipherable.

    (E) theoretical.

QUESTIONS 13–15 ARE BASED ON THE FOLLOWING PASSAGE.

Because of our federal system, voting rights for women were conferred and denied at different times in our history. Observers with a twenty-first century perspective might be quick to speculate that states with the most progressive reputations prior to the passage of the Nineteenth Amendment would have been the first to grant suffrage to women, but the first
5   state to confer full voting rights was Wyoming in 1890. In doing so, it was only following the forward-looking precedent it had itself set in 1869, when, as a territory, it granted women full voting rights. In fact, while the movement for suffrage seemed to have a decidedly East Coast epicenter, the West led the way in women's suffrage. Washington Territory had been the first to introduce a suffrage bill in 1848, and the West generally led the East in conferring
10 women's suffrage. In fact, in 1914, all states west of the Rockies had granted full suffrage, whereas only one state east of them had, and that was not an acknowledged progressive or liberal bastion such as New York or Massachusetts, but Kansas. It should, however, be noted that women in Illinois were granted the right to vote for president, but not full voting rights, in 1913. Among those states that granted full suffrage to women only after passage of
15 the Nineteenth Amendment were Virginia, Georgia, Alabama, Kentucky, and New Mexico.

> **FOR QUESTION 13, CONSIDER EACH ANSWER INDIVIDUALLY AND CHOOSE <u>ALL</u> THAT APPLY.**

13. What does the passage imply about why the West led the way in conferring women's suffrage prior to the Nineteenth Amendment?
    - (A) The West was acting in accordance with the mandates of our federal system.
    - (B) The region was more forward-looking in this regard than states that are often considered to be progressive today.
    - (C) The action was surprising, given that the political activism for suffrage was centered elsewhere.

14. Select the sentence in the passage that does NOT add to the support for the main idea of the passage.
    - (A) In doing so, it was only following the forward-looking precedent it had itself set in 1869, when, as a territory, it granted women full voting rights.
    - (B) In fact, in 1914, all states west of the Rockies had granted full suffrage, whereas only one state east of them had, and that was not an acknowledged progressive or liberal bastion such as New York or Massachusetts, but Kansas.
    - (C) Among those states that granted full suffrage to women only after passage of the Nineteenth Amendment were Virginia, Georgia, Alabama, Kentucky, and New Mexico.

15. In the passage, "federal" (line 1) most nearly means relating to
    - (A) a central government.
    - (B) the North in the Civil War.
    - (C) a military representative of the government.
    - (D) a government with strong central powers.
    - (E) a government with shared powers.

FOR QUESTIONS 16–19, CHOOSE THE <u>TWO</u> ANSWERS THAT BEST FIT THE MEANING OF THE SENTENCE AS A WHOLE AND RESULT IN TWO COMPLETED SENTENCES THAT ARE ALIKE IN MEANING.

---

16. In shuttering programs to reduce costs, the new CFO was _____ toward employees and refused to listen to their concerns and alternative suggestions.

    (A) arrogant
    (B) unkind
    (C) uncharitable
    (D) dismissive
    (E) contentious
    (F) confrontational

17. Green building, that is, the construction of new buildings and the renovation of existing ones to make them eco-friendly, is a fast-growing segment of the construction industry and one that ALLIED Builders hopes to _____ according to its five-year business plan.

    (A) promote
    (B) advance
    (C) capitalize on
    (D) upgrade
    (E) exploit
    (F) endorse

18. The original intention in creating NASA was to explore space, but many of the products people take for granted today such as cordless power tools and sunglasses with polarized lenses resulted from _____ research that NASA conducted for the space program.

    (A) far-reaching
    (B) wide-ranging
    (C) innovative
    (D) unusual
    (E) cutting-edge
    (F) conventional

19. Many researchers believe that _____ bacteria keep harmful bacteria from invading humans by using the material that harmful bacteria need to live.

    (A) helpful
    (B) malignant
    (C) pathogenic
    (D) benign
    (E) benevolent
    (F) beneficial

QUESTION 20 IS BASED ON THE FOLLOWING PASSAGE.

Emily Dickinson, a poet virtually unknown in her lifetime, wrote some of the most memorable lines in American poetry. Her poems are instantly recognizable for their brevity (they are often no longer than 20 lines) and their quirky punctuation and capitalization. Her frequent and often idiosyncratic use of the dash serves to emphasize many of her recurrent topics. A great
5   number of Dickinson's almost 1,800 poems deal with the themes of death and immortality, though her poems are also filled with joy and hope. Because of its unusual syntax and use of figurative language—imagery, metaphor, personification—Dickinson's poetry can seem to the uninitiated reader something of a puzzle. Present-day readers would do well to renounce a literal way of reading in order to truly appreciate Dickinson's poetry.

20. What does the author imply by the last statement in the passage?
    (A) Readers should not try to find literal meaning in Dickinson's poetry.
    (B) Readers of poetry today are not used to so much figurative language.
    (C) Readers should try to figure out what themes were most important to Dickinson.
    (D) Readers who try to unlock the mysteries of Dickinson's figurative language are doing themselves a disservice.
    (E) Readers of poetry today need to consider the context in which Dickinson's poetry was written.

STOP

> If you finish before the time is up, you may check your work in this section only.

SECTION 4: VERBAL REASONING

30 minutes • 20 questions

(The paper-and-pencil version will have 25 questions to be completed in 35 minutes.)

For each question, follow the specific directions and choose the best answer.

> **FOR QUESTIONS 1–5, CHOOSE <u>ONE</u> ANSWER FOR EACH BLANK. SELECT FROM THE APPROPRIATE COLUMN FOR EACH BLANK. CHOOSE THE ANSWER THAT BEST COMPLETES THE SENSE OF THE TEXT.**

1. Social networking is a marketing tool that many companies are harnessing to sell their products; however, it must be used _____ because the hard sell risks offending potential customers.

(A) with ease
(B) actively
(C) judiciously
(D) expeditiously
(E) efficiently

2. In composing "Scheherazade," Rimsky-Korsakov hoped to _____ the "magical spirit" of *One Thousand and One Nights*, a collection of exotic folk tales from the Middle East and South Asia.

(A) motivate
(B) induce
(C) inspire
(D) evoke
(E) provoke

3. Garraty states that the problems faced by private colleges in the 1820s and 1830s were of their own making to a degree. Many cities and towns wanted the (i) _____ of hosting a college, but the supply of colleges soon (ii) _____ the demand, that is, the number of potential students.

Blank (i)	Blank (ii)
(A) honor	(D) outperformed
(B) admiration	(E) outstripped
(C) character	(F) outshone

4. The nation-states of early modern Europe guarded their sovereignty (i) _____, finding countless reasons—real and (ii) _____—for wars. Peace (iii) _____ only when one nation managed to subdue its neighbors.

Blank (i)	Blank (ii)	Blank (iii)
(A) jealously	(D) feigned	(G) occurred
(B) intolerantly	(E) facetious	(H) mediated
(C) liberally	(F) deceptive	(I) intervened

5. The speaker, a former prosecutor turned politician, remains direct, candid, and (i) _____ in her assessment of policy, but she can also be (ii) _____ and offhand toward her colleagues. She is considered a/n (iii) _____ legislator.

Blank (i)	Blank (ii)	Blank (iii)
(A) frank	(D) rough	(G) very ambitious
(B) pragmatic	(E) brusque	(H) really approachable
(C) rigid	(F) brisk	(I) no-nonsense

FOR QUESTIONS 6–20, CHOOSE ONLY <u>ONE</u> ANSWER CHOICE UNLESS OTHERWISE INDICATED.

QUESTIONS 6–7 ARE BASED ON THE FOLLOWING PASSAGE.

Access to clean drinking water and sanitation systems are crucial global goals. This access constitutes a fundamental health and human dignity issue. Expanding sewage systems will also reduce contamination of soil, rivers, and oceans, thereby promoting biodiversity and decreasing land degradation. Furthermore, access to clean water will reduce geopolitical
5 conflict centered on water rights. In addition, commitment to clean water goals promotes investment in new technologies, such as desalination and water reuse.

Even though the United Nations reported that between 1990 and 2010, more than "2 billion people gained access to improved water sources, and 1.8 billion gained access to improved sanitation," a more recent global assessment warns that significant problems continue to
10 plague the world. Despite well-coordinated global initiatives, the latest U.N. report discusses factors that slow the progress toward clean water goals. These include the failure of some countries to set national hygiene standards, inadequate funding or poor absorption of existing funding, lack of skilled labor to implement change, and lack of political will. Only 80% of nations recognize the right to water; only some 50% recognize the right to sanitation.

6. Based on the passage, which of the following is NOT a factor that is delaying progress toward clean water goals?

(A) failure of some nations to set national hygiene standards

(B) inability to manage skilled labor resources at water sites

(C) inadequate funding for global water initiatives

(D) failure to properly use all available water funding

(E) reluctance of some nations to consider water as a right

FOR QUESTION 7, CONSIDER EACH ANSWER INDIVIDUALLY AND CHOOSE <u>ALL</u> THAT APPLY.

---

7. Select the sentence in the passage that is NOT a supporting detail for a central idea.

   (A) This access constitutes a fundamental health and human dignity issue.

   (B) Expanding sewage systems will also reduce contamination of soil, rivers, and oceans, thereby promoting biodiversity and decreasing land degradation.

   (C) Despite well-coordinated global initiatives, the latest U.N. report discusses factors that slow the progress toward clean water goals.

QUESTIONS 8 AND 9 ARE BASED ON THE FOLLOWING PASSAGE.

Propaganda on the U.S. home front took many forms during World War I. Encouraging the public to buy bonds to fund the war, getting young men to enlist, and inspiring anyone who could to volunteer were not its only motives. For example, a poster called "20 at Home to 1 in the Trenches," published by the National Industrial Conservation Movement in 1918,
5   clearly sends the message that "American industry can and will win this war for human liberty." Through words and pictures, it describes the multiple and monumental efforts required at home to food, clothe, and arm each U.S. soldier abroad. But it also intersperses the admonition that "Breeders of industrial war at home must be eliminated" before ending with "National co-operation is the slogan to insure victory for Democracy over Autocracy."
10 In this poster and other publications, the National Industrial Conservation Movement sought to celebrate the so-called "fair-minded working man" who, it assured its audience, wanted no friction between labor and capital.

8. Select the statement that restates the premise of the author's argument.

   (A) Propaganda merged the interests of big business with the higher ideals of the war effort.

   (B) Americans who worked in industry during World War I tended to be both fair-minded and patriotic.

   (C) Propaganda subverted the interests of the war effort to the interests of American business.

   (D) Americans were subjected to anti-democratic and autocratic propaganda.

   (E) Propaganda took many forms on the home front during World War I.

FOR QUESTION 9, CONSIDER EACH ANSWER INDIVIDUALLY AND CHOOSE <u>ALL</u> THAT APPLY.

---

9. Which of the following, if it were true, would weaken the author's argument?

   (A) During World War I, many Americans went to work in factories producing military supplies.

   (B) The majority of American workers supported the war effort and the role of big business in feeding, clothing, and arming soldiers.

   (C) The National Industrial Conservation Movement also published many posters that did not promote big business or send anti-union messages.

QUESTIONS 10–12 ARE BASED ON THE FOLLOWING PASSAGE.

The increasing awareness of lighting inefficiency and the billions of dollars of potential annual energy savings that can be achieved by switching to LED lighting has resulted in many government-funded research initiatives around the world. In addition, governments in the United States, Canada, Europe, and Australia have responded to the growing need for energy
5   conservation by passing legislation that regulates or eliminates the sale of incandescent and halogen light bulbs by a certain date. However, though increasing consumers' awareness of the inefficiency of other light sources can help increase the adoption of LED lighting, regulations that focus on enforcing energy-efficient lighting are likely to work better. One example is California's Energy Efficiency Standards for Residential and Nonresidential Buildings, or
10   Title 24, that provides a set of mandatory regulations covering all aspects of new building construction. The Residential Lighting section of Title 24 requires that a high-efficiency light source be used in several areas of the home, including the kitchen and bathrooms, and that all outdoor light fixtures must either use energy-efficient bulbs, or must be controlled by light and motion sensors.

10. This passage achieves all of the following purposes EXCEPT it

   (A) implies that LED lighting will become a necessity of the future.

   (B) explains one way governments are forcing people to switch to LED lighting.

   (C) cites a regulation that enforces the use of high-efficiency light sources.

   (D) describes how LED lighting is more energy efficient than incandescent lighting.

   (E) implies that government-funded research on energy efficiency is essential.

11. The author introduces California's Title 24 in order to

   (A) support the concept that the government needs to set rules to increase the adoption of LED lighting.

   (B) provide a possible explanation for why more Americans have adopted LED lighting.

   (C) reinforce the concept that other methods of lighting are less efficient than LED lighting.

   (D) introduce the idea that governments need to enforce rules about high-efficiency lighting in residential buildings.

   (E) cast doubt on studies that show that Americans are not eager to switch to LED lighting.

12. "Mandatory" (line 10) most nearly means

   (A) provisional.

   (B) permanent.

   (C) predetermined.

   (D) discretionary.

   (E) obligatory.

> **FOR QUESTIONS 13–15, CHOOSE THE <u>TWO</u> ANSWERS THAT BEST FIT THE MEANING OF THE SENTENCE AS A WHOLE AND RESULT IN TWO COMPLETED SENTENCES THAT ARE ALIKE IN MEANING.**

13. If life did exist on other planets, scientists theorize that it would not _____ life on Earth. For example, depending on the wavelengths of light given off by the plant, plants could be red, yellow, or green.

    (A) epitomize

    (B) mimic

    (C) illustrate

    (D) typify

    (E) imitate

    (F) reflect

14. Scientists believe that unlocking the genome is _____; it will forever change the way we diagnose, treat, and someday even prevent disease.

    (A) modernization

    (B) reforming

    (C) revolutionary

    (D) transformative

    (E) huge

    (F) corrective

15. Many of his critics complain that once they finish reading his books with their convoluted plot lines, they are no wiser and their brains perhaps even more _____.

    (A) befogged

    (B) taxed

    (C) muddled

    (D) weakened

    (E) wary

    (F) heedful

QUESTIONS 16–18 ARE BASED ON THE FOLLOWING PASSAGE.

The use of specially designed eye-tracking technology for measuring the response of children ages two months to twenty-four months old has recently yielded valuable information for those hoping for earlier intervention in autism spectrum disorder (ASD). Using the technology to discern changes not apparent with the naked eye, researchers studied responses to social,
5 facial cues from a friendly caregiver or mother-like figure. Infants in the study were siblings of children on the autism spectrum; such children are at high risk for ASD. While levels of eye contact were the same initially among the youngest experimental subjects, eye contact steadily declined among those who were later diagnosed with autism, but it increased for those who were not. Study results suggest that diagnoses of ASD, or more specifically, signs
10 pointing toward an ASD diagnosis, might now be detected at between two and six months of age; the disorder is now more typically diagnosed when a child is between the ages of three and five years.

16. Which of the following best describes the author's opinion of the research she reports?

    (A) Unbiased objectivity

    (B) Guarded optimism

    (C) Unchecked enthusiasm

    (D) Slight pessimism

    (E) Complete negativity

17. Which of the following opinions does the passage most clearly support?

    (A) It is now possible to diagnose ASD at the age of two months.

    (B) Siblings of children with ASD are more likely to be diagnosed with ASD.

    (C) Significantly earlier detection of signs of ASD is now possible.

    (D) Siblings of children with ASD are more likely to increase their emotional responses over time.

    (E) Changes in emotional response are discernible by caregivers and mother-like figures.

FOR QUESTION 18, CONSIDER EACH ANSWER INDIVIDUALLY AND CHOOSE <u>ALL</u> THAT APPLY.

---

18. What function does the descriptive information, "ages two months to twenty-four months old," (line 2) serve in the passage?

    (A) It characterizes the group in which early signs of ASD can now be discerned.

    (B) It defines the group with which the study was conducted.

    (C) It identifies the age group most at risk for an ASD diagnosis.

QUESTIONS 19 AND 20 ARE BASED ON THE FOLLOWING PASSAGE.

Unpleasant and even distasteful as they can be, attack ads actually serve a purpose in our culture: they illuminate issues of character, and the character of our public officials does, in fact, matter. Recently pinpointed by political columnist Matt Bai as originating in 1987 with presidential candidate Gary Hart, the era of scandal journalism, into which the attack
5 ad so neatly fits, ended the era of "good old boy" conspiracy, when the media often knew of the many sins and personal peccadilloes of the president, presidential candidate, or other elected official, but chose to keep that information secret. While attack ads may divert the electorate from issues to matters of personal choice and lifestyle and even adversely affect voter turnout, they nevertheless expose moral and significant choices made by the potential
10 leader of the free world, congressional representative, or other candidate or nominee. If used judiciously with other ads that focus on issues, attack ads and so-called "scandal journalism" that expose questionable moral and individual choices show the media wielding its First Amendment right and serving the purposes of the electorate. More pragmatically, campaigns may be induced to employ attack ads because they work. Unfortunately, practicality is no
15 endorsement, for even when the right or better-qualified candidate assumes public office, undesirable means do not justify the end.

19. The word "wielding" (line 12) most nearly means

   (A) bearing.
   (B) abusing.
   (C) intoning.
   (D) exerting.
   (E) misapplying.

20. Which of the following expresses the author's thesis about attack ads?

   (A) They adversely affect voter attitudes and turnout.
   (B) They serve a useful, rightful purpose in our elections.
   (C) They have ended an era of conspiratorial and negative secrecy.
   (D) They are both granted and restricted by the First Amendment.
   (E) They are generally negative as the end cannot justify the means.

STOP

If you finish before the time is up, you may check your work in this section only.

SECTION 5: QUANTITATIVE REASONING

35 minutes • 20 questions

(The paper-and-pencil version will have 25 questions to be completed in 40 minutes.)

For each question, follow the specific directions and choose the best answer.

The test-maker provides the following information that applies to all questions in the Quantitative Reasoning section of the GRE®:

- All numbers used are real numbers.

- All figures are assumed to lie in a plane unless otherwise indicated.

- Geometric figures, such as lines, circles, triangles, and quadrilaterals, *are not necessarily* drawn to scale. That is, you should *not* assume that quantities such as lengths and angle measures are as they appear in a figure. You should assume, however, that lines shown as straight are actually straight, points on a line are in the order shown, and more generally, all geometric objects are in the relative positions shown. For questions with geometric figures, you should base your answers on geometric reasoning, not on estimating or comparing quantities by sight or by measurement.

- Coordinate systems, such as *xy*-planes and number lines, *are* drawn to scale. Therefore, you can read, estimate, or compare quantities in such figures by sight or by measurement.

- Graphical data presentations, such as bar graphs, circle graphs, and line graphs, *are* drawn to scale. Therefore, you can read, estimate, or compare data values by sight or by measurement.

FOR QUESTIONS 1–8, COMPARE QUANTITY A AND QUANTITY B. SOME QUESTIONS WILL HAVE ADDITIONAL INFORMATION ABOVE THE TWO QUANTITIES TO USE IN DETERMINING YOUR ANSWER.

1.

Quantity A	Quantity B
0.324875	$\dfrac{10}{31}$

- (A) Quantity A is greater.
- (B) Quantity B is greater.
- (C) The two quantities are equal.
- (D) The relationship cannot be determined from the information given.

2.

Quantity A	Quantity B
$|x|$	$|y|$

(A) Quantity A is greater.

(B) Quantity B is greater.

(C) The two quantities are equal.

(D) The relationship cannot be determined from the information given.

Mary is twice as old as Stephen. Stephen is 5 years older than Joe. Joe is $\dfrac{3}{4}$ of Mary's age. All three were born in the twenty-first century.

3.

Quantity A	Quantity B
Mary's birth year	Joe's birth year

(A) Quantity A is greater.

(B) Quantity B is greater.

(C) The two quantities are equal.

(D) The relationship cannot be determined from the information given.

A try is worth 5 points. A conversion is worth 2 points. A penalty goal is worth 3 points.

4.

Quantity A	Quantity B
3 tries, 2 conversions, 1 penalty	24

(A) Quantity A is greater.

(B) Quantity B is greater.

(C) The two quantities are equal.

(D) The relationship cannot be determined from the information given.

5.	Quantity A	Quantity B
x	115

(A) Quantity A is greater.

(B) Quantity B is greater.

(C) The two quantities are equal.

(D) The relationship cannot be determined from the information given.

6.	Quantity A	Quantity B
$-\dfrac{15}{16}$	$-\dfrac{16}{15}$

(A) Quantity A is greater.

(B) Quantity B is greater.

(C) The two quantities are equal.

(D) The relationship cannot be determined from the information given.

There are 15 players on Team 1. There are 22 players on Team 2.

There are more offensive players than defensive players on each team.

7.	Quantity A	Quantity B
Number of goalies on Team 1	Number of goalies on Team 2

(A) Quantity A is greater.

(B) Quantity B is greater.

(C) The two quantities are equal.

(D) The relationship cannot be determined from the information given.

$$\frac{y}{x} = 3$$

$$x, y \neq 0$$

8.

Quantity A	Quantity B
x	y

(A) Quantity A is greater.

(B) Quantity B is greater.

(C) The two quantities are equal.

(D) The relationship cannot be determined from the information given.

Questions 9–20 have several formats. Unless the directions state otherwise, choose one answer choice. For the Numeric Entry questions, follow the instructions below.

Numeric Entry Questions

The following items are the same for both the computer-based version of the test and the paper-and-pencil version. However, those taking the computer-based version will have additional information about entering answers in decimal and fraction boxes on the computer screen. Those taking the paper-and-pencil version will have information about entering answers on answer grids.

- Your answer may be an integer, a decimal, or a fraction, and it may be negative.

- If a question asks for a fraction, there will be two boxes. One box will be for the numerator and one will be for the denominator.

- Equivalent forms of the correct answer, such as 2.5 and 2.50, are all correct.

- Enter the exact answer unless the question asks you to round your answers.

9. Evaluate the function $f(x) = 5x^3 + 4x^2 + 8x + 1$, when $x = 2$.

   (A) 73

   (B) –11

   (C) 183

   (D) 117

   (E) –73

10. Solve the equation $4xy + 8y = 128$ for x, when $y = 4$.

   (A) $x = 10$

   (B) $x = 6$

   (C) $x = 1$

   (D) $x = 12$

   (E) $x = 32$

11. If $\dfrac{3}{x-1} = \dfrac{6}{3x+6}$, then $x =$

   (A) −8
   (B) −1
   (C) 0
   (D) 1
   (E) 8

12. A new model hybrid car gets 45 miles per gallon for city driving and 20% more for highway driving. How many miles per gallon does the hybrid get for highway driving?

   (A) 34
   (B) 46
   (C) 51
   (D) 54
   (E) 58

FOR QUESTION 13, ENTER YOUR ANSWER IN THE BOX.

---

13. Find the area of the trapezoid.

QUESTIONS 14–16 REFER TO THE TABLE BELOW.

Number of Children per Family in a Neighborhood

Number of Children	Number of Families
1	19
2	36
3	21
4+	9
0	15

14. What is the total number of families that have no more than two children?
    (A) 19
    (B) 36
    (C) 55
    (D) 70
    (E) 81

15. What is the percentage of families who have no children?
    (A) 9%
    (B) 12%
    (C) 15%
    (D) 18%
    (E) 21%

16. What percentage of the families has 6 children?
    (A) 19
    (B) 9
    (C) 15
    (D) 12
    (E) unknown

17. In the xy-plane, what is the slope of a line that is perpendicular to the line whose equation is $x + 2y = 5$?
    (A) –2
    (B) $-\dfrac{1}{2}$
    (C) $\dfrac{1}{2}$
    (D) 2
    (E) 5

18. What is the *x*-coordinate of the point at which the graphs of the equations $x + 2y = 4$ and $y - x = 2$ intersect?

(A) –8

(B) –2

(C) 0

(D) 2

(E) 16

FOR QUESTION 19, CHOOSE <u>ALL</u> THE ANSWERS THAT APPLY.

---

19. In triangle *ABC*, the length of side *AB* is 4 cm and the length of side *BC* is 8 cm. Which of the following could be the length of side *AC*?

(A) 2 cm

(B) 4 cm

(C) 6 cm

(D) 8 cm

(E) 10 cm

(F) 12 cm

FOR QUESTION 20, ENTER YOUR ANSWER IN THE BOXES.

---

20. If *AB* and *BD* are equal lengths and *ABDC* is a rectangle, what is the ratio of the area of triangle *CED* to the area of rectangle *ABDC*?

Give your answer as a fraction.

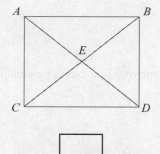

STOP

If you finish before the time is up, you may check your work in this section only.

ANSWER KEY AND EXPLANATIONS

Section 1: Analytical Writing

Analyze an Issue

Model: 6 points out of 6

It no doubt sounds ideal that every citizen of the United States know and understand the fundamental document on which our nation is based. After all, the U.S. Constitution is the principle document from which we derive our rights and freedoms as citizens. The Constitution encapsulates the workings of a great democracy that has become a beacon and a model to many other countries. Its words represent the wisdom of our founders and the ideals of our leaders and citizens.

Yet, is it really necessary to informed citizenship to know every article of the Constitution so well and pass a test on it? Does informed citizenship rely on this and this alone? It seems to me that anyone can Google and read the Constitution at any time. Whatever the issue may be, whether it is the right to bear arms, the meaning of due process, or the history of prohibition, the exact words of the Constitution on that topic are just a few clicks away. With the tendency to carry mobile devices for accessing information becoming ever more common, there is less and less need to know information about the Constitution or any other topic just for the sake of knowing it; all one really needs to know is how to find and interpret information. Furthermore, if we spend time in our schools on memorizing documents, even very important ones, that is less time we have to spend on more important skills such as finding information, and analyzing, interpreting, and evaluating it. Knowing and spitting back information on a test is not enough; a student must process and draw his or her own conclusions. An exam based on the Constitution with specific questions on each article is highly unlikely to require or foster such skills.

Moreover, is informed citizenship necessarily good citizenship or the best citizenship? I would argue that engaged, active citizenship is just as important as informed citizenship, and that one can engage in cleaning up one's community or other good-citizen tasks quite effectively without knowing even one article or word of the central document of our democracy. In addition, all citizens can exercise their duties as citizens by voting thoughtfully and responsibly; performing jury duty; paying taxes; and serving one's country in the military if called upon without knowing every article—or perhaps any article—of the Constitution. There are, naturally, exceptions, and those who seek a career in public service should know the Constitution well. But does a person who designs landscape, performs physical therapy, or creates apps need complete familiarity with the Constitution? It would scarcely seem so. And even if that landscape designer, physical therapist, or app creator could rattle off every article on command, just exactly how enriched would our democracy be by that? If we want more informed and better citizens, let's spend more time, not less, on the thinking skills that actually matter.

This essay scores 6 out of 6 because it

- **answers the task.** It clearly tells the extent to which it disagrees with the claim (that all U.S. students should read and learn the U.S. Constitution well enough to be able to pass an exam), and it competently disputes the reason on which it is based (that such an exam would produce better informed citizens or that being better informed about the Constitution makes a better citizen).

- **is well supported.** The essay offers specific, accurate examples of what one might know about the Constitution, as well as persuasive examples of what a citizen might do well without knowing about the Constitution. Throughout the essay, support and development are abundant, clear, and convincing.

- **is well organized.** Paragraph 1 leads smoothly into the main attack on the claim; paragraphs 2 and 3 effectively refute the reason for the claims, thereby refuting the claim itself. Each paragraph is a well organized, discrete, and unified unit, with the third paragraph leading smoothly to closure. Several transitional words and phrases help create coherence.

- **is fluid, precise, and graceful.** Sentences are varied throughout, with many effective uses of questions. Words are precise and varied.

- **observes the conventions of Standard Written English.**

Model: 1 point out of 6

It is very important to know and understand the constitution, it is the most important document of our nation and a very important document in the world. It is very wrong when some politicians do not know about the constitution. They do not know what freedoms it gives us. They do not know about freedom of speech and religion and so on.

I would be proud of a study of the constitution and know about the constitution and to answer questions about every article. I think this should be the part of the education of every student because it will make all better informed. I think it would make all proud to know the constitution and it's articles, too.

We will know more about the jobs in goverment of the differant people at the voting, so we will be able to chose better people for the jobs. We will also understand the news better when the supreme court decides constitutional or unconstitutional. We will also better understand what is happening when congress makes laws or the President takes actions.

This essay scores 1 out of 6 because it

- **answers only part of the task and reflects little or no insight.** It conveys the extent to which it disagrees with the claim (that all U.S. students should read and learn the U.S. Constitution well enough to be able to pass an exam), but it offers little or no meaningful insight into how that would make people better informed.

- **is poorly supported.** The essay is seriously limited and flawed in terms of support. In fact, it does not support claims. Rather, it basically repeats the prompt and supplies simple, illogical, or unsubstantiated support. For example, it suggests that being able to pass a test on the Constitution would make people able to vote in a more informed matter (why would that be so? and would it apply to state and local elections?) and able to understand the constitutionality of issues before the Supreme Court (would that necessarily be the case? why?). Its claims go unanswered.

- **is not organized well.** While paragraphs 1 and 2 exhibit some unity and coherence, the information in paragraph 3 consists of examples that should be used to support sentence 2 of paragraph 2. Both the opening and closing lack the sophistication and focus of a higher-scoring essay.

- **has poorly constructed sentences.** There is little variety in sentence structure and many sentences begin with "I" and "We."

- **has some major and minor errors in the conventions of Standard Written English.** Despite these problems, the low score does not result mainly from problems with conventions; rather, it results mainly from lack of insight and development; most fundamentally, the essay lacks content.

Analyze an Argument

Model: 6 points out of 6

Upbeat and affirmative, Skybold (or its representative) appears to want to sound as visionary, decisive, and forward-looking in this argument as its name suggests. Certainly, it presents and "envisions" ideas that many readers could wish were true. What company would not want to institute a policy with such desirable and money-saving benefits? Yet, many questions must be answered in order to evaluate the conclusion that "Skybold's new telecommunicating policy is clearly a win-win situation."

First among questions to be addressed are those that probe the exact statistics about fewer sick days and personal days. By what precise number or percent have the number of sick and personal days diminished? Could that diminishment be due to factors other than the new work-at-home policy? Furthermore, over what span of time has this diminishment been measured? For example, if the policy has been in place for three months, and the absenteeism rate has truly dropped significantly over that period of time, could that not be accounted for by the fact that the policy is new? Once it is in place for a year or several years, will the same rates hold true? For the claims to have logical weight, the results surely should have held true for some long span of time, such as a year or more. These answers would help evaluate the conclusion that the policy is a "win" for Skybold.

Specific questions must also be asked in order to interpret the fabulous, though unsubstantiated, claims of greater employee satisfaction and enhanced employee loyalty. Have employees completed questionnaires about greater satisfaction? How many employees are actually more satisfied? Exactly how was the assertion of greater employee loyalty arrived at? Or does Skybold just assume this to be true? Is there any quantifiable data that exists to substantiate these claims? Finally, even if the claims are true, one must consider the dampening effects on satisfaction and loyalty should an employee have his or her desk removed at work and, consequently, be forced to share a space, or use someone else's space, on those days when he or she does not telecommute. Would he or she experience "greater employee satisfaction" then? The answers to all the questions raised in this paragraph would help evaluate the conclusion that the policy is a "win" for employees.

Perhaps the most important questions of all have to do with the writer's motivation and point of view. Was this argument written by the person who instituted the policy, perhaps as a bit of self-aggrandizement? What is the purpose, and just exactly who is the audience for this seeming self-congratulation? The answers to these questions might help peel away the outer layers of argument to expose a propagandistic core.

This essay scores 6 out of 6 because it

- **answers the task.** With sophistication and perceptiveness, the response raises questions that would have to be answered in order to evaluate the conclusion and the reasons on which it is based. The questions are not only apt, but they are offered in abundance.

- **is well supported.** In this case, the support is the questions, as well as the way in which they are introduced, explained, and related back to the writer's evaluative purpose. Although there are many other questions that could be asked, the ones that appear here are logically sound and presented with clarity and rhetorical effect.

- **is well organized.** The essay is a tour de force of good organization, with its attention-provoking opening that not only draws the reader in, but clearly states the claim of the argument. The three remaining paragraphs offer discrete, well-developed analyses of major points and concerns, and lead skillfully to the final "most important" issues of author, purpose, and audience.

- **is fluid, precise, and graceful.** Sentences are varied throughout, with many effective uses of questions. The essay is a trove of particularly well-chosen words and phrases, from "visionary," "institute," and "probe" to the "propagandistic core" and its accompanying metaphor.

- **observes the conventions of Standard Written English.**

Model: 2 points out of 6

Many questions must be asked about the many claims made in this argument. The first about if there was a remarkable surge in productivity. This being an interesting claim that is not explained. In order to evaluate if there was a remarkable surge in productivity, you should ask how much the production of the creative staff people had went up and basing that on the before and after figures of production of those workers, so that you would know if productivity doubled, or if it went up by 50% or if it went up by .05%, the exact amount being crucial to knowing if the policy resulted in a remarkable surge in productivity. Other questions you must ask and answer being about why Skybold brought about its new policy, after all, if the employees were upset that they couldn't ever telecommute, as so many employees do these days, then it only stands to reason that they were happier when they could finally get to telecommute. This would also help you evaluate the claim that there was a remarkable surge in productivity because the telecommuters now felt better about getting to telecommute after not being let to work from there homes before.

This essay scores 2 out of 6 because it

- **does not fully answer the task.** This essay never evaluates the conclusion that Skybold's new telecommuting policy is a win-win situation. While it does begin to raise and support interesting and logical questions about the reasons on which that conclusion is based, it falls well short of presenting a full analysis.

- **lacks organization.** This single paragraph lacks one clear focus. The response fails to divide main ideas into separate, cogent units of discourse.

- **has poorly constructed sentences.** Sentences are convoluted, lacking punctuation and subordination that result in meaningless jumbles of words.

- **contains major errors in the conventions of Standard Written English.** Some of these errors are serious enough to obstruct meaning.

Section 2: Quantitative Reasoning

1. A	11. B, D, G	16. E
2. C	12. D	17. B
3. C	13. A	18. D
4. D	14. B	19. 105
5. B	15. A, C, F, H	20. C
6. A		
7. B		
8. D		
9. B		
10. D		

Question

1.

Quantity A	Quantity B
$6\dfrac{7}{8}$	$3.42(2)$

(A) Quantity A is greater.

(B) Quantity B is greater.

(C) The two quantities are equal.

(D) The relationship cannot be determined from the information given.

Answer Explanation

The correct answer is (A).

$6\dfrac{7}{8} = 6.875$

$3.42(2) = 6.84$

Quantity A is greater.

QUESTIONS 2–4 REFER TO THE DIAGRAM BELOW.

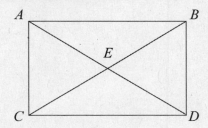

Question

ABCD is a rectangle.

E is the intersection of *AD* and *BC*.

2.   <u>Quantity A</u>   <u>Quantity B</u>
                  the area of △*CED*   the area of △*AEC*

(A) Quantity A is greater.
(B) Quantity B is greater.
(C) The two quantities are equal.
(D) The relationship cannot be determined from the information given.

Answer Explanation

The correct answer is (C). Any values that are assigned to the side lengths of the figure will result in the two areas being equal. This is true for both whole and fractional values.

Question

3.   <u>Quantity A</u>   <u>Quantity B</u>
              m∠*ACD* + m∠*CDB*   m∠*AEC* + m∠*CED*

(A) Quantity A is greater.
(B) Quantity B is greater.
(C) The two quantities are equal.
(D) The relationship cannot be determined from the information given.

Answer Explanation

The correct answer is (C). Angles in the corners of rectangles are equal to 90°, so any two added together will equal 180°. Angles formed by the bisection of a line by another line equal 180°; so Quantity A is equal to Quantity B.

Question

4.   Quantity A   Quantity B
     $(AB)^2 + (BD)^2$ AD

(A) Quantity A is greater.

(B) Quantity B is greater.

(C) The two quantities are equal.

(D) The relationship cannot be determined from the information given.

Answer Explanation

The correct answer is (D). If whole number values are assigned to the side lengths of this right triangle, then answer choice (A) would be correct. If fractional or decimal values (less than 1) are assigned to the side lengths of this right triangle, then answer choice (B) would be correct. Therefore the correct answer is (D).

Question

$$y < x < 0$$

5.   Quantity A   Quantity B
     $|x|$ $|y|$

(A) Quantity A is greater.

(B) Quantity B is greater.

(C) The two quantities are equal.

(D) The relationship cannot be determined from the information given.

Answer Explanation

The correct answer is (B). Since y is less than x which is less than 0, when we take the absolute value of x and y, y will always be greater than x.

Question

$$a > b > 0$$

6.   Quantity A   Quantity B
     $a^2 - b^2$ $(3a + 3b)(-2a + 2b)$

(A) Quantity A is greater.

(B) Quantity B is greater.

(C) The two quantities are equal.

(D) The relationship cannot be determined from the information given.

Answer Explanation

The correct answer is (A). Factor Quantity A and multiply Quantity B to find the comparison:

$$a^2 - b^2 = (a + b)(a - b)$$

$$(3a + 3b)(-2a + 2b) = -6(a + b)(a - b) = -6(a^2 - b^2)$$

Since $a > b > 0$, $a^2 - b^2$ will always be positive, and $-6(a^2 - b^2)$ will always be negative.

Question

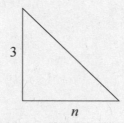

The area of the triangle is 15.

7.   Quantity A   Quantity B
                         n 12

(A) Quantity A is greater.

(B) Quantity B is greater.

(C) The two quantities are equal.

(D) The relationship cannot be determined from the information given.

Answer Explanation

The correct answer is (B). The area of a triangle is $\frac{1}{2} b \times h$ so using the working backwards strategy:

$\frac{1}{2}$ (3)(n) = 15, so n = 10

Question

$$x^2 = 9$$

8.   Quantity A   Quantity B
                         x −3

(A) Quantity A is greater.

(B) Quantity B is greater.

(C) The two quantities are equal.

(D) The relationship cannot be determined from the information given.

Answer Explanation

The correct answers is (D).

$x^2 = 9$

$x^2 - 9 = 0$

$(x + 3)(x - 3) = 0$

$x = 3, -3$

Since x can be either 3 or −3, Quantity A can be both equal to and less than Quantity B.

Question

9. The local pastry shop sells its doughnuts for $1.90 each, and the shop owner makes an 8% profit on each. How much profit would the owner make if she sold 15 doughnuts?

   (A) $0.15
   (B) $2.28
   (C) $28.50
   (D) $1.12
   (E) $3.45

Answer Explanation

The correct answer is (B). This is a question where turning verbose or abstract language into something concise and concrete will help you.

$15 \times \$1.90 \times 0.08 = \$2.28$

Question

10. A regular, six-sided die is rolled three times. What is the probability that each of the three rolls will produce an odd number?

   (A) $\frac{1}{2}$

   (B) $\frac{1}{3}$

   (C) $\frac{1}{6}$

   (D) $\frac{1}{8}$

   (E) $\frac{1}{216}$

Answer Explanation

The correct answer is (D). Three of the die's six sides feature odd numbers, so the probability that any given roll will produce an odd number is $\frac{3}{6}$, or $\frac{1}{2}$. Each roll of the die is independent of the others, so the probability that each of the three rolls will produce an odd number is $\frac{1}{2} \times \frac{1}{2} \times \frac{1}{2}$, or $\frac{1}{8}$.

Question

11. Find the next 3 numbers in the sequence. 1, 1, 2, 3, 5, 8, ….

- (A) 12
- (B) 13
- (C) 14
- (D) 21
- (E) 22
- (F) 33
- (G) 34
- (H) 55

Answer Explanation

The correct answers are (B), (D), and (G). You can find the next number by adding the last two numbers in the sequence.

$5 + 8 = 13$

$8 + 13 = 21$

$13 + 21 = 34$

Question

12. Let $f(x) = 2x^3 - x^2 + 7$. Find $f(3)$.

- (A) 25
- (B) 19
- (C) 16
- (D) 52
- (E) 54

Answer Explanation

The correct answer is (D). To evaluate the function $f(x) = 2x^3 - x^2 + 7$ for $f(3)$:

$$f(3) = 2x^3 - x^2 + 7$$
$$= 2(27) - 9 + 7$$
$$= 54 - 9 + 7$$
$$= 52$$

Question

13. Solve: $4(3x - 5) = x + 3$

 (A) $x = \dfrac{23}{11}$

 (B) $x = \dfrac{8}{11}$

 (C) $x = \dfrac{2}{3}$

 (D) $x = -4$

 (E) $x = 23$

Answer Explanation

The correct answer is (A). Solve the equation $4(3x - 5) = x + 3$.

$12x - 20 = x + 3$

$11x = 23$

$x = \dfrac{23}{11}$

Question

14. Find the value of x.

 (A) $55°$
 (B) $35°$
 (C) $90°$
 (D) $145°$
 (E) $125°$

Answer Explanation

The correct answer is (B).

$90 = 55 + x$

$35 = x$

Question

15. List all the factors of 51.

 (A) 1
 (B) 2
 (C) 3
 (D) 7
 (E) 16
 (F) 17
 (G) 48
 (H) 51

Answer Explanation

The correct answers are (A), (C), (F), and (H). 51 is odd, so eliminate answers (B), (E), and (G). That leaves 1, 3, 7, 17, and 51. Divide 51 by each:

$51 \div 1 = 51$, so 1, 51 are factors.

$51 \div 3 = 17$, so 3, 17 are factors.

$51 \div 7 = 7.3$, not a factor.

QUESTIONS 16–18 ARE BASED ON THE FOLLOWING DATA.

Annual State Budgets (in millions of dollars)

	2009	2010	2011	2012	2013	2014, est
State A	53.0	75.9	85.5	101.6	131.2	142.1
State B	14.4	14.5	20.0	19.0	39.2	43.5

Question

16. What is the ratio of the total (State A and State B) estimated budget of 2014 to 2009's budget?

 (A) 33.7 : 92.8
 (B) 142.1 : 53.0
 (C) 43.5 : 14.4
 (D) 14.4 : 43.5
 (E) 92.8 : 33.7

Answer Explanation

The correct answer is (E).
$142.1 + 43.5 = 185.6$
$53.0 + 14.4 = 67.4$
$\dfrac{185.6}{67.4} = \dfrac{92.8}{33.7} = 92.8 : 33.7$

Question

17. What is the total budget for State A for 2009, 2010, and 2013?
    - (A) 68.1
    - (B) 260.1
    - (C) 268
    - (D) 276.4
    - (E) 308.7

Answer Explanation

The correct answer is (B).

$53.0 + 75.9 + 131.2 = 260.1$

Question

18. What year had the biggest percentage increase from the previous year in State B and what was the percentage increase?
    - (A) 2011, 138%
    - (B) 2013, 206%
    - (C) 2011, 37%
    - (D) 2013, 106%
    - (E) 2014, 11%

Answer Explanation

The correct answer is (D). Estimate the difference from year to year, and then calculate the percentage. The difference between 2012 and 2013 is more than double and none of the other amounts is even close, so 2013 is the year.

$39.2 - 19.0 = 20.2$
$20.2 \div 19.0 = 106\%$

Question

19. Mary went to the convenience store with $20. She wanted to buy a newspaper for $1.25, a magazine for $6.50, a soda for $1.75, and then spend the rest of her $20 on dime candy. How many pieces would she get?

$$\boxed{}$$

Answer Explanation

The correct answer is 105.

$20 - (1.25 + 6.50 + 1.75) =$ amount spent on candy

$20 - (9.50) = 10.50$

$10.50 \div 0.10 = 105$

answers diagnostic test

Question

20. If p is the greatest prime number that is a factor of 51, and q is the smallest prime number that is a factor of 58, then $p + q =$

(A) 5
(B) 17
(C) 19
(D) 32
(E) 46

Answer Explanation

The correct answer is (C). The factors of 51 are 1, 3, 17, and 51, so the greatest prime number that is a factor of 51 is 17. Next, the smallest prime number that is a factor of 58 is 2 because 58 is an even number. The sum of 17 and 2 is 19.

Section 3: Verbal Reasoning

1. C	11. D	16. A, D
2. B, F	12. E	17. C, E
3. A, F	13. B, C	18. C, E
4. B, D, G	14. C	19. A, F
5. B, C	15. E	20. B
6. E		
7. A		
8. D		
9. A		
10. B		

Question

1. The unsophisticated nature of research tools affects the _____ and validity of market research into the potential market for products and programs.

(A) accountability
(B) acceptability
(C) reliability
(D) liability
(E) approval

Answer Explanation

The correct answer is (C). "Reliability" means "dependability and consistency," both characteristics required for sound, or valid, market research data. Choice (A), "accountability," means "capable of being accountable" as a person is for her/his actions. It doesn't fit the context, nor does choice (B), "acceptability," which means "satisfactory or merely adequate." The meaning is not strong enough to balance "valid." Choice (D), "liability," makes no sense because it means either "an obligation" or "a handicap." Choice (E), "approval," is also incorrect; it means "the formal agreement" of something. Substituting the answer choices in the blanks can help you determine the correct answer.

Question

2. That Jane Austen's satiric wit is lost on some readers is (i) _____ because it is so (ii) _____ as to become caricature; for example, consider the Rev. Collins in *Pride and Prejudice*.

Blank (i)
(A) logical
(B) understandable
(C) inexplicable

Blank (ii)
(D) flashy
(E) showy
(F) overdrawn

Answer Explanation

The correct answers are (B) and (F). Answer Blank (i): Choice (A), "logical," means "capable of reasoning in a clear and consistent manner" and may seem correct. But choice (B), "understandable," is a better choice between the two because it means "capable of being understood." In the context of the sentence, the writer is not reasoning something out, but stating his/her opinion. Choice (C), "inexplicable," means "impossible to explain, incomprehensible." It is the opposite of "understandable." In the context of the entire sentence, the word does not fit the meaning, and so, is incorrect.

Answer Blank (ii): In choosing answers for text completion items, consider the style and tone of the text. Choices (D) and (E), "flashy" and "showy," don't fit either. Only choice (F), "overdrawn," meaning "exaggerated" fits the meaning.

Question

3. As a result of overconfidence and a number of (i) _____ errors in judgment to employ a(n) (ii) _____, the majority party in the state legislature became the minority party in the last election.

Blank (i)
(A) embarrassing
(B) inconvenient
(C) upsetting

Blank (ii)
(D) paradox
(E) aphorism
(F) euphemism

Answer Explanation

The correct answers are (A) and (F). Answer Blank (i): Choice (B), "inconvenient," means "hard to reach" in one sense and "troublesome or difficult" in another sense. In this instance, it would be a euphemism for a stronger qualifier. The same is true of "upsetting," choice (C). Neither are strong enough descriptors based on the information in the sentence.

Answer Blank (ii): Choice (D), "paradox," means "something that is contradictory." It doesn't fit the context. An aphorism, choice (E), is a saying or adage, so it's incorrect because "error in judgment" isn't an aphorism, but it is a euphemism, substituting a mild or inoffensive term for a harsh or blunt term.

Question

4. One consequence of the desire among modern playwrights to bring (i) _____ to the theater has been the diminution of poetry as a dramatic language. On the other hand, realism in language has brought a (ii) _____ end to rant and rhetoric upon the stage. As one critic wrote, modern playwrights have been pushed to develop plays that are (iii) _____ and convincing when they could no longer rely on "verbal pyrotechnics."

Blank (i)	Blank (ii)	Blank (iii)
(A) vibrancy	(D) welcome	(G) more forceful
(B) verisimilitude	(E) final	(H) more cerebral
(C) resemblance	(F) limited	(I) more believable

Answer Explanation

The correct answers are (B), (D), and (G). Answer Blank (i): Context will help you complete this blank. This is also an instance when you might find it easier to begin by filling in one of the other blanks. Choice (A) doesn't make sense in the context because poetry would add vibrancy to the theater, but the sentence says that the position of poetry has been diminished in modern plays. Choices (B) and (C) are somewhat similar in meaning, but choice (C), "resemblance," doesn't make sense if you read it in the sentence. Choice (B), "verisimilitude," meaning "something that has the appearance of being real," is the answer by the process of elimination.

Answer Blank (ii): Choice (E), "final," is redundant; an end is final. Choice (F), "limited," doesn't make sense; how can you have a limited end? Choice (D), "welcome," is the correct answer by the process of elimination, but more importantly because it means "giving pleasure."

Answer Blank (iii): The word that you're looking for has to balance "convincing." Choice (I), "more believable," is similar to "more convincing," so choosing it would be redundant. There is nothing in the passage to indicate that modern plays should be "more cerebral" [choice (H)] because playwrights can't use rant and rhetoric. Choice (G), "more forceful," meaning "effective," is the best choice.

QUESTIONS 5–7 ARE BASED ON THE FOLLOWING PASSAGE.

The *New York Times* has boldly declared the end of the car culture in the United States. It based its claim on a few salient facts. The number of miles driven dropped steadily between 2005 and 2013. Over an even more extended period, rates of automobile ownership declined. The *Times* also charted changing attitudes toward driving and car ownership by young people,
5　quoting one study that showed a 23-percent decrease in driving among young people. Car sharing, bikes, and public transit were among the reasons cited for this decrease.

But is the automobility of American culture actually over, or is it just in the slow lane? It is true that the era of massive road building projects not only seems to be over, but also actually peaked as long ago as 1980. It is also true that environmental and social factors, as well as
10　the overcrowding of our roads and highways, are shaping new attitudes across all segments of society. During the past two decades, public transportation use has grown at a far faster rate than the population. Another significant factor in the declining number of miles driven has to do with our aging population; over many years, the number of miles driven has been shown to decline by age 45. Vehicle costs as a percentage of income have also been rising
15　since the mid-90s. While all of these data do not prove the end of cars, they may point to the end of the driving boom that characterized twentieth-century America.

Question

5. The passage suggests that the decline in driving is authenticated by which of the following?

   (A) A 23-percent decline in car ownership among young people

   (B) The end of the era of massive road building projects

   (C) The steady drop in the number of miles driven

Answer Explanation

The correct answers are (B) and (C). The passage explicitly states that the era of massive road-building projects peaked in 1980 and has been in decline since then, so choice (B) is correct. The author also explicitly presents a steady drop in the number of miles driven in recent years, so choice (C) is also correct. Choice (A) is incorrect because the passage says that there is a 23-percent drop in driving, not car ownership, among young people.

Question

6. It can be inferred from the passage that the author most likely thinks that the *Times* writer used the term "the end of car culture" because it

   (A) offered the clearest wording to contradict the phrase "automobility of American culture."

   (B) generalized the facts about U.S. driving trends in the most succinct and appropriate way.

   (C) created a new and appropriate catchphrase for referring to changes in driving.

   (D) summarized a number of recent studies and elucidated their results accurately.

   (E) reflected some current data and employed enough hyperbole to create interest.

Answer Explanation

The correct answer is (E). The author's contention is most likely that car culture isn't over, but rather that the twentieth-century boom in driving is over. Nevertheless, the author is not discrediting the *Times*'s facts; instead, the author is suggesting that the conclusions drawn from them are overblown. The reader might also infer that a dramatic phrase such as "the end of car culture" was meant to attract attention. Choice (A) is incorrect because nothing in the passage suggests or implies it. Choice (B) could be true, but does not explain the sensational phrase "end of the car culture." Choice (C) is not supported by passage facts. Choice (D) is tempting because the data presented by the *Times* sounds reasonable enough, but it is incorrect because such data do not justify the term "end of the car culture."

Question

7. In the second paragraph, the author is primarily concerned with

   (A) mitigating the *Times*'s assertion that car culture is at an end.

   (B) explaining why the number of miles driven has declined recently.

   (C) presenting reasons for a changing demographic of car ownership.

   (D) disputing the claim that car ownership is in significant decline.

   (E) offering further proof for the *Times*'s claim that the car culture is over.

Answer Explanation

The correct answer is (A). The author begins the paragraph with a question and ends it with an assertion about the end of the twentieth-century boom in driving, rather than the end of the car culture. In between, the author offers many facts about the decline, rather than the end, of the automobile. Choices (B), (C), and (D) are all incorrect because the paragraph does not elucidate any single point presented by the *Times*. Instead, it offers new facts about the decline of the automobile. Choice (E) is tempting because the paragraph does offer further proof; nevertheless, all the proof it offers is bracketed by sentences that suggest that the *Times*'s conclusion about the end of the automobile needs to be mitigated, moderated, or softened.

QUESTIONS 8 AND 9 ARE BASED ON THE FOLLOWING PASSAGE.

The connections between the brain, the digestive system, and food behaviors have been subject to increasing scrutiny and the focus of much research over the past few years. It is now understood that the brain is updated via signals from the digestive system's own enteric nervous system (ENS) about both nutrient content and fullness. Influenced by the central
5 nervous system (CNS), the ENS relies on many CNS neurotransmitters to send chemical signals about digestion and to affect ongoing food intake. Different nerve endings transmit varying information to the brain, some of which provide information about stretch or tension, in response to food volume, and some of which provide information about nutrient content. CNS and ENS cross connections ensure not only that the gut informs the CNS but that signals
10 from outside the nervous system can be relayed back to the gut. In addition, it is known that different peptides may be released in the presence of certain nutrients and play different feedback roles to the brain. **As Abigail Pepin of the National Institute of Health notes, "There are multiple interactions among systems that coordinate overall gastrointestinal (GI) function leading to changing GI states."**

Question

8. This passage suggests that the sensation of fullness is the result of which of the following?
   (A) Stretching and tension that result from too much eating
   (B) CNS reliance on ENS neurotransmitters
   (C) The role of the CNS in monitoring nutrient content
   (D) Chemical signals that travel to the brain
   (E) Varying ENS nutrient-content signals

Answer Explanation

The correct answer is (D). Sentence 3 says that the ENS sends chemical signals about digestion (which, as the context makes clear, includes food volume); sentence 1 says that these chemical signals are sent to the brain and influence food behaviors. Choice (A) is incorrect because, while the passage says that stretching and tension occur in response to volume, it also says that there is an intervening transmission of information that must be received by the brain. Choice (B) may seem correct, but the passage says the ENS relies on many CNS transmitters and not vice versa. Choices (C) and (E) are incorrect because the passage distinguishes nutrient content from fullness.

Question

9. Which of the following best characterizes the function of the boldfaced sentence in lines x–x of the passage?

(A) It provides evidence on which a theory is based.

(B) It presents a specific application of a general concept.

(C) It restates a point made earlier in the passage.

(D) It disproves a commonly accepted theory.

(E) It summarizes general passage information.

Answer Explanation

The correct answer is (E). This statement sums up the passage because, as it names "interactions among systems," it suggests ENS and CNS interaction; specific nerve-ending and brain interactions; and feedback roles played by the presence of peptides. Choice (A) is incorrect because it does not give evidence. Choice (B) is incorrect because there is no application. Choice (C) is incorrect because overall summary terms such as "gastrointestinal (GI) function" are used. Choice (D) is incorrect because the information suggests fact, not theory.

QUESTIONS 10–12 ARE BASED ON THE FOLLOWING PASSAGE.

Dutch artist M.C. Escher's work covers a variety of subjects, though he is probably best known for the pieces that he drew from unusual perspectives, which result in enigmatic effects. During the course of his life, Escher adopted a highly mathematical approach, using special notations that he invented himself, including a system for categorizing shapes, colors,
5 and symmetrical properties. Looking at his work, you can see clearly that mathematics played an important role in the development of his distinctive style, yet though he studied and admired various mathematical theories over the years, Escher did not consider himself a mathematician. However, this lack of formal training allowed him to explore mathematics in a unique way, without having to adhere to any set rules or restrictions. In 1958, he wrote:
10 "In mathematical quarters, the regular division of the plane has been considered theoretically . . . . [Mathematicians] have opened the gate leading to an extensive domain, but they have not entered this domain themselves. By their very nature they are more interested in the way in which the gate is opened than in the garden lying behind it."

Question

10. What material would help to support the intersection of art and mathematics in Escher's work?

(A) Escher's notebooks containing his mathematical notations

(B) A painting of Escher's demonstrating his use of mathematical principles in his art

(C) Art criticism of Escher's works

Answer Explanation

The correct answer is (B). One of Escher's paintings would prove that his art went beyond the theories of mathematics and actually expressed the beauty of it. Choice (A) is incorrect because they would not demonstrate how Escher created art from theories of mathematics. Choice (C) might or might not indicate an awareness of the mathematical underpinnings of Escher's work and, therefore, is not a viable answer.

Question

11. From the passage, what is Escher's view of mathematicians?
    - (A) They do not grasp how mathematics and art are interconnected.
    - (B) They will never have the ability to appreciate Escher's art.
    - (C) They cannot translate their theories into their own personalized notations.
    - (D) They will never be able to translate their theories into art.
    - (E) They cannot see the beauty that is inherent in their theories.

Answer Explanation

The correct answer is (E). By saying that mathematicians are only interested in the way the gate is opened but not the garden lying behind it, Escher is pointing out that they are only interested in how their theories work but not in how their theories can be expressed artistically. Choices (A) and (B) are incorrect because even if they might be true about some mathematicians, Escher does not imply this in the quote. Choice (C) is incorrect because Escher never addresses the personalized notations of other mathematicians. Choice (D) is incorrect because although Escher believes that mathematical theories can be expressed artistically, he does not imply that mathematicians need to do this, just that they are not interested in doing so.

Question

12. In the passage, "enigmatic" (line 2) means
    - (A) rational.
    - (B) inscrutable.
    - (C) comprehensible.
    - (D) decipherable.
    - (E) theoretical.

Answer Explanation

The correct answer is (B). "Enigmatic" in this passage means "inscrutable, or mysterious." Choice (A) is incorrect because something can be enigmatic without being rational. Choices (C) and (D) are incorrect because if something is comprehensible or decipherable, it is easy to read and not mysterious. Choice (E) is incorrect because "theoretical" means "hypothetical or speculative," which is not the same as inscrutable.

QUESTIONS 13–15 ARE BASED ON THE FOLLOWING PASSAGE.

Because of our federal system, voting rights for women were conferred and denied at different times in our history. Observers with a twenty-first century perspective might be quick to speculate that states with the most progressive reputations prior to the passage of the Nineteenth Amendment would have been the first to grant suffrage to women, but the first
5 state to confer full voting rights was Wyoming in 1890. In doing so, it was only following the forward-looking precedent it had itself set in 1869, when, as a territory, it granted women full voting rights. In fact, while the movement for suffrage seemed to have a decidedly East Coast epicenter, the West led the way in women's suffrage. Washington Territory had been the first to introduce a suffrage bill in 1848, and the West generally led the East in conferring

10   women's suffrage. In fact, in 1914, all states west of the Rockies had granted full suffrage,
     whereas only one state east of them had, and that was not an acknowledged progressive
     or liberal bastion such as New York or Massachusetts, but Kansas. It should, however, be
     noted that women in Illinois were granted the right to vote for president, but not full voting
     rights, in 1913. Among those states that granted full suffrage to women only after passage of
15   the Nineteenth Amendment were Virginia, Georgia, Alabama, Kentucky, and New Mexico.

Question

13. What does the passage imply about why the West led the way in conferring women's suffrage
    prior to the Nineteenth Amendment?
    (A) The West was acting in accordance with the mandates of our federal system.
    (B) The region was more forward-looking in this regard than states that are often considered
        to be progressive today.
    (C) The action was surprising, given that the political activism for suffrage was centered
        elsewhere.

Answer Explanation

The correct answers are (B) and (C). The passage does suggest that the actions of the West might
have been more reasonably expected, at least from a twenty-first century perspective, to have arisen
in the East. The passage also calls the East the epicenter of the women's suffrage movement. Choice
(A) is incorrect because the federal system did not require or mandate such an action, or any action
in this regard, on the part of any Western state at that time in history.

Question

14. Select the sentence in the passage that does NOT add to the support for the main idea of the
    passage.
    (A) In doing so, it was only following the forward-looking precedent it had itself set in 1869,
        when, as a territory, it granted women full voting rights.
    (B) In fact, in 1914, all states west of the Rockies had granted full suffrage, whereas only
        one state east of them had, and that was not an acknowledged progressive or liberal
        bastion such as New York or Massachusetts, but Kansas.
    (C) Among those states that granted full suffrage to women only after passage of the
        Nineteenth Amendment were Virginia, Georgia, Alabama, Kentucky, and New Mexico.

Answer Explanation

The correct answer is (C). The reference to New Mexico, a Western state, does not support the thesis
that the West was, curiously, where the earliest women's suffrage was granted. Choice (A), which
refers to the Western state of Wyoming as granting early suffrage, and Choice (B) both explain and
support the thesis. Remember that to answer a "NOT" question, like an "EXCEPT" question, you
need to find the answer that doesn't match the information.

Question

15. In the passage, "federal" (line 1) most nearly means relating to
    (A) a central government.
    (B) the North in the Civil War.
    (C) a military representative of the government.
    (D) a government with strong central powers.
    (E) a government with shared powers.

Answer Explanation

The correct answer is (E). The context makes it clear that the federal system allowed states to make laws independently of one another. Choice (A) is incorrect because a single, unified, or national system would have meant the conferring of suffrage all at once. Choices (B) and (C) are legitimate meanings of "federal," but they do not make sense in the context. Choice (D) is incorrect because states clearly acted separately and not as a single, centralized power.

Question

16. In shuttering programs to reduce costs, the new CFO was _____ toward employees and refused to listen to their concerns and alternative suggestions.
    (A) arrogant
    (B) unkind
    (C) uncharitable
    (D) dismissive
    (E) contentious
    (F) confrontational

Answer Explanation

The correct answers are (A) and (D). Choice A, "arrogant," means "displaying an exaggerated opinion of one's self-worth; being self-important" and choice (D), "dismissive," means "showing disregard, being disdainful of others." Both fit the context of the sentence. Choices (B) and (C) are also synonym pairs, and while the new CFO was undoubtedly "unkind" and "uncharitable" toward employees, the word "refused" in the sentence indicates that these two words are not strong enough; they also aren't typically used to describe business dealings. Choices (E) and (F) are also synonym pairs, but the word "refused" indicates that the CFO cut off communication so that there was no occasion for being either "contentious" or "confrontational," both of which mean "argumentative and quarrelsome."

Question

17. Green building, that is, the construction of new buildings and the renovation of existing ones to make them eco-friendly, is a fast-growing segment of the construction industry and one that ALLIED Builders hopes to _____ according to its five-year business plan.

(A) promote

(B) advance

(C) capitalize on

(D) upgrade

(E) exploit

(F) endorse

Answer Explanation

The correct answers are (C) and (E). "Capitalize on" and "exploit," choices (C) and (E), mean "take advantage of, make the most of." Choices (A) and (B), "promote" and "advance," both mean "to put forward, to aid the growth of." In the context of a business plan, the pair don't fit the sense. Choices (D) and (E) are not synonyms, and neither is a synonym of the other words in the list. "Upgrade" means "to improve," and "endorse" means "to approve."

Question

18. The original intention in creating NASA was to explore space, but many of the products people take for granted today, such as cordless power tools and sunglasses with polarized lenses, resulted from _____ research that NASA conducted for the space program.

(A) far-reaching

(B) wide-ranging

(C) innovative

(D) unusual

(E) cutting-edge

(F) conventional

Answer Explanation

The correct answers are (C) and (E). Although you may be confused that the answer choices contain three synonyms: innovative, unusual, and cutting-edge, choices (C), (D), and (E), you can eliminate choice (D) because the characteristic of being unusual is not so strong as being either innovative or cutting edge, the correct answers. Choice (A), "far-reaching," and choice (B), "wide-ranging," are synonyms, but the implication from the first part of the sentence is that NASA conducted research related to the space program, so that it wasn't doing research over a wide number of fields of study. You can eliminate choice (F) because NASA by the nature of its program wouldn't be conducting conventional research.

Question

19. Many researchers believe that _____ bacteria keep harmful bacteria from invading humans by using the material that harmful bacteria need to live.

    (A) helpful
    (B) malignant
    (C) pathogenic
    (D) benign
    (E) benevolent
    (F) beneficial

Answer Explanation

The correct answers are (A) and (F). From the context of the sentence, you can tell that choices (B) and (C), "malignant" and "pathogenic," are incorrect. The blank that you need to complete must be the opposite of the word "harmful," and both "malignant" and "pathogenic" are harmful. Choice (D), "benign," is incorrect because it means "harmless, having little or no effect, showing mildness." Choice (E) is incorrect because "benevolent" means "doing good, showing goodwill" and refers to people and organizations. The context requires two words that have a good effect, choices (A) and (F), "helpful" and "beneficial."

QUESTION 20 IS BASED ON THE FOLLOWING PASSAGE.

Emily Dickinson, a poet virtually unknown in her lifetime, wrote some of the most memorable lines in American poetry. Her poems are instantly recognizable for their brevity (they are often no longer than 20 lines) and their quirky punctuation and capitalization. Her frequent and often idiosyncratic use of the dash serves to emphasize many of her recurrent topics. A great
5 number of Dickinson's almost 1,800 poems deal with the themes of death and immortality, though her poems are also filled with joy and hope. Because of its unusual syntax and use of figurative language—imagery, metaphor, personification—Dickinson's poetry can seem to the uninitiated reader something of a puzzle. Present-day readers would do well to renounce a literal way of reading in order to truly appreciate Dickinson's poetry.

Question

20. What does the author imply by the last statement in the passage?

    (A) Readers should not try to find literal meaning in Dickinson's poetry.

    (B) Readers of poetry today are not used to so much figurative language.

    (C) Readers should try to figure out what themes were most important to Dickinson.

    (D) Readers who try to unlock the mysteries of Dickinson's figurative language are doing themselves a disservice.

    (E) Readers of poetry today need to consider the context in which Dickinson's poetry was written.

Answer Explanation

The correct answer is (B). Choice (B) most closely describes what the author implies: modern readers are not used to figurative language and could have a difficult time making sense of Dickinson's work. Choice (A) is incorrect because the author doesn't suggest that modern readers should not look for literal meaning in Dickinson's work, just that it might be a little difficult to do so. The author would likely agree with choice (C), but it doesn't reflect the last statement in the passage. Choice (D) contradicts what the author is implying in the last sentence. Choice (E) doesn't relate to anything in the passage.

Section 4: Verbal Reasoning

1. C	11. A	16. B
2. D	12. E	17. C
3. A, E	13. B, E	18. B
4. A, D, I	14. C, D	19. D
5. B, E, I	15. A, C	20. B
6. B		
7. C		
8. A		
9. C		
10. D		

Question

1. Social networking is a marketing tool that many companies are harnessing to sell their products; however, it must be used _____ because the hard sell risks offending potential customers.

(A) with ease
(B) actively
(C) judiciously
(D) expeditiously
(E) efficiently

Answer Explanation

The correct answer is (C). The clue to the correct answer is the phrase "hard sell"; the context of the sentence indicates that you need to find the word that indicates some opposite action. Choice (C), "judiciously," means "showing good judgment, being prudent," and matches the sense. Choice (A), "with ease," doesn't quite fit the sense; you can do a hard sell easily. The same problem occurs with choice (B), "actively." Choice (D), "expeditiously," means "efficiently and quickly," and is incorrect because doing a hard sell efficiently and quickly doesn't make it any more palatable to the consumer. Nor does being simply efficient, choice (E).

Question

2. In composing "Scheherazade," Rimsky-Korsakov hoped to _____ the "magical spirit" of *One Thousand and One Nights*, a collection of exotic folk tales from the Middle East and South Asia.

(A) motivate
(B) induce
(C) inspire
(D) evoke
(E) provoke

Answer Explanation

The correct answer is (D). To evoke, choice (D), means "to bring to mind or suggest," in this case metaphorically. Choice (A), "motivate," which means "to provide an incentive," doesn't make sense in the context of the sentence. Nor does choice (B), "induce," meaning "to lead or cause to happen." Inspiring the spirit doesn't make sense either, so eliminate choice (C). To provoke, choice (E), means "to incite or irritate," which doesn't make sense.

Question

3. Garraty states that the problems faced by private colleges in the 1820s and 1830s were of their own making to a degree. Many cities and towns wanted the (i) _____ of hosting a college, but the supply of colleges soon (ii) _____ the demand, that is, the number of potential students.

Blank (i)	Blank (ii)
(A) honor	(D) outperformed
(B) admiration	(E) outstripped
(C) character	(F) outshone

Answer Explanation

The correct answers are (A) and (E). Answer Blank (i): "Honor" means "respect, distinction, privilege" and fits the sense of the sentence. Choice (B), "admiration," means "a feeling of pleasure or approval," but doesn't fit in the sentence because the context usually references the source of the admiration, that is, "towns wanted the admiration of other cities for hosting a college." In the sentence, however, it's the college that admires the town, which makes no sense. Choice (C) is incorrect because none of the many meanings of "character" fits the sense.

Answer Blank (ii): Choice (E), "outstripped," means "to surpass, to grow greater or faster and leave behind," which fits the sense. Choice (D) is incorrect because "outperform" means "to perform better" and the sense of the discussion of supply and demand requires a quantitative response. The same reason makes choice (F), "outshone," incorrect.

Question

4. The nation-states of early modern Europe guarded their sovereignty (i) _____, finding countless reasons—real and (ii) _____—for wars. Peace (iii) _____ only when one nation managed to subdue its neighbors.

Blank (i)	Blank (ii)	Blank (iii)
(A) jealously	(D) feigned	(G) occurred
(B) intolerantly	(E) facetious	(H) mediated
(C) liberally	(F) deceptive	(I) intervened

Answer Explanation

The correct answers are (A), (D), and (I). Answer Blank (i): Choice (A), "jealously," meaning in this case "vigilantly," fits the sense of fighting to keep one's authority and territory. Choice (B) is incorrect because "intolerantly" means "unwilling to tolerate, that is, allow or respect, differences" and is not strong enough to match the context of warfare, though intolerance led to warfare. Choice (C) can mean "freely" in the sense of giving freely or generous and so doesn't match the context.

Answer Blank (ii): Choice (D), "feigned," means "fake, made up, fictitious" and counterbalances "real" in the parenthetical expression. Choice (E), "facetious," means "humorous, playful" and is a distractor for "fictitious." Choice (F), "deceptive," though meaning "capable of deceiving" doesn't necessarily mean fake.

Answer Blank (iii): This set of answers is a good example of why you should read all the answers. You might jump at choice (G), "occurred," because it does make sense in the context that peace occurred, but choice (I), "intervened," is a better choice because it identifies peace as happening in between bouts of warfare. Choice (H) is incorrect because "mediate" means "to resolve differences or bring about a settlement between two parties."

Question

5. The speaker, a former prosecutor turned politician, remains direct, candid, and (i) _____ in her assessment of policy, but she can also be (ii) _____ and offhand toward her colleagues. She is considered a/n (iii) _____ legislator.

Blank (i)	Blank (ii)	Blank (iii)
(A) frank	(D) rough	(G) very ambitious
(B) pragmatic	(E) brusque	(H) really approachable
(C) rigid	(F) brisk	(I) no-nonsense

Answer Explanation

The correct answers are (B), (E), and (I). Answer Blank (i): You're looking for a word that logically completes the description of the speaker. Eliminate choice (A) because "frank" means the same as "candid." Choice (C), "rigid," doesn't have the same sense as "direct" and "candid," which leave "pragmatic," meaning "practical, guided by experience and observation." One synonym is "hard-nosed."

Answer Blank (ii): In this set of descriptors, you need one that fits with "offhand." Choice (D), "rough," in this sense means "coarse, rude, inconsiderate" which may seem to fit, but choice (E), "brusque," meaning "abrupt or blunt in manner or speech," fits better with the earlier description and with "offhand," which it is meant to balance. Choice (F), "brisk," means "lively, quick" and doesn't fit the context.

Answer Blank (iii): The speaker may be very ambitious, choice (G), but there is nothing in the passage to support this, so eliminate it. Everything about the description, especially the second set of descriptors, indicates that the speaker is not approachable, choice (H). That leaves choice (I), "no-nonsense," that completes the passage logically.

QUESTIONS 6 AND 7 ARE BASED ON THE FOLLOWING PASSAGE.

Access to clean drinking water and sanitation systems are crucial global goals. This access constitutes a fundamental health and human dignity issue. Expanding sewage systems will also reduce contamination of soil, rivers, and oceans, thereby promoting biodiversity and decreasing land degradation. Furthermore, access to clean water will reduce geopolitical
5 conflict centered on water rights. In addition, commitment to clean water goals promotes investment in new technologies, such as desalination and water reuse.
    Even though the United Nations reported that between 1990 and 2010, more than "2 billion people gained access to improved water sources, and 1.8 billion gained access to improved sanitation," a more recent global assessment warns that significant problems continue to
10 plague the world. Despite well-coordinated global initiatives, the latest U.N. report discusses factors that slow the progress toward clean water goals. These include the failure of some countries to set national hygiene standards, inadequate funding or poor absorption of existing funding, lack of skilled labor to implement change, and lack of political will. Only 80% of nations recognize the right to water; only some 50% recognize the right to sanitation.

Question

6. Based on the passage, which of the following is NOT a factor that is delaying progress toward clean water goals?
    (A) failure of some nations to set national hygiene standards
    (B) inability to manage skilled labor resources at water sites
    (C) inadequate funding for global water initiatives
    (D) failure to properly use all available water funding
    (E) reluctance of some nations to consider water as a right

Answer Explanation

The correct answer is (B). Choices (A), (C), (D), and (E) are all mentioned in the passage as factors that are delaying progress toward clean water goals. The passage mentions that not enough skilled labor is available, and not that there is a problem in managing skilled labor. Remember: for "NOT" questions, you're looking for the answer choice that doesn't fit.

Question

7. Select the sentence in the passage that is NOT a supporting detail for a central idea.

   (A) This access constitutes a fundamental health and human dignity issue.

   (B) Expanding sewage systems will also reduce contamination of soil, rivers, and oceans, thereby promoting biodiversity and decreasing land degradation.

   (C) Despite well-coordinated global initiatives, the latest U.N. report discusses factors that slow the progress toward clean water goals.

Answer Explanation

The correct answer is (C). This information, while important, is actually a main idea and the topic sentence of the second paragraph. Choices (A) and (B) are both important points that support the topic sentence of the first paragraph: access to clean water and sanitation are crucial global goals.

QUESTIONS 8 AND 9 ARE BASED ON THE FOLLOWING PASSAGE.

Propaganda on the U.S. home front took many forms during World War I. Encouraging the public to buy bonds to fund the war, getting young men to enlist, and inspiring anyone who could to volunteer were not its only motives. For example, a poster called "20 at Home to 1 in the Trenches," published by the National Industrial Conservation Movement in 1918,
5   clearly sends the message that "American industry can and will win this war for human liberty." Through words and pictures, it describes the multiple and monumental efforts required at home to food, clothe, and arm each U.S. soldier abroad. But it also intersperses the admonition that "Breeders of industrial war at home must be eliminated" before ending with "National co-operation is the slogan to insure victory for Democracy over Autocracy."
10 In this poster and other publications, the National Industrial Conservation Movement sought to celebrate the so-called "fair-minded working man" who, it assured its audience, wanted no friction between labor and capital.

Question

8. Select the statement that restates the premise of the author's argument.

   (A) Propaganda merged the interests of big business with the higher ideals of the war effort.

   (B) Americans who worked in industry during World War I tended to be both fair-minded and patriotic.

   (C) Propaganda subverted the interests of the war effort to the interests of American business.

   (D) Americans were subjected to anti-democratic and autocratic propaganda.

   (E) Propaganda took many forms on the home front during World War I.

Answer Explanation

The correct answer is (A). The author's argument is that propaganda did not just support the war effort, but took other forms as well. The poster it describes promotes the workingman's effort in service of the political goal but also sends an anti-labor, anti-unionist message that is good for big business. While the National Industrial Conservation Movement appealed to the worker as "fair-minded," Choice (B), the author uses this as a detail in support of the idea of propaganda. Choice (C) is tempting, but the author suggests that the propaganda both supported the war effort and the interests of big business/industry. Choice (D) is contradicted by the poster quotation, which celebrates democracy over autocracy. Choice (E), while true, is a detail used to lead into the main idea and not the main idea itself.

Question

9. Which of the following, if it were true, would weaken the author's argument?

(A) During World War I, many Americans went to work in factories producing military supplies.

(B) The majority of American workers supported the war effort and the role of big business in feeding, clothing, and arming soldiers.

(C) The National Industrial Conservation Movement also published many posters that did not promote big business or send anti-union messages.

Answer Explanation

The correct answer is (C). If the National Industrial Conservation Movement had simply promoted the war, it would have still published propaganda, but not self-interested propaganda that rode on the coattails of patriotic feeling. Choice (A) is neutral or supportive: it merely contributes the idea that many Americans were the potential audience of such propaganda. Choice (B) neither weakens nor strengthens the argument because it does not address either National Industrial Conservation Movement propaganda or the workers' susceptibility to its specific underlying anti-union, pro-business message.

QUESTIONS 10–12 ARE BASED ON THE FOLLOWING PASSAGE.

The increasing awareness of lighting inefficiency and the billions of dollars of potential annual energy savings that can be achieved by switching to LED lighting has resulted in many government-funded research initiatives around the world. In addition, governments in the United States, Canada, Europe, and Australia have responded to the growing need for energy
5 conservation by passing legislation that regulates or eliminates the sale of incandescent and halogen light bulbs by a certain date. However, though increasing consumers' awareness of the inefficiency of other light sources can help increase the adoption of LED lighting, regulations that focus on enforcing energy-efficient lighting are likely to work better. One example is California's Energy Efficiency Standards for Residential and Nonresidential Buildings, or
10 Title 24, that provides a set of mandatory regulations covering all aspects of new building construction. The Residential Lighting section of Title 24 requires that a high-efficiency light source be used in several areas of the home, including the kitchen and bathrooms, and that all outdoor light fixtures must either use energy-efficient bulbs, or must be controlled by light and motion sensors.

Question

10. This passage achieves all of the following purposes EXCEPT it

(A) implies that LED lighting will become a necessity of the future.

(B) explains one way governments are forcing people to switch to LED lighting.

(C) cites a regulation that enforces the use of high-efficiency light sources.

(D) describes how LED lighting is more energy efficient than incandescent lighting.

(E) implies that government-funded research on energy efficiency is essential.

Answer Explanation

The correct answer is (D). The passage doesn't describes how LED lighting works and what makes it more energy efficient than incandescent lighting, so choice (D) is the correct answer. Choices (A), (B), (C), and (E) are all achieved in the passage.

Question

11. The author introduces California's Title 24 in order to
    (A) support the concept that the government needs to set rules to increase the adoption of LED lighting.
    (B) provide a possible explanation for why more Americans have adopted LED lighting.
    (C) reinforce the concept that other methods of lighting are less efficient than LED lighting.
    (D) introduce the idea that governments need to enforce rules about high efficiency lighting in residential buildings.
    (E) cast doubt on studies that show that Americans are not eager to switch to LED lighting.

Answer Explanation

The correct answer is (A). The author's point is that government needs to set rules to increase the adoption of LED lighting and uses Title 24 as an example of states' doing this. Choice (B) is incorrect because Title 24 doesn't explain why more Americans have adopted LED lighting; instead it illustrates how it can be done. Choice (C) is incorrect because although LED lighting is more efficient, this is not why the author specifically introduces Title 24. Choice (D) is incorrect because the author never specifically states anything about the importance of high efficiency lighting in residential buildings; this is merely described by Title 24. Choice (E) is incorrect because studies showing Americans are not eager to switch to LED lighting are not introduced in this passage.

Question

12. "Mandatory" (line 10) most nearly means
    (A) provisional.
    (B) permanent.
    (C) predetermined.
    (D) discretionary.
    (E) obligatory.

Answer Explanation

The correct answer is (E). "Mandatory" means about the same as "obligatory," meaning "compulsory or required." Choice (A) is incorrect because "provisional" means "temporary," which is not the same as "required." Choice (B) is incorrect because "permanent" means "fixed," which is also not the same as "required." Choice (C) is incorrect because "predetermined" means "determine in advance or to influence in a certain way," which doesn't fit the context. Choice (D) is incorrect because "discretionary" means "optional," which is the opposite of mandatory.

Question

13. If life did exist on other planets, scientists theorize that it would not _____ life on Earth. For example, depending on the wavelengths of light given off by the plant, plants could be red, yellow, or green.

    (A) epitomize

    (B) mimic

    (C) illustrate

    (D) typify

    (E) imitate

    (F) reflect

Answer Explanation

The correct answers are (B) and (E). Choices (B) and (E), the synonyms "mimic" and "imitate," mean "to copy, to resemble." Choices (A) and (D) are a synonym pair, meaning "to be a typical example of," which is not exactly the same as imitating, which fits the sense better. Choice (C), "illustrate," means "to clarify, to present an example" and doesn't fit the sense, nor does it have a synonym among the answer choices. Choice (F), "reflect," meaning "to make apparent or show an image of," has neither a synonym in the list nor fits the sense.

Question

14. Scientists believe that unlocking the genome is _____; it will forever change the way we diagnose, treat, and someday even prevent disease.

    (A) modernization

    (B) reforming

    (C) revolutionary

    (D) transformative

    (E) huge

    (F) corrective

Answer Explanation

The correct answers are (C) and (D). The phrase "forever change" in the second part of the sentence is the clue that identifies "revolutionary" and "transformative," choices (C) and (D). Both indicate radical change. Choice (A), "modernization," is also a form of change, but it doesn't fit the context. Choice (B), "reforming," may seem correct because it means "to change for the better," but it doesn't have the connotation of radical change that is implied in the sentence. Choice (E), "huge," is a vague word that doesn't indicate the nature of the change. Choice (F) is incorrect because "corrective" implies that something was wrong and needed to be fixed, and that's not what is implied in the sentence.

Question

15. Many of his critics complain that once they finish reading his books with their convoluted plot lines, they are no wiser and their brains perhaps even more _____.

(A) befogged

(B) taxed

(C) muddled

(D) weakened

(E) wary

(F) heedful

Answer Explanation

The correct answers are (A) and (C). The sense of the sentence is that reading convoluted books doesn't make the reader any more intelligent, but it does make his/her brain tired or confused. Choices (A) and (C), "befogged" and "muddled," fit the sense of confused. Choice (B), "taxed," fits the idea of tired, but there is no synonym for it in the list of answer choices, so eliminate it. Don't be fooled by choice (E), "wary," which on a fast read might look like "weary"; "wary" means "cautious." "Heedful" is a loose synonym of "wary," but neither makes sense. Choice (D), "weakened," might work, but there is no synonym for it in the list.

QUESTIONS 16–18 ARE BASED ON THE FOLLOWING PASSAGE.

The use of specially designed eye-tracking technology for measuring the response of children ages two months to twenty-four months old has recently yielded valuable information for those hoping for earlier intervention in autism spectrum disorder (ASD). Using the technology to discern changes not apparent with the naked eye, researchers studied responses to social,
5 facial cues from a friendly caregiver or mother-like figure. Infants in the study were siblings of children on the autism spectrum; such children are at high risk for ASD. While levels of eye contact were the same initially among the youngest experimental subjects, eye contact steadily declined among those who were later diagnosed with autism, but it increased for those who were not. Study results suggest that diagnoses of ASD, or more specifically, signs
10 pointing toward an ASD diagnosis, might now be detected at between two and six months of age; the disorder is now more typically diagnosed when a child is between the ages of three and five years.

Question

16. Which of the following best describes the author's opinion of the research she reports?

(A) Unbiased objectivity

(B) Guarded optimism

(C) Unchecked enthusiasm

(D) Slight pessimism

(E) Complete negativity

Answer Explanation

The correct answer is (B). Through the use of the phrase "yielded valuable information" and the contrast presented in the final sentence about detection, the author subtly embraces the results; yet, she maintains a serious, not jubilant tone, and refrains from the use of word choices that exult. Therefore, she exhibits guarded optimism. Choice (A) seems like the correct choice, except that the judgment word "valuable" would be missing from a completely unbiased report. Choice (C) is incorrect because the tone is not celebratory, and Choices (D) and (E) are incorrect because the author does not exhibit even a trace of negativity or pessimism.

Question

17. Which of the following opinions does the passage most clearly support?
    (A) It is now possible to diagnose ASD at the age of two months.
    (B) Siblings of children with ASD are more likely to be diagnosed with ASD.
    (C) Significantly earlier detection of signs of ASD is now possible.
    (D) Siblings of children with ASD are more likely to increase their emotional responses over time.
    (E) Changes in emotional response are discernible by caregivers and mother-like figures.

Answer Explanation

The correct answer is (C). The passage clearly states, in the final sentence, that signs of ASD can now be detected at between two and six months of age and, by means of contrast, shows that this is "significantly" earlier than the current norm of between three and five years. Choice (A) might seem correct, but earliest detection appears to occur within a range of ages and not necessarily always at two months of age. Choice (B) is not an opinion; it is presented as a fact that underpinned the experimental procedure. Choice (D) is wrong not only because the passage suggests the opposite, but also because it is presented as a finding rather than an opinion. Choice (E) confounds passage details: caregivers and mother-like figures were used in the study, but they were not discerning changes.

Question

18. What function does the descriptive information, "ages two months to twenty-four months old," (line 2) serve in the passage?
    (A) It characterizes the group in which early signs of ASD can now be discerned.
    (B) It defines the group with which the study was conducted.
    (C) It identifies the age group most at risk for an ASD diagnosis.

Answer Explanation

The correct answer is (B). The first age group mentioned in the passage is the one that was tested rather than the one to whom the findings are applicable, Choice (A). Choice (C) is incorrect because, among other reasons, the group most at risk for an ASD diagnosis is defined otherwise in the passage.

QUESTIONS 19 AND 20 ARE BASED ON THE FOLLOWING PASSAGE.

Unpleasant and even distasteful as they can be, attack ads actually serve a purpose in our culture: they illuminate issues of character, and the character of our public officials does, in fact, matter. Recently pinpointed by political columnist Matt Bai as originating in 1987 with presidential candidate Gary Hart, the era of scandal journalism, into which the attack
5 ad so neatly fits, ended the era of "good old boy" conspiracy, when the media often knew of the many sins and personal peccadilloes of the president, presidential candidate, or other elected official, but chose to keep that information secret. While attack ads may divert the electorate from issues to matters of personal choice and lifestyle and even adversely affect voter turnout, they nevertheless expose moral and significant choices made by the potential
10 leader of the free world, congressional representative, or other candidate or nominee. If used judiciously with other ads that focus on issues, attack ads and so-called "scandal journalism" that expose questionable moral and individual choices show the media wielding its First Amendment right and serving the purposes of the electorate. More pragmatically, campaigns may be induced to employ attack ads because they work. Unfortunately, practicality is no
15 endorsement, for even when the right or better-qualified candidate assumes public office, undesirable means do not justify the end.

Question

19. The word "wielding" (line 12) most nearly means
    (A) bearing.
    (B) abusing.
    (C) intoning.
    (D) exerting.
    (E) misapplying.

Answer Explanation

The correct answer is (D). In this context, "wielding" means about the same as "exerting" or "exercising." Choice (A) is incorrect because "wield" means to bear in the sense of authority, and not simply to bear, as in to carry, or any of the word's other meanings. Choice (B) is incorrect because the context makes it clear that what is justifiably or appropriately wielded is a right. Choice (C) is incorrect because "intoning" has to do with utterances or a song, which does not match the context clues of using something to expose moral and individual choices. Choice (E) is incorrect because "misapplying" suggests the opposite of judiciously using a First Amendment right.

Question

20. Which of the following expresses the author's thesis about attack ads?
    (A) They adversely affect voter attitudes and turnout.
    (B) They serve a useful, rightful purpose in our elections.
    (C) They have ended an era of conspiratorial and negative secrecy.
    (D) They are both granted and restricted by the First Amendment.
    (E) They are generally negative as the end cannot justify the means.

Answer Explanation

The correct answer is (B). The thesis or main idea presented by the author is that, despite some problems, attack ads are useful, important, and legitimate. Choices (A) and (C) are tempting, but both name supporting details rather than the overall main idea or thesis, and this question requires you to focus on the word "thesis." Choice (D) is incorrect because the author does not state or suggest that attack ads should be restricted; rather, the author only invokes the First Amendment right to their use. Choice (E) is tempting because the author suggests the problem of the end not justifying the means, but the author characterizes the use of attack ads as generally positive rather than generally negative.

Section 5: Quantitative Reasoning

1. A	11. A	16. E
2. D	12. D	17. D
3. B	13. 48	18. C, D, E
4. B	14. D	19. A, F
5. C	15. C	20. $\frac{1}{4}$
6. A		
7. D		
8. D		
9. A		
10. B		

Question

1.

Quantity A	Quantity B
0.324875	$\frac{10}{31}$

(A) Quantity A is greater.

(B) Quantity B is greater.

(C) The two quantities are equal.

(D) The relationship cannot be determined from the information given.

Answer Explanation

The correct answer is (A). Change $\frac{10}{31}$ into a decimal: 0.32258, which is less than 0.324875.

Question

2.

Quantity A	Quantity B
$|x|$	$|y|$

(A) Quantity A is greater.

(B) Quantity B is greater.

(C) The two quantities are equal.

(D) The relationship cannot be determined from the information given.

Answer Explanation

The correct answer is (D). With no parameters set for x or y, there is no way to determine a relationship between the two.

Question

Mary is twice as old as Stephen. Stephen is 5 years older than Joe. Joe is $\frac{3}{4}$ of Mary's age. All three were born in the twenty-first century.

3.   Quantity A   Quantity B
          Mary's birth year   Joe's birth year

(A) Quantity A is greater.

(B) Quantity B is greater.

(C) The two quantities are equal.

(D) The relationship cannot be determined from the information given.

Answer Explanation

The correct answer is (B). Because Mary is the oldest, she will have a birth year that is less than either Joe or Stephen.

Question

A try is worth 5 points. A conversion is worth 2 points. A penalty goal is worth 3 points.

4.   Quantity A   Quantity B
      3 tries, 2 conversions, 1 penalty   24

(A) Quantity A is greater.

(B) Quantity B is greater.

(C) The two quantities are equal.

(D) The relationship cannot be determined from the information given.

Answer Explanation

The correct answer is (B). Evaluate each quantity:

$3(5) + 2(2) + 3 = 15 + 4 + 3 = 22$

22 is less than 24.

Question

5.   Quantity A   Quantity B
                 x 115

(A) Quantity A is greater.

(B) Quantity B is greater.

(C) The two quantities are equal.

(D) The relationship cannot be determined from the information given.

Answer Explanation

The correct answer is (C). Supplementary angles equal 180°.

$180° = 65° + x$

$115° = x$

Question

6.   Quantity A   Quantity B

           $-\dfrac{15}{16}$ $-\dfrac{16}{15}$

(A) Quantity A is greater.

(B) Quantity B is greater.

(C) The two quantities are equal.

(D) The relationship cannot be determined from the information given.

Answer Explanation

The correct answer is (A). $-\dfrac{15}{16}$ is greater than -1 and $-\dfrac{16}{15}$ is less than -1.

Question

There are 15 players on Team 1. There are 22 players on Team 2.
There are more offensive players than defensive players on each team.

7.   Quantity A   Quantity B
          Number of goalies on Team 1   Number of goalies on Team 2

(A) Quantity A is greater.

(B) Quantity B is greater.

(C) The two quantities are equal.

(D) The relationship cannot be determined from the information given.

Answer Explanation

The correct answer is (D). There is no way to know the number of goalies on each team.

Question

$$\frac{y}{x} = 3$$

$$x, y \neq 0$$

8.   Quantity A   Quantity B
                          x y

(A) Quantity A is greater.

(B) Quantity B is greater.

(C) The two quantities are equal.

(D) The relationship cannot be determined from the information given.

Answer Explanation

The correct answer is (D). Pick some numbers and evaluate:

If $y = 12$, then $x = 4$. If $y = -12$, then $x = -4$

Question

9. Evaluate the function $f(x) = 5x^3 + 4x^2 + 8x + 1$, when $x = 2$.

   (A) 73

   (B) −11

   (C) 183

   (D) 117

   (E) −73

Answer Explanation

The correct answer is (A). Evaluate the function:

$$f(x) = 5x^3 + 4x^2 + 8x + 1$$
$$f(2) = 5(8) + 4(4) + 8(2) + 1$$
$$f(2) = 40 + 16 + 16 + 1$$
$$f(2) = 73$$

Question

10. Solve the equation $4xy + 8y = 128$ for x, when $y = 4$.

    (A) $x = 10$

    (B) $x = 6$

    (C) $x = 1$

    (D) $x = 12$

    (E) $x = 32$

Answer Explanation

The correct answer is (B). Solve for x:

$$4xy + 8y = 128$$
$$4x(4) + 8(4) = 128$$
$$16x + 32 = 128$$
$$16x = 96$$
$$x = 6$$

Question

11. If $\dfrac{3}{x-1} = \dfrac{6}{3x+6}$, then $x =$

    (A) -8

    (B) -1

    (C) 0

    (D) 1

    (E) 8

Answer Explanation

The correct answer is (A). Solve for x:

$$\frac{3}{x-1} = \frac{6}{3x+6}$$

$$3(3x+6) = 6(x-1)$$

$$9x + 18 = 6x - 6$$

$$3x = -24$$

$$x = -8$$

Or, work backwards from the answer choices:

$$\frac{3}{x-1} = \frac{6}{3x+6}$$

$$\frac{3}{-8-1} = \frac{6}{-24+6}$$

$$\frac{3}{-9} = \frac{6}{-18}$$

$$-\frac{1}{3} = -\frac{1}{3}$$

Question

12. A new model hybrid car gets 45 miles per gallon for city driving and 20% more for highway driving. How many miles per gallon does the hybrid get for highway driving?

   (A) 34
   (B) 46
   (C) 51
   (D) 54
   (E) 58

Answer Explanation

The correct answer is (D). Turn the verbose language into concise and concrete terms to help you solve this problem.

$$45(0.20) = 9$$

$$45 + 9 = 54$$

Question

13. Find the area of the trapezoid.

Answer Explanation

The correct answer is 48. Redraw the diagram to show all the information that you need.

$$6 \times 6 = 36$$
$$\frac{1}{2} 6 \times 4 = 12$$
$$36 + 12 = 48$$

QUESTIONS 14–16 REFER TO THE TABLE BELOW.

Number of Children per Family in a Neighborhood

Number of Children	Number of Families
1	19
2	36
3	21
4+	9
0	15

Question

14. What is the total number of families that have no more than two children?

(A) 19

(B) 36

(C) 55

(D) 70

(E) 81

Answer Explanation

The correct answer is (D). Using the information from the table, add the families having 0, 1, and 2 children:

$$19 + 36 + 15 = 70$$

Question

15. What is the percentage of families who have no children?

(A) 9%

(B) 12%

(C) 15%

(D) 18%

(E) 21%

Answer Explanation

The correct answer is (C). Using the information from the table, there are $19 + 36 + 21 + 9 + 15$ = 100 total families and there are 15 families with no children, so $\frac{15}{100} = 0.15$, or 15%.

Question

16. What percentage of the families has 6 children?

(A) 19

(B) 9

(C) 15

(D) 12

(E) unknown

Answer Explanation

The correct answer is (E). There is no information given on the number of families with 6 children.

Question

17. In the xy-plane, what is the slope of a line that is perpendicular to the line whose equation is $x + 2y = 5$?

    (A) -2

    (B) $-\dfrac{1}{2}$

    (C) $\dfrac{1}{2}$

    (D) 2

    (E) 5

Answer Explanation

The correct answer is (D). Since the lines are perpendicular, the product of their slopes must equal -1.

First, rewrite the given equation in slope-intercept form:

$$x + 2y = 5$$
$$2y = -x + 5$$
$$y = -\frac{1}{2}x + \frac{5}{2}$$

The given equation's slope is $-\dfrac{1}{2}$, the coefficient of x. Therefore, the slope you're looking for is 2.

Question

18. What is the x-coordinate of the point at which the graphs of the equations $x + 2y = 4$ and $y - x = 2$ intersect?

    (A) -8

    (B) -2

    (C) 0

    (D) 2

    (E) 16

Answer Explanation

The correct answer is (C). The point at which the two lines intersect lies on the graph of both equations. Therefore, you have a system of two linear equations, and you're looking for the value of x in the solution to the system. First, solve the second equation for y: $y - x = 2 \Rightarrow y = x + 2$. Now substitute this expression of y into the first equation:

$$x + 2y = 4$$
$$x + 2(x + 2) = 4$$
$$x + 2x + 4 = 4$$
$$3x = 0$$
$$x = 0$$

Question

19. In triangle *ABC*, the length of side *AB* is 4 cm and the length of side *BC* is 8 cm. Which of the following could be the length of side *AC*?

(A) 2 cm

(B) 4 cm

(C) 6 cm

(D) 8 cm

(E) 10 cm

(F) 12 cm

Answer Explanation

The correct answers are (C), (D), and (E). Let *x* be the length of side *AC*. According to the triangle inequality, *x* is greater than (and not equal to) the positive difference of the lengths of the other two sides, and it is less than (and not equal to) the sum of the lengths of the other two sides:

$$8 - 4 < x < 8 + 4$$
$$4 < x < 12$$

Question

20. If *AB* and *BD* are equal lengths and *ABDC* is a rectangle, what is the ratio of the area of triangle *CED* to the area of rectangle *ABDC*?

Give your answer as a fraction.

Answer Explanation

The correct answer is $\frac{1}{4}$. Since *ABDC* is a rectangle and sides *AB* and *BD* are equal, *ABDC* is a square. The diagonals of a square form 4 equivalent triangles, so the ratio of triangle *CED* to the rectangle *ABDC* is $\frac{1}{4}$.

PART III

ANALYTICAL WRITING

The Issue Task

OVERVIEW

- Basic information about the Issue Task
- Understand the prompt: the issue
- Understand the prompt: the writing instructions
- Understand the scoring rubric
- Review the anatomy of an issue essay
- Create your writing plan
- A final note of caution
- Issue prompt with six model responses, scoring, and analyses
- Summing it up

The Analytical Writing section of the GRE® revised General Test measures both your ability to think and your ability to write in response to two kinds of prompts: the Issue Task and the Argument Task. The Issue Task assesses how well you can develop and support your own position on an issue, and the Argument Task evaluates how well you can analyze someone else's argument. This chapter will focus on the Issue Task.

To respond to the Issue Task, you will need to take a position either agreeing or disagreeing with an issue and defend your position with evidence. As part of that defense, you may be required to counter potential arguments of others. The issue prompt presents you with a brief statement of a general issue and sets the conditions under which you can respond to it. That is, you may agree or disagree with the statement, but you must discuss certain aspects of the issue based on the accompanying instructions. The issue will be one that anyone can respond to, such as whether or not it's morally justifiable to spend resources on a pet.

This chapter describes the Issue Task and the possible instructions that may accompany it and reviews the components of a successful issue essay. The chapter ends with a sample Issue Task and six models that are analyzed and scored using a rubric based on the GRE® rubric for the Issue Task.

chapter 4

BASIC INFORMATION ABOUT THE ISSUE TASK

The Analytical Writing section is always first in any administration of the GRE® revised General Test. For many test-takers, it is probably a relief to have it out of the way early so they no longer have to worry about it. However, reviewing the basics of the Issue Task, as well as the basic organization and development of a response, will help your confidence and your score.

Type of Question

The Issue Task presents you with one issue that you may agree or disagree with, but you must do one or the other. You can't be neutral, and you will have no choice of issues from which to choose. The purpose of the Issue Task is to measure how well you can stake out a position and develop your reasoning to support it. That support has to be developed according to certain conditions contained in a set of instructions that accompany the prompt. The instructions, which are described in more detail later in this chapter, may require you to

- explain how the issue might or might not hold true in some cases.
- examine examples that could be used to challenge your position on an issue.
- discuss why you disagree with a claim and the reasoning that underpins the claim.

Typically, the issue statement is very short compared to the argument prompt. The issue is usually stated in a single sentence, and it's always of a general nature that anyone could respond to. No special knowledge is required. ETS states that the claim made in the issue statement is one that can be discussed "from various perspectives" and applied "to many different situations or conditions."

Time Limit and Software

The Issue Task, like the Argument Task, has a time limit of 30 minutes. This is the same for both the computer-based version and the paper-and-pencil version.

The word processing program on the computer version allows the test-taker to insert and delete text, cut and paste text, and undo actions. A spell checker and grammar checker are not included. Similarly, those taking the paper-and-pencil version will not have access to dictionaries or grammar handbooks during the test.

Scoring

The Issue Task has its own rubric. You'll work through the rubric for the Issue Task later in this chapter. Like the Argument Task, Issue Tasks are scored on a scale from 0 to 6. The average of the two scores is taken to arrive at a combined score from 0 to 6 in half-point increments. This is the score that is reported to graduate and business schools.

UNDERSTAND THE PROMPT: THE ISSUE

The issue prompt has two parts, and you'll probably see a line of space between the two parts. The first part of the issue prompt states one side of an issue. For example, it might suggest that everyone start paying entrance fees to the public museums and institutions that are currently free in Washington, D.C. The issue will be stated briefly and simply, most likely in just one sentence.

UNDERSTAND THE PROMPT: THE WRITING INSTRUCTIONS

The second part of the prompt is the instructions that set the conditions for your response. It begins with the words "Write a response. . . ." The instructions will ask you (1) to take a position, qualifying it, as you want to or need to, by extent or degree and (2) to explain and support your position. The prompt may also ask you to explain your position in relation to one of the following:

- Conditions/circumstances under which the statement of your position might not be true
- Circumstances when the recommendation would not have the intended results
- Likely and major challenges to your position
- Views both for and against your position
- The reason on which the claim is based
- The possible consequences of taking action based on your position

The actual wording of the sets of instructions will be somewhat similar to the following:

- Discuss how much you agree or disagree with the statement and why, as well as considering how the statement might or might not always be true and how these considerations affect your point of view.
- Discuss how much you agree or disagree with the recommendation and why. Using specific examples, explain how the circumstances under which the recommendation could be adopted would or would not be advantageous. In developing and supporting your viewpoint, explain how these specific circumstances affect your point of view.
- Discuss how much you agree or disagree with the claim and include the most compelling reasons and/or examples that someone could use to dispute your point of view.
- While addressing both viewpoints provided, discuss which more closely aligns with your own. Explain your reasoning for holding this position in developing and providing evidence for your response.
- Discuss how much you agree or disagree with the claim and the reasoning used to support that claim.
- Discuss your viewpoint on the proposed policy and the reasons for your point of view. Take into consideration the potential consequences of implementing the policy and the extent to which these consequences influence your viewpoint in developing and supporting your response.

As with the argument prompt, you must take care to focus on the specific requirements in the instructions. You could present a well-reasoned and well-supported position, but if you fail to present views both for and against your position as the prompt asks, you won't earn a high score.

UNDERSTAND THE SCORING RUBRIC

Before we go any further, let's look at the scoring rubric for the Issue Task against which your response will be evaluated. Like your argument essay, your issue essay will be scored on a 6-point

ALERT!

ETS states that the goal of the Analytical Writing section on the GRE® revised General Test is to elicit "more focused responses" from test-takers, so beware of generalizing in your response.

NOTE

As you can see by the writing instructions, you'll need to be specific in presenting your response to the issue. As ETS states, you'll need to "support ideas with relevant reasons and examples" in "a well-focused, coherent discussion."

scale by two readers. These readers are your audience, and your purpose in writing this essay is to earn the best score that you can. Six is the maximum score your response can earn. The scale ranges in 1-point increments from 6 to 0.

6 Points

To earn 6 points, your response should exhibit these characteristics:

- A clear, focused position on the issue and an overall response to the specific writing task that is thorough, cogent, and sophisticated.

- Fully developed, persuasive support for the position, including, but not limited to, particularly apt or well-chosen examples, facts, and other illustrations, as well as an explanation that clearly and effectively links the support to the specific requirements of the writing task.

- A rhetorically effective method of organization, such as one that organizes support by order of importance and saves the most effective reasons for last. Connections between and among ideas are logical and may also be as subtle as they are effective.

- A formal grace that is a product primarily of well-constructed, varied sentences and exact and rhetorically effective word choices.

- Adherence to almost all the conventions of Standard Written English, including grammar, usage, and mechanics. If there are any errors, they are minor.

5 Points

To earn 5 points, your response will likely have these characteristics, though it may exceed one or more of them yet fall short on another:

- A clear, focused position on the issue and a thoughtful, complete response to the specific writing task.

- Persuasive support for the position, including, but not limited to, examples, facts, and other illustrations, as well as an explanation that clearly links the support to the specific requirements of the writing task.

- An effective method of organization with logical connections between and among all ideas.

- Well-constructed, varied sentences and appropriate word choices that help create clarity as well as interest.

- Adherence to almost all the conventions of Standard Written English, including grammar, usage, and mechanics. If there are any errors, they should be minor.

4 Points

To earn 4 points, a response will have these characteristics:

- A clear position on the issue and a generally complete response to the specific writing task.

- Support for the position, as well as an explanation that links the support to the specific require-ments of the writing task.

- A logical method of organization.

- Sentences and word choices that generally create clarity.

- General adherence to the conventions of Standard Written English. Some errors may occur.

3 Points

Your response will earn only 3 points if it has *one or more* of the following characteristics:

- A generally clear position and a response to the specific writing task that may be limited in scope or marred by occasional vagueness, extraneous detail, repetition, or other flaws.
- Limited or inadequate support for the position or a limited or inadequate explanation that links the support to the specific requirements of the writing task.
- Lapses in organization or confusing organization and/or lack or misuse of transitional words and phrases.
- Sentences and word choices that occasionally interfere with clarity.
- One or more errors in the conventions of Standard Written English that are so significant that they obstruct meaning.

2 Points

Your response will earn only 2 points if it has *one or more* of the following characteristics:

- A wandering, unclear, or limited response characterized by an unclear or not fully articulated position and a response to the specific writing task that is limited or inadequate in scope or marred by vagueness, extraneous detail, repetition, or other flaws.
- Inadequate support and explanation.
- Confusing organization and/or general lack or misuse of transitional words and phrases.
- Sentences and word choices that interfere with clarity.
- Repeated errors in the conventions of Standard Written English that are so significant that they obstruct meaning.

1 Point

Your response will earn only 1 point if it has *one or more* of the following characteristics:

- An unclear position and almost no response to, or minimal understanding of, the specific task.
- A total lack of support or only illogical or flawed support for the main point or points; a total lack of explanation or only illogical or flawed explanation of the main points of your argument in relation to the specific details of the task.
- No pattern of organization or confusing organization.
- Sentences and word choices that interfere with clarity.
- So many errors in the conventions of Standard Written English that they obstruct meaning throughout the response.

0 Points

This score is possible under the following circumstances:

- The response does not answer the task in any way.
- The response is written in a foreign language.
- The response simply copies the argument.
- The response is not legible.
- The response is nonverbal.

From these criteria, you can draw or reaffirm the following four conclusions about your task:

❶ You must meet the requirements stated in the prompt completely.

❷ You need a clear statement of your position; substantial, thoughtful support; and explanations that link your support to the specific task requirements.

❸ You can make minor errors in grammar, usage, and mechanics without seriously jeopardizing your score, but remember that errors in these areas can affect the clarity of your writing, so be sloppy at your own peril.

❹ The length of your response is in no way a deciding factor in your score. But don't assume that brevity is a virtue. According to the rubric, you'll have to produce a response of sufficient length to support your position in adequate, if not dense, detail. Although there is no magic number for success, aim to make at least three points in favor of your position—and aim to elaborate them fully.

REVIEW THE ANATOMY OF AN ISSUE ESSAY

In addition to keeping track of time—and using it wisely—there are some priorities that you can set and skills you can review and practice to help you write a successful response. Obviously, it takes time to develop superior—6-point—writing skills; however, staying focused on a few simple guidelines can lead to a bump up of a point or more in your score. Think about putting these recommendations to work for you.

State a Thesis, and State It Early

Don't make your reader guess what side of the issue you're on. There is nothing to be gained by being timid or staying on the middle of the fence. A thesis statement that makes your view on the issue absolutely unmistakable should appear somewhere in the first paragraph. Don't worry about being too obvious or even leading off with your thesis. You can, in fact, score a 6 if you state your point of view in the very first sentence. Of course, you must be sure that the thesis is clear and that it adequately reflects the content that follows.

Use a Standard Pattern of Organization

ETS makes it clear that test-takers don't need to employ a standard pattern of organization to succeed. But think critically about that advice. That doesn't mean that standard patterns of organization won't succeed for either the issue or the argument response. A standard pattern of organization helps to lead your reader smoothly from point to point. In addition, such patterns help create fluency.

Order Paragraphs Effectively

Now you've got your overall structure, but how do you hang your ideas on that structure so that your paragraphs flow in logical order? Possibly the best organizational model for the issue response (and the argument response, too) is order of importance. You could order the paragraphs in the body of your response either from the most important reason to the least important reason, or from the least important reason to the most important reason. The latter is the more effective technique. It often results in a strong or memorable ending.

In crafting your paragraphs, don't begin the first two body paragraphs with something like "The first reason in support of my thesis is…" and "The second reason in support of my thesis is…" Similarly, don't end with "In conclusion" or "As I have said." Use transitional words and phrases. They can provide a smooth link from one paragraph to another—and from one sentence to another—by identifying and emphasizing the relationships between ideas. In its analysis of the scoring of sample papers, as well as in its rubrics, ETS stresses the value of transitional words and phrases. In addition to helping you create coherence, transitions can help you vary the beginnings of your sentences.

TIP

Using a standard pattern of organization has an added benefit. If you decide ahead of time how to set up your response, you can save time when faced with writing the actual response on test day.

TRANSITIONS

Review the following lists of transitional words and phrases and use them as you practice writing responses to the tasks in the practice tests. Then they will come more easily as you write the actual response.

Transitions to Introduce or Link Opinions and Reasons

because	*evidently*	*indeed*
besides	*for this reason*	*on the other hand*
by comparison	*furthermore*	*since*
consequently	*however*	*therefore*

Transitions that Introduce or Link Examples

for example	*in this case*	*one type*
for instance	*in this situation*	*to illustrate this point*

Transitions that Create Emphasis or Add Information

after all	*furthermore*	*more important*
again	*in addition*	*moreover*
besides	*indeed*	*similarly*
certainly	*in fact*	*what's more*

Transitions that Introduce Opposing Views

although this may be true	*naturally*	*on the other hand*
even though	*nevertheless*	*undeniably*
evidently	*notwithstanding*	*unquestionably*
it may be said	*of course*	*without a doubt*

Use a Standard Pattern of Paragraphing

Try a traditional structure for developing the paragraphs within the body of your response.

Topic Sentence: The topic sentence states the main idea of the paragraph. In an issue response, the topic sentence of each body paragraph can state a reason that supports your point of view, or a likely "challenge," or reason, against your point of view. For example, if you're arguing that it is, in fact, a reasonable policy to insist that visitors to the nation's museums in Washington, D.C., pay an entrance fee, a topic sentence might suggest that by having to pay, people will place a greater value on their visit.

Support and Development: Once you've written the topic sentence for your paragraph, you have several choices for how to develop the meat of the paragraph. You can choose restriction (a qualification or other way of narrowing and focusing the topic sentence), explanation, and/or evidence. Your job in this part of the paragraph is to make your topic sentence convincing by developing it with supporting points. In discussing paid-entry to national museums in Washington, you might talk about how families visiting for a long weekend from faraway might not come if they had to pay for two adults and several children at three museums. You could emphasize the loss of first-hand access to our nation's history for those children and how seeing, for example, the original Constitution can foster patriotism. Try to make this part of your paragraph full and dense with detail.

Final Summary or Clincher Statement: This last sentence is optional in body paragraphs, but it can give a final rhetorical punch to the paragraph. You could ask a rhetorical question or restate the idea of the paragraph in a fresh way. What you want is a way to give final emphasis to the idea developed in the paragraph. If you can't think of an original and effective clincher, don't add anything to the paragraph. Go on to the next paragraph, using a transition.

If, however, this is your final paragraph in your response, think hard for a memorable final statement. You want to end your response in way that gives closure to your thoughts and emphasizes your points. You could rephrase the thesis, summarize the main points, or direct the reader to a larger issue. The concluding paragraph should tie up all loose ends so that the reader doesn't finish with a sigh of "so what?"

Successful paragraphs can certainly deviate from this order. The important thing to keep in mind, however, is that paragraphs are themselves discrete units of discourse that require organization. It's not enough to organize the paragraphs of your essay logically. The sentences of each paragraph must be organized logically, too.

Develop Each Paragraph Fully

A huge factor in the success or relative failure of your essay will be the kinds and amount of support you provide. Never, ever write a one-sentence paragraph. If you have two-sentence paragraphs, the chances are good that they need more substance. Of course, you can't just add words for the sake of their own sake, nor should you repeat yourself. What you need is more examples, illustrations, or other evidence, as well as the explanation that relates them back to the topic sentence or to the thesis and connect them to the next ideas. If your paragraphs lack details, ask yourself if you can add any of the following:

Facts: Facts are always the best choice for support. Statistics are one kind of fact that lend credibility to an argument. You aren't expected to pull sophisticated facts and statistics out of the air on the GRE® nor should you ever make up any! But you may know some general facts such as the typical miles per gallon of an SUV versus a subcompact or a domestic car brand versus a Japanese brand if you're writing a response to a policy issue on raising emissions standards. Incorporate as many facts as you can. This is one method of appealing to your reader's reason.

Authoritative Opinions or Human Interest: You may not be able to call a quote to mind, yet you may recall a famous person's idea or point of view about your topic. For example, for a response on whether government should fund the arts, you might paraphrase the chair of the National Endowment for the Arts on the value of arts to the economy or a local restaurant owner on how much the theater down the street drives business to her establishment. This kind of support is best used sparingly, especially if the quotation or opinion appeals more to emotion than to reason. In some cases, however, appeals to emotion are as effective as appeals to reason.

Observations: Your own first-hand observations about life can be useful evidence of a point of view. In fact, since you cannot use source material on the GRE®, this type of evidence is extremely helpful as it is available to you in abundance. Observations may appeal to either reason or emotion.

An Anecdote: Occasionally, a brief story not only enlivens your writing, it also adds evidence. Use an anecdote to illustrate some general truth such as how schools rely on parent volunteers. This is another technique that should be used sparingly—most likely just once in a response. Like observations, anecdotes may appeal to either reason or emotion; occasionally, they appeal to both.

Examples: Multiple examples or illustrations of an idea, such as how scandals have led to government reform, will add substance and support to a position that agrees with this claim. Use examples generously to support your points; they are usually very effective appeals to reason.

Take Care with Tone and Person

ETS makes no mention of tone in its scoring rubrics. Nevertheless, you should strive to sound reasonable. You may be forceful and impassioned at the same time, but don't cross the line into harangue or diatribe. The most successful arguments rely on valid reasoning and sophisticated support, both of which can be undercut by a shrill, overly strident, or whining voice.

Similarly, ETS makes no mention of person. Using the third person is your safest bet for both types of tasks, but there may be times when you might want to, or should, incorporate the first person (*I, me, my, myself, mine*) in your essay. It's certainly better to say *I* or *me* than to try to maintain the third person by referring to yourself as "this writer" or in any other self-conscious way. That said, refer to yourself only as necessary and don't, for example, use obvious lead-ins such as "In my humble opinion."

As Time Permits, Add Extras

Should you take time for style or craft? Yes, by all means, once you've got the substance of your ideas completely down on paper. (Of course, it's much easier for computer-based users to follow this advice than paper test-takers.) Be sure, however, to view all of the following as add-ons. You can have, for example, the most interesting and well-written introduction in the world and not do well

TIP

If you think you might use the first person, brush up on when you use *I* (subject) versus *me* (object) and when using *myself* is appropriate (either as reflexive or intensive pronoun).

on the task if you don't have time to develop the key points that support your opinion, or you don't have time to answer the task fully because you never deal with the key challenges to your position.

Interest-Grabbing Opening

If you have time, create an interesting lead by posing a question or offering a surprising or startling fact. Or craft a formal introduction that establishes some background or context for your position. As a review of the sample essays from ETS show, you can succeed without crafting a formal opening.

Apt Word Choice

As time permits, you should also review and revise your word choice:

- Avoid simple, overused words such as *very*, *really*, *good*, *bad*, *interesting*, *fun*, *great*, *awesome*, *incredible*, and *unbelievable*.

- Replace state of being verbs, such as *was* and *are* with active verbs.

- Edit out clichés. (For example, don't begin an essay on dogs with "A dog is man's best friend.")

- Whenever you know a more precise, forceful, or connotatively rich word that will accurately convey your meaning, use it, BUT don't go for the big word, just because it's big.

Varied Sentence Structure

If you want a 6, you have to show some style by varying your sentences. There are many ways to do this:

- Intersperse an occasional short sentence in a paragraph of long sentences.

- Vary your sentences by type by occasionally inserting a question where appropriate. (A word of caution: avoid exclamatory sentences and exclamation points. These are almost never appropriate.)

- Vary your sentences by structure, using compound, complex, and simple sentences.

- Create sentence variation by beginning sentences in different ways, that is, make sure all sentences in a paragraph don't begin with "The" followed by the subject. Begin sentences with conjunctions, prepositions, and transitions.

A Final Word of Advice

Think of the organization for your response as the box that holds your product. Although that box is absolutely necessary, chances are you won't sell that product—no matter how good it is—in a plain cardboard box. Instead, you'll need an attractive outer layer, a packaging that says "Buy me! Buy me!" That's why you must also strive for qualities such as original and sophisticated word choice, sentence variation, and rhetorical devices in your essay. ETS readers will not give a 5 or 6 to a plain cardboard box.

CREATE YOUR WRITING PLAN

You'll have just 30 minutes to read and respond to the issue prompt. But don't read the prompt and start writing. You need a plan to attack the task and that plan has three parts: prewriting, drafting, and proofreading. Of the 30 minutes, set aside 2 to 3 minutes at the end to review and proofread your response. The bulk of the 30 minutes—say 23 or so minutes—should be spent in the actual writing of your response. The first 4 to 5 minutes should be spent in planning and prewriting.

Prewriting

The prewriting part of your writing plan has three steps that will help you focus on the task, gather your ideas, and plan the development of your response. They are tailored to the Issue Task and are slightly different from the prewriting steps for responding to the Argument Task.

Because your time is so short, you may be tempted to overlook prewriting. This is inadvisable for several reasons. First, with prewriting, you're actually testing your position to see if it will work; that is, in the few minutes you spend prewriting, you will be finding out whether you have good ideas or not. Second, organization is dependent on ideas. If you have a few ideas jotted down when you start to write, it will be much easier to order your ideas effectively. It's a trick that experienced writers use because it's much easier to start writing with a short list of ideas in front of you than no ideas at all.

Restate the Prompt: Although the issue prompt is easier to read and understand than the argument prompt, don't overlook this first step. Be sure the issue is clear to you.

Think About Reasons on Both Sides of the Issue: Understanding and being able to develop both sides of the issue are necessary in crafting a successful response. There are two main reasons for this. First, you don't need—nor are you expected—to express your truest feelings. Instead, you need to choose the side of the issue for which you can present the most convincing, well-developed argument of your own. Second, to be successful with most variations of the prompt, you need to anticipate and refute the opposing point of view.

Jot a "Quick Write": Begin by briefly identifying your position on the issue and then listing reasons that support your position. Strive for the most persuasive reasons.

If the specific instructions ask for challenges, both sides of the issue, advantages or disadvantages, or other considerations related to the opposite viewpoint, list reasons that could be given to oppose your position.

The flow of ideas won't come in any particular order so reread your list and number the reasons in the order that you want to use them. You may also find that some ideas don't fit with the majority of your ideas, or that you have too many ideas, or some are weak. Don't be afraid to cross off ones that don't fit or are the least convincing.

Drafting

You'll actually be drafting and revising simultaneously because of the time limitation. To get the most of your actual writing time, keep these priorities in mind:

TIP

Those taking the computer-based test will be given scrap paper for making notes, so if you're taking the computer version, consider jotting down the key requirements of the instructions. If you're taking the paper-based test, you may want to underline the key requirements.

NOTE

Both those taking the test on computer and those taking the paper-and-pencil test will have scrap paper available for making notes.

Answer the Task: Be sure that you answer the task. This may seem obvious, but in the hurry to write down your ideas, don't let your ideas take you on a line of thinking that doesn't respond to the issue and the task. Even though you have a "quick write" to work from, new ideas will come as you write. Be sure to go back to the last few lines of the prompt to be sure you aren't just agreeing or disagreeing with the issue, but also addressing both points of view, citing and refuting possible challenges, or doing whatever else the task specifically requires you to do.

Organize Your Response: The following pattern is a standard, or traditional, way to organize your overall response. It leads your reader smoothly through your response by eliminating confusion and guesswork. In addition, it helps to create fluency—or the illusion of it. If you're a writer who has trouble with organization, this pattern gives you a structure to develop your ideas around:

- Opening paragraph: thesis or clear statement of your position
- Body paragraph 1: Reason 1 for your position, fully explained and supported
- Body paragraph 2: Reason 2 for your position, fully explained and supported
- Body paragraph 3: A statement of the most effective counterargument, an acknowledgment of its reasonableness, and your fully explained and supported response; or any other specific and developed point needed to address the writing task instructions
- Closing paragraph: Reason 3 (another key challenge or another main point) that directly responds to the specific writing instructions; support as needed; plus a detail, statement, question, or other device that delivers closure

NOTE

A run-on sentence is two clauses of equal weight joined only by a comma; for example, *A run-on sentence looks like this, it detracts from meaning.* Fix it by making the two clauses separate sentences, making one clause dependent on the other, using a semicolon, or adding a coordinating conjunction (*and, but, or*).

Suppose you use this pattern of organization. How do you decide what reason to use first, second, and third? Often, the best way to organize points for an argument is by order of importance. You could choose your most significant reason to be first or last. If you use your most powerful, that is, strongest, support as the third and final point, your readers will take away from your response your most impressive piece of argument.

Provide Ample, Thoughtful, Well-Developed Support: Developing sufficient support is the key element for success on the Issue Task. The most foolproof method of organization you can use in an issue essay is to begin with a clear statement of your opinion in your opening and to develop each well-chosen point of support paragraph by paragraph.

Link Ideas Clearly: Your organization doesn't have to be traditional, or based in any way on typical instruction in college writing classes, but it does have to be logical and help to create overall coherence. Based on reviewing sample analyses, ETS values transitional words and phrases, so link paragraphs and ideas appropriately as you write. Also, don't overlook the value of a topic sentence in providing an organizational boost to your essay.

Consider Style

If you're aiming for a top score, vary your sentences and word choices. Rubric criteria specify varied, well-constructed sentences; for this test, they are an important index of your sophistication as a writer. ETS readers are also looking for appropriateness, precision, and rhetorical effectiveness in word choice.

Proofreading

When you go back over your essay in the 2 or 3 minutes you may have remaining, keep the following priorities in mind, which are based on the scoring rubric:

Check Your Thesis: Make sure you've stated it and that it's clear. Make sure it also adequately reflects the content of your essay.

Look for Omitted Words: When you're writing in a hurry, it's easy to leave out words. One omitted word can, however, destroy the sense of an entire sentence, and sentence sense is an important rubric criterion.

Check for Sentence Faults: At this stage, you want to make certain that you eliminate any ineffective fragments, any run-on sentences, and any fused sentences or comma splices. Because grammar counts? No, because poor grammar can obscure your meaning and bring down your score.

Don't Spend Your Time on Spelling or Commas: Keep in mind that the rubric doesn't mention spelling. It evidently has "minor error" status for the readers. Likewise, a missing comma here or there shouldn't affect your score.

A FINAL NOTE OF CAUTION

ETS wants its computer-based users to know that their responses will be subjected to analysis by software that searches for similarities to published information. It warns that it will "cancel" a score if it contains any unacknowledged use of sources. In addition, ETS will cancel a response if an essay or any part of it has been prepared by another person. Finally, a score will be canceled if it includes language that is "substantially" similar to the language in one or more other test responses.

ISSUE PROMPT WITH SIX MODEL RESPONSES, SCORING, AND ANALYSES

Use this prompt as a practice opportunity, and compare your response with the samples, scoring, and analyses that follow.

Time yourself and follow these 6 steps. In the real test, you will have 30 minutes.

1. Read the prompt.
2. Follow the prewriting steps.
3. Stop! Compare your "quick write" plan with the sample that follows the prompt to see different ideas (perhaps more sophisticated, perhaps less) that you might have thought of.
4. Draft your response.
5. Read each model that follows the sample "quick write." Determine the positive and negative qualities of each sample response before you read its scoring analysis.
6. Score your response against the rubric on pages 130–131. Be honest in your analysis.

Issue Task

In a world filled with significant challenges, owning pets, and especially owning costly, resource-consuming dogs, is an irresponsible use of time and money.

Write a response in which you discuss how much you agree or disagree with the claim and include the most compelling reasons and/or examples that someone could use to dispute your point of view.

Sample "Quick Write"

The 6-point response to this prompt began with just 3 minutes of prewriting and planning. It looked like this:

TIP

Note how specific the "quick write" is. The writer is off to a good start for developing a response that is grounded in specific details to support any generalizations that he or she may make.

> My opinion
> (1) Dog owning not irresponsible
> reasons
> loveable
> people's best friends
> (3) doing good for your town government or charitable org.
> by getting dog off street or out of shelter—you pay for medical, food, etc.
> (2) homeless dogs starving
> (2a) dogs have feelings
> Challenges
> (4b) don't take care of dogs, take care of people
> waste of $ on such things as home-made dog treats
> (4c) dogs use too many resources (time? money?)
> (4a) dogs too pampered

Making Your Plan Work

In many ways, the success of the 6-point essay based on this prewriting is due to some of the thought processes demonstrated in this plan. First, notice how the plan addresses the prompt. It has two clear parts: reasons for the position and challenges to the position. Second, notice that the writer decides not to develop all the ideas generated in the prewriting. The writer makes a judgment to develop ideas that he or she perhaps feels can be treated with deeper analysis, or are less predictable answers to the prompt.

Return to this planning guide after you read the sample 6-point model below. Notice how the prewriting does not, in fact, show the eventual order of organization. Note also that there are more details than the "quick write" includes. Once the writer began to write, ideas began to flow, affirming the idea that writing is a generative process. This should be a comforting fact to remember as you prepare to take the Analytical Writing section. You don't need to list all your ideas in a "quick write"; believe that more ideas will come as you write. However, it's also important to check your "quick write" and the task instructions to make sure that your flow of ideas isn't taking you off the track of responding accurately and adequately to the task.

Furthermore, you don't want to spend the kind of time on the prewriting process that extensive planning would require. The main goal of prewriting during a timed writing test is to be sure that you've got good points to make before you begin your writing. If you don't, quickly scratch out your first plan and make another.

Model 1: 6 points out of 6

It is not irresponsible to own a dog. In fact, the truth is quite the opposite. Owning a dog is an act of generosity and compassion—as long as the dog was once homeless or most likely would have been homeless.

There is a huge overpopulation of homeless dogs in the United States. It is estimated that some 5 million dogs and cats are euthanized each year because no one has adopted them. The reality is that the number of homeless dogs is far greater than that, because many homeless animals are not identified or counted, or they spend time in, or languish in, shelters. Dogs, like other animals, are sentient beings. Dogs without homes and proper care suffer. Some starve for food; others are starved for the love and compassion on which they thrive. As many vets and animal behaviorists have explained, dogs do have emotional lives, even if those lives are different from our own.

Of course, some will counter that if we are going to relieve the suffering of the homeless, why not relieve the suffering of homeless people? That, too, is a worthy cause. I would say that those equipped with the time, money, or inclination to deal with the suffering of homeless people should devote their resources to such a cause, and those equipped to deal with the suffering of homeless dogs, even if just by adopting a single dog, should devote their resources to that cause.

Adopting a dog is not just compassionate to the dog or gratifying to its owner, it is a generous act on behalf of society. A person who adopts a dog may be taking responsibility for an animal that might otherwise roam the streets, do damage, or spread disease. After all, shelters can only accommodate so many dogs. If people do not move existing dogs out of shelters, then more animals must wait on the streets or in the wild. A person who adopts a dog from a shelter is also taking responsibility off the public for that dog's food, medical care, spaying or neutering, or, in too many cases, euthanasia and disposal. While some people might counter that saving dogs only adds to the dog population, and perhaps the very popularity of dogs as pets, every dog that is adopted is one less dog on the public or charitable dole.

In general, of course, people may argue that there are more important ways to use private or public resources than by spending them on dogs. They are correct. There are more important uses of our time and money, such as feeding the hungry. But does one worthy cause, such as feeding the hungry, invalidate all other worthy causes, such as teaching the illiterate? Cannot some people devote themselves to some worthy causes that touch or move them personally, while others devote their resources to different worthy causes? I believe we can have compassion for the least among us, including our four-footed friends, as well as for those people who do, indeed, lay a more significant moral claim upon us.

Scoring Analysis

This essay scores 6 out of 6 because it

- **answers the task.** With care and considerable sophistication, this essay not only gives cogent reasons for disagreement, but it also responds thoughtfully to the most likely and compelling challenges.

- **is well supported.** Support for dog ownership is abundant and well explained. The writer acknowledges the validity of counterarguments, yet weakens them with provocative questions and logical reasoning or with ample and persuasive support.

- **is well organized.** The writer uses the opening paragraph to state and qualify the position and uses subsequent, discrete, and well-constructed paragraphs to counter challenges and reinforce the position. All ideas lead logically and smoothly to a satisfying conclusion.

- **is fluid, precise, and graceful.** The capable prose includes short sentences that are interspersed with longer ones for dramatic effect. Sophisticated word choices include *languish, sentient,* and *invalidate*. The tone and style help the reader form an opinion of the writer as objective and thoughtful.

- **observes the conventions of Standard Written English.**

Other observations: While the opening could create interest, or more points could be made in support of the position, the essay nevertheless meets all the criteria for a score of 6. ETS readers do not expect perfection in 30 minutes; nor do they expect you to cover the entire waterfront of your topic. What they do expect, however, are reasonably sophisticated, well-supported, well-organized, and fluent responses within the time constraints.

Write Your Observations About Model 1

Model 2: 5 points out of 6

Dogs are loveable creatures that almost no one wishes to malign. It is also true that dog owners can be responsible, morally upright human beings. Yet, it is the inescapable truth that dogs consume resources, and that we can make better use of our time, our money, and our love than by lavishing them on dogs. Coming from a family in which a pet was always like a family member, this is a statement I make with deep personal regret. Therefore, I would not go so far as to brand all dog ownership as irresponsible.

If you own a dog, you may be spending quite a lot of your time on that animal. You may exercise it two or more times a day, as well attend to its other needs to go out. You may spend time brushing it, grooming it, or taking it to be groomed, and taking it to the vet. You may have to make arrangements for it when you will be gone for a long stretch, such as more than eight hours. If you are a good dog owner, then you are also spending time training your dog and giving it the attention and love that it craves. Now think about how those hours might be spent in other ways, such as tutoring people learning English, helping an elderly person to get groceries or meet other needs, or advocating for cleaner water or air. Which is the worthiest of these causes? Of the causes mentioned, to me, the dog finishes last.

If you own a dog, you must also spend quite a bit of money on it. Sums will vary with the dog and the owner, but some dog owners report spending well over $1,000 per year on their pet. One must think about where that money could have gone, such as to homeless people, the local food pantry, or medical research aimed at finding cures for cancer. Is it really better to spend your $1,000 on Fluffy or Mitten or Max than it is to help cure cancer? I think not.

Furthermore, dogs do use up resources. The pet industry is huge in America, cranking out as it does all kinds of unnecessary items for dogs ranging from luxury dog beds to Halloween hats and costumes. Page through almost any catalog and you will find items such as luxury dog beds and designer sweaters. Furthermore, dogs soil our roads and parks. If a dog owner is responsible and cleans up, each of the nation's millions of dogs is then responsible for the use of thousands of plastic bags. A dog consumes other resources as well, such as food and water. Therefore, no matter how loveable they may be, dogs do not merit the many resources that we lavish on them.

Scoring Analysis

This essay scores 5 out of 6 because it

- **answers the task.** Both good and some excellent reasons are given for agreeing with the position. The essay also capably addresses counterarguments, such as all the hours spent on animals that might be spent more responsibly or productively.

- **is well supported.** For example, the final paragraph that bulwarks the writer's position offers capable, persuasive support. Other paragraphs also contain ample, detailed, and well-developed support.

- **is generally well organized.** A few organizational missteps mar the essay by failing to make the position as clear as possible from the outset and by articulating counterclaims or challenges (such as dogs being loveable) less clearly and centrally than they could have been. (Attention to topic sentences might have cured this problem.) For the most part, however, the flow of ideas is logical.

- **is fluid.** Words and sentences are clear; some words, such as *malign, inescapable,* and *advocating* are quite sophisticated. The sentences are, in general, more serviceable than elegant. (Compare them with the sentences in the 6-point essay.)

- **observes the conventions of Standard Written English.** There are a few minor errors that do not interfere with meaning.

Other observations: In an issue essay, be sure your position is clearly stated from the outset. If a personal statement such as the one about family might somehow obfuscate that position, leave it out. Note how the writer never really develops the qualification at the end of that final line of the first paragraph. In addition, there is no transition between that statement and the following paragraph. These failings contribute to the essay's scoring a 5 instead of a 6.

Write Your Observations About Model 2

_____

_____

_____

_____

_____

_____

_____

_____

_____

_____

_____

_____

_____

_____

_____

_____

_____

_____

_____

_____

_____

_____

_____

_____

_____

_____

_____

_____

_____

_____

_____

_____

_____

_____

_____

_____

_____

_____

_____

_____

Model 3: 4 points out of 6

Individuals and families who own dogs know what a financial drain it is to have such a pet. For a big dog, food costs alone can run $50 per month. In addition, there are vet bills for everything from routine vaccinations to heartworm medication to occassional illness or injury. There are leashes, bowls, collars, licences, whistles, and dog beds to buy. In addition, some people buy dog toys, dog sweaters and booties, and even high-end dog biscuits. Most people have to board their dogs at least from time to time, while others board them often, hire dog walkers, or send their dogs to day care. That means spending anywhere from approximately $1,000 per year to upwards of $10,000 per year, on their dog. Some of these owners pass by the homeless people on the street, or go through poor neighborhoods with children who are not eating right, with their purebred, just-groomed dog decked out in it's lovely new handnit sweater. This fabulous waste of money is common in our country, where dog ownership seems to be on the rise. Going hand in hand with that waste of money is the time they waste on caring for, walking, and toting around dogs when we might be involved in feeding the hungry, working for a cleaner enviroment or taking steps to end global warming, or addressing other really important challenges.

Pets, of course, are not useless, and they do bring joy into peoples' lives. Pets must be used as guide dogs for some people. They may also be important in mental or psychological healing. For example, when used to provide therapy to children or others who have experienced grave loss or other tramma. Also, a visit from a well-trained dog at a nursing home, children's ward, or other place where such companions are both welcome and useful has many beneficial affects. Indeed, a dog can be a light in the life of any lonely or sick person.

Those who feel their lives are not complete without a pet certainly have a right to one. But do they need a designer dog? Do they need doggie daycare? And do they need two dogs, or three, or five? Furthermore, could such people not also look outward at the world, and spend some of their energy on tasks that need doing, instead of so much energy on loving and pampering their dogs? In my humble opinion, it is far better to help the people of this world then to spend our presious time and resources on cute, but unnecessary, animal friends.

Scoring Analysis

This essay scores 4 out of 6 because it

- **answers the task.** This essay clearly takes a position and supports the position. It is less effective on responding to the possible challenges to that position.

- **supports the position well but is limited in terms of explaining and countering challenges.** Examples are appropriate and various, but responses to likely challenges are not so clearly explained or developed as they should be. In fact, the writer does a better job of agreeing with the challenges than refuting them in any way.

- **lacks strong organization.** The argument starts immediately before the position is clear; paragraph 1 needs reorganization. Paragraph 2 could also be more clearly and fluidly linked to both the paragraph that precedes it and the one that follows it.

- **is generally clear.** Most points are clear, but paragraph 2 should also be more sharply focused to reflect and specifically refute challenges to the writer's position. The tone at times verges on the harangue.

- **observes the conventions of Standard Written English.** There are several minor flaws, but they do not interfere with meaning. They do, however, help contribute to the score of 4.

Other observations: This response contains a wealth of insights, but the critical thinking outshines the writing. Because the reader almost has to remind herself or himself of the side of the question that he or she supports, the entire essay looses its persuasiveness. This problem is exemplified by the ending, where meaningful questions are raised and qualifying circumstances considered, but the level of clarity and focus is not such that the reader can be perfectly certain of where the writer is going with them. The "over-the-top" rhetoric also gets in the way of the seriousness of some of the writer's points. Notice, too, how much weaker the vocabulary (as evidenced by choices such as "really important") and sentences are in this essay than they are in the 5- and 6-point essays.

Write Your Observations About Model 3

_____

_____

_____

_____

_____

_____

_____

_____

_____

_____

_____

_____

_____

_____

_____

_____

_____

_____

_____

_____

_____

_____

_____

_____

_____

_____

_____

_____

_____

_____

_____

_____

_____

_____

_____

_____

_____

_____

_____

_____

_____

_____

_____

_____

_____

Model 4: 3 points out of 6

Face it, America! Owning a dog is egotistical. An indulgence of the most selfish people for the most selfish reasons. Dogs are everywhere where a lot of people don't want them. There's always people who are ignoring leash laws or cleanup laws and letting their dogs run up to and frighten people and children who do not like dogs and never wanted them around in the first place. Letting their dogs make a mess in parks and on the streets, too, and just leaving that behind. Or letting their dogs use other peoples' lawns and killing bushes or green areas through repeated use. These people somehow think their dogs deserve rights, that their dog has the right to be on someone else's property as long as it is attached to their leash. There, however, being no bill of rights for dogs.

Plus, look at the money people spend on their dogs, and not just on the necessary things like a license and rabies shots but on crazy things like designer collars and bows and ribbons and special haircuts. People are making themselves, not there dogs, feel good with these things.

Some people will say that pets help you out when you are lonely and give you friend when you need one. I say why not a person for a friend instead of a dog.

Some people will also say that people should have dogs to help out blind people or to serve as guide dogs. I have no problem with that. But those dogs aren't pets. They are specially trained animals for a special service, not indulged, spoiled animals owned by selfish people.

Scoring Analysis

This essay scores 3 out of 6 because it

- **answers task in a limited way.** This essay makes its position very clear, but barely touches on the challenges to the writer's position. Only one challenge is actually dealt with—that dogs can dispel loneliness or be friends—and that challenge is treated quite simplistically and ineffectively.

- **offers inadequate support.** Support is present, especially in the first paragraph, but it could have been more effectively used in service of the writer's position had it not been presented as a laundry list of the irresponsible deeds of some dog owners. There is inadequate support to rebut the challenges to the writer's position.

- **lacks organization.** The response would benefit from a true introductory paragraph and placing much of the current paragraph 1 in a second, well-developed paragraph as support for a clearly stated topic sentence.

- **is fluid, but not precise.** Ideas flow in a variety of sentence structures, including sentence fragments, and the latter are effective in places, but the overall impression is a writer writing at break-neck speed to finish in 30 minutes.

- **observes the conventions of Standard Written English.** There are several consistent flaws, some of which interfere with meaning.

Other observations: Try to avoid the personal and name-calling approach taken here. It's fine to express passion for your point of view; you may even create a distinctive voice. But remember that an argument is most effective when it creates the appearance of objectivity. Edit out any name-calling, gratuitous judgments, or vitriol.

Write Your Observations About Model 4

_____

_____

_____

_____

_____

_____

_____

_____

_____

_____

_____

_____

_____

_____

_____

_____

_____

_____

_____

_____

_____

_____

_____

_____

_____

_____

_____

_____

_____

_____

_____

_____

_____

_____

_____

_____

_____

_____

_____

_____

_____

_____

_____

_____

_____

Model 5: 2 points out of 6

If you want unconditional love, you need a dog. A dog will love you when no one else cares. A dog will always be there for you. A dog will help you get through the times when you are sad or lonely.

The best thing about owning a dog is coming home from a hard day and theres your dog so happy to see you and wag its tail and jump all over you like you are the greatest person in the world.

You should also own a dog because there are so many unwanted dogs in the world and some of them are going to die or be put to death in shelters and other places because no one wants them.

You should also own a dog because no animal should have to have it's life cut short when there are so many people out there who would gain so much from having a dog, even though it is expensive and takes time from you.

If someone tells you its not right to own a dog because dogs don't do anything for the world, you can tell them how much your dog does for you.

Scoring Analysis

This essay scores 2 out of 6 because it

- **answers only part of the task.** The position is clear, and, indeed, the last point is a good one, but challenges to the position are not developed.

- **lacks support.** The assertions are either not backed up or are backed up with extremely simple or inadequate support.

- **is poorly written.** Most "paragraphs" are just one sentence. No single idea is explored in depth. Variety of sentence structure and word choice are not apparent.

- **observes the conventions of Standard Written English.** There are a several minor grammatical errors that add to the overall impression that this piece was poorly conceived and written.

Other observations: This writer could probably have scored an extra point or more by paying more attention to structuring and developing paragraphs.

Write Your Observations About Model 5

_____

_____

_____

_____

_____

_____

_____

_____

_____

_____

_____

_____

_____

_____

_____

_____

_____

_____

_____

_____

_____

_____

_____

_____

_____

_____

_____

_____

_____

_____

_____

_____

Model 6: 1 point out of 6

If there's one thing people have a real, 100% right to in this nation, it's there property, and a dog is a kind of property. Therefore, no one has the right to take that property away or to say a person cannot own a dog.

It's fine for a person to own a dog because a dog meets that person's needs or wants in some way. The dog might make the person feel good or more loved. The dog might make the person feel like someone or something on this earth depends on him and would not be the same without him. The dog might even be trained to fetch the person's slippers for him or do some other job. There has even been times when dogs have saved their owner's lifes. It is not right for anyone without a dog to say that someone with a dog can't have that dog. No one has the right to do that.

Scoring Analysis

This essay scores 1 out of 6 because it

- **answers only part of the task.** This essay takes a clear position while failing to respond to challenges. The first paragraph is off task.

- **lacks support.** There is almost no support; the support that appears is simple and predictable.

Other observations: In addition to other flaws that sink the essay, the final two lines also present the reader with an example of circular reasoning—saying something is so because it is so. Avoid this kind of reasoning in your own response.

Write Your Observations About Model 6

_____
_____
_____
_____
_____
_____
_____
_____
_____
_____
_____
_____
_____
_____
_____
_____
_____
_____
_____
_____
_____
_____
_____
_____
_____
_____
_____
_____
_____
_____
_____
_____
_____
_____
_____

SUMMING IT UP

- The Issue Task of the Analytical Writing portion of the GRE® revised General Test measures how well you can develop and support your own position on an issue.

- The Issue Task is of a general nature, and no special knowledge is required to analyze and form an opinion about it.

- The issue will be accompanied by a set of instructions that establishes the conditions or requirements for the response.

- You will be presented with one issue to write about. You won't have a choice of issues from which to select one.

- The Issue Task is part of the Analytical Writing section, which is always first in an administration of the GRE®. The time limit for the Issue Task is 30 minutes.

- If you're taking the computer version of the GRE®, you'll use specially designed word processing software that allows the user to insert and delete text, cut and paste text, and undo actions. There is no spell or grammar checker.

- The Issue Task is scored against a rubric using a 0 to 6 range in 1-point increments. The scores for the Issue Task and the Argument Task are averaged and reported as a combined score ranging from 0 to 6 in half-point increments.

- Follow these steps when writing the Issue Task:
  - State the thesis early.
  - Use a standard pattern of organization, namely order of importance.
  - Order paragraphs effectively.
  - Use a standard pattern of paragraphing: topic sentence, support and development, final summary statement.
  - Develop each paragraph fully: use facts, authoritative opinions or human interest, observations, anecdote, and examples.

- While spelling is not included in the scoring rubric, transitions are, so be sure to include them as you draft your response. If time permits, you can add extras to the response such as an interest-grabbing opener, apt word choice, and varied sentence structure.

- Your writing plan should consist of:
  - Prewriting: restate the prompt, think about reasons on both sides of the issue, jot a quick write
  - Drafting: answer the task, organize your response, provide well-developed support, consider style, link ideas clearly, take care with tone and person
  - Proofreading: check your thesis, look for omitted words, check for sentence faults, don't spend time on spelling or commas

- While you shouldn't spend time on spelling or minor mechanical errors, remember that misspelled words and lack of punctuation or wrong punctuation can detract from meaning.

The Argument Task

chapter 5

OVERVIEW

- Basic information about the Argument Task
- Understand the prompt: the argument
- Understand the prompt: the writing instructions
- Understand the scoring rubric
- Review the basics of argumentation
- Learn the flaws in arguments
- Create your writing plan
- A final note of caution
- Argument prompt with six model responses, scoring, and analyses
- Summing it up

The Analytical Writing section of the GRE® revised General Test measures both your ability to think and your ability to write in response to two kinds of prompts. The second of these prompts is the Argument Task. It presents you with a very brief argument and then states your task. Depending on the question, you'll have one of eight sets of directions explaining how you should construct your response. This chapter describes the prompt and sets of writing instructions and walks you through strategies that will aid you in crafting a successful response. To help you put it all together, the chapter ends with a sample Argument Task and six responses complete with analyses based on the GRE® rubric for Argument Tasks.

BASIC INFORMATION ABOUT THE ARGUMENT TASK

You will find the Analytical Writing section always first in any administration of the GRE® revised General Test. For many test-takers, it is probably the most stressful part of the test, so evidently the test-maker slots it first so anxious test-takers can get it out of the way.

Type of Question

For the Argument Task, you must write a response to an argument within certain guidelines set by the instructions that accompany the argument. The task for an argument response is not to craft your own opinion about the argument, but to analyze the argument. The instructions, which are described in more detail later in this chapter, may require that you

- explain how certain evidence would make a claim stronger or weaker.
- examine stated and unstated assumptions to explain how much the argument depends on them, as well as what the argument loses if the assumptions are not valid or correct.
- present and discuss alternative explanations that could reasonably compete with the proposed explanation.

The content of the argument will be drawn from a wide range of subject areas. You might find a prompt about funding for the fine arts, a policy to monitor employee Internet use, a health study's recommendation, or a government plan for land use. Topics are drawn from the physical and social sciences, the fine arts, and the humanities. However, no special knowledge of the subject is necessary to develop a well-reasoned and well-written response. The topics are general in nature, and the goal of the exercise is to enable test-takers to demonstrate "complex thinking and persuasive writing" ability.

Unlike other essay portions of standardized tests that you may have taken, there is only one prompt. You won't get a choice of arguments from which to choose one to write about.

Time Limit and Software

TIP

If you're taking the paper-and-pencil version and there is enough space on the sheets of paper, write on every other line. That will leave you space to insert additions and neatly make deletions. If your handwriting isn't legible, try printing, but practice ahead of time so that you can print quickly and legibly.

The Argument Task and the Issue Task are each allotted 30 minutes to complete. The time limit is the same on both the computer-based version and the paper-and-pencil version.

The computer version has a word processing program that allows the test-taker to edit by inserting and deleting text, cutting and pasting text, and undoing actions. There is no spell checker or grammar checker. This is similar to the restrictions placed on those taking the paper-and-pencil version. They will have no access during the test to dictionaries or grammar handbooks.

Scoring

Both the Argument Task and the Issue Task have their own rubrics. You'll work through the rubric for the Argument Task later in this chapter. Both tasks share the same score scale, which ranges from 0 to 6. The average of the two scores is taken to arrive at a combined score from 0 to 6 in half-point increments. This is the score that is reported to graduate and business schools.

UNDERSTAND THE PROMPT: THE ARGUMENT

All the prompts in the Argument Task have two parts: the argument and the specific instructions. The first part of the prompt states a brief argument, expressed completely in just a few sentences, which may end with a conclusion, a recommendation, a bit of advice, or a prediction. For example, the argument might suggest how funds are to be spent, a new policy that should be instituted, or why things would go better if a particular plan or action were implemented.

Think about this description of the first part of the prompt. An argument expressed in just a few sentences has to lack evidence—or enough evidence. Indeed, it has to be big on assertions and small on explanation and development. In short, it has to be a flawed argument.

Don't be fooled if the prompt has numbers, percentages, or other statistics. Their function is to support the argument—or to appear to support the argument. They may actually reveal a flaw in the argument that you can build on in your own line of reasoning.

UNDERSTAND THE PROMPT: THE WRITING INSTRUCTIONS

The second part of the prompt states the task or special instructions that define your response. These instructions will begin with the words "Write a response. . ." and then explain how that response should be shaped. Typically, you'll be told to be specific in explaining your analysis, that is, you'll need to provide examples, reasons, questions to answer, or alternative explanations, depending on the prompt. The sets of instructions for responding to an Argument Task will have wording similar to the following:

- Discuss the evidence needed to assess the argument. Include specific examples and an explanation of how the evidence might weaken or strengthen the argument.

- Discuss the stated and/or unstated assumptions and explain how the argument is based on these assumptions and the implications for the argument if the assumptions are shown to be unjustified.

- Discuss the questions that need to be asked and answered to determine if the recommendation and its argument are reasonable. As part of your response, describe how the answers would help in the evaluation process.

- Discuss the questions that need to be asked and answered to determine if the advice and its argument are reasonable. As part of your response, explain how the answers would help in the evaluation process.

- Discuss the questions that need to be asked and answered to determine if the recommendation is likely to result in the outcome that is projected. As part of your response, explain how the answers would help in the evaluation process.

- Discuss the questions that need to be asked and answered to determine if the prediction and its argument are reasonable. As part of your response, explain how the answers would help in the evaluation process.

- Presented with an explanation, discuss one or more alternative explanations that could reasonably compete with the proposed explanation. Explain how your explanation(s) account for the facts in the argument that is proposed.

- Discuss the questions that need to be asked and answered to determine if the conclusion and the argument it is derived from are reasonable. As part of your response, explain how the answers would help in the evaluation process.

If the task asks you to raise questions, don't fail to raise them. If it asks you to provide alternative explanations, be sure you include them. And, above all, remember that you're being asked to analyze and evaluate a flawed or, at best, an incomplete argument. That knowledge can help you focus your thinking.

NOTE

You can see by the writing instructions that you're being directed to respond in specific terms to the presented argument. In the words of ETS, you'll need to "support ideas with relevant reasons and examples" in "a well-focused, coherent discussion."

UNDERSTAND THE SCORING RUBRIC

Before we go any further, let's look at the scoring rubric for the Argument Task against which your response will be evaluated. Two readers will read and analyze your response using a six-point scale. The readers are your audience, and scoring high is your purpose. Scores range from 6 as the maximum to 0. Scores are whole numbers.

6 Points

To earn 6 points, your response should exhibit these characteristics:

- A logically sound, well-focused answer to the specific task that is particularly insightful, thoughtful, deep, or sophisticated.

- Fully developed, persuasive support for the main point or points of your response. At this high level of response, examples and other illustrations are particularly apt or well chosen, and their relationship to the focus of your analysis is extremely clear and/or well articulated.

- A method of organization that complements the main ideas of the analysis by effectively creating a flow of well-organized paragraphs and easing the reader's progress through the paper from first word to last. Connections between and among ideas are logical and may also be as subtle as they are effective.

- A formal grace that is a product primarily of well-constructed, varied sentences and exact and rhetorically effective word choices.

- Adherence to almost all the conventions of Standard Written English, including grammar, usage, and mechanics. If there are any errors, they are minor.

5 Points

To earn 5 points, your response will likely have these characteristics, though it may exceed one or more of them yet fall short on another:

- A logically sound, focused answer to the specific task that reflects insight and evidences some deep thought.

- Well-developed, persuasive support for the main point or points of your response. Examples and other illustrations are well chosen, and their relationship to the focus of your analysis are clear.

- A method of organization that complements main ideas and connects ideas clearly and in a logical order.

- Well-constructed, varied sentences and appropriate word choices that help create clarity as well as interest.

- Adherence to almost all the conventions of Standard Written English, including grammar, usage, and mechanics. If there are any errors, they are minor.

4 Points

To earn 4 points, a response will have these characteristics:

- A generally focused answer to the specific task.

- Varying degrees of adequate and inadequate support.

- A logical method of organization, although some linkages may be missing or unclear.

- Sentences and word choices that generally create clarity, though some problems may exist with structure or usage.

- General adherence to the conventions of Standard Written English. Some errors may occur.

3 Points

Your response will earn only 3 points if it has *one or more* of the following characteristics:

- An inadequate answer to the specific task. It may not quite respond to the task or all aspects of it; it may be limited in its scope or number of points, or it may be vague or confusing in places.

- Inadequate support for the main point or points of your response or support that is illogical.

- A pattern of organization that does not complement the main ideas or causes confusion for the reader.

- Sentences and word choices that occasionally interfere with clarity.

- One or more errors in the conventions of Standard Written English that are so significant that they obstruct meaning or very frequent minor errors.

2 Points

Your response will earn only 2 points if it has *one or more* of the following characteristics:

- An inadequate or unclear answer to the specific task. It may not quite respond to the task or all aspects of it, or it may be too vague or confusing to answer the task adequately.

- Little, if any, support or support that is illogical.

- Confusing or inadequate organization.

- Sentences and word choices that interfere with clarity.

- Repeated errors in the conventions of Standard Written English that are so significant that they obstruct meaning.

1 Point

Your response will earn only 1 point if it has *one or more* of the following characteristics:

- Almost no response to, or minimal understanding of, the specific task.

- A total lack of support or only illogical or flawed support.

- No pattern of organization or confusing organization.

- Many sentences and word choices that interfere with clarity.

- So many errors in the conventions of Standard Written English that they obstruct meaning throughout the response.

0 Points

This score is possible under the following circumstances:

- The response does not answer the task in any way.

- The response is written in a foreign language.

- The response simply copies the argument.

- The response is not legible.

- The response is nonverbal.

From these criteria, you can draw or reaffirm the following four conclusions about your task:

1 You must answer the prompt completely.

2 Your ideas, support, and analysis must be in-depth, sophisticated, and well-developed to earn the highest score.

3 To dramatically affect your score, grammar, usage, and mechanics errors must be both numerous and serious. (However, that doesn't mean you can be sloppy.)

4 The quality of your ideas is far more important than the quantity. However, in order to identify significant problems or flaws and to examine them in adequate, if not dense, detail, you'll need to write a response of some length. Although there is no magic number for success, aim for well-elaborated coverage of at least three flaws in the argument.

REVIEW THE BASICS OF ARGUMENTATION

The good news about the GRE® Argument Task is that you don't need any knowledge of formal argument. You don't have to identify an argument as deductive or inductive, or worry about syllogisms. The purpose of the Argument Task, according to ETS, is to assess your analytical writing skills and your informal reasoning skills. Nevertheless, a quick review of what an argument is and what it does may prove useful in helping you tease out the assumptions, supposed facts, explanations, etc., on which an argument prompt is based.

Basic Argument Facts

The following basic facts define an argument:

An Argument, or the Claim or Thesis at the Center of the Argument, Can Be Simple or Complex. In the prompts you are presented with, your job is always to find the claim, and treat it like a claim, not a fact, no matter how simple or "fact-like" it may appear.

An Argument Persuades. At the heart of an argument is the purpose of causing someone to think in a new way or adopt a new way of acting. Arguments may well inform, but if they don't also at least seek to persuade, they aren't arguments.

Arguments Rely on Evidence. Evidence can consist of everything from a simple anecdote to complex statistics. Examples, illustrations, and facts are all evidence. Evidence alone is never enough, however. The best arguments explain and interpret the evidence and successfully relate that support back to the claim. Because the arguments you will be presented with on the GRE® are so brief, this kind of interpretation will be entirely missing from them. Furthermore, most arguments will lack evidence of any kind—or they will present only flawed or problematic evidence.

There is one additional fact about arguments that you won't find present in the short argument statements on the GRE®, but that you can use to your advantage in writing your response:

A Successful Argument Often Depends, at Least in Part, on Rhetorical Devices to Engage and Sway the Audience. An argument may use rhetorical devices while leading into the claim, reasserting it, or explaining the evidence that supports it. Exploiting the rich connotations of words for their emotional effect, luring the reader in through an engaging opening, or using devices such as parallelism, inversion, or figures of speech to transport the reader smoothly down the road of the argument are some of the rhetorical devices that writers use. Such devices are uncommon in GRE® argument prompts because they are too short. However, in developing your response, you will be framing a long analysis, which is essentially an argument for your point of view, and you can use these devices most effectively for that purpose.

Rhetorical Devices

There are a variety of rhetorical devices that you could employ in your response. The following are perhaps the most useful in this case:

- **Rhetorical question as a lead-in to your introductory paragraph:** Are libraries dead?
- **Metaphor:** A library's after-school programs are a beacon of hope for children of working parents.
- **Simile:** A library's after-school programs are like a magnet that draws the children of working parents to homework clubs and fun reading groups.
- **Understatement:** A library is home to the children of working parents.
- **Overstatement:** With fewer than 400 books a month being borrowed, the city library's circulation of books is dead!
- **Sound devices:** ssssshhhh or click-click, tap, tap—which are the sounds of the modern library?
- **Parallel structure:** I came to the library, I saw its collection of DVDs and CDs, and I was captured by the possibilities of free entertainment.

The Basic Language of Argumentation

In dissecting the argument, it will be helpful if you know what you're looking for. The following is a quick review of the parts and qualities of arguments:

The Claim: The claim is the main idea, proposition, or thesis statement of the argument. As you read the argument part of the prompt, look for the claim, that is, what the argument is about.

The Conclusion: The conclusion is the idea that is reached in the argument. Ask yourself: What's the conclusion arrived at by the end of the argument?

Premise/Assumption: The reasoning process to reach the conclusion begins with premises (or statements assumed to be true). Some people use the word "premise" as a synonym for an "assumption," which is any statement set forth as true or presumed to be true and may be stated or implied. The premises, or assumptions, are the meat of the argument. They lay out the support for the claim, proposition, or thesis. Responding to them will be the major part of your writing.

Counterargument: All argument writers should expect someone to counter their ideas, or present an opinion that opposes their own. In an extended argument, a good writer will anticipate and address counterarguments. The argument prompt is too short for any extended counterarguments; in writing your Argument Task you're in effect countering the argument made in the prompt.

Assessing an Argument as Sound, Valid, Logical: These are three terms that are standard ways to convey that a point is reasonable, logical, or substantiated.

Assessing an Argument as Unsound, Invalid, Illogical: Similarly, these are three terms that brand an argument as unreasonable or that identify it as untrue.

The Perspective or Point of View: As you respond to the Argument Task, consider the perspective or point of view from which the argument is made. As you analyze the premises, ask yourself if the information provided is one-sided, reflecting a bias, or if it presents several sides to the argument. If it's one-sided, which is likely because of space limitations and the need of item writers to provide something for test-takers to write about, what is that point of view? Then, consider what some other points of view about the topic might be and who might hold those other views. That information should help you develop your response.

LEARN THE FLAWS IN ARGUMENTS

The GRE® will present you with flawed arguments. Remember that it's not your job to agree or disagree with the claim, but to expose those flaws. The most common flaws you'll find will be embedded in statements of, or references to, the following:

Unreliable Opinion Polls, Surveys, Questionnaires

You can expose the potential flaws or unreliability of an opinion poll, a survey, a questionnaire, or similar instrument by asking or speculating about the following:

- How many people took part?
- Was it a representative sample?
- Was it a random sample, self-selected, or handpicked?
- What questions were asked?
- Did the wording of the question contribute to a certain answer? (Consider that some questions are leading questions. Consider, too, that some questions do not allow for the full range of possible answers.)

In addition, instruments that are intended to measure change may not account for novelty, that is, initial responses to a change or new policy may be different over time. Also, those who design and analyze surveys, opinion polls, and questionnaires can leap to conclusions that aren't borne out by the data. They overstate or overgeneralize from the data.

Faulty Cause-and-Effect Relationships

Always examine cause-and-effect relationships in the argument. Sometimes, the prompt will confuse a correlation or an association with a cause, or propose a false cause. For example, an argument might suggest that every inch of space in a building is in use; therefore, a new building is needed. But you might be able to undercut this argument by conjecturing about how the space is being used. It may be storing useless equipment or supplies that should be discarded or recycled. You could then point out that the cause is not lack of space, but bad use of space.

False Generalizations

Even if a set of evidence does logically lead to a valid conclusion, it is possible to overgeneralize. That is, it's possible to suggest the data applies to more situations or to more people than it actually does. Another term for this is sweeping generalization.

More common, perhaps, is the hasty generalization that bases a conclusion, a recommendation, advice, or a prediction on too small a sample or an unrepresentative sample. For example, an argument might suggest that because a few public libraries in the state are failing to keep up with technology, all public libraries have the same problem and state government should fund upgrades for all libraries in the state.

False Analogies

If two or more things are alike in one or more ways, it's illogical to suggest that, on the basis of that similarity, they are alike in other ways. For example, if the city funded a new city hall last year, a good choice that met with overwhelming approval, the argument may make a false analogy by suggesting that the new public safety building will be a similarly good choice and meet with the same overwhelming approval.

Either-Or Thinking

This line of "reasoning" suggests that if one thing is true, the other cannot be true, as in "Either we build the new public safety building now, or we act with wanton disregard for the safety of every citizen in this community." Either-or thinking may be used to argue that two courses of action cannot exist at the same time or lead as effectively to the same result at the same time.

Assumptions

ETS rolls many of the specific flaws described above, as well as others, into the blanket term "assumptions." For example, ETS calls faulty cause-and-effect, or the fact that one thing is said to cause another but didn't necessarily, a flawed assumption. Therefore, feel free to use "faulty," "incorrect," or "illogical assumption" to identify most flaws you find, or expose the flaws without naming their type.

A statement such as "One problem with the argument is . . ." is perfectly acceptable based on the models that ETS presents. What will make or break your response is not the language you use to identify flaws, but the ability to recognize flaws, explain the problems with their supposed "support" of the argument, and relate the flaws back to the specific writing instructions.

CREATE YOUR WRITING PLAN

Now that you know what to expect in an Argument Task, it's time to create a plan for attacking it. Think of it as three-pronged: prewriting, drafting, and proofreading. You'll have just 30 minutes to do all this, so you should plan to spend the bulk of that time—say 23 or so minutes—drafting. However, you need to know what you're going to write, so don't skip prewriting.

Prewriting

The prewriting part of your writing plan has these steps that will help you focus on the task, gather your ideas, and plan the development of your response.

TIP

Those taking the computer-based test will be given scrap paper for making notes, so if you're taking the computer version, consider jotting down the key requirements of the instructions. If you're taking the paper-based test, you may want to underline the key requirements.

Restate the Prompt: Read the entire prompt carefully and then restate it in your own words to make certain that you understand the argument and the specific instructions.

Identify the Claim/Issue and Any Statements Based on the Claim: Next, find the claim. Sometimes the word "claim" is actually used in the prompt, but most of the time it is not. Remember that the claim is the main idea or proposition. Statements based on the claim may include advice, recommendations, predictions, explanations, and conclusions. Ask:

- Is the main claim true?

- Is it true in all cases?

- Under what circumstances would it not be true?

Ask some "what if" questions about situations or circumstances in which the claim would be weakened or invalidated. Then decide whether the conclusion, recommendation, prediction, explanation, or advice logically follows from the claim. Ask yourself why.

Examine the Claim/Issue from Different Perspectives: For example, a town is deciding whether it needs a new public safety building to replace its old fire and police station.

Think about this question from the point of view of

- a person who works in the station every day.

- people who will make money from the new construction.

- people who will feel more important if a new station is built.

- taxpayers, some of whom may be burdened by high taxes, unemployment, or both.

- people who think the old building is just fine and it's better to renovate than build new.

ALERT!

The conclusion, recommendation, prediction, explanation, or advice will never be totally logical or completely unassailable!

Jot a "Quick Write": Spend 2 or 3 minutes jotting down your ideas. (Computer-based test-takers will be able to use scrap paper that is provided for this purpose.) This isn't a full outline, but just a list of flaws in the argument, main points, and few supporting ideas for each main point. Ideas won't come in any particular order, so list them as they flow. Then cross out ideas that don't seem as though they fit, and number ideas you want to use in the order in which you want to use them.

The most sophisticated ideas earn the highest scores on the analytical writing measure; therefore, don't just plan on developing the first ideas that pop into your head! Instead, use the best, least simplistic, and most original ideas for your response, ideas that you can substantiate in meaty, persuasive ways. If possible, position your best idea at the end of your essay for greatest rhetorical effect. If you can, also come up with an idea for the opening that will appeal to your audience—with drama, human interest, vivid detail.

Some Tried-and-True Sentence Starters

You can use the basic language of analyzing an argument in sentence starters such as those on the following list. You'll find fleshed-out examples of several of these starters in the sample essays later in this chapter. These sentence starters can help bring clarity to your writing, as well as give your writing an organizational boost by providing transitions between sentences and paragraphs:

- The first problem/the most fundamental problem/an obvious flaw in this argument is . . .

- The statement/prediction/conclusion that XXX is an unjustified assumption because . . .

- A problem with this reasoning is . . .

- It is arguable that . . .

- What if . . .

- The writer/author/argument implies that . . .

- Nothing in this argument actually tells/explains/supports . . .

- This argument asserts that . . .

- This assertion is illogical because . . .

Drafting

In reality, you won't just be drafting: you'll be drafting and revising simultaneously because there's no time to do them as separate steps. To get the most out of your limited time, keep these priorities in mind as you draft:

Answer the Task: Some test-takers produce competent essays that fail to answer the task and, therefore, sink them. After you write your opening or first paragraph, glance briefly back at the task to be sure you are addressing it or are on track to addressing it. (Computer-based users can do this by clicking on "Question Directions" at the top of the screen.) As you answer the task, be as thoughtful and insightful as you can be. Be sure you focused on the flaws in the argument.

Organize Your Response: The following pattern is a standard, or traditional, way to organize your overall response. It leads your reader smoothly through your response by eliminating confusion and guesswork. In addition, it helps to create fluency—or the illusion of it. If you're a writer who has trouble with organization, this pattern gives you a structure to develop your ideas around:

- Opening paragraph: Thesis or clear statement of your position

- Body paragraph 1: Reason 1 for your position, fully explained and supported

- Body paragraph 2: Reason 2 for your position, fully explained and supported

- Body paragraph 3: A statement of the most effective counterargument, an acknowledgment of its reasonableness, and your fully explained and supported response; or any other specific and developed point needed to address the writing task instructions

- Closing paragraph: Reason 3 (another key challenge or another main point) that directly responds to the specific writing instructions; provides support as needed; plus a detail, statement, question, or other device that delivers closure to your response

TIP

Using a standard pattern of organization has an added benefit. If you decide ahead of time how to set up your response, you can save time when faced with writing the actual response on test day.

Suppose you use this pattern of organization. How do you decide what reason to use first, second, and third? Often, the best way to organize points for an argument is by order of importance. You could choose your most significant reason to be first or last. If you use your most powerful, that is, strongest, support as the third and final point, your readers will take away from your response your most impressive piece of argument.

Provide Ample, Thoughtful, Well-Developed Support: As you lay out each main point of your response, be sure you support it fully with the best evidence, and be sure you explain that evidence clearly enough so that it actually does evaluate the recommendation, advice, prediction, explanation, or conclusion. All the topics are meant to be general enough that anyone can answer them. For example, a prompt may ask you to discuss the questions that would need to be asked in order to decide if a recommendation to adopt honor codes by colleges and universities is reasonable. No special knowledge is required to respond to this prompt, but if you have experience with an honor code, you could incorporate that experience. Observations, such as your own experience, facts, authoritative opinions, examples, and human interest stories can and should be used liberally to support your points.

Link Ideas Clearly: Your organization doesn't have to be traditional, or based in any way on typical instruction in college writing classes, but it does have to be logical and help to create overall coherence. Based on reviewing sample analyses, ETS values transitional words and phrases, so link paragraphs and ideas appropriately as you write. Also, don't overlook the value of a topic sentence in providing an organizational boost to your essay.

Consider Style: If you're aiming for a top score, vary your sentences and word choices. Note that transitional words and phrases not only help you create coherence, but they can help you vary the beginnings of sentences as well.

TIP

If you have enough time, look for ways to increase the style quotient of your response by making your opening more attention getting, tweaking word choice so that it's stronger or more vivid, and varying your sentences.

TRANSITIONS

Review the following lists of transitional words and phrases and use them as you practice writing responses to the tasks in the practice tests. In that way, you can integrate them into your writing style so they flow as you write your actual responses on test day.

Transitions to Introduce or Link Opinions and Reasons

because	*evidently*	*indeed*
besides	*for this reason*	*on the other hand*
by comparison	*furthermore*	*since*
consequently	*however*	*therefore*

Transitions that Introduce or Link Examples

for example	*in this case*	*one type*
for instance	*in this situation*	*to illustrate this point*

Transitions that Create Emphasis or Add Information

after all	*furthermore*	*more important*
again	*in addition*	*moreover*
besides	*indeed*	*similarly*
certainly	*in fact*	*what's more*

Transitions that Introduce Opposing Views

although this may be true	*naturally*	*on the other hand*
even though	*nevertheless*	*undeniably*
evidently	*notwithstanding*	*unquestionably*
it may be said	*of course*	*without a doubt*

Proofreading

Save 2 or 3 minutes for proofreading and fine-tuning your essay. An omitted word could invalidate a good point by making the sentence in which it appears unclear or nonsensical. Look specifically for the following:

Check Your Thesis: Make sure that you've stated it and stated it clearly. Make sure your response reflects this statement.

Look for Omitted Words: When you're writing in a hurry, it's easy to leave out what could be a crucial word.

Check for Sentence Faults: At this stage, you want to make certain that you eliminate any ineffective fragments, any run-on sentences, and any fused sentences or comma splices.

Don't Spend Time on Spelling or Commas: Keep in mind that the rubric doesn't mention spelling. Spelling evidently has "minor error" status for ETS readers. Likewise, ETS readers aren't concerned with errors such as a missing comma here or there.

NOTE

Correct a fused sentence by making two sentences, or, if the sentences are closely related in meaning, by replacing the comma with a semicolon.

A FINAL NOTE OF CAUTION

ETS wants its computer-based users to know that their responses will be subjected to analysis by software that searches for similarities to published information. It warns that it will "cancel" a score if it contains any unacknowledged use of sources. In addition, ETS will cancel a response if an essay or any part of it has been prepared by another person. Finally, a score will be cancelled if it includes language that is "substantially" similar to the language in one or more other test responses.

ARGUMENT PROMPT WITH SIX MODEL RESPONSES, SCORING, AND ANALYSES

Use this prompt as a practice opportunity and compare your response with the samples, scoring, and analyses that follow.

Time yourself; in the real test, you will have 30 minutes.

1. Read the prompt.
2. Follow the prewriting steps.
3. Stop! Compare your "quick write" plan with the sample that follows the prompt to see different ideas (perhaps more sophisticated, perhaps less) that you might have thought of.
4. Draft your response.
5. Read each model that follows the sample "quick write." Determine the positive and negative qualities of each sample response before you read its scoring analysis.
6. Score your response against the rubric on pages 160–161. Be honest in your analysis.

Argument Task

In our fast-paced, digital world, the public library has long been on the way out. In Springfield, where the population voted for a library expansion in 2001, 42 percent of residents opposed the expansion at that time. One can be certain that figure has grown by leaps and bounds since then, especially now that Springfield can no longer maintain its library at its previous financial levels. Therefore, the city should accept the offer of Infogenesys to run the library with its dusty books and tattered magazines as a for-profit business. The city will divest itself of a costly burden, and residents who are still using such fast disappearing methods for getting information will retain the option of getting that information at what Infogenesys promises will be a nominal cost.

Write a response in which you discuss the stated and/or unstated assumptions, and explain how the argument is based on these assumptions and the implications for the argument if the assumptions are shown to be unjustified.

Sample "Quick Write"

The 6-point response to this prompt began with a process like the one that follows. First, the writer identified flaws. Notice that not every flaw in the argument is recorded here. Notice also, however, that the writer found many flaws and, therefore, a firm basis for analysis.

> Flaws
>
> public library not on way out: library probably digital
>
> 2001 isn't now; 58% were in favor
>
> "certain" that figure has grown—no evidence
>
> dusty books/tattered magazines—true?
>
> Who is Infogenesys? Why should city accept offer?
>
> library is a burden?

TIP

Note how specific the "quick write" is. The writer is off to a good start for developing a response that is grounded in specific details to support any generalizations that the writer may make.

Now look at the plan the writer quickly made:

①　all? libraries digital

①ⓑ　online catalog, big variety of databases

①ⓐ　busy: meetings, tutoring, art exhibits, lectures,

　　　　children's summer reading program, book sales

　　　so busy can't park at Melville Library

③　burden—would people who use it say that?

②　2001 isn't now

②ⓐ　58% were in favor

②ⓑ　vote about expansion, not whether to have a free public

　　　　library

Making Your Plan Work

As you'll see when you read the 6-point essay based on this prewriting activity, some of the success of the response is due directly to ideas listed here. First, notice how the plan isn't a formal outline; it doesn't need to be. There is no five-paragraph organization of intro, body, conclusion expressed in the quick write. Instead, the plan goes to the heart of the 30-minute Argument Task and reflects a great variety of evidence for exposing the flaws in the argument. You'll see in the response how this planning leads to a dense, richly supported analysis that effectively undermines the argument.

Notice how, even in the prewriting, the writer goes beyond the obvious ideas (that 2001 isn't now and that 58 percent of people were in favor of the expansion) to think a little more deeply about the nature of the vote and its implications.

When you read the resulting essay, you'll also see that the writer didn't use every idea here. For example, the writer left out the idea about parking, which was probably a good choice because it was one of the less thoughtful kinds of support he or she could have provided.

Furthermore, there are many more ideas in the essay than appear in this simple plan. Remember that fact when you make your plan. You don't have to come up with every possible idea during prewriting. Writing is a generative process; ideas come to writers as they write. Trust that they will come to you, too. The secrets to successful prewriting are mainly the following:

- Quickly generate more ideas than you think you need.

- Edit out the least significant, the simplest, or the most predictable ideas.

- Know when to stop: try not to spend more than 3 minutes on prewriting.

Model 1: 6 points out of 6

Someone who refers to the public library as a collection of dusty books and tattered magazines inadvertently exposes a complete ignorance of today's public libraries—of which the Springfield library may be entirely representative—whose circulation figures are now heavily comprised of digital items and whose services are as much about meeting a wide range of community needs, including job searching, as they are about making print items available. This argument needs a firmer basis in reality before it can successfully argue that the people of Springfield should hand their library over to a for-profit company.

First, it is highly arguable that the public library, or any public library, is on its way out or that it has not kept up with the changing times. In general, public libraries today have a large variety of functions that have nothing to do with print items. They provide meeting places for large groups, such as public or nonprofit committees, and small groups, such as one-on-one or one-on-two tutoring. They offer ways for new community members to learn about their town or city and its services. They provide a wide range of databases, from local and national newspapers, to encyclopedias, to health and wellness databases, to business databases that permit the user to do everything from invest wisely in a mutual fund to determine whether the refrigerator he or she is about to buy is worth the price and really does what it claims to do. Not all of this information is available to private Internet users; much of it exists in costly, subscription databases. Some public libraries hang art exhibits, offer programs on everything from gathering local grasses and herbs to the nation's history, and encourage literacy by establishing summer reading and other reading programs for children and adults. They also sponsor book groups for adults, Yet, the writer of this argument assumes that none of this is happening in the Springfield public library—when all of it and much more might be. Instead, the writer peremptorily decides that it is a place where books and magazines molder untouched.

Moreover, the prediction that people would vote overwhelmingly to rid themselves of the public library is an unjustified assumption. Even if past performance were a guarantee of future results, which it is not, the statistics do not show that people voted overwhelmingly against their library in the past; rather, they show that the people voted for it. Nor do the statistics reveal under what circumstances even 42 percent of the city voted against the new addition. Some of those people could have been in favor of expanding the library, yet waiting for a more optimal time to expand, such as when state funding might increase or during a year when Springfield was not also investing heavily in, as one possibility, its water works. Most fundamentally, a vote against expansion is not the same as a vote for no free, public library at all.

As for the library's being a costly burden to the city, a detailed cost-benefit analysis might well prove this assumption incorrect. Such an analysis might compare the cost and benefits of the Springfield Public Library with other institutions in the city; it might also more fairly and fundamentally probe the potential losses to the community if the library were no longer a free, public institution. Until such an analysis is done, the word "burden," with all its connotations of onerous, unwanted weight and responsibility, should not be used. It forms a misleading part of yet another of the unsubstantiated statements on which this illogical argument is based.

Scoring Analysis

This essay scores 6 out of 6 because it

- **answers the task.** The writer examines several statements that form the basis of the argument for their implications and for their reasonableness. In doing so, the author probes deeply to create a thoughtful analysis of several unsubstantiated statements and their implications.

- **is well supported.** The writer offers numerous examples of what today's library, and therefore, the Springfield library by inference, might be, do, and offer, thereby refuting the reasonableness of the premise that all public libraries are now a place where books gather dust. Other points are likewise well substantiated.

- **is well organized.** There is a clear opening and an effective closing, and the body paragraphs are logically organized. All ideas lead logically from one to the next.

- **is fluid, precise, and graceful.** Sentences and word choices (such as "peremptorily" and "molder") are varied and, at times, quite sophisticated and graceful. Statements are placed effectively at the ends of paragraphs for clincher effect. The tone and style are appropriate to the task.

- **observes the conventions of Standard Written English.**

Other observations: Notice how this response doesn't try to refute every statement and implication—nor does it need to in order to be successful. Notice, too, how deeply it probes. For example, it moves from the obvious flaw that 42 percent against expansion still means 58 percent for expansion (an easy problem to spot) to a more sophisticated analysis of the possible implications of that statistic. Also, examine how rich, varied, and dense the support is for the idea that public libraries are vital places.

Write Your Observations About Model 1

_____
_____
_____
_____
_____
_____
_____
_____
_____
_____
_____
_____
_____
_____
_____
_____
_____
_____
_____
_____
_____
_____
_____
_____
_____
_____
_____
_____
_____
_____
_____
_____
_____
_____
_____
_____
_____
_____
_____

Model 2: 5 points out of 6

The writer of this argument is both 100 percent certain and clear. But has s/he presented us with a reasoned, logical argument? A few questions can quickly begin to tear holes in this argument.

What if it was true that circulation rates are actually climbing at public libraries across the nation including at the Springfield Public Library? What if it was the case that the books on the shelves of the Springfield Public Library are not the least bit dusty and being read all the time instead? What if it was true that the magazines are, in fact, tattered, but they're tattered because they're being used all the time? These facts would help rip apart the argument that Springfield should give its library over to Infogenesys as a for-profit business.

Also, since when aren't libraries fast paced and digital? The writer implies that libraries in general and the Springfield library in particular aren't keeping up with the world because of not being digital or fast paced, but the argument doesn't have evidence to support that idea. Libraries across the country are filled with terminals, and usually there is a sign-up sheet for using them because every single one is occupied and so there has to be a fair way of sharing them. What if in fact many, many Springfield citizens are accessing their library catalog or databases remotely and getting services and information that way that they couldn't get on their own computers at home?

Finally, how do we know who wrote this argument. If a representative of Infogenesys, which might stand to make a very good deal by getting the library and all its assets and turning them into a business, wrote it, then many statements here might be biased or one-sided and the whole argument a lot less then valid. In fact, the argument doesn't give the background, aims, and goals of Infogenesys, and they could include buying the library, operating it short term for profit, and then selling the property it stands on (which could be prime Main Street property) for a huge redevelopment profit.

Scoring Analysis

This essay scores 5 out of 6 because it

- **answers the task.** The writer examines some statements that form the basis of the argument for their implications and for their reasonableness. The analysis raises many thoughtful points.

- **is well supported.** The writer offers competent what-if questions that expose the possible flaws in statements that form the basis of the argument. The writer also offers clear examples, although not in depth.

- **is well organized.** The ideas lead logically from one to the next.

- **is fluid and precise.** Sentences and word choices are varied, although many of the word choices are more serviceable than sophisticated. The tone and style are for the most part appropriate to the task, though a bit overwrought at times.

- **observes the conventions of Standard Written English.**

Other observations: Notice that while this response touches on many ideas, it actually examines and develops fewer statements and implications than the 6-point essay does. The opening is competent, but quite predictable. Compare the opening, as well as the body paragraphs, with the 6-point essay to see differences in the quality of both the thinking and the writing.

Write Your Observations About Model 2

Model 3: 4 points out of 6

When was the last time the writer of this arguement was really in a public library? It sounds like he never goes there at all! Public libraries I have used include Montvale Public Library, where I grew up, a branch of the New York public library where my family moved after I went to college, the Madison public library where I went to undergraduate school, and the small, but pretty busy Deansville library where I now live. All of these public libraries keep changing as the times change, they offer people the tools they need now. They are busy places with many uses. I think that many people are in them really often. I can't imagine how much people would loose if any of these libraries charged people for it's services. It would be a terrible thing if any of them had to close or be taken over by a private company like Infogenesys.

The writer of this arguement insults the users of public libraries by saying that they are people who are still using outdated methods for getting information. Implying that they are technophobes or computer illiterite. Well, what if all the people in the public library are really the smartest people in Springfield? They are in there library getting more and better information then they can get at home. Maybe they are even there getting information on Infogenesys and how it operates. All of this being left unclear by the writer who really doesn't want us knowing who Infogenesys is or what it's past is. Nevertheless, it insults the people of Springfield by saying that the people in the library are the ones who can't get information any other way.

My sense in the Montvale Public Library, where I grew up, the branch of the New York public library I used sometimes, the Madison public library and the Deansville library is that more people are using them then ever before. If the writer of this arguement ever went inside a library maybe he could see that for himself. Otherwise maybe he could get some circulation figures about these libraries or the Springfield library. The circulation figures might tell that the use of the library is going up and up and up and pretty much wreck his argument. The Springfield Library might also keep counts of how many people come thru there doors each and everyday. That would probably tell the writer that the Springfield library really is an important place in the city and not a place just to give away to some company that wants to make a profit off it.

But the writer is too busy insulting the people of Springfield, while he is actually writing an arguement that also insults the intelligence of the readers of the arguement. Being as he uses a ridiculous statistic in favor of his idea when that statistic is really against his idea. The statistic is that 42% of the people were against adding on to the library in 2001. That means that 58% of the people were for it. Last I knew 58% was a majority. So the writer is not just insulting the people of Springfield and trying to make them loose out their public library but he is also insulting the readers of this arguement.

Finally, charging people to get into their own library is a bad idea with bad consequences. It's definately going to hurt the poor people. And nobody is going to want to pay for something that use to be free. So maybe all those books and magazines and everything else that the people of Springfield paid for over all the years they had a library really is going to get dusty on the shelves. An important place for meeting and learning in the city is going to be an empty place so that some private company can profit off of it. This arguement is an insult to the people of Springfield and to the readers of the arguement.

Scoring Analysis

This essay scores 4 out of 6 because it

- **generally answers the task.** That is, it probes the argument both for what it says directly and what it implies. It identifies weaknesses in the argument that seriously undermine it.

- **is supported, but often simply and repetitively.** The examples of the writer's own libraries do form support, but that support is simple, weak, and tangential. Some ideas are repeated. Assertions about use going up and many people using the library are simplistic and vague.

- **is organized.** In general, the ideas flow in an acceptable order, though some repeated ideas should have been deleted. There is no transition between the opening paragraph and the second paragraph.

- **is sufficiently clear.** The sentences and words are mainly serviceable, though they lack sophistication. A number of sentences are convoluted and difficult to understand though they do not detract from the meaning of the paragraphs.

- **observes the conventions of Standard Written English.** There are several errors here, but, in general, they do not interfere with meaning.

Other observations: This is an example of a very long essay that doesn't succeed on the basis of its length. In fact, its length is part of its problem. The response would have been more cogent had repeated ideas and vague assertions been deleted. While ETS gives no indication in its scoring rubrics of how informal diction and a less than objective tone might undercut a score, it is probably safe to assume that the writer's choices in these regards in no way enhance this essay and may well undermine it by contributing to the scorer's sense of inadequate word choice or unconventional usage in respect to the purpose, audience, and writing occasion.

Write Your Observations About Model 3

_____

_____

_____

_____

_____

_____

_____

_____

_____

_____

_____

_____

_____

_____

_____

_____

_____

_____

_____

_____

_____

_____

_____

_____

_____

_____

_____

_____

_____

_____

_____

_____

_____

_____

_____

_____

_____

_____

_____

_____

_____

_____

_____

_____

_____

Model 4: 3 points out of 6

As a person who has pretty much stopped using libraries, I more or less agree that many public libraries have outworn their usefulness. They may have been a crucial nineteenth century institution. They may have even served our nation well into most of the twentieth century. But with the coming of the Internet, the public library is now an obsolete institution. If businesses can make a profit out of them while still extending some outdated services to the members of a community, that is a reasonable course of action.

There are, however, some flaws in this argument that make it less than sound. The flaws have mainly to do with things that are left out of the argument. The argument lacks evidence for most things that it says. There is no explanation and evidence for the idea that the percentage of residents who would want to vote against a public library has grown by "leaps and bounds" between 2001 and the present. Someone would actually have to do a poll to see if that were true. If it were not true, then the argument would be affected in a negative way. In addition, more explanation is needed for a reader to believe that the people who voted for expansion in 2001 would want to lose their library now. Also, what is the evidence that Springfield can "no longer maintain" its library? There might, for example, be some evidence to suggest that Springfield could actually reallocate funds from other sources for its library, if there is enough political will to do so, and that also would affect the argument in a negative way.

Scoring Analysis

This essay scores 3 out of 6 because it

- **answers the task in a very limited way.** The first paragraph is well written, but off course as it offers agreement with the argument instead of launching immediately into an analysis of it. The second paragraph does offer three acceptable insights.

- **is not well supported.** All insights in this essay are crammed into two paragraphs without much support. Sentences 2 and 3 of paragraph 2 offer more repetition than support. Statements such as "Someone would actually have to do a poll to see if that were true" begin to provide support, but only vague support.

- **lacks organization.** Paragraph 2 should have been split into separate paragraphs and each main idea developed more thoroughly.

- **is fluid and precise.** Unfortunately, good word choice and sentence construction as well as appropriate style and tone do not outrate poor critical analysis.

- **observes the conventions of Standard Written English.** Unfortunately, excellent command of the conventions of Standard Written English do not outrate poor critical analysis.

Other observations: This is an example of how a well-written response doesn't score high because the quality (or extent) of the thinking is not on the same level as the quality of the word choice or sentence construction. The writer may have run out of ideas or out of time.

Write Your Observations About Model 4

Model 5: 2 points out of 6

This argument suggests that Springfield and its residents would be a lot better off if its libary were in private not public hands. So the first thing to examine is the private hands. Who is Infogenesys and have they bought libaries before and what were the results in the communities where they bought the libaries? Did they really continue to provide the people of the city with a libary and was it acceptable to them and what was the nominal price they charged for using it and was the nominal price really nominal? Or did that price turn out to be pretty high for some people who didn't get the information they wanted or needed as a result? The answers affect the argument by showing that things might not go well if Infogenesys gets the library and starts charging a high price and people stop using the libary as a result.

Scoring Analysis

This essay scores 2 out of 6 because it

- **answers the task in a very limited way.** It identifies for analysis just two ideas in the argument: the motives and history of Infogenesys and the nominal price it will supposedly charge. It does, however, ask good questions.

- **is not supported.** While the writer shows some insight in the ideas selected for analysis, these ideas are, mainly, not explained and developed.

- **lacks organization.** A single paragraph is not an essay.

- **has poorly constructed sentences.** Most of the sentences coordinate one or more ideas that should be subordinated.

- **observes the conventions of Standard Written English.** While not committing obvious grammatical errors, the writer shows a lack of command of sentence construction.

Write Your Observations About Model 5

(blank ruled lines)

Model 6: 1 point out of 6

Selling the public libraries of our nation is a new idea that some communities are considering now, especially when their budgets are stretched. This sale may well have some validity for Springfield and its residents, especially since everyday we are getting more and more information from the Internet via our home and work computers. It is true that no one really and truly needs a library anymore, unless they don't have a computer, they are traveling and didn't bring their computer, or their computer is broken or out for repair.

Scoring Analysis

This essay scores 1 out of 6 because it

- **it does not answer the task.** Instead, it agrees with a premise in the prompt.

Write Your Observations About Model 6

SUMMING IT UP

- The Argument Task of the Analytical Writing portion of the GRE® revised General Test measures how well test-takers can analyze an argument, including the evidence to support that argument, and then discuss their analysis using examples from the given argument.

- The argument will be of a general nature, and no special knowledge will be required to analyze and discuss it.

- The prompt will be accompanied by a set of instructions that establishes the conditions or requirements for your response.

- You will be presented with one argument. You won't have a choice from which to select.

- The Argument Task is part of the Analytical Writing section, which is always first in an administration of the GRE®. The time limit for the Argument Task, like the Issue Task, is 30 minutes.

- Those taking the computer version of the GRE® will use specially designed word processing software that allows the user to insert and delete text, cut and paste text, and undo actions. There is no spell or grammar checker.

- Like the Issue Task, the argument is scored against a rubric using a 0 to 6 range in 1-point increments. The scores for the Argument Task and the Issue Task are averaged and reported as a combined score ranging from 0 to 6 in half-point increments.

- The basic facts of argumentation are the following:
  o An argument can be simple or complex.
  o An argument is meant to persuade.
  o An argument relies on evidence.
  o A successful argument often depends on rhetorical devices to sway the audience.

- The basic language of an argument is claim, conclusion, premise/assumption, counterargument, assessment of an argument (sound, valid, logical; unsound, invalid, illogical), perspective, or point of view.

- The flaws in an argument can be based on unreliable opinion polls, surveys, and questionnaires; faulty cause-and-effect relationships; false generalizations; false analogies; either-or thinking; or assumptions.

- Your writing plan should consist of:
  o Prewriting: restate the prompt, identify the claim/issue and any statements based on it, examine the claim/issue from different perspectives, jot a quick write
  o Drafting: answer the task, organize your response, provide well-developed support, link ideas clearly, consider style
  o Proofreading: check your thesis, look for omitted words, check for sentence faults, don't spend time on spelling or commas

- While spelling is not included in the scoring rubric, transitions are, so be sure to include them as you draft your response.

- While you shouldn't spend time on spelling or minor mechanical errors, remember that misspelled words and lack of punctuation or wrong punctuation can detract from meaning.

PART IV
VERBAL REASONING

Strategies for Reading Comprehension Questions

OVERVIEW

- Basic information about reading comprehension questions
- Active reading
- General strategies for answering multiple-choice questions
- Additional strategies for multiple-choice questions—select one or more answer choices
- Strategies for select-in-passage questions
- Practice questions
- Answer key and explanations
- Summing it up

Chapter 6 describes the reading comprehension questions on the GRE®. These questions make up about half of each Verbal Reasoning section. The majority of reading comprehension questions are multiple-choice questions—select one answer choice. However, there are two other formats for reading comprehension questions: select-in-passage questions and multiple-choice questions—select one or more answer choices. In addition to basic information about the reading comprehension section, Chapter 6 offers useful strategies to help you answer reading comprehension questions in all three formats quickly and competently.

BASIC INFORMATION ABOUT READING COMPREHENSION QUESTIONS

The reading comprehension questions on the Verbal Reasoning section of the GRE® assess your ability to understand, analyze, and apply information found in the types of reading you will encounter in graduate school. About half the questions on the verbal section of the GRE® are reading comprehension questions.

The Passages

There are approximately ten reading comprehension passages on the GRE®. They are based on information found in a wide range of scholarly and everyday sources from nonfiction books to popular periodicals to scholarly journals. The arts and humanities, physical sciences, biological sciences, social sciences, and business are all content areas that may be represented in the passages.

The passages may be from one to several paragraphs in length. Most, however, will be one paragraph; only one or two will be longer. Some passages will inform. Others will analyze. Still others will argue a point and seek to persuade. As in all real-world writing, a single passage may reflect more than one mode of exposition.

Each reading comprehension question appears on a separate screen with the passage on which it is based. If the passage is too long to display legibly on a single screen, as in the case of multi-paragraph passages, you will be able to scroll through the passage without changing screens.

Directly before the start of the passage is a statement of how many questions each passage has, for example:

QUESTIONS 1–3 ARE BASED ON THE FOLLOWING PASSAGE.

A direction line appears from time to time during the questions—not each and every time—telling you how many answers to select, for example:

> **FOR QUESTIONS 1–3, CHOOSE ONLY <u>ONE</u> ANSWER CHOICE UNLESS OTHERWISE INDICATED.**

A Word to the Wise: Put Aside Your Personal Views

When it comes to the content of the passages, ETS notes that occasionally "your own views may conflict with those presented in a passage." That is, you may have a reaction to the content of a passage that runs the gamut from mild disagreement to outrage. Don't let these reactions interfere with your analysis. To succeed, temporarily shelve any feelings and get on with answering the question(s) about the passage.

Question-and-Answer Formats

Each passage is followed by one to six questions. There are three formats that questions and answers may take for reading comprehension questions:

1 Multiple-choice questions—select one answer choice

2 Multiple-choice questions—select one or more answer choices

3 Select-in-passage

Most reading comprehension questions ask you to select *one* answer from a list of five possible answer choices. The answer choices for these questions will be preceded by *ovals*.

You will find a few multiple-choice questions that ask you to select *one or more answers* from a list of three possible choices. One, two, or all three answers may be correct. You have to select all the correct possibilities to earn credit for that question. The answer choices for these questions are preceded by *squares*.

You will find only a few questions that ask you to *select a particular sentence* in the passage as your answer. To do this, you will highlight your answer choice by clicking on the sentence. If you are working with a passage of several paragraphs, the paragraph or paragraphs that the question refers to will be marked with an arrow at the beginning and end of the subject paragraphs. Clicking on a sentence in any other part of the passage will not highlight it.

For your convenience in working through this book, we are marking answer choices as (A), (B), (C), and so on.

Skills

The purpose of the GRE® is to predict success in graduate school. Therefore, the questions on the test are meant to assess the preparedness of potential graduate school students. You will find questions that ask you to use the skills and abilities that are expected of students in graduate school. To answer questions on the reading comprehension section of the GRE®, you will need to be able to

- identify or infer the main idea, or major point, of a passage.

- distinguish between main and subordinate ideas (major and minor points in GRE® parlance).

- summarize information.

- reason from incomplete data to infer missing information.

- determine the relationship of ideas to one another and/or to the passage in which they appear.

- analyze a text.

- draw conclusions from information.

- identify the author's assumptions or perspective.

- identify the strengths and weaknesses of a position.

- develop and assess alternative ideas.

- determine the meaning of individual words, sentences, and paragraphs, and of longer pieces of writing.

Some questions require you to use more than one skill at a time. For example, you might need the main idea to answer a question, but to find it, you might have to distinguish between main ideas and subordinate or supporting details. Or you might have to find a relationship between ideas by both inferring information about main and subordinate ideas and using structural clues to understand meaning.

Recurring Question Types

The list of skills may seem daunting, but when put in the context of actual questions, they will seem much more familiar. For example, the question "Which of the following best restates the author's point of view?" asks for the main idea of the passage. To find it, you may need to infer it, or it may be directly stated, though probably not in a graduate-level piece of writing.

You will find that certain categories of questions recur among the reading comprehension questions. The common question types are the following:

- **Main Idea Questions:** These questions require you to identify or infer the main idea (or major point), summarize the passage, draw conclusions from complete or incomplete information about the main idea, and infer relationships between the main idea and subordinating details. You will find this to be a common question type, both in this book and on the GRE®. Sample questions might be:

  o Which of the following does the passage most clearly support?

  o What was the underlying cause of the financial crisis?

o   What qualities of the painter's style most influenced the critic's view?

o   The passage implies that the president's actions were based on...

o   Select the sentence that restates the premise of the author's argument.

- **Supporting or Subordinate Details Questions:** These questions ask you to identify subordinate details, infer subordinate details, summarize the passage, draw conclusions about subordinate details, or infer relationships between two or more subordinate details.

  o   The passage mentions financial regulations in order to...

  o   You can infer that the president's actions were based on...

  o   The passage notes each of the following causes EXCEPT...

  o   Based on the passage, which of the following was excluded from the experiment?

  o   The passage suggests that which set of data is the more compelling?

  o   The purpose of the sentence "Yet a close look . . . continents" is to...

  o   Select the sentence that restates the author's claim.

- **Author's Perspective Questions:** To answer these questions, you may need to infer the author's attitude or tone, or deduce the author's unstated assumptions. Not every question that mentions the author—or even the author's beliefs—is a perspective question. The question may, for example, be a main idea question such as the last example under Main Idea Questions.

  o   What was the underlying cause of the financial crisis, according to the author?

  o   The author attributes the early experimental results to...

  o   It can be inferred from the passage that the author believes that...

  o   The author of the passage most likely agrees with which historian's view as described in the passage?

  o   Select the sentence that best describes the author's attitude toward critics of Darwin.

- **Application Questions:** These test items ask you to evaluate the strengths and weaknesses of an argument, develop alternative explanations, hypothesize about the relationship of new ideas to stated or implied ideas, and use structural clues to determine or infer meaning. As their name suggests, these questions will often require you to apply or build on what you have already identified or inferred about the main idea, supporting details, or the author's perspective in earlier questions in the set for a particular passage and then apply that information to a different idea or situation.

  o   Which of the following, if it were true, would weaken the author's argument?

  o   Select the sentence that best describes the opinions of the anthropologists who actually examined the skeleton.

  o   What is the primary purpose of the two groups of words in bold type?

  o   Which of the following is most similar in reasoning to the ideas expressed in the final sentence?

  o   According to the passage, which is the correct sequence of events?

- **Word-Meaning Questions:** These questions are easy to spot because they're accompanied by line numbers to help you quickly pinpoint the word and the context. They require you to infer the meaning of a word from the specific context in which it appears. The phrase "specific context" is important because words have different meanings in different subject areas and as different parts of speech.
  - o "Verisimilitude" (line XX) most nearly means...
  - o In the passage, "obfuscate" means...

ACTIVE READING

This is a timed test, and you will—and should—feel the pressure of the clock. Nevertheless, you can't read a GRE® reading comprehension passage at the same rate at which you read the back of a cereal box or the latest posting to your favorite blog. In general, adjust your reading rate so that you're reading every passage with concentration and active participation. This can be hard to do when the clock is ticking, but it's your best bet to improve your comprehension, and it is especially good advice when the content is unfamiliar to you.

Just slowing down as you read won't help you much. You need to focus on what you are reading and participate actively in what you're reading. Participating actively includes the following steps:

- Identify the topic, main idea, thesis, or proposition.
- Clarify your understanding.
- Summarize what you've read.

To help you understand the process, skim the following reading comprehension passage to get an idea of its topic, main idea, and details.

Passage 1

Sculptor Henry Moore (born 1898) achieved prominence in the 1930s with his earliest recumbent figures. An English abstractionist, Moore has also been associated with romantic feeling in the relationship of his biomorphic forms to nature. His sculptures, which often consist of large flowing, rhythmic masses united by a common base, have been called universal
5 shapes by art historian Brian McAvera, who credits them with subconscious appeal to our essential humanity. Yet, this characterization is not entirely comforting, for the biomorphic figures, many of which are suggestive of the female figure, can both soothe and disturb as they evoke motherhood, sexuality, or even a surreal anxiety. Moreover, Moore can be said to have explained and celebrated the void as much as he explored the body in his sculptures,
10 which, as time marched forward and his fame grew, came to be modeled rather than carved and more the product of mass-production techniques than of exacting attention to every inch of every surface.

Identify the Topic, Main Idea, Thesis, or Proposition

The more unfamiliar the subject matter of the passage is, the more basic your approach must be. Furthermore, working step by step to find meaning can help you focus. Determine the main idea first. If you can't identify the main idea, then start by identifying the simple subject, or topic, of the passage. For example, the topic of Passage 1 is the sculptures of Henry Moore.

TIP

If you are running out of time, you could go through remaining passages looking for word-meaning questions. To answer the sentence, read the question, the sentence referred to in the question, and the sentences immediately before and after this sentence.

To get from topic or subject to thesis, main idea, or proposition, ask yourself what the author is saying about the topic or subject. If you can establish only part of that thesis, main idea, or proposition, do as much as you can. For example, you might begin identifying the thesis of Passage 1 as:

> The author is saying that Henry Moore's sculptures consist of large flowing masses, some of which are figures that both comfort and disturb.

Clarify Your Understanding

There are a variety of techniques for clarifying understanding. One is to ask and answer questions as you read. For example, you might ask yourself what a concept means or the meaning of a word in the context of the passage. As you read Passage 1 on Henry Moore, you might ask yourself what "biomorphic" means. At least one question on the reading comprehension test is almost certain to be about the meaning of a key word. Often, this word will convey a meaning that is specific to the context. Again, if you can establish only part of that meaning, do at least that much, using knowledge of word parts, context clues, or other applicable strategies. For example:

> In the passage, the term "biomorphic" seems to have a specific meaning that is related to shapes, figures, and nature. The word part *bio-* suggests humans or animals; the word part *morph-* suggests forms or shapes.

Another way to clarify understanding is by stopping to restate or paraphrase information. This usually involves rereading the previous sentence or perhaps a couple of sentences. For example, you might stop and ask yourself just exactly what the second sentence in the passage is saying. Restate whatever you can. Don't worry if you can't restate everything. Your thinking might be something like the following:

> The second sentence of the test passage says that Moore's work was abstract; that is, he didn't represent things as they really are. It says his shapes are biomorphic, or forms of humans and animals. It says his sculptures had a relationship to nature.

Summarize

Quickly summarize the passage to yourself after you have read it, but before you begin answering the question(s). This strategy can also help you clarify your understanding.

GENERAL STRATEGIES FOR ANSWERING MULTIPLE-CHOICE QUESTIONS

The purposes, structures, and content of the reading comprehension passages and questions you will encounter on the GRE® will vary widely, and, unfortunately, there is no single strategy and no magic bullet that can guarantee success with all. In addition to active reading, the following ten general strategies will help you answer reading comprehension multiple-choice questions, whether you need to select one answer choice or more than one answer choice:

1 Restate the question.

2 Try answering the question before you read the answer choices.

3 Read all the answers before you choose.

4 Compare answer choices to each other and the question.

5 Avoid selecting an answer you don't fully understand.

6 Choose the *best* answer.

7 Pay attention to structure and structural clues.

8 Don't select an answer just because it's true.

9 Substitute answer choices in word meaning questions.

10 Choose the answer that *doesn't* fit for EXCEPT questions.

This list may seem like a huge number of strategies to remember and use on test day, but there are two things to remember about the strategies:

1 Not all strategies will work for all questions. That said, the first three strategies will work for any question. If you've taken the SAT or AP subject tests, you've used these strategies.

2 The more you practice using the strategies as you work through this book, the easier they will be to remember, to figure out which are the appropriate strategies to use for different questions, and to apply on test day.

For the first six strategies in this section, you will focus on a single reading comprehension passage and a single question. There is an additional strategy later in the chapter for multiple-choice questions—select one or more answer choices.

If you're reading a physical book, you will want to mark the page with the passage and the question with a sticky note or other bookmark so that you can refer to it easily. If you are using an e-book reader, you will want to mark the page for reference.

QUESTION 1 IS BASED ON THE FOLLOWING PASSAGE.

Sculptor Henry Moore (born 1898) achieved prominence in the 1930s with his earliest recumbent figures. An English abstractionist, Moore has also been associated with romantic feeling in the relationship of his biomorphic forms to nature. His sculptures, which often consist of large flowing, rhythmic masses united by a common base, have been called universal
5   shapes by art historian Brian McAvera, who credits them with subconscious appeal to our essential humanity. Yet, this characterization is not entirely comforting, for the biomorphic figures, many of which are suggestive of the female figure, can both soothe and disturb as they evoke motherhood, sexuality, or even a surreal anxiety. Moreover, Moore can be said to have explained and celebrated the void as much as he explored the body in his sculptures,
10 which, as time marched forward and his fame grew, came to be modeled rather than carved and more the product of mass-production techniques than of exacting attention to every inch of every surface.

FOR QUESTION 1, CHOOSE ONLY <u>ONE</u> ANSWER CHOICE.

---

1. The passage suggests that the main quality of Moore's work is most nearly which of the following?
   - (A) A romantic presentation of human or animal forms
   - (B) An attempt to reinvent abstraction as a mirror of nature
   - (C) A soothing evocation of the often recumbent female figure
   - (D) A blend of artisan craft and mass production techniques
   - (E) A use of flowing forms with universal appeal but diverse response

---

Time Out for Some Advice on Unfamiliar Material

If you come across a passage like this that is totally unfamiliar to you—whether it is about fine arts, political geography, or any other subject—don't leap to the conclusion that the passage is too difficult for you. Instead, master your emotions and proceed logically by using your strategies. As the GRE website says, "Do not be discouraged if you encounter unfamiliar material; all the questions can be answered on the basis of the information provided in the passage."

You may be tempted to "mark" a passage like this to come back to later without giving it an active reading. Although the format of the test makes it easy to mark a question and return to it, use this strategy only if you are still stumped after having given the passage a purposeful, focused reading and have at least attempted to answer one or more of the questions. This is especially true when a reading comprehension passage is accompanied by more than one question.

Think about it. If you save for later a passage with three questions, and you are doing a typical test with twenty questions, you have just delayed answering approximately 15 percent of the test. Putting off large chunks of the test until later can lead to increased anxiety. Saving, returning, and, most of all, rereading also eats into your precious time. Sometimes you may have no choice, but give the passage and its questions a good try first.

Restate the Question

Here again is the question that accompanies the passage on Henry Moore.

> **FOR QUESTION 1, CHOOSE ONLY <u>ONE</u> ANSWER CHOICE.**

1. The passage suggests that the main quality of Moore's work is most nearly which of the following?
   - (A) A romantic presentation of human or animal forms
   - (B) An attempt to reinvent abstraction as a mirror of nature
   - (C) A soothing evocation of the often recumbent female figure
   - (D) A blend of artisan craft and mass production techniques
   - (E) A use of flowing forms with universal appeal but diverse response

Read the direction line and the question. What does the direction line ask you to do?

The direction line says to select one answer. On the computer version of the test, the ovals that precede the answer choices convey the same information.

In addition to verifying what you must select, paraphrase or restate the question to be sure that you know what you are being asked to find:

- The question asks what the main quality of Moore's work is.

- You need to find and weigh all the characteristics of Moore's work that are presented in the passage and decide which is most important. Although this strategy may seem to involve looking for supporting details, you're actually really looking for the main idea, or topic, of the passage.

Try Answering the Question Before You Read the Answer Choices

This strategy is especially useful when you feel confident that you understand the passage. But it is also a useful strategy when you feel unsure of your understanding. By trying to answer the question in your own words first, you can get part of the way toward the correct answer. When you check the answers, you'll either find an answer that's the same as your idea, but in different words, or no answer that is even close to yours, so you know you've missed the point. Coming up with your own answer or a partial answer is, in fact, a way to clarify your understanding in relation to the specific question you have to answer.

Again, returning to Question 1, come up with the best answer you can before you begin to eliminate choices. For example, you might come up with this answer:

The passage emphasizes forms and shapes that suggest humans or animals and their effects on the viewer. The viewer has an immediate recognition because the shapes are "universal," but recognition doesn't always mean comfort or a good feeling.

ALERT!

Don't rely on outside information to answer questions. Base your answers solely on the information in the passage. You may know that mannerism was a Renaissance art style, but in this passage mannerism is used in its twentieth-century sense.

Read All the Answers Before You Choose

After you've developed some idea of the correct answer, read all the answer choices listed. Don't read the first one and, if it seems correct, choose it and go on to the next question. Keep in mind that a well-constructed test will have answers that are close approximations of the correct answer.

For example, you might jump to the conclusion that the right answer to the question about the main quality of Moore's work is choice (A). Reading carefully through all the answers, and eliminating them one by one, however, may lead you to a different choice.

Compare Answer Choices to Each Other and the Question

Suppose you eliminate three answer choices, but cannot eliminate one of the two remaining choices. If you are crunched for time, you can make your best guess at this point. If you have time, however, don't guess before you try this strategy: Compare the choices to each other and to the question. The following is based on Question 1 and assumes that you've eliminated choices (B), (C), and (D):

- Choice (A) is very different from choice (E). Choice (A) does get to the heart of Moore's work by mentioning human or animal, or biomorphic, forms. Yet it calls them "romantic," an idea that a later detail about mass production seems to refute. In comparison, choice (E) also presents the fundamental idea of forms while incorporating more of the fundamental facts: first, that the forms are universal, and second, that they evoke diverse responses, which the passage explains can range from soothing to disturbing.

- The question asks for a main quality. Choice (E) encompasses the notion of universal appeal; of abstract, flowing forms; and of "diverse" responses of the viewer. In comparison, the key word in choice (A) seems to be "romantic," which, in the context of the passage, is a less important quality that is not developed, or perhaps even contradicted or limited, by the author. Therefore, choice (E) is the best answer. **The correct answer is (E).**

Avoid Selecting an Answer You Don't Fully Understand

Again, suppose you have eliminated three choices, but you're at a loss to eliminate one of the two remaining answers. As you reread the choices, avoid selecting the one that is more confusing or unintelligible to you. You might work your way through your dilemma something like this:

- Choice (A) is hard to understand. The passage implies that a romantic feeling is evoked by Moore's forms, but the term "romantic" isn't really ever defined in the passage, and it seems to relate to only some of his work.

- Choice (E) is easier to understand, and it also clearly sums up more of the ideas in the paragraph. Therefore, choice (E) is more likely to be correct.

Choose the *Best* Answer

Once again, suppose you have been able to eliminate three choices, but are having trouble eliminating one of the two remaining answers. As you try to choose, remember that your goal is to select the *best* answer. Therefore, if both answers appear reasonable or possibly correct to you, your task is to choose the better—more reasonable—of the two:

- Choice (E) sums up the ideas in the paragraph. It summarizes essential or main qualities of Moore's work: universality, abstract forms, and diverse response.

- On the other hand, choice (A) seems as if it could possibly be correct, but it definitely doesn't sum up most of the main ideas that the passage's author attributes to Moore.

- You're looking for the main idea of the passage, so choice (E) is more likely to be correct (because it encompasses more key information).

For the next four strategies, you will focus on a multi-paragraph passage and four questions to learn to apply the strategies. Once again, it is probably wise to mark the passage for easy reference as you try out the various strategies.

Passage 2 differs in three significant ways from the first passage you read. First, it has four paragraphs. While most passages you encounter on the test will be a single paragraph in length, at least one passage is likely to be longer. Second, notice also that this passage contains some information in bold type. Figure that this must be important information to pay close attention to as you read. Finally, note that the passage contains two arrows. These arrows relate to the select-in-passage question type covered later in this chapter.

FOR QUESTIONS 2–6, CHOOSE ONLY <u>ONE</u> ANSWER CHOICE UNLESS OTHERWISE INDICATED.

QUESTIONS 2–6 ARE BASED ON THE FOLLOWING PASSAGE.

Americans take a profound interest in wildlife, as long as that wildlife is in other people's backyards. American Audubon societies strive mightily to save Central America's jaguar while schoolchildren across the nation focus on China's endangered panda and the African elephant. But when it comes to America's own most pressing wildlife problem, deer, the
5 public is curiously—and dangerously—somnolent.

→Adaptable to a wide range of habitats, including the paved roads and manicured, pesticide-rich lots of suburban America, white-tailed deer live in at least part of every state except for, possibly, Hawaii, Alaska, and Utah. And just about everywhere, as their numbers increase yet their habitat decreases, the animals are wreaking havoc: **destroying public and**
10 **private landscape; eating row crops and nursery stock; and, most significantly, carrying with increasingly alarming frequency tick-borne pathogens that cause Lyme disease, babesiosis, and other newly emerging diseases.**

While states pretend to deal with these animals by establishing hunting seasons to harvest populations, as well as by offering information on control, the problem escalates. One reason
15 for this may be that deer populations were endangered in the 1930s and brought back, leading wildlife agencies to trumpet the success of "sustainable hunting." Another more disturbing reason may be that Americans think deer are cute. Called "charismatic" animals on at least one website, tick-infested deer are seemingly beloved for their fluffy white tails; their large, dark eyes; their lithe and graceful prancing motions; and, perhaps, most of all, their reticence
20 for retreat in the face of human contact. ←

But what are the economics of cuteness? Just a few annual costs include $2 billion borne by U.S. farmers and 150 human fatalities plus $3.8 billion in insurance payouts to drivers who hit deer. Additionally, there's the approximately $11,000 *per case* of Lyme disease—and all of these costs will rise dramatically as deer populations grow. These costs alone show **the**
25 **necessity of stopping deer in their tracks.**

TIP
Before reading the answers, remember to try answering the question in your own words.

TIP

In reading the
question, remember to
• restate the question
in your own words.
• check the number
of answer choices.
• double check if
squares or ovals
precede the
answers.

Now, read Question 2.

2. What function do the two groups of words in bold type serve in this argument?

(A) The first anticipates the argument's conclusion; the second provides support for that conclusion.

(B) The first supports the proposition or opinion; the second states the proposition or opinion.

(C) The first presents the proposition or opinion; the second presents the final support for the proposition or opinion.

(D) The first serves as an intermediate conclusion; the second serves as a definitive conclusion.

(E) The first presents the argument; the second restates and reinforces the argument.

Pay Attention to Structure and to Structural Clues

When you read actively, you should be drawing a conclusion about the author's purpose. Many passages inform, but the purpose of this particular passage is to persuade. As part of reading actively, you should also be looking for the main idea, proposition, or thesis of the passage. The point of view of this passage is that more has to be done to stop the problems caused by deer. Once you know you are reading a persuasive piece—an argument, in other words—and once you determine the thesis or proposition, begin the work of tracing the argument's development and separating claims from evidence, opinions, and judgments.

- The first segment in bold type presents a series of effects caused by deer; these facts support the opinion that strong measures are necessary to stop the problems caused by deer.

- The second segment in bold type states the opinion.

TIP

Before you try any
other strategy,
remember to eliminate
any answer that you
know is wrong. Each
of the answers has
two parts. Each part
characterizes one
group of bold words.
If you can eliminate
either part of the
answer choice, the
whole answer is wrong.

Persuasive writing is often organized inductively in order to lead the reader through a process of reasoning. With this method of organization, the conclusion often presents the opinion for the first time; it may also draw a final conclusion or present a clincher statement that reinforces the opinion or proposition. Therefore, while a proposition, or thesis, may be stated at the beginning of an argument both for clarity and clout, stating it at the end of an argument, as if it were the most logical conclusion possible, is also rhetorically effective.

- The first segment in bold type presents facts about the dangerous and costly effects of deer as supporting evidence for the idea that stronger measures for controlling deer are necessary.

- The intermediate claim "the animals are wreaking havoc," which leads up to the facts and signals a list with its closing colon, suggests that support for the claim will follow.

- The factual claims about land destruction, crop damage, and disease are evidence that supports the intermediate claim as well as the conclusion drawn by the final sentence, and the final sentence clearly states the proposition, or argument. Therefore, choice (B) is correct. **The correct answer is (B).**

Sometimes structural clues reveal the writer's thinking over the course of an entire paragraph. For example, a passage from the GRE® online sample questions reveals the following structure, and clues to meaning, embedded in it:

- Sentence 1: "According to . . ."
- Sentence 2: "In this view . . ."
- Sentence 3: "... however . . ."

These clues tell you that you're reading one view—stated and explained in sentences 1 and 2. In sentence 3, you're reading its rebuttal or some significant qualification of it (beginning with "however") in the remainder of the paragraph.

In another sample passage, there are no structural clues until the passage's midway point. These structural clues follow:

- Sentence 4: "It follows that . . ."
- Sentence 6: "Therefore, . . ."

These clues tell you that you're most likely reading an argument.

To give you more practice with argument questions, try Question 3, which is based on the same passage as Question 2. The GRE® showcases the following type of question more than once in its practice materials.

3. Which of the following, if it were true, would most seriously weaken the argument?
   (A) Expenditures for landscape damages include losses of plantings and foundations, as well as costs of fencing, netting, and repellants.
   (B) Controversial deer culling proposals tend to elicit organized resistance from anti-hunting constituencies.
   (C) The highest cost of automobile accidents involving deer is reported by the states of Pennsylvania and Michigan, with annual price tags of $343 and 339 million respectively.
   (D) In its most recent report, the CDC states that 95% of all cases of Lyme disease originated in just thirteen states.
   (E) Hunting in the United States, mainly deer, generates some $67 billion in business revenues and creates approximately 1 million jobs annually.

This question asks you to find the relationship between a hypothetical or an alternative idea and the ideas in the passage. This is an application question because you're applying information from one situation to other situations. You will use a variety of reading comprehension skills to answer the question, including making inferences, drawing conclusions, and evaluating hypotheses.

Try answering Question 3 on your own before you read the following answer rationale:

The argument is that stronger measures are needed to stop the problems presented by the white-tailed deer in America.

- You can eliminate choice (A) because this information supports the idea that damage to the landscape from deer is significant and costly.
- You can eliminate choice (B) because it neither weakens nor strengthens the argument; instead, it heads off in a new direction by anticipating, but not countering, opposition to the thesis.

www.petersons.com

TIP

Make a mental note of transitional words and phrases as you read. Transitions can show time order, add information, indicate cause and effect, and show comparisons and contrasts.

- Choice (C) is incorrect because it adds increased specificity to the costs of crashes with deer, which is already reported in paragraph 4 and strengthened by this information.

- Choice (D) is tempting, but also incorrect, because this fact does not necessarily clash in any way with facts in the passage that point to the increasing incidence and cost of Lyme disease.

- Choice (E) shows the great economic benefit of deer. This idea contradicts the thesis, or controlling opinion. Therefore, choice (E) is correct. **The correct answer is (E).**

Don't Select an Answer Just Because It's True

You want to choose an answer because it answers the question. Some answers may be true, but that doesn't mean that they answer the question. With a question like the following, restating the question is especially useful. It will help you to anchor your thoughts before you dive into the details of the answer choices.

4. The passage suggests which of the following as a cause of American insensitivity to the problems created by white-tailed deer?
    (A) White-tailed deer thrive even in conditions that are seemingly hostile to them.
    (B) Americans prefer to focus on the wildlife issues of other countries and continents.
    (C) Hunting has proven to be an inadequate means of controlling the deer population.
    (D) A self-congratulatory stance derived from past wildlife management efforts prevails.
    (E) The white-tailed deer does not pose equal threats in every state in the nation.

Try answering this question on your own first. Remember to read all the answer choices before you choose one.

- Choice (A) is true, but the author does not suggest it as a cause of insensitivity.

- Even though this statement is used to open the argument, the author never states a cause-effect relationship between this focus and insensitivity to the problems posed by deer. Instead, the author suggests the irony of the two co-existing attitudes, so choice (B) is incorrect.

- While the author implies the truth of choice (C), that hunting has been an inadequate means of control, hunting is not given as a reason for insensitivity.

- Paragraph 3 presents two key reasons why the deer problem escalates, and, by implication, goes unsolved. Choice (D) is true, but keep reading to the end of the answer choices.

- While passage facts permit the reader to infer the truth of Choice (E) (How can states without deer be as threatened by them as states with them?), it does not suggest this as a reason for failure to deal with the problems presented by deer.

Each of the five answers has some truth to it. But only choice (D) correctly answers the question of cause. Choice (D) is true, and it's the *best* answer because it's consistent with the cause-effect relationships stated or implied by the passage. **The correct answer is (D).**

Substitute Answer Choices in Word-Meaning Questions

Word-meaning questions may appear more than once on the GRE®. The context in which the word is used will help you choose the correct answer. Reading the answer choices may not be enough to get you to the correct answer because often a word will have several meanings and you need to find the meaning of the word as it is used in the passage. To do this, substitute each answer choice for the word in the passage.

5. In the passage, "lithe" (line 19) most nearly means
   (A) light.
   (B) supple.
   (C) alacritous.
   (D) labored.
   (E) ambulatory.

You may already know that "lithe" means "nimble, supple, or graceful," choice (B). If you don't know its meaning, however, you could substitute each answer choice in the sentence: "Called 'charismatic' animals on at least one website, tick-infested deer are seemingly beloved for their fluffy white tails; their large, dark eyes; their _____ and graceful prancing motions; and, perhaps, most of all, their reticence or retreat in the face of human contact."

- While lithe movements might appear light, this is not the full, exact, or correct meaning of "lithe," so choice (A) is incorrect.

- Neither was the movements described as quick, so choice (C) doesn't work.

- The context suggests movements that are the opposite of labored, so you can eliminate choice (D).

- Choice (E) doesn't work because "ambulatory" means "capable of movement" and does not describe the movement itself. **The correct answer is (B).**

Choose the Answer That Doesn't Fit for EXCEPT Questions

You may find one or two EXCEPT questions. These questions ask you to find the answer choice that doesn't fit with the other answer choices. That is, you're looking for the wrong answer as your right answer. If you took the SAT or any AP subject tests, you'll remember this question type.

6. All of the following support the claim of "cute," likable, or endearing deer EXCEPT their
   (A) association with nursery stock.
   (B) physiognomy.
   (C) agility.
   (D) seeming shyness.
   (E) avoidance of human beings.

The article mentions damage to nursery stock as evidence of the problems caused by deer, so choice (A) does not support the claim of cuteness. Choices (B), (C), (D), and (E) are developed with details about the appearance and behavior of deer. Physiognomy, or facial appearance, is touched on with details about the deer's eyes, agility is implied by descriptive details about movement, and shyness and avoidance are expressed by the passage details of "reticence" and "retreat." Only choice (A) fails to support the claim. **The correct answer is (A).**

NOTE

Remember to use other strategies for multiple-choice questions such as restate the questions and try to come up with an answer on your own.

ADDITIONAL STRATEGIES FOR MULTIPLE-CHOICE QUESTIONS—SELECT ONE OR MORE ANSWER CHOICES

You will find a few multiple-choice questions on the GRE® that may require one or more answers to be correct. We say "may" because only one answer may be correct, or two, or all three choices. The direction for the question will state that you are to choose "all that apply." If you choose only choice (A), and choice (C) is also correct, you won't get credit for the question. To get credit, you need to select "all that apply." Half or a third of a correct answer is zero correct.

The multiple-choice questions—select one or more answer choices questions have only three choices listed as possible answers. Each choice is preceded by a square rather than an oval. For your convenience in checking answers, we have used (A), (B), and (C) to signal the answer choices.

The major strategy that you need to remember for answering questions that use the format of multiple-choice questions—select one or more answer choices is *choose an answer that answers the question on its own.*

Choose an Answer that Answers the Question on Its Own

Each answer choice has to answer the question on its own. Don't make the mistake of thinking that because there may be more than one answer, combining partial answer choices gives you a complete answer. Always assess each answer as a standalone. Is it accurate? Is it complete? Then move on to the next answer and ask yourself the same questions.

QUESTION 7 IS BASED ON THE FOLLOWING PASSAGE.

Telematics, a science that will, conceivably, by the year 2025, allow every car to be connected to the Internet, should be used to stop or significantly reduce the 1.48 million crashes now estimated to result from texting or other cellphone use while driving. Through a combination of GPS and knowledge of individual drivers' habits and their typical locations during the day
5   gathered in part from mobile carriers, telematics has the potential both to block handheld use of phones and texting, as well as to shut down a driver's phone when a text or call comes in. While insurance companies as well as many mobile carriers have become ardent opponents of texting while driving, a network-level technology solution, not to mention the Big Brother-style encroachment on civil rights, gives significant pause. Will millions of lives hang in the
10   balance, then, until the self-driving car makes the issue moot?

FOR QUESTION 7, CONSIDER EACH ANSWER INDIVIDUALLY AND CHOOSE <u>ALL</u> THAT APPLY.

---

7. The second-to-last sentence "While insurance . . . significant pause." (lines 7–9) serves which of the following purposes in the passage?

    (A) It counters the argument expressed in the first sentence.

    (B) It provides evidence for the positive effect of telematics.

    (C) It suggests the limitation of freedom imposed by telematics.

The first sentence argues that telematics should be employed to cut the accident rate resulting from cellphone use and texting. Although the second-to-last sentence begins with a kind of reassertion of the thesis, that sentence mainly brings up a problem with telematics, or the "network-level solution" involving mobile carriers: drivers being monitored and controlled "Big Brother" style. Therefore, the second-to-last sentence counters, or raises a point in opposition to, the first sentence, so choice (A) is correct. Choice (B) is incorrect because the next-to-the-last sentence does not supply evidence and is mainly about a negative consequence. Choice (C) is, however, correct because, ultimately, the use of telematics described here is a surveillance system that curtails the freedom of the driver. **The correct answers are (A) and (C).**

STRATEGIES FOR SELECT-IN-PASSAGE QUESTIONS

Select-in-passage questions ask you to choose a sentence within a passage as the correct answer. You will have a direction line, but no listing of multiple-choice answers (unless you're taking the paper-and-pencil test). For a passage that is a single paragraph, any sentence in the entire paragraph is fair game for the answer. For multi-paragraph passages, arrows [→] mark the beginning and end of the text from which you should select the sentence. To make your choice, click on any part of the sentence that you determine to be the answer. If you click on a sentence that is not between the arrows, it will not be highlighted and will not register as an answer.

This may seem silly, but don't lose track of where a marked section begins and ends. You don't want to waste time analyzing sentences in a part of the passage that isn't the subject of the question. If you try to click on a sentence in the unmarked portion of the passage, it won't highlight, so your answer won't be wrong, but you will have wasted precious time.

Similar to answering questions with the multiple-choice questions—select one or more answer choices format, you need to assess each sentence in the marked section of a passage as a stand-alone sentence.

The special strategy that applies to select-in-passage questions is *match the sentence to the information.*

Match the Sentence to the Information

The GRE® information materials about the test note two facts about select-in-passage questions. First, a select-in-passage question contains the description of a sentence—content, tone, purpose, author's perspective, or similar aspect. In answering the question, you must look for the sentence that contains that information. However, you should not select a sentence if any part of the information in the sentence doesn't match the question.

This relates to the second caveat for select-in-passage questions: A question may not necessarily describe all aspects of the sentence for the sentence to be the correct answer. Sentences in GRE® passages may be long and complicated. A question may focus on one or two aspects of a sentence. The sentence you choose just can't contradict the description in the question.

NOTE

For international students taking the paper-and-pencil test, you will find the multiple-choice questions—select one answer choice version of select-in-passage questions.

QUESTION 8 IS BASED ON THE FOLLOWING PASSAGE.

Fareed Zakaria notes in *The Post-American World* that there really is no such thing as Asia; he calls Asia a Western cultural construct. In other words, Zakaria suggests that Asia isn't really a continent, which calls for an examination of the term *continent*. If continents are defined as discrete landmasses separated by large bodies of water, then North and South
5   America should be one American continent, as the canal that separates them is neither a large nor natural body of water. Furthermore, if continents are described as large landmasses separated by large bodies of water, then Greenland, one of Earth's largest islands, is rather arbitrarily defined as an island instead of a continent.

Other problems with the historical and cultural constructs that underlie the classification
10 of continents include the classification of smaller islands, especially those located beyond the continental shelf of their so-called "continent," such as Hawaii. Clearly, political constructs also affect historical classification. Indeed, a close look at how the word *continent* is applied proves Zakaria's point and shows that the meaning of the word has more to do with the conventions long established to identify the somewhat agreed-upon number of continents
15 on Earth than it has to do with strict geographical or other criteria.

FOR QUESTION 8, CHOOSE ONLY <u>ONE</u> ANSWER CHOICE.

---

8. In which sentence does the author state the main idea of the paragraph?

(A) The first sentence ("Fareed Zakaria … construct")

(B) The second sentence ("In other words, . . . *continent*")

(C) The fifth sentence ("Other problems . . . Hawaii")

(D) The sixth sentence ("Clearly . . . classification")

(E) The last sentence ("Indeed, a close . . . criteria")

Zakaria's assertion that Asia is not a discrete or unified continent leads into the topic of continents and how they are defined. Therefore, the first sentence is not a main idea, and choice (A) should be eliminated. Whereas the second sentence does clarify the first, it doesn't yet get to the central focus of the entire passage, which goes beyond the example of Asia, so choice (B) is also incorrect. Choice (C) is incorrect because it's an example that supports the main idea. Choice (D) must also be eliminated because it supports the main idea rather than states it. Choice (E) alone provides an overview idea that encapsulates the many ideas of the paragraph. Therefore, choice (E) is the correct answer. Notice how choice (E) does a bit more than state the main idea. It also affirms Zakaria's idea. Although Zakaria's point about Asia is a minor rather than major one, the remainder of the sentence does state the main idea. **The correct answer is (E).**

PRACTICE QUESTIONS

FOR QUESTIONS 1–15, CHOOSE <u>ONE</u> ANSWER CHOICE UNLESS OTHERWISE DIRECTED.

QUESTION 1 IS BASED ON THE FOLLOWING PASSAGE.

Prosopagnosia, or face blindness, was lately given a boost in long-overdue recognition as a genetic disorder when the distinguished professor of neurology and best-selling author Oliver Sacks described his own affliction with the disease. Like other proposagnosiacs, Sacks has a fundamental inability to recognize faces, and not just the faces of random strangers or
5 people he met for the first time last week. One index to the profundity of Sacks's problem is reflected in a study that found that proposagnosiacs who looked at photos of their own family members were unable to recognize 30% of the faces. Sacks himself admits that he often does not recognize a person whom he has met just five minutes before.

1. The passage achieves all of the following purposes EXCEPT

  (A) explain why prosopagnosia was given recognition as a genetic disorder.

  (B) tell or imply how prosopagnosia manifests itself.

  (C) cite research that helps define the challenges faced by prosopagnosiacs.

  (D) personalize and humanize the disorder known as prosopagnosia.

  (E) imply the severity of the challenges faced by prosopagnosiacs.

QUESTIONS 2–4 ARE BASED ON THE FOLLOWING PASSAGE.

Does a double standard dictate the average American response to breaches of privacy? Of course, few Americans maintain much, if any illusion, about the degree of privacy they actually enjoy, especially if they frequently use search engines, shop online, or belong to social networks. As the well-known saying goes, when a product is free—such as a "free"
5 gmail account, a "free" Facebook membership, or a "free" Bing Internet search—you are actually the product. With every keystroke you make, your data is being lifted, charted, analyzed, and redirected. Yet, despite our glib acceptance of website terms of agreement, often at the rate of many websites per day, and all the personal data we willingly unleash in that way, revelations that surfaced in 2013 about the kinds and scope of data about individuals
10 collected by the National Security Agency (NSA) brought serious and sustained outcries.

    For many citizens for whom it was and remains absolutely acceptable for an Internet company to gather information from their every e-mail and Internet search, the same was not true for the U.S. government. No matter, it seems, that the search engine's motive appears to be, elementally, corporate millions and the government's appears to be, fundamentally, pre-
15 venting acts of terrorism, Americans were and are outraged. Of course, unlike many Internet companies (which are essentially surveillance groups), the NSA never requested permission or revealed its operations or scope. The NSA, unlike the online giants whose trespasses we forgive daily, seems to have indulged in the ridiculous notion that, for the success of its mission, secrecy was important.
20   Why do we constantly forgive the participants of the new California Gold Rush, whose actions include not only infringement of our most basic rights, but also the creation of a new class of super-rich that undermines our democracy just as certainly as any practice on Wall Street does? In part, this phenomenon derives from the fact that we actually trust our government to do the right thing, at least eventually, while we actually expect corporations
25 to achieve their goals at our expense.

FOR QUESTION 2, CONSIDER EACH ANSWER INDIVIDUALLY AND CHOOSE <u>ALL</u> THAT APPLY.

---

2. Which is the first sentence in this passage to clearly reflect the author's perspective on a question posed earlier in the passage?

   (A) Sentence 3 ("As the well-known . . . the product.")

   (B) Sentence 6 ("For many citizens . . . U.S. government.")

   (C) Sentence 9 ("The NSA . . . secrecy was important.")

3. In this passage, "glib" (line 7) most nearly means

   (A) spoken sarcastically or with a bitter tone.

   (B) performed with a natural ease or grace.

   (C) accomplished too easily or carelessly.

   (D) characterized by agility or spryness.

   (E) marked by insincerity or superficiality.

FOR QUESTION 4, CONSIDER EACH ANSWER INDIVIDUALLY AND CHOOSE <u>ALL</u> THAT APPLY.

---

4. It can be inferred from the passage that the author believes

   (A) the public prefers to hold government, not corporations, accountable.

   (B) the government may be justified in its secret surveillance procedures.

   (C) certain online companies engage in less morally ambiguous actions than Wall Street does.

QUESTIONS 5–7 ARE BASED ON THE FOLLOWING PASSAGE.

The precipitate rise in the incidence of type 1, or juvenile, diabetes, as well as the startling decrease in average age at onset, has led to a nearly commensurate rise in causation hypotheses. The single factor that scientists have most commonly and consistently linked with the rise of cases of type 1 diabetes is weight gain, and, indeed, children's weights are increasing

5 generation by generation, and the greater BMI (body mass index), the younger the child is likely to be at the age of onset. Other factors linked to this rise in incidence and decrease in average of age of onset and tracked with varying degrees of success in recent studies include psychological stress, the increased wealth of the homes in which the children reside, the increased levels of hygiene in the homes in which the children reside, and nourishment

10 by infant formula during the first six months of life. Some of these theories have garnered more academic support than others, but, no matter how much support they have received, correlation is not causation.

5. The writer mentions greater BMI at earlier ages in this paragraph in order to

   (A) introduce a common causation hypothesis.

   (B) provide support for an implied argument.

   (C) reinforce the importance of a healthful diet for children.

   (D) provide a possible explanation for the confusion of cause and correlation.

   (E) cast doubt on studies that collect data on wealth and hygiene.

6. Which of the following, if it were true, would most seriously weaken the import of a specific data set suggesting a correlation?

(A) The average age at onset of type 1 diabetes decreased by one year over a period of just five years.

(B) Nourishment by baby formula has not been correlated to a rise in BMI.

(C) Among stress factors, only poor performance in school and divorce have been shown to correlate with increased incidence of type 1 diabetes.

(D) The incidence of type 1 diabetes is rising at a slower rate among children who are not overweight.

(E) There is a higher rate of type 1 diabetes in households with incomes of more than $80,000 than in households with lower incomes.

7. Which of the following statements does the passage most clearly support?

(A) The weight-gain theory originated before the other theories.

(B) There are reasons to give the stress, hygiene, wealth, and formula theories less credence than the weight-gain theory.

(C) None of the theories has shown a significant correlation with rising incidence.

(D) Only one of the theories has been linked to younger age at onset.

(E) The weight-gain theory is universally accepted by scientists.

QUESTIONS 8–9 ARE BASED ON THE FOLLOWING PASSAGE.

Robert Frost is often categorized as an anti-Romantic writer, that is, as a poet whose poetry contradicts the ideals of Romanticism as embodied in the works of Wordsworth, Keats, Shelley, and others. **Simultaneously, he is categorized as an anti-modernist, a poet who has little in common with his contemporaries, Eliot, Pound, Joyce, Woolf, and others.**
5   Nevertheless, because modernists declared that modernism was, among other things, the rejection of Romanticism, there can be only partial validity in the claim that Frost was both anti-Romantic and anti-modernist. **Instead, as the poems bear out, Frost was at once neither and a bit of both, and one does not have to look far in the poems for substantiation.** Whether the reader is "Stopping by Woods" or out among the "Birches," nature and wildness
10   are the gateways to introspection and imagination, even if emotion receives short shrift. At the same time, modernism asserts itself—albeit in traditional poetic form—in poems such as "After Apple Picking," with its evocation of a transitional state of consciousness; and in "The Death of the Hired Man," "Desert Places," and "Acquainted with the Night" with their experience of alienation, loss, and despair.

8. It can be inferred that the author judges which of the following characteristics as most clearly defining or epitomizing Romanticism?

(A) The reliance on traditional poetic forms

(B) The rejection of modernism

(C) Nature and wildness as the gateway to introspection and imagination

(D) Poems such as "Stopping by Woods" and "Birches"

(E) Poems that evoke a transitional state of consciousness

9. In the passage, what is the primary purpose of the two groups of words in boldface type?

(A) The first provides contrast to the sentence that precedes it; the second expands upon and elucidates the sentence that precedes it.

(B) The first provides background information that leads up to the argument; the second presents the argument.

(C) The first reinforces the argument through contrast; the second explains the argument through explanation and expansion.

(D) The first states a position that the argument as a whole contradicts; the second presents the argument.

(E) The first provides contrast to the sentence that precedes it; the second provides evidence that supports the argument.

QUESTIONS 10–11 ARE BASED ON THE FOLLOWING PASSAGE.

When explaining the issues of urbanization in Africa of the late twentieth century, some textbooks conflate effects of the phenomenon with effects of urbanization in the newly industrialized cities of England in the early nineteenth century. That is, some historians restrict their analysis to the problems of overcrowding, lack of sanitation, and inadequate
5 housing that occur in the wake of rapid mass movement from rural to urban areas. Their analysis ignores arguments, such as those put forth by the 1996 UN Habitat II conference, suggesting that economies of scale are preferable for the delivery of health care, clean water, electricity, and other needs. It further overlooks the freedoms available to women in the cities, where they may escape tribal or religious practices, or find fulfillment in both traditional
10 and nontraditional roles.

10. The author of the passage would most likely consider which of the following ideas most similar to the reasoning of historians mentioned in lines 3–5?

(A) Economies of scale is a relatively recent economic concept that suggests, not entirely accurately, that bigger is always better.

(B) The problems of overcrowding, lack of sanitation, and inadequate housing also occurred in major U.S. cities during the Industrial Revolution.

(C) The increased disparity in economic class in today's Mumbai cannot be attributed to globalization alone.

(D) Urbanization has a negative effect on traditional social mores and usually proves disruptive to cultural unity.

(E) The recent economic crises in Ireland may best be explained by examining financial crises in the United States in the late nineteenth century.

11. Which of the following, if it were true, most seriously undermines the support that the final sentence provides for the claim?

(A) Urban women are more likely than men to have to deal directly with the problems of lack of sanitation.

(B) Women in large urban centers often achieve a higher level of education than they achieve in rural areas.

(C) Many rural women find fulfillment through local tribal and religious practices.

(D) Inadequate housing in the cities often offers more advantages than adequate housing in rural areas.

(E) Women in large urban centers often work in the marketplace.

QUESTIONS 12–14 ARE BASED ON THE FOLLOWING PASSAGE.

Andrew Dickson White famously asserted that Darwin's *Origin of the Species* came "into the theological world like a plough into an ant-hill." At all costs, the anthill had to be rebuilt with some ants reconstructing the same structure and others making only slight alterations to it. Among the many ants rebuilding the hill was Teilhard de Chardin, who, among other
5 things, posited (without so much as a wink!) that the descent of man was actually the ascent of man. His new anthill took shape in *The Phenomenon of Man,* which Julian Huxley would subsequently hail as the synthesis of the "whole of knowable reality" and a triumph of human significance. Yet, the phrase "whole of knowable reality" is, along, of course, with Teilhard's fatuous scientific arguments, a clue to just how scientifically unpalatable this
10 particular philosophically respected, yet scientifically incoherent reconstruction of the anthill was. For example, P. B. Medawar found such flowery, unscientific, and abstract language "suffocating"—and the very obfuscation of sense.

FOR QUESTION 12, CONSIDER EACH ANSWER INDIVIDUALLY AND CHOOSE <u>ALL</u> THAT APPLY.

---

12. The sentence "Among the many . . . the ascent of man" (lines 4–6) serves which of the following purposes in the passage?

    (A) It counters the argument expressed in the preceding sentence.

    (B) It provides evidence for the central argument or proposition of the passage.

    (C) It makes an assertion that subsequent sentences will contradict.

13. It can be inferred that P. B. Medawar took issue with all of the following aspects of *The Phenomenon of Man* EXCEPT the

    (A) blurring of scientific fact.

    (B) attempt to rebuild the anthill.

    (C) lack of concreteness and specificity.

    (D) rebuttal of Darwin's ideas in poetic language.

    (E) obfuscation of sense.

14. In the passage, "hail" (line 7) most nearly means

    (A) be a native of.

    (B) call for.

    (C) greet.

    (D) acclaim.

    (E) precipitate.

QUESTION 15 IS BASED ON THE FOLLOWING PASSAGE.

The pivotal considerations affecting the design of any stationary robotic arm are the central tasks and workspace, which will, in turn, affect the desired degrees of freedom (DOF). A relatively simple design might have just 3 DOFs—not counting any additional DOFs on the end effector or gripper. When designers create an FBD (free body diagram) for a new robotic
5   arm, other considerations reflected in that diagram will include the limitations of each DOF, which should be accounted for in the FBD by annotations showing maximum joint angles and exact arm link lengths. Engineers commonly use a coordinate system known as the Denavit-Hartenberg (D-H) Convention for this purpose.

15. According to the information in this passage, in what order would these steps in the design of a robotic arm most likely take place?

(A) Determine DOFs, plan for D-H, draw FBD.

(B) Determine maximum joint angles, draw FBD, add end effector or gripper.

(C) Draw FBD, annotate joints according to D-H system, determine DOFs.

(D) Identify robotic task(s), determine DOFs, create FBD with D-H.

(E) Create FBD, determine DOFs, add end effector DOF.

ANSWER KEY AND EXPLANATIONS

1. A	6. D	11. C
2. B	7. B	12. B
3. C	8. C	13. B
4. A, B	9. B	14. D
5. A	10. E	15. D

QUESTION 1 IS BASED ON THE FOLLOWING PASSAGE.

Prosopagnosia, or face blindness, was lately given a boost in long-overdue recognition as a genetic disorder when the distinguished professor of neurology and best-selling author Oliver Sacks described his own affliction with the disease. Like other proposagnosiacs, Sacks has a fundamental inability to recognize faces, and not just the faces of random strangers or
5 people he met for the first time last week. One index to the profundity of Sacks's problem is reflected in a study that found that proposagnosiacs who looked at photos of their own family members were unable to recognize 30% of the faces. Sacks himself admits that he often does not recognize a person whom he has met just five minutes before.

Passage Summary: The passage introduces the phenomenon of prosopagnosia to the general reader through the lens of Oliver Sacks's experience of the disease. It briefly explains what prosopagnosia, or face blindness, is.

Question

1. The passage achieves all of the following purposes EXCEPT

   (A) explain why prosopagnosia was given recognition as a genetic disorder.

   (B) tell or imply how prosopagnosia manifests itself.

   (C) cite research that helps define the challenges faced by prosopagnosiacs.

   (D) personalize and humanize the disorder known as prosopagnosia.

   (E) imply the severity of the challenges faced by prosopagnosiacs.

Answer Explanation

The correct answer is (A). This question involves main idea and supporting details. The passage briefly tells how prosopagnosia manifests itself (through the inability to recognize faces), choice (B); cites research, choice (C); personalizes and humanizes the issue by attaching a famous name to it, choice (D); and suggests the severity of the disease, choice (E), by suggesting that subjects don't recognize their own family members or people they've met five minutes earlier. Therefore, choices (B), (C), (D), and (E) are incorrect answers to the question. What the passage doesn't tell is why the disease received attention as a genetic order, choice (A). (It implies the disease has, in the past, received more attention as a disease arising from other causes.)

QUESTIONS 2–4 ARE BASED ON THE FOLLOWING PASSAGE.

Does a double standard dictate the average American response to breaches of privacy? Of course, few Americans maintain much, if any illusion, about the degree of privacy they actually enjoy, especially if they frequently use search engines, shop online, or belong to social networks. As the well-known saying goes, when a product is free—such as a "free"
5   gmail account, a "free" Facebook membership, or a "free" Bing Internet search—you are actually the product. With every keystroke you make, your data is being lifted, charted, analyzed, and redirected. Yet, despite our glib acceptance of website terms of agreement, often at the rate of many websites per day, and all the personal data we willingly unleash in that way, revelations that surfaced in 2013 about the kinds and scope of data about individuals
10   collected by the National Security Agency (NSA) brought serious and sustained outcries.

For many citizens for whom it was and remains absolutely acceptable for an Internet company to gather information from their every e-mail and Internet search, the same was not true for the U.S. government. No matter, it seems, that the search engine's motive appears to be, elementally, corporate millions and the government's appears to be, fundamentally, pre-
15   venting acts of terrorism, Americans were and are outraged. Of course, unlike many Internet companies (which are essentially surveillance groups), the NSA never requested permission or revealed its operations or scope. The NSA, unlike the online giants whose trespasses we forgive daily, seems to have indulged in the ridiculous notion that, for the success of its mission, secrecy was important.

20   Why do we constantly forgive the participants of the new California Gold Rush, whose actions include not only infringement of our most basic rights, but also the creation of a new class of super-rich that undermines our democracy just as certainly as any practice on Wall Street does? In part, this phenomenon derives from the fact that we actually trust our government to do the right thing, at least eventually, while we actually expect corporations
25   to achieve their goals at our expense.

FOR QUESTION 2, CONSIDER EACH ANSWER INDIVIDUALLY AND CHOOSE <u>ALL</u> THAT APPLY.

---

2. Which is the first sentence in this passage to clearly reflect the author's perspective on a question posed earlier in the passage?

    (A) Sentence 3 ("As the well-known . . . the product.")

    (B) Sentence 6 ("For many citizens . . . U.S. government.")

    (C) Sentence 9 ("The NSA . . . secrecy was important.")

Answer Explanation

The correct answer is (B). This question asks about author's perspective. Choice (B) most clearly answers the question by implying the affirmative response that there is a double standard and by elucidating the two sides: government and certain online companies. The opening sentence poses a question about whether a double standard exists in terms of breaches of privacy. Sentence 3 doesn't answer that question; instead, it helps makes the claim, spurious or otherwise, that online companies invade our privacy, so eliminate choice (A). Sentence 9 makes a statement that clarifies and strengthens the author's position, but it doesn't answer the question, so eliminate choice (C).

Question

3. In this passage, "glib" (line 7) most nearly means
   (A) spoken sarcastically or with a bitter tone.
   (B) performed with a natural ease or grace.
   (C) accomplished too easily or carelessly.
   (D) characterized by agility or spryness.
   (E) marked by insincerity or superficiality.

Answer Explanation

The correct answer is (C). This is an easy-to-spot word-meaning question. Choice (C) alone conveys the thoughtless, offhanded, and easy way in which, according to the author, people accept terms of agreement. In the context in which it appears, "glib" has nothing to do with natural ease, grace, spryness, or agility—so eliminate choices (B) and (D). You can also eliminate choice (A) because the context refers to an action, not a statement, and choice (E), because the context does not suggest superficiality.

FOR QUESTION 4, CONSIDER EACH ANSWER INDIVIDUALLY AND CHOOSE <u>ALL</u> THAT APPLY.

---

4. It can be inferred from the passage that the author believes
   (A) the public prefers to hold government, not corporations, accountable.
   (B) the government may be justified in its secret surveillance procedures.
   (C) certain online companies engage in less morally ambiguous actions than Wall Street does.

Answer Explanation

The correct answers are (A) and (B). This question tests your ability to understand the main idea of the passage and is also a multiple-choice question requiring one or more answer choices. Choice (A) is correct because this idea is implied by various details throughout the passage, including the final sentence that states that the public expects the government to "do the right thing," while it has no such expectations for corporations. Choice (B) is also implied by the passage when the author states the government's motivations for secrecy (preventing terrorism) and suggests, albeit through sarcasm, that secrecy may well be needful in such cases. Choice (C) is incorrect because, in paragraph 3, the author claims that certain online companies undermine our democracy just as much as any Wall Street practice does.

QUESTIONS 5–7 ARE BASED ON THE FOLLOWING PASSAGE.

The precipitate rise in the incidence of type 1, or juvenile, diabetes, as well as the startling decrease in average age at onset, has led to a nearly commensurate rise in causation hypotheses. The single factor that scientists have most commonly and consistently linked with the rise of cases of type 1 diabetes is weight gain, and, indeed, children's weights are increasing
5 generation by generation, and the greater BMI (body mass index), the younger the child is likely to be at the age of onset. Other factors linked to this rise in incidence and decrease

in average of age of onset and tracked with varying degrees of success in recent studies include psychological stress, the increased wealth of the homes in which the children reside, the increased levels of hygiene in the homes in which the children reside, and nourishment 10 by infant formula during the first six months of life. Some of these theories have garnered more academic support than others, but, no matter how much support they have received, correlation is not causation.

Passage Summary: This passage mentions various theories, or causation hypotheses, for the rise in incidence, or decrease in age of onset of type 1 diabetes. It begins with what has been shown to be the most common and consistent correlation with the rise of the disease, weight gain; it also presents the correlation between BMI and early onset. The writer goes on to mention other correlations, some of which have more support than others: psychological stress, household wealth, household cleanliness, and infant formula. Yet, the author warns, none of these correlations is necessarily a cause.

Question

5. The writer mentions greater BMI at earlier ages in the paragraph in order to

    (A) introduce a common causation hypothesis.

    (B) provide support for an implied argument.

    (C) reinforce the importance of a healthful diet for children.

    (D) provide a possible explanation for the confusion of cause and correlation.

    (E) cast doubt on studies that collect data on wealth and hygiene.

Answer Explanation

The correct answer is (A). Like many of the questions on the GRE®, this question is about main idea and supporting details. The passage implies that scientists have most consistently explored weight gain as a cause of type 1 diabetes; weight gain is most commonly and consistently linked with the rise in incidence. While scientists have found that the increased incidence correlates with this rise, not that it causes the disease, this idea nevertheless constitutes a causation hypothesis, choice (A). Choice (B) can be eliminated because this paragraph is informational; there is no implied argument. The passage does not state or imply anything about a healthful diet, so choice (C) is incorrect. Choice (D) is also incorrect because the passage clearly states that psychological stress, increased wealth, increased levels of hygiene, and infant formula have all been linked either to the rise in incidence or to the decrease in average age of onset of the disease. The passage does not cast doubt on any studies, so choice (E) is also wrong.

Question

6. Which of the following, if it were true, would most seriously weaken the import of a specific data set suggesting a correlation?

    (A) The average age at onset of type 1 diabetes decreased by one year over a period of just five years.

    (B) Nourishment by baby formula has not been correlated to a rise in BMI.

    (C) Among stress factors, only poor performance in school and divorce have been shown to correlate with increased incidence of type 1 diabetes.

    (D) The incidence of type 1 diabetes is rising at a slower rate among children who are not overweight.

    (E) There is a higher rate of type 1 diabetes in households with incomes of more than $80,000 than in households with lower incomes.

Answer Explanation

The correct answer is (D). This is an application question. Both choices (A) and (E) would strengthen the correlation, so they should be eliminated. Choice (B) should also be eliminated because, among other reasons, the question refers to a single data set. Choice (C) is also incorrect because the cited forms of stress do fall under the category of psychological stress. Even though the incidence of type 1 diabetes is rising at a slower rate among children who are not overweight, it is still rising; therefore, choice (D) undercuts or weakens the correlation between being overweight and developing the disease.

Question

7. Which of the following statements does the passage most clearly support?
   - (A) The weight-gain theory originated before the other theories.
   - (B) There are reasons to give the stress, hygiene, wealth, and formula theories less credence than the weight-gain theory.
   - (C) None of the theories has shown a significant correlation with rising incidence.
   - (D) Only one of the theories has been linked to younger age at onset.
   - (E) The weight-gain theory is universally accepted by scientists.

Answer Explanation

The correct answer is (B). This is another application question. There is no evidence in the passage to suggest that the weight-gain theory arose before other theories, or that the weight-gain theory is universally accepted by scientists, so eliminate choices (A) and (E). The passage does, however, say that the weight-gain theory has been most commonly and consistently linked with the rise of type 1 diabetes. Because all of the theories have shown a significant correlation with rising incidence, choice (C) is incorrect. Choice (D) is incorrect because it's not clear which, or if only one, of the theories among the final theories discussed has been linked to the rise in incidence or the decrease in average age of onset.

QUESTIONS 8–9 ARE BASED ON THE FOLLOWING PASSAGE.

Robert Frost is often categorized as an anti-Romantic writer, that is, as a poet whose poetry contradicts the ideals of Romanticism as embodied in the works of Wordsworth, Keats, Shelley, and others. **Simultaneously, he is categorized as an anti-modernist, a poet who has little in common with his contemporaries, Eliot, Pound, Joyce, Woolf, and others.**
5 Nevertheless, because modernists declared that modernism was, among other things, the rejection of Romanticism, there can be only partial validity in the claim that Frost was both anti-Romantic and anti-modernist. **Instead, as the poems bear out, Frost was at once neither and a bit of both, and one does not have to look far in the poems for substantiation.** Whether the reader is "Stopping by Woods" or out among the "Birches," nature and wildness
10 are the gateways to introspection and imagination, even if emotion receives short shrift. At the same time, modernism asserts itself—albeit in traditional poetic form—in poems such as "After Apple Picking," with its evocation of a transitional state of consciousness; and in "The Death of the Hired Man," "Desert Places," and "Acquainted with the Night" with their experience of alienation, loss, and despair.

Passage Summary: The author argues that while some people call Frost anti-Romantic and others call him anti-modern, both labels can apply—and both labels don't apply. The author then provides evidence to show that Frost was Romantic, at least in one sense, while admitting that the poems cited are not true to all aspects of Romanticism. The writer also provides evidence that Frost was modern, at least in one sense, while also admitting that Frost was traditional in terms of poetic form.

Question

8. It can be inferred that the author judges which of the following characteristics as most clearly defining or epitomizing Romanticism?

(A) The reliance on traditional poetic forms

(B) The rejection of modernism

(C) Nature and wildness as the gateway to introspection and imagination

(D) Poems such as "Stopping by Woods" and "Birches"

(E) Poems that evoke a transitional state of consciousness

Answer Explanation

The correct answer is (C). This question asks only about supporting details. Choices (D) and (E) can be eliminated because poems are not characteristics. The phrase about "traditional poetic forms" is couched in the discussion of what modernism is "not," so choice (A) is unlikely to be the answer. Nothing in the passage suggests that Romanticism is the rejection of modernism, so choice (B) is incorrect. The answer to this question appears in the sentence directly following the second boldfaced sentence. Here, the author is explaining why Frost "was at once neither and a bit of both." Since the second of the two sentences that follow is about modernism, it can be inferred that the first is about Romanticism. That is where the words about nature and wildness appear.

Question

9. In the passage, what is the primary purpose of the two groups of words in boldface type?

(A) The first provides contrast to the sentence that precedes it; the second expands upon and elucidates the sentence that precedes it.

(B) The first provides background information that leads up to the argument; the second presents the argument.

(C) The first reinforces the argument through contrast; the second explains the argument through explanation and expansion.

(D) The first states a position that the argument as a whole contradicts; the second presents the argument.

(E) The first provides contrast to the sentence that precedes it; the second provides evidence that supports the argument.

ALERT!

Remember not to apply any knowledge that you already have about a subject in answering questions on the GRE. Rely solely on the information in the passages.

Answer Explanation

The correct answer is (B). Did you notice that the question is asking you to apply information to come up with your answer? While choice (A) provides an accurate description of what the sentences do in the passage, it doesn't describe the primary purpose of the two groups of words in bold type. You can also eliminate choices (C), (D), and (E) because they don't accurately explain the purpose of the word groups. Choice (B) is the best answer—the most accurate answer—but only reading through all the answer choices will assure you of this.

QUESTIONS 10–11 ARE BASED ON THE FOLLOWING PASSAGE.

When explaining the issues of urbanization in Africa of the late twentieth century, some textbooks conflate effects of the phenomenon with effects of urbanization in the newly industrialized cities of England in the early nineteenth century. That is, some historians restrict their analysis to the problems of overcrowding, lack of sanitation, and inadequate
5 housing that occur in the wake of rapid mass movement from rural to urban areas. Their analysis ignores arguments, such as those put forth by the 1996 UN Habitat II conference, suggesting that economies of scale are preferable for the delivery of health care, clean water, electricity, and other needs. It further overlooks the freedoms available to women in the cities, where they may escape tribal or religious practices, or find fulfillment in both traditional
10 and nontraditional roles.

Passage Summary: The passage says that some textbooks mistakenly merge the issues of urbanization in late twentieth-century Africa with the issues of urbanization in the industrialized cities of England during the early nineteenth century. That is, they explain a contemporary or recent problem by providing the same explanations that have been given for a much different time and place. According to the author, these historians ignore twentieth-century ideas such as economies of scale and the changed and changing status of women.

Question

10. The author of the passage would most likely consider which of the following ideas most similar to the reasoning of historians mentioned in lines 3–5?

(A) Economies of scale is a relatively recent economic concept that suggests, not entirely accurately, that bigger is always better.

(B) The problems of overcrowding, lack of sanitation, and inadequate housing also occurred in major U.S. cities during the Industrial Revolution.

(C) The increased disparity in economic class in today's Mumbai cannot be attributed to globalization alone.

(D) Urbanization has a negative effect on traditional social mores and usually proves disruptive to cultural unity.

(E) The recent economic crises in Ireland may best be explained by examining financial crises in the United States in the late nineteenth century.

Answer Explanation

The correct answer is (E). This is another application question. The passage makes it clear that historians don't take into account the notion of economies of scale, so choice (A) is incorrect. Choices (B), (C), and (D) take the ideas of the passage off into entirely new directions, unrelated to the reasoning specified in the question, so they should be eliminated. Only choice (E) suggests a line of reasoning in which the problems of today are explained by the events of the past.

Question

11. Which of the following, if true, most seriously undermines the support that the final sentence provides for the claim?

    (A) Urban women are more likely than men to have to deal directly with the problems of lack of sanitation.

    (B) Women in large urban centers often achieve a higher level of education than they achieve in rural areas.

    (C) Many rural women find fulfillment through local tribal and religious practices.

    (D) Inadequate housing in the cities often offers more advantages than adequate housing in rural areas.

    (E) Women in large urban centers often work in the marketplace.

Answer Explanation

The correct answer is (C). How did you do with this application question? The claim is that some textbooks erroneously suggest that urbanization in Africa today leads to the same problems as it did, or is much the same phenomenon as it was, during the Industrial Revolution. The final sentence of the paragraph supports that claim by suggesting that women in particular benefit from urbanization (that is, it's not necessarily the nineteenth-century England industrial scourge) because their movement from rural areas to the cities can liberate women from tribal and religious practices, which, the passage implies, can oppress them or diminish their sphere of influence. Therefore, to undermine the claim, the correct answer has to say something about how women are not diminished by tribal life, or that city life oppresses them. Choice (D) can be immediately eliminated because it doesn't relate to women. Choices (A) and (E) neither support nor weaken the claim, whereas choice (B) strengthens it. Choice (C) is then the only correct answer because it claims that many rural women are fulfilled through local tribal and religious practices.

QUESTIONS 12–14 ARE BASED ON THE FOLLOWING PASSAGE.

Andrew Dickson White famously asserted that Darwin's *Origin of the Species* came "into the theological world like a plough into an ant-hill." At all costs, the anthill had to be rebuilt with some ants reconstructing the same structure and others making only slight alterations to it. Among the many ants rebuilding the hill was Teilhard de Chardin, who, among other
5 things, posited (without so much as a wink!) that the descent of man was actually the ascent of man. His new anthill took shape in *The Phenomenon of Man,* which Julian Huxley would subsequently hail as the synthesis of the "whole of knowable reality" and a triumph of human significance. Yet, the phrase "whole of knowable reality" is, along, of course, with Teilhard's fatuous scientific arguments, a clue to just how scientifically unpalatable this
10 particular philosophically respected, yet scientifically incoherent reconstruction of the anthill was. For example, P. B. Medawar found such flowery, unscientific, and abstract language "suffocating"—and the very obfuscation of sense.

Passage Summary: The passage begins with White's famous response to Darwin's *Origin of the Species*, which suggests that Darwin's huge, new, powerful ideas completely upset the little world of ants—that is, people who were used to thinking a certain way and simply could not accept the fundamental shift in worldview that Darwin presented. The implied claim is that ants began rebuilding the anthill, or that "little" people with little ideas began to refute Darwin's colossal ideas. One philosopher the passage maligns for "rebuilding," and, therefore, misreading or subverting Darwin, is Pierre Teilhard de Chardin. The passage also mentions responses to Teilhard de Chardin: there was Julian Huxley who lavishly praised the work, and R. P. Medawar who disliked it immensely, in large part because of Teilhard de Chardin's flowery language.

Question

12. The sentence "Among the many . . . the ascent of man" (lines 4–6) serves which of the following purposes in the passage?
    (A) It counters the argument expressed in the preceding sentence.
    (B) It provides evidence for the central argument or proposition of the passage.
    (C) It makes an assertion that subsequent sentences will contradict.

Answer Explanation

The correct answer is (B). Application question stems can take a variety of forms. This is also a multiple-choice question—select one or more answer choices. The anthill simile suggests the response to Darwin. The parenthetical "without so much as a wink" shows the attitude of the writer: he or she is stunned—and disdainful—that Teilhard de Chardin could get away with turning Darwin's ideas upside down to fit his own. Choice (A) is incorrect because the argument is not expressed in Sentence 2. Choice (C) is also incorrect because the subsequent sentences help explain and support the target sentence. On the other hand, choice (B) is correct because the target sentence does provide explanation for the central argument by providing an example of an "ant" and suggesting a response to Darwin that was, at least seemingly, illogical and something that the author clearly regards as ridiculous.

Question

13. It can be inferred that P. B. Medawar took issue with all of the following aspects of *The Phenomenon of Man* EXCEPT the
    (A) blurring of scientific fact.
    (B) attempt to rebuild the anthill.
    (C) lack of concreteness and specificity.
    (D) rebuttal of Darwin's ideas in poetic language.
    (E) obfuscation of sense.

Answer Explanation

The correct answer is (B). Supporting details are the subject of this EXCEPT question. The passage states directly that Teilhard de Chardin's *The Phenomenon of Man* contains absurd scientific arguments and is also scientifically unpalatable because of the very "flowery" way in which the work is written. When the author calls Teilhard's work an "incoherent reconstruction," he or she is stating that it lacked sense. Medawar also takes issue with how the book obfuscates sense. Eliminate both choices (A) and (E). Medawar's complaint about the flowery language eliminates choices (C) and (D) as well. Medawar does not, however, object to Teilhard's or anyone else's attempt to "rebuild the anthill"—or rebut Darwin, so choice (B) is correct.

Question

14. In the passage, "hail" (line 7) most nearly means

(A) be a native of.

(B) call for.

(C) greet.

(D) acclaim.

(E) precipitate.

Answer Explanation

The correct answer is (D). Choice (A), "be a native of," doesn't relate to the context in any way. Because Huxley didn't "call for" Teilhard de Chardin's work (instead, he responded to it), choice (B) is also incorrect. Choice (C) should be eliminated because it doesn't suggest the positive response alluded to in the passage. Any of the meanings of "precipitate" don't make sense in the context of a critical response to a work, so choice (E) is incorrect. "Acclaim," choice (D), fits the context because it suggests a positive response.

QUESTION 15 IS BASED ON THE FOLLOWING PASSAGE.

The pivotal considerations affecting the design of any stationary robotic arm are the central tasks and workspace, which will, in turn, affect the desired degrees of freedom (DOF). A relatively simple design might have just 3 DOFs—not counting any additional DOFs on the end effector or gripper. When designers create an FBD (free body diagram) for a new robotic
5 arm, other considerations reflected in that diagram will include the limitations of each DOF, which should be accounted for in the FBD by annotations showing maximum joint angles and exact arm link lengths. Engineers commonly use a coordinate system known as the Denavit-Hartenberg (D-H) Convention for this purpose.

Passage Summary: The passage presents a few of the basic concepts in the design of a robotic arm, including identifying the central tasks and the workspace, determining the degrees of freedom, making a diagram, and labeling that diagram with coordinates.

Question

15. According to the information in this passage, in what order would these steps in the design of a robotic arm most likely take place?

(A) Determine DOFs, plan for D-H, draw FBD.

(B) Determine maximum joint angles, draw FBD, add end effector or gripper.

(C) Draw FBD, annotate joints according to D-H system, determine DOFs.

(D) Identify robotic task(s), determine DOFs, create FBD with D-H.

(E) Create FBD, determine DOFs, add end effector DOF.

Answer Explanation

The correct answer is (D). To give you more practice, here is another application question. The passage implies that the first considerations in this design are the central tasks and the workspace; these must be known in order to determine the degrees of freedom (DOF) that the robotic arm must have. Although it may not be clear on first reading, the order of information in the paragraph is basically sequential; therefore, choices (A), (B), (C), and (E) do not follow the paragraph order and so must be eliminated.

SUMMING IT UP

- There are approximately ten reading comprehension passages on the Verbal Reasoning sections of the GRE®.

- Most passages will be one paragraph in length, though you will find one or two passages that have multiple paragraphs.

- Passages may be informational, analytical, or persuasive.

- There are three formats for questions: multiple-choice questions—select one answer choice, multiple-choice questions—select one or more answer choices, and select-in-passage answers.

- The select-in-passage questions on the computerized test will require students to choose a sentence within the passage to highlight as the answer. For international students taking the paper-and-pencil version, the select-in-passage questions will be in the form of multiple-choice questions—select one answer choice questions.

- Computer versions of the GRE® will have approximately 20 questions for each of the two Verbal Reasoning sections, of which perhaps more than half will be reading comprehension questions. The time limit is 30 minutes. Students taking the paper-and-pencil version will have 25 questions to be completed in 35 minutes.

- Multiple-choice questions—select one answer choice questions are preceded by ovals. Multiple-choice questions—select one or more answer choices are preceded by squares.

- Multiple-choice questions—select one answer choice questions are followed by a list of five possible answer options. Multiple-choice questions—select one or more answer choices are followed by a list of only three answers.

- Answer all questions based only on the information contained in the passage. Don't use anything from your own experience or outside knowledge.

- Don't allow your own opinions to enter into your selection of an answer.

- You will find that certain types of questions recur among the reading comprehension questions: main idea (major point), supporting details (minor points), author's perspective, application, and word meaning.

- Remember to use the following active reading strategies when reading the passages:
  o Identify the topic, main idea, thesis, or proposition.
  o Clarify your understanding.
  o Summarize what you've read.

- The following strategies can be helpful for both kinds of multiple-choice questions:
  o Restate the question.
  o Try answering the question before you read the answer choices.
  o Read all the answers before you choose.
  o Compare answer choices to each other and the question.
  o Avoid selecting an answer you don't fully understand.
  o Choose the *best* answer.

- o　Pay attention to structure and structural clues.
- o　Don't select an answer just because it's true.
- o　Substitute answer choices in word meaning questions.
- o　Choose the answer that doesn't fit for EXCEPT questions.
- The following strategy applies to multiple-choice questions—select more than one answer choice questions: *choose an answer that answers the question on its own.*
- In addition to choosing an answer that stands on its own, the following strategy can be helpful for answering select-in-passage questions: *match the sentence to the information.*

Strategies for Text Completion Questions

chapter 7

OVERVIEW

- Basic information about text completion questions
- Strategies for text completion
- Practice questions
- Answer key and explanations
- Summing it up

The GRE® revised General Test has at least two Verbal Reasoning sections. Reading comprehension, text completion, and sentence equivalence questions are mixed within the Verbal Reasoning sections. This chapter describes the question formats for text completion test items and also provides a discussion of strategies to help you answer this question type.

BASIC INFORMATION ABOUT TEXT COMPLETION QUESTIONS

The text completion questions on the GRE® assess your ability not only to actively interpret and evaluate what you read, but also to supply words and phrases whose meaning is consistent with the ideas that are presented. You will complete text by choosing among three to five options to fill in one, two, or three blanks in a passage. You can expect around one quarter to one third of the questions on each verbal section of the GRE® to be text completion questions, that is, five to seven questions.

The text completion items (as well as the sentence equivalence items) test your vocabulary. (In some ways, they take the place of the antonyms and analogies questions that used to be on the GRE®.) To do well on these questions, you need to know "big" words—words such as *refulgent, dissimulation,* and *deleterious.* Not all the words are a test of the size of one's vocabulary, however. Some items will involve words that are close in meaning or an unusual meaning of a familiar word.

As you will see in reading this chapter, the text completion items are not just about vocabulary. They also test your reading comprehension skills. Furthermore, you may also have to apply your knowledge of grammar and usage in order to choose the best answers.

Regardless of the number of blanks, each question is worth one point. All the blanks for a test item must be answered correctly in order to earn a point for that question.

Passages and Question Formats

Unlike the reading comprehension questions, the text completion items offer a predictable sameness of format. Overall, the text completion passages are much less intimidating. Generally speaking, you will need to spend less time with a text completion passage than with a reading comprehension passage, and, of course, the shorter length of a text completion passage, compared to the typical reading comprehension passage, also contributes significantly to greater ease of reading.

Text completion questions are fill-in-the-blank questions. The blanks are embedded in passages of different lengths, ranging from one sentence to approximately five sentences.

- In single sentences, you will typically be required to fill in just one blank. There are, however, exceptions.

- In passages that consist of multiple sentences, you will most likely be required to fill in two or three blanks.

Text completion items are interspersed with the other test items in the Verbal Reasoning sections. Each text completion question appears on a separate screen. All passages are short enough to display on a single screen; you won't need to scroll or change screens to answer a text completion question.

The Direction Line and Answer Choices

Text completion items have only one type of direction, which is worded something like the following:

> **FOR QUESTIONS 1–10, CHOOSE <u>ONE</u> ANSWER FOR EACH BLANK. SELECT FROM THE APPROPRIATE COLUMN FOR EACH BLANK. CHOOSE THE ANSWER THAT BEST COMPLETES THE SENSE OF THE TEXT.**

In most cases, you will be selecting a single word for each blank. Occasionally, you will be presented with a list of phrases or group of words from which to select the answer.

- If the sentence or passage contains only *one blank,* there will be five answer choices listed in a single column.

- If the sentence or passage contains *two blanks,* you will choose the first answer from a column of three choices (Blank (i)) and the second from a second column of three choices (Blank (ii)).

- If the sentence or passage contains *three blanks,* you will choose each answer from one of three columns—Blank (i), Blank (ii), Blank (iii)—with three choices each.

To select an answer, you will click on the cell that contains your answer choice. If you change your mind, clicking on another cell will change your answer.

Using the "Mark" Option

Depending on how the test is going for you, you might consider using the "Mark" option more readily on the text completion and sentence equivalence items than you would on reading comprehension items. Both text completion and sentence equivalence items are quicker to revisit than reading comprehension items. They're shorter and less time-consuming to read and answer.

In addition, each text completion is only one question. When you mark a text completion item to return to, no matter how many blanks it has, you're making a commitment to revisit only about 4 percent of the test section. This is not a huge task to put off until near the end and, therefore, a reasonable strategy to use when your confidence or attention wavers on a question. But be careful that you don't use it too often, or you could find yourself circling back to a quarter of the test.

STRATEGIES FOR TEXT COMPLETION

Text completion questions lend themselves to a variety of specific strategies. As you read through the following strategies, note that the first four are really commonsense reminders.

1 Try answering the question before you read the answer choice(s).

2 Focus on one blank at a time.

3 If there is more than one blank, complete the blanks in the order that makes sense to you.

4 Check your answer(s) in place.

The last four strategies ask you to make use of what you once learned in English composition classes.

1 Use structural clues.

2 Consider tone and style.

3 Consider grammar and usage.

4 Avoid selecting a word or phrase that you don't fully understand or is unfamiliar.

In addition, remember to apply the four test-taking strategies discussed in Chapter 1.

1 Anticipate and use the clock.

2 Skip and return to questions.

3 Eliminate answer choices you know are incorrect.

4 Use educated guessing.

Try Answering the Question Before You Read the Answer Choice(s)

As you read a passage, try to get a clear sense of what the passage is about. Then, before you read the answer choices, fill in the answer blank(s) in your own words. What you come up with doesn't need to be sophisticated or polysyllabic. It just needs to be a word or words that capture the meaning of the sentence. With your answer in mind, check the list of answers, and choose the one that seems to best match your idea.

Try this now with Question 1 below.

> **FOR QUESTION 1, CHOOSE <u>ONE</u> ANSWER FOR THE BLANK. CHOOSE THE ANSWER THAT BEST COMPLETES THE SENSE OF THE TEXT.**

1. Emerging African democracies of the 1960s and 1970s faced insurmountable problems that ranged from lack of infrastructure to borders that ignored ethnic conflict: in fact, these _____ governments were destined to fail.

(A) despotic
(B) ephemeral
(C) incompetent
(D) deteriorating
(E) fledgling

TIP

Remember that there is no penalty for wrong answers. If you absolutely cannot decide on an answer even through the process of elimination, make your best guess based on what you do know.

ALERT!

If you find test time running out and you still have a number of questions to answer, go quickly through the test looking for text completion and sentence equivalence questions. They're quicker to answer than reading comprehension questions, and a point is a point, no matter what question you answer to earn it.

ALERT!

Both the computer version of the GRE and the paper-and-pencil version for international test-takers have two scored sections of Verbal Reasoning questions. Each section of the computer version will have approximately 20 questions with a time limit of 30 minutes. Each section of the paper-and-pencil version will consist of 25 questions with a time limit of 35 minutes.

If you try to fill the blank before you read the answers, you might come up with either the word "new" or "democratic." You can safely eliminate "democratic" because it's highly unlikely that ETS is going to make the answer that simple. That is, the test-item writer isn't going to repeat a word, or form of a word, that already appears in the passage as the correct answer. Your next step, then, is to look for a word in the list that means the same as, or close to the same as, new. "Fledgling" means "young and inexperienced," which suggests the meaning of "new." "Fledgling" is most often applied to birds leaving the nest and trying their wings for the first time, just as the new democracies referred to in the passage were beginning to grow, develop, or "take flight" in a metaphorical sense. **The correct answer is (E).**

Focus on Only One Blank at a Time

The majority of the text completion items will present you with either two blanks or three blanks to fill. When you have multiple blanks to fill, it is best to arrive at the answers by concentrating on just one blank at a time. Try out this strategy as you read the following two-blank item.

> **FOR QUESTION 2, CHOOSE <u>ONE</u> ANSWER FOR EACH BLANK. SELECT FROM THE APPROPRIATE COLUMN FOR EACH BLANK. CHOOSE THE ANSWER THAT BEST COMPLETES THE SENSE OF THE TEXT.**

2. A major part of the body's immune system, the lymphatic system is responsible for producing, maintaining, and distributing lymphocytes (white blood cells that attack bacteria in blood and take the form of T cells and B cells) in the body, as well as for defending the body against pathogens. Besides removing waste, dead blood cells, and toxins from cells and the tissues between them, the lymphatic system also works in concert with the circulatory system to deliver oxygen, nutrients, and hormones from the blood to the cells. The (i) _____ role of the lymphatic system in fighting disease and maintaining homeostasis (ii) _____.

Blank (i)	Blank (ii)
(A) pivotal	(D) must not be trivial
(B) autonomous	(E) cannot be gainsaid
(C) hypothetical	(F) will not be equivocated

Starting with the first blank might lead you to a word that conveys the importance or centrality of the lymphatic system. You might, for example, come up with the words "key," "major," "necessary," or "central." Reading down the list of answers for Blank (i), you find choice (A), "pivotal," which means "key" or "essential," so this is the answer for Blank (i). But read all the answer choices for Blank (i) just to be sure "pivotal" is the best choice. Once the first blank is filled, it can be easier to come up with the second answer. For example, it makes no sense to say that "the pivotal role must not be trivial." Neither does it make sense to say that "the pivotal role will not be equivocated," meaning "using vague language." Therefore, the correct answer for the second blank is choice (E), "cannot be gainsaid." "Gainsaid" means "denied." **The correct answers are (A) and (E).**

If There Is More Than One Blank, Complete the Blanks in the Order That Makes Sense to You

Don't assume that you need to fill the first blank first, the second blank second, and the third blank third. Begin by filling in the blank that is easiest or most obvious to you. Try this strategy now with the following three-blank item.

FOR QUESTION 3, CHOOSE <u>ONE</u> ANSWER FOR EACH BLANK. SELECT FROM THE APPROPRIATE COLUMN FOR EACH BLANK. CHOOSE THE ANSWER THAT BEST COMPLETES THE SENSE OF THE TEXT.

---

3. Those calling for the regulation of commodities trading are, at best, uninformed. Instead of (i) _____ traders for spikes in prices of wheat, oil, and metals, as well as for the bubbles, legislators would be wiser to consider how speculators help to create (ii) _____ by injecting cash into markets—which contributes to market efficiency. Furthermore, legislators who are gung-ho to rein in traders might bother to note that speculators have little or no effect on the production, and only (iii) _____ effect on the consumption, of goods.

Blank (i)	Blank (ii)	Blank (iii)
(A) regulating	(D) liquidity	(G) minimal
(B) scapegoating	(E) activity	(H) negative
(C) castigating	(F) inventory	(I) lasting

Suppose you read the passage and know that injecting, or moving, cash into markets creates liquidity, so you mark choice (D) for Blank (ii). With "liquidity" in place for Blank (ii), you can now move back to Blank (i) or on to Blank (iii). In either case, you can use the concept of liquidity to help you make sense of the rest of the passage. The more words you fill in, the easier it will be for you to come up with the answer that is most difficult for you. For the record, the correct answer for Blank (i) is choice (B), "scapegoating." Scapegoating means "blaming unfairly." The correct answer for Blank (iii) is choice (G), "minimal." **The correct answers are (B), (D), and (G).**

You will revisit Question 3 and read a more detailed analysis later in this chapter.

Check Your Answer(s) in Place

When you've chosen your answer(s), it's a good idea to reread the question quickly with the answers in place. All the words together should create a unified whole: that is, the meanings should all work together; everything should be grammatically correct; and the tone and style should be consistent.

Use Structural Clues

Many text completion items will take the form of organizational structures for writing that are familiar to you and that you can use to help you determine the correct answer. These structures include sentences and paragraphs that compare, contrast, restate, show causes and/or effects, and present main idea and supporting details. Some of these passages will contain what the test-maker calls "signposts," that is, trigger, signal, or transitional words and phrases to help you understand the meaning of the passage—more specifically, the relationship of ideas in that passage.

You can use the following types of structural clues to help you determine meaning and fill in the blanks of many text completion questions. As you work through various examples, you will note that, in some cases, a single sentence or passage may contain more than one type of structure and structural clue. The following clues can help you identify answers:

- Restatement
- Cause and effect
- Contrast
- Comparison or similarity structure
- Main idea and details

Restatement

Restatement is a presentation of an idea in words other than those used the first time the idea is presented; an amplification or clarification of an idea; or the presentation of an example of the idea. A sentence or passage that uses restatement will most often have two independent clauses joined by a colon, a semicolon, or a correlative conjunction such as *moreover.* Or, a restatement might take the form of two sentences, the second of which begins with a signal word for restatement. (See the box below for signal words.)

Depending on the restatement structure used, one of the following will be apparent:

- Sentence 2 or clause 2 presents in other words the meaning of sentence 1 or clause 1.
- Sentence 2 or clause 2 amplifies or clarifies sentence 1 or clause 1. This is a more likely combination than mere repetition of an idea in other words.
- Sentence 2 or clause 2 exemplifies sentence or clause 1. That is, sentence 2 or clause 2 provides a single example or illustration.

Signals for Restatement

Among the words and phrases that can signal restatement relationships are the following:

for example	*in other words*	*that is*
for instance	*in short*	*this means*
in fact	*namely*	*thus*

Often, you may have to infer the words and phrases that signal restatement, amplification, clarification, or illustration. For an example of restatement, we'll look again at Question 1. You should be able to identify a restatement signal before you read the analysis that follows the question.

FOR QUESTION 1, CHOOSE <u>ONE</u> ANSWER FOR THE BLANK. CHOOSE THE ANSWER THAT BEST COMPLETES THE SENSE OF THE TEXT.

---

1. Emerging African democracies of the 1960s and 1970s faced insurmountable problems that ranged from lack of infrastructure to borders that ignored ethnic conflict: in fact, these _____ governments were destined to fail.

(A) despotic
(B) ephemeral
(C) incompetent
(D) deteriorating
(E) fledgling

A thought process to work through Question 1 might go something like this:

- Note that the signal phrase "in fact," along with the second clause more or less restating or amplifying the first, signals a restatement.

- Knowing that you're working with restatement, next restate, paraphrase, or summarize the item. Focus on only the parts of the passage that reflect the restatement you want to zero in on. Eliminate extraneous wording. For this passage, you would concentrate on the two main clauses and eliminate the clause that begins with "that ranged from . . . ." You might arrive at this summary: "New African governments faced huge problems; these _____ governments could do nothing but fail."

- The omission of extra words helps make it clear that the word that fits the blank must be a synonym for emerging or new, or it must in some way express a similar or close meaning.

- To arrive at the correct answer, use the process of elimination. The first four choices are not synonyms for new, nor do they evoke something new. Therefore, the correct answer is choice (E), "fledgling."

Go back to Question 1 above and drop out the words "in fact." Reread the passage without those words and you'll see that you're still dealing with restatement, even though it's not quite so apparent. **The correct answer is (E).**

Cause and Effect

A sentence or passage with a cause-and-effect structure expresses the reason(s) someone did something or something occurred, or it expresses the result(s) of an action or event. A cause-and-effect relationship can be expressed in one sentence or in a longer passage.

> **Cause-and-Effect Signals**
>
> Cause-and-effect relationships may or may not include signal words. Among the words and phrases that can signal cause-and-effect relationships are the following:
>
> | | | |
> |---|---|---|
> | *as a result* | *in order to* | *so that* |
> | *because* | *reason why* | *therefore* |
> | *consequently* | *since* | *thus* |
> | *for* | *so* | *why* |

Sometimes, you will have to infer cause-and-effect relationships. For example, Question 4 below begins with the infinitive phrase "To defeat the English. . . ." You can and should reasonably infer that this phrase means "[In order to] defeat the English. . . ." or "[Because he wanted to] defeat the English. . . ." This is your first step.

FOR QUESTION 4, CHOOSE ONE ANSWER FOR THE BLANK. CHOOSE THE ANSWER THAT BEST COMPLETES THE SENSE OF THE TEXT.

---

4. To defeat the English, Metacomet, whom the English called King Philip, knew he had to bring disparate and sometimes warring groups together into a _____.

(A) battalion
(B) community
(C) legation
(D) confederation
(E) hierarchy

An analysis of Question 4 could take this shape:

- Once you know that you're working with cause and effect, begin by restating, paraphrasing, or summarizing the item in a way that reflects your understanding of the cause-and-effect relationship. For example, you might arrive at this loose paraphrase or summary: "In order to defeat the English, Metacomet had to bring together different and warring groups into a _____.

- This summary, which leaves out the clause "whom the English called King Philip" and which is extraneous to the cause-and-effect relationship, makes it clear that the reason, or cause, for bringing together the groups was defeat of the English. So the word that goes into the blank must be one that names a group that can defeat someone or something. That immediately leaves out the all-too-peaceable or scientific sounding "community," as well as the diplomatic and also peaceful "legation." It also leaves out "hierarchy": a hierarchy alone wouldn't get the job of defeating someone accomplished.

- Using cause-and-effect clues in this case quickly narrows down the possible choices to choice (A), "battalion," and choice (D), "confederation."

- To reach the correct answer, try a general strategy, such as comparing two answers against each other and against the passage. A confederation brings many different groups together, which is the point of the sentence; therefore, choice (D) is correct. **The correct answer is (D).**

Contrast

A sentence or passage with a contrast structure expresses differences. This commonly used structure is probably very familiar to you.

Contrast Signals

Like other structures, contrasts of information may or may not include signal words. Among the words and phrases that can be used to signal contrasts are the following:

although	*however*	*on the contrary*
as opposed to	*in contrast*	*on the other hand*
but	*in spite of*	*otherwise*
by contrast	*instead*	*still*
conversely	*nevertheless*	*unlike*
despite	*nonetheless*	*yet*

Most often, you will have to infer contrasts or the words and phrases that signal them. Question 5, however, does contain a contrast word.

FOR QUESTION 5, CHOOSE <u>ONE</u> ANSWER FOR THE BLANK. CHOOSE THE ANSWER THAT BEST COMPLETES THE SENSE OF THE TEXT.

5. Judging by the various glances exchanged, the statistics Mai offered during the meeting struck everyone in attendance as _____; later, however, she managed to authenticate most of them in her expansive written analysis.

(A) valid
(B) inconsequential
(C) spurious
(D) unexpurgated
(E) superfluous

An analysis of the contrast relationship in Question 5 could look something like this:

- Once you have identified the structure as a contrast, restate, paraphrase, or summarize the item in a way that reflects your understanding of the contrast relationship. For example, you might arrive at this paraphrase: "The glances showed people thought Mai's statistics were _____; later, her analysis showed they were authentic."

- This loose paraphrase makes it clear that the answer must express the opposite, or near opposite, of "authentic."

- Through the process of elimination, choices (A), (B), (D), and (E) should all be ruled out because they don't show or suggest the opposite of authentic. Choice (A), "valid," means "just, producing the desired results, or legally binding," all somewhat similar to "authentic." Choice (B), "inconsequential," is incorrect because it isn't the opposite of "authentic." Choice (D) is incorrect because "unexpurgated" refers to removing offensive material from something. Choice (E) is incorrect because "superfluous" means "unnecessary, more than what is required." Therefore, choice (C), "spurious," meaning "false," is the correct answer.

Try rereading the passage after eliminating the signal word "however" to help familiarize yourself with an alternative way in which a contrast passage might appear. **The correct answer is (C).**

Comparison or Similarity Structure

Like a sentence or passage expressing contrasting ideas, a sentence or passage expressing a comparison or similarity should also be familiar to you. Such a structure expresses how two or more things are alike.

> **Comparison Signals**
>
> Among the words and phrases that can signal a comparison are the following:
>
> | | | |
> |---|---|---|
> | *also* | *in comparison* | *moreover* |
> | *and* | *in the same way* | *same* |
> | *another* | *like* | *similarly* |
> | *as* | *likewise* | *too* |
> | *by the same token* | | |

FOR QUESTION 6, CHOOSE <u>ONE</u> ANSWER FOR THE BLANK. CHOOSE THE ANSWER THAT BEST COMPLETES THE SENSE OF THE TEXT.

---

6. Debussy is regarded as the germinal musical impressionist who created color through the use of individual instruments in the orchestra; by the same token, Monet's use of blocks of color, in lieu of line, was a _____ influence on impressionism in art. There, however, the similarity between the two "impressionists" ends.

(A) imperative
(B) seminal
(C) discernable
(D) super
(E) formidable

An analysis of the comparison in Question 6 could look something like this:

- Note that the signal phrase "by the same token" along with the word "similarity" indicate a comparison.

- The next step is to restate, paraphrase, or summarize the item in a way that reflects your understanding of the comparison relationship, or structure. For example, you might arrive at this summary: "Debussy had great influence in music because of his use of color; likewise, Monet was a _____ influence in art because of how he used color."

- This summary significantly reduces the original in order to focus on the comparison. It makes clear that the word that belongs in the blank must be an adjective that suggests great influence.

- At this point, you might use the process of elimination. Choice (A) should be eliminated because "imperative" means "absolutely necessary." Choice (C) is also incorrect because the similarity suggests that Monet had more than a discernable, or noticeable, influence on art; he had a great influence. Choice (D) is likewise incorrect because "super," which can mean "particularly excellent," is too informal for this passage. Finally, choice (E) is incorrect because "formidable," while suggesting a meaning that fits, does not exactly match the meaning expressed by the first clause. The context makes it clear that the effect of each artist on his discipline was not only huge or formidable, it was also influential. Choice (B), "seminal," is the only word that conveys something formative or something that shaped, influenced, or decided what was to come. **The correct answer is (B).**

Now try analyzing Question 6 without the signal words in the passage.

If you look back at Question 1, you'll see that it could also be approached as a comparison, but without any signal words. Structures can be combined or overlapped in a single sentence or passage. Your task is not to identify the "right" structure, but to identify and use structures that will best help you find the answer.

Main Idea and Details

Main ideas and details as an organizing structure consist of more than one sentence. The main idea may be stated at the beginning of the passage, in the middle, or at the end. The main idea may also be implied through the details in the passage. Although passages may occasionally contain signal words and phrases such as "for example" to help you identify details, you will most likely have to infer the main idea based on the content of the passage.

Take a look again at Question 2. See if you can identify its main ideas and details before you read the analysis.

> **FOR QUESTION 2, CHOOSE <u>ONE</u> ANSWER FOR EACH BLANK. SELECT FROM THE APPROPRIATE COLUMN FOR EACH BLANK. CHOOSE THE ANSWER THAT BEST COMPLETES THE SENSE OF THE TEXT.**

2. A major part of the body's immune system, the lymphatic system is responsible for producing, maintaining, and distributing lymphocytes (white blood cells that attack bacteria in blood and take the form of T cells and B cells) in the body, as well as for defending the body against pathogens. Besides removing waste, dead blood cells, and toxins from cells and the tissues between them, the lymphatic system also works in concert with the circulatory system to deliver oxygen, nutrients, and hormones from the blood to the cells. The (i) _____ role of the lymphatic system in fighting disease and maintaining homeostasis (ii) _____.

Blank (i)	Blank (ii)
(A) pivotal	(D) must not be trivial
(B) autonomous	(E) cannot be gainsaid
(C) hypothetical	(F) will not be equivocated

An analysis of the main idea and supporting details in a passage to help you answer a text completion question might look like this for Question 2:

- Begin by finding the main idea (the last sentence) and the details that support it (everything that precedes the last sentence).

- Then, once again, restate, paraphrase, or summarize the part or parts of the passage containing the blank or blanks you must fill in. For example, you might arrive at this summary: "The _____ part played by the lymphatic system in the body _____."

- This summary depends, of course, on the details for correct completion, so now reread the details. The details inform you of the various and important roles the lymphatic system plays in the body. Therefore, the first blank must have to do with importance, or being essential.

- The word that comes closest in meaning to important is "pivotal." "Pivotal," choice (A), is the correct answer for Blank (i).

- To complete Blank (ii), work with the more complete version of your summary: "The pivotal part played by the lymphatic system in the body _____." If you come up with your own answer for this blank, you might say "cannot be (or must not be or will not be) denied." Therefore, look for the answer choice that means "denied," choice (E).

If you don't know the meaning of all the words—or even if you do—remember to use the process of elimination. "Trivial" doesn't mean "denied." Neither does "equivocated." So, while you may not know that choice (E), "gainsaid," means "denied," by the process of elimination, it must be the correct answer. **The correct answers are (A) and (E).**

Consider Tone and Style

Although this strategy won't apply to every passage, some passages will carry a distinctive tone that you can use as a clue to meaning. For example, the author's attitude may be sympathetic, indignant, questioning, mournful, celebratory, or praising. If there is an obvious tone, don't overlook it as a clue to the words that belong in the blanks. Look again at Question 3 and see if you can identify the tone of the passage for Blanks (i) and (ii).

> **FOR QUESTION 3, CHOOSE <u>ONE</u> ANSWER FOR EACH BLANK. SELECT FROM THE APPROPRIATE COLUMN FOR EACH BLANK. CHOOSE THE ANSWER THAT BEST COMPLETES THE SENSE OF THE TEXT.**

3. Those calling for the regulation of commodities trading are, at best, uninformed. Instead of (i) _____ traders for spikes in prices of wheat, oil, and metals, as well as for the bubbles, legislators would be wiser to consider how speculators help to create (ii) _____ by injecting cash into markets—which contributes to market efficiency. Furthermore, legislators who are gung-ho to rein in traders might bother to note that speculators have little or no effect on the production, and only (iii) _____ effect on the consumption, of goods.

Blank (i)	Blank (ii)	Blank (iii)
(A) regulating	(D) liquidity	(G) minimal
(B) scapegoating	(E) activity	(H) negative
(C) castigating	(F) inventory	(I) lasting

An analysis of the question based on tone would be something like this:

- The critical, almost indignant, tone of this passage is signaled by two groups of words that denigrate legislators: "at best, uninformed" and "legislators who are gung-ho to rein in traders . . ."

- This critical tone tells you that the author is not going to choose particularly moderate or measured word choices. Instead, at least some of the words that are most consistent with the message will be words with strong negative connotations. Of all the answer choices, choice (B), "scapegoating," has the most negative connotations. It is, in fact, the correct answer for Blank (i).

- Based on this assessment of the tone and sense of the passage, the best choice for the second blank is choice (D), "liquidity."

Similarly, considering the author's style might help you arrive at a correct answer. **The correct answers are (B) and (D).**

Read Question 6 again, but this time pay attention to the writer's style.

> **FOR QUESTION 6, CHOOSE <u>ONE</u> ANSWER FOR THE BLANK. CHOOSE THE ANSWER THAT BEST COMPLETES THE SENSE OF THE TEXT.**

6. Debussy is regarded as the germinal musical impressionist who created color through the use of individual instruments in the orchestra; by the same token, Monet's use of blocks of color, in lieu of line, was a _____ influence on impressionism in art. There, however, the similarity between the two "impressionists" ends.

(A) imperative
(B) seminal
(C) discernable
(D) super
(E) formidable

The style of the passage is formal and academic; therefore, the word that fits in the blank must be the same in order to work with that style. A quick read-through of the answer choices comes across "super." Though it means "particularly excellent" and might at first appear to be correct, "super" is an informal word appropriate to an informal context. It doesn't fit the style of this passage, so choice (D) can be eliminated. That leaves you four other choices with which to use the process of elimination.

Use Grammar and Usage

You will be able to eliminate some answer choices because they violate the rules of grammar or do not match the customary way in which a word or phrase is used. For example, look again at Question 3, Blank (iii):

> **FOR QUESTION 3, CHOOSE <u>ONE</u> ANSWER FOR EACH BLANK. SELECT FROM THE APPROPRIATE COLUMN FOR EACH BLANK. CHOOSE THE ANSWER THAT BEST COMPLETES THE SENSE OF THE TEXT.**

3. Those calling for the regulation of commodities trading are, at best, uninformed. Instead of (i) _____ traders for spikes in prices of wheat, oil, and metals, as well as for the bubbles, legislators would be wiser to consider how speculators help to create (ii) _____ by injecting cash into markets—which contributes to market efficiency. Furthermore, legislators who are gung-ho to rein in traders might bother to note that speculators have little or no effect on the production, and only (iii) _____ effect on the consumption, of goods.

Blank (i)	Blank (ii)	Blank (iii)
(A) regulating	(D) liquidity	(G) minimal
(B) scapegoating	(E) activity	(H) negative
(C) castigating	(F) inventory	(I) lasting

Notice that both "negative" and "lasting" actually require the article *a* before them. Only "minimal" fits in the space as it is worded. Therefore, choice (H), "negative," and choice (I), "lasting," must both be eliminated. **The correct answer is (G).**

Avoid Selecting the Word or Phrase You Don't Fully Understand or Is Unfamiliar

Look again at Question 4 and its answer choices.

> **FOR QUESTION 4, CHOOSE <u>ONE</u> ANSWER FOR THE BLANK. CHOOSE THE ANSWER THAT BEST COMPLETES THE SENSE OF THE TEXT.**

4. To defeat the English, Metacomet, whom the English called King Philip, knew he had to bring disparate and sometimes warring groups together into a _____.

(A) battalion
(B) community
(C) legation
(D) confederation
(E) hierarchy

Suppose you have no idea what "legation" means. In most cases, you should not leap to choose this word or any other unfamiliar word. "Legation," which means "a permanent diplomatic mission," is incorrect in the context of Question 4. Of course, if you have clearly eliminated every other choice, then an unfamiliar word may be correct.

PRACTICE QUESTIONS

> FOR QUESTIONS 1–10, CHOOSE <u>ONE</u> ANSWER FOR EACH BLANK. SELECT FROM
> THE APPROPRIATE COLUMN FOR EACH BLANK. CHOOSE THE ANSWER THAT
> BEST COMPLETES THE SENSE OF THE TEXT.

1. The stock character known as Harlequin in commedia dell'arte invariably appeared in a diamond-patterned suit; a half-mask and a ruff were other unmistakable parts of his _____ dress.

(A) inventive
(B) flamboyant
(C) signature
(D) unusual
(E) disturbing

2. In terms of material goods, contemporary humans may well be more acquisitive than any group or society before them. Or, it may just be that contemporary patterns of acquisition are entirely consistent with the far-reaching _____ for new and different goods that characterized so many early societies.

(A) tenet
(B) grasp
(C) tussle
(D) quest
(E) yearning

3. Architects and sound engineers routinely use sound-absorbing materials on ceilings and walls. In addition, they have sometimes tried to create optimal acoustics by building the ceilings and walls of concert halls with rippled or (i) _____ surfaces, so that the sound is reflected and (ii) _____ at many angles.

Blank (i)	Blank (ii)
(A) invariably rigid	(D) distorted
(B) highly polished	(E) diffused
(C) slightly undulating	(F) auditory

4. When oblique, rather than vertical, rays of the sun pass through the atmosphere, they must (i) _____ pierce a greater part of that atmosphere, thereby lessening the (ii) _____ of their heat.

Blank (i)	Blank (ii)
(A) necessarily	(D) relativity
(B) largely	(E) delivery
(C) regularly	(F) intensity

5. The investigative panel was nothing short of outraged by the bus driver's negligence and lack of remorse. It determined that the driver had failed to follow the established (i) _____. As a result, she had compromised the safety of the passengers. More fundamentally, however, she had actually and effectively (ii) _____ at least two of her riders' rights.

Blank (i)	Blank (ii)
(A) code of conduct	(D) abrogated
(B) rules of engagement	(E) renounced
(C) terms of use	(F) negated

6. The playwright created atmosphere in part through the (i) _____ afternoon on which he set the scene. The cloying humidity seemed at once to (ii) _____ the characters' physical energy and play devil's advocate to their sense of morality.

Blank (i)	Blank (ii)
(A) sultry	(D) sap
(B) unsettled	(E) beguile
(C) bone-chilling	(F) intensify

7. Is the most spineless method of delivering the news of a breakup by means of a text message? A recent survey based on Facebook data found that 14% of those born after 1984 are likely to choose this most expedient of methods. Of course, expedience alone may not explain this choice, but the study offers no other explanation for why respondents act in such a (i) _____ manner. Readers of the study are left to infer why the perpetrators of such spineless behavior (ii) _____ the more dignified, if not relatively (iii) _____, face-to-face meeting.

Blank (i)	Blank (ii)	Blank (iii)
(A) muted	(D) disavow	(G) decorous
(B) unreliable	(E) eschew	(H) imposing
(C) craven	(F) denounce	(I) outdated

8. Is understanding your stature in relation to the universe ultimately a psychic (i) _____ of your sense of self? On the one hand, gauging your own experience of space and time in relation to the space and time of galaxies can make you feel (ii) _____ small. On the other hand, sensing you are one with this great universe, or even knowing that its cosmic rays pass through you, may in some ways (iii) _____ that sense of smallness.

Blank (i)	Blank (ii)	Blank (iii)
(A) raveling	(D) antithetically	(G) mitigate
(B) diminution	(E) debilitatingly	(H) expropriate
(C) misappropriation	(F) infinitesimally	(I) enervate

9. The peasants portrayed in Pieter Brueghel the Elder's renowned paintings performed physical labor from sunup to sundown and lived grim, short lives. In *The Wedding Dance,* Pieter Brueghel depicts a nearly frenzied release from that daily round of (i) _____ and (ii) _____ in which peasants dance and (iii) _____ to the music of the bagpipes.

Blank (i)	Blank (ii)	Blank (iii)
(A) employment	(D) inanity	(G) unwind
(B) privation	(E) woe	(H) carouse
(C) mediocrity	(F) striving	(I) sing

10. In part by personifying them, and in larger part through a selection of detail, children's books do nothing less than (i) _____ cars and trucks. The trucks are big, mighty, fearless, and friendly behemoths that happily get the job done. Cars are speedy, bright, often open conveyances that delight their drivers and passengers on similarly open roads without traffic, congestion, or exhaust fumes. Such storybook portrayals begin the process of (ii) _____ that preserves and protects the (iii) _____ of the automobile in American culture.

Blank (i)	Blank (ii)	Blank (iii)
(A) extol	(D) indoctrination	(G) desultory consequences
(B) infantilize	(E) validation	(H) eternal aggrandizement
(C) venerate	(F) vindication	(I) unquestioned dominance

ANSWER KEY AND EXPLANATIONS

1. C	6. A, D
2. D	7. C, E, G
3. C, E	8. B, F, G
4. A, F	9. B, E, H
5. A, F	10. A, D, I

Question

1. The stock character known as Harlequin in commedia dell'arte invariably appeared in a diamond-patterned suit; a half-mask and a ruff were other unmistakable parts of his _____ dress.

(A) inventive
(B) flamboyant
(C) signature
(D) unusual
(E) disturbing

Answer Explanation

The correct answer is (C). This item is structured as a restatement. The first clause tells how the Harlequin was "invariably" dressed: in a diamond-patterned suit. The second half of the sentence, or the restatement/exemplification part, further explains that invariable, or characteristic, parts of the Harlequin's dress also included a half-mask and ruff. Therefore, the multiple-meaning word "signature" is used here to mean "characteristic," or something that serves to identify. Choices (A), (B), (D), and (E) are incorrect because, while the dress of a harlequin may seem inventive, flamboyant, unusual, or even possibly disturbing to today's viewer, the sentence makes it clear that it was characteristic, as well as invariable, at the time.

Question

2. In terms of material goods, contemporary humans may well be more acquisitive than any group or society before them. Or, it may just be that contemporary patterns of acquisition are entirely consistent with the far-reaching _____ for new and different goods that characterized so many early societies.

(A) tenet
(B) grasp
(C) tussle
(D) quest
(E) yearning

Answer Explanation

The correct answer is (D). A quest is a search or pursuit that would have preceded the acquisition of goods for early societies. Choice (A) should be eliminated because "tenet," which means "opinion, belief, or principle," doesn't make sense. Choice (B) also doesn't make sense; furthermore, it can be eliminated because "grasp for" is nonstandard usage. Choice (C) is incorrect because the meaning of a scuffle, or disorderly fighting, doesn't fit the context. While choice (E) makes some sense, it's not the best answer because yearning for something is not so close to acquiring it as questing, that is, searching, for it is.

Question

3. Architects and sound engineers routinely use sound-absorbing materials on ceilings and walls. In addition, they have sometimes tried to create optimal acoustics by building the ceilings and walls of concert halls with rippled or (i) _____ surfaces, so that the sound is reflected and (ii) _____ at many angles.

Blank (i)	Blank (ii)
(A) invariably rigid	(D) distorted
(B) highly polished	(E) diffused
(C) slightly undulating	(F) auditory

Answer Explanation

The correct answers are (C) and (E). For the first blank, the phrase with the closest meaning to "rippled" is what you're looking for. Eliminate choice (A), "invariably rigid," which means the opposite of "rippled," and choice (B), "highly polished," which makes no sense in the sentence. For the second blank, choice (E) is correct because a rippled surface would diffuse the sound "at many angles" to create the desired effect. Distortion is the opposite of the desired effect, so choice (D) is incorrect. Choice (F) should also be eliminated because "auditory" means "related to the process of hearing," not "able to be heard" or "audible."

Question

4. When oblique, rather than vertical, rays of the sun pass through the atmosphere, they must (i) _____ pierce a greater part of that atmosphere, thereby lessening the (ii) _____ of their heat.

Blank (i)	Blank (ii)
(A) necessarily	(D) relativity
(B) largely	(E) delivery
(C) comparatively	(F) intensity

Answer Explanation

The correct answers are (A) and (F). Although this passage is structured as a cause-and-effect item, notice that there is also a contrast here. The contrast is between oblique and vertical rays.

Therefore, the clause with the first blank means, by inference, "oblique rays must _____ pierce a greater part of that atmosphere than vertical rays do." Choice (A), "necessarily," is correct for the first blank because it best shows this contrast. Choice (B), "largely," is incorrect because it doesn't make sense, and choice (C) is incorrect because "comparatively" creates ineffective repetition or redundancy; the comparing word "greater" already appears in the sentence. For Blank (ii), choice (D), "relativity," doesn't make sense, so eliminate it. It's a good distracter, though, because it sounds "sciency." Choice (E), "delivery," is incorrect because lessening the delivery of something doesn't make sense. Choice (F), "intensity," is the correct choice because intensity is a quality and so can be increased or decreased.

Question

5. The investigative panel was nothing short of outraged by the bus driver's negligence and lack of remorse. It determined that the driver had failed to follow the established (i) _____. As a result, she had compromised the safety of the passengers. More fundamentally, however, she had actually and effectively (ii) _____ at least two of her riders' rights.

Blank (i)	Blank (ii)
(A) code of conduct	(D) abrogated
(B) rules of engagement	(E) renounced
(C) terms of use	(F) negated

Answer Explanation

The correct answers are (A) and (F). Choice (A) is correct for Blank (i) because a "code of conduct" is a set of principles and practices outlined for an individual, group, or organization. "Rules of engagement," choice (B), generally outline when and how force should be used, and "terms of use," choice (C), often establish a relationship between a company's product and its user; therefore, choices (B) and (C) are incorrect. For Blank (ii), choice (F) is correct because this blank requires a synonym or near synonym for "denied." Choice (D), "abrogated," can be eliminated because an abrogation is an official or legislative annulment or cancellation. Eliminate choice (E) also because "renounced" makes no sense in this context.

Question

6. The playwright created atmosphere in part through the (i) _____ afternoon on which he set the scene. The cloying humidity seemed at once to (ii) _____ the characters' physical energy and play devil's advocate to their sense of morality.

Blank (i)	Blank (ii)
(A) sultry	(D) sap
(B) unsettled	(E) beguile
(C) bone-chilling	(F) intensify

Answer Explanation

The correct answers are (A) and (D). "Sultry" means "excessively hot or humid," which matches the "cloying humidity" mentioned in Sentence 2; therefore, choice (A) is correct. You can eliminate choices (B) and (C), because neither "unsettled" nor "bone-chilling" suggests excessive humidity. Choice (D) is the correct answer for the second blank, as "sap" means "to exhaust" or "to deplete." This is the only answer that makes sense in the context of lessening physical energy or moral fortitude. Choices (E) and (F), "beguile" and "intensify," make no sense.

Question

7. Is the most spineless method of delivering the news of a breakup by means of a text message? A recent survey based on Facebook data found that 14% of those born after 1984 are likely to choose this most expedient of methods. Of course, expedience alone may not explain this choice, but the study offers no other explanation for why respondents act in such a (i) _____ manner. Readers of the study are left to infer why the perpetrators of such spineless behavior (ii) _____ the more dignified, if not relatively (iii) _____, face-to-face meeting.

Blank (i)	Blank (ii)	Blank (iii)
(A) muted	(D) disavow	(G) decorous
(B) unreliable	(E) eschew	(H) imposing
(C) craven	(F) denounce	(I) outdated

Answer Explanation

The correct answers are (C), (E), and (G). For Blank (i), choice (C) is correct because "craven" can mean "cowardly," and the author clearly implies a negative judgment about the behavior that the word describes and equates it with spinelessness. Neither choices (A) nor (B), "muted" and "unreliable," make sense in the context. Although "unreliable" has a negative connotation, it's not strong enough to match the intensity of "spineless."

Choice (E) is correct for Blank (ii) because the meaning conveyed by "eschew" is "to shun" or "avoid deliberately." Choice (D), "disavow," makes no sense because, according to the passage, those who break up by text message don't disclaim knowledge or refuse to acknowledge another person. Similarly, choice (F), "denounce," must be eliminated because those who break up by text message aren't speaking out against anything.

Choice (G) is the correct choice for the third blank because "decorous" behavior is marked by propriety and dignity, which creates the correct contrast to the implied impropriety and indignity of breakup via text message. Choice (H) is incorrect because it's redundant. "Imposing" can mean "dignified," so the sentence would read "the more dignified, if not relatively dignified. . . ." While some test-takers might leap to choice (I), "outdated," it's incorrect because the passage in no way implies that the face-to-face meeting is outdated. After all, given the facts in the passage, it is possible that up to 86% of the survey respondents born after 1984 still use this method.

Question

8. Is understanding your stature in relation to the universe ultimately a psychic (i) _____ of your sense of self? On the one hand, gauging your own experience of space and time in relation to the space and time of galaxies can make you feel (ii) _____ small. On the other hand, sensing you are one with this great universe, or even knowing that its cosmic rays pass through you, may in some ways (iii) _____ that sense of smallness.

Blank (i)	Blank (ii)	Blank (iii)
(A) raveling	(D) antithetically	(G) mitigate
(B) diminution	(E) debilitatingly	(H) expropriate
(C) misappropriation	(F) infinitesimally	(I) enervate

Answer Explanation

The correct answers are (B), (F), and (G). For the first blank, choice (B) is correct because the context implies some kind of a reduction or diminishment. Choice (A) can be eliminated because "raveling" suggests an undoing rather than a decrease in size, as is clearly conveyed by Sentence 2. Choice (C), "misappropriation," makes no sense and can be eliminated. For the second blank, choice (F) is correct because "infinitesimally" conveys the sense of extreme smallness. Eliminate choice (D), "antithetically," meaning "in direct opposition," because it makes no sense, and choice (E), "debilitatingly," suggests weakening rather than diminishment and can be eliminated. Choice (G) is the correct choice for Blank (iii) because, as the signal phrase "on the other hand" suggests, this blank calls for a word that suggests a decrease or lessening of the sense of smallness. Eliminate both choices (H) and (I), "expropriate" meaning "to deprive someone of something" and "enervate" meaning "to weaken or destroy strength," because neither suggest a decrease or reduction as "mitigate" does.

Question

9. The peasants portrayed in Pieter Brueghel the Elder's renowned paintings performed physical labor from sunup to sundown and lived grim, short lives. In *The Wedding Dance,* Pieter Brueghel depicts a nearly frenzied release from that daily round of (i) _____ and (ii) _____ in which peasants dance and (iii) _____ to the music of the bagpipes.

Blank (i)	Blank (ii)	Blank (iii)
(A) employment	(D) inanity	(G) unwind
(B) privation	(E) woe	(H) carouse
(C) mediocrity	(F) striving	(I) sing

Answer Explanation

The correct answers are (B), (E), and (H). To restate the grim daily round of physical labor from sunup to sundown, choice (B) for Blank (i), "privation," and choice (E) for Blank (ii), "woe," are the best choices. For Blank (i), the words "employment" and "mediocrity," choices (A) and (C), are not only inaccurate, but they're also not negative enough. For Blank (ii), choices (D) and (F), "inanity" and "striving," are similarly insufficiently negative as well as inaccurate. For Blank (iii), choice (H), "carouse," is correct because the passage says the peasants are depicted as in "a nearly frenzied release." Neither choice (G), "unwind," nor choice (I), "sing," expresses the meaning conveyed by choice (H), "carouse": "to engage in noisy, drunken, boisterous, or even riotous merrymaking."

Question

10. In part by personifying them, and in larger part through a selection of detail, children's books do nothing less than (i) _____ cars and trucks. The trucks are big, mighty, fearless, and friendly behemoths that happily get the job done. Cars are speedy, bright, often open conveyances that delight their drivers and passengers on similarly open roads without traffic, congestion, or exhaust fumes. Such storybook portrayals begin the process of (ii) _____ that preserves and protects the (iii) _____ of the automobile in American culture.

Blank (i)	Blank (ii)	Blank (iii)
(A) extol	(D) indoctrination	(G) desultory consequences
(B) infantilize	(E) validation	(H) eternal aggrandizement
(C) venerate	(F) vindication	(I) unquestioned dominance

Answer Explanation

The correct answers are (A), (D), and (I). Choice (A), "extol," is the correct answer for Blank (i) because the author's perspective is that children's books glorify and celebrate cars and trucks. Choice (B) is incorrect because cars and trucks cannot be infantilized, or reduced to the status of an infant. Choice (C) is also incorrect because "venerate" means "to adore," and although this is close in meaning to "extol," it's not the same.

Choice (D) is the correct choice for Blank (ii) because the author suggests that the typical portrayal in children's books results in a kind of one-sided belief that cars and trucks are great. Choice (E) and choice (F), while close in meaning, are not so accurate: both a validation and a vindication (defense against criticism) fall short of an indoctrination as a way of extolling and furthering the dominance of the automobile.

For Blank (iii), choice (I), "unquestioned dominance," is the correct answer because indoctrination generally results in an unquestioning faith or loyalty in or toward something. Choice (G) should be eliminated because "desultory," which means "jumping from idea to idea," makes no sense. While choice (H) is close to the correct meaning because aggrandizement is an increase in power or the act of making something seem greater than it actually is, it's incorrect when coupled with the word "eternal." Usage can also help you eliminate this answer: there is no need to preserve and protect something eternal.

SUMMING IT UP

- Text completion questions assess your ability to interpret and evaluate what you read and supply words or phrases whose meaning is consistent with the ideas presented.

- Text completion questions have from one to three blanks to be filled in.

- Test items that have one blank offer a list of five options. Test items with two or three blanks offer lists of three options for each blank.

- Some test items will revolve around words that are close in meaning or ask for an unusual meaning of a familiar word. Some items may involve less familiar words.

- Passages for the text completion test items tend to have lighter concept loads than those for reading comprehension questions on the GRE®.

- The following strategies for answering text completion questions involve both common sense and knowledge gained in English composition classes:

  o Try answering the questions before you read the answer choice(s).

  o Focus on only one blank at a time.

  o If there is more than one blank, complete the blanks in the order that makes sense to you.

  o Check your answer(s) in place.

  o Use structural clues: restatement, cause and effect, contrast, comparison, main idea, and details.

  o Consider tone and style.

  o Consider grammar and usage.

  o Avoid selecting a word or phrase that you don't fully understand or that is unfamiliar.

- General test-taking strategies that are also helpful include:

  o Anticipate and use the clock.

  o Skip and return to questions.

  o Eliminate answer choices you know are incorrect.

  o Use educated guessing.

Strategies for Sentence Equivalence Questions

OVERVIEW

- Basic information about sentence equivalence questions
- Strategies for sentence equivalence questions
- Practice questions
- Answer key and explanations
- Summing it up

Sentence equivalence questions ask you to determine how a sentence should be completed—in two ways. You will need to pick two words that are close in meaning. This chapter describes the purpose of the sentence equivalence test items and offers strategies to help you do well on these questions.

BASIC INFORMATION ABOUT SENTENCE EQUIVALENCE QUESTIONS

Like text completion items, sentence equivalence questions on the GRE® test your ability both to interpret what you read and to supply words whose meaning is consistent with the ideas presented in the test item. Unlike text completion items, however, sentence equivalence items place more emphasis on the meaning of the completed sentence.

Also, like text completion items, sentence equivalence items test your vocabulary. Therefore, knowing "big" words—such as *dichotomous* and *prescient*—can help you do well, but that's not the only way to score points. Learning and using a few key strategies can help you as well.

Question Format

Each sentence equivalence question is a single sentence with one blank and six answer choices. This is the simplest of the verbal formats and is the same each and every time. From the list of six options, you must choose two answers for each question. You have to choose two answers that have similar (equivalent) meaning so that they both complete the sentence with a similar (equivalent) meaning.

There is only one type of direction line for the text completion items. It will be worded something like this:

> **FOR QUESTIONS 1–2, CHOOSE THE <u>TWO</u> ANSWERS THAT BEST FIT THE MEANING OF THE SENTENCE AS A WHOLE AND RESULT IN TWO COMPLETED SENTENCES THAT ARE ALIKE IN MEANING.**

You can expect perhaps one quarter or fewer—maybe 5 or 6—of the items on the Verbal Reasoning section to be sentence equivalence items. These items are interspersed with the other items on each of the two scored verbal sections of the test.

Each sentence equivalence item appears on a separate screen. All passages are short enough to display on a single screen, so you won't need to scroll or change screens. In fact, these short items require the least from you of any of the verbal items and should be done the most quickly.

Selecting Answers

When you have decided on an answer to a question, click on your choice. The oval preceding your selection will completely darken. Remember for sentence equivalence test items to click on two choices. Once you are satisfied with your two answers, hit the "Next" icon.

To earn credit for a sentence equivalence test item, you must choose both correct answers. Choosing only one correct answer of the pair will not gain you any credit.

Consider using the "Mark" option more readily on the sentence equivalence items than you might use it for reading comprehension items. Because sentence equivalence items are shorter and less time-consuming, they're easier to revisit than reading comprehension items. When you mark a sentence equivalence item, you are making a commitment to revisit only approximately 4 percent of the test. This is not a huge task to put off until later and, therefore, a reasonable strategy to use with challenging items.

If you're running out of time, go through the section looking for any unanswered sentence equivalence questions. You can answer them quickly and earn credit.

STRATEGIES FOR SENTENCE EQUIVALENCE QUESTIONS

You will be using many of the same strategies for sentence equivalence items that you may use for other Verbal Reasoning questions on the test. Strategies for sentence equivalence test items can be grouped into two categories: those that are general commonsense ideas and those that you learned in English composition class. The first group includes the following three strategies:

1 Read the item stem first.

2 Come up with your own answer.

3 Check your answers in place.

More specific language strategies include the following four strategies:

1 Use signal words and structural clues.

2 Avoid leaping at the first pair of synonyms.

③ Examine connotations.

④ Consider grammar and usage.

Remember to apply the following four test-taking strategies as well:

① Anticipate and use the clock.

② Skip and return to questions.

③ Eliminate answer choices that you know are not correct.

④ Use educated guessing.

Notice how these review strategies are integrated into the approaches for answering each of the sample items in this chapter.

Read the Item Stem First

Read through the entire sentence before you do anything else. Get a clear sense of what it's about first. The answers are deliberately structured with multiple pairs of synonyms and with close meanings that might appear correct at first glance, so you want to be sure that you understand the meaning of the incomplete sentence.

Come Up with Your Own Answer

Coming up with your own answer before you read the answer choices can be one of the most efficient methods you can use with sentence equivalence items. Try this now with Question 1 below.

> **FOR QUESTION 1, CHOOSE THE <u>TWO</u> ANSWERS THAT BEST FIT THE MEANING OF THE SENTENCE AS A WHOLE AND RESULT IN TWO COMPLETED SENTENCES THAT ARE ALIKE IN MEANING.**

1. Jade could not keep her negativity or aggression to herself; it seemed that everywhere she went, some kind of _____ ensued.
   - (A) kerfuffle
   - (B) insurgency
   - (C) insurrection
   - (D) rebellion
   - (E) demonstration
   - (F) disturbance

Working through the answer process might take this shape:

- Read the sentence first and try to figure out your own answer. Using this strategy, you come up with either the word "problems" or the word "difficulty."

- Step 2 is to look for a pair of words in the list that mean the same as, or close to the same as, problems or difficulty.

- "Kerfuffle" means "disturbance" or "minor outburst or tumult." It is a state of commotion rather than complete uproar like choices (B), (C), and (D). A kerfuffle is not so intense or serious as an insurgency, insurrection, or rebellion.

- In the context of the completed sentence, "disturbance" means the same thing. Therefore, the correct answers are choice (A), "kerfuffle," and choice (F), "disturbance." For the record, "demonstration" connotes a protest, usually large in nature, so choice (E) is incorrect also. **The correct answers are (A) and (F).**

Check Your Answers in Place

You aren't finished when you select your two answer choices. Remember that the answers must create equivalence, so the last step in the process of completing this type of test item is an evaluation of meaning. To do this, read the item quickly twice, first with the first answer you have chosen in the blank, and the second time with the second answer in place. Ask yourself: Do the two sentences mean the same? Weigh the meaning of the completed sentences against each other before you click on the answer choices.

Use Signal Words and Structural Clues

Many sentence equivalence items will include transitions—signal words and phrases—such as *consequently, because, on the other hand, although, moreover, however,* and *in fact.* These words signal a relationship between ideas in the sentence. Pay close attention to them. They can help you decide whether the answer should show cause and effect, contrast, comparison, or restatement. Familiar signal words for different types of structures are included in the following boxes:

Signals for Restatement

Among the words and phrases that can signal restatement relationships are the following:

for example	*in other words*	*that is*
for instance	*in short*	*this means*
in fact	*namely*	*thus*

Cause-and-Effect Signals

Cause-and-effect relationships may or may not include signal words. Among the words and phrases that can signal cause-and-effect relationships are the following:

as a result	*in order to*	*so that*
because	*reason why*	*therefore*
consequently	*since*	*thus*
for	*so*	*why*

NOTE

Restatement is a presentation of an idea in words other than those used the first time the idea is presented; an amplification or clarification of an idea; or the presentation of an example of the idea.

Contrast Signals

Like other structures, contrasts of information may or may not include signal words. Among the words and phrases that can be used to signal contrasts are the following:

although	*however*	*on the contrary*
as opposed to	*in contrast*	*on the other hand*
but	*in spite of*	*otherwise*
by contrast	*instead*	*still*
conversely	*nevertheless*	*unlike*
despite	*nonetheless*	*yet*

Comparison Signals

Among the words and phrases that can signal a comparison are the following:

also	*by the same token*	*moreover in comparison*
and	*in the same way*	*same*
another	*like*	*similarly*
as	*likewise*	*too*

Not all test items for sentence equivalence will have signal words and phrases. You will need to recognize clues to organizational structures such as restatement and cause and effect without the help of transitional words and phrases.

To practice identifying and using structural clues with sentence equivalence items, read Question 1 again and then read through the analysis that follows based on the sentence's restatement structure.

FOR QUESTION 1, CHOOSE THE <u>TWO</u> ANSWERS THAT BEST FIT THE MEANING OF THE SENTENCE AS A WHOLE AND RESULT IN TWO COMPLETED SENTENCES THAT ARE ALIKE IN MEANING.

---

1. Jade could not keep her negativity or aggression to herself; it seemed that everywhere she went, some kind of _____ ensued.
   - (A) kerfuffle
   - (B) insurgency
   - (C) insurrection
   - (D) rebellion
   - (E) demonstration
   - (F) disturbance

Reading this sentence, you may decide that it has a restatement structure. The second part of the sentence (the part following the semicolon) amplifies the information in the first part of the sentence (the part preceding the semicolon). No signal word or phrase is present. Structural analysis helps you determine that the pair of words you are looking for must name something that results from negativity or aggression. Insurgency, insurrection, and rebellion are all actions that go well beyond negativity or aggression. They don't express the same minor degree of problem, commotion, or upset that is conveyed by the first part of the sentence, so eliminate choices (B), (C), and (D). Choice (E), "demonstration," is usually used in conjunction with a large group, so it is incorrect as well. Negativity and aggression might both lead to a disturbance. The only synonym or near synonym on the list for disturbance is "kerfuffle." Therefore, the correct answers are choice (A), "kerfuffle," and choice (F), "disturbance." **The correct answers are (A) and (F).**

It's also reasonable to think that this sentence is structured as a cause-and-effect relationship. The following is one way you might work through it looking for an effect of Jade's attitude:

- If you begin by restating the item with cause and effect in mind, you might arrive at this paraphrase: "Because Jade could not keep her negativity or aggression in check, she caused some kind of _____ everywhere she went."

- Structural analysis helps you determine that the pair of words you are looking for must name something that results from negativity or aggression.

- The rest of the analysis is the same as above, so the correct answers are choice (A), "kerfuffle," and choice (F), "disturbance."

Avoid Leaping at the First Pair of Synonyms

You might think it's a good idea just to find the pair of synonyms among the answer choices, wrap up an item at lightning speed, and move on to the next item. You would be wrong. First, many answer sets contain more than one set of synonyms. Second, as the test-maker warns, even if a word is a synonym for the correct choice, it doesn't necessarily lead to the same meaning in the completed sentence. Finally, two words may be synonyms, but they may have different connotations.

Take a look at Question 1 again.

> **FOR QUESTION 1, CHOOSE THE <u>TWO</u> ANSWERS THAT BEST FIT THE MEANING OF THE SENTENCE AS A WHOLE AND RESULT IN TWO COMPLETED SENTENCES THAT ARE ALIKE IN MEANING.**

1. Jade could not keep her negativity or aggression to herself; it seemed that everywhere she went, some kind of _____ ensued.

   (A) kerfuffle
   (B) insurgency
   (C) insurrection
   (D) rebellion
   (E) demonstration
   (F) disturbance

Master the GRE® 23rd Edition

The first pair of synonyms in the answer choices for Question 1 is "insurgency" and "rebellion," choices (B) and (C). The meaning of these words, however, suggests an outcome that would arise from problems that are far greater than negativity. Note also that choices (B), (C), and (D) are similar. If you chose two answers just by looking for synonym pairs in the list of answer choices, you would have a dilemma on your hands. Which two should you choose?

Examine Connotations

In choosing answers, think about the connotations that the words carry. As you read Question 2, for example, consider just exactly what kind of walking is meant.

FOR QUESTION 2, CHOOSE THE <u>TWO</u> ANSWERS THAT BEST FIT THE MEANING OF THE SENTENCE AS A WHOLE AND RESULT IN TWO COMPLETED SENTENCES THAT ARE ALIKE IN MEANING.

---

2. Kierkegaard said that he had "walked himself into his best thoughts"; in fact, research links exercise with heightened states of _____ experience.
   (A) examining
   (B) pensive
   (C) thoughtful
   (D) meditative
   (E) generative
   (F) contemplative

The walking in this sentence led to thinking, so it was likely solitary and prolonged walking. That information may help you in considering the connotations of the answer choices. Even though "pensive" and "meditative" are synonyms, they don't quite result in equivalence in the sentence. "Pensive," choice (B), has to be eliminated because it suggests a deep or melancholy thoughtfulness, an inward kind of experience that would not likely yield the "best thoughts" or be generative. Similarly, "contemplative" and "thoughtful" are synonyms. Choice (F), "contemplative," carries connotations of prolonged thought, the kind of thought that might arise over the course of a long walk. However, "thoughtful," choice (C), doesn't have that connotation, so eliminate it. Choice (E), "generative," must be eliminated because there is no similar word that would result in equivalence. Choice (A), "examining," is also incorrect in terms of usage and has no twin. Through elimination, that leaves as the correct answers, choice (D), "meditative," and choice (F), "contemplative." They are synonyms and have similar connotations. **The correct answers are (D) and (F).**

Consider Grammar and Usage

As with the text completion items, the words you select for sentence equivalence must result in correct grammar and standard usage when inserted into the sentence. Look again at Question 2 and the first answer choice.

> **FOR QUESTION 2, CHOOSE THE TWO ANSWERS THAT BEST FIT THE MEANING OF THE SENTENCE AS A WHOLE AND RESULT IN TWO COMPLETED SENTENCES THAT ARE ALIKE IN MEANING.**

2. Kierkegaard said that he had "walked himself into his best thoughts"; in fact, research links exercise with heightened states of _____ experience.

    (A) examining

You can eliminate choice (A) because, even though the form of the word "examining" makes it appear as if it could be an adjective, it results in an ambiguous and nonstandard usage in the sentence "in fact, research links exercise with heightened states of examining experience."

PRACTICE QUESTIONS

> **FOR QUESTIONS 1–10, CHOOSE THE <u>TWO</u> ANSWERS THAT BEST FIT THE MEANING OF THE SENTENCE AS A WHOLE AND RESULT IN TWO COMPLETED SENTENCES THAT ARE ALIKE IN MEANING.**

1. Deep in credit card debt, Dylan changed his view of his grandparents, whom he had once regarded as _____, but now thought of as wise.
   - (A) nitpicking
   - (B) penurious
   - (C) censorious
   - (D) parsimonious
   - (E) disingenuous
   - (F) quibbling

2. Even though the senator's speeches were marked by an admirable _____, he was not always able to translate his insight into legislation.
   - (A) alacrity
   - (B) acuity
   - (C) astuteness
   - (D) perspicacity
   - (E) ingenuity
   - (F) erudition

3. One explanation for the nearly _____ use of the very American "okay" is that it's phonetically familiar; almost every language has sounds that approximate a long *o* followed by a quick *k* sound followed by a long *a*.
   - (A) catholic
   - (B) cosmic
   - (C) global
   - (D) pandemic
   - (E) planetary
   - (F) universal

4. The appetite of the venture capitalist for a quick and lucrative killing could only be described as _____.
   - (A) avaricious
   - (B) grasping
   - (C) voracious
   - (D) unslaked
   - (E) indomitable
   - (F) rapacious

5. While Milly conducted herself with a sort of unflappable grace even in challenging circumstances, her husband Ned could often be both _____ and petty.

(A) peevish

(B) inimical

(C) irritable

(D) despicable

(E) contemptible

(F) pusillanimous

6. The woman could scarcely have been more disparaging about her ex-husband's participation in family life and responsibilities; she accused him of both physical laziness and _____.

(A) lethargy

(B) apathy

(C) petulance

(D) decrepitude

(E) turpitude

(F) languor

7. If modern art had a personality, it might be said to be forward or fresh; it might even be said to be sassy or _____.

(A) impudent

(B) extemporaneous

(C) insolent

(D) impromptu

(E) malevolent

(F) malapropos

8. As the play progressed, Molière could see that his tragedy was falling flat, so he moved quickly to transform the developing _____ into a farce.

(A) travail

(B) flop

(C) drudgery

(D) composition

(E) fiasco

(F) creation

9. Modern monopolies or near monopolies such as Microsoft and Amazon should be embraced rather than criticized—as with earlier monopolies such as Western Union and AT&T, their universal, convenient, and _____ innovations would scarcely have been possible had there been competition.

(A) gargantuan

(B) far-reaching

(C) promethean

(D) game-changing

(E) Lilliputian

(F) sundry

10. Members of the audience practically writhed in their seats as they endured the speaker's _____.

    (A) jeremiad

    (B) oratory

    (C) exhortation

    (D) harangue

    (E) declamation

    (F) tirade

ANSWER KEY AND EXPLANATIONS

1. B, D	6. A, F
2. C, D	7. A, C
3. C, F	8. B, E
4. C, F	9. B, D
5. A, C	10. D, F

Question

1. Deep in credit card debt, Dylan changed his view of his grandparents, whom he had once regarded as _____, but now thought of as wise.
   - (A) nitpicking
   - (B) penurious
   - (C) censorious
   - (D) parsimonious
   - (E) disingenuous
   - (F) quibbling

Answer Explanation

The correct answers are (B) and (D). This item is structured as a contrast; it contains the clue "but." However, the answer is not the opposite of "wise," but the opposite of the behavior that lands a person in credit card debt. "Penurious" and "parsimonious," choices (B) and (D), meaning "extremely or excessively unwilling to spend money," fit this sentence and result in the same meaning in the two completed sentences. Choices (A) and (C), "nitpicking" and "censorious," which both mean "overly critical," don't make sense. Choices (E) and (F) are also incorrect: "disingenuous" means "fake or deceptive" and "quibbling" means "arguing over little or petty things."

Question

2. Even though the senator's speeches were marked by an admirable _____, he was not always able to translate his insight into legislation.
   - (A) alacrity
   - (B) acuteness
   - (C) astuteness
   - (D) perspicacity
   - (E) ingenuity
   - (F) erudition

Answer Explanation

The correct answers are (C) and (D). With this question, you should be looking for a comparison or similarity to "insight." Don't be fooled by the word "not." "Astuteness" and "perspicacity," choices (C) and (D), can both mean shrewdness, but they both can also mean "intellectual sharpness or keenness," depending on the context, so they are correct in this sentence. Choice (A) should be eliminated because "alacrity" means "eagerness, liveliness, or quickness" and doesn't make sense. Choice (B) is incorrect because "acuteness" refers to sensitivity, not insight. Choice (E), "ingenuity," often means "cleverness," which isn't the same as insight. Choice (F) can also be eliminated because "erudition" is scholarly or deep learning, which isn't the same as insight. It also has no twin in the list.

Question

3. One explanation for the nearly _____ use of the very American "okay" is that it's phonetically familiar; almost every language has sounds that approximate a long *o* followed by a quick *k* sound followed by a long *a*.

    (A) catholic
    (B) cosmic
    (C) global
    (D) pandemic
    (E) planetary
    (F) universal

Answer Explanation

The correct answers are (C) and (F). Whether you view this item as having a restatement or contrast structure, your analysis should hinge on the phrase "every language," because that's what makes "the very American okay" universal and global. Notice how similar all the choices are here; each could be used in a certain context to mean "universal." So try the process of elimination. Choice (A), "catholic," isn't correct. It may suggest a certain universality, but cannot be used in every context because it most often refers to a "catholicity of tastes" or to the Roman Catholic religion. You can eliminate choices (B) and (E), "cosmic" and "planetary," because these usages are generally reserved for references to the universe in the sense of the solar system or cosmos. Similarly, while choice (D), "pandemic," can mean "universal," it is mainly used only in the sense of something unwanted that is widespread, such as the outbreak of deadly disease. That leaves choices (C) and (F), "global" and "universal."

Question

4. The appetite of the venture capitalist for a quick and lucrative killing could only be described as _____.

    (A) avaricious
    (B) grasping
    (C) voracious
    (D) unslaked
    (E) indomitable
    (F) rapacious

Answer Explanation

The correct answers are (C) and (F). This is a question that hinges on word usage. "Voracious" and "rapacious" both mean "having an insatiable appetite for something," so they both match the word "appetite." Choices (A) and (B) are incorrect because even though "avaricious" and "grasping" mean "greedy," an appetite cannot be correctly described as avaricious or grasping. Choice (D) is incorrect because a thirst, not an appetite, is slaked (or left unslaked), and choice (E) is incorrect because "indomitable" is not applied to an appetite; furthermore, it doesn't fit the meaning of the sentence.

Question

5. While Milly conducted herself with a sort of unflappable grace even in challenging circumstances, her husband Ned could often be both _____ and petty.

   (A) peevish

   (B) inimical

   (C) irritable

   (D) despicable

   (E) contemptible

   (F) pusillanimous

Answer Explanation

The correct answers are (A) and (C). In this contrast item, Ned's peevish and irritable as well as petty behavior forms a loose opposite to Milly's "unflappable grace." Choice (B), "inimical," which suggests unfriendliness, provides insufficient contrast to Milly's imperturbable grace. Choices (D) and (E), "despicable" and "contemptible," which constitute a second pair of synonyms meaning "mean" or "vile," convey behavior that is too extreme to be an appropriate contrast in the sentence. "Pusillanimous," choice (F), is incorrect because cowardliness is not the opposite, or even a loose opposite, of grace.

Question

6. The woman could scarcely have been more disparaging about her ex-husband's participation in family life and responsibilities; she accused him of both physical laziness and _____.

   (A) lethargy

   (B) apathy

   (C) petulance

   (D) decrepitude

   (E) turpitude

   (F) languor

Answer Explanation

The correct answers are (A) and (F). Both "lethargy" and "languor" denote an extreme lack of energy or state of physical weakness or listlessness, so they match "physical laziness." You can eliminate choice (B), "apathy," which means "lack of interest"; choice (C), "petulance," which means "irritability"; choice (D), "decrepitude," which means "a state of deterioration due to old age"; and choice (E), "turpitude," which means "baseness or depravity."

Question

7. If modern art had a personality, it might be said to be forward or fresh; it might even be said to be sassy or _____.
   - (A) impudent
   - (B) extemporaneous
   - (C) insolent
   - (D) impromptu
   - (E) malevolent
   - (F) malapropos

Answer Explanation

The correct answers are (A) and (C). In this sentence, the second independent clause amplifies the first independent clause. Therefore, you can expect both words to be intensifications of the adjectives "forward" and "fresh," used in this sense to mean "showing a lack of restraint" or "improperly bold." Both "impudent" and "insolent," choices (A) and (C), ratchet up, or amplify, that sense of impropriety to downright rudeness. The second pair of synonyms presented by choices (B) and (D), "extemporaneous" and "impromptu," are incorrect because they mean "offhand" or "without preparation," neither of which accurately describes a personality or fits the context. Choice (E), "malevolent," meaning "displaying ill will," and choice (F), "malapropos," meaning "out of place" or "inappropriate," should also be ruled out.

Question

8. As the play progressed, Molière could see that his tragedy was falling flat, so he moved quickly to transform the developing _____ into a farce.
   - (A) travail
   - (B) flop
   - (C) drudgery
   - (D) composition
   - (E) fiasco
   - (F) creation

Answer Explanation

The correct answers are (B) and (E). Comparison or similarity clues in this item tip you off to the fact that what was "developing" was also falling flat, or failing to have the desired effect on the audience. Therefore, what was developing was a flop, choice (B), or a fiasco, choice (E), words that are not synonyms (a fiasco is more disastrous than a flop), but which both result in nearly the same meaning for the sentence as a whole. Choices (A) and (C), "travail" and "drudgery," which are near synonyms, make no sense in terms of usage and don't provide the proper comparison. The third set of near synonyms or possible synonyms, choices (D) and (F), "composition" and "creation," must also be eliminated because they don't convey the sense of something falling flat, or failing.

Question

9. Modern monopolies or near monopolies such as Microsoft and Amazon should be embraced rather than criticized—as with earlier monopolies such as Western Union and AT&T, their universal, convenient, and _____ innovations would scarcely have been possible had there been competition.

   (A) gargantuan
   (B) far-reaching
   (C) promethean
   (D) game-changing
   (E) Lilliputian
   (F) sundry

Answer Explanation

The correct answers are (B) and (D). Both cause and comparison ideas are at play in this item, whose answers are not synonyms; yet, the answers create equivalence in the completed sentence. Choices (A), (C), and (E) are all incorrect because the emphasis in the statement is not on the size of the innovations—"gargantuan," "promethean," "Lilliputian"—which makes no sense, but on their effect, which was both far-reaching and game-changing. Choice (F) is also incorrect because "sundry," meaning "various," doesn't express the same magnitude of greatness in relation to the innovations as the words "far-reaching" and "game-changing" do, choices (B) and (D).

Question

10. Members of the audience practically writhed in their seats as they endured the speaker's _____.
   (A) jeremiad
   (B) oratory
   (C) exhortation
   (D) harangue
   (E) declamation
   (F) tirade

Answer Explanation

The correct answers are (D) and (F). The cause in this item is the speaker's "harangue" or "tirade," and the effect is the audience's great discomfort. Choice (A) isn't so likely an answer because a "jeremiad" is often mournful; it may go on and on and may look gloomily at the future, but it is much less likely to make its listeners so physically or visibly uncomfortable as a tirade or harangue would. Mere "oratory," choice (B), or even "declamation," choice (E), which can be both pompous and excessively loud, would also not result in such great discomfort; in fact, they could as likely be uplifting, so choices (B) and (E) are also incorrect. Similarly, "exhortation" alone, no matter how forceful, is less likely to elicit the physical response of writhing with discomfort than a harangue or tirade is, so choice (C) is also incorrect.

SUMMING IT UP

- Sentence equivalence test items assess your ability to interpret what you read and to supply words whose meaning is consistent with the ideas presented in the test item.

- The emphasis is on the meaning of the complete sentence for sentence equivalence test items.

- Each sentence equivalence test item is a single sentence with one blank and six answer choices. From the six answer choices, you must select two answers for the question that will result in two sentences with a similar—equivalent—meaning.

- Both answer choices must be correct in order to earn credit for the question.

- Commonsense strategies for answering sentence equivalence questions are the following:

    o   Read the item stem first.

    o   Come up with your own answer.

    o   Check your answers in place.

- More specific language strategies are the following:

    o   Use signal words and structural clues.

    o   Avoid leaping at the first pair of synonyms.

    o   Examine connotations.

    o   Consider grammar and usage.

- General test-taking strategies that are also helpful include:

    o   Anticipate and use the clock.

    o   Skip and return to questions.

    o   Eliminate answer choices you know are incorrect.

    o   Use educated guessing.

PART V

QUANTITATIVE REASONING

Strategies for Multiple-Choice Questions

OVERVIEW

- Basic information about multiple-choice question types
- Math conventions
- Strategies for selecting one answer choice
- Strategies for selecting one or more answer choices
- Strategies for multiple-choice questions in data interpretation sets
- Practice questions
- Answer key and explanations
- Summing it up

The Quantitative Reasoning section of the GRE® evaluates test-takers' understanding of basic math concepts in arithmetic, algebra, geometry, and data analysis and their ability to apply these concepts to analyze and interpret real-world scenarios. This may sound daunting if you haven't had math for several years, but working through the strategies and the practice questions in this and the next two chapters should reassure you that the math on the GRE® is not that difficult.

In this chapter, you will find an introduction to the two types of multiple-choice questions on the GRE® and to certain strategies that will help you answer these questions correctly and quickly.

BASIC INFORMATION ABOUT MULTIPLE-CHOICE QUESTION TYPES

On the GRE® revised General Test, there are two formats for multiple-choice questions:

- Multiple-choice questions—select one answer choice
- Multiple-choice questions—select one or more answer choices

You may find multiple-choice questions as stand-alone items, or they may be part of a group of questions that refer to the same tables, graphs, or other form of data presentation. In the latter case, they are known as data interpretation questions.

Most multiple-choice questions on the GRE® are of the familiar multiple-choice questions—select one answer choice type. These questions are accompanied by five answer choices, each with an oval beside it. These questions have only one correct answer, as you would surmise from the name.

Multiple-choice questions—select one or more answer choices are accompanied by a varying number of answer choices. Each answer choice has a square beside it, which is a reminder that the question is a multiple-choice question that may have more than one correct answer, as the name suggests.

The following notes apply to "one or more answer choice" questions:

- The number of answer choices is not always the same—though typically you will see at least three choices.

- The number of correct answer choices is also not always the same. It may be that only one answer choice is correct, or two, or three, or all of them.

- Usually, the question asks you to select all correct answer choices. Sometimes, though, a question will instruct you to select a certain number of answer choices—in which case, of course, you should select exactly that number of choices.

- In order to answer a question correctly, you must select all the correct answer choices, and only those.

  o You do not get any credit if you select some, but not all of the correct answer choices.

  o You do not get any credit if you select the correct number of answer choices, but not all the choices you have selected are correct. (That is, if three out of five answer choices are correct, and you select two of the correct ones as well as the incorrect one, you don't get any credit.)

Although in this book we refer to answer choices as (A), (B), (C), and so on, the answer choices are not labeled on the actual GRE®. The oval or square beside each answer choice is blank.

MATH CONVENTIONS

The test-maker provides the following information that applies to all questions in the Quantitative Reasoning section of the GRE®:

- All numbers used are real numbers.

- All figures are assumed to lie in a plane unless otherwise indicated.

- Geometric figures, such as lines, circles, triangles, and quadrilaterals, *are not necessarily* drawn to scale. That is, you should *not* assume that quantities such as lengths and angle measures are as they appear in a figure. You should assume, however, that lines shown as straight are actually straight, points on a line are in the order shown, and more generally, all geometric objects are in the relative positions shown. For questions with geometric figures, you should base your answers on geometric reasoning, not on estimating or comparing quantities by sight or by measurement.

- Coordinate systems, such as *xy*-planes and number lines, *are* drawn to scale. Therefore, you can read, estimate, or compare quantities in such figures by sight or by measurement.

- Graphical data presentations, such as bar graphs, circle graphs, and line graphs, *are* drawn to scale. Therefore, you can read, estimate, or compare data values by sight or by measurement.

The On-Screen Calculator

The GRE® revised General Test provides you with an on-screen calculator. You may use the calculator at any point during the Quantitative Reasoning sections, but you may find it particularly useful with the numeric entry questions. Before we talk about how you may use the calculator, let's discuss when you should and should not use it.

In general, you *should use* the on-screen calculator if you need to perform difficult calculations. However, most calculations on the GRE® are not that complicated, so most of the time you will not need the calculator. In particular, you *should not use* it in the following cases:

- when the required calculations are simple to perform mentally or on scratch paper.

- when you need to give the answer as a fraction rather than a decimal (either in numeric entry questions or in multiple-choice ones).

- when estimating will suffice (for instance, in certain quantitative comparison or data interpretation questions).

The following are a few notes on using the calculator. Learn them before test day to relieve some of the stress you may experience on that day.

- Unlike some other calculators, this one follows the order of operations. So, for instance, if you type in sequence "1", "+", "3", "×", "5", "=" the GRE® calculator will yield "16" as the answer because it will perform the multiplication of 3 by 5 first and then add 1 to the result. If, however, you need to compute $(1+3) \times 5$ instead, then you must type the following sequence: "(", "1", "+", "3", ")", "×", "5", "=". Alternatively, you may type "1", "+", "3", "=", "×", "5", "=". However, it is easy to make mistakes if you try to perform a lengthy combination of operations as a single sequence on the calculator. It may be better to perform each individual computation on its own, use your scratch paper to note intermediate results, and then perform new computations on these results. In the above example, calculate $1+3$ first, note the result ("4") on your scratch paper, clear the calculator display by pressing the "C" button, and finally calculate 4×5.

> • When you click the memory sum button ("M+"), the number in the calculator display is placed in the calculator's memory bank, and the letter "M" appears to the left of the display. When you later click "M+" again, the number in the calculator's display is added to the number in the memory bank. When you click the memory recall button ("MR"), the number in the calculator's memory bank at that time appears in the display area. The memory clear button ("MC") clears the memory.
>
> • In numeric entry questions, you may click the calculator's "Transfer Display" button in order to transfer the number displayed on the calculator to the answer box. You cannot use the "Transfer Display" feature if the answer is a fraction. Note that if you click "Transfer Display" on a question that asks you to round your answer to a certain degree of accuracy, you may need to edit the number in the answer box so that it is appropriately rounded up or down.

STRATEGIES FOR SELECTING ONE ANSWER CHOICE

TIP

Don't forget these four test-taking strategies listed in Chapter 1: (1) anticipate and use the clock, (2) skip and return to questions, (3) eliminate answer choices that you know are incorrect, and (4) use educated guessing.

Reviewing the math principles that are covered in the GRE® is an important part of preparing to take the test. However, using test-specific strategies can help you move through the test more quickly and with greater confidence. The following four strategies work especially well for multiple-choice questions that require only one answer:

1 Pick and plug numbers.

2 Work backwards from the answer choices.

3 Turn verbose or abstract language into concise and concrete wording.

4 Estimate.

Pick and Plug Numbers

Picking and plugging numbers can be a useful strategy IF

- a question and its answer choices contain variables, but you're not certain how to solve the question directly.

- you are dealing with a question about percents.

- you are not certain about a particular number property—such as whether the product of two odd numbers is odd or even.

Apply the strategy by

- picking simple numbers so that calculations are reasonable.

- plugging these numbers into the answer choices.

- eliminating any choices that don't produce the desired result.

FOR THIS QUESTION, CHOOSE <u>ONE</u> ANSWER CHOICE.

Example 1

Susan can run $2x$ miles in y hours. In 75 minutes, how many miles will Susan run?

(A) $\dfrac{5y}{8x}$

(B) $\dfrac{2x}{75y}$

(C) $\dfrac{150x}{y}$

(D) $\dfrac{5xy}{2}$

(E) $\dfrac{5x}{2y}$

You can solve this question directly: if Susan runs $2x$ miles in y hours, then she runs $\dfrac{2x}{y}$ miles per hour. Thus, in 75 minutes, that is, in $\dfrac{5}{4}$ hours, she will run $\dfrac{2x}{y} \times \dfrac{5}{4} = \dfrac{5x}{2y}$ miles. If you don't feel comfortable solving directly, you have an alternative.

Let $x = 4$ and $y = 1$.

Susan can run 8 miles in 1 hour (60 minutes), so in 75 minutes Susan will run 10 miles: one-and-a-quarter as many miles as she can run in 1 hour. Now, plug the values $x = 4$ and $y = 1$ into the answer choices and see which of them yield(s) 10.

(A) $\dfrac{5 \times 1}{8 \times 4} = \dfrac{5}{32}$ Eliminate.

(B) $\dfrac{2 \times 4}{75 \times 1} = \dfrac{8}{75}$ Eliminate.

(C) $\dfrac{150 \times 4}{1} = 600$ Eliminate.

(D) $\dfrac{5 \times 4 \times 1}{2} = 10$ This option is a possibility. Hold on to it and choose option (E).

(E) $\dfrac{5 \times 4}{2 \times 1} = 10$ This option is also possible.

Since two answer choices produce the desired result, you need to check these choices again.

Pick different numbers—say, $x = 6$ and $y = 2$. Susan runs 12 miles every 2 hours, or 6 miles per hour. Therefore, in 75 minutes, Susan will run 7.5 miles.

(D) $\dfrac{5 \times 6 \times 2}{2} = 30$ Eliminate.

(E) $\dfrac{5 \times 6}{2 \times 2} = 7.5$ Correct.

The correct answer is (E).

Picking numbers can be a useful back-up tool if you're not confident that you can solve a question directly. However, when it comes to percentage increase/decrease problems, it is not only a good back-up, but an excellent way to find the right answer even more quickly than if you were solving directly. Consider the following example:

FOR THIS QUESTION, CHOOSE <u>ONE</u> ANSWER CHOICE.

Example 2

Mary sold her biology textbook to her friend John for a 40% discount compared with the price she paid to buy it. After completing his class, John sold the book on the Internet for 20% more than the price he paid Mary for the book. The price for which John sold the book is what percent of the price that Mary paid?

(A) 40

(B) 60

(C) 72

(D) 80

(E) 120

Pick the number $100 to represent the amount that Mary paid to buy the book. She then sold the book to John for a 40% discount of $100, or $100 − 40 = $60. John sold it for 20% more than the $60 he paid, so he sold it for $72.

What percent of $100 (the price Mary paid to buy the book) is $72 (the price John got when he sold it)?

$$\frac{72}{100} = \frac{x}{100} \Rightarrow x = 72$$

The correct answer is (C).

Work Backwards from the Answer Choices

In some cases, if there are numbers in the answer choices, and if, in order to solve directly, you may have to work through some complicated equations, you may choose to work backwards from the answer choices.

FOR THIS QUESTION, CHOOSE <u>ONE</u> ANSWER CHOICE.

Example 3

In city X, the first $30,000 of someone's annual income are taxed at the rate of 5%, while any income over $30,000 is taxed at the rate of 10%. If in a certain year Betty paid $2100 in city X taxes, what was her income that year?

(A) $32,000

(B) $33,000

(C) $34,000

(D) $35,000

(E) $36,000

In this example, you can turn the information in the question stem into an equation, and then solve that equation directly. Or, you can go straight to the answer choices, and, since the choices are listed from least to greatest, begin with choice (C), the middle one. If Betty's income had been $34,000, then she would have paid $\frac{5}{100}\$30,000 + \frac{10}{100}\$4000 = \$1500 + \$400 = \$1900$.

This amount is too low, so Betty must have earned more than $34,000. You can eliminate choices (A) and (B) in addition to choice (C), because they are less than choice (C). Next, check choice (D).

If Betty's income had been $35,000, then she would have paid $\frac{5}{100}\$30,000 + \frac{10}{100}\$5000 = \$2000$.

This amount, also, is too low, so you can eliminate choice (D). That leaves choice (E). **The correct answer is (E).**

Turn Verbose or Abstract Language into Concise and Concrete Wording

Sometimes it seems as though test-makers are trying to confuse you with wordy questions. Don't worry! You can always turn excessive verbiage into diagrams or mathematical expressions that are easier to understand and work with.

NOTE

Turning verbose or abstract language into concise and concrete wording is an important strategy to help you answer any math question.

FOR THIS QUESTION, CHOOSE <u>ONE</u> ANSWER CHOICE.

Example 4

Diana prepared a certain amount of a chemical solution and stored it in 10 right-cylindrical containers, each with a diameter of 8 inches and a height of 8 inches. Alternatively, she could have stored the same amount of the solution in 40 right-cylindrical containers, all of them with the same height as one another and with a radius of 2 inches. What is the height of these containers?

(A) 4
(B) 8
(C) 10
(D) 16
(E) 40

These are the two most important strategies for you to follow: Always read questions carefully, and reword confusing questions into concise and concrete language. You need to understand what a question is asking in order to answer it correctly.

Begin by writing down the given information, removing the clutter of any extraneous words. The dimensions of the first set of containers are $r = 4$ and $h = 8$. The dimensions of the second set of containers are $r' = 2$ and h'.

The volume of the solution equals 10 times the volume of each of the initial containers: $V_{total} = 10\pi r^2 h$. The volume also equals 40 times the volume of each of the alternate containers: $V_{total} = 40\pi r'^2 h'$. Equate these two expressions: $10\pi r^2 h = 40\pi r'^2 h'$.

Next substitute the values of r, h and r': $10\pi 4^2 \times 8 = 40\pi 2^2 h'$. Eliminate π from both sides of the equation and calculate the two squares: $10 \times 16 \times 8 = 40 \times 4h'$. Divide both sides by 160: $h' = 8$. **The correct answer is (B).**

Estimate

Estimating is a very valuable strategy for data interpretation questions as well as for quantitative comparisons. However, even in regular multiple-choice questions with a single correct answer, estimating may help, especially if you're running out of time.

FOR THIS QUESTION, CHOOSE <u>ONE</u> ANSWER CHOICE.

Example 5

Sixty percent of the 25 professors on a certain university's engineering department are male. If two male professors retire and two female professors are hired, what percent of the department's professors will be male? (Assume no other changes in the engineering faculty.)

(A) 48
(B) 52
(C) 56.5
(D) 60
(E) 68

It's best to solve this question directly. However, you should also note that, after the changes, the engineering department will have fewer male professors than it had before, but the same total number of professors. The percentage of its faculty that's male should drop from the original 60%. Thus, you can eliminate answer choices (D) and (E) because they are greater than 60%.

For the record, to solve this directly, first find the number of male professors before the changes:
$$\frac{60}{100} = \frac{x}{25} \Rightarrow x = \frac{60 \times 25}{100} \Rightarrow x = 15$$
After the changes, the department still has 25 professors, but this time 13 of them are male. Set up a proportion in order to turn 13 into a percentage: $\frac{13}{25} = \frac{x}{100} \Rightarrow x = 52$. **The correct answer is (B).**

STRATEGIES FOR SELECTING ONE OR MORE ANSWER CHOICES

Remember that the number of answer choices is not always the same for this multiple-choice format. You might have three answers to choose from—the basic number of choices—or as many as five or more. The number of correct answers that you can be asked to choose varies as well. If you don't choose all the correct answers, you will not get credit for the correct answers that you do choose.

Of the five strategies listed for multiple-choice questions that require only one answer, the strategy of picking numbers and working backwards from the answer choices is not so useful when you aren't told how many correct answer choices there are. Estimating can be very useful, especially in data interpretation questions, as you'll see later in this chapter. As for turning verbose language into something concise and concrete: It's always a helpful strategy in mathematics! However, the following strategies and notes are specific to multiple-choice questions with one or more correct answer choices:

- Calculate the least and greatest possible values.
- Make sure you're answering the correct question.
- Think through data sufficiency questions.

NOTE

If you decide to skip a question, make sure you click the "Mark" button so you can find it quickly on the "Review" screen later. Remember: There's no wrong-answer penalty, so don't leave any questions unanswered!

Calculate the Least and Greatest Possible Values

On some questions, it is helpful to calculate what the least and greatest possible values for the answer choices are, and then eliminate any choices that do not fit within that range.

FOR THIS QUESTION, INDICATE <u>ALL</u> THE ANSWERS THAT APPLY.

Example 6

A kiosk sells only the following snacks: cookies for $1.50 each, ice-cream bars for $2.50 each, and chips for $1.00 each. Clara bought four snacks at the kiosk. Which of the following could be the total amount that she paid?

Indicate <u>all</u> such amounts.

(A) $3.50
(B) $4.00
(C) $4.50
(D) $6.50
(E) $8.50
(F) $10.50

You should start by calculating the least and greatest possible values, in order to limit your options. If Clara bought four bags of chips, the cheapest item, then she spent $4.00. Thus, all answer choices that are an amount less than $4.00 are incorrect. If she bought four ice-cream bars, the most expensive item, she spent $10.00. Thus, all answer choices that feature an amount greater than $10.00 are incorrect.

You're left with the middle four answer choices, and indeed, all four of them are possible: $4.00 represents a purchase of four bags of chips; $4.50 represents a purchase of three bags of chips and one cookie; $6.50 represents a purchase of two cookies, one bag of chips, and one ice-cream bar; and $8.50 represents a purchase of three ice-cream bars and one bag of chips. **The correct answers are (B), (C), (D), and (E).**

Note in which of the following questions you MUST work backwards from the answer choices. Do not start by calculating all the possible amounts that Clara could have spent. The answer choices do not have to list all of these amounts, only some of them. For instance, Clara could have spent $7.50 if she had bought two ice-cream bars, one cookie, and one bag of chips. However, $7.50 is not one of the answer choices—so you don't want to waste your time making calculations that are unnecessary.

Make Sure You're Answering the Correct Question

This is always sound advice, of course, but it is of particular importance in answering questions with one or more correct answer choices. Most of these questions ask you to select <u>all</u> the correct answer choices. However, you may also come upon a question that asks you to select a specific number of answer choices. You have to read the questions carefully to be sure of what to do.

FOR THIS QUESTION, INDICATE <u>ALL</u> THE ANSWERS THAT APPLY.

NOTE
While you're making sure you're answering the correct question, also make sure to double-check your work.

Example 7

If p is a prime number, then the product of which <u>two</u> of the following numbers must be the square of an integer?

(A) $\dfrac{1}{p}$

(B) $\sqrt{p}$

(C) p^2

(D) p^3

Since you know that the product of only two of the answer choices is a perfect square, you may not need to check all the possible combinations. When you find the two answer choices that work, you can stop and move on to the next question. In this case, if you noticed early on that the product of $\dfrac{1}{p}$ and p^3 is p^2, a perfect square, you won't have to consider any other products. **The correct answers are (A) and (D).**

Think Through Data Sufficiency Questions

Example 8 is a data sufficiency question: a question that asks you to determine whether each answer choice is sufficient on its own to provide a definitive answer to the question. Sometimes, a data sufficiency question is of the yes/no variety (as is the case with this example). For such questions, an answer choice is sufficient

- if it provides a positive answer

OR

- if it provides a negative answer.

FOR THIS QUESTION, INDICATE <u>ALL</u> THE ANSWERS THAT APPLY.

Example 8

Angela is five years older than Melissa, who is two years younger than Heather. Which of the following statements <u>individually</u> provide(s) sufficient additional information to determine whether Heather is older than 23 years old?

Indicate <u>all</u> such statements.

(A) Angela is 27 year old.

(B) Melissa is younger than 21 years old.

(C) Heather is twice as old as Melissa was ten years ago.

Begin by reviewing the information in the question. If Angela is five years older than Melissa, and Melissa is two years younger than Heather, then Angela is three years older than Heather. It helps to write out these relationships as equations:

$$A = M + 5$$
$$H = M + 2$$
$$A = H + 3$$

Answer choice (A): If Angela is 27 years old, then Heather is 24 years old—in other words, she is older than 23 years old. Answer choice (A) is sufficient.

Answer choice (B): This tells you that Melissa is younger than 21 years old. Since $H = M + 2$, Heather is younger than 23 years old. Answer choice (B) is sufficient, as well.

Answer choice (C): Write out this statement as an equation:

$$H = 2(M - 10) \Rightarrow$$
$$H = 2M - 10$$

You now have two equations that relate H and M (the other one is $H = M + 2$). These two equations are distinct—that is, one is not a multiple of the other—so it is possible to solve these equations and find a unique solution for H and M. Therefore, the third answer choice is also sufficient. **The correct answers are (A), (B), and (C).**

STRATEGIES FOR MULTIPLE-CHOICE QUESTIONS IN DATA INTERPRETATION SETS

In each Quantitative Reasoning section, you should expect to see one set of questions that are grouped together and refer to the same data presentation—such as a graph or table. The questions will be either multiple-choice (both types) or numeric entry. The following strategies are helpful in solving data interpretation sets:

- Scan the data quickly.
- Make sure you're answering the correct question.
- Estimate.

The last two are useful for all types of questions in the Quantitative Reasoning section.

Quickly Scan the Data

When you first encounter a data interpretation set, scan the data in order to get a general idea of the information presented. Just as you do when reading a Reading Comprehension passage, don't waste time on the details. There will be time for the details when you look at the actual questions. Rather, note the following:

- What kind of data—such as sales figures, population trends, etc.—are presented?
- Do the graphs/tables give actual values or percentages?
- If more than one table or graph is presented, how are they related? For instance, does one table give actual values, whereas the other gives percentages?
- What units are used (for example, millions vs. billions of dollars)?
- Are there any notes above or below the data that give additional information?

The following example is a straightforward bar graph. It compares enrollment by male and female students majoring in science, engineering, and mathematics. The information is presented in real numbers.

EXAMPLES 9–10 ARE BASED ON THE FOLLOWING DATA.

NUMBER OF STUDENTS AT UNIVERSITY K MAJORING IN SCIENCE, ENGINEERING, AND MATHEMATICS

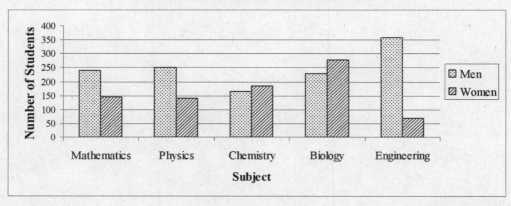

TIP

The GRE does not penalize wrong answers, so educated guessing could raise your score.

Make Sure You're Answering the Correct Question

Don't make careless mistakes when considering the questions. If a question asks about June sales figures, don't look in the July column of the table by mistake. If you're asked to find a percentage, don't look for or calculate actual values.

FOR THIS QUESTION, CHOOSE <u>ONE</u> ANSWER CHOICE.

Example 9

    If a total of 12,049 students are enrolled in University K, approximately what percentage of these students is majoring in engineering?

    (A) 0.5

    (B) 3

    (C) 3.5

    (D) 17

    (E) 20

This question is not particularly difficult, as long as you don't make any careless mistakes. Make sure you look at the bars representing the engineering majors, not any of the other four sets of bars. Also, make sure you consider both male and female engineering majors, not just male or just female students.

The number of male engineering majors is approximately 355. The number of female engineering majors is approximately 70. Thus, the total number of engineering majors is approximately 425. Solve a proportion in order to find what percent of the total student population 425 is: $\dfrac{425}{12,049} = \dfrac{x}{100} \Rightarrow x \approx 3.53$. **The correct answer is (C).**

Estimate

For some questions, you only need to find approximate values. Don't waste time performing exact calculations if you don't have to. In particular, remember that graphs are drawn to scale, so you can use them to estimate values. Consider the following:

FOR THIS QUESTION, INDICATE <u>ALL</u> THE ANSWERS THAT APPLY.

Example 10

Which of the following statements about science majors at University K must be true?

Indicate <u>all</u> such statements.

(A) The absolute value of the difference of male to female physics majors was greater than the absolute value of the difference of male to female mathematics majors.

(B) More students, male and female, majored in biology than in engineering.

(C) The number of students who majored in mathematics is closer to the number of students who majored in physics than it is to the number of students who majored in biology.

Answer choice (A): From the graph you can tell that there were slightly more male physics majors than male mathematics majors, but slightly fewer female physics majors than female mathematics majors. You don't need to worry about their exact numbers. The visual evidence is sufficient to tell you that when you subtract the number of female physics majors from the number of male physics majors, you get a larger number than you do when you subtract the number of female mathematics majors from the number of male mathematics majors. Answer choice (A) is true.

Answer choice (B): The number of students who majored in biology was approximately 225 (male) + 275 (female) = 500. In example 9, you approximated the number of engineering students as 425. Again, the visual evidence is sufficient, even if your estimates are not perfect. Answer choice (B) is true.

Answer choice (C): Once again, you can estimate from the graph that the number of students who majored in mathematics is slightly less than 400, which is similar to the number of students who majored in physics. You've already estimated the number of students who majored in biology as 500. Thus, answer choice (C) is true, as well.

The correct answers are (A), (B), and (C).

PRACTICE QUESTIONS

> **FOR QUESTIONS 1–15, UNLESS THE DIRECTIONS STATE OTHERWISE, CHOOSE ONE ANSWER CHOICE.**

1. If the sum of two consecutive integers is 87 and the difference of their squares is 87, what is the larger integer?

   (A) 44
   (B) 46
   (C) 54
   (D) 69
   (E) 87

2. Each year between 2001 and 2011, an Italian winemaker in Montalcino used between 75% and 80% of his grapes to produce his Brunello di Montalcino wine, and the rest to produce his Rosso di Montalcino wine. If in 2011 he produced 2,500 cases of Brunello, which of the following could have been the total number of cases of wine he produced that year?

   Indicate <u>all</u> such numbers of cases.

   (A) 3,128
   (B) 3,153
   (C) 3,241
   (D) 3,308
   (E) 3,334

3. If a is a positive even integer less than 10, b is a negative even integer greater than -10, and c is a positive odd integer between 2 and 10, which of the following cannot be an integer?

   (A) $\dfrac{bc}{a}$

   (B) $\dfrac{ac}{b}$

   (C) $\dfrac{ab}{c}$

   (D) $\dfrac{ab}{c^2}$

   (E) $\dfrac{2ab}{c^3}$

4. A drawer contains 20 pairs of socks: some white, some black, and the rest brown. Picking at random, one has a 0.4 probability of removing a white pair. If 1 white pair, 1 brown pair, and 3 black pairs are added, and no pairs are removed, what is the probability that one will pick at random either a black or a brown pair?

(A) 0.36

(B) 0.4

(C) 0.6

(D) 0.64

(E) 0.8

5. The average (arithmetic mean) weight of a football team's offensive linemen is 320 pounds, while the average weight of the team's defensive linemen is 300 pounds. If the team has at least 50% more defensive linemen than offensive linemen, which of the following could be the average weight of all of the team's offensive and defensive linemen, combined?

Indicate all such weights.

(A) 304

(B) 305

(C) 306

(D) 307

(E) 308

(F) 309

6. *ABCD* is a quadrilateral, with side *AB* parallel to side *CD*. Which of the following statements individually provide(s) sufficient additional information to determine whether *ABCD* is a rectangle or not?

Indicate all such statements.

(A) The diagonals *AC* and *BD* are of equal length.

(B) The diagonals *AC* and *BD* are not of equal length.

(C) The measure of angle *CDA* is 90°, and both pairs of opposite angles are equal.

7. In a high school orchestra, 40% of the string players are violinists, 20% are violists, 25% are cellists, and 15% are bassists. If 2 violinists, 1 violist, 1 cellist, and 1 bassist are added, what will be the percentage of violinists in the orchestra? (Assume no other changes to the orchestra's string section.)

(A) 30%

(B) 35%

(C) 40%

(D) 45%

(E) It cannot be determined.

8. If a and b are two of the solutions of the equation $x^3 - x^2 - 6x = 0$, with $a \neq 0$ and $a \neq b$, then which of the following could be the graph of $\dfrac{x}{a} > b$?

Indicate <u>all</u> such graphs.

(A)

    0

(B)

    0

(C)

    0

(D)

    0

9. Each of the managers of a 20-person technical support team received $3000 as a year-end bonus, whereas each of the nonmanagers received $1200 as a year-end bonus. If the total amount that the 20 employees received was $31,200, how many of the team's members are managers?

(A) 1

(B) 2

(C) 3

(D) 4

(E) 5

QUESTIONS 10–12 ARE BASED ON THE FOLLOWING DATA.

INCOME DATA FOR TOWN X's FOUR NEIGHBORHOODS: A, B, C, and D.

Annual Income in 2011	Percent of Neighborhood Populations			
	A	B	C	D
$0–$24,999	14%	4%	17%	13%
$25,000–$49,999	30%	19%	34%	31%
$50,000–$74,999	26%	29%	27%	32%
$75,000–$99,999	19%	28%	15%	18%
$100,000–$249,999	9%	14%	6%	5%
> $250,000	2%	6%	1%	1%

10. In the neighborhood with the smallest percentage of six-figure earners in 2011, what percent of the population earned less than $50,000 that year?

    (A) 23

    (B) 31

    (C) 34

    (D) 44

    (E) 51

11. If the percentage of people who resided in neighborhood B in 2011 and earned between $0 and $24,999 was 20% less than the percentage of people who resided in neighborhood B in 2001 and earned between $0 and $24,999, and if the latter percentage was 20% less than the percentage of people who resided in neighborhood B in 1991 and earned between $0 and $24,999, what percent of the people who resided in neighborhood B in 1991 earned between $0 and $24,999 that year?

    (A) 4

    (B) 5

    (C) 6

    (D) 6.25

    (E) 6.67

12. Which of the following statements must be true?

    Indicate <u>all</u> such statements.

    (A) In 2011, the neighborhood with the highest average income was neighborhood B.

    (B) 12% of the people living in town X in 2011 earned less than $25,000 that year.

    (C) If in 2011 more than twice as many people lived in neighborhood A as in neighborhood B, then the number of people who lived in neighborhood A and earned $100,000 or more was greater than the number of people who lived in neighborhood B and earned $100,000 or more.

13. Which of the following graphs intersect(s) the graph of $y = x$?

    Indicate <u>all</u> such graphs.

    (A) The graph of $y = 2x + 2$

    (B) The graph of $y = |2x + 2|$

    (C) The graph of $y = -x + 2$

14. Streetlamps are to be placed along one side of a 1-kilometer-long road. Each streetlamp has a diameter of 50 centimeters. If the distance between streetlamps is 29.5 meters, and the first streetlamp is placed at one end of the road, how many streetlamps will be needed? (1 meter equals 100 centimeters. 1 kilometer equals 1,000 meters.)

    (A) 30

    (B) 31

    (C) 32

    (D) 33

    (E) 34

15. If x and y are integers such that $|x - y| = 1$, which of the following statements individually provide(s) sufficient additional information to determine what x is?

Indicate <u>all</u> such statements.

(A) x and y are the solutions of the equation $a^2 + 7a + 12 = 0$

(B) $y = 3$

(C) x and y are both prime numbers, and y is odd

ANSWER KEY AND EXPLANATIONS

1. A	9. D
2. A, B, C, D	10. D
3. E	11. D
4. D	12. C
5. A, B, C, D, E	13. A, C
6. B, C	14. E
7. C	15. C
8. A, B, D	

Question

1. If the sum of two consecutive integers is 87 and the difference of their squares is 87, what is the larger integer?

   (A) 44
   (B) 46
   (C) 54
   (D) 69
   (E) 87

Answer Explanation

The correct answer is (A). Turn the abstract into an equation and solve:

$$x + (x + 1) = 87$$
$$2x + 1 = 87$$
$$2x = 86$$
$$x = 43$$
$$x + 1 = 44$$

Question

2. Each year between 2001 and 2011, an Italian winemaker in Montalcino used between 75% and 80% of his grapes to produce his Brunello di Montalcino wine, and the rest to produce his Rosso di Montalcino wine. If in 2011 he produced 2,500 cases of Brunello, which of the following could have been the total number of cases of wine he produced that year?

   Indicate all such numbers of cases.

   (A) 3,128
   (B) 3,153
   (C) 3,241
   (D) 3,308
   (E) 3,334

Answer Explanation

The correct answers are (A), (B), (C), and (D). For this question, the strategy "calculate the least and greatest possible values" is the most helpful. Calculate the least and greatest values and then select all the choices that fall between them. The 2,500 cases of Brunello that the winemaker produced in 2011 are between $\frac{3}{4}$ and $\frac{4}{5}$ of his total production.

If P is his total production that year, then $\frac{3}{4}P < 2,500 < \frac{4}{5}P$.

The first inequality yields $P < 3,333.\overline{3}$.

The second yields $P > 3,125$.

Any answer choice that falls between these two numbers is correct.

Question

3. If a is a positive even integer less than 10, b is a negative even integer greater than -10, and c is a positive odd integer between 2 and 10, which of the following cannot be an integer?

   (A) $\dfrac{bc}{a}$

   (B) $\dfrac{ac}{b}$

   (C) $\dfrac{ab}{c}$

   (D) $\dfrac{ab}{c^2}$

   (E) $\dfrac{2ab}{c^3}$

Answer Explanation

The correct answer is (E). "Which of the following cannot be" means that you can eliminate any answer choice for which you can find at least one example that *can* be true. In other words, it does not matter if, let's say, for choice (A), the fraction $\dfrac{bc}{a}$ is sometimes not an integer. As long as it can be an integer at least once, then (A) is not the correct answer choice.

First, turn the abstract language into more concrete wording.

- If a is a positive even integer less than 10, then a may be 2, 4, 6, or 8.

- If b is a negative even integer greater than -10, then b may be $-2, -4, -6,$ or -8.

- If c is a positive odd integer between 2 and 10, then c may be 3, 5, 7, or 9.

Next, move on to the answer choices:

   (A) As long as $a = 2$, then $\dfrac{bc}{a}$ will be an integer, no matter what the other two numbers are. Eliminate it.

(B) As long as $b = -2$, then $\dfrac{ac}{b}$ will be an integer, no matter what the other two numbers are. Eliminate it.

(C) If $c = 3$ and either $a = 6$ or $b = -6$ (or both), then $\dfrac{ab}{c}$ will be an integer. Eliminate it.

(D) If $c = 3$, $a = 6$ and $b = -6$, then $\dfrac{ab}{c^2}$ will be an integer. Eliminate it.

(E) 5 and 7 are not part of the prime factorization of any of the possible values that a and b may take, so if $c = 5$ or $c = 7$, $\dfrac{2ab}{c^3}$ cannot be an integer. If $c = 3$, raising it to the third power will produce three 3s in the denominator. At best, the numerator will have two 3s as factors (if $a = 6$ and $b = -6$, so $\dfrac{2ab}{c^3}$ cannot be an integer if $c = 3$. Finally, if $c = 9$, the denominator will have even more 3s. Thus, $\dfrac{2ab}{c^3}$ cannot be an integer.

Question

4. A drawer contains 20 pairs of socks: some white, some black, and the rest brown. Picking at random, one has a 0.4 probability of removing a white pair. If 1 white pair, 1 brown pair, and 3 black pairs are added, and no pairs are removed, what is the probability that one will pick at random either a black or a brown pair?

   (A) 0.36
   (B) 0.4
   (C) 0.6
   (D) 0.64
   (E) 0.8

Answer Explanation

The correct answer is (D). If one has a 0.4 probability of picking a white pair out of the 20 pairs in the drawer, then there must be $0.4 \times 20 = 8$ pairs in the drawer. When the new pairs are added, the result is 9 white pairs out of 25 total pairs. Since you're asked for the probability of picking either a black or a brown pair, do not worry about the specific numbers for black and brown. You only need to treat black and brown pairs as one group: the nonwhite pairs of socks.

If there are 9 white pairs, then there are 16 nonwhite ones. Thus, the probability of picking a nonwhite pair out of the 25 is $\dfrac{16}{25} = 0.64$.

Question

5. The average (arithmetic mean) weight of a football team's offensive linemen is 320 pounds, while the average weight of the team's defensive linemen is 300 pounds. If the team has at least 50% more defensive linemen than offensive linemen, which of the following could be the average weight of all of the team's offensive and defensive linemen, combined?

Indicate <u>all</u> such weights.

(A) 304

(B) 305

(C) 306

(D) 307

(E) 308

(F) 309

Answer Explanation

The correct answers are (A), (B), (C), (D), and (E). Calculate the greatest possible value and then select all the choices that fall between it and 300. If the team has exactly 50% more defensive linemen than offensive linemen, then for every 3 defensive linemen there are 2 offensive linemen. In this scenario, the average of the weights is the following weighted average:

$$\frac{2 \times 320 + 3 \times 300}{5} = 308$$

If the team has more than 50% defensive linemen, then that average will be even lower.

Question

ALERT!

This is a data sufficiency question—and remember that an answer statement is sufficient if it tells you that *ABCD* certainly IS a rectangle, or certainly IS NOT a rectangle.

6. *ABCD* is a quadrilateral, with side *AB* parallel to side *CD*. Which of the following statements individually provide(s) sufficient additional information to determine whether *ABCD* is a rectangle or not?

Indicate <u>all</u> such statements.

(A) The diagonals *AC* and *BD* are of equal length.

(B) The diagonals *AC* and *BD* are not of equal length.

(C) The measure of angle *CDA* is 90°, and both pairs of opposite angles are equal.

Answer Explanation

The correct answers are (B) and (C). The first statement mentions a property that rectangles have: diagonals of equal length. However, rectangles are not the only quadrilaterals with this property. Isosceles trapezoids also have diagonals of equal length:

The first statement is insufficient to show whether the quadrilateral is a rectangle, so eliminate it.

The second statement, however, is sufficient to show that *ABCD* is not a rectangle: If *ABCD*'s diagonals are not equal to each other, *ABCD* cannot be a rectangle.

The final statement gives you the most information yet. Because the opposite angles are equal in pairs, *ABCD* is a parallelogram. Further, since one of the angles is a right angle, all four of them are right. Thus, *ABCD* is a rectangle, and this statement is sufficient also.

Question

7. In a high school orchestra, 40% of the string players are violinists, 20% are violists, 25% are cellists, and 15% are bassists. If 2 violinists, 1 violist, 1 cellist, and 1 bassist are added, what will be the percentage of violinists in the orchestra? (Assume no other changes to the orchestra's string section.)

    (A) 30%
    (B) 35%
    (C) 40%
    (D) 45%
    (E) It cannot be determined.

Answer Explanation

The correct answer is (C). This is a tricky question. Answer choice (E) seems correct, since you know only the starting percentages of string players but not their exact numbers. On the other hand, choice (E) may be a trap. If you don't feel confident, you can skip this question and revisit it later. However, working from what you know, you can make the information more concrete, and arrive at the correct answer. Five new string players are added, and two of them are violinists. In other words, 40% of the new players are violinists. Because 40% of the original string players were violinists, and 40% of the ones added are violinists, the percentage of violinists remains intact.

Question

8. If *a* and *b* are two of the solutions of the equation $x^3 - x^2 - 6x = 0$, with $a \neq 0$ and $a \neq b$, then which of the following could be the graph of $\frac{x}{a} > b$?

    Indicate <u>all</u> such graphs.

    (A)

    (B)

(C)

0

(D)

0

Answer Explanation

The correct answers are (A), (B), and (D). Begin by scanning the answer choices in order to see what type of answers to look for. Next, work out the math in the question, and see which answer choices fit your results.

First, manipulate the equation $x^3 - x^2 - 6x = 0$. Factor out an x from each term:

$x(x^2 - x - 6) = 0$

Then factor the quadratic expression, using reverse FOIL (First, Outside, Inside, Last). Remember that $x^2 - x - 6 = (x + a)(x + b)$, where $ab = -6$ and $a + b = -1$, the coefficient of x. The numbers 2 and -3 for a and b are the only ones that qualify, so the expression becomes $x(x + 2)(x - 3) = 0$.

Thus, the possible solutions of the equation are $x = 0$, $x = -2$, and $x = 3$. All three of these solutions are possible values for b and the possible values for a are -2 or 3.

Next, move on to the inequality $\dfrac{x}{a} > b$. There are four different possibilities:

1. If $a = -2$ and $b = 0$, then $x < 0$. (Remember that multiplying both sides of an inequality by a negative number reverses the direction of the inequality.) The graph of this inequality appears in answer choice (A).

2. If $a = -2$ and $b = 3$, then $x < -6$. The graph of this inequality appears in choice (B).

3. If $a = 3$ and $b = 0$, then $x > 0$. The graph of this inequality is not listed.

4. If $a = 3$ and $b = -2$, then $x > -6$. The graph of this inequality appears in choice (D).

Question

9. Each of the managers of a 20-person technical support team received $3000 as a year-end bonus, while each of the nonmanagers received $1200. If the total amount that the 20 employees received was $31,200, how many of the team's members are managers?

(A) 1

(B) 2

(C) 3

(D) 4

(E) 5

TIP

When you are working backwards, start with the middle answer choice. That way, if the answer is wrong, you will know if you need to check the answers that are more or less than the middle answer.

Answer Explanation

The correct answer is (D). Work backwards, starting with choice (C). If there are 3 managers, then together they received $9000. The remaining 17 employees received $20,400. These two amounts add up to $29,400, which is too low. Thus, there are more than 3 managers. Move on to choice (D). If there are 4 managers, then together they received $12,000. The remaining 16 employees received $19,200. These two add up to $31,200.

Master the GRE® 23rd Edition

QUESTIONS 10–12 ARE BASED ON THE FOLLOWING DATA.

INCOME DATA FOR TOWN X's FOUR NEIGHBORHOODS: A, B, C, and D.

Annual Income in 2011	Percent of Neighborhood Populations			
	A	B	C	D
$0–$24,999	14%	4%	17%	13%
$25,000–$49,999	30%	19%	34%	31%
$50,000–$74,999	26%	29%	27%	32%
$75,000–$99,999	19%	28%	15%	18%
$100,000–$249,999	9%	14%	6%	5%
> $250,000	2%	6%	1%	1%

Question

10. In the neighborhood with the smallest percentage of six-figure earners in 2011, what percent of the population earned less than $50,000 that year?

   (A) 23
   (B) 31
   (C) 34
   (D) 44
   (E) 51

Answer Explanation

The correct answer is (D). Make sure you're answering the correct question. "Six-figure earners" means that you have to look at the bottom two rows, not just the bottom row. Also, "less than $50,000" means you should add the top two rows in the appropriate column. So, first, identify the neighborhood with the smallest percentage of six-figure earners: that's neighborhood D, 5 + 1 = 6% of its residents earn $100,000 or more. Next, add the percentages of D residents who earned between $0 and $49,999: 13 + 31 = 44.

Question

11. If the percentage of people who resided in neighborhood B in 2011 and earned between $0 and $24,999 was 20% less than the percentage of people who resided in neighborhood B in 2001 and earned between $0 and $24,999, and if the latter percentage was 20% less than the percentage of people who resided in neighborhood B in 1991 and earned between $0 and $24,999, what percent of the people who resided in neighborhood B in 1991 earned between $0 and $24,999 that year?

   (A) 4
   (B) 5
   (C) 6
   (D) 6.25
   (E) 6.67

✝ ## Answer Explanation

The correct answer is (D). First, translate English into math:

The percentage of B residents who earned between $0 and $24,999 in 2011 is 4.

20% fewer B residents earned between $0 and $24,999 in 2011 than in 2001. Hence, if X is the percentage of those folks who earned between $0 and $24,999 in 2001, then $4 = \dfrac{80}{100}X \Rightarrow X = \dfrac{400}{80}$.

20% fewer B residents earned between $0 and $24,999 in 2001 than in 1991. Hence, if Y is the percentage of those folks who earned between $0 and $24,999 in 1991, then $X = \dfrac{80}{100}Y \Rightarrow \dfrac{400}{80} = \dfrac{80}{100}Y$. Solve for Y to get $Y = 6.25$.

Question

12. Which of the following statements must be true?
    Indicate all such statements.

    (A) In 2011, the neighborhood with the highest average income was neighborhood B.

    (B) 12% of the people living in town X in 2011 earned less than $25,000 that year.

    (C) If in 2011 more than twice as many people lived in neighborhood A as in neighborhood B, then the number of people who lived in neighborhood A and earned $100,000 or more was greater than the number of people who lived in neighborhood B and earned $100,000 or more.

Answer Explanation

The correct answer is (C). Do not conclude hastily that statement 1 (A) is true. It may be, for instance, that all of the B residents earned at the lowest end of their income range (e.g., all the $250,000+ earners actually earned $250,000), while the A residents earned at the highest end of their income range. In this scenario, the residents in neighborhood A had a higher average income than the residents in neighborhood B.

Statement 2 (B) takes the straight average of the percentages of residents in the four neighborhoods who earned between $0 and $24,999. However, if all four neighborhoods did not have the same number of people in 2011, you need a weighted average—and such an average may be different from 12%. Thus, statement 2 (B) is not necessarily true.

Finally, evaluate statement 3 (C). In 2011, 11% of the residents in neighborhood A earned $100,000 or more, and 20% of the B residents did also. If P_A is the total number of A residents in 2011 and P_B is the total number of B residents in 2011, then $P_A > 2P_B$. Thus, 11% of P_A is greater than 20% of P_B and statement 3 (C) is true.

Question

13. Which of the following graphs intersect(s) the graph of $y = x$?

Indicate <u>all</u> such graphs.

(A) The graph of $y = 2x + 2$

(B) The graph of $y = |2x + 2|$

(C) The graph of $y = -x + 2$

Answer Explanation

The correct answers are (A) and (C). There are several ways to solve this question. You may treat it as a question that asks you to solve two equations simultaneously, you may choose to work with slopes and intercepts, you may pick numbers, or you may draw diagrams.

Solving a system of two equations is simple algebra, so it's an easy way to evaluate choices (A) and (C). First, choice (A), $y = 2x + 2$, solves a system of two equations.

If $y = x$ and $y = 2x + 2$ intersect, then there is an (x, y) pair that satisfies them both. Let the two ys be equal to each other, and see if that leads to a possible value of x:

$$2x + 2 = x \Rightarrow x = -2$$

For both equations, when x equals -2, y equals -2, so the two lines intersect.

You can evaluate choice (C) in the same way:

$$-x + 2 = x \Rightarrow x = 1$$

For both equations, when x equals 1, y equals 1, so the two lines intersect.

The absolute value in choice (B) makes the system of equations approach trickier. Instead, draw a diagram in order to make things more concrete:

The graph of $y = x$ is easy to plot. As for the graph of $y = |2x+2|$, four points are sufficient to plot it: when $x = 0$, $y = 2$; when $x = 1$, $y = 4$; when $x = -1$, $y = 0$; and when $x = -2$, $y = 2$. You can see from the diagram that the graphs of these two equations do not intersect.

Question

14. Streetlamps are to be placed along one side of a 1-kilometer-long road. Each streetlamp has a diameter of 50 centimeters. If the distance between streetlamps is 29.5 meters, and the first streetlamp is placed at one end of the road, how many streetlamps will be needed? (1 meter equals 100 centimeters. 1 kilometer equals 1,000 meters.)

(A) 30

(B) 31

(C) 32

(D) 33

(E) 34

Answer Explanation

The correct answer is (E). Rather than trying to work out this question in the abstract, draw a diagram in order to get a clearer picture of what's going on:

So, one streetlamp will be placed at every 30-meter mark, starting with one lamp at the 0-meter mark. Now set up a proportion in order to find the number of streetlamps required for 1,000 meters:

$\frac{1}{30} = \frac{x}{1,000} \Rightarrow x = 33.3$. There will be 33 streetlamps plus the 1 at the zero mark. The total will be

34 streetlamps.

Question

15. If x and y are integers such that $|x - y| = 1$, which of the following statements individually provide(s) sufficient additional information to determine what x is?

Indicate <u>all</u> such statements.

(A) x and y are the solutions of the equation $a^2 + 7a + 12 = 0$

(B) $y = 3$

(C) x and y are both prime numbers, and y is odd

Answer Explanation

The correct answer is (C). This is another data sufficiency question. First, you need to understand the question stem.

If $|x - y| = 1$, then either $x - y = 1$ or $x - y = -1$.

x and y are consecutive integers (since the absolute value of their difference is 1), but otherwise, the range of possibilities for x and y is infinite. There's nothing more you can do with the question stem alone.

Step 2 is to consider the first statement, (A). Factor the quadratic equation:

$a^2 + 7a + 12 = 0 \Rightarrow (a + 4)(a + 3) = 0$. The two solutions are $a = -4$ and $a = -3$. However, you do not know which of the two solutions is x and which is y, so this answer choice is not sufficient for you to determine what the value of x is. (Plug in $x = -4$ and $y = -3$, and then $x = -3$ and $y = -4$ into the absolute value equation in the question stem, and you'll see that both options work.)

The second statement, (B), pins down the value of y. However, that is still not sufficient: The absolute value equation is satisfied if $x = 4$ as well as if $x = 2$.

Moving on to the third statement, (C), because x and y are consecutive integers (as you determined above), and if both are prime, then they have to be the numbers 2 and 3. (All other prime numbers are odd, so the only way to get two consecutive integers that are both prime is if one of the two is the number 2.) Additionally, y is odd, which means that $x = 2$. This statement is sufficient.

SUMMING IT UP

- There are two types of multiple-choice questions on the Quantitative Reasoning section of the GRE®:
  - o   Multiple-choice—select one answer choice
  - o   Multiple-choice—select one or more answer choices
- Multiple-choice questions may be structured separately or they may be part of a data interpretation set, which includes several questions built around presentation of data such as a table or graph.
- Multiple-choice questions that require only one answer have five answer choices to select from. Each answer choice is preceded by an oval.
- Multiple-choice questions that ask for one or more answer choices are accompanied by a varying number of answer choices. These answer choices are preceded by squares, not ovals, as a signal to choose one or more answer choices.
- Strategies that are useful for all math questions are the following:
  - o   Make sure you're answering the correct question.
  - o   Skip and come back to questions—used sparingly.
- Strategies specific to multiple-choice questions—select one answer choice are the following:
  - o   Pick and plug numbers.
  - o   Work backwards from the answer choices.
  - o   Turn verbose or abstract language into concise and concrete wording
  - o   Estimate.
- Strategies specific to multiple-choice questions—select one or more answer choices are the following:
  - o   Calculate the least and greatest possible values.
  - o   Make sure you're answering the correct question.
  - o   Think through data sufficiency questions.
- Strategies for data interpretation sets are the following:
  - o   Scan the data quickly.
  - o   Make sure you're answering the correct question.
  - o   Estimate.

Strategies for Numeric Entry Questions

OVERVIEW

- **Answer format for numeric entry questions**
- **A reminder about using the on-screen calculator**
- **Strategies for numeric entry questions**
- **Practice questions**
- **Answer key and explanations**
- **Summing it up**

This chapter describes the answer format for numeric entry questions and provides the following three useful strategies for solving numeric entry questions:

1 Turn verbose or abstract language into concise and concrete wording.

2 Make sure you're answering the correct question.

3 Round correctly.

Like multiple-choice questions, numeric entry questions may be stand-alone items, or they may be part of a data interpretation set: a group of questions that refer to the same tables, graphs, or other form of data presentation. Strategies for data interpretation, other than estimating, apply to numeric entry questions, as well.

Finally, remember also that you can always skip a question and return to it if you find that you're having trouble figuring out what it's asking or you think it will take too long to answer.

ANSWER FORMAT FOR NUMERIC ENTRY QUESTIONS

Numeric entry questions do not offer any answer choices from which you can choose. Rather, they present you with a question and

- one answer box, if the answer is an integer or decimal.
- two answer boxes, if the answer is a fraction.

You have to use your keyboard to input your answer in the appropriate answer box. If the answer is a fraction, type the numerator in the top box and the denominator in the bottom box.

Entering Answers

Here are a few instructions about entering answers that you should be familiar with before you take the test. Knowing how to enter answers will ease some of the stress you may experience on test day.

- To erase a numeral in the answer box, use the "backspace" key.
- To enter a negative sign, type a hyphen.
- To remove the negative sign, type the hyphen again.
- To enter a decimal point, type a period. Note that you cannot use decimal points in fractions.
- Equivalent forms of the answer, such as 2.5 and 2.50, are all correct.
- You do not need to reduce fractions to lowest terms.

A REMINDER ABOUT USING THE ON-SCREEN CALCULATOR

The on-screen calculator can be especially useful in answering numeric entry questions. One feature that can save you a few seconds—and keep you from making an entry mistake—is the "Transfer Display" function. You may click this button to transfer the number displayed on the calculator to the answer box. However, you cannot use the "Transfer Display" feature if the answer is a fraction.

Note that if you click "Transfer Display" on a question that asks you to round your answer to a certain degree of accuracy, you may need to edit the number in the answer box so that it is appropriately rounded up or down.

STRATEGIES FOR NUMERIC ENTRY QUESTIONS

Because numeric entry questions don't provide any answer choices, you will not be able to use some of the strategies—such as working backwards from the answer choices and eliminating incorrect ones—that are helpful on multiple-choice questions. On the other hand, you will not be tempted by trap answer choices, those that are the result of using incorrect processes or faulty computations. Let's review what you can—and should—do in order to answer numeric entry questions correctly.

Turn Verbose or Abstract Language into Concise and Concrete Wording

Remember to write out equations or draw diagrams when the question does not provide any, in order to get a clearer picture. In this respect, numeric entry questions are no different from multiple-choice questions.

> **FOR THIS QUESTION, ENTER YOUR ANSWER IN THE BOX.**

Example 1

Dominic bought a pair of shoes for $90, two t-shirts for $20 each, and four pairs of socks. If he paid 8% sales tax on the entire purchase, and if the total amount of the tax he paid was $12, what was the cost of each pair of socks?

Instead of trying to think this through in the abstract, write out the information you have as an equation. Let S be the cost of each pair of socks. Then, before tax, Dominic paid $90 + 2 \times \$20 + 4S$. The amount of tax he paid was 8% of $90 + 2 \times \$20 + 4S$, or $\frac{8}{100}(\$90 + 2 \times \$20 + 4S)$. Equate this to $12 and solve for S:

$$\frac{8}{100}(\$90 + 2 \times \$20 + 4S) = \$12 \Rightarrow$$

$$\frac{2}{100}(\$90 + 2 \times \$20 + 4S) = \$3$$

$$\frac{2}{100}\$130 + \frac{2}{100}4S = \$3 \Rightarrow$$

$$\frac{2}{100}4S = \$0.4 \Rightarrow$$

$$S = \$5$$

The correct answer is $5.

Make Sure You're Answering the Correct Question

Your worst enemy on numeric entry questions, especially if you feel you have to race against the clock, is careless mistakes—such as confusing the diameter for the radius or giving an answer in the wrong units (e.g., minutes instead of hours, or feet instead of inches). To avoid such mistakes, always read the question carefully and double-check your work.

> **FOR THIS QUESTION, ENTER YOUR ANSWER IN THE BOX.**

Example 2

What is the median of the first ten positive integers?

This is not a hard question, but one that invites two kinds of careless mistakes. When a question asks for the mean, median, or mode, make sure you don't mistakenly calculate the wrong one. Second, don't answer hastily. In this case, don't answer "5," thinking that the middle number among the first ten positive integers will be 5. After more reasoned thinking, you would realize that because there are ten numbers—that is, an even number of numbers—the median will be the average of the middle two numbers: 5 and 6. **The correct answer is 5.5 (or equivalent).**

ALERT!
One way to be sure that you are answering the right question is to double-check your answer against the question. Did you solve for the correct variable or the proper units?

NOTE
An equivalent form of the correct answer 5.5 such as 5.50 and 5.500 will be considered correct. This is especially useful to remember when answering questions for which the answer is a fraction. You might enter this as 8/10 and someone else might enter it as 4/5. Both will be counted as correct unless you are specifically told to reduce it.

FOR THIS QUESTION, ENTER YOUR ANSWER IN THE BOXES.

Example 3

> If 12 of the 20 members of Springfield's city council are male, what is the ratio of female council members to male council members?
>
> Give your answer as a fraction.

$$\frac{\boxed{}}{\boxed{}}$$

Here you are asked to find a part-to-part ratio: female-to-male council members. Do not provide a part-to-whole ratio (e.g., female-to-total council members), or the wrong part-to-part ratio (male-to-female council members).

If there are 20 council members and 12 are male, the remaining 8 are female. The ratio you're looking for is $\frac{8}{12}$. Since fractions do not need to be reduced to lowest terms, you do not need to reduce $\frac{8}{12}$ to $\frac{2}{3}$. **The correct answer is $\frac{8}{12}$ (or any equivalent fraction).**

Round Correctly

Sometimes, a numeric entry question will ask you to round your answer to a certain degree of accuracy. Once you've performed the necessary calculations, don't lose sight of that instruction. For instance, if you're asked to round your answer to the nearest integer, and your calculations yield 13.6, type "14" in the answer box.

Make sure, however, that you don't round any numbers until the very end. For instance, let's say that in the process of computing the answer, you have to multiply 11.2 by 3. That product is 33.6, which, rounded to the nearest integer, is 34. However, if before performing the final calculation you had rounded 11.2 down to 11, you would have given your answer as "33," which would have been incorrect.

FOR THIS QUESTION, ENTER YOUR ANSWER IN THE BOX.

Example 4

> In 2012, the sales of The Cranston Computer Company, a manufacturer of desktop and laptop computers, increased by 20% compared with 2011. In 2013, Cranston's sales decreased by 20% compared with 2012. Cranston's 2011 sales were what percent of its 2013 sales?
>
> Give your answer to the nearest 0.1.

$$\boxed{}$$

Pick the number 100 to represent the company's sales in 2011.

Then, the 2012 sales were 120 and the 2013 sales were $120 - \dfrac{20}{100}(120) = 96$.

Now you need to find what percent of 96 (the 2013 sales) is 100 (the 2011 sales). Set up and solve a proportion—remembering that you need to round your answer to the nearest tenth of a percent:

$$\dfrac{100}{96} = \dfrac{x}{100} => x = \dfrac{10,000}{96} => x = 104.1\overline{6}$$

The correct answer is 104.2% (or equivalent).

Note that the calculator will give you the answer as 104.16667, and this is the number that will be placed into the answer box if you use the calculator's "Transfer Display" feature. In that case, you must then click onto the answer box and change "104.16667" to "104.2." If you don't, your answer will be marked incorrect.

TIP

Always read questions carefully. This plus turning confusing questions into concise and concrete wording may be the two most important strategies you can use. You need to understand what a question is asking in order to answer it correctly.

PRACTICE QUESTIONS

> **FOR QUESTIONS 1–10, ENTER YOUR ANSWER IN THE BOXES.**

1. The average (arithmetic mean) of the salaries that four siblings earned last year is $50,000. If one of the siblings earned $80,000 and another earned $60,000, what is the average (arithmetic mean) of the salaries that the remaining two siblings earned last year?

$ [_____]

2. The perimeter of a square with a side of 4 inches is equal to the perimeter of a rectangle with a height of 3 inches. What fraction of the rectangle's area is the square's area?

Give your answer as a fraction.

[_____]
[_____]

3. Justin bought 160 shares of company A and 50 shares of company B for a total purchase price of $2450. At the same per-share prices, Susan bought 40 shares of company A and 50 shares of company B, for a total purchase price of $1250. How much did Justin pay in total for his shares of company A?

$ [_____]

4. Line l is perpendicular to line $2x = 3y - 6$. If the point $(0,2)$ lies on line l, what is the x-intercept of line l?

Give your answer as a fraction.

[_____]
[_____]

5. For all numbers a and b, $a \Diamond b = a^2 b$. What is the value of $\left[(-2) \Diamond (-3) \right] \Diamond (-2)$?

[_____]

6. Company A, a widget manufacturer, has eight stores in town X. The average (arithmetic mean) number of widgets these stores sold in March 2014 is 150. Not including the company's flagship store in town X, the average (arithmetic mean) number of widgets the remaining seven stores sold in March 2014 is 130. How many widgets did the flagship store sell in March 2014?

[_____]

QUESTIONS 7–8 ARE BASED ON THE FOLLOWING DATA.

SALES OF NEW CARS IN COUNTRY A, BY CATEGORY, IN 2010

AVERAGE HIGHWAY FUEL CONSUMPTION, BY CATEGORY, FOR NEW CARS SOLD IN 2010

Category	Average Fuel Consumption
Compact Cars	32
Family Sedans	28
Luxury Sedans	24
Sports Cars	24
SUVs	23
Pickup Trucks	21

7. If in 2010 the total number of new cars that were sold across all categories was 1,621,018, how many categories of cars had sales of fewer than 250,000 cars?

8. What was the average fuel consumption on the highway for all cars sold in 2010?

   Give your answer to the nearest 0.1.

9. Working alone at its constant rate, Machine A produces 15 widgets every 90 minutes. Working alone at its constant rate, Machine B produces widgets twice as quickly as does Machine A. If the two machines work together at their respective constant rates, how many hours will it take them to produce 75 widgets?

   _____ hours

10. Two of the eight lawyers who work at a law firm are partners, while the rest are associates. If a team of five lawyers is to be selected randomly from among these eight lawyers, what is the probability that more than 80% of the lawyers on the team will be associates?

    Give your answer to the nearest 0.01.

ANSWER KEY AND EXPLANATIONS

1. $30,000	6. 290
2. $\dfrac{16}{15}$	7. 2
3. $1600	8. 26.3
4. $\dfrac{4}{3}$	9. 2.5
5. −288	10. 0.11

Question

1. The average (arithmetic mean) of the salaries that four siblings earned last year is $50,000. If one of the siblings earned $80,000 and another earned $60,000, what is the average (arithmetic mean) of the salaries that the remaining two siblings earned last year?

$$\$\ \boxed{}$$

Answer Explanation

The correct answer is $30,000. Read the question carefully and double-check your calculations along the way in order to avoid careless mistakes. If the four siblings earned $50,000 on average, then together they earned $50,000 × 4 = $200,000.

Two of the siblings earned $140,000 of that $200,000, so the remaining two siblings together earned $200,000 − $140,000 = $60,000. Thus, the average of the salaries for these two siblings is $60,000 ÷ 2 = $30,000.

Question

2. The perimeter of a square with a side of 4 inches is equal to the perimeter of a rectangle with a height of 3 inches. What fraction of the rectangle's area is the square's area?

Give your answer as a fraction.

$$\boxed{}$$
$$\boxed{}$$

Answer Explanation

The correct answer is $\dfrac{16}{15}$ (or any equivalent fraction). Make sure you're answering the correct question: the rectangle's area should go in the denominator, and the square's area in the numerator.

The perimeter of the square is 4 × 4 = 16 inches.

If the width of the rectangle is y inches, and because its perimeter is also 16 inches (equal to the square's perimeter), then $2y + 2 \times 3 = 16 \Rightarrow y = 5$.

Next, find the areas of the two shapes.

The square's area is $4 \times 4 = 16$ sq. inches.

The rectangle's area is $3 \times 5 = 15$ sq. inches.

Thus, the square's area is $\dfrac{16}{15}$ of the rectangle's area.

Question

3. Justin bought 160 shares of company A and 50 shares of company B for a total purchase price of $2450. At the same per-share prices, Susan bought 40 shares of company A and 50 shares of company B, for a total purchase price of $1250. How much did Justin pay in total for his shares of company A?

$$\$ \boxed{}$$

Answer Explanation

The correct answer is $1600. Turn the question's words into concrete equations. Let A be the per-share price for company A and B be the per-share price for company B. Write out equations for Justin's and Susan's purchases.

Justin's purchase: $160A + 50B = \$2,450$.

Susan's purchase: $40A + 50B = \$1,250$.

Subtract the second equation from the first one and solve for A: $120A = \$1,200 \Rightarrow A = \$10$.

So Justin paid $10 for each share of company A. Since he bought 160 such shares, he paid $1600 for them, in total.

Question

4. Line l is perpendicular to line $2x = 3y - 6$. If the point $(0,2)$ lies on line l, what is the x-intercept of line l?

Give your answer as a fraction.

Answer Explanation

The correct answer is $\dfrac{4}{3}$ (or any equivalent fraction). This question requires several steps of equation manipulation, so solve carefully and double-check your work before you move on. Also make sure you do not answer the wrong question: You're looking for the x-intercept, not the y-intercept or the slope.

Perpendicular lines have slopes that are negative reciprocals of each other, that is, slopes whose product is –1. Rewrite $2x = 3y - 6$ in the slope-intercept form, $y = mx + b$, where m is the line's slope and b its y-intercept:

$$y = \frac{2}{3}x + 2$$

Therefore, the slope of $2x = 3y - 6$ is $\frac{2}{3}$, and so line l has a slope of $-\frac{3}{2}$.

Next, consider point $(0,2)$. Because this point lies on line l, the y-intercept of line l (that is, the y-value of the point at which the line crosses the y-axis) is 2.

Now write line l in slope-intercept form: $y = -\frac{3}{2}x + 2$.

You're looking for the line's x-intercept, that is, the x-value of the point at which the line crosses the x-axis. Set $y = 0$ and solve for x:

$$0 = -\frac{3}{2}x + 2 \Rightarrow x = \frac{4}{3}$$

Question

5. For all numbers a and b, $a \lozenge b = a^2 b$. What is the value of $[(-2) \lozenge (-3)] \lozenge (-2)$?

Answer Explanation

The correct answer is –288. Here, too, you should solve carefully and double-check your work before you move on. Perform the calculations, starting with the operation in brackets to the left.

$$[(-2) \lozenge (-3)] \lozenge (-2) = [(-2)^2 \times (-3)] \lozenge (-2)$$
$$= [4 \times (-3)] \lozenge (-2)$$
$$= (-12) \lozenge (-2)$$
$$= (-12)^2 \times (-2)$$
$$= 144 \times (-2)$$
$$= -288$$

Question

6. Company A, a widget manufacturer, has eight stores in town X. The average (arithmetic mean) number of widgets these stores sold in March 2014 is 150. Not including the company's flagship store in town X, the average (arithmetic mean) number of widgets the remaining seven stores sold in March 2014 is 130. How many widgets did the flagship store sell in March 2014?

Answer Explanation

The correct answer is 290. Turn words into equations. The eight stores together sold $150 \times 8 = 1200$ widgets.

The seven stores other than the flagship store averaged 130 widgets, so together they sold $130 \times 7 = 910$.

Thus, the flagship store sold $1200 - 910 = 290$ widgets.

QUESTIONS 7–8 ARE BASED ON THE FOLLOWING DATA.

SALES OF NEW CARS IN COUNTRY A, BY CATEGORY, IN 2010

AVERAGE HIGHWAY FUEL CONSUMPTION, BY CATEGORY, FOR NEW CARS SOLD IN 2010

Category	Average Fuel Consumption
Compact Cars	32
Family Sedans	28
Luxury Sedans	24
Sports Cars	24
SUVs	23
Pickup Trucks	21

Question

7. If in 2010 the total number of new cars that were sold across all categories was 1,621,018, how many categories of cars had sales of fewer than 250,000 cars?

Answer Explanation

The correct answer is 2. Find what percent of 1,621,018 is 250,000:

$$\frac{250,000}{1,621,018} = \frac{x}{100} \Rightarrow x \approx 15.42$$

There were only two categories whose sales were less than 15.42% of the total: luxury sedans and sports cars. Make sure that you don't mistakenly answer 4, the number of categories of cars with sales of more than 15.4% of the total.

Question

8. What was the average highway fuel consumption for all cars sold in 2010? Give your answer to the nearest 0.1.

Answer Explanation

The correct answer is 26.3. For this question, you need to use the two data displays together. Additionally, in the end you must remember to round correctly. The question asks you for a weighted average. Assume there were 100 cars sold, 32 of which were family sedans, 21 of which were compact cars, and so on. Then, multiply the number of cars in each category by that category's average fuel consumption. Finally, divide this product by 100, the total number of cars sold:

$$\frac{32 \times 28 + 21 \times 32 + 18 \times 23 + 16 \times 21 + 8 \times 24 + 5 \times 24}{100} = 26.3$$

Question

9. Working alone at its constant rate, Machine A produces 15 widgets every 90 minutes. Working alone at its constant rate, Machine B produces widgets twice as quickly as does Machine A. If the two machines work together at their respective constant rates, how many hours will it take them to produce 75 widgets?

[   ] hours

Answer Explanation

The correct answer is 2.5. Make the information in this question more concrete. You need to start by finding how many widgets each machine produces in an hour. If Machine A produces 15 widgets every 90 minutes, then it produces two-thirds of that number, or 10 widgets, every hour.

Machine B is twice as fast, so it produces $2 \times 10 = 20$ widgets every hour. Thus, the two machines working together produce $10 + 20 = 30$ widgets every hour. To find how many hours the two machines together will need in order to produce 75 widgets, set up and solve the proportion: $\frac{30}{1} = \frac{75}{x} \Rightarrow x = 2.5$

Question

10. Two of the eight lawyers who work at a law firm are partners, while the rest are associates. If a team of five lawyers is to be selected randomly from among these eight lawyers, what is the probability that more than 80% of the lawyers on the team will be associates?

Give your answer to the nearest 0.01.

[   ]

Answer Explanation

The correct answer is 0.11. Make the information in the question more concrete, so that you get a better understanding of what you're looking for. If more than 80%—that is, more than four out of five—of the lawyers on the team are associates, then all five of them will be associates. To find the probability that all five of the lawyers on the team will be associates, divide the number of desirable outcomes (the total number of ways five associates can be selected from the firm's six associates) by the number of all possible outcomes (the total number of ways five lawyers can be selected from the firm's eight lawyers).

The total number of ways five associates can be selected from the firm's six associates is $_6C_5 = \dfrac{6!}{5! \times 1!}$, which equals 6.

The total number of ways five lawyers can be selected from the firm's eight lawyers is $_8C_5 = \dfrac{8!}{5! \times 3!}$. Simplify this fraction: $_8C_5 = \dfrac{8!}{5! \times 3!} = \dfrac{8 \times 7 \times 6 \times 5!}{5! \times 3 \times 2} = 56$

Thus, the probability that more than 80% of the lawyers on the team will be associates is $\dfrac{6}{56}$. That fraction is equal to 0.107…. Make sure you round correctly: rounded to the nearest hundredth, 0.107… equals 0.11.

SUMMING IT UP

- Numeric entry questions do not offer lists of possible answers. Instead, you will be presented with a question and one or two answer boxes.
    - o   If the answer should be an integer or a decimal, there will be one answer box.
    - o   If the answer should be in the form of a fraction, there will be two answer boxes, one over the other for numerator and denominator.
- Some numeric entry questions may be part of a data interpretation set.
- The screen will show a calculator for you to use.
    - o   To erase numerals in an answer box, use the "backspace" key.
    - o   To enter a negative sign, type a hyphen, and to erase a negative sign, type the hyphen again.
    - o   To enter a decimal point, use a period.
- Equivalent forms of an answer are correct.
- Fractions don't need to be reduced to lowest terms, but some directions may instruct you to round decimals up or down.
- The three specific strategies to use for solving numeric entry questions are the following:
    - o   Turn verbose or abstract language into concise and concrete wording.
    - o   Make sure you're answering the correct question.
    - o   Round correctly.

Strategies for Quantitative Comparison Questions

chapter 11

OVERVIEW

- Basic information about quantitative comparison questions
- Strategies for quantitative comparison questions
- Practice questions
- Answer key and explanations
- Summing it up

In this chapter, you will find an introduction to the quantitative comparison questions that you will find on the GRE® as well as a discussion of strategies to help you answer these questions quickly and competently. A few of these strategies will be familiar to you from the chapters on multiple-choice questions and numeric entry questions. Most, however, are specific to answering quantitative comparison questions. The strategies are:

- Pick and plug numbers.
- Simplify the quantities.
- Avoid unnecessary calculations.
- Estimate.
- Redraw the figure.
- Recognize when the answer cannot be choice (D). The relationship cannot be determined from the information given.

The one thing you won't find in the quantitative comparison section of the GRE® is data sets. Each quantitative comparison question is a stand-alone item.

BASIC INFORMATION ABOUT QUANTITATIVE COMPARISON QUESTIONS

Quantitative comparisons present you with two Quantities, A and B. Your task is to compare these quantities and choose one of the following answers:

- Quantity A is greater.
- Quantity B is greater.
- The two quantities are equal.
- The relationship cannot be determined from the information given.

These answer choices, *in this exact order,* appear with all quantitative comparison questions. Memorize the answers in order, so you don't waste time reading them for each question.

On the official GRE®, these answer choices are not labeled (A), (B), and so on. They are merely listed in this order, each with an oval to its left. For your convenience in this book, we've labeled the ovals (A), (B), (C), and (D).

There are two other points of information to remember.

1 Some questions feature additional information centered above the two quantities. You should use this information to help you determine the relationship between the two quantities.

2 Any symbol that appears more than once in a question (e.g., one that appears in Quantity A and in the centered information) has the same meaning throughout the question.

STRATEGIES FOR QUANTITATIVE COMPARISON QUESTIONS

In addition to the strategies explained here, remember that you can always skip and return to a question. You have to click the "Mark" button so that you can find the question quickly in the "Review" screen when you are ready to give it another try. However, you can only go back to a question in the section you are currently working on.

Pick and Plug Numbers

Picking and plugging numbers to represent variables is a powerful strategy if you are asked to compare expressions that contain variables. You pick numbers to represent the variables, and then plug these numbers into the expressions given in Quantities A and B. Work quickly, but also thoroughly. Depending on the question, you should choose

- not only positive, but also negative numbers.
- not only integers, but also fractions (in particular fractions between 0 and 1, and 0 and −1).
- the numbers 1 and 0.

FOR THIS QUESTION, COMPARE QUANTITY A AND QUANTITY B. THIS QUESTION HAS ADDITIONAL INFORMATION ABOVE THE TWO QUANTITIES TO USE IN DETERMINING YOUR ANSWER.

Example 1

$$\frac{x}{y} = 3$$

$$y \neq 0$$

Quantity A	Quantity B
x	y

(A) Quantity A is greater.

(B) Quantity B is greater.

(C) The two quantities are equal.

(D) The relationship cannot be determined from the information given.

First, rewrite the centered information as $x = 3y$, which is easier to work with.

This question features variables in both quantities, so picking numbers is likely to get you to the right answer quickly. Choose different numbers for y, and see what results you get for x, as well as what the relationship between the two quantities is. To keep track of the results, draw a table on your scratch paper.

y		x
1	<	3
2	<	6
$\frac{1}{3}$	<	1

So, when y equals 1, x equals 3; when y equals 2, x equals 6; and when, y equals $\frac{1}{3}$, x equals 1. In all three cases x is greater than y, so you may be tempted to conclude that Quantity A will always be greater than Quantity B. However, you have not tested a sufficient variety of numbers so far, so you should not jump to a conclusion yet. (In fact, testing $y = 2$ in particular was a waste of time because there was no reason to think that it would have yielded a different result than did $y = 1$.) In order to be thorough, you should also test numbers that have some different properties.

y		x
-1	>	-3

In this example, picking a negative number for y results in y being greater than x. Because you have now found at least one instance in which x is greater than y, as well as at least one instance in which y is greater than x, you are finished. **The correct answer is (D).**

> **FOR THIS QUESTION, COMPARE QUANTITY A AND QUANTITY B. THIS QUESTION HAS ADDITIONAL INFORMATION ABOVE THE TWO QUANTITIES TO USE IN DETERMINING YOUR ANSWER.**

Example 2

$$\frac{x}{y} = 3$$

$$y \neq 0$$

Quantity A	Quantity B
$|x|$	$|y|$

(A) Quantity A is greater.
(B) Quantity B is greater.
(C) The two quantities are equal.
(D) The relationship cannot be determined from the information given.

TIP

The GRE does not penalize wrong answers, so educated guessing could raise your score.

This question is similar to Example 1, but there is one important difference. You are now being asked to compare the absolute values of the two variables, not the variables themselves.

Again, start by rewriting the centered information in the following form: $x = 3y$

Pick numbers, again.

y	x	$|y|$		$|x|$
1	3	1	<	3
-1	-3	1	<	3
$\dfrac{1}{6}$	$\dfrac{1}{2}$	$\dfrac{1}{6}$	<	$\dfrac{1}{2}$

This time, because the absolute values eliminate the minus signs, the pattern that emerges is reliable. Because x equals 3 times y and because you're asked to compare the absolute values of x and y, no matter what value you pick for y, the absolute value of x will always be greater than the absolute value of y. **The correct answer is (A).**

When to Use Pick and Plug and When Not

Picking numbers is a useful strategy, but you should keep in mind that it doesn't always answer the question definitively.

- It is best used when it reveals quickly two different relationships between the quantities, in which case you have proved that the answer is choice (D).

- It is also helpful if the possible values that the variables may take are few, and you are able to test them all.

However, if the possible values that the variables may take are infinite—or if they are finite, but too many for you to check in any reasonable amount of time—then you cannot use this strategy alone to answer the question. Even if you test many numbers, all of which produce the same result, it's entirely possible that some other numbers, which you have not tested yet, may produce a different result.

That said, even in such a case, picking numbers may be useful if you are stuck and do not know how to proceed. After you've picked a few numbers and examined the results, you may notice a pattern that you may not have noticed previously, and that will help you compare the quantities.

Simplify the Quantities

Sometimes, test-item writers present you with expressions—either in the two quantities or in the centered information—that appear complicated, thus making your job harder. In such cases you can help yourself by

- simplifying each quantity in order to make it easier to evaluate on its own.

- manipulating one quantity in such a way as to make it easier to compare with the other quantity.

- simplifying the centered information so that you end up with a new piece of information that's easier to interpret.

TIP

Always read questions carefully. This plus turning confusing questions into concise and concrete wording may be the two most important strategies you can use. You need to understand what a question is asking in order to answer it correctly.

FOR THIS QUESTION, COMPARE QUANTITY A AND QUANTITY B.

Example 3

Quantity A	Quantity B
$4x^2 - 8x + 4$	$(2x - 2)^2$

(A) Quantity A is greater.

(B) Quantity B is greater.

(C) The two quantities are equal.

(D) The relationship cannot be determined from the information given.

As written, these quantities are hard to compare. However, you can manipulate either quantity so that it resembles the other one. For instance, if you distribute Quantity B, you get:

$(2x - 2)^2 = 4x^2 - 8x + 4$

Thus, Quantity A is the distributed form of Quantity B, so the quantities are equal. **The correct answer is (C).**

FOR THIS QUESTION, COMPARE QUANTITY A AND QUANTITY B. THIS QUESTION HAS ADDITIONAL INFORMATION ABOVE THE TWO QUANTITIES TO USE IN DETERMINING YOUR ANSWER.

Example 4

$$-1 < x < y < 0$$

Quantity A	Quantity B
xy	$\dfrac{x}{y}$

(A) Quantity A is greater.

(B) Quantity B is greater.

(C) The two quantities are equal.

(D) The relationship cannot be determined from the information given.

In this question, you should simplify the two quantities together in order to arrive at something that's easier to compare. Start by assuming that one quantity is larger than the other, and simplify the inequality until you arrive at a statement that you can evaluate. If that statement is correct, then your initial assumption was correct. If that statement is incorrect, your initial assumption was incorrect. Let's see this process at work.

Begin by assuming that Quantity A is larger than Quantity B:

$$xy > \frac{x}{y}$$

Next, cancel x from both sides of the inequality—that is, divide both sides by x. You can do this for two reasons: First, because $x \neq 0$, division by x is permissible; second, because $x < 0$, you know that division by x will reverse the sign of the inequality. (If you don't know whether a variable is positive or negative, you cannot multiply or divide both sides of the inequality by that variable.) So, you are left with $y < \frac{1}{y}$.

Now evaluate whether this statement is correct or not. Since y is a fraction between 0 and -1 (such as $-\frac{1}{2}$), its reciprocal will also be a negative number, but one smaller than -1 (such as -2). Thus, y is greater than $\frac{1}{y}$, and the inequality $y < \frac{1}{y}$ is incorrect. This means that the initial assumption that Quantity A is larger than Quantity B was also incorrect.

Since it turns out that $y > \frac{1}{y}$, you should reverse the sign of the inequality for each one of the prior steps, thus arriving at $xy < \frac{x}{y}$. **The correct answer is (B).**

Eliminating Terms When Simplifying Quantities

This example also illustrates another helpful tool when you simplify two expressions together: You can eliminate any term that appears on both expressions, as long as you keep the following rules in mind:

- You can add or subtract any term to or from both quantities. For instance, if both quantities feature the term $3y$, you can subtract it from both of them.

- You can multiply or divide both quantities by any nonzero term, as long as you know whether this term is positive or negative.

Avoid Unnecessary Calculations

Remember that you do not always need to find the exact value of the two quantities in order to compare them. This will save you time.

FOR THIS QUESTION, COMPARE QUANTITY A AND QUANTITY B.

Example 5

Quantity A	Quantity B
The average (arithmetic mean) of all odd integers between 10 and 30	The average (arithmetic mean) of all even integers between 11 and 31

(A) Quantity A is greater.

(B) Quantity B is greater.

(C) The two quantities are equal.

(D) The relationship cannot be determined from the information given.

To answer this question, you could, of course, list all the odd integers between 10 and 30, add them up, and find their average in order to determine the exact value of Quantity A. Then you could do the same for the even integers in Quantity B. However, that would be a very time-consuming process. Luckily, you don't have to do all that.

Instead, think about what the two quantities are. Quantity A is the average of ten integers, starting with the number 11 and ending with the number 29. Quantity B is also the average of ten such integers, this time starting with 12 and ending with 30. Notice that both quantities feature the same number of terms.

Next, you should note that the smallest term in Quantity B is larger than the smallest term in Quantity A; the second smallest term in Quantity B is larger than the second smallest term in Quantity A; and so on, for each of the ten terms in the two quantities, since in both cases the numbers increase by 2.

Thus, the sum of the terms in Quantity B is larger than the sum of the terms in Quantity A, and, therefore, the average of the terms in Quantity B is also larger than the average of the terms in Quantity A. No further work is needed. **The correct answer is (B).**

Estimate

One particular way of avoiding unnecessary calculations is estimating.

FOR THIS QUESTION, COMPARE QUANTITY A AND QUANTITY B.

Example 6

Quantity A	Quantity B
$65 \times \dfrac{6}{5}$	47% of 130

(A) Quantity A is greater.

(B) Quantity B is greater.

(C) The two quantities are equal.

(D) The relationship cannot be determined from the information given.

Avoid the temptation to use the calculator. As a quantitative comparison, the question asks you to compare the two quantities, not to evaluate them fully.

First, look at Quantity A. The fraction $\frac{6}{5}$ is greater than 1. That means that Quantity A is greater than 65. Stop there for the moment, and move on to Quantity B.

Quantity B features a number that is less than 50% of 130. 50% of 130 is 65, so Quantity B is less than 65.

In other words, Quantity A is greater than 65, whereas Quantity B is less than 65, which means that Quantity A is greater than Quantity B. **The correct answer is (A).**

Redraw the Figure

TIP

Redrawing the figure can be useful in answering other question formats as well.

Remember that geometric figures on the GRE® are not necessarily drawn to scale. When in doubt, you can always redraw a figure on your scratch paper, altering any quantities such as side lengths or angle measures that have not been defined fully. Doing so may reveal additional information about the figure that may not have been obvious from the figure that the test-maker provided.

> **FOR THIS QUESTION, COMPARE QUANTITY A AND QUANTITY B. THIS QUESTION HAS ADDITIONAL INFORMATION ABOVE THE TWO QUANTITIES TO USE IN DETERMINING YOUR ANSWER.**

Example 7

Quantity A	Quantity B
$2x$	y

(A) Quantity A is greater.
(B) Quantity B is greater.
(C) The two quantities are equal.
(D) The relationship cannot be determined from the information given.

As the figure is drawn, you may be tempted to assume that $x°$ is an acute angle and $y°$ is an obtuse angle. Further, you may be tempted to estimate the value of the two angles and try to compare the two quantities that way. Don't!

The figure is not necessarily drawn to scale, and you have no further information to help you evaluate the angles. You can redraw the figure on your scratch paper in order to see this latter point visually:

The only thing that the original figure tells you definitively is that $x°$ and $y°$ are supplementary angles—that is, that they add up to $180°$. Thus, the relationship between the two quantities cannot be determined. **The correct answer is (D).**

Recognize When the Answer Cannot Be (D)

The answer in a quantitative comparison question cannot be (D) if the two quantities are defined fully. That happens

- when there are no variables in either quantity.

- when there are variables, but each of the variables may take only one value.

FOR THIS QUESTION, COMPARE QUANTITY A AND QUANTITY B. THIS QUESTION HAS ADDITIONAL INFORMATION ABOVE THE TWO QUANTITIES TO USE IN DETERMINING YOUR ANSWER.

Example 8

$$x - 3 = 2$$
$$3y = x + 7$$

Quantity A	Quantity B
x	y

(A) Quantity A is greater.

(B) Quantity B is greater.

(C) The two quantities are equal.

(D) The relationship cannot be determined from the information given.

Even though the quantities feature variables, these variables are defined absolutely because of the two equations in the centered information. The first equation yields a unique value for x, and that value, when substituted into the second equation, yields a unique value for y. Because both quantities are fully defined, a definitive comparison between them is possible. In this case, $x = 5$ and $y = 4$. **The correct answer is (A).**

PRACTICE QUESTIONS

FOR QUESTIONS 1–15, COMPARE QUANTITY A AND QUANTITY B. SOME
QUESTIONS WILL HAVE ADDITIONAL INFORMATION ABOVE THE TWO
QUANTITIES TO USE IN DETERMINING YOUR ANSWER.

$$\frac{x}{y} - 4 = 0$$

$$x \neq 0, y \neq 0$$

1.

Quantity A	Quantity B
$\dfrac{1}{x}$	$\dfrac{1}{y}$

(A) Quantity A is greater.

(B) Quantity B is greater.

(C) The two quantities are equal.

(D) The relationship cannot be determined from the information given.

$$x < y$$

2.

Quantity A	Quantity B
$-x^2$	xy

(A) Quantity A is greater.

(B) Quantity B is greater.

(C) The two quantities are equal.

(D) The relationship cannot be determined from the information given.

3.

Quantity A	Quantity B
The units digit of $23^8 \times 67^8 \times 89^8$	$\dfrac{4^{11} + 4^{10} + 4^9}{3 \times 4 \times 7} \times \left(4^{-4}\right)^2$

(A) Quantity A is greater.

(B) Quantity B is greater.

(C) The two quantities are equal.

(D) The relationship cannot be determined from the information given.

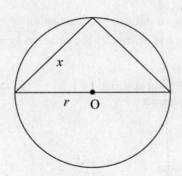

4.   Quantity A   Quantity B

The circumference of the circle with $4x$
center O and radius r

(A) Quantity A is greater.

(B) Quantity B is greater.

(C) The two quantities are equal.

(D) The relationship cannot be determined from the information given.

5.   Quantity A   Quantity B
                  $b - a$ $c - a$

(A) Quantity A is greater.

(B) Quantity B is greater.

(C) The two quantities are equal.

(D) The relationship cannot be determined from the information given.

Line *l* is defined by the equation $2x + y = 2$.

Line *k* is defined by the equation $3x + y = 4$.

6.

Quantity A	Quantity B
The *x*-coordinate of the point at which the two lines intersect	The slope of line *l*

(A) Quantity A is greater.

(B) Quantity B is greater.

(C) The two quantities are equal.

(D) The relationship cannot be determined from the information given.

7.

Quantity A	Quantity B
The sum of all multiples of 5 between 450 and 550, inclusive	The sum of all multiples of 10 between 400 and 600, inclusive

(A) Quantity A is greater.

(B) Quantity B is greater.

(C) The two quantities are equal.

(D) The relationship cannot be determined from the information given.

$$\frac{2x - xy}{3} = y - \frac{1}{3}xy$$

8.

Quantity A	Quantity B
$2x$	$2y$

(A) Quantity A is greater.

(B) Quantity B is greater.

(C) The two quantities are equal.

(D) The relationship cannot be determined from the information given.

9.

Quantity A	Quantity B
$\sqrt{230}$	The average (arithmetic mean) of all prime numbers between 10 and 20

(A) Quantity A is greater.

(B) Quantity B is greater.

(C) The two quantities are equal.

(D) The relationship cannot be determined from the information given.

10.

Quantity A	Quantity B
$\left(\dfrac{14}{42}\right)^4$	$\dfrac{1}{3} \times \dfrac{2}{9} \times \dfrac{3}{(-6)} \times \dfrac{(-1)}{3}$

(A) Quantity A is greater.

(B) Quantity B is greater.

(C) The two quantities are equal.

(D) The relationship cannot be determined from the information given.

ABC is a right triangle with legs of length $\dfrac{x}{y}$ and y.

11.

Quantity A	Quantity B
$\dfrac{x\left(5 - \sqrt{17}\right)\left(\sqrt{17} + 5\right)}{\sqrt{256}}$	The area of triangle ABC

(A) Quantity A is greater.

(B) Quantity B is greater.

(C) The two quantities are equal.

(D) The relationship cannot be determined from the information given.

12.

Quantity A	Quantity B
The number of prime numbers between 1 and 100	The number of multiples of 3 between 1 and 100

(A) Quantity A is greater.

(B) Quantity B is greater.

(C) The two quantities are equal.

(D) The relationship cannot be determined from the information given.

$$xy^2 z^3 > 0$$
$$xyz < 0$$

13.

Quantity A	Quantity B
y	xz

(A) Quantity A is greater.

(B) Quantity B is greater.

(C) The two quantities are equal.

(D) The relationship cannot be determined from the information given.

Point P (a, b) lies in quadrant I of the rectangular coordinate system. Point Q (m,n) is $180°$ rotationally symmetric to point P about the origin O.

14.   <u>Quantity A</u>   <u>Quantity B</u>

The distance between points P and Q $\left[\left(|a|+|n|\right)^2 - 2|bm|\right]^{\frac{1}{2}}$

(A) Quantity A is greater.

(B) Quantity B is greater.

(C) The two quantities are equal.

(D) The relationship cannot be determined from the information given.

M and N are two right cylinders, such that the height of cylinder M is 10% greater than the height of cylinder N, and the radius of cylinder M is 10% less than the radius of cylinder N.

15.   <u>Quantity A</u>   <u>Quantity B</u>
The surface area of cylinder M   The surface area of cylinder N

(A) Quantity A is greater.

(B) Quantity B is greater.

(C) The two quantities are equal.

(D) The relationship cannot be determined from the information given.

ANSWER KEY AND EXPLANATIONS

1. D	6. A	11. C
2. D	7. C	12. B
3. C	8. D	13. B
4. D	9. A	14. A
5. A	10. C	15. B

Question

$$\frac{x}{y} - 4 = 0$$

$$x \neq 0, y \neq 0$$

1.   <u>Quantity A</u>   <u>Quantity B</u>

$$\frac{1}{x}$$ $$\frac{1}{y}$$

(A) Quantity A is greater.
(B) Quantity B is greater.
(C) The two quantities are equal.
(D) The relationship cannot be determined from the information given.

Answer Explanation

The correct answer is (D). Begin by manipulating the centered information:
$\frac{x}{y} - 4 = 0 \Rightarrow \frac{x}{y} = 4 \Rightarrow x = 4y$

Now pick numbers for y, and see what the relationship between the two quantities is.

y	x	$\frac{1}{x}$		$\frac{1}{y}$
1	4	$\frac{1}{4}$	<	1
−1	−4	$-\frac{1}{4}$	>	−1

Clearly, the relationship between the two quantities cannot be determined from the information given.

Question

$$x < y$$

2.   Quantity A   Quantity B
                        $-x^2$ xy

   (A) Quantity A is greater.
   (B) Quantity B is greater.
   (C) The two quantities are equal.
   (D) The relationship cannot be determined from the information given.

Answer Explanation

The correct answer is (D). You cannot simplify the two quantities any more than they already are. You might be tempted to divide both quantities by x; however, that would be wrong. If x equals 0, then division by x would not be permissible. Additionally, you don't know whether x is positive or negative, so you don't know whether dividing by x would change the direction of the inequality or not. Instead, pick numbers for x and y right away.

x	y	$-x^2$		xy
2	3	-4	$<$	6
0	Any positive number	0	$=$	0

When $x = 2$ and $y = 3$, Quantity B is greater than Quantity A, whereas when $x = 0$ and $y =$ any number, then the two quantities are equal.

Question

3.   Quantity A   Quantity B
      The units digit of $23^8 \times 67^8 \times 89^8$ $\dfrac{4^{11} + 4^{10} + 4^9}{3 \times 4 \times 7} \times \left(4^{-4}\right)^2$

   (A) Quantity A is greater.
   (B) Quantity B is greater.
   (C) The two quantities are equal.
   (D) The relationship cannot be determined from the information given.

Answer Explanation

The correct answer is (C). Consider Quantity A first. In order to find the units digit of any number that is the product of two integers, you only need to multiply the units digits of those two integers. For instance, the units digit of 23×23 is equal to $3 \times 3 = 9$. Use this trick—albeit several times—to simplify Quantity A quickly. Calculate the units digit of the eighth power of each of the three numbers, and then multiply those three units digits together.

First, write out the units digits of the first few powers of 3, 7, and 9, to see if you can discern any pattern.

The units digit of 3^1 is 3.

The units digit of 3^2 is $3 \times 3 = 9$.

The units digit of 3^3 is the units digit of $3 \times 9 = 27$, that is, 7.

The units digit of 3^4 is the units digit of $3 \times 7 = 21$, that is, 1.

The units digit of 3^5 is $3 \times 1 = 3$.

So, the units digits of successive powers of 3 follow the pattern 3, 9, 7, 1, 3. . . . With this approach, you also find that the units digits of successive powers of 7 follow the pattern 7, 9, 3, 1, 7...; and the units digits of successive powers of 9 follow the pattern 9, 1, 9. . . .

In other words, the fourth, eighth, twelfth, and so on, powers of 3 end in 1. So do the fourth, eighth, twelfth, and so on, powers of 7, while all even powers of 9 end in 1. Therefore, Quantity A equals $1 \times 1 \times 1 = 1$.

Next, simplify Quantity B. Begin by writing the terms in the numerator as multiples of 4^9:

$$\frac{4^2 \times 4^9 + 4 \times 4^9 + 4^9}{3 \times 4 \times 7} \times \left(4^{-4}\right)^2$$

Combine the terms in the numerator:

$$\frac{\left(4^2 + 4 + 1\right) \times 4^9}{3 \times 4 \times 7} \times \left(4^{-4}\right)^2 = \frac{21 \times 4^9}{3 \times 4 \times 7} \times \left(4^{-4}\right)^2$$

Remove the parentheses and move $(4^{-4})^2$ to the denominator:

$$\frac{21 \times 4^9}{3 \times 4 \times 7} \times 4^{-8} = \frac{21 \times 4^9}{3 \times 4 \times 7 \times 4^8}$$

Finally, combine the terms in the denominator, and eliminate:

$$\frac{21 \times 4^9}{21 \times 4 \times 4^8} = \frac{21 \times 4^9}{21 \times 4^9} = 1$$

Question

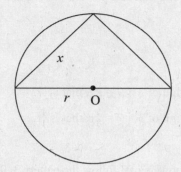

4. Quantity A   Quantity B
    The circumference of the circle with   4x
    center O and radius r

(A) Quantity A is greater.

(B) Quantity B is greater.

(C) The two quantities are equal.

(D) The relationship cannot be determined from the information given.

Answer Explanation

The correct answer is (D). Even though the triangle inscribed in the circle appears to be isosceles, don't assume that it is. The triangle is definitely a right one, since one of its sides is a diameter of the circle; however, you cannot tell anything about its two legs. Each of them may be of any length between (but not including) 0 and $2r$. For instance, here is one way that you may legitimately redraw the figure:

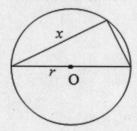

So how do we compare the two quantities? First, consider Quantity A. The circumference of the circle is $2\pi r$, and since $\pi \approx 3.14$, the circumference is approximately equal to $6.28r$.

Next, examine a couple of different possibilities for Quantity B. If the triangle were isosceles, it would be a 45–45–90 right triangle, and x would equal $r\sqrt{2}$. $\sqrt{2}$ is somewhat smaller than 1.5, so $r\sqrt{2}$ is somewhat smaller than $1.5r$, and $4x$ is somewhat smaller than $6r$. In this scenario, Quantity A is greater. However, x can be almost as large as the diameter. Therefore, $4x$ can be almost as large as $4 \times 2r$, or $8r$—so Quantity B may be greater than Quantity A.

Question

5.   Quantity A   Quantity B
                       $b - a$ $c - a$

(A) Quantity A is greater.

(B) Quantity B is greater.

(C) The two quantities are equal.

(D) The relationship cannot be determined from the information given.

Answer Explanation

The correct answer if (A). By looking at the graph, you can estimate the relationship of the three numbers to one another—and this estimate will be enough because you don't need to find exact values in order to answer the question correctly:

b, the y-coordinate of point L, is greater than a, the y-coordinate of point K because point L is farther up than point K. That is, $b > a$, so $b - a > 0$, and Quantity A is positive.

a, the x-coordinate of point L, is greater than c, the x-coordinate of point K because point L is farther to the right than point K. That is, $a > c$, so $c - a < 0$, and Quantity B is negative.

Thus, Quantity A is larger than Quantity B.

Question

Line l is defined by the equation $2x + y = 2$.

Line k is defined by the equation $3x + y = 4$.

6.   Quantity A   Quantity B
            The x-coordinate of the point at   The slope of line l
              which the two lines intersect

(A) Quantity A is greater.

(B) Quantity B is greater.

(C) The two quantities are equal.

(D) The relationship cannot be determined from the information given.

Answer Explanation

The correct answer is (A). Think of this purely as an algebra question. Quantity A asks for the value of x that is a solution of both equations. In other words, it asks you to solve the simultaneous equations for x. The combination method is fastest here. Subtract the first equation from the second:

$$3x + y = 4$$
$$-(2x + y = 2)$$
$$x = 2$$

So the value of Quantity A is 2.

For Quantity B, rewrite the equation for line l in slope-intercept form:

$y = mx + b$, where m is the slope of the line.

$y = -2x + 2$

The coefficient of x is the slope, so Quantity B is –2.

Question

7.

Quantity A	Quantity B
The sum of all multiples of 5 between 450 and 550, inclusive	The sum of all multiples of 10 between 400 and 600, inclusive

- (A) Quantity A is greater.
- (B) Quantity B is greater.
- (C) The two quantities are equal.
- (D) The relationship cannot be determined from the information given.

Answer Explanation

The correct answer is (C). There are 21 multiples of 5 between 450 and 550, inclusive. Ten of them are less than 500, ten of them are greater than 500, and one of them is 500. Since the list consists of all multiples of a certain number, and there is an odd number of such multiples in the list, the average (arithmetic mean) of all these numbers is equal to the middle number: 500. Thus, instead of adding up all 21 numbers in order to find their sum, you should multiply their average by the number of terms in the list: The value of Quantity A is 500×21.

Similarly, there are 21 multiples of 10 between 400 and 600, inclusive, and their average is also 500. Thus, the value of Quantity B is 500×21.

Question

$$\frac{2x - xy}{3} = y - \frac{1}{3}xy$$

8.

Quantity A	Quantity B
$2x$	$2y$

(A) Quantity A is greater.

(B) Quantity B is greater.

(C) The two quantities are equal.

(D) The relationship cannot be determined from the information given.

Answer Explanation

The correct answer is (D). Begin by simplifying the centered information:

$$\frac{2x - xy}{3} = y - \frac{1}{3}xy$$

Multiply both sides by 3:
$$2x - xy = 3y - xy$$

Add xy to both sides:
$$2x = 3y$$

Finally, divide both sides by 2:
$$x = \frac{3}{2}y$$

It would be nice if the question asked you to compare $2x$ to $3y$. However, it asks you to compare $2x$ to $2y$—in other words, to compare x to y—so there's another step you have to take. Pick numbers for y and see what values these produce for x:

y		x
1	$<$	$\frac{3}{2}$
-1	$>$	$-\frac{3}{2}$

Thus, the relationship between the two quantities cannot be determined from the information given.

Question

9.

Quantity A	Quantity B
$\sqrt{230}$	The average (arithmetic mean) of all prime numbers between 10 and 20

(A) Quantity A is greater.

(B) Quantity B is greater.

(C) The two quantities are equal.

(D) The relationship cannot be determined from the information given.

Answer Explanation

The correct answer is (A). On this question, you may use the calculator or estimate. If you estimate, you should recall that 225 is the square of 15, so Quantity A is slightly larger than 15. For Quantity B, list all the primes between 10 and 20: 11, 13, 17 and 19. The average of these four numbers is exactly 15. Thus, Quantity A is larger.

Question

10.

Quantity A	Quantity B
$\left(\dfrac{14}{42}\right)^4$	$\dfrac{1}{3} \times \dfrac{2}{9} \times \dfrac{3}{(-6)} \times \dfrac{(-1)}{3}$

- (A) Quantity A is greater.
- (B) Quantity B is greater.
- (C) The two quantities are equal.
- (D) The relationship cannot be determined from the information given.

Answer Explanation

The correct answer is (C). Simplifying the two quantities is the strategy to use here. First, work on Quantity A, the simpler one of the two: $\dfrac{14}{42} = \dfrac{1}{3}$, so $\left(\dfrac{14}{42}\right)^4 = \left(\dfrac{1}{3}\right)^4$. Don't calculate any further: you may not have to. If, after simplifying Quantity B, you still need to simplify Quantity A further, you can do so then. Move on to Quantity B and see what that simplifies to.

First, cancel out the minus signs from the numerator and denominator:

$$\frac{1}{3} \times \frac{2}{9} \times \frac{3}{6} \times \frac{1}{3}$$

Then, rearrange the terms:

$$\frac{1}{3} \times \frac{1}{3} \times \frac{2}{6} \times \frac{3}{9}$$

Next, simplify the last two fractions:

$$\frac{1}{3} \times \frac{1}{3} \times \frac{1}{3} \times \frac{1}{3}$$

And finally, write the product as a power of the fraction $\dfrac{1}{3}$:

$$\left(\frac{1}{3}\right)^4$$

The two quantities are equal.

Question

ABC is a right triangle with legs of length $\dfrac{x}{y}$ and y.

11.

Quantity A	Quantity B
$\dfrac{x\left(5-\sqrt{17}\right)\left(\sqrt{17}+5\right)}{\sqrt{256}}$	The area of triangle ABC

(A) Quantity A is greater.

(B) Quantity B is greater.

(C) The two quantities are equal.

(D) The relationship cannot be determined from the information given.

Answer Explanation

The correct answer is (C). Simplify the quantities in order to compare them more easily. Start with Quantity B, which is more straightforward. The area of this triangle is given by:

$$A = \frac{1}{2}\frac{x}{y}y = \frac{1}{2}x$$

Next, simplify Quantity A. Notice that the two terms in parentheses on the numerator are the factored form of the special product $a^2 - b^2$, where $a = 5$ and $b = \sqrt{17}$:

$$\frac{x\left(5-\sqrt{17}\right)\left(\sqrt{17}+5\right)}{\sqrt{256}} = \frac{\left(5^2 - \left(\sqrt{17}\right)^2\right)x}{\sqrt{256}} = \frac{(25-17)x}{\sqrt{256}} = \frac{8x}{\sqrt{256}}$$

As for the denominator, you should recognize that 256 is the square of 16. Thus, the fraction becomes:

$$\frac{8x}{16} = \frac{1}{2}x$$

Thus, Quantity A is equal to Quantity B.

Question

12.

Quantity A	Quantity B
The number of prime numbers between 1 and 100	The number of multiples of 3 between 1 and 100

(A) Quantity A is greater.

(B) Quantity B is greater.

(C) The two quantities are equal.

(D) The relationship cannot be determined from the information given.

Answer Explanation

The correct answer is (B). Quantity A is the harder of the two to deal with, so start with Quantity B: $99 = 33 \times 3$, so there are 33 multiples of 3 between 1 and 100.

Returning to Quantity A, you now have an easier task. You don't have to find the exact number of primes between 1 and 100. You only need to determine whether there are fewer or more prime numbers than 33. In other words, estimate! There are 98 integers between 1 and 100. Forty-nine of them are even, and none of those, other than the number 2, is prime. Thus, you are already down to $98 - 48 = 50$ numbers remaining: The number 2 and all the odd numbers in the range.

Next, you can eliminate all the odd multiples of 3 (other than 3 itself) because these are not prime. (Do not eliminate all multiples of 3 because the even ones are included in the 48 even numbers you eliminated in the previous step.) There are 33 multiples of 3 between 1 and 100, and both the first one (3) and the last one (99) are odd. Therefore, of these 33 multiples, 17 are odd and 16 are even. Subtract 16 of the 17 odd ones (that is, all of them other than 3) from the 50 remaining numbers: $50 - 16 = 34$.

At this point, if you can find at least two additional nonprime numbers, you are finished. Look for nonprime numbers that are neither even nor multiples of 3. The numbers 25 and 55 are two such numbers (not even, not multiples of 3, and not prime), so you can remove them from the list, as well. You are now left with, at most, 32 numbers; in other words, the number of primes between 1 and 100 is definitely smaller than 33. (The number is 25.)

Question

$$xy^2z^3 > 0$$
$$xyz < 0$$

13.

Quantity A	Quantity B
y	xz

(A) Quantity A is greater.
(B) Quantity B is greater.
(C) The two quantities are equal.
(D) The relationship cannot be determined from the information given.

Answer Explanation

The correct answer is (B). On first look, this question may appear rather complicated to solve directly. If you're running out of time, or you don't feel too confident about how you should approach this question, you may wish to skip it—clicking the "Mark" button so that you can revisit the question easily at a later point.

That said, if you dissect methodically the centered information using the properties of positives and negatives, as well as those of exponents, you'll be able to find the right answer.

First, examine the first inequality: $xy^2 z^3 > 0$. y^2 is positive, so the product of x and z^3 must also be positive (if xz^3 were negative, then you'd have a negative number multiplied by a positive number to produce another positive number, which is impossible).

Now, for xz^3 to be positive, x and z have to be either both positive or both negative. That's as far as you can go with this inequality alone.

Next, examine the second inequality: $xyz < 0$. Because xz^3 is positive (based on the first inequality), xz must also be positive. Therefore, for xyz to be negative, y must be negative. You can now answer the question! You have proven that Quantity A is negative, while Quantity B is positive.

Question

Point $P\ (a,b)$ lies in quadrant I of the rectangular coordinate system. Point $Q\ (m,n)$ is 180° rotationally symmetric to point P about the origin O.

14.

Quantity A	Quantity B
The distance between points P and Q.	$\left[\left(\lvert a\rvert+\lvert n\rvert\right)^{2}-2\lvert bm\rvert\right]^{\frac{1}{2}}$

(A) Quantity A is greater.

(B) Quantity B is greater.

(C) The two quantities are equal.

(D) The relationship cannot be determined from the information given.

Answer Explanation

The correct answer is (A). This question also seems difficult at first. For one thing, Quantity B appears complicated. For another, the question tests more than one area of mathematical knowledge. So this may be another candidate for skipping and revisiting.

Nonetheless, let's see how you would solve this question. Start by interpreting the centered information. If points P and Q are symmetric about the origin, then their x- and y-coordinates are opposites of each other. In other words, $a = -m$ and $b = -n$. Also, since P lies in quadrant I, then a and b are positive numbers, while m and n are negative.

Next, examine Quantity A. Drawing a diagram helps:

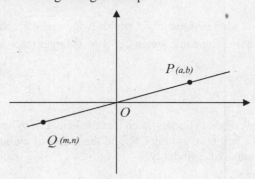

The distance between P and Q is equal to the length of line segment PO plus the length of line segment OQ. This sum is equal to two times the length of the segment PO, since $PO = OQ$.

PO is the hypotenuse of a right triangle with legs PR and OR (see the following figure). The length of PR is b (the y-coordinate of P), and the length of OR is a (the x-coordinate of R).

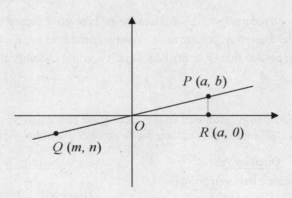

You can use the Pythagorean theorem to find the length of segment PO:
$$PO = \sqrt{a^2 + b^2}$$

Thus, the length of PQ is twice the length of PO: $PQ = 2\sqrt{a^2 + b^2}$.

Now, move on to Quantity B. First, tackle the absolute value signs so you can simplify the expression. Since a is positive, $|a| = a$. Additionally, since $b = -n$ and b is positive, $|n| = b$. Next, $|bm| = |b| \times |m|$, and since $m = -a$, $|bm| = |b| \times |a|$. Further, since a and b are both positive, $|bm| = a \times b$.

Now you're ready to transform the expression, so that $\left[\left(|a| + |n|\right)^2 - 2|bm|\right]^{\frac{1}{2}}$ becomes:
$$\sqrt{(a+b)^2 - 2ab}$$

Distribute the first term:
$$\sqrt{a^2 + b^2 + 2ab - 2ab}$$

Finally, cancel the two $2ab$:
$$\sqrt{a^2 + b^2}$$

Quantity B equals $\sqrt{a^2 + b^2}$, whereas Quantity A equals twice $\sqrt{a^2 + b^2}$. Since $\sqrt{a^2 + b^2}$ is a positive number (it's the length of a line segment), twice $\sqrt{a^2 + b^2}$ is larger than once $\sqrt{a^2 + b^2}$, so Quantity A is larger.

Question

M and N are two right cylinders, such that the height of cylinder M is 10% greater than the height of cylinder N, and the radius of cylinder M is 10% less than the radius of cylinder N.

15.   Quantity A   Quantity B
     The surface area of cylinder M   The surface area of cylinder N

(A) Quantity A is greater.

(B) Quantity B is greater.

(C) The two quantities are equal.

(D) The relationship cannot be determined from the information given.

Answer Explanation

The correct answer is (B). This is a wordy question that needs translation into mathematical expressions. First, you need to recall the definition of the surface area of a cylinder: $A = 2\pi r^2 + 2\pi rh$, where r is the radius of the circular base as well as the circular top of the cylinder, while h is the height of the cylinder.

Next, write out mathematical expressions to represent the centered information:

$$h_M = 1.1h_N \text{ and } r_M = 0.9r_N$$

Now find the surface area of cylinder M with respect to r_N and h_N, in order to see whether a direct comparison with the surface area of cylinder N is possible. Start by writing the equation for the surface area of cylinder M in terms of its own radius and height:

$$A_M = 2\pi r_M^2 + 2\pi r_M h_M$$

Replace r_M with $0.9r_N$, and h_M with $1.1h_N$:

$$A_M = 2\pi(0.9r_N)^2 + 2\pi(0.9r_N)1.1h_N$$

Perform the various calculations:

$$A_M = 2\pi 0.81 r_N^2 + 1.8\pi r_N 1.1h_N \Rightarrow$$
$$A_M = 1.62\pi r_N^2 + 1.98\pi r_N h_N$$

Next, write out the expression for the surface area of cylinder N:

$$A_N = 2\pi r_N^2 + 2\pi r_N h_N$$

You have simplified Quantity A in such a way that you can now compare it with Quantity B. Notice that each of the two terms in the expression for Quantity B is larger than its corresponding term in the expression for Quantity A: that is, $2\pi r_N^2$ is larger than $1.62\pi r_N^2$, and $2\pi r_N h_N$ is larger than $1.98\pi r_N h_N$. Therefore, Quantity B is larger.

Alternatively, you could have determined this by subtracting Quantity A from Quantity B:

$$A_N - A_M = 2\pi r_N^2 + 2\pi r_N h_N - 1.62\pi r_N^2 - 1.98\pi r_N h_N \Rightarrow$$
$$A_N - A_M = 0.38\pi r_N^2 + 0.02\pi r_N h_N$$

The difference is a positive number, so A_N is larger than A_M.

SUMMING IT UP

- Quantitative comparison questions present two Quantities, A and B, that you must compare. To select an answer, you choose one answer from the following list:
  - o   Quantity A is greater.
  - o   Quantity B is greater.
  - o   The two quantities are equal.
  - o   The relationship cannot be determined from the information given.

- Some questions feature additional information centered above the two quantities. You should use this information to help you determine the relationship between the two quantities.

- Any symbol that appears more than once in a question (e.g., one that appears in Quantity A and in the centered information) has the same meaning throughout the question.

- Specific strategies for quantitative comparison questions are the following:
  - o   Pick and plug numbers.
  - o   Simplify the quantities.
  - o   Avoid unnecessary calculations.
  - o   Estimate.
  - o   Redraw the figure.
  - o   Recognize when the answer cannot be (D). The relationship cannot be determined from the information given.

- Data interpretation sets are not used for quantitative comparison questions.

PART VI
THREE PRACTICE TESTS

PRACTICE TEST 2 ANSWER SHEETS

Section 1: Analytical Writing

Analyze an Issue

FOR PLANNING

answer sheet

ANALYZE AN ISSUE RESPONSE

_____
_____
_____
_____
_____
_____
_____
_____
_____
_____
_____
_____
_____
_____
_____
_____
_____
_____
_____
_____
_____
_____
_____
_____
_____
_____
_____
_____
_____
_____
_____
_____
_____
_____
_____
_____
_____
_____
_____
_____

ANALYZE AN ISSUE RESPONSE

answer sheet

ANALYZE AN ISSUE RESPONSE

_____
_____
_____
_____
_____
_____
_____
_____
_____
_____
_____
_____
_____
_____
_____
_____
_____
_____
_____
_____
_____
_____
_____
_____
_____
_____
_____
_____
_____
_____
_____
_____
_____
_____
_____
_____
_____
_____
_____
_____
_____

ANALYZE AN ISSUE RESPONSE

_____
_____
_____
_____
_____
_____
_____
_____
_____
_____
_____
_____
_____
_____
_____
_____
_____
_____
_____
_____
_____
_____
_____
_____
_____
_____
_____
_____
_____
_____
_____
_____

answer sheet

Analyze an Argument

FOR PLANNING

ANALYZE AN ARGUMENT RESPONSE

answer sheet

ANALYZE AN ARGUMENT RESPONSE

_____
_____
_____
_____
_____
_____
_____
_____
_____
_____
_____
_____
_____
_____
_____
_____
_____
_____
_____
_____
_____
_____
_____
_____
_____
_____
_____
_____
_____
_____
_____
_____
_____
_____
_____
_____
_____
_____
_____
_____

ANALYZE AN ARGUMENT RESPONSE

_____
_____
_____
_____
_____
_____
_____
_____
_____
_____
_____
_____
_____
_____
_____
_____
_____
_____
_____
_____
_____
_____
_____
_____
_____
_____
_____
_____
_____
_____
_____

answer sheet

ANALYZE AN ARGUMENT RESPONSE
_____
_____
_____
_____
_____
_____
_____
_____
_____
_____
_____
_____
_____
_____
_____
_____
_____
_____
_____
_____
_____
_____
_____
_____
_____
_____
_____
_____
_____
_____
_____
_____
_____
_____
_____
_____
_____
_____
_____

Section 2: Quantitative Reasoning

1. Ⓐ Ⓑ Ⓒ Ⓓ
2. Ⓐ Ⓑ Ⓒ Ⓓ
3. Ⓐ Ⓑ Ⓒ Ⓓ
4. Ⓐ Ⓑ Ⓒ Ⓓ
5. Ⓐ Ⓑ Ⓒ Ⓓ
6. Ⓐ Ⓑ Ⓒ Ⓓ
7. Ⓐ Ⓑ Ⓒ Ⓓ
8. Ⓐ Ⓑ Ⓒ Ⓓ
9. Ⓐ Ⓑ Ⓒ Ⓓ Ⓔ
10. Ⓐ Ⓑ Ⓒ Ⓓ Ⓔ

11. Ⓐ Ⓑ Ⓒ Ⓓ Ⓔ
12. Ⓐ Ⓑ Ⓒ Ⓓ Ⓔ
13. Ⓐ Ⓑ Ⓒ Ⓓ Ⓔ
14. Ⓐ Ⓑ Ⓒ Ⓓ Ⓔ
15. Ⓐ Ⓑ Ⓒ Ⓓ Ⓔ Ⓕ Ⓖ
16. Ⓐ Ⓑ Ⓒ Ⓓ Ⓔ Ⓕ Ⓖ Ⓗ
17. ☐

18. ☐/☐
19. ☐/☐
20. Ⓐ Ⓑ Ⓒ Ⓓ Ⓔ

Section 3: Quantitative Reasoning

1. Ⓐ Ⓑ Ⓒ Ⓓ
2. Ⓐ Ⓑ Ⓒ Ⓓ
3. Ⓐ Ⓑ Ⓒ Ⓓ
4. Ⓐ Ⓑ Ⓒ Ⓓ
5. Ⓐ Ⓑ Ⓒ Ⓓ
6. Ⓐ Ⓑ Ⓒ Ⓓ
7. Ⓐ Ⓑ Ⓒ Ⓓ
8. Ⓐ Ⓑ Ⓒ Ⓓ
9. Ⓐ Ⓑ Ⓒ Ⓓ
10. Ⓐ Ⓑ Ⓒ Ⓓ

11. Ⓐ Ⓑ Ⓒ Ⓓ Ⓔ
12. Ⓐ Ⓑ Ⓒ Ⓓ Ⓔ
13. Ⓐ Ⓑ Ⓒ Ⓓ Ⓔ
14. Ⓐ Ⓑ Ⓒ Ⓓ Ⓔ
15. Ⓐ Ⓑ Ⓒ Ⓓ Ⓔ

16. Ⓐ Ⓑ Ⓒ Ⓓ Ⓔ Ⓕ Ⓖ Ⓗ
17. Ⓐ Ⓑ Ⓒ Ⓓ Ⓔ Ⓕ Ⓖ Ⓗ
18. ☐
19. ☐
20. Ⓐ Ⓑ Ⓒ Ⓓ Ⓔ Ⓕ Ⓖ Ⓗ

Section 4: Verbal Reasoning

1. Ⓐ Ⓑ Ⓒ Ⓓ Ⓔ
2. Ⓐ Ⓑ Ⓒ Ⓓ Ⓔ
3. Ⓐ Ⓑ Ⓒ Ⓓ Ⓔ Ⓕ
4. Ⓐ Ⓑ Ⓒ Ⓓ Ⓔ Ⓕ
5. Ⓐ Ⓑ Ⓒ Ⓓ Ⓔ Ⓕ Ⓖ Ⓗ Ⓘ
6. Ⓐ Ⓑ Ⓒ Ⓓ Ⓔ
7. Ⓐ Ⓑ Ⓒ
8. Ⓐ Ⓑ Ⓒ Ⓓ Ⓔ
9. Ⓐ Ⓑ Ⓒ Ⓓ Ⓔ
10. Ⓐ Ⓑ Ⓒ Ⓓ Ⓔ

11. Ⓐ Ⓑ Ⓒ
12. Ⓐ Ⓑ Ⓒ Ⓓ Ⓔ
13. Ⓐ Ⓑ Ⓒ Ⓓ Ⓔ
14. Ⓐ Ⓑ Ⓒ Ⓓ Ⓔ
15. Ⓐ Ⓑ Ⓒ Ⓓ Ⓔ
16. Ⓐ Ⓑ Ⓒ Ⓓ Ⓔ Ⓕ

17. Ⓐ Ⓑ Ⓒ Ⓓ Ⓔ Ⓕ
18. Ⓐ Ⓑ Ⓒ Ⓓ Ⓔ Ⓕ
19. Ⓐ Ⓑ Ⓒ Ⓓ Ⓔ Ⓕ
20. Ⓐ Ⓑ Ⓒ Ⓓ Ⓔ

answer sheet

Section 5: Verbal Reasoning

1. Ⓐ Ⓑ Ⓒ Ⓓ Ⓔ
2. Ⓐ Ⓑ Ⓒ Ⓓ Ⓔ Ⓕ
3. Ⓐ Ⓑ Ⓒ Ⓓ Ⓔ Ⓕ
4. Ⓐ Ⓑ Ⓒ Ⓓ Ⓔ Ⓕ
5. Ⓐ Ⓑ Ⓒ Ⓓ Ⓔ Ⓕ Ⓖ Ⓗ Ⓘ
6. Ⓐ Ⓑ Ⓒ Ⓓ Ⓔ
7. Ⓐ Ⓑ Ⓒ
8. Ⓐ Ⓑ Ⓒ Ⓓ Ⓔ
9. Ⓐ Ⓑ Ⓒ Ⓓ Ⓔ
10. Ⓐ Ⓑ Ⓒ Ⓓ Ⓔ

11. Ⓐ Ⓑ Ⓒ Ⓓ Ⓔ
12. Ⓐ Ⓑ Ⓒ Ⓓ Ⓔ
13. Ⓐ Ⓑ Ⓒ
14. Ⓐ Ⓑ Ⓒ Ⓓ Ⓔ
15. Ⓐ Ⓑ Ⓒ Ⓓ Ⓔ
16. Ⓐ Ⓑ Ⓒ Ⓓ Ⓔ

17. Ⓐ Ⓑ Ⓒ Ⓓ Ⓔ Ⓕ
18. Ⓐ Ⓑ Ⓒ Ⓓ Ⓔ Ⓕ
19. Ⓐ Ⓑ Ⓒ Ⓓ Ⓔ Ⓕ
20. Ⓐ Ⓑ Ⓒ Ⓓ Ⓔ Ⓕ

Practice Test 2

The test begins with general information about the number of sections on the test (six for the computer version, including the unidentified unscored section or an identified research section, and five for the paper-and-pencil version) and the timing of the test (approximately 3 hours and 45 minutes including one 10-minute break after Section 3, 1-minute breaks after the other sections for the computer version, and 3 hours and 30 minutes for the paper-and-pencil version with similar breaks). The following practice test contains the five scored sections.

Each section has its own time allocation and, during that time period, you may work on only that section.

Next, you will read ETS's policy on scoring the Analytical Writing responses. Each essay is read by experienced readers, and ETS may cancel any test scores that show evidence of unacknowledged use of sources, unacknowledged collaboration with others, preparation of the response by another person, and language that is "substantially" similar to the language in one or more other test responses.

Each section has specific instructions for that section.

You will be told when to begin.

practice test 2

SECTION 1: ANALYTICAL WRITING

Analyze an Issue

30 minutes

The time for this task is 30 minutes. You must plan and draft a response that evaluates the issue given below. If you do not respond to the specific issue, your score will be zero. Your response must be based on the accompanying instructions, and you must provide evidence for your position. You may use support from reading, experience, observations, and/or course work.

> In an era of steadily decreasing voter participation, Jackson County should remind all citizens within its jurisdiction, preferably by phone or by home visit, and preferably one week before elections, that their number one responsibility to their nation, their state, and their community is to vote.
>
> Write an essay that takes a position on this proposed policy. As you explain and support your position, also discuss how possible alternatives to the policy and/or likely results or consequences of the policy help to shape your position.

Your response will be read by experienced readers who will assess your ability to do the following:

- Follow the set of task instructions.
- Analyze the complexities involved.
- Organize, develop, and explain ideas.
- Use pertinent reasons and/or illustrations to support ideas.
- Adhere to the conventions of Standard Written English.

You will be advised to take some time to plan your response and to leave time to reread it before the time is over. Those taking the paper-and-pencil version of the GRE® will find a blank page in their answer booklet for making notes and then four ruled pages for writing their actual response. Those taking the computer version will be given scrap paper for making notes.

STOP

> If you finish before the time is up, you may check your work in this section only.

Analyze an Argument
30 minutes

The time for this task is 30 minutes. You must plan and draft a response that evaluates the argument given below. If you do not respond to the given argument, your score will be zero. Your response must be based on the accompanying instructions, and you must provide evidence in support of your analysis.

You should not present your views on the subject of the argument but on the strengths or weakness of the argument.

The constant use by children of computers, computer games, and devices such as smart phones that integrate computer technology is perilously diminishing the attention spans of the students at Medville Elementary. A coalition of concerned parents and teachers hereby recommends the banning of computers, computer games, and cell phones in Medville School (except when a phone must be used for necessary communication with parents/guardians or other caregivers at designated times and in designated areas), and the judicious use of computers only when necessary to teach fundamental skills, such as searching for information. All of us want to educate children who can maintain the kind of sustained, focused attention that will be necessary for success in the 21st-century workplace.

Write an essay that raises questions that would have to be answered in order to evaluate the reasonableness of the recommendation and the argument on which it is based. Be sure to explain how the answers to the questions would help to determine whether the argument and recommendation are reasonable.

Your response will be read by experienced readers who will assess your ability to do the following:

- Follow the set of task instructions.
- Analyze the complexities involved.
- Organize, develop, and explain ideas.
- Use pertinent reasons and/or illustrations to support ideas.
- Adhere to the conventions of Standard Written English.

You will be advised to take some time to plan your response and to leave time to reread it before the time is over. Those taking the paper-and-pencil version of the GRE® will find a blank page in their answer booklet for making notes and then four ruled pages for writing their actual response. Those taking the computer version will be given scrap paper for making notes.

STOP

If you finish before the time is up, you may check your work in this section only.

INSTRUCTIONS FOR THE VERBAL REASONING AND QUANTITATIVE REASONING SECTIONS

You will find information here on the question formats for the Verbal Reasoning and Quantitative Reasoning sections as well as information about how to use the software program, or, if you're taking the paper-and-pencil version, how to mark your answers in the answer booklet.

Perhaps the most important information is a reminder about how these two sections are scored. Every correct answer earns a point, but wrong answers don't subtract any points. The advice from ETS is to guess if you aren't sure of an answer. ETS says that this is better than not answering a question.

All multiple-choice questions in the computer-based test will have answer options preceded by either blank ovals or blank squares, depending on the question type. The paper-and-pencil test will follow the same format of answer choices, but it will use letters instead of ovals or squares for answer choices.

For your convenience in answering questions and checking answers in this book, we use (A), (B), (C), etc. By using letters with parentheses, you will find it easy to check your answers against the answer key and explanation sections.

SECTION 2: QUANTITATIVE REASONING

35 minutes • 20 questions

(The paper-and-pencil version will have 25 questions to be completed in 40 minutes.)

For each question, follow the specific directions and choose the best answer.

The test-maker provides the following information that applies to all questions in the Quantitative Reasoning section of the GRE®:

- All numbers used are real numbers.

- All figures are assumed to lie in a plane unless otherwise indicated.

- Geometric figures, such as lines, circles, triangles, and quadrilaterals, *are not necessarily* drawn to scale. That is, you should *not* assume that quantities such as lengths and angle measures are as they appear in a figure. You should assume, however, that lines shown as straight are actually straight, points on a line are in the order shown, and more generally, all geometric objects are in the relative positions shown. For questions with geometric figures, you should base your answers on geometric reasoning, not on estimating or comparing quantities by sight or by measurement.

- Coordinate systems, such as *xy*-planes and number lines, *are* drawn to scale. Therefore, you can read, estimate, or compare quantities in such figures by sight or by measurement.

- Graphical data presentations, such as bar graphs, circle graphs, and line graphs, *are* drawn to scale. Therefore, you can read, estimate, or compare data values by sight or by measurement.

FOR QUESTIONS 1–8, COMPARE QUANTITY A AND QUANTITY B. SOME QUESTIONS WILL HAVE ADDITIONAL INFORMATION ABOVE THE TWO QUANTITIES TO USE IN DETERMINING YOUR ANSWER.

1.

Quantity A	Quantity B
$6(4)\left(\dfrac{1}{2}\right)^2$	6

(A) Quantity A is greater.

(B) Quantity B is greater.

(C) The two quantities are equal.

(D) The relationship cannot be determined from the information given.

$$xy = 12$$

2.

Quantity A	Quantity B
$(3x)(2y)$	60

(A) Quantity A is greater.

(B) Quantity B is greater.

(C) The two quantities are equal.

(D) The relationship cannot be determined from the information given.

3.

Quantity A	Quantity B
40% of $\dfrac{5}{8}$	60% of $\dfrac{3}{4}$

(A) Quantity A is greater.

(B) Quantity B is greater.

(C) The two quantities are equal.

(D) The relationship cannot be determined from the information given.

$$x \neq 0$$

4.

Quantity A	Quantity B
$\dfrac{5}{x}$	$5x$

(A) Quantity A is greater.

(B) Quantity B is greater.

(C) The two quantities are equal.

(D) The relationship cannot be determined from the information given.

$$x + 3 = 4x - 2$$
$$5y - 2 = 2y + 1$$

5.   Quantity A   Quantity B
          $3x$ $6y$

(A) Quantity A is greater.
(B) Quantity B is greater.
(C) The two quantities are equal.
(D) The relationship cannot be determined from the information given.

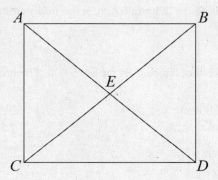

6.   Quantity A   Quantity B
   The area of *AEC*   The area of *CED*

(A) Quantity A is greater.
(B) Quantity B is greater.
(C) The two quantities are equal.
(D) The relationship cannot be determined from the information given.

7.   Quantity A   Quantity B
                  5x   180

(A) Quantity A is greater.

(B) Quantity B is greater.

(C) The two quantities are equal.

(D) The relationship cannot be determined from the information given.

A 2,475-square-foot house sells for $475,000. The broker's fee is 6%.

8.   Quantity A   Quantity B
            The broker's fee $31,000

(A) Quantity A is greater.

(B) Quantity B is greater.

(C) The two quantities are equal.

(D) The relationship cannot be determined from the information given.

Questions 9–20 have several formats. Unless the directions state otherwise, choose one answer choice. For the Numeric Entry questions, follow the instructions below.

Numeric Entry Questions

The following items are the same for both the computer-based version of the test and the paper-and-pencil version. However, those taking the computer-based version will have additional information about entering answers in decimal and fraction boxes on the computer screen. Those taking the paper-and-pencil version will have information about entering answers on answer grids.

- Your answer may be an integer, a decimal, or a fraction, and it may be negative.

- If a question asks for a fraction, there will be two boxes. One box will be for the numerator and one will be for the denominator.

- Equivalent forms of the correct answer, such as 2.5 and 2.50, are all correct.

- Enter the exact answer unless the question asks you to round your answers.

QUESTIONS 9–11 REFER TO THE CHART BELOW.

Sales by type 2010

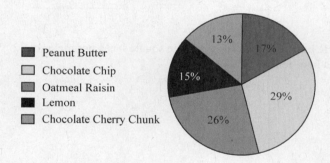

- ◼ Peanut Butter
- ◻ Chocolate Chip
- ◼ Oatmeal Raisin
- ◼ Lemon
- ◼ Chocolate Cherry Chunk

9. The two most popular types of cookies were what percentage of sales?

(A) 26

(B) 29

(C) 42

(D) 44

(E) 55

10. How many different types of cookies do NOT have chocolate in them?

(A) 1

(B) 2

(C) 3

(D) 4

(E) 5

11. If total sales for the year were $94,480, what was the total amount sold of the third most popular cookie?

(A) $12,543

(B) $16,062

(C) $17,727

(D) $24,980

(E) $27,589

12. The above circle has a diameter of 8, and the square has a perimeter of 32. What is the difference in the area between the two?

(A) 11.82

(B) 12.96

(C) 13.33

(D) 13.76

(E) 15.97

13. Lacy receives 45% of the commission of every painting she sells. If she recently sold a painting for $256,000 and received a commission of $7,488, what was the total rate of commission?

(A) 0.016

(B) 0.029

(C) 0.065

(D) 0.067

(E) 0.076

14. The expression $(4x+7y)^2 - (2x-3y)^2$ is equivalent to

   (A) $4(3x^2 + 17xy + 10y^2)$
   (B) $16x^2 + 10y^2$
   (C) $12x^2 + 12xy - 9y^2$
   (D) $x^2 + 12xy + 40y^2$
   (E) None of the above

FOR QUESTIONS 15 AND 16, INDICATE <u>ALL</u> THE ANSWERS THAT APPLY.

---

15. If *ab* and *cd* are parallel, what other angles are equal to 115º?

   (A) 1
   (B) 2
   (C) 3
   (D) 4
   (E) 5
   (F) 6
   (G) 7

16. What are the next three numbers in the sequence 0, 1, 3, 7, 15, 31,…

(A) 57

(B) 63

(C) 72

(D) 111

(E) 127

(F) 295

(G) 255

(H) 511

17. The average (arithmetic mean) score of Sanjay's six biology tests is 88. The sum of the scores of his first four tests is 332. What is the average score of his last two tests?

(A) 83

(B) 93

(C) 98

(D) 196

(E) The average score cannot be determined from the information given.

FOR QUESTIONS 18 AND 19, ENTER YOUR ANSWERS IN THE BOXES.

---

18. $\dfrac{1}{2}+\dfrac{1}{3}+\dfrac{3}{4}+\dfrac{5}{6}=$

Give your answer as a fraction.

19. On a rugby team of 15 players, the ratio of forwards to backs is $\dfrac{8}{7}$. What is the ratio of backs to total number of players?

Give your answer as a fraction.

20. If an acre is equal to 43,560 square feet, how many acres are there in 362,985 square feet?

   (A) 6.33
   (B) 7.33
   (C) 8.33
   (D) 9.33
   (E) 10.33

STOP

If you finish before the time is up, you may check your work in this section only.

SECTION 3: QUANTITATIVE REASONING

35 minutes • 20 questions

(The paper-and-pencil version will have 25 questions to be completed in 40 minutes.)

For each question, follow the specific directions and choose the best answer.

The test-maker provides the following information that applies to all questions in the Quantitative Reasoning section of the GRE®:

- All numbers used are real numbers.

- All figures are assumed to lie in a plane unless otherwise indicated.

- Geometric figures, such as lines, circles, triangles, and quadrilaterals, *are not necessarily drawn to scale.* That is, you should *not* assume that quantities such as lengths and angle measures are as they appear in a figure. You should assume, however, that lines shown as straight are actually straight, points on a line are in the order shown, and more generally, all geometric objects are in the relative positions shown. For questions with geometric figures, you should base your answers on geometric reasoning, not on estimating or comparing quantities by sight or by measurement.

- Coordinate systems, such as *xy*-planes and number lines, *are* drawn to scale. Therefore, you can read, estimate, or compare quantities in such figures by sight or by measurement.

- Graphical data presentations, such as bar graphs, circle graphs, and line graphs, *are* drawn to scale. Therefore, you can read, estimate, or compare data values by sight or by measurement.

FOR QUESTIONS 1–8, COMPARE QUANTITY A AND QUANTITY B. SOME QUESTIONS WILL HAVE ADDITIONAL INFORMATION ABOVE THE TWO QUANTITIES TO USE IN DETERMINING YOUR ANSWER.

$$\frac{5}{8}x = \frac{1}{12}$$

1.　　　　　Quantity A　　　　　　　　　Quantity B

　　　　　　　　　　x　　　　　　　　　　　$\dfrac{2}{15}$

(A) Quantity A is greater.

(B) Quantity B is greater.

(C) The two quantities are equal.

(D) The relationship cannot be determined from the information given.

2.

Quantity A	Quantity B
$\dfrac{0.00008}{0.00006}$	0.75

(A) Quantity A is greater.
(B) Quantity B is greater.
(C) The two quantities are equal.
(D) The relationship cannot be determined from the information given.

3.

Quantity A	Quantity B
The area of the trapezoid	80

(A) Quantity A is greater.
(B) Quantity B is greater.
(C) The two quantities are equal.
(D) The relationship cannot be determined from the information given.

4.

Quantity A	Quantity B
The mean of angles x, y, z	60

(A) Quantity A is greater.
(B) Quantity B is greater.
(C) The two quantities are equal.
(D) The relationship cannot be determined from the information given.

5.

	Quantity A	Quantity B
	$\sqrt{(66)(27)}$	$(8)(4.9)$

(A) Quantity A is greater.

(B) Quantity B is greater.

(C) The two quantities are equal.

(D) The relationship cannot be determined from the information given.

$$xy = 3.2$$

6.

	Quantity A	Quantity B
	$1.5x(4.6y)$	22.08

(A) Quantity A is greater.

(B) Quantity B is greater.

(C) The two quantities are equal.

(D) The relationship cannot be determined from the information given.

7.

Quantity A	Quantity B
Time it takes a bicycle to travel 15 miles	Time it takes a car to travel 60 miles

(A) Quantity A is greater.

(B) Quantity B is greater.

(C) The two quantities are equal.

(D) The relationship cannot be determined from the information given.

An apple costs $0.25. An orange costs $0.35. A pear costs $\frac{1}{2}$ of the sum of an apple and an orange.

8. <u>Quantity A</u> <u>Quantity B</u>

    5 apples and 5 oranges 12 pears

(A) Quantity A is greater.

(B) Quantity B is greater.

(C) The two quantities are equal.

(D) The relationship cannot be determined from the information given.

Questions 9–20 have several formats. Unless the directions state otherwise, choose one answer choice. For the Numeric Entry questions, follow the instructions below.

Numeric Entry Questions

The following items are the same for both the computer-based version of the test and the paper-and-pencil version. However, those taking the computer-based version will have additional information about entering answers in decimal and fraction boxes on the computer screen. Those taking the paper-and-pencil version will have information about entering answers on answer grids.

- Your answer may be an integer, a decimal, or a fraction, and it may be negative.

- If a question asks for a fraction, there will be two boxes. One box will be for the numerator and one will be for the denominator.

- Equivalent forms of the correct answer, such as 2.5 and 2.50, are all correct.

- Enter the exact answer unless the question asks you to round your answers.

---

9. A card player selects two cards at random and without replacement from a standard deck of 52 playing cards. What is the probability that the player will select at least one ace?

(A) $\frac{1}{1326}$

(B) $\frac{33}{221}$

(C) $\frac{188}{221}$

(D) $\frac{144}{169}$

(E) $\frac{12}{13}$

10. What is the solution to the inequality $(4 - 2x)\frac{1}{2} \leq \frac{1-x}{3}$.

(A) $x \leq \frac{5}{2}$

(B) $x > \frac{5}{2}$

(C) $x \geq \frac{5}{2}$

(D) $x \geq 2$

(E) $x \geq \frac{2}{5}$

QUESTIONS 11–13 REFER TO THE GRAPH BELOW.

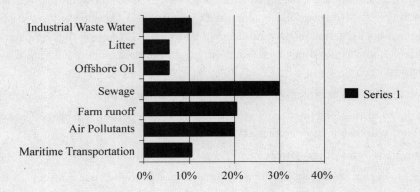

Pollutants Entering the Ocean

11. What is the percentage of offshore oil compared to all pollutants?
(A) 5%
(B) 10%
(C) 15%
(D) 20%
(E) 30%

12. Sewage, litter, and air pollution make up what percentage of the whole?
(A) 5%
(B) 15%
(C) 30%
(D) 45%
(E) 55%

13. If air pollution is eliminated from the graph, what percentage would sewage be of the new graph "Water-Born Pollutants Entering the Ocean"?

(A) 24%

(B) 28%

(C) 37.5%

(D) 40%

(E) 44.5%

14. A receptionist greeted the following numbers of people during one work week: 4, 19, 21, 18, 23. What is the mean of the number of people she greeted?

(A) 17

(B) 19

(C) 20

(D) 21

(E) 85

15. A farmer owns a square property and wants to sell a lot formed by dividing the lot in half, both lengthwise and widthwise. If the resulting lot has a perimeter of 888,000 feet, what is the area of the original lot?

(A) 179,936,000,000 sq. ft.

(B) 185,926,000,000 sq. ft.

(C) 197,136,000,000 sq. ft.

(D) 200,000,000,000 sq. ft.

(E) 212,386,000,000 sq. ft.

FOR QUESTIONS 16 AND 17, CHOOSE <u>ALL</u> THE ANSWERS THAT APPLY.

---

16. If p and q are integers, and n is an odd integer that is a factor of both $2p$ and q, then n is a factor of which of the following?

(A) $p + q$

(B) p

(C) $\dfrac{pq}{n}$

(D) $|2p - q|$

17. The local baseball team employs at least 3 times as many pitchers as catchers, but never more than 11 players total. Pitchers make an average of $45,000, and catchers make an average of $30,000. Which of the following amounts are the possible averages for all the pitchers and catchers, rounded to the nearest dollar?

(A) 30,000

(B) 35,899

(C) 40,375

(D) 41,250

(E) 41,956

(F) 42,273

(G) 43,743

(H) 45,000

FOR QUESTIONS 18 AND 19, ENTER YOUR ANSWERS IN THE BOXES.

---

18. $\dfrac{\left(\left(2^3\right)^2\right)^2}{\left(2^2\right)^3} = \boxed{}$

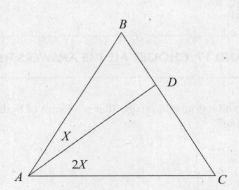

19. If ABC is an equilateral triangle, what is the measure of angle BAD?

$\boxed{}$

20. A bowling league is made up of 36 players in total, three-quarters of whom are adults. If 15 of the adults are men, what is the ratio of the number of adult women to the total number of players in the league?

(A) $\dfrac{1}{4}$

(B) $\dfrac{1}{3}$

(C) $\dfrac{5}{12}$

(D) $\dfrac{7}{12}$

(E) $\dfrac{4}{3}$

STOP

If you finish before the time is up, you may check your work in this section only.

SECTION 4: VERBAL REASONING

30 minutes • 20 questions

(The paper-and-pencil version will have 25 questions to be completed in 35 minutes.)

For each question, follow the specific directions and choose the best answer.

FOR QUESTIONS 1–5, CHOOSE <u>ONE</u> ANSWER FOR EACH BLANK. SELECT FROM THE APPROPRIATE COLUMN FOR EACH BLANK. CHOOSE THE ANSWER THAT BEST COMPLETES THE SENSE OF THE TEXT.

---

1. Myanmar's path to unity is complicated by its physical geography. Mountains and plateaus _____ contacts among different regions within the nation and with its neighbors, making commerce, communication, and human movement difficult.

(A) bar
(B) exhaust
(C) hamper
(D) blockade
(E) harm

2. Although there is much talk about the value of entrepreneurship, less is said about intrapreneurship, or entrepreneurial activity within an existing business. The creation of the iPhone by Apple is an example of intrapreneurship. The innovative spirit within Apple has produced a number of such _____ products.

(A) similar
(B) exceptional
(C) innovative
(D) excellent
(E) breakthrough

3. Although the scientific evidence for human activity as the cause of climate change appears (i) _____, many remain (ii) _____ that it's simply part of the natural climate cycle. One wonders in that case if they have considered the possibility of an Ice Age.

Blank (i)	Blank (ii)
(A) urgent	(D) implacable
(B) irrefutable	(E) inflexible
(C) uncontrollable	(F) adamant

4. Setting an eighteenth-century opera in the twenty-first century can make the opera seem both (i) _____ in some ways and (ii) _____ at the same time. How many modern households have servants popping out of closets singing?

Blank (i)
(A) strangely mundane
(B) really interesting
(C) definitively secular

Blank (ii)
(D) humorous
(E) diverting
(F) farcical

5. The (i) _____ nature of modern pop culture makes it easy to think of it as throwaway culture, here today and gone in "15 minutes," in a(n) (ii) _____ to Andy Warhol. However, it is possible that some elements of it may indeed be (iii) _____.

Blank (i)
(A) imperceptible
(B) discernible
(C) inconsequential

Blank (ii)
(D) illusion
(E) allusion
(F) paraphrase

Blank (iii)
(G) memorable
(H) prestigious
(I) prominent

FOR QUESTIONS 6–20, CHOOSE ONLY <u>ONE</u> ANSWER CHOICE UNLESS OTHERWISE INDICATED.

QUESTIONS 6–8 ARE BASED ON THE FOLLOWING PASSAGE.

In a *Washington Post* column, Abigail Trafford raised a question about the reportage of the health of presidents and presidential candidates. She noted that the past has made us cautious about White House cover-ups regarding presidents' illnesses. Yet she pointed to an interesting dilemma: that of the confidentiality of the doctor–patient relationship. How
5 can we reconcile the public's right to know with a public figure's right to this confidential relationship? Trafford brings up a suggestion posed by historian Robert H. Ferrell that "the personal physicians of the president be scrutinized by Congress." Ferrell believes that this would deter physicians from saying anything untruthful regarding the president's health. But Trafford points out that this would cause many doctors to reconsider becoming the
10 president's doctor if it meant being questioned by Congress. Robert S. Robins, a professor of political science at Tulane University, is quoted in the column as believing that this could result in the president's ending up with a choice he doesn't want. Robins says, "This could lead a president to forgo treatment rather than see his doctor or to secretly consult people he trusts." Trafford herself believes that some information from medical reports can also be
15 misleading if they are not followed up on.

6. This passage implies that if Congress were involved in the choice of the president's doctor, the

(A) president would no longer be able to consult Congress on certain crucial issues.

(B) American public would no longer need to know so many specific details about the health of the president.

(C) White House could no longer need to cover up incriminating details about the health of the president.

(D) president's doctor would totally respect the confidentiality of the president.

(E) president would not agree to accept the choice of doctor.

FOR QUESTION 7, CONSIDER EACH ANSWER CHOICE SEPARATELY AND SELECT <u>ALL</u> ANSWER CHOICES THAT APPLY.

---

7. Select the sentence in the passage that expresses an opinion of Abigail Trafford.

   (A) Yet she pointed to an interesting dilemma: that of the confidentiality of the doctor–patient relationship.

   (B) Trafford brings up a suggestion posed by historian Robert H. Ferrell that "the personal physicians of the president be scrutinized by Congress."

   (C) But Trafford points out that this would cause many doctors to reconsider becoming the president's doctor if it meant being questioned by Congress.

8. The author of the passage most likely agrees with which view as described in the passage?

   (A) Personal physicians of the president should be scrutinized by Congress.

   (B) The current system of choosing a doctor for the president is flawed.

   (C) The White House no longer covers up the health of the president quite so much as it used to.

   (D) There would probably be a smaller pool of doctors to choose from if Congress had a say in the choice of doctors for the president.

   (E) The press publishes too much information about the health of the president.

QUESTIONS 9 AND 10 ARE BASED ON THE FOLLOWING PASSAGE.

Contemporary forms of mixed media art have their genesis in some of the early twentieth-century works of Pablo Picasso and Georges Braque, who first called these works *collage*. Interestingly, the combination, or even agglutination, of visual media has been around at least since Byzantine artists added gold leaf to their paintings. Nevertheless, for the Cubist
5 practitioners, the new combinatory methods challenged old notions of what a painting could be, and the new freedoms they embodied served as approaches either to further fragmentation of the picture plane or to adding a third dimension, through texture and layering, to the two-dimensional surface. By introducing what Braque called displaced objects, such as pieces of cloth or multiple layers of newspaper, and what later artists called found objects,
10 early collage makers, as well as contemporary artists, pushed the painting envelope to ask new questions such as whether art could be made with already existing materials, to what extent the process of making art superseded or was of equal importance to the product, and to what degree art and the objects of real life were, indeed, separate. Scores of later artists further developed these questions and added new ones, including Marcel Duchamp, the great
15 conceptual artist; Robert Rauschenberg, a pioneer in the use of materials traditionally thought to be beyond the realm of art; and Rosemarie Trockel, producer of the first machine-knitted pictures, among other groundbreaking mixed media works.

9. Which of the following, if it were true, would weaken the author's argument?

(A) Leonardo DaVinci consciously mixed dry and wet visual media in order to make a statement about the limitations of Italian art.

(B) William Blake employed an early form of mixed media when he added vibrant watercolor washes to his prints.

(C) As early as the twelfth century, Japanese artists employed collage methods to make paper for painting.

(D) Rosemarie Trockel stretched knitted woolens over a frame to create some of her mixed media art.

(E) Duchamp, most famously known for Dadaism, proclaimed the purpose of art to be to please the mind, not the eye.

10. In the passage, "fragmentation" (lines 6–7) most nearly means

(A) pulverization.

(B) atomization.

(C) disruption.

(D) reducing.

(E) fracturing.

QUESTIONS 11–13 ARE BASED ON THE FOLLOWING PASSAGE.

Officially completed in 2003, the Human Genome Project was an international research collaboration that sought to identify the 20,000 to 25,000 genes of the human genome, to map the sequence of those genes, and to make that information freely available for scientific research. While these goals were largely met, the Project simultaneously opened a tap from
5 which a flood of ethical and legal questions poured.

For example, in 2013, knowledge derived from the Human Genome Project helped both to revive and put to rest issues related to the HeLa cell line. This cell line, derived from the tissue of a 1951 cancer patient without her consent or knowledge, was widely disseminated and has been in use for more than sixty years. This use was never without its ethical com-
10 plexities. Still, when researchers who had benefited from knowledge gained through the Human Genome Project posted the HeLa genome online in 2013, the situation became even more complicated because, by making the descendants' genetic information known to all, scientists further violated privacy rights. The problem was solved by placing the information in a controlled-access database that ensured its availability to researchers, yet also limited
15 it to specific terms of use.

In another case, the Supreme Court ruled in 2013 that naturally occurring DNA cannot be patented. Using information uncovered by the Human Genome Project, scientists and private companies have spent considerable resources extracting and sequencing human DNA that might help cure breast cancer and other diseases. The question arose of who owned such
20 extracted DNA in which genes are encoded. In the same decision, the Court acknowledged the importance of private research by deciding that modified DNA sequences are patent eligible.

FOR QUESTION 11, CONSIDER EACH ANSWER CHOICE SEPARATELY AND SELECT _ALL_ ANSWER CHOICES THAT APPLY.

---

11. What was significant about the Supreme Court's decision regarding DNA?
    (A) It repudiated some of the findings of the Human Genome Project.
    (B) It decided that companies could not patent naturally occurring DNA.
    (C) It decided ownership of human DNA.

12. The point of this passage is to
    (A) elucidate the timeline and sequence of accomplishments of the Human Genome Project.
    (B) detail two legal issues that arose as a result of findings of the Human Genome Project.
    (C) explain why the Human Genome Project continues to be an ethical minefield.
    (D) inform the reader about the purpose of the Human Genome Project and how it has changed international research.
    (E) delineate the conflict between private and public interest related to findings of the Human Genome Project.

13. Select the sentence in the passage that does NOT add support to the main idea.

(A) The question arose of who owned such extracted DNA in which genes are encoded.

(B) Still, when researchers who had benefited from knowledge gained through the Human Genome Project posted the HeLa genome online in 2013, the situation became even more complicated because, by making the descendants' genetic information known to all, scientists further violated privacy rights.

(C) The problem was solved by placing the information in a controlled-access database that ensured its availability to researchers, yet also limited it to specific terms of use.

(D) Officially completed in 2003, the Human Genome Project was an international research collaboration that sought to identify the 20,000 to 25,000 genes of the human genome, to identify the sequence of those genes, and to make that information freely available for scientific research

(E) Using information uncovered by the Human Genome Project, scientists and private companies have spent considerable resources extracting and sequencing human DNA that might help cure breast cancer and other diseases.

QUESTIONS 14 AND 15 ARE BASED ON THE FOLLOWING PASSAGE.

Historians are often drawn to studies of African American migration as a way of understanding the black urban experience, both past and present. But as Gretchen Lemke-Santangelo points out in her book *Abiding Courage*, black urban migration studies frequently focus on just the first two decades of the twentieth century and most often on the experiences of men.
5 Lemke-Santangelo sets out to generate "new perspectives on where and how social change takes place." Therefore, the subjects of her study are black Southern women who migrated to California's East Bay community during World War II. In this way, Lemke-Santangelo introduces the reader to a much lesser known (but no less important) aspect of African American migration history, namely the move from the South to the West, which occurred
10 with increasing frequency during the 1940s. Also, by underscoring the experience of women, Lemke-Santangelo demonstrates the importance of female participation in the migration process and the subsequent organization of the new community.

14. "Underscoring" (line 10) most nearly means

(A) overrating.

(B) accentuating.

(C) facilitating.

(D) recommending.

(E) obfuscating.

15. Select the sentence that restates the premise of the author's argument.

(A) African American women in the 1940s migrated in much greater numbers to the West than was previously understood.

(B) The experience of African American men in the Great Migration is entirely limited.

(C) Urban migration studies are not complete if they only focus on certain experiences.

(D) The first two decades of the twentieth century saw the greatest movement of African Americans out of the South.

(E) African American women were instrumental in organizing new communities in the West.

FOR QUESTIONS 16–19, CHOOSE THE TWO ANSWERS THAT BEST FIT THE MEANING OF THE SENTENCE AS A WHOLE AND RESULT IN TWO COMPLETED SENTENCES THAT ARE ALIKE IN MEANING.

---

16. Because of _____ wording in the press release, some people thought that the CEO was being ousted because of irregularities in accounting when it was the CFO who was fired.

    (A) explicit

    (B) mystifying

    (C) inscrutable

    (D) ambiguous

    (E) impressionable

    (F) equivocal

17. The particularly _____ caricature done by the artist's wife showed her intense, though sub-conscious, dislike of her husband.

    (A) amateurish

    (B) grotesque

    (C) imitative

    (D) bizarre

    (E) incompetent

    (F) mocking

18. The brainstorming activity resulted in _____ ideas for how to improve morale and boost productivity—but in the evaluative process, most were found not to be viable.

    (A) satisfactory

    (B) sufficient

    (C) requisite

    (D) elective

    (E) abundant

    (F) copious

19. The team's proposal was still in its early stages, but one could see from the _____ ideas how the study would take shape and probably result in useful conclusions.

    (A) inchoate

    (B) incipient

    (C) incoherent

    (D) incongruous

    (E) immutable

    (F) obtuse

QUESTION 20 IS BASED ON THE FOLLOWING PASSAGE.

Despite the seeming benefits to the environment that electric cars provide, there are still several challenges that need to be addressed if fully electric vehicles can be realistically expected to replace fuel-powered cars or hybrids in the foreseeable future. Currently, electric cars are limited by the output of their batteries and the current technology that uses energy produced

5   while braking to partly recharge the batteries. This technology would have to be improved in order to allow drivers to travel long distances. In addition, most plug-in electric cars take hours to recharge, which is another serious hindrance to their long-term use. Finally, in order for electric cars to become a truly workable option, charging and battery-exchange stations will have to be put in place everywhere cars are driven. These stations will also have to be

10   designed in such a way that their operation would not drain the power from municipal power grids. There is also the question of electricity production. As long as electric power plants continue to run on nonrenewable fossil fuels, such as coal, recharging electric cars will still release carbon emissions into the atmosphere, which is not a benefit to the environment.

20. What is the author's opinion about the future of electric cars?

(A) There are serious pros and cons to this issue.

(B) It is probably not a realistic option.

(C) Technology simply needs to improve.

(D) Electric cars do not solve the problem of carbon emissions in the atmosphere.

(E) The production of electricity will continue to rely on fossil fuels.

STOP

If you finish before the time is up, you may check your work in this section only.

SECTION 5: VERBAL REASONING

30 minutes • 20 questions

(The paper-and-pencil version will have 25 questions to be completed in 35 minutes.)

For each question, follow the specific directions and choose the best answer.

FOR QUESTIONS 1–5, CHOOSE <u>ONE</u> ANSWER FOR EACH BLANK. SELECT FROM THE APPROPRIATE COLUMN FOR EACH BLANK. CHOOSE THE ANSWER THAT BEST COMPLETES THE SENSE OF THE TEXT.

---

1. The _____ nature of the prototype site was apparent in that it kept crashing.

(A) immature
(B) rudimentary
(C) sophisticated
(D) elemental
(E) primal

2. Though (i) _____, the conclusions are based on actual economic activities as surveyed by a(n) (ii) _____ outside research team.

Blank (i)	Blank (ii)
(A) certainly credible	(D) impartial
(B) actually impervious	(E) interested
(C) seemingly implausible	(F) nonpartisan

3. In 1961, putting a man on the moon by 1970 seemed not only (i) _____, but also not (ii) _____ in the time frame.

Blank (i)	Blank (ii)
(A) improbable	(D) serviceable
(B) unusual	(E) feasible
(C) fortuitous	(F) durable

4. The (i) _____ of ideas for reforming the pension system was matched only by the (ii) _____ promises to do something—at some point.

Blank (i)	Blank (ii)
(A) sparsity	(D) keen
(B) derisory	(E) fatuous
(C) paucity	(F) vacuous

5. The success of the show's previews (i) _____ the need for reworking the script. However, the male lead (ii) _____ the playwright to expand his role, but the playwright (iii) _____ and nothing happened.

Blank (i)	Blank (ii)	Blank (iii)
(A) reduced	(D) taunted	(G) condescended
(B) obviated	(E) persisted	(H) demurred
(C) discarded	(F) importuned	(I) patronized

FOR QUESTIONS 6–20, CHOOSE ONLY ONE ANSWER CHOICE UNLESS OTHERWISE INDICATED.

QUESTIONS 6–8 ARE BASED ON THE FOLLOWING PASSAGE.

Demoralization and malaise resulting from factors as disparate as the loss of the war in Vietnam, the humiliation of the Watergate scandal, and inflation all prepared and fertilized the ground for what is now sometimes called the Reagan Revolution, a turning back of the clock on the dominant liberalism that had characterized the nation's politics almost since
5 FDR first took power. Elected and re-elected in the 1980s, Reagan preached a new and simplified conservative doctrine that included American exceptionalism as well as a focus on the problems of big government, or the "welfare state" as characterized by conservatives.

One might ask, however, how consistently conservative Reagan was, as he questioned, as early as 1964, and in an era of New Deal saturation in Washington, whether Americans
10 might "abandon the American Revolution and confess that a little intellectual elite in a far-distant capital can plan our lives for us better than we can plan them ourselves." At the same time, Reagan focused endlessly on two great threats to the United States: communism abroad and radicalism within. The radicalism, of course, often existed on college campuses and was the province of the "intellectual elite." Rising crime rates in U.S. cities also informed
15 and motivated his political policies. Less government, stronger defense, and renewed U.S. prestige were stated goals of the conservative revolution, while an anti-intellectual current often coursed fast and hard below its surface.

6. Select the sentence in the passage that is least central to the main idea.

(A) Elected and re-elected in the 1980s, Reagan preached a new and simplified conservative doctrine that included American exceptionalism as well as a focus on the problems of big government or the "welfare state" as characterized by conservatives.

(B) One might ask, however, how consistently conservative Reagan was, as he questioned, as early as 1964, and in an era of New Deal saturation in Washington, whether Americans might "abandon the American Revolution and confess that a little intellectual elite in a far-distant capital can plan our lives for us better than we can plan them ourselves."

(C) At the same time, Reagan focused endlessly on two great threats to United States: communism abroad and radicalism within.

(D) The radicalism, of course, existed often on college campuses, and was the province of the "intellectual elite."

(E) Rising crime rates in U.S. cities also informed and motivated his political polices.

FOR QUESTION 7, CONSIDER EACH ANSWER INDIVIDUALLY AND CHOOSE <u>ALL</u> THAT APPLY.

---

7. Which of the following, if it were true, would weaken the author's argument?

   (A) Reagan joined in and enlarged the battle against Great Society liberalism.

   (B) Reagan viewed antiwar and other protestors as antipatriotic naysayers.

   (C) Reagan turned often to conservative think tanks to provide ideological underpinning for his agenda.

8. The passage implies that Reagan would have said that

   (A) taxes needed to be cut for the sake of fairness.

   (B) the United States was the greatest country in the world.

   (C) recent advances resulting from the Civil Rights Movement had humanized and democratized America.

   (D) the Founders were representative Americans with representative American hopes and aspirations.

   (E) Soviet expansionism could not be tamed by force alone.

QUESTIONS 9 AND 10 ARE BASED ON THE FOLLOWING PASSAGE.

The evidence is manifold for why gene therapy is now used only for those diseases that have no cures. By means of gene therapy, a technique that is still in its infancy, researchers and medical geneticists seek to cure illness without drugs or surgery. They believe this might be accomplished in various ways, **such as through the inactivation of a mutated gene or**
5 **the replacement of a mutated gene with a healthy copy of that gene.** Theoretically, gene therapy surpasses all current medical science in both eloquence of promise and elegance of design. Yet, in its execution, results have been mixed at best, **as some patients have not rallied and at least one has died as a result.** Furthermore, even when gene therapy appears to be at its most promising, its cost is prohibitive. For example, the European Commission
10 recently approved a gene therapy treatment for a rare lipoprotein disease, but it will have an estimated cost of $1.6 million for a single patient.

9. Based on the passage, the author evidently believes that

   (A) there needs to be more funding for gene therapy.

   (B) gene therapy research and treatments should be abandoned.

   (C) replacement genes cannot be effective in curing disease.

   (D) the use of gene therapy should be expanded to more diseases.

   (E) the promise of gene therapy has not yet been realized.

10. What function do the two groups of words in bold type serve in this argument?

   (A) The first provides an explanation of evidence; the second provides an example of an argument.

   (B) The first supports an argument; the second provides an example of evidence.

   (C) The first provides support for the author's conclusion; the second confirms the support for the conclusion.

   (D) The first provides an example of evidence; the second provides an explanation of evidence.

   (E) The first presents an argument; the second provides evidence to support the argument.

QUESTIONS 11–13 ARE BASED ON THE FOLLOWING PASSAGE.

According to its own website, Wikipedia is "a free, web-based, collaborative, multilingual encyclopedia project." The obvious advantage of an online encyclopedia is that it can instantly produce articles on up-to-the-minute topics. However, unlike traditional encyclopedias, the millions of articles on Wikipedia can be edited by anyone who visits the website. Not
5 surprisingly, this means that a lot of information on Wikipedia is incorrect or biased, or has no other sources to back it up.

   If you use Wikipedia for research, you must proceed with caution. Some articles may contain serious factual errors, and some may be in the process of being edited. Some articles are deficient, presenting only one side of a controversial issue or detailing only certain parts
10 of a person's life. In addition, many contributors to Wikipedia do not cite their sources, which can make it difficult to judge the credibility of what is written. Sometimes Wikipedia articles reference other resources, such as news articles, which can be helpful, but these should be verified. In many cases, Wikipedia can provide a good starting point from which to begin your research, but it should never be your only source of information.

11. Select the sentence from the passage that best exemplifies the main point of the author.

   (A) Not surprisingly, this means that a lot of information on Wikipedia is incorrect, or biased, or has no other sources to back it up.

   (B) The obvious advantage of an online encyclopedia is that it can instantly produce articles on up-to-the-minute topics.

   (C) In many cases, Wikipedia can provide a good starting point from which to begin your research, but it should never be your only source of information.

   (D) In addition, many contributors to Wikipedia do not cite their sources, which makes it difficult to judge the credibility of what is written.

   (E) Some articles are deficient, presenting only one side of a controversial issue or detailing only certain parts of a person's life.

12. The passage implies all of the following statements EXCEPT

   (A) Wikipedia articles can contain useful information.

   (B) Wikipedia articles never provide backup source material.

   (C) you should not write a paper using only Wikipedia research.

   (D) contributors to Wikipedia articles may or may not cite their sources.

   (E) if sources are cited on Wikipedia, you might still not be able to tell who wrote each article.

FOR QUESTION 13, CONSIDER EACH ANSWER CHOICE INDIVIDUALLY AND CHOOSE <u>ALL</u> THAT APPLY.

13. Based on the article, how should a person use Wikipedia when doing research on a particular topic?

(A) Start with Wikipedia and then move on to more academic sources.

(B) Not use Wikipedia unless there is no other information to be found on the topic.

(C) Should only use those Wikipedia articles that contain citations.

QUESTIONS 14–16 ARE BASED ON THE FOLLOWING PASSAGE.

Of the novels published in the late eighteenth and early nineteenth centuries, Jane Austen's are among the few to survive to the present day. However, during her lifetime, Austen's novels were not read widely and were noted by just a few critics who reviewed them, mostly favorably. Not long after Austen died in 1817, most of her novels were all but forgotten.
5   This changed in 1870 with the publication of *Memoir of Jane Austen*, written by her nephew James Edward Austen-Leigh. Although his portrayal of Austen was somewhat misleading, the biography marked the beginning of a new appreciation of Jane Austen's works, both in scholarly and popular circles. Austen-Leigh portrayed his Aunt Jane as a woman who recorded the domestic rural life she lived in just as she saw it—with all its domestic crises
10 and affairs of the heart. This memoir had an immeasurable effect on the public perception of Jane Austen, and it dramatically increased her popularity. The publication of the memoir also spurred the reissue of Austen's novels, which became popular classics and in the twentieth century, popular movies and television programs.

14. Without publication of the *Memoir of Jane Austen*, which of the following would likely be true?

(A) Modern readers would not still be reading the works of Jane Austen.

(B) People's opinions of Jane Austen would not be based on misleading information.

(C) Jane Austen's books would not have been reissued.

(D) People would not know much about the lives of women in the nineteenth century.

(E) Modern readers would know much less about Jane Austen's life.

15. Based on the passage, what was the most significant result of the publication of the memoir?

(A) It introduced the reading public to the works of Jane Austen.

(B) It changed the public's perception of Jane Austen.

(C) It made her works a critical and popular success.

(D) It gave Austen's fans a glimpse into the real life of their beloved author.

(E) It recorded the details of late eighteenth-century rural life.

16. In the passage, "immeasurable" (line 10) means

(A) incalculable.

(B) monstrous.

(C) infinitesimal.

(D) intricate.

(E) convoluted.

practice test

FOR QUESTIONS 17–20, CHOOSE THE <u>TWO</u> ANSWERS THAT BEST FIT THE MEANING OF THE SENTENCE AS A WHOLE AND RESULT IN TWO COMPLETED SENTENCES THAT ARE ALIKE IN MEANING.

17. The sales revenue lost during the economic downturn can be _____ if every sales representative contacts one former or current customer and three new customers every day.

   (A) redeemed

   (B) returned

   (C) remediable

   (D) recovered

   (E) remediated

   (F) rectified

18. Wildlife in urban areas includes such non-typical city creatures as foxes that have increased as restaurants with their treat-filled garbage bags have _____.

   (A) gotten along

   (B) proliferated

   (C) progressed

   (D) advanced

   (E) multiplied

   (F) thrive

19. Big box stores cause anxiety among small towns and cities because they appear to be the harbingers of the _____ of the downtown business area as shoppers forsake local small businesses for the big discounters.

   (A) decline

   (B) degradation

   (C) depreciation

   (D) obsolescence

   (E) deterioration

   (F) retrogression

20. Some of the more unforgettable characters in literature are _____. Who can forget the servile, groveling, and fawning Uriah Heep or the Reverend Collins?

   (A) enthralling

   (B) curmudgeonly

   (C) surly

   (D) gruff

   (E) sycophantic

   (F) obsequious

STOP

If you finish before the time is up, you may check your work in this section only.

ANSWER KEY AND EXPLANATIONS

Section 1: Analytical Writing

Analyze an Issue

Model: 6 points out of 6

While increasing voter participation is a laudable goal, instituting a costly process of reminders to achieve this goal is as shortsighted as it is misdirected. There are two main reasons to oppose this policy. First, there are more important and more easily achievable goals, as well as "number one" responsibilities, of good citizenship to work toward. Second, it is fiscally irresponsible for the county government to invest resources in a misguided method of encouraging voter participation.

Voting is a vital responsibility in a democracy, but it is not necessarily the most important or "number one" responsibility of a democratic society or, more narrowly, of the citizens of Jackson County. If Jackson County is to undertake a costly, and most likely, complex process of reminding citizens of their civic duty, it might be more effective to focus on these civic duties: (1) participation in the community through active engagement, such as by doing volunteer work or becoming more responsible family members and neighbors; and (2) increasing the quality of community interactions by encouraging politeness in all actions and exchanges in the community, from driving in traffic to waiting one's turn in lines. After all, what would instill more civic pride in Jackson County: a once-a-year trip to the voting polls, or a more engaged populace, willing to turn its back on a few hours of TV a week to feed the hungry or improve the schools? What would raise the level of civility and, along with it, civic pride, more in Jackson County: fulfilling one's civic duty to vote at every election or the willing, open, and civil exchange of ideas between community members who disagree? Yes, getting people to the polls and in the habit of exercising their civic duty could be a source of civic pride; yet, there are actions that could demonstrate much more civic pride and, at the same time, have real and profound positive effects on the quality of life in Jackson County.

Furthermore, to carry out a program of voting reminders would be costly, as each and every household would have to be visited or called, and some would have to be called or visited repeatedly as many people are not home, do not answer calls from unknown or unfamiliar numbers, or do not answer their door. Besides, is the real goal of a good citizen simply to show up at the polls and pull a lever, or is the real goal to arrive at the voting booth fully informed? A system of reminders would do nothing to make sure that people are voting in an informed and thoughtful manner. A better way to involve voters would be to educate them on the ways in which the decision matters to them, or to make them aware of how much "skin" they have in the "game." If voters can be educated on the issues and see their relationship to their own needs and wants, as well as to the present and future of the place where they live, they are more likely to vote, and vote in an informed manner.

This essay scores 6 out of 6 because it

- **answers the task.** With thought and care, this essay clearly presents and explains the writer's views on the policy. It delves deep into the issue as it logically and persuasively develops alternatives to it and likely consequences of it.

- **is well supported.** The writer offers perceptive and persuasive support for why the proposed Jackson County initiative, just getting people out to vote, might not be a worthy goal. The author also offers thoughtful and well-developed support for why the program might be too costly and lead to results that are not worth the program's expense.

- **is well organized.** The opening paragraph clearly and concisely presents the writer's point of view in sentence one, and suggests the essay's structure in sentences two and three. Paragraphs two and three each develop one clear reason in support of the writer's point of view. Appropriate connections help unify the ideas, connect sentences and paragraphs, and ease the reader's passage through the response. While the essay lacks a formal conclusion, it also avoids repetition by coming to a logical close.

- **is fluid.** Word choices are sophisticated and effective, while sentences demonstrate qualities of directness and variety as well as parallelism.

- **observes the conventions of Standard Written English.**

Model: 1 point out of 6

At this point in time, the level of voter participation in America is truely embarassing. I read online that the United States ranked only 28th in the world in voter turnout at elections, and this ranking includes nations such as South Africa. A real problem for our democracy seeing as so few people are participating in the important decisions about who gets elected to office and runs our goverment as well as sevral issues that can be on the ballet at any given point in time. This is one reason why it is a **very good** idea to run a reminder program like the one suggested for Jackson County, it will finely bring alot of voters to the polls. More than that, as a reminder to anyone that might have forgot to vote that todays' the day when they need to go the polls. Another good reason for having a system of reminders being that people really do want to vote but can get mixed up about where and when.

This essay scores 1 out of 6 because it

- does not answer the task. While the writer does state a position, it is not fully explained, and possible alternatives to the policy or consequences of implementing it are omitted.

- lacks support and development. There is only one simple idea that might be categorized as support.

- has multiple errors in standard written English. While a few errors matter little in a well- organized and well-developed essay, the many and serious errors in this piece greatly hinder comprehension.

Analyze an Argument

Model: 6 points out of 6

Many questions would have to be answered before this argument could be considered even vaguely reasonable. The first of these questions relates to the nature of an attention span. For example, what is an attention span? Has anyone ever measured one? How can the parents and teachers make a recommendation based on something that no one has the first idea of how to quantify or track? Even if attention span were quantifiable or trackable, wouldn't the school have to have conducted baseline studies and then have collected statistics suggesting diminishment for students before drawing the conclusion that attention spans are diminishing? This fundamental question of what, actually, constitutes an attention span, and its so-called diminishment, is a fundamental problem with the argument, which undercuts the recommendation based on it. It is also just the first of the argument's multiple problems.

An almost equally fundamental problem with this argument is the assumption of a cause-and-effect relationship between "computers, computer games, and devices such as smart phones that integrate computer technology" and a perilous drop in attention spans. Again, just exactly who has measured this? More fundamentally, is such a cause and effect even measurable? Educators and parents may so dislike computer games or so gravely suspect them to be impediments to learning that they leap to the conclusion that one thing causes the other. Yet, is there actual evidence that this is the case? The question of actual cause and effect must also be answered before this recommendation can be logically evaluated.

In addition, the argument asserts that the parents and teachers who are making the recommendation to ban computers are motivated by the desire to prepare children for the serious work of the 21st century workplace. This part of the argument, too, leaves many questions unanswered. The parents and teachers seem to assume that workers will need to sustain a single focus to do the jobs of the future, but isn't it possible that the best skill set for the jobs ahead in a fast-changing world will include skills that allow workers to instantly switch their focus from one task to the next, to switch rapidly from idea to idea or situation to situation? Could it be possible that instead of intense concentration, or perhaps in addition to it, a certain distractibility or willingness to follow new links and ideas to wherever they lead will also be crucial for success? In other words, what is the evidence that the skills learned by playing computer games or communicating almost instantly are not going to be the necessary skills, or among the necessary skills, for success in future employment? The answers to these questions may completely contradict the recommendation or render it totally illogical.

In fact, nowhere does this argument actually tell what the effects of using computers actually are. Instead, the argument implies that this behavior is negative and rushes to the conclusion that it is putting students at risk. The argument then suggests banning certain computer technology under almost all circumstances. Thus the argument remains unreasonable even after questions of what constitutes an attention span are answered.

This essay scores 6 out of 6 because it

- **answers the task.** The writer poses and discusses many important questions that would have to be answered to decide whether the recommendation and the argument on which it is based are reasonable. The essay also explains how the answers to these questions will help to evaluate the argument.

- **is well supported.** Questions of what an attention span is, and the inability to measure it, are insightful, logical, and effective. The reader clearly sees how this central problem with the argument devalues the recommendation based on it. Other cogent discussion is offered throughout the essay. Particularly insightful are supporting details and explanation related to twenty-first-century workplace skills.
- **is well organized.** All four substantial paragraphs are logically organized and lead smoothly one to the next. The essay concludes as sure-footedly as it begins. Transitions and other elements of coherence ease the reader's passage through the essay.
- **is fluid and precise.** The writing is clear and direct; the voice is clear and assertive; the tone is appropriate. Word choices are apt and sentences are varied.
- **observes the conventions of Standard Written English.**

Model: 1 point out of 6

I am in complete agreement that attention spans are going down and educaters and parents need to do something drastic about it as soon as possible and not just in one school but across our hole nation. My main reason for agreeing with this view point is that I have a little brother who has been taking medication for attention deficit disorder for sevral years now. He was playing computer games before he was two years old and is totally obsessed with computers and technology now. But he is very antisocial and shows behaviors that are concerning to my parents and to his teachers, such as occasional outbursts that have harmed other kids he played with. Even his placement in the public school is in jepardy being due to his attention deficit disorder. I believe strongly that technology brung on his problems and therefore it should be banned. Not completely, but definitely in the classroom if it isn't absolutely necessary, such as in teaching search skills.

Their are so many students just like my little brother! When I went to elementry school, maybe one out of every five or six kids at least were taking some kind of medicine to un-hyper them. I recently read that now about 25% of all students in U.S. elementry schools take a drug for there attention deficit disorder. It is troubling to think of young children on these meds. When all we really need to do is pull the plug on the computer games and get back to traditional reading and other focused things in our classrooms. Kids will still get plenty of exposure to technology, such as computers, computer games, and cellphones, at home, and they will still keep up with there world. I'm not saying that technology isn't important or shouldn't be used. I'm not saying computer games aren't fun. But school should be a place, instead, for concentration on just one thing at a time. That being learning the skills needed for success in the 21st century workplace.

This essay scores 1 out of 6 because it

- **does not answer the task.** While an issue task requires you to agree or disagree, with or without qualification, an argument task requires you to evaluate the argument in some way. This essay does not do that. It ignores the instructions accompanying the prompt by raising no questions about the validity of the position. A response that does not answer the task completely cannot be successful no matter what other qualities it may demonstrate. This writer does show a certain fluency with the written word, but his or her lack of complete compliance with the instructions cannot earn more than a 1.

Section 2: Quantitative Reasoning

1. C	11. B	16. B, E, G
2. A	12. D	17. C
3. B	13. C	18. $\dfrac{29}{12}$
4. D	14. A	
5. B	15. A, D, E	19. $\dfrac{7}{15}$
6. D		20. C
7. B		
8. B		
9. E		
10. C		

Question

1.

Quantity A	Quantity B
$6(4)\left(\dfrac{1}{2}\right)^2$	6

(A) Quantity A is greater.

(B) Quantity B is greater.

(C) The two quantities are equal.

(D) The relationship cannot be determined from the information given.

Answer Explanation

The correct answer is (C). Simplify $6(4)\left(\dfrac{1}{2}\right)^2$.

$$6(4)\left(\frac{1}{2}\right)^2$$
$$= 6(4)\left(\frac{1}{4}\right)$$
$$= 6$$

So, both quantities are the same, 6.

Question

$$xy = 12$$

2.   Quantity A   Quantity B
        $(3x)(2y)$ 60

(A) Quantity A is greater.

(B) Quantity B is greater.

(C) The two quantities are equal.

(D) The relationship cannot be determined from the information given.

Answer Explanation

The correct answer is (A). Simplify and substitute.

$(3x)(2y)$

$= 6xy$

$= 6(12)$

$= 72$

So, 72 is greater than 60.

Question

3.   Quantity A   Quantity B

        40% of $\dfrac{5}{8}$ 60% of $\dfrac{3}{4}$

(A) Quantity A is greater.

(B) Quantity B is greater.

(C) The two quantities are equal.

(D) The relationship cannot be determined from the information given.

Answer Explanation

The correct answer is (B). Evaluate:

$\left(\dfrac{2}{5}\right)\left(\dfrac{5}{8}\right) = \dfrac{10}{40} = \dfrac{1}{4}$

$\left(\dfrac{3}{5}\right)\left(\dfrac{3}{4}\right) = \dfrac{9}{20}$

Question

$$x \neq 0$$

4.

Quantity A	Quantity B
$\dfrac{5}{x}$	$5x$

(A) Quantity A is greater.

(B) Quantity B is greater.

(C) The two quantities are equal.

(D) The relationship cannot be determined from the information given.

Answer Explanation

The correct answer is (D). Pick numbers to find the answer. Be sure to pick a positive, a negative, and a fraction to test all possibilities.

$x = 1$

$\dfrac{5}{1} = 5$ and $5(1) = 5$, which are equal.

$x = -1$

$\dfrac{5}{-1} = -5$ and $5(-1) = -5$, which are equal.

$x = \dfrac{1}{5}$

$\dfrac{5}{\frac{1}{5}} = 25$ and $5\left(\dfrac{1}{5}\right) = 5$, which are not equal.

Question

$$x + 3 = 4x - 2$$
$$5y - 2 = 2y + 1$$

5.

Quantity A	Quantity B
$3x$	$6y$

(A) Quantity A is greater.

(B) Quantity B is greater.

(C) The two quantities are equal.

(D) The relationship cannot be determined from the information given.

Answer Explanation

The correct answer is (B). Solve the equations:

$$x + 3 = 4x - 2$$
$$-3x = -5$$
$$x = \frac{5}{3}$$
$$5y - 2 = 2y + 1$$
$$3y = 3$$
$$y = 1$$

$$3x = 3\left(\frac{5}{3}\right) = 5$$
$$6y = 6(1) = 6$$

Question

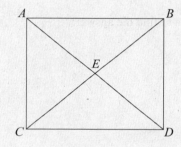

6.   Quantity A   Quantity B
      The area of *AEC*   The area of *CED*

(A) Quantity A is greater.
(B) Quantity B is greater.
(C) The two quantities are equal.
(D) The relationship cannot be determined from the information given.

Answer Explanation

The correct answer is (D). Because there are no parameters given for the shape *ABCD*, the areas can't be determined.

Question

7.   <u>Quantity A</u>   <u>Quantity B</u>
                         5x   180

   (A) Quantity A is greater.

   (B) Quantity B is greater.

   (C) The two quantities are equal.

   (D) The relationship cannot be determined from the information given.

Answer Explanation

The correct answer is (B). Solve to find the answer:

$x + 2x + 75 = 180$

$\quad 3x + 75 = 180$

$\qquad\quad 3x = 105$

$\qquad\quad\ x = 35$

$5x = 5(35) = 175$

Question

A 2,475-square-foot house sells for $475,000. The broker's fee is 6%.

8.   <u>Quantity A</u>   <u>Quantity B</u>
                  The broker's fee $31,000

   (A) Quantity A is greater.

   (B) Quantity B is greater.

   (C) The two quantities are equal.

   (D) The relationship cannot be determined from the information given.

Answer Explanation

The correct answer is (B). Estimate 6% of $475,000 which will be a little less than 6% of $500,000, which is $30,000 which is less than $31,000.

QUESTIONS 9–11 REFER TO THE GRAPH BELOW.

Sales by type 2010

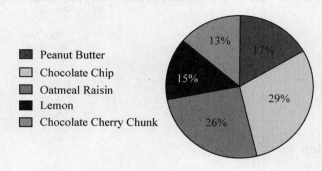

Peanut Butter
Chocolate Chip
Oatmeal Raisin
Lemon
Chocolate Cherry Chunk

Question

9. The two most popular types of cookies were what percentage of sales?

   (A) 26
   (B) 29
   (C) 42
   (D) 44
   (E) 55

Answer Explanation

The correct answer is (E). Evaluate:

$$29 + 26 = 55$$

Question

10. How many different types of cookies do NOT have chocolate in them?

    (A) 1
    (B) 2
    (C) 3
    (D) 4
    (E) 5

Answer Explanation

The correct answer is (C). Peanut butter, oatmeal raisin, and lemon are chocolate-less. This may seem like a simple question, but some people will try to figure out the shadings on the graph so they can work out percentages before they realize what the question is asking; others will look for the cookies with chocolate chips and select "2" as the answer.

Question

11. If total sales for the year were $94,480, what was the total amount sold of the third most popular cookie?

    (A) $12,543

    (B) $16,062

    (C) $17,727

    (D) $24,980

    (E) $27,589

Answer Explanation

The correct answer is (B). Turn the words into equations, using the information from the pie chart.

17% of $94,480 = 0.17(94,480) = $16,062

Question

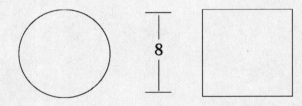

12. The above circle has a diameter of 8, and the square has a perimeter of 32. What is the difference in the area between the two?

    (A) 11.82

    (B) 12.96

    (C) 13.33

    (D) 13.76

    (E) 15.97

Answer Explanation

The correct answer is (D). Find the areas of the two figures and subtract.

Area of a square $h(w)$:

$8(8) = 64$

Area of a circle πr^2:

$3.14(4)^2$

$3.14(16) = 50.24$

$64 - 50.24 = 13.76$

Question

13. Lacy receives 45% of the commission of every painting she sells. If she recently sold a painting for $256,000 and received a commission of $7,488, what was the total rate of commission?

    (A) 0.016
    (B) 0.029
    (C) 0.065
    (D) 0.067
    (E) 0.076

Answer Explanation

The correct answer is (C). Turn the problem into equations and solve:

$$7,488 \div 0.45 = 16,640$$
$$16,640 \div 256,000 = 0.065$$

Question

14. The expression $(4x + 7y)^2 - (2x - 3y)^2$ is equivalent to
    (A) $4(3x^2 + 17xy + 10y^2)$
    (B) $16x^2 + 10y^2$
    (C) $12x^2 + 12xy - 9y^2$
    (D) $x^2 + 12xy + 40y^2$
    (E) None of the above

Answer Explanation

The correct answer is (A). You can simplify the expression:

$$(4x + 7y)^2 - (2x - 3y)^2$$
$$= 16x^2 + 56xy + 49y^2 - (4x^2 - 12xy + 9y^2)$$
$$= 16x^2 + 56xy + 49y^2 - 4x^2 + 12xy - 9y^2$$
$$= 12x^2 + 68xy + 40y^2$$
$$= 4(3x^2 + 17xy + 10y^2)$$

Or do small parts of the math and check the answers:

$$16x^2 - 4x^2 = 12x^2 = 4(3x^2)$$

Choices (A) and (C) have this. Now do another part of the math:

$$48y^2 - 9y^2 = 40y^2 = 4(10y^2)$$

Of choices (A) and (C), only choice (A) has this.

Question

15. If *ab* and *cd* are parallel, what other angles are equal to 115°?

 (A) 1
 (B) 2
 (C) 3
 (D) 4
 (E) 5
 (F) 6
 (G) 7

Answer Explanation

The correct answers are (A), (D), and (E). The other angles equal to 115° are 1, 4, 5.

Question

16. What are the next three numbers in the sequence 0, 1, 3, 7, 15, 31,…

- (A) 57
- (B) 63
- (C) 72
- (D) 111
- (E) 127
- (F) 295
- (G) 255
- (H) 511

Answer Explanation

The correct answers are (B), (E), and (G). Determine the relationship of the sequence:

$$2^{n-1} - 1$$

$$2^{7-1} - 1 = 2^6 - 1 = 64 - 1 = 63$$

$$2^{8-1} - 1 = 2^7 - 1 = 128 - 1 = 127$$

$$2^{9-1} - 1 = 2^8 - 1 = 256 - 1 = 255$$

Question

17. The average (arithmetic mean) score of Sanjay's six biology tests is 88. The sum of the scores of his first four tests is 332. What is the average score of his last two tests?

- (A) 83
- (B) 93
- (C) 98
- (D) 196
- (E) The average score cannot be determined from the information given.

Answer Explanation

The correct answer is (C). The average of all six test scores is 88, so the combined score for the six tests is 88×6, or 528. Subtracting 332 from 528 leaves 196, the combined score for the last two tests. Thus, the average score for those two tests is 196 divided by 2, which equals 98.

Question

18. $\dfrac{1}{2} + \dfrac{1}{3} + \dfrac{3}{4} + \dfrac{5}{6} =$

Give your answer as a fraction.

Answer Explanation

The correct answer is $\dfrac{29}{12}$. Solve: $\dfrac{1}{2} + \dfrac{1}{3} + \dfrac{3}{4} + \dfrac{5}{6} = \dfrac{6}{12} + \dfrac{4}{12} + \dfrac{9}{12} + \dfrac{10}{12} = \dfrac{29}{12}$

Question

19. On a rugby team of 15 players, the ratio of forwards to backs is $\dfrac{8}{7}$. What is the ratio of backs to total number of players?

Give your answer as a fraction.

Answer Explanation

The correct answer is $\dfrac{7}{15}$. The ratio is 7 backs to 15 players.

Question

20. If an acre is equal to 43,560 square feet, how many acres are there in 362,985 square feet?
    (A) 6.33
    (B) 7.33
    (C) 8.33
    (D) 9.33
    (E) 10.33

Answer Explanation

The correct answer is (C). $362{,}985 \div 43{,}560 = 8.33$

Section 3: Quantitative Reasoning

1. C	11. A	16. A, B, C, D
2. A	12. E	17. D
3. A	13. C	18. 64
4. C	14. A	19. 20
5. A	15. C	20. B
6. C		
7. D		
8. B		
9. B		
10. C		

Question

$$\frac{5}{8}x = \frac{1}{12}$$

1.
Quantity A	Quantity B
x	$\frac{2}{15}$

(A) Quantity A is greater.

(B) Quantity B is greater.

(C) The two quantities are equal.

(D) The relationship cannot be determined from the information given.

Answer Explanation

The correct answer is (C). Work backwards to find the answer.

$$x = \frac{5}{8}\left(\frac{2}{15}\right) = \frac{10}{120} = \frac{1}{12}$$

Question

2.   Quantity A   Quantity B
                    $\dfrac{0.00008}{0.00006}$ 0.75

  (A) Quantity A is greater.

  (B) Quantity B is greater.

  (C) The two quantities are equal.

  (D) The relationship cannot be determined from the information given.

Answer Explanation

The correct answer is (A). Evaluate to find the answer.

$$\dfrac{0.00008}{0.00006} = 1.333$$

Question

3.   Quantity A   Quantity B
                    The area of the trapezoid   80

  (A) Quantity A is greater.

  (B) Quantity B is greater.

  (C) The two quantities are equal.

  (D) The relationship cannot be determined from the information given.

Answer Explanation

The correct answer is (A). Calculate the area:

$$area = h\left(\dfrac{b_1 + b_2}{2}\right)$$

$$= 9\left(\dfrac{6 + 14}{2}\right) = 9(10) = 90$$

Question

4.   Quantity A   Quantity B

        The mean of angles x, y, z 60

(A) Quantity A is greater.

(B) Quantity B is greater.

(C) The two quantities are equal.

(D) The relationship cannot be determined from the information given.

Answer Explanation

The correct answer is (C). Work backwards:

$180 = x + y = z$

$\dfrac{180}{3} = 60$

Question

5.   Quantity A   Quantity B

          $\sqrt{(66)(27)}$ (8)(4.9)

(A) Quantity A is greater.

(B) Quantity B is greater.

(C) The two quantities are equal.

(D) The relationship cannot be determined from the information given.

Answer Explanation

The correct answer is (A). Use your calculator:

$\sqrt{(66)(27)} > \sqrt{(64)(25)}$

$\sqrt{(64)(25)} = (8)(5)$

$\quad(8)(5) > (8)(4.9)$

Question

$$xy = 3.2$$

6.   Quantity A   Quantity B
                    $1.5x(4.6y)$ 22.08

(A) Quantity A is greater.

(B) Quantity B is greater.

(C) The two quantities are equal.

(D) The relationship cannot be determined from the information given.

Answer Explanation

The correct answer is (C). Simplify and substitute:

$xy = 3.2$

$1.5x(4.6y) =$

$\quad 6.9xy =$

$\quad 6.9(3.2) = 22.08$

Question

7.   Quantity A   Quantity B
         Time it takes a bicycle to travel   Time it takes a car to travel
                    15 miles   60 miles

(A) Quantity A is greater.

(B) Quantity B is greater.

(C) The two quantities are equal.

(D) The relationship cannot be determined from the information given.

Answer Explanation

The correct answer is (D). Because there are no parameters given for the problem, no relationship can be determined.

Question

An apple costs $0.25. An orange costs $0.35. A pear costs $\frac{1}{2}$ of the sum of an apple and an orange.

8.

Quantity A	Quantity B
5 apples and 5 oranges	12 pears

(A) Quantity A is greater.

(B) Quantity B is greater.

(C) The two quantities are equal.

(D) The relationship cannot be determined from the information given.

Answer Explanation

The correct answer is (B). Set up expressions and evaluate:

A pear costs $\frac{.25 + .35}{2} = .30$

5 apples and 5 oranges cost $5(.25) + 5(.35) = \$3.00$

12 pears cost $12(.30) = \$3.60$

Question

9. A card player selects two cards at random and without replacement from a standard deck of 52 playing cards. What is the probability that the player will select at least one ace?

(A) $\frac{1}{1326}$

(B) $\frac{33}{221}$

(C) $\frac{188}{221}$

(D) $\frac{144}{169}$

(E) $\frac{12}{13}$

Answer Explanation

The correct answer is (B). The probability you're looking for equals 1 minus the probability that the player selects no aces at all. On the first draw, the probability that he does not select an ace is $\frac{48}{52}$, and on the second draw that probability is $\frac{47}{51}$. Thus, the probability you're looking for is:

$$P(\text{at least 1 ace}) = 1 - P(\text{no ace})$$
$$= 1 - \frac{48}{52} \times \frac{47}{51}$$
$$= 1 - \frac{12}{13} \times \frac{47}{51}$$
$$= 1 - \frac{4}{13} \times \frac{47}{17}$$
$$= 1 - \frac{188}{221}$$
$$= \frac{33}{221}$$

Question

10. What is the solution to the inequality $(4-2x)\dfrac{1}{2} \le \dfrac{1-x}{3}$?

(A) $x \le \dfrac{5}{2}$

(B) $x > \dfrac{5}{2}$

(C) $x \ge \dfrac{5}{2}$

(D) $x \ge 2$

(E) $x \ge \dfrac{2}{5}$

Answer Explanation

The correct answer is (C). Solve the inequality:

$$(4-2x)\frac{1}{2} \le \frac{1-x}{3}$$
$$2 - x \le \frac{1-x}{3}$$
$$6 - 3x \le 1 - x$$
$$2x \ge 5$$
$$x \ge \frac{5}{2}$$

QUESTIONS 11–13 REFER TO THE BAR GRAPH BELOW.

Pollutants Entering the Ocean

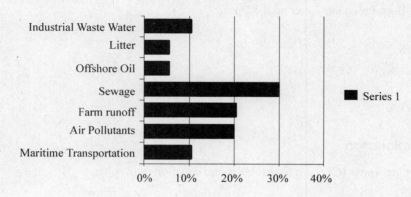

Question

11. What is the percentage of offshore oil compared to all pollutants?

    (A) 5%

    (B) 10%

    (C) 15%

    (D) 20%

    (E) 30%

Answer Explanation

The correct answer is (A). To find the answer, read the graph: 5%.

Question

12. Sewage, litter, and air pollution make up what percentage of the whole?

    (A) 5%

    (B) 15%

    (C) 30%

    (D) 45%

    (E) 55%

Answer Explanation

The correct answer is (E).

$30\% + 5\% + 20\% = 55\%$

Question

13. If air pollution is eliminated from the graph, what percentage would sewage be of the new graph "Water-Born Pollutants Entering the Ocean"?

(A) 24%

(B) 28%

(C) 37.5%

(D) 40%

(E) 44.5%

Answer Explanation

The correct answer is (C). Turn the problem into equations and solve:

$$\frac{x}{100} = \frac{30}{80}$$
$$x = \frac{3000}{80}$$
$$x = 37.5$$

Question

14. A receptionist greeted the following numbers of people during one work week: 4, 19, 21, 18, 23. What is the mean of the number of people she greeted?

(A) 17

(B) 19

(C) 20

(D) 21

(E) 85

Answer Explanation

The correct answer is (A). The mean is the average. The sum of the numbers is 85. There are 5 data points. Dividing the sum by the number of data points results in 17.

Question

15. A farmer owns a square property and wants to sell a lot formed by dividing the lot in half, both lengthwise and widthwise. If the resulting lot has a perimeter of 888,000 feet, what is the area of the original lot?

(A) 179,936,000,000 sq. ft.

(B) 185,926,000,000 sq. ft.

(C) 197,136,000,000 sq. ft.

(D) 200,000,000,000 sq. ft.

(E) 212,386,000,000 sq. ft.

Answer Explanation

The correct answer is (C). Drawing a diagram will help you to visualize the problem. Then calculate:

$888,000 \div 4 = 222,000$

$444,000 \times 444,000 = 197,136,000,000$ or 197.136 billion

Question

16. If p and q are integers, and n is an odd integer that is a factor of both $2p$ and q, then n is a factor of which of the following?

    (A) $p+q$

    (B) p

    (C) $\dfrac{pq}{n}$

    (D) $|2p-q|$

Answer Explanation

The correct answers are (A), (B), (C), and (D). Note that, if $2p$ is divisible by n, an odd integer, then p is divisible by n as well, since 2 is not divisible by n. Thus, choice (B) is correct. You can rewrite choice (A) as $n\left(\dfrac{p}{n}+\dfrac{q}{n}\right)$, where $\dfrac{p}{n}$ and $\dfrac{q}{n}$ are both integers since n is a factor of both p and q. Thus, choice (A) also is correct. The same is true of choice (C): the product of p and q contains at least two factors of n, so dividing pq by n removes only one of those two factors, leaving a number that has another factor of n. Finally, you can see that choice (D) is correct by factoring n out of $|2p-q|$ to arrive at $\left|n\left(\dfrac{2p}{n}-\dfrac{q}{n}\right)\right|$, where both $\dfrac{2p}{n}$ and $\dfrac{q}{n}$ are integers.

Question

17. The local baseball team employs at least 3 times as many pitchers as catchers, but never more than 11 players total. Pitchers make an average of $45,000, and catchers make an average of $30,000. Which of the following amounts are the possible averages for all the pitchers and catchers, rounded to the nearest dollar?

   (A) 30,000

   (B) 35,899

   (C) 40,375

   (D) 41,250

   (E) 41,956

   (F) 42,273

   (G) 43,743

   (H) 45,000

Answer Explanation

The correct answer is (D). The only combination of pitchers and catchers that apply are 3 pitchers/1 catcher and 6 pitchers/2 catchers. Both combinations leave you with the same answer: 41,250.

$$\frac{3(45,000) + 30,000}{3 + 1}$$

$$= \frac{135,000 + 30,000}{4}$$

$$= \frac{165,000}{4}$$

$$= 41,250$$

$$\frac{6(45,000) + 2(30,000)}{6 + 2}$$

$$= \frac{270,000 + 60,000}{8}$$

$$= \frac{330,000}{8}$$

$$= 41,250$$

The answer must be 41,250.

Question

18. $\dfrac{\left(\left(2^3\right)^2\right)^2}{\left(2^2\right)^3} = \boxed{}$

Answer Explanation

The correct answer is 64. Calculate:

$$\frac{\left(\left(2^3\right)^2\right)^2}{\left(2^2\right)^3}$$

$$=\frac{\left(8^2\right)^2}{\left(4\right)^3}$$

$$=\frac{64^2}{64}$$

$$=64$$

Question

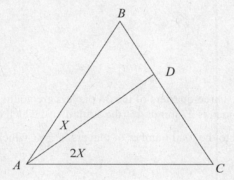

19. If ABC is an equilateral triangle, what is the measure of angle BAD?

Answer Explanation

The correct answer is 20. Turn the information into an equation and solve.

The angles in an equilateral triangle are equal to 60, so:

$60 = 2x + x$

$60 = 3x$

$x = 20$

Question

20. A bowling league is made up of 36 players in total, three-quarters of whom are adults. If 15 of the adults are men, what is the ratio of the number of adult women to the total number of players in the league?

   (A) $\dfrac{1}{4}$

   (B) $\dfrac{1}{3}$

   (C) $\dfrac{5}{12}$

   (D) $\dfrac{7}{12}$

   (E) $\dfrac{4}{3}$

Answer Explanation

The correct answer is (B). Three-quarters of the 36 players are adults, so the number of adults is 27. The number of adult women is 27 minus 15 (the adult men), which equals 12. Thus, the ratio of the number of adult women to the total number of players is $\dfrac{12}{36}$, which equals $\dfrac{1}{3}$.

Section 4: Verbal Reasoning

1. C	11. B, C	16. D, F
2. E	12. B	17. B, D
3. A, F	13. D	18. E, F
4. A, F	14. B	19. A, B
5. C, E, G	15. C	20. A
6. C		
7. C		
8. D		
9. A		
10. E		

Question

1. Myanmar's path to unity is complicated by its physical geography. Mountains and plateaus _____ contacts among different regions within the nation and with its neighbors, making commerce, communication, and human movement difficult.

(A) bar
(B) exhaust
(C) hamper
(D) blockade
(E) harm

Answer Explanation

The correct answer is (C). Choice (A), "bar," is incorrect because the final part of the second sentence indicates that carrying on commerce, communication, and human movement is difficult, but not impossible, which it would be if they were barred, or blocked, from occurring. For this reason, choice (D), "blockade" is also incorrect; it means "to block, to keep from passing" and often has a legal or quasi-legal meaning. Choice (B), "exhaust," may be true about trekking over mountains, but it doesn't fit the context, so eliminate it. Choice (E) is incorrect because "harm" means "to injure in some way, physically, morally, or mentally," and that doesn't fit with the effects of geography.

Question

2. Although there is much talk about the value of entrepreneurship, less is said about intrapreneurship, or entrepreneurial activity within an existing business. The creation of the iPhone by Apple is an example of intrapreneurship. The innovative spirit within Apple has produced a number of such _____ products.

(A) similar
(B) exceptional
(C) innovative
(D) excellent
(E) breakthrough

Answer Explanation

The correct answer is (E). Tone will help you answer this question. While choice (A), "similar," makes sense, it doesn't fit with the tone of the phrase "innovative spirit" or the idea of entrepreneurship. Choice (B), "exceptional," also makes sense and is closer to the sense of "innovative spirit," so it might work. However, choice (E), "breakthrough," meaning "a major achievement," better fits the tone of the sentence. Choice (C), "innovative," might work to create parallelism, but breakthrough indicates a higher level of creativity and importance. Choice (D), "excellent," indicates quality, but not necessarily inventiveness.

Question

3. Although the scientific evidence for human activity as the cause of climate change appears (i) _____, many remain (ii) _____ that it's simply part of the natural climate cycle. One wonders in that case if they have considered the possibility of an Ice Age.

Blank (i)	Blank (ii)
(A) urgent	(D) implacable
(B) irrefutable	(E) inflexible
(C) uncontrollable	(F) adamant

Answer Explanation

The correct answers are (A) and (F). Answer Blank (i): When you consider the two blanks, it becomes apparent that choice (A), "urgent," meaning "requiring immediate action" fits the sense of the sentence, which is about differences in opinion, not the need for action. Choice (B), "irrefutable," which means "impossible to disprove, unassailable," doesn't fit the sense. Climate change may or may not be "uncontrollable," but that's not the point of the sentence.

Answer Blank (ii): Choice (F), "adamant," meaning "firm, stubbornly unyielding, not open to reason or persuasion" fits the sense. Choice (D), "implacable," means "not capable of pleasing, unforgiving" and doesn't fit the sense. "Inflexible," choice (E), is a synonym of "implacable" and, therefore, can be eliminated. Note also that choices (D) and (E) don't sound "right" to the ear; both are usually followed by a preposition, not a clause.

Question

4. Setting an eighteenth-century opera in the twenty-first century can make the opera seem both (i) _____ in some ways and (ii) _____ at the same time. How many modern households have servants popping out of closets singing?

Blank (i)
(A) strangely mundane
(B) really interesting
(C) definitively secular

Blank (ii)
(D) humorous
(E) diverting
(F) farcical

Answer Explanation

The correct answers are (A) and (F). Answer Blank (i): This is a question where it may make more sense to complete the second blank first to help you figure out the first. In that case, you would be able to eliminate "really interesting" because it doesn't counterbalance choice (F), "farcical," the answer for the second blank. Choice (C), "definitively secular," meaning "worldly, earthly," doesn't make sense.

Answer Blank (ii): While choice (D), "humorous," might fit the sense, choice (F), "farcical," is a better answer considering the next sentence, which describes a situation that you might find in a farce; a farce tells its story through exaggerated situations and characters, improbable plot lines, and slapstick. Choice (E) is incorrect because "diverting" indicates something that might be only mildly humorous, and the context indicates something much funnier.

Question

5. The (i) _____ nature of modern pop culture makes it easy to think of it as throwaway culture, here today and gone in "15 minutes," in a(n) (ii) _____ to Andy Warhol. However, it is possible that some elements of it may indeed be (iii) _____.

Blank (i)
(A) imperceptible
(B) discernible
(C) inconsequential

Blank (ii)
(D) illusion
(E) allusion
(F) paraphrase

Blank (iii)
(G) memorable
(H) prestigious
(I) prominent

Answer Explanation

The correct answers are (C), (E), and (G). Answer Blank (i): Choices (A) and (B) are opposites, so either both are incorrect, or one is correct. In this case both are incorrect. Choice (A), "imperceptible," means "difficult to perceive or subtle" and choice (B), "discernible," means "able to perceive." Neither fits the sense that modern pop culture is so insubstantial that it can be easily forgotten. Choice (C), "inconsequential," fits this sense.

Answer Blank (ii): Choice (E), "allusion," is "an indirect reference to someone or something." An "illusion," choice (D), is "a mistaken perception of reality" and doesn't make sense in the sentence. Choice (F), a "paraphrase," is a restating in your own words of what someone else said and is incorrect because the phrase "15 minutes" is quoted.

Answer Blank (iii): Because of the reference to time in the first sentence, choice (G), "memorable," meaning "lasting, worth remembering," matches the sense. Neither choices (H) nor (I) include the sense of time. Choice (H), "prestigious," means "being esteemed or honored," and choice (I), "prominent," means "to stand out, be widely known."

QUESTIONS 6–8 ARE BASED ON THE FOLLOWING PASSAGE.

In a *Washington Post* column, Abigail Trafford raised a question about the reportage of the health of presidents and presidential candidates. She noted that the past has made us cautious about White House cover-ups regarding presidents' illnesses. Yet she pointed to an interesting dilemma: that of the confidentiality of the doctor–patient relationship. How
5   can we reconcile the public's right to know with a public figure's right to this confidential relationship? Trafford brings up a suggestion posed by historian Robert H. Ferrell that "the personal physicians of the president be scrutinized by Congress." Ferrell believes that this would deter physicians from saying anything untruthful regarding the president's health. But Trafford points out that this would cause many doctors to reconsider becoming the
10 president's doctor if it meant being questioned by Congress. Robert S. Robins, a professor of political science at Tulane University, is quoted in the column as believing that this could result in the president's ending up with a choice he doesn't want. Robins says, "This could lead a president to forgo treatment rather than see his doctor or to secretly consult people he trusts." Trafford herself believes that some information from medical reports can also be
15 misleading if they are not followed up on.

Question

6. This passage implies that if Congress were involved in the choice of the president's doctor, the
   (A) president would no longer be able to consult Congress on certain crucial issues.
   (B) American public would no longer need to know so many specific details about the health of the president.
   (C) White House would no longer need to cover up incriminating details about the health of the president.
   (D) president's doctor would totally respect the confidentiality of the president.
   (E) president would not agree to accept the choice of doctor.

Answer Explanation

The correct answer is (C). The passage implies that if Congress chose the president's doctor, the doctor would tell the truth about the president's health so the White House would not be able to cover up serious health issues. Choice (A) is incorrect because nowhere in the passage does it discuss how the president would consult with Congress on other issues. Choice (B) is incorrect because this is not implied in the passage and actually contradicts its main point. Choice (D) might seem correct because it is very likely true, but it is not what is implied by the statement presented in the question. Choice (E) is incorrect because the passage neither says nor implies that the president's doctor would be chosen by any one other than the president. The passage only says Congress would question the doctor, not confirm him.

Question

7. Select the sentence in the passage that expresses an opinion of Abigail Trafford.

   (A) Yet she pointed to an interesting dilemma: that of the confidentiality of the doctor–patient relationship.

   (B) Trafford brings up a suggestion posed by historian Robert H. Ferrell that "the personal physicians of the president be scrutinized by Congress."

   (C) But Trafford points out that this would cause many doctors to reconsider becoming the president's doctor if it meant being questioned by Congress.

Answer Explanation

The correct answer is (C). Trafford expresses an opinion by presuming that doctors would reconsider becoming the president's doctor. This cannot be proven. Choices (A) and (B) are incorrect because they are merely pointing out information, not stating her opinion.

Question

8. The author of the passage most likely agrees with which view as described in the passage?

   (A) Personal physicians of the president should be scrutinized by Congress.

   (B) The current system of choosing a doctor for the president is flawed.

   (C) The White House no longer covers up the health of the president quite so much as it used to.

   (D) There would probably be a smaller pool of doctors to choose from if Congress had a say in the choice of doctors for the president.

   (E) The press publishes too much information about the health of the president.

Answer Explanation

The correct answer is (D). Based on the opinions of the people quoted in the article, we can draw the conclusion that the author feels that if Congress could question the president's doctor, fewer doctors would want the job. Choice (A) is incorrect because though this is presented as an opinion in the passage, there is no indication that the author agrees with it. Choice (B) seems correct, except that nowhere in the passage does it suggest that at this time doctors are *chosen* for the president. Choice (C) is not addressed in the passage, and choice (E) is incorrect because this is not implied in the passage.

QUESTIONS 9 AND 10 ARE BASED ON THE FOLLOWING PASSAGE.

Contemporary forms of mixed media art have their genesis in some of the early twentieth-century works of Pablo Picasso and Georges Braque, who first called these works *collage*. Interestingly, the combination, or even agglutination, of visual media has been around at least since Byzantine artists added gold leaf to their paintings. Nevertheless, for the Cubist
5   practitioners, the new combinatory methods challenged old notions of what a painting could be, and the new freedoms they embodied served as approaches either to further fragmentation of the picture plane or to adding a third dimension, through texture and layering, to the two-dimensional surface. By introducing what Braque called displaced objects, such as pieces of cloth or multiple layers of newspaper, and what later artists called found objects,
10 early collage makers, as well as contemporary artists, pushed the painting envelope to ask new questions such as whether art could be made with already existing materials, to what extent the process of making art superseded or was of equal importance to the product, and to what degree art and the objects of real life were, indeed, separate. Scores of later artists further developed these questions and added new ones, including Marcel Duchamp, the great
15 conceptual artist; Robert Rauschenberg, a pioneer in the use of materials traditionally thought to be beyond the realm of art; and Rosemarie Trockel, producer of the first machine-knitted pictures, among other groundbreaking mixed media works.

Question

9. Which of the following, if it were true, would weaken the author's argument?

(A) Leonardo DaVinci consciously mixed dry and wet visual media in order to make a statement about the limitations of Italian art.

(B) William Blake employed an early form of mixed media when he added vibrant watercolor washes to his prints.

(C) As early as the twelfth century, Japanese artists employed collage methods to make paper for painting.

(D) Rosemarie Trockel stretched knitted woolens over a frame to create some of her mixed media art.

(E) Duchamp, most famously known for Dadaism, proclaimed the purpose of art to be to please the mind, not the eye.

Answer Explanation

The correct answer is (A). The passage argues that mixed media generally and collage specifically challenged the ideas of what a painting was or could be. The only choice that suggests this same kind of breaking of the "rules" or transcendence of limits is the example of DaVinci. Choices (B) and (C) are incorrect because these methods are much like adding goldleaf: yes, they resulted in mixed media, but, at least insofar as the choices are worded, neither can be interpreted as a conscious rebellion against existing art. Choices (D) and (E) help explain the author's argument about how and why mixed media challenged existing artistic limitations.

Question

10. In the passage, "fragmentation" (lines 6–7) most nearly means

(A) pulverization.

(B) atomization.

(C) disruption.

(D) reducing.

(E) fracturing.

Answer Explanation

The correct answer is (E). This reference to the picture plane suggests it is broken up in a way that makes it no longer flat or no longer consistent with traditional perspective; "fractured" best suggests this breaking up of both line and expectation. Choice (A) is wrong because it suggests destruction; choices (B) and (D) are wrong because they state or suggest reduction. Choice (C) is incorrect because there is no sense of interrupting progress or of aiming specifically to create disorder.

QUESTIONS 11–13 ARE BASED ON THE FOLLOWING PASSAGE.

Officially completed in 2003, the Human Genome Project was an international research collaboration that sought to identify the 20,000 to 25,000 genes of the human genome, to map the sequence of those genes, and to make that information freely available for scientific research. While these goals were largely met, the Project simultaneously opened a tap from

5　which a flood of ethical and legal questions poured.

　　For example, in 2013, knowledge derived from the Human Genome Project helped both to revive and put to rest issues related to the HeLa cell line. This cell line, derived from the tissue of a 1951 cancer patient without her consent or knowledge, was widely disseminated and has been in use for more than sixty years. This use was never without its ethical com-

10　plexities. Still, when researchers who had benefited from knowledge gained through the Human Genome Project posted the HeLa genome online in 2013, the situation became even more complicated because, by making the descendants' genetic information known to all, scientists further violated privacy rights. The problem was solved by placing the information in a controlled-access database that ensured its availability to researchers, yet also limited

15　it to specific terms of use.

　　In another case, the Supreme Court ruled in 2013 that naturally occurring DNA cannot be patented. Using information uncovered by the Human Genome Project, scientists and private companies have spent considerable resources extracting and sequencing human DNA that might help cure breast cancer and other diseases. The question arose of who owned such

20　extracted DNA in which genes are encoded. In the same decision, the Court acknowledged the importance of private research by deciding that modified DNA sequences are patent eligible.

Question

11. What was significant about the Supreme Court's decision regarding DNA?

(A) It repudiated some of the findings of the Human Genome Project.

(B) It decided that companies could not patent naturally occurring DNA.

(C) It decided ownership of human DNA.

Answer Explanation

The correct answers are (B) and (C). In this case, the Supreme Court ruled on questions related to a new ethical and legal issue: who owns DNA? It decided that if a company spends considerable resources extracting and studying DNA, it still does not own or cannot patent that DNA. Instead, companies can only patent those DNA sequences that they have modified. Choice (A) is incorrect because the passage does not state or imply that anything the Supreme Court did in any way invalidated or repudiated the findings of the Human Genome Project.

Question

12. The point of this passage is to
    (A) elucidate the timeline and sequence of accomplishments of the Human Genome Project.
    (B) detail two legal issues that arose as a result of findings of the Human Genome Project.
    (C) explain why the Human Genome Project continues to be an ethical minefield.
    (D) inform the reader about the purpose of the Human Genome Project and how it has changed international research.
    (E) delineate the conflict between private and public interest related to findings of the Human Genome Project.

Answer Explanation

The correct answer is (B). This passage explains in paragraph 1 that the Human Genome Project resulted in a flood of legal and ethical issues and then details two of those issues in paragraphs 2 and 3. Choices (A) and (D) are incorrect because the central idea of the passage is not about the purposes or accomplishments of the Human Genome Project; instead, it is primarily about what happened in its wake. Choice (C) is tempting but incorrect because the bulk of the passage is about two specific cases and not about why, in general, the Human Genome Project has led to ethical and legal issues. Choice (E) is incorrect because this conflict is a relatively minor detail treated only in part of the last paragraph.

Question

13. Select the sentence in the passage that does NOT add support to the main idea.
    (A) The question arose of who owned such extracted DNA in which genes are encoded.
    (B) Still, when researchers who had benefited from knowledge gained through the Human Genome Project posted the HeLa genome online in 2013, the situation became even more complicated because, by making the descendants' genetic information known to all, scientists further violated privacy rights.
    (C) The problem was solved by placing the information in a controlled-access database that ensured its availability to researchers, yet also limited it to specific terms of use.
    (D) Officially completed in 2003, the Human Genome Project was an international research collaboration that sought to identify the 20,000 to 25,000 genes of the human genome, to identify the sequence of those genes, and to make that information freely available for scientific research
    (E) Using information uncovered by the Human Genome Project, scientists and private companies have spent considerable resources extracting and sequencing human DNA that might help cure breast cancer and other diseases.

Answer Explanation

The correct answer is (D). All the other choices are significant details that support the thesis of the passage. But choice (D), though true, does not support the idea that the accomplishments of the Human Genome Project led to complex legal and ethical issues. Instead, it briefly sums up what the Human Genome Project was.

QUESTIONS 14 AND 15 ARE BASED ON THE FOLLOWING PASSAGE.

Historians are often drawn to studies of African American migration as a way of understanding the black urban experience, both past and present. But as Gretchen Lemke-Santangelo points out in her book *Abiding Courage*, black urban migration studies frequently focus on just the first two decades of the twentieth century and most often on the experiences of men.
5 Lemke-Santangelo sets out to generate "new perspectives on where and how social change takes place." Therefore, the subjects of her study are black Southern women who migrated to California's East Bay community during World War II. In this way, Lemke-Santangelo introduces the reader to a much lesser known (but no less important) aspect of African American migration history, namely the move from the South to the West, which occurred
10 with increasing frequency during the 1940s. Also, by underscoring the experience of women, Lemke-Santangelo demonstrates the importance of female participation in the migration process and the subsequent organization of the new community.

Question

14. "Underscoring" (line 10) most nearly means
    - (A) overrating.
    - (B) accentuating.
    - (C) facilitating.
    - (D) recommending.
    - (E) obfuscating.

Answer Explanation

The correct answer is (B). "Underscoring" means the same as "accentuating," meaning "emphasizing." Choice (A) is incorrect because "overrating" means "overvaluing," and that is the opposite of the author's opinion of Lemke-Santangelo's work. Choice (C) is incorrect because "facilitating" means "helping," which is not the same as emphasizing. Choice (D) is incorrect because "recommending" means "praising," which is not the same as emphasizing. Choice (E) is incorrect because "obfuscating" means "disguising or making something confused," which is the opposite of emphasizing.

Question

15. Select the sentence that restates the premise of the author's argument.

   (A) African American women in the 1940s migrated in much greater numbers to the West than was previously understood.

   (B) The experience of African American men in the Great Migration is entirely limited.

   (C) Urban migration studies are not complete if they only focus on certain experiences.

   (D) The first two decades of the twentieth century saw the greatest movement of African Americans out of the South.

   (E) African American women were instrumental in organizing new communities in the West.

Answer Explanation

The correct answer is (C). The author's thesis is that African American urban migration studies tend to focus on the experience of only one group (men) and only during a certain time period (first two decades of the twentieth century) and are, therefore, incomplete. Choices (A), (D), and (E) may all be true statements, but these points are not what the author is arguing in the passage. Choice (B) is incorrect because this point is not raised in the passage.

Question

16. Because of _____ wording in the press release, some people thought that the CEO was being ousted because of irregularities in accounting when it was the CFO who was fired.

   (A) explicit

   (B) mystifying

   (C) inscrutable

   (D) ambiguous

   (E) impressionable

   (F) equivocal

Answer Explanation

The correct answers are (D) and (F). Lack of clarity caused confusion, so choice (D), "ambiguous," and choice (F), "equivocal," are the correct answers. They mean "unclear, open to different interpretations." Had the wording been explicit, choice (A), that is, clearly stated, there would have been no confusion. Choices (B) and (C), "mystifying" and "inscrutable," are synonyms; "inscrutable" means "unclear, difficult to understand," "mystifying" means to involve in mystery or obscurity which doesn't apply in this sentence. The ambiguous press release may have made an impression, but it wasn't impressionable, choice (E), that is, nothing made an impression or influenced the press release.

Question

17. The particularly _____ caricature done by the artist's wife showed her intense, though sub-conscious, dislike of her husband.

(A) amateurish

(B) grotesque

(C) imitative

(D) bizarre

(E) incompetent

(F) mocking

Answer Explanation

The correct answers are (B) and (D). "Grotesque," choice (B), describes something that is mis-shapen or distorted in a strange or horrifying way, which could indicate intense dislike. Choice (D), "bizarre," means something "grotesquely strange." Choices (A) and (E), "amateurish" and "incompetent," are synonyms but don't fit the sense of intense dislike the way grotesque and bizarre do. Nor does choice (F), "mocking," meaning "to make fun of." Choice (C), "imitative," might work except that it doesn't fit the sense either.

Question

18. The brainstorming activity resulted in _____ ideas for how to improve morale and boost productivity—but in the evaluative process, most were found not to be viable.

(A) satisfactory

(B) sufficient

(C) requisite

(D) elective

(E) abundant

(F) copious

Answer Explanation

The correct answers are (E) and (F). Choices (E) and (F), "abundant" and "copious," mean "plentiful, ample" and fit within the context. Choice (A), "satisfactory," might seem like a reasonable answer on a quick read, but it doesn't fit with the fact that the ideas weren't viable; if they weren't viable, they couldn't have been satisfactory. Choice (B),"sufficient," meaning "enough," could fit the sense, but it has no synonym in the list of answers. Neither do choice (C), "requisite," meaning "required," nor choice (D), "elective," meaning "optional."

Question

19. The team's proposal was still in its early stages, but one could see from the _____ ideas how the study would take shape and probably result in useful conclusions.

    (A) inchoate

    (B) incipient

    (C) incoherent

    (D) incongruous

    (E) immutable

    (F) obtuse

Answer Explanation

The correct answers are (A) and (B). "Inchoate," choice (A), means "at an early stage," similar to the meaning of "incipient," choice (B), meaning "emerging, coming into being." Choice (C), "incoherent," means "muddled, confused" and doesn't fit the context of ideas taking shape. Choice (D), "incongruous," means "conflicting, contradictory, or even inappropriate" and doesn't fit the sense of ideas coming together. Choice (E), "immutable," means "unchanging." Choice (F), "obtuse," means "slow to understand, lacking in intelligence or quickness." Both have to do with ideas or concepts but are neither appropriate in this sentence nor synonymous.

QUESTION 20 IS BASED ON THE FOLLOWING PASSAGE.

Despite the seeming benefits to the environment that electric cars provide, there are still several challenges that need to be addressed if fully electric vehicles can be realistically expected to replace fuel-powered cars or hybrids in the foreseeable future. Currently, electric cars are limited by the output of their batteries and the current technology that uses energy produced
5 while braking to partly recharge the batteries. This technology would have to be improved in order to allow drivers to travel long distances. In addition, most plug-in electric cars take hours to recharge, which is another serious hindrance to their long-term use. Finally, in order for electric cars to become a truly workable option, charging and battery-exchange stations will have to be put in place everywhere cars are driven. These stations will also have to be
10 designed in such a way that their operation would not drain the power from municipal power grids. There is also the question of electricity production. As long as electric power plants continue to run on nonrenewable fossil fuels, such as coal, recharging electric cars will still release carbon emissions into the atmosphere, which is not a benefit to the environment.

Question

20. What is the author's opinion about the future of electric cars?

    (A) There are serious pros and cons to this issue.

    (B) It is probably not a realistic option.

    (C) Technology simply needs to improve.

    (D) Electric cars do not solve the problem of carbon emissions in the atmosphere.

    (E) The production of electricity will continue to rely on fossil fuels.

Answer Explanation

The correct answer is (A). We can infer from the passage that the author thinks there are serious issues to be worked out to determine the future of electric cars. Choice (B) is incorrect because the author never implies this. Choice (C) is incorrect because the author does not conclude that technology is the only solution. Choice (D) is incorrect because the author never implies this. Instead the author says that at the current time, this is true. Choice (E) is incorrect because the author does not make any conclusions about this fact.

Section 5: Verbal Reasoning

1. B	11. C	16. A
2. C, D	12. B	17. A, D
3. A, E	13. A	18. B, E
4. C, F	14. E	19. A, E
5. B, F, H	15. B	20. E, F
6. A		
7. C		
8. B		
9. E		
10. D		

Question

1. The _____ nature of the prototype site was apparent in that it kept crashing.

(A) immature
(B) rudimentary
(C) sophisticated
(D) elemental
(E) primal

Answer Explanation

The correct answer is (B). "Rudimentary," choice (B), means "at the earliest stages of development" and fits the sense of the sentence. Choice (A), "immature," means "not fully developed," but usage will help you decide that it's not the correct answer. "Immature" is typically used to describe an animate being, not an inanimate object. Choice (C) is incorrect because "sophisticated" doesn't fit the prototype as described, though it might describe the concept of the site. Choice (D), "elemental," means "basic or essential" and doesn't make sense; had the choice been "elementary," that would fit the context. Choice (E), "primal," is similar in meaning to "elemental" so it's incorrect, too.

Question

2. Though (i) _____, the conclusions are based on actual economic activities as surveyed by a(n) (ii) _____ outside research team.

Blank (i)	Blank (ii)
(A) certainly credible	(D) impartial
(B) actually impervious	(E) interested
(C) seemingly implausible	(F) nonpartisan

Answer Explanation

The correct answers are (C) and (D). Answer Blank (i): This set of answers is a good reason to read the sentence and all the answer choices carefully. "Certainly credible," choice (A), could be the answer except that it doesn't fit the sense. The sentence needs the opposite of "credible" because the word "though" sets up a contrast relationship. Choice (B), "actually impervious," means "unaffected, invulnerable, unmoved" and makes no sense. Choice (C), "seemingly implausible," means "difficult to believe, unlikely" and fulfills the contrast relationship in the sentence.

Answer Blank (ii): It might have been easier to fill the second blank first to help you identify the contrast relationship. The clue for this part of the sentence is the word "outside." Choice (D) is correct because "impartial" means "unbiased, unprejudiced, fair." Choice (E), "interested," doesn't fit the sense because an interested party would be one that showed some interest or connection to the survey. Choice (F), "nonpartisan," is incorrect because it refers to political parties, and no parties are mentioned in the sentence.

Question

3. In 1961, putting a man on the moon by 1970 seemed not only (i) _____, but also not (ii) _____ in the time frame.

Blank (i)	Blank (ii)
(A) improbable	(D) serviceable
(B) unusual	(E) feasible
(C) fortuitous	(F) durable

Answer Explanation

The correct answers are (A) and (E). Answer Blank (i): Once you figure out all the negatives in the sentence, you'll see that you need two words that balance each other. Choice (A), "improbable," means "unlikely to happen." Choice (B), "unusual," meaning "out of the ordinary, odd" doesn't strike the right significance in describing putting a human on the moon. Choice (C) is incorrect because "fortuitous" means "happening by chance, unplanned," the opposite of requirements for the space program.

Answer Blank (ii): Choice (E), "feasible," meaning "possible, viable" balances "improbable" when you add the "not" from the sentence in front of "feasible." Choice (D), "serviceable," means "usable, capable of lasting for a long time." The latter definition makes it a synonym for choice (F), "durable," but you're not looking for synonyms, and those words don't make sense in the context.

Question

4. The (i) _____ of ideas for reforming the pension system was matched only by the (ii) _____ promises to do something—at some point.

Blank (i)	Blank (ii)
(A) sparsity	(D) keen
(B) derisory	(E) fatuous
(C) paucity	(F) vacuous

Answer Explanation

The correct answers are (C) and (F). Answer Blank (i): You're looking for two words that balance each other. Choice (A) is incorrect because "sparsity" refers to "thinly scattered, not densely populated or crowded," so it doesn't make sense in the context of ideas. Choice (B) is incorrect because "derisory" is an adjective meaning "laughable, ridiculous," and while the ideas might be that, the word doesn't make sense in the construction (it has no noun to modify). Choice (C), "paucity" meaning "scarcity, small number" makes sense.

Answer Blank (ii): The phrase "to do something—at some point" indicates an unwillingness or inability to act and coupled with "paucity" in the first part of the sentence makes choice (F), "vacuous," meaning "lacking in substance or meaning or ideas" the correct choice. Choice (D), "keen," means "intellectually sharp, quick-witted" and is the opposite of the sense that the phrase plus the word "paucity" create. "Fatuous," choice (E), means "foolish, silly in a self-satisfied way" and doesn't fit the sense of the sentence.

Question

5. The success of the show's previews (i) _____ the need for reworking the script. However, the male lead (ii) _____ the playwright to expand his role, but the playwright (iii) _____ and nothing happened.

Blank (i)	Blank (ii)	Blank (iii)
(A) reduced	(D) taunted	(G) condescended
(B) obviated	(E) persisted	(H) demurred
(C) discarded	(F) importuned	(I) patronized

Answer Explanation

The correct answers are (B), (F), and (H). Answer Blank (i): Choice (B), "obviated," means "to have made unnecessary," and presumably successful preview performances would have made any rewrites unnecessary. Choice (A), "reduced," is incorrect based on the sense that if something was successful, no changes would be necessary, not just fewer. Choice (C), "discarded," means "to have thrown out, to have gotten rid of," and doesn't quite fit the sense of the sentence.

Answer Blank (ii): This is another instance where usage can help you determine the answer. Choice (E), "persisted," means "to have been insistent, to have held firm to a purpose"; however, "persisted" doesn't take an object, so "persisted him" doesn't make sense (the clause would need to read "persisted in asking the playwright . . ."). If the actor wanted the playwright to rewrite his role, he would hardly taunt him, that is, try to provoke him by mocking him or criticizing him, so eliminate choice (D). Choice (F), "importuned," means "to have repeatedly asked for, to plead," so it's the correct answer.

Answer Blank (iii): "To demur" is "to object to something that a person doesn't want to do, to be reluctant" so choice (H) is the best answer. Choice (G), "condescended," means "to patronize someone, to act graciously toward someone considered beneath one's social or economic level" and there is no indication of that in the passage. Choice (I), "patronized," is similar to "condescended" and is, therefore, incorrect.

QUESTIONS 6–8 ARE BASED ON THE FOLLOWING PASSAGE.

Demoralization and malaise resulting from factors as disparate as the loss of the war in Vietnam, the humiliation of the Watergate scandal, and inflation all prepared and fertilized the ground for what is now sometimes called the Reagan Revolution, a turning back of the clock on the dominant liberalism that had characterized the nation's politics almost since
5 FDR first took power. Elected and re-elected in the 1980s, Reagan preached a new and simplified conservative doctrine that included American exceptionalism as well as a focus on the problems of big government, or the "welfare state" as characterized by conservatives.

One might ask, however, how consistently conservative Reagan was, as he questioned, as early as 1964, and in an era of New Deal saturation in Washington, whether Americans
10 might "abandon the American Revolution and confess that a little intellectual elite in a far-distant capital can plan our lives for us better than we can plan them ourselves." At the same time, Reagan focused endlessly on two great threats to the United States: communism abroad and radicalism within. The radicalism, of course, often existed on college campuses and was the province of the "intellectual elite." Rising crime rates in U.S. cities also informed
15 and motivated his political policies. Less government, stronger defense, and renewed U.S. prestige were stated goals of the conservative revolution, while an anti-intellectual current often coursed fast and hard below its surface.

Question

6. Select the sentence in the passage that is least central to the main idea.

   (A) Elected and re-elected in the 1980s, Reagan preached a new and simplified conservative doctrine that included American exceptionalism as well as a focus on the problems of big government or the "welfare state" as characterized by conservatives.

   (B) One might ask, however, how consistently conservative Reagan was, as he questioned, as early as 1964, and in an era of New Deal saturation in Washington, whether Americans might "abandon the American Revolution and confess that a little intellectual elite in a far-distant capital can plan our lives for us better than we can plan them ourselves."

   (C) At the same time, Reagan focused endlessly on two great threats to United States: communism abroad and radicalism within.

   (D) The radicalism, of course, existed often on college campuses, and was the province of the "intellectual elite."

   (E) Rising crime rates in U.S. cities also informed and motivated his political polices.

Answer Explanation

The correct answer is (E). All the other choices are significant points that explain Reagan's conservative policies, but Choice (E), rising crime rates, is not specific to a conservative agenda. Although Choice (A) veers a bit to show a somewhat radical disagreement with founding principles, it is used to lead up to the anti-intellectualism of Reagan's presidency and part of the conservative revolution.

Question

7. Which of the following, if it were true, would weaken the author's argument?

   (A) Reagan joined in and enlarged the battle against Great Society liberalism.

   (B) Reagan viewed antiwar and other protestors as antipatriotic naysayers.

   (C) Reagan turned often to conservative think tanks to provide ideological underpinning for his agenda.

Answer Explanation

The correct answer is (C). A person who regards intellectuals as suspect would not logically turn to them to develop or bolster his own ideology. Choice (A) is consistent with the idea of Reagan turning "back the clock" on "dominant liberalism." Choice (B) is broadly supportive of passage ideas about squelching protest.

Question

8. The passage implies that Reagan would have said that
    (A) taxes needed to be cut for the sake of fairness.
    (B) the United States was the greatest country in the world.
    (C) recent advances resulting from the Civil Rights Movement had humanized and democratized America.
    (D) the Founders were representative Americans with representative American hopes and aspirations.
    (E) Soviet expansionism could not be tamed by force alone.

Answer Explanation

The correct answer is (B). The author says that Reagan was a proponent of U.S. exceptionalism, which, while suggestive of many meanings related to U.S. democracy, is often used to mean "greatest country." The author also says that the restoration of U.S. prestige was a goal of the conservative revolution that Reagan spearheaded. Choice (A) might seem correct, but the passage suggests the motive would be cutting big government and not liberal fair-mindedness. Choice (C) might also seem correct, but this was never implied in the passage. Choices (D) and (E) run counter to passage facts, which suggest that the Founders were not like ordinary people and that the communist threat could be tamed by means of "stronger defense."

QUESTIONS 9 AND 10 ARE BASED ON THE FOLLOWING PASSAGE.

The evidence is manifold for why gene therapy is now used only for those diseases that have no cures. By means of gene therapy, a technique that is still in its infancy, researchers and medical geneticists seek to cure illness without drugs or surgery. They believe this might be accomplished in various ways, **such as through the inactivation of a mutated gene or**
5   **the replacement of a mutated gene with a healthy copy of that gene.** Theoretically, gene therapy surpasses all current medical science in both eloquence of promise and elegance of design. Yet, in its execution, results have been mixed at best, **as some patients have not rallied and at least one has died as a result.** Furthermore, even when gene therapy appears to be at its most promising, its cost is prohibitive. For example, the European Commission
10   recently approved a gene therapy treatment for a rare lipoprotein disease, but it will have an estimated cost of $1.6 million for a single patient.

Question

9. Based on the passage, the author evidently believes that
   (A) there needs to be more funding for gene therapy.
   (B) gene therapy research and treatments should be abandoned.
   (C) replacement genes cannot be effective in curing disease.
   (D) the use of gene therapy should be expanded to more diseases.
   (E) the promise of gene therapy has not yet been realized.

Answer Explanation

The correct answer is (E). Although the author's opinion is not explicitly stated, we can infer, based on the details presented, that the author sees many problems with the use of gene therapy, including its cost and its failures. Choice (A) is incorrect because funding isn't addressed in the passage. Choice (B) might seem correct because the author clearly names problems of gene therapy; however, the author does not go so far as to suggest its abandonment. Choices (C) and (D) are incorrect because they are not stated or implied in the passage.

Question

10. What function do the two groups of words in bold type serve in this argument?
    (A) The first provides an explanation of evidence; the second provides an example of an argument.
    (B) The first supports an argument; the second provides an example of evidence.
    (C) The first provides support for the author's conclusion; the second confirms the support for the conclusion.
    (D) The first provides an example of evidence; the second provides an explanation of evidence.
    (E) The first presents an argument; the second provides evidence to support the argument.

Answer Explanation

The correct answer is (D). The first section in bold is an example of evidence, and the second bold portion is an explanation of evidence. Choice (A) is incorrect because it has these reversed. Choice (B) is incorrect because the first section helps define gene therapy through examples. Choice (C) is incorrect because neither portion in bold type deals with the author's conclusion. Choice (E) is incorrect because, while the second portion in bold supports the author's argument, the first portion does not present the argument.

QUESTIONS 11–13 ARE BASED ON THE FOLLOWING PASSAGE.

According to its own website, Wikipedia is "a free, web-based, collaborative, multilingual encyclopedia project." The obvious advantage of an online encyclopedia is that it can instantly produce articles on up-to-the-minute topics. However, unlike traditional encyclopedias, the millions of articles on Wikipedia can be edited by anyone who visits the website. Not
5 surprisingly, this means that a lot of information on Wikipedia is incorrect or biased, or has no other sources to back it up.

If you use Wikipedia for research, you must proceed with caution. Some articles may contain serious factual errors, and some may be in the process of being edited. Some articles are deficient, presenting only one side of a controversial issue or detailing only certain parts
10 of a person's life. In addition, many contributors to Wikipedia do not cite their sources, which can make it difficult to judge the credibility of what is written. Sometimes Wikipedia articles reference other resources, such as news articles, which can be helpful, but these should be verified. In many cases, Wikipedia can provide a good starting point from which to begin your research, but it should never be your only source of information.

Question

11. Select the sentence from the passage that best exemplifies the main point of the author.

   (A) Not surprisingly, this means that a lot of information on Wikipedia is incorrect, or biased, or has no other sources to back it up.

   (B) The obvious advantage of an online encyclopedia is that it can instantly produce articles on up-to-the-minute topics.

   (C) In many cases, Wikipedia can provide a good starting point from which to begin your research, but it should never be your only source of information.

   (D) In addition, many contributors to Wikipedia do not cite their sources, which makes it difficult to judge the credibility of what is written.

   (E) Some articles are deficient, presenting only one side of a controversial issue or detailing only certain parts of a person's life.

Answer Explanation

The correct answer is (C). This is the main point of the passage. The other choices are all important details about Wikipedia, but only choice (C) clearly states the thesis that Wikipedia, while useful as a starting point for research, should never be the only source of information.

Question

12. The passage implies all of the following statements EXCEPT

   (A) Wikipedia articles can contain useful information.

   (B) Wikipedia articles never provide backup source material.

   (C) you should not write a paper using only Wikipedia research.

   (D) contributors to Wikipedia articles may or may not cite their sources.

   (E) if sources are cited on Wikipedia, you might still not be able to tell who wrote each article.

Answer Explanation

The correct answer is (B). The passage implies that *sometimes* Wikipedia articles do not provide valid backup source material, but it does not imply that this is always the case. The other choices are all incorrect because each one is true and can be proven using the details of the passage.

Question

13. Based on the article, how should a person use Wikipedia when doing research on a particular topic?

 (A) Start with Wikipedia and then move on to more academic sources.

 (B) Not use Wikipedia unless there is no other information to be found on the topic.

 (C) Should only use those Wikipedia articles that contain citations.

Answer Explanation

The correct answer is (A). The passage suggests you can start with Wikipedia at first, but always move on to other sources. Choice (B) is incorrect because the point of the article is that Wikipedia should never be the only source to use. Choice (C) is incorrect because the passage points out that Wikipedia articles are a good starting point as long as other sources are used.

QUESTIONS 14–16 ARE BASED ON THE FOLLOWING PASSAGE.

Of the novels published in the late eighteenth and early nineteenth centuries, Jane Austen's are among the few to survive to the present day. However, during her lifetime, Austen's novels were not read widely and were noted by just a few critics who reviewed them, mostly favorably. Not long after Austen died in 1817, most of her novels were all but forgotten.
5 This changed in 1870 with the publication of *Memoir of Jane Austen*, written by her nephew James Edward Austen-Leigh. Although his portrayal of Austen was somewhat misleading, the biography marked the beginning of a new appreciation of Jane Austen's works, both in scholarly and popular circles. Austen-Leigh portrayed his Aunt Jane as a woman who recorded the domestic rural life she lived in just as she saw it—with all its domestic crises
10 and affairs of the heart. This memoir had an immeasurable effect on the public perception of Jane Austen, and it dramatically increased her popularity. The publication of the memoir also spurred the reissue of Austen's novels, which became popular classics and in the twentieth century, popular movies and television programs.

Question

14. Without publication of the *Memoir of Jane Austen*, which of the following would likely be true?

 (A) Modern readers would not still be reading the works of Jane Austen.

 (B) People's opinions of Jane Austen would not be based on misleading information.

 (C) Jane Austen's books would not have been reissued.

 (D) People would not know much about the lives of women in the nineteenth century.

 (E) Modern readers would know much less about Jane Austen's life.

Answer Explanation

The correct answer is (E). The *Memoir* gave details about Austen's life, and it is likely that without this material from her nephew we would not know so much about Austen. Choices (A) and (C) are incorrect because there is no way of knowing if other events would have sparked a renewed interest in Jane Austen. Choice (B) is incorrect because it is impossible to know what precisely people's opinions of Jane Austen would be based on. Choice (D) is incorrect because there are other works that would have told us about women's lives in the nineteenth century.

Question

15. Based on the passage, what was the most significant result of the publication of the memoir?
    (A) It introduced the reading public to the works of Jane Austen.
    (B) It changed the public's perception of Jane Austen.
    (C) It made her works a critical and popular success.
    (D) It gave Austen's fans a glimpse into the real life of their beloved author.
    (E) It recorded the details of late eighteenth-century rural life.

Answer Explanation

The correct answer is (B). The change in the public's perception of Austen was the most *significant* result of the publication of the memoir, which, in turn, made them more interested in reading her work. Choices (A) and (C) are incorrect because although true, these were effects of the change in the public's perception and their consequent reading of her novels. Choice (D) is incorrect because the passage suggests that the memoir was somewhat misleading and also assumes that her fans read the *Memoir*, whereas the passage indicates that the *Memoir* created her fans. Choice (E) is incorrect because the memoir recorded details of Jane Austen's life, which may have touched on eighteenth-century rural life, but that was not the topic of the work.

Question

16. In the passage, "immeasurable" (line 10) means
    (A) incalculable.
    (B) monstrous.
    (C) infinitesimal.
    (D) intricate.
    (E) convoluted.

Answer Explanation

The correct answer is (A). "Immeasurable" means about the same as "incalculable," meaning "limitless." Choice (B) is incorrect because "monstrous," meaning in this case "huge, colossal," is not the same as "limitless." Choice (C) is incorrect because "infinitesimal" means "insignificant," the opposite of "immeasurable." Choices (D) and (E) are incorrect because "intricate" and "convoluted" mean "complicated," which is not the same as "limitless."

Question

17. The sales revenue lost during the economic downturn can be _____ if every sales representative contacts one former or current customer and three new customers every day.

(A) redeemed

(B) returned

(C) remediable

(D) recovered

(E) remediated

(F) rectified

Answer Explanation

The correct answers are (A) and (D). Choice (A), "redeemed," may mean "made up for," and choice (D), "recovered," may mean "returned to or regained a previous state or condition." Both fit the idea that the revenue that was lost, that is, not generated, can be made up by hard work. Choice (B), "returned," doesn't fit because the money was not lost in the sense of "being mislaid or misplaced." Choices (C) and (D) are similar and incorrect. "Remediable," choice (C), means "capable of being remedied or redressed" and doesn't fit the sense. Choice (E), "remediated," meaning "correcting a fault or a flaw" doesn't fit the sense because lost revenue isn't a flaw. Choice (F), "rectified," meaning "having set right or corrected something," is similar to choices (C) and (E) and incorrect for the same reason.

Question

18. Wildlife in urban areas includes such non-typical city creatures as foxes that have increased as restaurants with their treat-filled garbage bags have _____.

(A) gotten along

(B) proliferated

(C) progressed

(D) advanced

(E) multiplied

(F) thrive

Answer Explanation

The correct answers are (B) and (E). "Proliferated" means "to grow in number rapidly" and is similar to "multiplied," meaning "to increase in number," so choices (B) and (E) are synonyms and the correct answers. Choice (A), "gotten along," means "make progress" and is similar to "thrive," choice (F), meaning "to make progress, to succeed," but neither includes the idea of increasing in number implicit in the balance set up by the phrase "increase as restaurants . . . have . . ." Choices (C) and (D), "progressed" and "advanced," are also synonym pairs and mean "to move forward, to improve," but they lack the idea of increasing in number.

Question

19. Big box stores cause anxiety among small towns and cities because they appear to be the har-bingers of the _____ of the downtown business area as shoppers forsake local small businesses for the big discounters.

    (A) decline
    (B) degradation
    (C) depreciation
    (D) obsolescence
    (E) deterioration
    (F) retrogression

Answer Explanation

The correct answers are (A) and (E). Choice (E), "deterioration," is a synonym for choice (A), "decline," and also means "a lessening in value, a weakening." Choice (D), "obsolescence," meaning "falling into disuse, becoming outdated," would also be a good choice, but it has no synonym among the answer options. Choice (B), "degradation," means "to move to a lower level, or a state of dis-honor or disgrace," neither of which fit the sense. Choice (C), "depreciation," means "a decrease in worth" and is an economics term. Choice (F), "retrogression," means "returning to a former state, regression," and doesn't make sense.

Question

20. Some of the more unforgettable characters in literature are _____. Who can forget the servile, groveling, and fawning Uriah Heep or the Reverend Collins?

    (A) enthralling
    (B) curmudgeonly
    (C) surly
    (D) gruff
    (E) sycophantic
    (F) obsequious

Answer Explanation

The correct answers are (E) and (F). "Servile, groveling, and fawning" actually describe choices (E) and (F), "sycophantic" and "obsequious." Choice (A), "enthralling," which means "appealing, beguiling, enchanting," doesn't fit the description. Choice (B), "curmudgeonly," is another type of obnoxious character, but one who is ill-tempered, stubborn, and resentful, which is similar to "surly," choice (C), and "gruff," choice (D).

PRACTICE TEST 3 ANSWER SHEETS

Section 1: Analytical Writing

Analyze an Issue

FOR PLANNING

answer sheet

ANALYZE AN ISSUE RESPONSE

_____
_____
_____
_____
_____
_____
_____
_____
_____
_____
_____
_____
_____
_____
_____
_____
_____
_____
_____
_____
_____
_____
_____
_____
_____
_____
_____
_____
_____
_____
_____
_____
_____
_____
_____
_____
_____
_____

ANALYZE AN ISSUE RESPONSE

_____
_____
_____
_____
_____
_____
_____
_____
_____
_____
_____
_____
_____
_____
_____
_____
_____
_____
_____
_____
_____
_____
_____
_____
_____
_____
_____
_____
_____
_____
_____

answer sheet

ANALYZE AN ISSUE RESPONSE

_____
_____
_____
_____
_____
_____
_____
_____
_____
_____
_____
_____
_____
_____
_____
_____
_____
_____
_____
_____
_____
_____
_____
_____
_____
_____
_____
_____
_____
_____
_____
_____
_____
_____
_____
_____
_____
_____
_____

ANALYZE AN ISSUE RESPONSE

_____
_____
_____
_____
_____
_____
_____
_____
_____
_____
_____
_____
_____
_____
_____
_____
_____
_____
_____
_____
_____
_____
_____
_____
_____
_____
_____
_____

answer sheet

Analyze an Argument

FOR PLANNING

ANALYZE AN ARGUMENT RESPONSE

_____

_____

_____

_____

_____

_____

_____

_____

_____

_____

_____

_____

_____

_____

_____

_____

_____

_____

_____

_____

_____

_____

_____

_____

_____

_____

_____

_____

_____

answer sheet

ANALYZE AN ARGUMENT RESPONSE

ANALYZE AN ARGUMENT RESPONSE

_____
_____
_____
_____
_____
_____
_____
_____
_____
_____
_____
_____
_____
_____
_____
_____
_____
_____
_____
_____
_____
_____
_____
_____
_____
_____
_____
_____
_____
_____
_____
_____
_____

answer sheet

ANALYZE AN ARGUMENT RESPONSE

_____
_____
_____
_____
_____
_____
_____
_____
_____
_____
_____
_____
_____
_____
_____
_____
_____
_____
_____
_____
_____
_____
_____
_____
_____
_____
_____
_____
_____
_____
_____
_____
_____
_____
_____
_____

Section 2: Verbal Reasoning

1. (A) (B) (C) (D) (E)
2. (A) (B) (C) (D) (E)
3. (A) (B) (C) (D) (E) (F)
4. (A) (B) (C) (D) (E) (F) (G) (H) (I)
5. (A) (B) (C) (D) (E) (F) (G) (H) (I)
6. (A) (B) (C) (D) (E)
7. (A) (B) (C) (D) (E)
8. (A) (B) (C)
9. (A) (B) (C) (D) (E)
10. (A) (B) (C) (D) (E)

11. (A) (B) (C) (D) (E)
12. (A) (B) (C) (D) (E)
13. (A) (B) (C) (D) (E)
14. (A) (B) (C)
15. (A) (B) (C) (D) (E)

16. (A) (B) (C) (D) (E) (F)
17. (A) (B) (C) (D) (E) (F)
18. (A) (B) (C) (D) (E) (F)
19. (A) (B) (C) (D) (E) (F)
20. (A) (B) (C) (D) (E)

Section 3: Verbal Reasoning

1. (A) (B) (C) (D) (E)
2. (A) (B) (C) (D) (E)
3. (A) (B) (C) (D) (E) (F)
4. (A) (B) (C) (D) (E) (F) (G) (H) (I)
5. (A) (B) (C) (D) (E) (F) (G) (H) (I)
6. (A) (B) (C) (D) (E)
7. (A) (B) (C) (D) (E)
8. (A) (B) (C) (D) (E)
9. (A) (B) (C) (D) (E)
10. (A) (B) (C) (D) (E)

11. (A) (B) (C) (D) (E)
12. (A) (B) (C)
13. (A) (B) (C) (D) (E)
14. (A) (B) (C) (D) (E)
15. (A) (B) (C)

16. (A) (B) (C) (D) (E) (F)
17. (A) (B) (C) (D) (E) (F)
18. (A) (B) (C) (D) (E) (F)
19. (A) (B) (C) (D) (E) (F)
20. (A) (B) (C) (D) (E)

Section 4: Quantitative Reasoning

1. (A) (B) (C) (D)
2. (A) (B) (C) (D)
3. (A) (B) (C) (D)
4. (A) (B) (C) (D)
5. (A) (B) (C) (D)
6. (A) (B) (C) (D)
7. (A) (B) (C) (D)
8. (A) (B) (C) (D)
9. (A) (B) (C) (D) (E)
10. (A) (B) (C) (D) (E)

11. (A) (B) (C) (D) (E)
12. (A) (B) (C) (D) (E)
13. (A) (B) (C) (D) (E)
14. (A) (B) (C) (D) (E)
15. (A) (B) (C) (D) (E)

16. (A) (B) (C) (D) (E)
17. (A) (B) (C) (D) (E) (F)
18. (A) (B) (C) (D) (E)
19. [ ]
20. [ ]

answer sheet

Section 5: Quantitative Reasoning

1. Ⓐ Ⓑ Ⓒ Ⓓ
2. Ⓐ Ⓑ Ⓒ Ⓓ
3. Ⓐ Ⓑ Ⓒ Ⓓ
4. Ⓐ Ⓑ Ⓒ Ⓓ
5. Ⓐ Ⓑ Ⓒ Ⓓ
6. Ⓐ Ⓑ Ⓒ Ⓓ
7. Ⓐ Ⓑ Ⓒ Ⓓ
8. Ⓐ Ⓑ Ⓒ Ⓓ
9. Ⓐ Ⓑ Ⓒ Ⓓ Ⓔ
10. Ⓐ Ⓑ Ⓒ Ⓓ Ⓔ Ⓕ Ⓖ Ⓗ

11. ☐

12. Ⓐ Ⓑ Ⓒ Ⓓ Ⓔ
13. Ⓐ Ⓑ Ⓒ Ⓓ Ⓔ
14. Ⓐ Ⓑ Ⓒ Ⓓ Ⓔ
15. Ⓐ Ⓑ Ⓒ Ⓓ Ⓔ

16. Ⓐ Ⓑ Ⓒ Ⓓ Ⓔ
17. Ⓐ Ⓑ Ⓒ Ⓓ
18. Ⓐ Ⓑ Ⓒ Ⓓ Ⓔ Ⓕ Ⓖ Ⓗ

19. ☐

20. ☐

Practice Test 3

The test begins with general information about the number of sections on the test (six for the computer version, including the unidentified unscored section or an identified research section, and five for the paper-and-pencil version) and the timing of the test (approximately 3 hours and 45 minutes including one 10-minute break after Section 3, 1-minute breaks after the other sections for the computer version, and 3 hours and 30 minutes for the paper-and-pencil version with similar breaks). The following practice test contains the five scored sections.

Each section has its own time allocation and, during that time period, you may work on only that section.

Next, you will read ETS's policy on scoring the Analytical Writing responses. Each essay is read by experienced readers, and ETS may cancel any test scores that show evidence of unacknowledged use of sources, unacknowledged collaboration with others, preparation of the response by another person, and language that is "substantially" similar to the language in one or more other test responses.

Each section has specific instructions for that section.

You will be told when to begin.

practice test 3

SECTION 1: ANALYTICAL WRITING

Analyze an Issue
30 minutes

The time for this task is 30 minutes. You must plan and draft a response that evaluates the issue given below. If you do not respond to the specific issue, your score will be zero. Your response must be based on the accompanying instructions, and you must provide evidence for your position. You may use support from reading, experience, observations, and/or course work.

The American public education system is broken and only drastic changes can save it.

Write an essay that takes and explains a position on this issue. As you present, develop, and explain your position, discuss when and how the statement might or might not hold true. Explain how those possibilities provide support for your own point of view.

Your response will be read by experienced readers who will assess your ability to do the following:

- Follow the set of task instructions.
- Analyze the complexities involved.
- Organize, develop, and explain ideas.
- Use pertinent reasons and/or illustrations to support ideas.
- Adhere to the conventions of Standard Written English.

You will be advised to take some time to plan your response and to leave time to reread it before the time is over. Those taking the paper-and-pencil version of the GRE® will find a blank page in their answer booklet for making notes and then four ruled pages for writing their actual response. Those taking the computer version will be given scrap paper for making notes.

STOP

If you finish before the time is up, you may check your work in this section only.

Analyze an Argument
30 minutes

The time for this task is 30 minutes. You must plan and draft a response that evaluates the argument given below. If you do not respond to the given argument, your score will be zero. Your response must be based on the accompanying instructions, and you must provide evidence in support of your analysis.

You should not present your views on the subject of the argument but on the strength or weakness of the argument.

> During a recent opinion poll, citizens of our town noted that one of the town's most pressing needs was a new public safety building. The old building was erected in 1961 and was, at the time, merely a police and fire station. It is now overcrowded and unable to accommodate the additional and necessary functions of a 911 communications center, an emergency management center, and an emergency management office; it also cannot accommodate the new environmental safety team. Furthermore, there are insufficient garages for all the police vehicles, and the latest-model ambulances do not fit in the station bays. For all these reasons, a new building, which residents clearly support, and which will help ensure a greater level of safety in our town, must be constructed.
>
> Write an essay that identifies and explains the specific evidence required to determine whether the argument is reasonable. Discuss how that evidence would weaken or strengthen the argument.

Your response will be read by experienced readers who will assess your ability to do the following:

- Follow the set of task instructions.
- Analyze the complexities involved.
- Organize, develop, and explain ideas.
- Use pertinent reasons and/or illustrations to support ideas.
- Adhere to the conventions of Standard Written English.

You will be advised to take some time to plan your response and to leave time to reread it before the time is over. Those taking the paper-and-pencil version of the GRE® will find a blank page in their answer booklet for making notes and then four ruled pages for writing their actual response. Those taking the computer version will be given scrap paper for making notes.

STOP

> If you finish before the time is up, you may check your work in this section only.

INSTRUCTIONS FOR THE VERBAL REASONING AND QUANTITATIVE REASONING SECTIONS

You will find information here on the question formats for the Verbal Reasoning and Quantitative Reasoning sections as well as information about how to use the software program, or, if you're taking the paper-and-pencil version, how to mark your answers in the answer booklet.

Perhaps the most important information is a reminder about how these two sections are scored. Every correct answer earns a point, but wrong answers don't subtract any points. The advice from ETS is to guess if you aren't sure of an answer. ETS says that this is better than not answering a question.

All multiple-choice questions in the computer-based test will have answer options preceded by either blank ovals or blank squares, depending on the question type. The paper-and-pencil test will follow the same format of answer choices, but it will use letters instead of ovals or squares for answer choices.

For your convenience in answering questions and checking answers in this book, we use (A), (B), (C), etc. By using letters with parentheses, you will find it easy to check your answers against the answer key and explanation sections.

SECTION 2: VERBAL REASONING

30 minutes • 20 questions

(The paper-and-pencil version will have 25 questions to be completed in 35 minutes.)

For each question, follow the specific directions and choose the best answer.

FOR QUESTIONS 1–5, CHOOSE <u>ONE</u> ANSWER FOR EACH BLANK. SELECT FROM THE APPROPRIATE COLUMN FOR EACH BLANK. CHOOSE THE ANSWER THAT BEST COMPLETES THE SENSE OF THE TEXT.

---

1. One of the major concerns as states pulled themselves out of the deficits created during the Great Recession was whether they would return to their _____ spending habits once the good times began to roll again.

(A) decadent
(B) profligate
(C) parsimonious
(D) immoral
(E) licentious

2. To the board of directors, it appeared that the only way to placate _____ stockholders was to remove the CEO.

(A) seditious
(B) subversive
(C) insubordinate
(D) disobedient
(E) disgruntled

3. In discussing the vanishing ecosystem of the Grand Canyon, the speaker spoke (i) _____ and passionately about his subject. It was obvious that the (ii) _____ of the natural environment caused him grave concern.

Blank (i)	Blank (ii)
(A) eloquently	(D) mutilation
(B) emotionally	(E) reparation
(C) prominently	(F) destruction

4. The epic heroes who undergo a series of (i) _____ challenges to attain a goal are (ii) _____ feature of many national cultural identities. Many of the challenges involve some (iii) _____ feat of daring.

Blank (i)	Blank (ii)	Blank (iii)
(A) extraordinary	(D) an underlying	(G) intrepid
(B) copious	(E) an external	(H) steadfast
(C) massive	(F) a conventional	(I) resolute

5. Among the health scams that the FDA warns the (i) _____ public about are (ii) _____ cancer-treatment products and weight-loss programs with FDA (iii) _____ ingredients.

Blank (i)	Blank (ii)	Blank (iii)
(A) wary	(D) trick	(G) unsanctioned
(B) circumspect	(E) mock	(H) unmeasured
(C) credulous	(F) deceptive	(I) characteristic

FOR QUESTIONS 6–20, CHOOSE ONLY <u>ONE</u> ANSWER CHOICE UNLESS OTHERWISE INDICATED.

QUESTIONS 6–8 ARE BASED ON THE FOLLOWING PASSAGE.

In the year 1901, Spanish painter Pablo Picasso entered what is now referred to as his Blue Period. At the time Picasso was just 20 years old, living in Paris as a relatively unknown artist. Up to this point, the paintings Picasso produced were vibrantly colored, expressing the decadent life he and his friend Carlos Casagemas had been leading together in Paris. But
5 the suicide of Casagemas in 1901 was a major trigger for Picasso's Blue Period, in which Picasso began to paint in various shades of blue, giving the paintings a haunting and melancholy feel. The recurring theme of the Blue Period paintings is the desolation of outsiders, which included beggars, prisoners, and circus people. By 1904, Picasso had emerged from the Blue Period and began what is known as the Rose Period, characterized by bright colors,
10 and featuring acrobats and harlequins. A few years later, Picasso began to explore Cubism, which broke completely from the traditional three-dimensional representation of objects, and for which he became famous. The Blue and Rose Periods can be viewed as transitional times for Picasso in which he moved from the traditional art of his youth to the iconoclastic art of his adulthood.

6. Based on the passage the author evidently believes that

(A) the Rose Period is less significant a time period than the Blue Period in the artistic development of Picasso.

(B) the suicide of Casagemas had an effect on Picasso that would haunt him for the rest of his life.

(C) if Picasso had not gone through the Blue and Rose Periods he would have never been ready to explore a new form of art.

(D) there is no way to understand Cubism without seeing the artistic road that led Picasso to it over the course of his work.

(E) the Blue Period was how Picasso expressed himself artistically during a difficult time of his life.

7. In this passage, "iconoclastic" (line 13) means

(A) eclectic.

(B) eccentric.

(C) consequential.

(D) revolutionary.

(E) conservative.

FOR QUESTION 8, CONSIDER EACH ANSWER INDIVIDUALLY AND SELECT <u>ALL</u> CHOICES THAT APPLY.

---

8. Which of the following ideas are clearly supported in this passage?

    (A) After the Blue Period, Picasso no longer painted pictures of desolation.

    (B) Picasso is best known for his Cubist works.

    (C) The Rose Period was just as significant as the Blue Period in terms of Picasso's growth as an artist.

QUESTIONS 9 AND 10 ARE BASED ON THE FOLLOWING PASSAGE.

Although the quality of smartphone photos varies by manufacturer, smartphone camera manufacturers are nevertheless putting camera companies out of business. Smartphones offer sophisticated technology in lenses, sensors, flashes, image stabilization, video, and playback. While small gradations in image quality now separate smartphone competitors, a
5   more fundamental difference lies in each smartphone's organization, storage, and transformational capabilities. Companies that offer organization by capabilities such as face and other recognition, as well as more streamlined sharing to all devices, have a definite advantage over those who force the user to make fundamental organization and storage choices. Some of these manufacturers even distinguish superior shots, in terms of lighting and composition,
10 from inferior ones, streamlining the selection and deletion process that many smartphone owners must now undertake laboriously by hand. Superior smartphone cameras also have the capability to transform related single shots into an animated GIF.

9. All of the following are stated or implied in this passage EXCEPT

    (A) Smartphone camera image quality and storage vary by manufacturer.

    (B) Small differences in the quality of images now separate smartphone cameras.

    (C) Some smartphone cameras flag or otherwise differentiate good images from bad ones.

    (D) Smartphone cameras offer only slightly better lenses and sensors than traditional cameras do.

    (E) Smartphone camera capability includes creating the appearance of motion from successive shots.

10. Which of the following statements expresses the author's opinion about smartphone cameras?

    (A) Consumers should select those cameras that offer the highest image quality.

    (B) Smartphones camera sales now outstrip traditional camera sales, even though smartphone images are not any better.

    (C) The best smartphone cameras offer advanced discrimination, animation, and other capacities.

    (D) Facial recognition is the most advanced capability in smartphone cameras today.

    (E) Consumers should select those cameras that can organize photos by topic.

QUESTIONS 11 AND 12 ARE BASED ON THE FOLLOWING PASSAGE.

The use of solar energy to produce electricity can be an excellent alternative to using fossil fuels. Solar panels give off no pollution, and, unlike other alternative energy sources like wind turbines, are silent. One big advantage of solar energy is that it can harness electricity in remote locations that are not connected to a national grid. One example of this is in space,
5   where high-efficiency solar cells are used to power satellites. Although the initial investment for solar cells is high, once they are installed, they provide free electricity. Yet unfortunately this initial cost is one reason people are hesitant to embrace solar energy as an alternative energy source. Currently, a single solar cell can cost more than $1000, and some households may need more than one. Also, solar cells do not generate electricity 24 hours a day, so
10 excess electricity needs to be captured during daylight time for later use. The weather and pollution levels can also affect a solar cell's efficiency, which could have a huge impact on solar panels installed in cities. However, cost is still considered the main deterrent. Because fossil fuels still cost less than the initial investment for solar panels, it will likely be some time before we see a significant shift toward solar energy use.

11. Select the sentence that is NOT a major detail that supports the author's opinion.

   (A) One example of this is in space, where high-efficiency solar cells are used to power satellites.

   (B) The weather and pollution levels can also affect a solar cell's efficiency, which could have a huge impact on solar panels installed in cities.

   (C) Currently, a single solar cell can cost more than $1000, and some households may need more than one.

   (D) Because fossil fuels still cost less than the initial investment for solar panels, it will likely be some time before we see a significant shift toward solar energy use.

   (E) The use of solar energy to produce electricity can be an excellent alternative to using fossil fuels.

12. Which of the following, if it were true, would weaken the author's conclusion?

   (A) Fossil fuels and solar energy cost about the same.

   (B) Solar panels will eventually be able to run 24 hours a day.

   (C) Solar panels can sometimes create more noise than wind turbines.

   (D) Many people who use solar panels are disappointed with the results.

   (E) There are many alternatives to solar energy that are much cheaper.

QUESTIONS 13–15 ARE BASED ON THE FOLLOWING PASSAGE.

In the arena of dietary advice, science has produced some nutty conclusions. For the past two decades, multiple studies have drawn similar conclusions linking nut consumption to reduced risk of certain diseases, including hypertension, type-2 diabetes mellitus, and colon cancer. Studies have also shown reductions among nut eaters in many common and significant
5   mediators of chronic diseases, such as inflammation, hyperglycemia, and insulin resistance.
   More significantly, a study recently reported by the *New England Journal of Medicine* has found that nut consumption is "inversely related with total and cause-specific mortality." The study was conducted over the 30-year period spanning 1980 and 2010; used a cohort of some 20,000 nurses and other health professionals; and tracked other dietary and lifestyle
10 factors, such as fruit and vegetable intake, meat and alcohol consumption, physical activity, age, and body mass index. The study's authors concluded that those who ate more nuts were also leaner, got more exercise, ate more fruits and vegetables, and drank more alcohol. The import of this and earlier studies is that nuts contribute to both good health and longevity.

Furthermore, these calorie-laden snacks have been shown to make their consumers leaner.

15 Questions as to why the study found this may be answered in various ways—consumers eat them instead of snacks with even more calories; the body may treat nut calories differently than other calories; and nut consumers may just be more active or nutritionally conscious—or they elude definitive answers. But even if the possibility of a clear cause-and-effect relationship between nut consumption and svelteness is not enough of an enticement for more nut eating,

20 the makeup of nuts should be. For example, nuts are an excellent source of omega-3 fatty acids that lower triglycerides, slow down the accretion of plaque, and lower blood pressure. They also contain phytochemicals and antioxidants thought to reduce the risk of certain cancers.

13. What is the most significant detail about the study reported by the *New England Journal of Medicine?*

(A) The study was conducted over a period of some thirty years.

(B) The study suggested a reduced rate of mortality for those who consumed nuts.

(C) The study suggested a decreased rate in the incidence of certain chronic diseases.

(D) The study suggested a cause-effect relationship between nut consumption and leanness.

(E) The study contradicted the claims of most nut studies conducted over the past two decades.

FOR QUESTION 14, CONSIDER EACH ANSWER INDIVIDUALLY AND SELECT <u>ALL</u> CHOICES THAT APPLY.

---

14. What does the author suggest about studies that predate the study reported by the *New England Journal of Medicine?*

(A) They drew unsubstantiated conclusions about the effects of consuming nuts.

(B) They showed how eating nuts contributes to the incidence of type-2 diabetes mellitus.

(C) They showed how eating nuts works against factors that may contribute to disease.

15. "Definitive" (line 18) most nearly means

(A) final.

(B) inconclusive.

(C) lexical.

(D) equivocal.

(E) defined.

FOR QUESTIONS 16–19, CHOOSE THE <u>TWO</u> ANSWERS THAT BEST FIT THE MEANING OF THE SENTENCE AS A WHOLE AND RESULT IN TWO COMPLETED SENTENCES THAT ARE ALIKE IN MEANING.

16. The gallery owner has a(n) _____ eye and an amazing ability to select the next hot artist from all the new artists who show him their portfolios.
    - (A) discerning
    - (B) discriminating
    - (C) detecting
    - (D) investigative
    - (E) observant
    - (F) understanding

17. _____ data from the traffic safety survey shows a 17 percent increase in nonfatal pedestrian accidents due to texting drivers. The final report will be available next year.
    - (A) Improvised
    - (B) Acting
    - (C) Interim
    - (D) Permanent
    - (E) Terminal
    - (F) Provisional

18. Scrooge has come to be considered the _____ miser from whom all similar characters are drawn.
    - (A) pattern
    - (B) eccentric
    - (C) archetypal
    - (D) unusual
    - (E) alternate
    - (F) classic

19. While economics may be exciting to some, the yawning student in the back of the room thought it _____.
    - (A) tedious
    - (B) sundry
    - (C) repetitive
    - (D) soporific
    - (E) disingenuous
    - (F) monotonous

QUESTION 20 IS BASED ON THE FOLLOWING PASSAGE.

For years astronomers could not figure out why the Sun's outer atmosphere, or corona, is millions of degrees hotter than its surface, but recently NASA scientists came up with an answer. The corona consists of loops of hot gas that are thousands of miles high, but from the Earth, the corona can only be seen during a total solar eclipse, which has made it difficult
5   to study. However, NASA scientists recently determined that nanoflares, tiny bursts of heat and energy, are what make the temperature so much hotter in the corona. The loops of gas are made up of bundles of smaller magnetic strands that can reach temperatures of several million degrees Kelvin, which is significantly hotter than the surface of the Sun. NASA scientists created a simulation to see how nanoflares might occur and determined that the
10 million-degree temperatures in the corona could only be produced by impulsive energy bursts. However, the magnetic strands cool very quickly, which explains why this phenomenon had been so difficult to detect.

20. Select the sentence that best explains the recent discovery about the Sun's corona.

(A) However, the magnetic strands cool very quickly, which explains why this phenomenon had been so difficult to detect.

(B) The corona consists of loops of hot gas that are thousands of miles high, but from the Earth, the corona can only be seen during a total solar eclipse, which has made it difficult to study.

(C) For years astronomers could not figure out why the Sun's outer atmosphere, or corona, is millions of degrees hotter than its surface, but recently NASA scientists came up with an answer.

(D) The loops of gas are made up of bundles of smaller magnetic strands that can reach temperatures of several million degrees Kelvin, which is significantly hotter than the surface of the Sun.

(E) However, NASA scientists recently determined that nanoflares, tiny bursts of heat and energy, are what make the temperature so much hotter in the corona.

STOP

If you finish before the time is up, you may check your work in this section only.

SECTION 3: VERBAL REASONING

30 minutes • 20 questions

(The paper-and-pencil version will have 25 questions to be completed in 35 minutes.)

For each question, follow the specific directions and choose the best answer.

> **FOR QUESTIONS 1–5, CHOOSE <u>ONE</u> ANSWER FOR EACH BLANK. SELECT FROM THE APPROPRIATE COLUMN FOR EACH BLANK. CHOOSE THE ANSWER THAT BEST COMPLETES THE SENSE OF THE TEXT.**

1. Even though technology has vastly improved the accuracy of weather forecasts, it is unlikely that technology will enhance forecasting enough to enable accurate forecasts for more than two weeks because weather is too _____.

| (A) unpredictable |
| (B) subjective |
| (C) arbitrary |
| (D) unreliable |
| (E) elusive |

2. The Library of Congress recordings of American African folk songs recorded on location in the Deep South are considered the _____ versions against which musicologists evaluate all other versions.

| (A) indispensable |
| (B) momentous |
| (C) explicit |
| (D) definitive |
| (E) scholarly |

3. At one end of the spectrum is Van Gogh's (i) _____ life driven by the demons of madness and at the other end is Monet's (ii) _____ life in his beloved garden at Giverny.

Blank (i)	Blank (ii)
(A) turbulent	(D) stoical
(B) rowdy	(E) tranquil
(C) boisterous	(F) bucolic

4. Ernest Hemingway was (i) _____ storyteller—an artist with words. He could paint (ii) _____ portrait of a proud young man locked in deadly combat with a ferocious bull and an equally (iii) _____ picture of a proud old man in his epic struggle with a giant fish.

Blank (i)	Blank (ii)	Blank (iii)
(A) an accomplished	(D) an impressive	(G) glittering
(B) a consummate	(E) an interesting	(H) riveting
(C) a perfect	(F) a stunning	(I) conspicuous

5. The anthropologist's explanation for the difference in cultural traits had always seemed (i) _____, but they were later deemed (ii) _____ after new discoveries. His entire life's work was (iii) _____ by the academic community and his career was in ruins.

Blank (i)	Blank (ii)	Blank (iii)
(A) desirable	(D) delusory	(G) reneged
(B) tenable	(E) deceptive	(H) annulled
(C) worthwhile	(F) specious	(I) repudiated

FOR QUESTIONS 6–20, CHOOSE ONLY <u>ONE</u> ANSWER CHOICE UNLESS OTHERWISE INDICATED.

QUESTIONS 6–8 ARE BASED ON THE FOLLOWING PASSAGE.

A meteoric rise in service sector jobs has characterized India's dynamic labor market over the past 15 years. In a paper for the National Bureau of Economic Research, Eichengreen and Gupta caution that this rise resulted from factors such as an extremely low starting point and dramatic increases in employment for those who are highly skilled, a group that makes up a
5　tiny proportion of India's population. The two economists note that without a concomitant rise in manufacturing jobs— a sector that Bloomberg News described in early 2013, in a generally gloomy look at India's employment future, as "stagnated"—similar rates of growth cannot be sustained. The Manpower Employment survey for the next quarter of 2013, however, projected a 46% increase in jobs in the retail and trade sector, with the services sector just
10　1 percentage point behind. The data, gathered from some 5,000 Indian employers, glowed with other similarly sunny figures for all sectors, including manufacturing.

6. Select the sentence that **most likely states the author's opinion.**

(A) New data make future meteoric growth in India's employment a certainty.

(B) Without an increase in manufacturing jobs, India's economy will most likely falter.

(C) Only high-tech service industry jobs are likely to solve India's employment problems.

(D) Projected employment rates suggest a reversal of India's employment trends for the last 15 years.

(E) Continued dramatic growth in India's employment rates may be illusory.

7. Which of the following sentences would serve as the **most logical and relevant addition to the paragraph?**

(A) India's economy has grown at one of the fastest rates in the world over the past fifteen years.

(B) India's economy must be dominated by the high-tech service industry.

(C) Data for actual employment rates in the next quarter may tell a significantly different story.

(D) Loss of manufacturing jobs to globalization has not negatively impacted all developing countries.

(E) India's "demographic dividend" cannot be cashed in unless more high-tech service sector jobs are created.

8. What would the author **most likely predict or advise on the subject of employment in India in the future?**

(A) Employment will continue to rise but at slightly less dramatic rates.

(B) Gains in employment for most people must come from a reversal of manufacturing employment trends.

(C) Employment in all sectors will remain stagnant no matter what some predictions say.

(D) Decreases in employment will occur as employment in the high-tech service industry is saturated.

(E) Employment will continue to rise in the manufacturing sector but not in the high-tech service industry.

QUESTIONS 9–11 ARE BASED ON THE FOLLOWING PASSAGE.

Until the late nineteenth century, a loophole in U.S. copyright law allowed publishers to reprint British books without paying royalties to the authors. Charles Dickens was among the many authors who were affected. Dickens was even more popular in the United States than he was in England, partly because of the availability of his works and their low prices in the
5 United States. When Dickens travelled to America for the first time in 1841, he wrote that "there never was a king or Emperor upon the Earth, so cheered, and followed by crowds." Even so, during this visit he gave speeches calling for an international copyright law. The U.S. press, whose papers readily took advantage of free British content, were outraged. Editors took up their pens in an effort to convince the public that Dickens was ungrateful and greedy.
10   When he returned to England, Dickens published a critical book about his travels called *American Notes,* which included his outrage over his experience with the press. He also began a new novel, *Martin Chuzzlewit,* that details the adventures of a young man seeking his fortune in the United States. Dickens used the novel to seek revenge on the U.S. press. It satirized U.S. customs as well as the press, which ironically ran serialized installments of
15 the novel without compensating Dickens. *Martin Chuzzlewit* sold poorly in England, perhaps because it was so obviously aimed at the U.S. audience.

9. "Compensating" (line 15) most nearly means

(A) remunerating.

(B) resolving.

(C) equivocating.

(D) extrapolating.

(E) ingratiating.

10. Based on the passage, what was Dickens's probable attitude toward Americans in general during his visit to the United States?

(A) indebtedness

(B) belligerence

(C) dislike

(D) merciful

(E) ingratitude

11. According to the passage, what was Dickens's main reason for writing *Martin Chuzzlewit*?

    (A) To write a book that would sell well in the United States

    (B) To make the United States change its existing copyright laws

    (C) To force U.S. publishers to sell his book in the United States

    (D) To attack Americans for their love of his novels

    (E) To show how he felt about the U.S. press

QUESTIONS 12 AND 13 ARE BASED ON THE FOLLOWING PASSAGE.

Journalists rarely elicit art commentary from Isa Genzken, the famously interview-phobic German artist whose work was recently the subject of a Museum of Modern Art retrospective. **Instead, Genzken's work must speak for her, though its message surely begins with the prefix *un-*, as in the word *unmonumental*, the title of an earlier show featuring**
5 **Genzken's work.** In its publicity for the recent show, MoMa extols Genzken, "who with a new language of found objects and collage, has created several bodies of work that have redefined assemblage for a new era." Indeed, objects on display were innovatory, if not generative. **No matter what the size of the display, however, viewers had to find their own language for parts that are not wholes, for pieces that appear not to be connected,**
10 **and for spaces that are seemingly not bounded.**

FOR QUESTION 12, CONSIDER EACH ANSWER INDIVIDUALLY AND SELECT <u>ALL</u> CHOICES THAT APPLY.

---

12. What do MoMa's words about "assemblage for a new era" suggest?

    (A) That the artwork is assembled in a new way from found objects

    (B) That the artwork will be reassembled in many new ways in the future

    (C) That the artwork is representative of the present

13. What function do the two groups of words in bold type serve in this passage?

    (A) The first presents an argument; the second presents support for the argument.

    (B) The first anticipates a conclusion; the second provides support for that conclusion.

    (C) The first presents an opinion; the second provides an additional opinion that supports the first.

    (D) The first serves as an intermediate conclusion; the second serves as the final conclusion.

    (E) The first supports an opinion; the second states the opinion.

QUESTIONS 14 AND 15 ARE BASED ON THE FOLLOWING PASSAGE.

The American electoral system is commonly called a "two-party system" because there have historically been only two major political parties dominating electoral politics. Today, the Republican and Democratic Parties are the major two, but there are more than 30 other political parties active in the United States. One major role of third parties in the United States
5   has been to refocus the two major parties on issues they may have not dealt with effectively. Sometimes this happens when one of the major parties fears that a third party is going to become a viable alternative to a major party candidate, or will at least siphon off votes from that candidate during an election. At that point, what often happens is that the major party that feels threatened will take on certain policy positions of the third party in order to lure
10   more voters to it or keep voters from abandoning it. Third parties may also strengthen the government by giving those unhappy with the status quo a legitimate platform for demanding reform. In addition, third parties can simply be a welcoming place for people who want to belong to a group of like-minded people.

14. The author's primary purpose in this passage is to

(A) encourage Americans to vote for third-party candidates in elections.

(B) explain how third parties affect the U.S. electoral system.

(C) emphasize the importance of third parties to the electoral process.

(D) suggest that the U.S. electoral system could not function without third parties.

(E) analyze various platforms of third parties in the United States.

FOR QUESTION 15, CONSIDER EACH ANSWER INDIVIDUALLY AND SELECT <u>ALL</u> CHOICES THAT APPLY.

---

15. The author of the passage implies that third parties in the United States function in the electoral system by

(A) allowing people to vote for the candidate they believe in.

(B) giving people a platform for radical ideas.

(C) making the major parties rethink some of their policies.

FOR QUESTIONS 16–19, CHOOSE THE <u>TWO</u> ANSWERS THAT BEST FIT THE
MEANING OF THE SENTENCE AS A WHOLE AND RESULT IN TWO COMPLETED
SENTENCES THAT ARE ALIKE IN MEANING.

---

16. The _____ doctor of internal medicine received an honorary degree from his alma mater in
    further recognition of his humanitarian work in Zambia.
    (A) humble
    (B) illustrious
    (C) brilliant
    (D) illustrative
    (E) celebrated
    (F) dignified

17. The Director of Marketing's _____ assistant kept making suggestions about how to shoot
    the product launch until the photographer finally told him to sit down and be quiet, which he
    did.
    (A) officious
    (B) overbearing
    (C) condescending
    (D) supercilious
    (E) meddlesome
    (F) diligent

18. The young people were not so _____ as their elders when it came to accepting the imposition
    of martial law including curfews beginning at 5 p.m.
    (A) alterable
    (B) resilient
    (C) amenable
    (D) adaptable
    (E) tractable
    (F) movable

19. At the end of the meeting, the participants released a joint statement pledging to continue their
    dialogue in an effort to improve the _____ relations over trade differences.
    (A) taut
    (B) stressed
    (C) tense
    (D) strained
    (E) difficult
    (F) demanding

QUESTION 20 IS BASED ON THE FOLLOWING PASSAGE.

Is the Fourth Estate, the theoretical fourth branch of the government that is the press, in jeopardy now that, first, overall news readership is declining even as online readership is increasing, and, second, digital media have gained apparent ascendancy over traditional print journalism? The answer may depend in part on whether the eye of the beholder views jour-
5   nalism, regardless of its form, largely as a disinterested public good, an evanescent medium for democratic comment, or a consumer product. Those holding to the highest ideal of the press as safeguard of our democracy will no doubt lament changes that make Twitter and the like as attractive as any news source. Those holding to the second vision will likely embrace the idea of up-to-the-minute, ever-fresh and evolving ideas and democratized commentary,
10   while those holding to the third conception will bank on the more recent journalistic brands such as Buzzfeed and Politico that "sell" what has always been a product of capitalism. No matter what the perspective, however, it is indisputable that online journalism shifts power away from the publication, which in the era of print functioned as a kind of sentry at the gate of truth, appropriateness, and corporate interest, and transfers that power to the user.

20. Which of the following can be inferred from this passage?

(A) In the current age of digital media, the processes and products of journalism are more transitory than ever before.

(B) The Fourth Estate has been eroded by new commercial interests that shift motivation from public good to profit.

(C) The idea that the Fourth Estate is currently diminished by the ascendancy of digital media depends on a subjective view of the role of the press.

(D) Journalism today exists largely beyond the realm of corporate interests and is characterized by a new democratizing impulse.

(E) Journalism, regardless of the form it takes, should have a central purpose of serving democratic principles.

STOP

> If you finish before the time is up, you may check your work in this section only.

SECTION 4: QUANTITATIVE REASONING

35 minutes • 20 questions

(The paper-and-pencil version will have 25 questions to be completed in 40 minutes.)

For each question, follow the specific directions and choose the best answer.

The test-maker provides the following information that applies to all questions in the Quantitative Reasoning section of the GRE®:

- All numbers used are real numbers.

- All figures are assumed to lie in a plane unless otherwise indicated.

- Geometric figures, such as lines, circles, triangles, and quadrilaterals, *are not necessarily* drawn to scale. That is, you should *not* assume that quantities such as lengths and angle measures are as they appear in a figure. You should assume, however, that lines shown as straight are actually straight, points on a line are in the order shown, and more generally, all geometric objects are in the relative positions shown. For questions with geometric figures, you should base your answers on geometric reasoning, not on estimating or comparing quantities by sight or by measurement.

- Coordinate systems, such as *xy*-planes and number lines, *are* drawn to scale. Therefore, you can read, estimate, or compare quantities in such figures by sight or by measurement.

- Graphical data presentations, such as bar graphs, circle graphs, and line graphs, *are* drawn to scale. Therefore, you can read, estimate, or compare data values by sight or by measurement.

FOR QUESTIONS 1–8, COMPARE QUANTITY A AND QUANTITY B. SOME QUESTIONS WILL HAVE ADDITIONAL INFORMATION ABOVE THE TWO QUANTITIES TO USE IN DETERMINING YOUR ANSWER.

1.   Quantity A   Quantity B

$$\frac{5}{\left(\frac{1}{5}\right)^2}$$ 125

(A) Quantity A is greater.
(B) Quantity B is greater.
(C) The two quantities are equal.
(D) The relationship cannot be determined from the information given.

2.

Quantity A	Quantity B
$\frac{1}{2} + \frac{1}{3} + \frac{1}{4} + \frac{1}{5}$	1

(A) Quantity A is greater.

(B) Quantity B is greater.

(C) The two quantities are equal.

(D) The relationship cannot be determined from the information given.

$$y \neq 0$$

3.

Quantity A	Quantity B
$\frac{5}{y}$	$5y$

(A) Quantity A is greater.

(B) Quantity B is greater.

(C) The two quantities are equal.

(D) The relationship cannot be determined from the information given.

$$a > b > 0 > c > d$$

4.

Quantity A	Quantity B
$a + d$	$b + c$

(A) Quantity A is greater.

(B) Quantity B is greater.

(C) The two quantities are equal.

(D) The relationship cannot be determined from the information given.

$$x > 0$$

5.

Quantity A	Quantity B
$x^3(x - 1)$	$x^4 + x^3$

(A) Quantity A is greater.

(B) Quantity B is greater.

(C) The two quantities are equal.

(D) The relationship cannot be determined from the information given.

6.   Quantity A   Quantity B
                      x 15

(A) Quantity A is greater.

(B) Quantity B is greater.

(C) The two quantities are equal.

(D) The relationship cannot be determined from the information given.

$$x \neq 0$$

7.   Quantity A   Quantity B

        $x^{-3}\left(x^3\right)$ $\dfrac{1}{x^{-3}\left(x^3\right)}$

(A) Quantity A is greater.

(B) Quantity B is greater.

(C) The two quantities are equal.

(D) The relationship cannot be determined from the information given.

Sam is 3 times as old as Sue. In 5 years Sam will be 12 years older than twice Sue's age.

8.   Quantity A   Quantity B
                  Sue's age   22

(A) Quantity A is greater.

(B) Quantity B is greater.

(C) The two quantities are equal.

(D) The relationship cannot be determined from the information given.

Questions 9–20 have several formats. Unless the directions state otherwise, choose one answer choice. For the Numeric Entry questions, follow the instructions below.

Numeric Entry Questions

The following items are the same for both the computer-based version of the test and the paper-and-pencil version. However, those taking the computer-based version will have additional information about entering answers in decimal and fraction boxes on the computer screen. Those taking the paper-and-pencil version will have information about entering answers on answer grids.

- Your answer may be an integer, a decimal, or a fraction, and it may be negative.

- If a question asks for a fraction, there will be two boxes. One box will be for the numerator and one will be for the denominator.

- Equivalent forms of the correct answer, such as 2.5 and 2.50, are all correct.

- Enter the exact answer unless the question asks you to round your answers.

QUESTIONS 9–11 REFER TO THE BAR GRAPH BELOW.

Average Daily Use Per Salesperson
(rounded to the nearest dollar)

9. If there are 33 salespeople in the company, what was the approximate total spent on food and gas for January?

   (A) $24,765
   (B) $25,575
   (C) $29,865
   (D) $35,805
   (E) $36,905

10. In February, the company had an outlay of $21,056 for food. How many salespeople did the company employ for the month?

   (A) 28

   (B) 47

   (C) 56

   (D) 73

   (E) 75

11. The projections for the coming year indicate an increase of 10 percent in the average cost of gas. How much more per day will the company pay out on average for gas for the first 6 months of next year?

   (A) $9

   (B) $12

   (C) $15

   (D) $18

   (E) $21

12. The frame shop has a rectangular mat 36" by 22". If a mat is cut from it that is 2" less all the way around, what is the area of the new mat?

   (A) 576

   (B) 680

   (C) 648

   (D) 792

   (E) 822

13. A right circular cylinder's dimensions are changed so that the cylinder's new height equals twice its original height, and the cylinder's new radius equals one-half its original radius. Which of the following describes correctly the resulting change, if any, to the cylinder's volume?

   (A) The cylinder's volume remains the same.

   (B) The cylinder's new volume equals twice the cylinder's original volume.

   (C) The cylinder's new volume equals one-half the cylinder's original volume.

   (D) The cylinder's new volume equals four times the cylinder's original volume.

   (E) The cylinder's new volume equals one-fourth the cylinder's original volume.

14. Find the perimeter of the figure.

(A) 7

(B) 8

(C) 14

(D) 16

(E) 30

15. The original price of a shirt was $40. It was marked down twice before it was sold. First it was marked down 20%, and then it was marked down 15% of its discounted price. What percentage of the original price did it sell for?

(A) 68%

(B) 48%

(C) 32%

(D) 85%

(E) 80%

16. What is the mean salary of 5 potters when two make $15.50 per hour, one makes $12 per hour, and the other two make $13.50 per hour?

(A) $10

(B) $12

(C) $14

(D) $16

(E) $17

FOR QUESTIONS 17 AND 18, CHOOSE <u>ALL</u> THE ANSWERS THAT APPLY.

---

17. The first term, r_1, of a sequence is 1, and the nth term of the sequence is given by the formula $r_n = r_{n-1} + 7$. Which of the following are terms of the sequence?

    (A) 7
    (B) 15
    (C) 20
    (D) 57
    (E) 63

18. If $x^2 - 11x - 12 = 0$, what are the two possible values for x?

    (A) −12
    (B) −1
    (C) 0
    (D) 1
    (E) 12

FOR QUESTIONS 19 AND 20, ENTER YOUR ANSWERS IN THE BOXES.

19. Lines 1 and 2 are parallel. What is the value of a?

20. In the barber shop, a haircut costs $22.50. How many haircuts must be done to cover the monthly rent of $1,276? Round the answer up to the nearest haircut.

STOP

If you finish before the time is up, you may check your work in this section only.

SECTION 5: QUANTITATIVE REASONING

35 minutes • 20 questions

(The paper-and-pencil version will have 25 questions to be completed in 40 minutes.)

For each question, follow the specific directions and choose the best answer.

> The test-maker provides the following information that applies to all questions in the Quantitative Reasoning section of the GRE®:
>
> - All numbers used are real numbers.
>
> - All figures are assumed to lie in a plane unless otherwise indicated.
>
> - Geometric figures, such as lines, circles, triangles, and quadrilaterals, *are not necessarily* drawn to scale. That is, you should *not* assume that quantities such as lengths and angle measures are as they appear in a figure. You should assume, however, that lines shown as straight are actually straight, points on a line are in the order shown, and more generally, all geometric objects are in the relative positions shown. For questions with geometric figures, you should base your answers on geometric reasoning, not on estimating or comparing quantities by sight or by measurement.
>
> - Coordinate systems, such as *xy*-planes and number lines, *are* drawn to scale. Therefore, you can read, estimate, or compare quantities in such figures by sight or by measurement.
>
> - Graphical data presentations, such as bar graphs, circle graphs, and line graphs, *are* drawn to scale. Therefore, you can read, estimate, or compare data values by sight or by measurement.

FOR QUESTIONS 1–8, COMPARE QUANTITY A AND QUANTITY B. SOME QUESTIONS WILL HAVE ADDITIONAL INFORMATION ABOVE THE TWO QUANTITIES TO USE IN DETERMINING YOUR ANSWER.

$$w < x < y < z$$

1.

Quantity A	Quantity B
$w + y$	$x + z$

(A) Quantity A is greater.

(B) Quantity B is greater.

(C) The two quantities are equal.

(D) The relationship cannot be determined from the information given.

2.

Quantity A	Quantity B
The number of dimes in $5.10	The number of pennies in 2 quarters

(A) Quantity A is greater.

(B) Quantity B is greater.

(C) The two quantities are equal.

(D) The relationship cannot be determined from the information given.

3.

Quantity A	Quantity B
$\frac{4}{3}\left(\frac{1}{2}\right)\left(\frac{11}{9}\right)$	$\frac{3}{4}\left(\frac{15}{16}\right)\left(\frac{15}{12}\right)$

(A) Quantity A is greater.

(B) Quantity B is greater.

(C) The two quantities are equal.

(D) The relationship cannot be determined from the information given.

$$\frac{x}{y} = 12$$

4.

Quantity A	Quantity B
x	y

(A) Quantity A is greater.

(B) Quantity B is greater.

(C) The two quantities are equal.

(D) The relationship cannot be determined from the information given.

Given triangle ABC

Where $AB = BC = CA$

5.

Quantity A	Quantity B
Value of an interior angle	$60°$

(A) Quantity A is greater.

(B) Quantity B is greater.

(C) The two quantities are equal.

(D) The relationship cannot be determined from the information given.

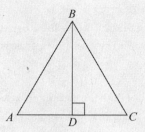

6.

Quantity A	Quantity B
$\angle A$	$\angle C$

(A) Quantity A is greater.

(B) Quantity B is greater.

(C) The two quantities are equal.

(D) The relationship cannot be determined from the information given.

The above shape is made up of 5 congruent squares. The area of the shape is 180.

7.

Quantity A	Quantity B
84	The perimeter of the shape

(A) Quantity A is greater.

(B) Quantity B is greater.

(C) The two quantities are equal.

(D) The relationship cannot be determined from the information given.

8.

Quantity A	Quantity B
$11^4 \times 11^5$	11^9

(A) Quantity A is greater.

(B) Quantity B is greater.

(C) The two quantities are equal.

(D) The relationship cannot be determined from the information given.

Questions 9–20 have several formats. Unless the directions state otherwise, choose one answer choice. For the Numeric Entry questions, follow the instructions below.

Numeric Entry Questions

The following items are the same for both the computer-based version of the test and the paper-and-pencil version. However, those taking the computer-based version will have additional information about entering answers in decimal and fraction boxes on the computer screen. Those taking the paper-and-pencil version will have information about entering answers on answer grids.

- Your answer may be an integer, a decimal, or a fraction, and it may be negative.
- If a question asks for a fraction, there will be two boxes. One box will be for the numerator and one will be for the denominator.
- Equivalent forms of the correct answer, such as 2.5 and 2.50, are all correct.
- Enter the exact answer unless the question asks you to round your answers.

9. If the salesperson receives a $5,500 commission on the sale of a yacht, how much did the yacht sell for if the commission rate is 5%?
   - (A) $110
   - (B) $1,100
   - (C) $11,000
   - (D) $110,000
   - (E) $1,100,000

10. Working at their respective rates, Masha can paint a given apartment in x hours, and Olga can paint it in y hours. If Masha and Olga work together, each at her own rate, in how many hours will they paint the apartment?
    - (A) $x + y$
    - (B) $\dfrac{x+y}{xy}$
    - (C) $\dfrac{xy}{x+y}$
    - (D) $\dfrac{1}{xy}$
    - (E) $\dfrac{1}{x+y}$

FOR QUESTION 11, ENTER YOUR ANSWER IN THE BOX.

---

11. The 20-person staff of a medical center consists of doctors and nurses. Sixty percent of the staff members are doctors, three-quarters of whom are general practitioners, while the rest are pediatricians. If 4 nurses and 4 pediatricians are added, and no other changes are made to the medical center's existing staff, what percentage of the medical center's staff will the pediatricians represent?

    (A) 7%

    (B) 15%

    (C) 20%

    (D) 25%

    (E) 33%

12. Evaluate $27^{\frac{2}{3}}$.

    (A) 3

    (B) 9

    (C) 18

    (D) 27

    (E) 81

QUESTIONS 13 AND 14 REFER TO THE FIGURE BELOW.

m is parallel to *n* and *k* is parallel to *l*

13. If m∠3 = 2x, and m∠10 = 63, find the value of *x*.

    (A) 58.5

    (B) 63

    (C) 72

    (D) 117

    (E) 119.5

14. In the parallelogram formed by the intersection of the lines, what is the sum of the measures of the interior angles?

(A) < 270

(B) < 360

(C) 360

(D) > 360

(E) > 540

QUESTION 15 REFERS TO THE TABLE BELOW.

PURCHASING-POWER PARITY (PPP)

Rank	Country	PPP Total (billion)	PPP/capita ($)	Population (million)
1.	European Union	10,840	28,600	379
2.	USA	10,400	37,600	290
3.	China	5,700	4,400	1,287
4.	Japan	3,550	28,000	127
5.	India	2,660	2,540	1,049
6.	Germany	2,180	26,600	82
7.	France	1,540	25,700	60
8.	Britain	1,520	25,300	60
9.	Italy	1,440	25,000	57
10.	Russia	1,350	9,300	144
11.	Brazil	1,340	7,600	182

15. Which country in the bottom 5 of population has the highest PPP Total?

(A) Italy

(B) Britain

(C) France

(D) Germany

(E) Japan

16. What is the first month's interest payment on a 1-year loan of $34,000 at 8.28%?

(A) $2346.00

(B) $281.52

(C) $234.60

(D) $2815.20

(E) $242.90

---

answers practice test 3

> **FOR QUESTIONS 17 AND 18, CHOOSE <u>ALL</u> THE ANSWERS THAT APPLY.**

17. If m, n, and p are positive integers, and m is a factor of n, and n is a factor of p, which of the following statements are true?

    (A) m is a factor of p

    (B) n is a factor of p^3

    (C) p is the product of $m(n)$

    (D) n is a factor of $m(p)$

18. Find the numbers in the sequence from t_5 to t_7, using the formula $t_n = n(n-2)$.

    (A) −1

    (B) 0

    (C) 3

    (D) 8

    (E) 15

    (F) 24

    (G) 35

    (H) 48

> **FOR QUESTIONS 19 AND 20, ENTER YOUR ANSWERS IN THE BOXES.**

19. It takes 3 electricians four 8-hour days to wire a house. If the general contractor wanted the house wired in three 8-hour days, how many electricians should he have hired?

    [   ]

20. David, Eric, and Justin are brothers. David is 6 years younger than Eric, and Justin is 3 years older than Eric. In 3 years, Justin will be twice as old as David. What is the current age of the oldest brother?

    [   ]

STOP

> If you finish before the time is up, you may check your work in this section only.

ANSWER KEY AND EXPLANATIONS

Section 1: Analytical Writing

Analyze an Issue

Model: 6 points out of 6

Who has not expressed their dissatisfaction with the American public school system? Every disappointment in American society is regularly laid at the doorstep of the public schools, which surely have gotten everything wrong from methods used to teach reading to policies related to discipline and detention. American public schools, it seems, don't just provide miserable educations. They also serve the wrong lunches, cannot teach math, provide inadequate preparation for the world of work, betray students who aspire to the best colleges and universities, have got it all wrong when it comes to physical education, and have turned the U.S. population into morons who neither understand simple scientific facts such as the seasons nor know simple civic facts such as the name of the current chief justice of the Supreme Court. Or so the story goes.

Are these the actual facts, however? The United States is one of the great powers of the world, one of the world leaders in everything from goods produced to standards of living to basic human rights. Was it our failing, inadequate, "broken" schools that produced this leadership? Perhaps it was schools that work, despite inevitable flaws, that helped propel the United States to the top over more than two centuries of remarkable achievement and progress.

The creation of a universal public education system is one of the great achievements of American democracy. Education isn't guaranteed by the Constitution; instead, this great right and privilege is based on abiding beliefs in fundamental equality: the right of everyone to achieve. And in that noble goal and commitment lie its flaws: if you are committed to democracy, truly committed to educating everyone, including children who may not speak English or are so severely handicapped that they perhaps need a year to develop skills that other children develop over the course of days or weeks, then it is difficult to also maintain the highest standards of achievement. This fundamental contradiction is at the heart of American education: we are committed both to democracy and high standards. No wonder that we sometimes don't quite make it on either count.

Yet, the relatively occasional failings are so often centerpieced, while the achievements of our system are overlooked or denigrated. Instead of thinking about all the constituencies that American education serves, and how many capable citizens it creates (are you, my reader, not one of them?) people focus instead on the shortcomings and inadequacies of our system. They then posit some kind of magic bullet, such as charter schools, as a cure for all the system's supposed ills. I do not argue here that charter schools are wrong or cannot be beneficial to students; what I do argue, however, is that it is not necessarily the case, as many statistics have shown, that even radically new schools and approaches end up producing better results than our American public schools do.

Furthermore, I do not argue that schools could not do better. There is no question that some populations remain underserved, such those as in areas in which a kind of de facto segregation exists—not by race but by income level. Again, however, what sprawling, many-faceted, complex institution could not do better? An admission that the American school system could make improvements is not an admission that is broken. Far from it. Over time, the American public school system has served more and more students and educated them at higher and higher levels. Yesterday's high school graduation rates are today's college graduation rates. Those who succeed in American society, and their numbers are legion, may credit their colleges or universities, their parents, and their own talents and drive, but surely the American public school system also played a key role in so many of those successes.

This essay scores 6 out of 6 because it

- **answers the task.** It follows specific instructions by disagreeing with the statement and supporting that disagreement; simultaneously, it thoughtfully reveals some of the complexities of the issue and how they help shape the writer's position.

- **is well supported.** The complex approach to the issue is best reflected in the clear and satisfying support, which draws on issues related to our Constitution and our democracy, as well as the problems of serving many constituencies. Examples are persuasive and developed.

- **is well organized.** The formal introduction creates interest; the body paragraphs provide thoughtful, focused support; and the essay concludes appropriately. Effective transitions between and within the paragraphs connect ideas.

- **is fluid.** Sentences are richly varied; constructions range from effective fragments to complex ideas linked by conjunctive adverbs to a sentence that uses a parenthetical element for rhetorical effect. Powerful, precise words characterize the writing throughout.

- **observes the conventions of Standard Written English.**

Model: 1 point out of 6

You have got that right. At Martindale High only a few kids ending up graduated. The numbers gone down each year, from freshmen year when maybe 1000 kids are in the school and then by sophmore year theres only 500 left and then by junior year theres only 250 till you get to senior year and a handful of kids get out with a diploma but then only some of them go on to college, or they can't afford to go anyway.

This essay scores 1 out of 6 because it

- **barely answers the task.** While the essay does take a position that agrees with the prompt, it could scarcely be more simple or inappropriate in the way it states that agreement.

- **is not supported.** The writer does offer one bit of evidence, but it is presented as a single run-on sentence. Furthermore, the evidence, based on one school, is not explained or broadened to support the position.

- **has no sense of sentence construction.** Of the three sentences in the paragraph, one is a very long series of unpunctuated ideas that are combined in one run-on sentence.

- **contains major errors in the conventions of Standard Written English.**

Analyze an Argument

Model: 6 points out of 6

The person who penned this argument clearly wants a new public safety building. But is this building truly needed and wanted?

Several types of evidence would be useful in evaluating whether a new building is necessary, including exact facts and figures of what the current building now accommodates and exact facts and figures relating to ideal or acceptable amounts of space required to integrate capacities that were never planned for in the 1961 building. For example, one would need to know how much space the current building has, and how much of that space is currently used, and for what. One might also ask whether the space in the 1961 building could be used better to accommodate more functions. In addition, one absolutely needs to know how much space, and what kind of space, is needed, either in ideal or baseline-acceptable terms, to accommodate the new environmental team, the 911 communications center, the emergency management center, and an emergency management office. One presumes, for instance, that the 1961 building already has some kind of arrangement and space allotment for dealing with 911 calls as well as for dealing with emergencies in general. After all, it currently performs these functions every day. Therefore, it is necessary to know if more space is actually needed for those functions, and if it is needed, how much more space, and why.

If evidence shows that the current building is too cramped or space is so inadequate that emergency calls cannot be met, or if current statistics point to a date in the near future when emergency calls cannot be met because of reasons of space, that evidence would seriously strengthen the argument. On the other hand, if data suggest that calls are being met, and trends suggest that they will continue to be met, that evidence would weaken the argument. In the same manner, if the facts show that emergency management computers, monitors, desks, and other equipment could be installed in spaces now crammed with items that could be discarded, or that the use of space in the 1961 building could be effectively redesigned at an acceptable cost, that would seriously weaken the argument for a new building.

The issue of public support for this building project also requires more evidence to strengthen the argument. No facts are given about the opinion poll, which may have listed 20 projects of importance to the town and which may not have limited the number that residents could list as important, high priority, or "pressing." This means that some residents could have marked all 20. Furthermore, the opinion poll may have been conducted only among a small group or among supporters of the project. If the evidence shows that only people who work in the current police and fire facility were polled, then the results are dramatically biased. If the evidence shows that only 3 percent of the town's population was polled, and of that number, only 51 percent identified a new public safety building as a "pressing need," then the results of that poll are not especially valid or credible. These results would, of course, seriously weaken the argument.

A final idea in the argument that is crying out for evidence or substantiation is the conclusion that the town will be safer once a new public safety building is built. To strengthen this argument, the writer could supply many types of evidence related to unsafe conditions that are a result, perhaps, of groups being unable to perform their jobs as well as they might perform them due to lack of proper facilities or adequate space. For example, if the environmental team cannot meet, or has no central or adequate office equipment available to each member, perhaps it cannot as carefully monitor water quality or toxic waste sites that do present a real and quantifiable threat to public health. These and other similar facts would seriously strengthen the conclusion of increased safety.

This essay scores 6 out of 6 because it

- **answers the task.** It discusses thoughtfully and logically the specific evidence that is needed to evaluate the argument, and it clearly explains how that evidence might strengthen or weaken the argument.

- **is well supported.** The explanation of evidence is specific and persuasive and drills down to key issues such as square footage, redesign of existing space, and possible percentages that might have constituted the opinion poll.

- **is well organized.** Paragraph 1 clearly states the focus, while the next paragraph begins with a clear and cogent topic sentence that is logically and coherently developed through the paragraph. Ideas for the ensuing paragraphs follow logically, and all the paragraphs are characterized by coherence and unity.

- **is fluid.** The sentences are sophisticated; no run-ons interfere with meaning or precision. There are a variety of sentence types and openers. Word choices are precise and appropriate.

- **observes the conventions of Standard Written English.**

Model: 1 point out of 6

This argument for a new public safety building lacks evidence. The argument says that theres not enough space for the police cars now or for the latest-model ambulance but it doesn't say how much space these cars need or how much bigger the new public safety building has to be. There should also be evidence about why the town needs all those new "functions of a 911 communications center, emergency management center, an emergency management office, and the new environmental safety team." What is the purpose of these teams and are they really needed has to be answered but isn't. This is not stated and it should be, including the evidence for needing these offices, centers, and teams. Many people in the town think that the new public safety building is necessary. That is not evidence to prove that the public safety building should be built. You have to do more than have the opinion that it is necessary, you have to have the facts that tell clearly why it is necessary. That is, what is concluded at the end does not necessarily follow from what is stated.

This essay scores 1 out of 6 because it

- **does not answer the task.** While this essay refers to the need for evidence, it provides no concrete examples of evidence that would actually weaken or strengthen the argument.

- **lacks organization.** The single paragraph lacks clear focus. The response fails to divide the main ideas into separate, cogent units of discourse.

- **offers illogical support.** The writer does try to say something specific about how much space the vehicles require, but this "evidence" would neither weaken nor strengthen the argument, as it is already a matter of fact stated in the argument that, for instance, the ambulance does not fit in its bay.

- **has poorly constructed sentences.** Run-on sentences and convoluted sentences interfere with coherence.

- **contains some errors in the conventions of Standard Written English.** In a better organized and written response, they would have stood out less.

Section 2: Verbal Reasoning

1. B	11. A	16. A, B
2. E	12. A	17. C, F
3. A, F	13. B	18. C, F
4. A, D, G	14. C	19. A, D
5. C, E, G	15. A	20. E
6. E		
7. D		
8. B, C		
9. D		
10. C		

Question

1. One of the major concerns as states pulled themselves out of the deficits created during the Great Recession was whether they would return to their _____ spending habits once the good times began to roll again.

(A) decadent
(B) profligate
(C) parsimonious
(D) immoral
(E) licentious

Answer Explanation

The correct answer is (B). "Profligate," choice (B), means "wildly extravagant, recklessly wasteful" as well as "dissolute." In this case, the first meanings fit the sense of the sentence. Usage will help you eliminate "decadent," choice (A), meaning "characterized by decay or decline" or "self-indulgent," because it is usually used to refer to persons. Choice (C), "parsimonious," means "frugal, penny-pinching" and the opposite of what is required by the context. Choice (D), "immoral," means "corrupt, against moral principles," and there is nothing to suggest that in the context. "Licentious," choice (E), can be eliminated for the same reason; it means "lacking moral discipline" and is usually used in reference to sexual promiscuity.

Question

2. To the board of directors, it appeared that the only way to placate _____ stockholders was to remove the CEO.

| (A) seditious |
| (B) subversive |
| (C) insubordinate |
| (D) disobedient |
| (E) disgruntled |

Answer Explanation

The correct answer is (E). Choice (E), "disgruntled," means "feeling or showing discontent or anger." Choice (A), "seditious," usually refers to inciting rebellion against civil authority, not a board of directors, so eliminate it. Choice (B), "subversive," might be applicable, but there is nothing to indicate that the stockholders were working to overthrow the governance of the company. Also, the word is usually used in reference to overthrowing a civil government. Choice (C), "insubordinate," is a synonym of "subversive" and means "refusal to submit to authority, disobedient." A person may be insubordinate to a boss, but stockholders don't answer to the board; it's the other way around, so eliminate choice (C). Choice (D), "disobedient," can also be eliminated because stockholders don't answer to the board.

Question

3. In discussing the vanishing ecosystem of the Grand Canyon, the speaker spoke (i) _____ and passionately about his subject. It was obvious that the (ii) _____ of the natural environment caused him grave concern.

Blank (i)		Blank (ii)
(A) eloquently		(D) mutilation
(B) emotionally		(E) reparation
(C) prominently		(F) destruction

Answer Explanation

The correct answers are (A) and (F). Answer Blank (i): You need to find the answer that balances the word "passionately." You can eliminate choice (B) because "emotionally" is similar to "passionately" so choice (B) would be redundant. Choice (C) is incorrect because "prominently" means "noticeably, remarkably" and doesn't fit the sense or usage so well as choice (A), "eloquently," meaning "articulately, vividly, movingly."

Answer Blank (ii): Sometimes, the simplest answer is the best answer. Choice (F), "destruction," means "destroying, or having been destroyed." Choice (D), "mutilation," means "to remove some essential part of a body, or to disfigure by damaging" and is usually used to refer to human disfigurement or something like a statue." Choice (E), "reparation," makes no sense because it means "making repairs or amends, or paying compensation."

Question

4. The epic heroes who undergo a series of (i) _____ challenges to attain a goal are (ii) _____ feature of many national cultural identities. Many of the challenges involve some (iii) _____ feat of daring.

Blank (i)	Blank (ii)	Blank (iii)
(A) extraordinary	(D) an underlying	(G) intrepid
(B) copious	(E) an external	(H) steadfast
(C) massive	(F) a conventional	(I) resolute

Answer Explanation

The correct answers are (A), (D), and (G). Answer Blank (i): Choice (A), "extraordinary," is the best answer. Choice (B), "copious," means "abundant, large quantity" and could fit the sense, but "series" implies "many," so to say "abundant" would be redundant. Choice (C), "massive," meaning "extremely large in amount, or large and heavy," doesn't make sense.

Answer Blank (ii): Choice (D), "underlying," means "lying beneath" literally, but it also means "hidden and significant, or essential," the appropriate meaning in this context. Choice (E), "external," means "coming from the outside, or suitable for use on the outside, or something outside the scope," and doesn't fit the sense. Choice (F), "conventional," means "socially accepted, customary, or established by general use or agreement," which doesn't fit the sense.

Answer Blank (iii): Choice (G), "intrepid," means "courageous" and fits the sense of daring feats. Choice (H), "steadfast," meaning "persistent, loyal, unwavering" may be true about epic heroes, but doesn't fit the sense. Nor does choice (I), "resolute," which means "firm in belief or purpose, or quickness."

Question

5. Among the health scams that the FDA warns the (i) _____ public about are (ii) _____ cancer-treatment products and weight-loss programs with FDA (iii) _____ ingredients.

Blank (i)	Blank (ii)	Blank (iii)
(A) wary	(D) trick	(G) unsanctioned
(B) circumspect	(E) mock	(H) unmeasured
(C) credulous	(F) deceptive	(I) characteristic

Answer Explanation

The correct answers are (C), (E), and (G). Answer Blank (i): If the public was "wary," choice (A), meaning "cautious, suspicious," the FDA might not need to warn it. Choice (B), "circumspect," is similar to "wary" in meaning and so doesn't fit. Choice (C), "credulous," meaning "gullible, trusting, naïve," fits the sense.

Answer Blank (ii): "Trick," choice (D), can mean "weak, defective, liable to fail; or designed for doing tricks," none of which fit the sense. Choice (E), "mock," as an adjective means "false, sham, imitative" and fits the context. Choice (F), "deceptive," might seem correct, but "deceptive" means "misleading," and these products are more than misleading—they're fake!

Answer Blank (iii): Choice (G), "unsanctioned," means "unapproved, unendorsed, unauthorized." The inclusion of "FDA" before the word is a clue. Choice (H), "unmeasured," might seem correct, but sense tips the answer toward "unsanctioned" as stronger and making better sense. Choice (I), "characteristic," doesn't make sense.

QUESTIONS 6–8 ARE BASED ON THE FOLLOWING PASSAGE.

In the year 1901, Spanish painter Pablo Picasso entered what is now referred to as his Blue Period. At the time Picasso was just 20 years old, living in Paris as a relatively unknown artist. Up to this point, the paintings Picasso produced were vibrantly colored, expressing the decadent life he and his friend Carlos Casagemas had been leading together in Paris. But
5 the suicide of Casagemas in 1901 was a major trigger for Picasso's Blue Period, in which Picasso began to paint in various shades of blue, giving the paintings a haunting and melancholy feel. The recurring theme of the Blue Period paintings is the desolation of outsiders, which included beggars, prisoners, and circus people. By 1904, Picasso had emerged from the Blue Period and began what is known as the Rose Period, characterized by bright colors,
10 and featuring acrobats and harlequins. A few years later, Picasso began to explore Cubism, which broke completely from the traditional three-dimensional representation of objects, and for which he became famous. The Blue and Rose Periods can be viewed as transitional times for Picasso in which he moved from the traditional art of his youth to the iconoclastic art of his adulthood.

Question

6. Based on the passage the author evidently believes that

(A) the Rose Period is less significant a time period than the Blue Period in the artistic development of Picasso.

(B) the suicide of Casagemas had an effect on Picasso that would haunt him for the rest of his life.

(C) if Picasso had not gone through the Blue and Rose Periods he would have never been ready to explore a new form of art.

(D) there is no way to understand Cubism without seeing the artistic road that led Picasso to it over the course of his work.

(E) the Blue Period was how Picasso expressed himself artistically during a difficult time of his life.

Answer Explanation

The correct answer is (E). The author explains that during Picasso's Blue Period he painted scenes of desolation because he was so affected by his friend's suicide. Choice (A) is incorrect because the author never states or implies that either period is more significant than the other. Choice (B) is incorrect because the author only implies that Casamegas's suicide affected Picasso during his Blue Period. Choice (C) is incorrect because although this might be a conclusion that could be drawn, the author of the passage doesn't draw this conclusion. Choice (D) is incorrect because although it might seem true, the author does not imply this in the passage.

Question

7. In this passage, "iconoclastic" (line 13) means
   (A) eclectic.
   (B) eccentric.
   (C) consequential.
   (D) revolutionary.
   (E) conservative.

Answer Explanation

The correct answer is (D). "Iconoclastic" means "revolutionary, one who attacks the status quo." Choice (A) is incorrect because "eclectic" means "diverse." Choice (B) is incorrect because "eccentric" means "unconventional," which is not so close in meaning as "revolutionary." Choice (C) is incorrect because "consequential" means "significant," which doesn't express the degree or quality of difference that "revolutionary" does. Choice (E) is incorrect because "conservative" means about the opposite of revolutionary.

Question

8. Which of the following ideas are clearly supported in this passage?
   (A) After the Blue Period, Picasso no longer painted pictures of desolation.
   (B) Picasso is best known for his Cubist works.
   (C) The Rose Period was just as significant as the Blue Period in terms of Picasso's growth as an artist.

Answer Explanation

The correct answers are (B) and (C). The passage states that Cubism made Picasso famous, and we can infer that he is best known for these works. The Rose and Blue Periods are both cited as artistic expressions Picasso explored in his youth. Choice (A) is incorrect because even if it were true, we have no way of knowing this from the details of the passage.

QUESTIONS 9 AND 10 ARE BASED ON THE FOLLOWING PASSAGE.

Although the quality of smartphone photos varies by manufacturer, smartphone camera manufacturers are nevertheless putting camera companies out of business. Smartphones offer sophisticated technology in lenses, sensors, flashes, image stabilization, video, and playback. While small gradations in image quality now separate smartphone competitors, a
5 more fundamental difference lies in each smartphone's organization, storage, and transformational capabilities. Companies that offer organization by capabilities such as face and other recognition, as well as more streamlined sharing to all devices, have a definite advantage over those who force the user to make fundamental organization and storage choices. Some of these manufacturers even distinguish superior shots, in terms of lighting and composition,
10 from inferior ones, streamlining the selection and deletion process that many smartphone owners must now undertake laboriously by hand. Superior smartphone cameras also have the capability to transform related single shots into an animated GIF.

Question

9. All of the following are stated or implied in this passage EXCEPT
    (A) Smartphone camera image quality and storage vary by manufacturer.
    (B) Small differences in the quality of images now separate smartphone cameras.
    (C) Some smartphone cameras flag or otherwise differentiate good images from bad ones.
    (D) Smartphone cameras offer only slightly better lenses and sensors than traditional cameras do.
    (E) Smartphone camera capability includes creating the appearance of motion from successive shots.

Answer Explanation

The correct answer is (D). All the statements except choice (D) are supported by information in the passage. No statement is made, however, that claims or implies a difference in the quality of lenses and sensors.

Question

10. Which of the following statements expresses the author's opinion about smartphone cameras?
    (A) Consumers should select those cameras that offer the highest image quality.
    (B) Smartphones camera sales now outstrip traditional camera sales, even though smartphone images are not any better.
    (C) The best smartphone cameras offer advanced discrimination, animation, and other capacities.
    (D) Facial recognition is the most advanced capability in smartphone cameras today.
    (E) Consumers should select those cameras that can organize photos by topic.

Answer Explanation

The correct answer is (C). The topic sentence, in the middle of the paragraph, states clearly that the author thinks that the more fundamental difference between competing cameras is not image quality, but the camera's ability to organize, store, and transform the photographs once they are taken. To do this, the best cameras discriminate, animate, and more. Choice (A) is incorrect because the author suggests other capabilities are more important. Choices (B), (D), and (E) misstate information in the passage.

QUESTIONS 11 AND 12 ARE BASED ON THE FOLLOWING PASSAGE.

The use of solar energy to produce electricity can be an excellent alternative to using fossil fuels. Solar panels give off no pollution, and, unlike other alternative energy sources like wind turbines, are silent. One big advantage of solar energy is that it can harness electricity in remote locations that are not connected to a national grid. One example of this is in space,
5   where high-efficiency solar cells are used to power satellites. Although the initial investment for solar cells is high, once they are installed, they provide free electricity. Yet unfortunately this initial cost is one reason people are hesitant to embrace solar energy as an alternative energy source. Currently, a single solar cell can cost more than $1000, and some households may need more than one. Also, solar cells do not generate electricity 24 hours a day, so

10 excess electricity needs to be captured during daylight time for later use. The weather and pollution levels can also affect a solar cell's efficiency, which could have a huge impact on solar panels installed in cities. However, cost is still considered the main deterrent. Because fossil fuels still cost less than the initial investment for solar panels, it will likely be some time before we see a significant shift toward solar energy use.

Question

11. Select the sentence that is NOT a major detail that supports the author's opinion.

(A) One example of this is in space, where high-efficiency solar cells are used to power satellites.

(B) The weather and pollution levels can also affect a solar cell's efficiency, which could have a huge impact on solar panels installed in cities.

(C) Currently, a single solar cell can cost more than $1000, and some households may need more than one.

(D) Because fossil fuels still cost less than the initial investment for solar panels, it will likely be some time before we see a significant shift toward solar energy use.

(E) The use of solar energy to produce electricity can be an excellent alternative to using fossil fuels.

Answer Explanation

The correct answer is (A). This is the only sentence that is a minor point in the discussion of the author's topic: There are pros and cons that are weighed in choosing solar energy. That solar cells power satellites in space is a specialized use of no relevance to the average consumer of power.

Question

12. Which of the following, if it were true, would weaken the author's conclusion?

(A) Fossil fuels and solar energy cost about the same.

(B) Solar panels will eventually be able to run 24 hours a day.

(C) Solar panels can sometimes create more noise than wind turbines.

(D) Many people who use solar panels are disappointed with the results.

(E) There are many alternatives to solar energy that are much cheaper.

Answer Explanation

The correct answer is (A). The author concludes the passage by stating that the main deterrent to widespread use of solar energy is cost and that fossil fuels cost less than the initial investment for solar panels. So, if they cost about the same, this would weaken the author's conclusion. Choices (B) and (C) are incorrect because even if they were true, they don't address the conclusion, which is the cost of solar panels. Choice (D) is incorrect because if it were true, it still doesn't address the cost of the solar panels. Choice (E) is incorrect because if it were true it would actually strengthen, not weaken, the author's argument.

QUESTIONS 13–15 ARE BASED ON THE FOLLOWING PASSAGE.

In the arena of dietary advice, science has produced some nutty conclusions. For the past two decades, multiple studies have drawn similar conclusions linking nut consumption to reduced risk of certain diseases, including hypertension, type-2 diabetes mellitus, and colon cancer. Studies have also shown reductions among nut eaters in many common and significant
5 mediators of chronic diseases, such as inflammation, hyperglycemia, and insulin resistance.

More significantly, a study recently reported by the *New England Journal of Medicine* has found that nut consumption is "inversely related with total and cause-specific mortality." The study was conducted over the 30-year period spanning 1980 and 2010; used a cohort of some 20,000 nurses and other health professionals; and tracked other dietary and lifestyle
10 factors, such as fruit and vegetable intake, meat and alcohol consumption, physical activity, age, and body mass index. The study's authors concluded that those who ate more nuts were also leaner, got more exercise, ate more fruits and vegetables, and drank more alcohol. The import of this and earlier studies is that nuts contribute to both good health and longevity.

Furthermore, these calorie-laden snacks have been shown to make their consumers leaner.
15 Questions as to why the study found this may be answered in various ways—consumers eat them instead of snacks with even more calories; the body may treat nut calories differently than other calories; and nut consumers may just be more active or nutritionally conscious—or they elude definitive answers. But even if the possibility of a clear cause-and-effect relationship between nut consumption and svelteness is not enough of an enticement for more nut eating,
20 the makeup of nuts should be. For example, nuts are an excellent source of omega-3 fatty acids that lower triglycerides, slow down the accretion of plaque, and lower blood pressure. They also contain phytochemicals and antioxidants thought to reduce the risk of certain cancers.

Question

13. What is the most significant detail about the study reported by the *New England Journal of Medicine?*

(A) The study was conducted over a period of some thirty years.

(B) The study suggested a reduced rate of mortality for those who consumed nuts.

(C) The study suggested a decreased rate in the incidence of certain chronic diseases.

(D) The study suggested a cause-effect relationship between nut consumption and leanness.

(E) The study contradicted the claims of most nut studies conducted over the past two decades.

Answer Explanation

The correct answer is (B). The study appears to be the first to claim that the consumption of nuts is inversely related to mortality. Choices (A) and (C) are incorrect because even though they are important facts about the study, they are not as significant or groundbreaking as the study's conclusions. Choice (D) is incorrect because leanness is not the most significant idea; neither is it decisively in the realm of cause and effect, as paragraph 3 makes clear. Choice (E) is incorrect; the study corroborated some prior claims and enlarged upon them.

Question

14. What does the author suggest about studies that predate the study reported by the *New England Journal of Medicine?*

(A) They drew unsubstantiated conclusions about the effects of consuming nuts.

(B) They showed how eating nuts contributes to the incidence of type-2 diabetes mellitus.

(C) They showed how eating nuts works against factors that may contribute to disease.

Answer Explanation

The correct answer is (C). The last sentence of paragraph 1 discusses the role of nut consumption and common mediators of disease. Choice (A) is incorrect because the passage neither states nor implies this idea; furthermore, the passage takes some pains to tell about sample size, the length of the study, and the range of dietary and lifestyle factors that were taken into account. Choice (B) is incorrect because the author says the study shows the opposite.

Question

15. "Definitive" (line 18) most nearly means

(A) final.

(B) inconclusive.

(C) lexical.

(D) equivocal.

(E) defined.

Answer Explanation

The correct answer is (A). In this context, "definitive" means "final." Choices (B) and (D) are incorrect because "inconclusive" and "equivocal" both suggest ambiguity, which is the near opposite of something definitive. Choice (C) is incorrect because, even though "lexical" refers to the lexicon or vocabulary, the meaning of "definitive" does not relate to defined words. Choice (E) is incorrect because "defined," while having meanings ranging from "gave the meaning of" to "marked the limits of," is not a precise synonym for "definitive."

Question

16. The gallery owner has a(n) _____ eye and an amazing ability to select the next hot artist from all the new artists who show him their portfolios.

(A) discerning

(B) discriminating

(C) detecting

(D) investigative

(E) observant

(F) understanding

Answer Explanation

The correct answers are (A) and (B). Choice (A), "discerning," means "good judgment, perceptive," and choice (B), "discriminating," also means "perceptive, showing careful judgment or good taste." Choice (C), "detecting," and choice (D), "investigative," are synonyms, but don't fit the sense. There is no indication that the gallery owner looks for these artists; they come to him. Choice (E), "observant," might work in the sentence, but it has no synonym in the list. The same is true for choice (F), "understanding," but that's not typically used to describe eyes.

Question

17. _____ data from the traffic safety survey shows a 17 percent increase in nonfatal pedestrian accidents due to texting drivers. The final report will be available next year.

   (A) Improvised
   (B) Acting
   (C) Interim
   (D) Permanent
   (E) Terminal
   (F) Provisional

Answer Explanation

The correct answers are (C) and (F). Choice (C), "interim," and choice (F), "provisional," mean "temporary, short-term," which counterbalance the second sentence discussing a "final" report. Choice (A), "improvised," means "invented, used what was available," and is not consistent with data from a survey; there also is no synonym for it in the list. Although choice (B), "acting," is sometimes a synonym for "interim," in this case, it doesn't make sense to say "acting data." "Acting" is typically used to describe a person, such as "acting head of the department." Choice (D), "permanent," is the opposite of "interim" and doesn't make sense in the sentence. Choice (E), "terminal," on a quick read might be confused with "temporary," but the choice is "terminal" and is incorrect. It means "an ending point or place or part."

Question

18. Scrooge has come to be considered the _____ miser from whom all similar characters are drawn.

   (A) pattern
   (B) eccentric
   (C) archetypal
   (D) unusual
   (E) alternate
   (F) classic

Answer Explanation

The correct answers are (C) and (F). Choice (C), "archetypal," means "original model from which others are patterned or an ideal example of something." In this case, the first meaning works. Choice (F), "classic," means "serving as a model or standard" and is, therefore, a synonym for "archetypal." Choice (A), "pattern," doesn't work based on usage; the construction would have to be "pattern for a miser" to be correct. Choice (B), "eccentric," is incorrect because "eccentric" means "not conventional, departing from the usual pattern," and although Scrooge might be eccentric in his views, that doesn't fit the context. "Unusual," choice (D), doesn't fit the context either. Choice (E), "alternate," meaning "other," doesn't make sense either.

Question

19. While economics may be exciting to some, the yawning student in the back of the room thought it _____.

    (A) tedious
    (B) sundry
    (C) repetitive
    (D) soporific
    (E) disingenuous
    (F) monotonous

Answer Explanation

The correct answers are (A) and (D). The context clue is "yawning." Choice (A), "tedious," means "causing mental fatigue, monotonous" and choice (D), "soporific," means "sleep inducing." Choice (B) is less likely to put someone to sleep because "sundry" means "varied" as well as "miscellaneous." Choice (C), "repetitive," could work with "tedious" because it means "characterized by repetition," which may be tedious and boring, but doesn't include the idea of sleep. On first reading, choice (F), "monotonous," also could seem as though it might work because it means "spoken in the same tone, lacking in variety, tedious," but "monotonous" doesn't have the element of sleep inducing, so it doesn't fit the context so well as "soporific." Choice (E), "disingenuous," means "insincere, calculating, not straightforward," which doesn't relate to the context.

QUESTION 20 IS BASED ON THE FOLLOWING PASSAGE.

For years astronomers could not figure out why the Sun's outer atmosphere, or corona, is millions of degrees hotter than its surface, but recently NASA scientists came up with an answer. The corona consists of loops of hot gas that are thousands of miles high, but from the Earth, the corona can only be seen during a total solar eclipse, which has made it difficult
5 to study. However, NASA scientists recently determined that nanoflares, tiny bursts of heat and energy, are what make the temperature so much hotter in the corona. The loops of gas are made up of bundles of smaller magnetic strands that can reach temperatures of several million degrees Kelvin, which is significantly hotter than the surface of the Sun. NASA scientists created a simulation to see how nanoflares might occur and determined that the
10 million-degree temperatures in the corona could only be produced by impulsive energy bursts. However, the magnetic strands cool very quickly, which explains why this phenomenon had been so difficult to detect.

Question

20. Select the sentence that best explains the recent discovery about the Sun's corona.

- (A) However, the magnetic strands cool very quickly, which explains why this phenomenon had been so difficult to detect.
- (B) The corona consists of loops of hot gas that are thousands of miles high, but from the Earth, the corona can only be seen during a total solar eclipse, which has made it difficult to study.
- (C) For years astronomers could not figure out why the Sun's outer atmosphere, or corona, is millions of degrees hotter than its surface, but recently NASA scientists came up with an answer.
- (D) The loops of gas are made up of bundles of smaller magnetic strands that can reach temperatures of several million degrees Kelvin, which is significantly hotter than the surface of the Sun.
- (E) However, NASA scientists recently determined that nanoflares, tiny bursts of heat and energy, are what make the temperature so much hotter in the corona.

Answer Explanation

The correct answer is (E). This sentence sums up why the corona is so much hotter than the surface of the Sun. Choice (A) is incorrect because it only explains why the phenomenon was difficult to detect, but not what the phenomenon is. Choice (B) is incorrect because it describes what the corona consists of, but it doesn't explain why the corona is hotter than the Sun's surface. Choice (C) is incorrect because though it poses the problem, it doesn't answer it. Choice (D) is incorrect because although it explains an important detail about the phenomenon, it doesn't fully explain the phenomenon.

Section 3: Verbal Reasoning

1. A	11. E	16. B, E
2. D	12. A, C	17. A, E
3. A, E	13. A	18. C, E
4. B, F, H	14. B	19. C, D
5. B, F, I	15. A, B, C	20. C
6. E		
7. C		
8. B		
9. A		
10. A		

Question

1. Even though technology has vastly improved the accuracy of weather forecasts, it is unlikely that technology will enhance forecasting enough to enable accurate forecasts for more than two weeks because weather is too _____.

(A) unpredictable
(B) subjective
(C) arbitrary
(D) unreliable
(E) elusive

Answer Explanation

The correct answer is (A). "Unpredictable," choice (A), means "not able to be foretold or foreseen," so it fits the context of not being able to forecast the weather. Choice (B), "subjective," meaning "based on or influenced by attitudes, opinions, or beliefs instead of on verifiable evidence," is incorrect; weather is not subjective—it's objective. Choice (C), "arbitrary," is incorrect because it means "determined or founded on personal whim or impulse, not reasoned" and is used in reference to people or actions of people. Choice (D), "unreliable," is incorrect because it means "not trustworthy, not to be relied on," which doesn't make sense. Choice (E), "elusive," means "difficult to describe, detect, or analyze," which may seem correct, but it doesn't have the idea of seeing into the future that "unpredictable" includes, so eliminate choice (E).

Question

2. The Library of Congress recordings of American African folk songs recorded on location in the Deep South are considered the _____ versions against which musicologists evaluate all other versions.

| (A) indispensable |
| (B) momentous |
| (C) explicit |
| (D) definitive |
| (E) scholarly |

Answer Explanation

The correct answer is (D). Choice (D), "definitive," means "the recognized authority, authoritative" and best fits the context. Choice (A), "indispensable," meaning "necessary, very useful," is a good candidate for the answer, but it doesn't quite fit with the context: that these versions are the ones against which other versions are evaluated. This implies they're the standard—the authoritative versions. Choice (B), "momentous," meaning "very important, significant," though another near choice, doesn't include the idea of being the standard. Choice (C), "explicit," means "clearly expressed or defined" and doesn't fit the sense. Choice (E), "scholarly," may on a fast read be the answer by default, but it doesn't fit the context: these are recordings of actual folk songs that were made on location. They're not scholarly works, so choice (E) is incorrect.

Question

3. At one end of the spectrum is Van Gogh's (i) _____ life driven by the demons of madness and at the other end is Monet's (ii) _____ life in his beloved garden at Giverny.

Blank (i)	Blank (ii)
(A) turbulent	(D) stoical
(B) rowdy	(E) tranquil
(C) boisterous	(F) bucolic

Answer Explanation

The correct answers are (A) and (E). Answer Blank (i): Choices (B) and (C) are similar. Although both "rowdy" and "boisterous" have other meanings, they mean "loud," so their similarity makes either suspect as the correct answer. Choice (A), "turbulent," meaning "having a chaotic or restless nature, agitated, disturbed," fits the idea of mental illness best.

Answer Blank (ii): Choice (D), "stoical," is incorrect because it means "unemotional, indifferent," and the clause states that Monet loved his garden, so he wasn't indifferent. Choice (F), "bucolic," means "pastoral, relating to the countryside," which describes where Monet lived, but choice (E) is a better answer. You need an answer that counterbalances the emotionalism of Van Gogh, and that's "tranquil," meaning "free of disturbance, not agitated," choice (E).

Question

4. Ernest Hemingway was (i) _____ storyteller—an artist with words. He could paint (ii) _____ portrait of a proud young man locked in deadly combat with a ferocious bull and an equally (iii) _____ picture of a proud old man in his epic struggle with a giant fish.

Blank (i)	Blank (ii)	Blank (iii)
(A) an accomplished	(D) an impressive	(G) glittering
(B) a consummate	(E) an interesting	(H) riveting
(C) a perfect	(F) a stunning	(I) conspicuous

Answer Explanation

The correct answers are (B), (F), and (H). Answer Blank (i): Choice (A), "accomplished," meaning "skilled," is true, but choice (B), "consummate," meaning "masterful, highly skilled," captures the sense of the sentence better. It's a matter of degree: Hemingway isn't just a good storyteller, he's also great at his craft. Choice (C) is incorrect because "perfect" means "without defect, complete" and doesn't quite make sense.

Answer Blank (ii): To answer the second and third blanks, you need to consider the choices together because the phrase "and an equally" indicates that you need to look for two words that balance each other (are equal). Choices (D), "impressive," and (E), "interesting," are somewhat similar, and based on the style of the passage, which is slightly ornate, not intense enough, so eliminate them. Choice (F), "stunning," meaning "commanding attention, or shocking, astonishing," fits the context.

Answer Blank (iii): In choosing your third answer, look for a word that is similar to "stunning." Choice (H), "riveting," means "holding attention," so it's the correct answer. Choice (G), "glittering," means "showy, dazzling," and may be true of the portrait, but doesn't balance "stunning." As a double-check, it doesn't balance "impressive" or "interesting": it's of a more intense degree than either word. Choice (I), "conspicuous," means "obvious, without attempting to hide anything" and doesn't fit the context.

Question

5. The anthropologist's explanation for the difference in cultural traits had always seemed (i) _____, but they were later deemed (ii) _____ after new discoveries. His entire life's work was (iii) _____ by the academic community and his career was in ruins.

Blank (i)	Blank (ii)	Blank (iii)
(A) desirable	(D) delusory	(G) reneged
(B) tenable	(E) deceptive	(H) annulled
(C) worthwhile	(F) specious	(I) repudiated

Answer Explanation

The correct answers are (B), (F), and (I). Answer Blank (i): Choice (B), "tenable," means "based on reasoning and evidence, believable, defensible." It's the only option that contains the idea of credibility and defensibility, which would be necessary in a scientific field. Choice (A), "desirable," means "worth having or valuable," and choice (C), "worthwhile," means "valuable, useful, rewarding."

Answer Blank (ii): Choice (F), "specious," means "seemingly true, but actually false; not true" and fits the context. Both choice (D), "delusory," and choice (E), "deceptive," include an element of "intending to mislead" or "likely to mislead," which is not borne out in the passage.

Answer Blank (iii): Choice (I), "repudiated," means "to reject something as untrue" and fits the context. Choice (G), "reneged," means "to fail to act on a promise" and doesn't make sense. Choice (H), "annulled," means "to declare invalid in a legal sense" and doesn't make sense.

QUESTIONS 6–8 ARE BASED ON THE FOLLOWING PASSAGE.

A meteoric rise in service sector jobs has characterized India's dynamic labor market over the past 15 years. In a paper for the National Bureau of Economic Research, Eichengreen and Gupta caution that this rise resulted from factors such as an extremely low starting point and dramatic increases in employment for those who are highly skilled, a group that makes up a
5   tiny proportion of India's population. The two economists note that without a concomitant rise in manufacturing jobs— a sector that Bloomberg News described in early 2013, in a generally gloomy look at India's employment future, as "stagnated"—similar rates of growth cannot be sustained. The Manpower Employment survey for the next quarter of 2013, however, projected a 46% increase in jobs in the retail and trade sector, with the services sector just
10   1 percentage point behind. The data, gathered from some 5,000 Indian employers, glowed with other similarly sunny figures for all sectors, including manufacturing.

Question

6. Select the sentence that **most likely states the author's opinion.**
   (A) New data make future meteoric growth in India's employment a certainty.
   (B) Without an increase in manufacturing jobs, India's economy will most likely falter.
   (C) Only high-tech service industry jobs are likely to solve India's employment problems.
   (D) Projected employment rates suggest a reversal of India's employment trends for the last 15 years.
   (E) Continued dramatic growth in India's employment rates may be illusory.

Answer Explanation

The correct answer is (E). The author's viewpoint must be carefully inferred. The author leads with two sources that are gloomy about employment prospects and then adds one source that is very optimistic, but the source that is optimistic is based on predictions for the future, not present facts, and is gathered from a smaller, more subjective sample than most economic reports rely on. Furthermore, the author seems to deride the Manpower report predictions through the use of word choices *glowed* and *sunny*. The likely greater credibility, reliability, and validity of the first two sources might also tip the reader off to the author's opinion. Choice (A) is incorrect because the author does not express any certainty. Choice (B) is incorrect because this paragraph is about employment and not the economy, which, while related, is not the same. Choice (C) is incorrect because the author does not suggest a need for more high-tech industry sector jobs. Choice (D) is incorrect because the quoted projected employment rates suggest the opposite of a reversal.

Question

7. Which of the following sentences would serve as the **most logical and relevant addition to the paragraph?**

    (A) India's economy has grown at one of the fastest rates in the world over the past fifteen years.

    (B) India's economy must be dominated by the high-tech service industry.

    (C) Data for actual employment rates in the next quarter may tell a significantly different story.

    (D) Loss of manufacturing jobs to globalization has not negatively impacted all developing countries.

    (E) India's "demographic dividend" cannot be cashed in unless more high-tech service sector jobs are created.

Answer Explanation

The correct answer is (C). The employment rates quoted are predictions; they are based on what employers guess; furthermore, they are at odds with two other sources. Therefore, it seems likely that the real rates will be different. Choice (A), while not unrelated to the topic of the paragraph, is not the best choice because it is a broad statement about the economy rather than a specific statement about employment. Choices (B), (D), and (E) all express unrelated or opposing ideas.

Question

8. What would the author **most likely predict or advise on the subject of employment in India in the future?**

    (A) Employment will continue to rise but at slightly less dramatic rates.

    (B) Gains in employment for most people must come from a reversal of manufacturing employment trends.

    (C) Employment in all sectors will remain stagnant no matter what some predictions say.

    (D) Decreases in employment will occur as employment in the high-tech service industry is saturated.

    (E) Employment will continue to rise in the manufacturing sector but not in the high-tech service industry.

Answer Explanation

The correct answer is (B). The first source suggests that manufacturing jobs have to increase to sustain rates of growth; the view that manufacturing is not growing now is corroborated by Bloomberg News. Furthermore, the author implies that meteoric rises in the employment rate have been among the highly skilled, which is usually the segment that benefits from high-tech jobs, and not manufacturing ones. Therefore, for broader-based employment, manufacturing jobs must increase. Choices (A) (C), (D), and (E) are incorrect because no evidence in the passage either states or implies these ideas.

QUESTIONS 9–11 ARE BASED ON THE FOLLOWING PASSAGE.

Until the late nineteenth century, a loophole in U.S. copyright law allowed publishers to reprint British books without paying royalties to the authors. Charles Dickens was among the many authors who were affected. Dickens was even more popular in the United States than he was in England, partly because of the availability of his works and their low prices in the
5 United States. When Dickens travelled to America for the first time in 1841, he wrote that "there never was a king or Emperor upon the Earth, so cheered, and followed by crowds." Even so, during this visit he gave speeches calling for an international copyright law. The U.S. press, whose papers readily took advantage of free British content, were outraged. Editors took up their pens in an effort to convince the public that Dickens was ungrateful and greedy.
10   When he returned to England, Dickens published a critical book about his travels called *American Notes,* which included his outrage over his experience with the press. He also began a new novel, *Martin Chuzzlewit,* that details the adventures of a young man seeking his fortune in the United States. Dickens used the novel to seek revenge on the U.S. press. It satirized U.S. customs as well as the press, which ironically ran serialized installments of
15 the novel without compensating Dickens. *Martin Chuzzlewit* sold poorly in England, perhaps because it was so obviously aimed at the U.S. audience.

Question

9. "Compensating" (line 15) most nearly means
   (A) remunerating.
   (B) resolving.
   (C) equivocating.
   (D) extrapolating.
   (E) ingratiating.

Answer Explanation

The correct answer is (A). "Remunerating," choice (A), means "paying." Choice (B) is incorrect because "resolving" means "finding a solution," and the solution may be paying someone, but it's not the same as compensating someone. Choice (C) is incorrect because "equivocating" means "vacillating, being unclear," which doesn't make sense. Choice (D) is incorrect because "extrapolating" means "inferring, drawing a conclusion" and makes no sense. Choice (E) is incorrect because "ingratiating" means "gaining favor" and makes no sense.

Question

10. Based on the passage, what was Dickens's probable attitude toward Americans in general during his visit to the United States?
    (A) indebtedness
    (B) belligerence
    (C) dislike
    (D) merciful
    (E) ingratitude

Answer Explanation

The correct answer is (A). The passage explains that Dickens enjoyed the crowds that he received during his visit and he likely felt indebtedness, or gratitude, for that. For the same reason, choice (C), "dislike," is incorrect. Choice (B) is incorrect because "belligerence" means "aggression," and though the passage explains that Dickens was upset about the copyright laws, "belligerence" seems too strong to describe how he felt about the press, and in addition, the question asks about Americans in general, not the press. Choice (D) is incorrect because there is nothing to indicate he would have had any reason to feel merciful toward the American audience. Choice (E) is incorrect because it was implied that he was, in fact, grateful to his U.S. audiences.

Question

11. According to the passage, what was Dickens's main reason for writing *Martin Chuzzlewit*?
    (A) To write a book that would sell well in the United States
    (B) To make the United States change its existing copyright laws
    (C) To force U.S. publishers to sell his book in the United States
    (D) To attack Americans for their love of his novels
    (E) To show how he felt about the U.S. press

Answer Explanation

The correct answer is (E). Dickens seemed to want to take out his anger on the U.S. press and writing the book was a way for him to do it. Choice (A) is incorrect because even if the book sold well, this apparently wasn't Dickens's motivation for writing it. Choice (B) is incorrect because although Dickens wanted the copyright laws changed, this is not mentioned as a motivation for writing the book. Choice (C) is incorrect because publishers were already printing his works. Choice (D) is incorrect because Dickens was not angered by Americans' love of his novels, but rather by attacks from the press.

QUESTIONS 12 AND 13 ARE BASED ON THE FOLLOWING PASSAGE.

Journalists rarely elicit art commentary from Isa Genzken, the famously interview-phobic German artist whose work was recently the subject of a Museum of Modern Art retrospective. **Instead, Genzken's work must speak for her, though its message surely begins with the prefix *un-*, as in the word *unmonumental*, the title of an earlier show featuring**
5 **Genzken's work.** In its publicity for the recent show, MoMa extols Genzken, "who with a new language of found objects and collage, has created several bodies of work that have redefined assemblage for a new era." Indeed, objects on display were innovatory, if not generative. **No matter what the size of the display, however, viewers had to find their own language for parts that are not wholes, for pieces that appear not to be connected,**
10 **and for spaces that are seemingly not bounded.**

FOR QUESTION 12, CONSIDER EACH ANSWER INDIVIDUALLY AND SELECT <u>ALL</u> CHOICES THAT APPLY.

---

12. What do MoMa's words about "assemblage for a new era" suggest?
- (A) That the artwork is assembled in a new way from found objects
- (B) That the artwork will be reassembled in many new ways in the future
- (C) That the artwork is representative of the present

Answer Explanation

The correct answers are (A) and (C). The word *assemblage* suggests assembly, or the putting together of things. The quotation tells the reader that Genzken's assemblage is made from found objects and collage. The words "for a new era" suggest that Genzken's work goes beyond the similar work of other artists in the past. Choice (B) is incorrect because the quotation does not suggest reassembling Genzken's work.

Question

13. What function do the two groups of words in bold type serve in this passage?
- (A) The first presents an argument; the second presents support for the argument.
- (B) The first anticipates a conclusion; the second provides support for that conclusion.
- (C) The first presents an opinion; the second provides an additional opinion that supports the first.
- (D) The first serves as an intermediate conclusion; the second serves as the final conclusion.
- (E) The first supports an opinion; the second states the opinion.

Answer Explanation

The correct answer is (A). The first statement is the author's argument that Genzken's art is best characterized by what it is not, as suggested by the prefix *un-*; the second sentence supports this argument by explaining what the work is not: not (at least seemingly) whole, not connected, not bounded. Choices (B) and (D) are incorrect because there are no conclusions to be drawn from these statements. Choice (C) is incorrect because the first statement is the author's main claim, and the second statement is not an opinion; instead, it offers explanation and examples for the claim. Choice (E) is incorrect because the first is the opinion and the second is the support.

QUESTIONS 14 AND 15 ARE BASED ON THE FOLLOWING PASSAGE.

The American electoral system is commonly called a "two-party system" because there have historically been only two major political parties dominating electoral politics. Today, the Republican and Democratic Parties are the major two, but there are more than 30 other political parties active in the United States. One major role of third parties in the United States
5 has been to refocus the two major parties on issues they may have not dealt with effectively. Sometimes this happens when one of the major parties fears that a third party is going to become a viable alternative to a major party candidate, or will at least siphon off votes from that candidate during an election. At that point, what often happens is that the major party that feels threatened will take on certain policy positions of the third party in order to lure
10 more voters to it or keep voters from abandoning it. Third parties may also strengthen the government by giving those unhappy with the status quo a legitimate platform for demanding reform. In addition, third parties can simply be a welcoming place for people who want to belong to a group of like-minded people.

Question

14. The author's primary purpose in this passage is to
    (A) encourage Americans to vote for third-party candidates in elections.
    (B) explain how third parties affect the U.S. electoral system.
    (C) emphasize the importance of third parties to the electoral process.
    (D) suggest that the U.S. electoral system could not function without third parties.
    (E) analyze various platforms of third parties in the United States.

Answer Explanation

The correct answer is (B). The author's purpose is to explain how third parties work in the U.S. electoral system. Choice (A) is incorrect because the author doesn't encourage or discourage anyone's vote. Choice (C) may seem correct, but the point of the passage is less to show how important third parties are than to explain how they work. Choice (D) is incorrect because the author assumes third parties as a given and doesn't consider what it would be like without them. Choice (E) is incorrect because no platforms are analyzed in this passage.

Question

15. The author of the passage implies that third parties in the United States function in the electoral system by
    (A) allowing people to vote for the candidate they believe in.
    (B) giving people a platform for radical ideas.
    (C) making the major parties rethink some of their policies.

Answer Explanation

The correct answers are (A), (B), and (C). All three answer choices are presented in the passage as functions of third parties in the U.S. electoral system.

Question

16. The _____ doctor of internal medicine received an honorary degree from his alma mater in further recognition of his humanitarian work in Zambia.

    (A) humble
    (B) illustrious
    (C) brilliant
    (D) illustrative
    (E) celebrated
    (F) dignified

Answer Explanation

The correct answers are (B) and (E). Choices (B) and (E) are synonymous and fit the sense of the sentence. While the doctor may be choice (A), humble; choice (D), brilliant; and choice (F), dignified, there are no synonyms for any of them in the list and so can't be correct answers. Choice (C), illustrative, might confuse you on a quick read of the answers because it means "exemplifying, instructive."

Question

17. The Director of Marketing's _____ assistant kept making suggestions about how to shoot the product launch until the photographer finally told him to sit down and be quiet, which he did.

    (A) officious
    (B) overbearing
    (C) condescending
    (D) supercilious
    (E) meddlesome
    (F) diligent

Answer Explanation

The correct answers are (A) and (E). Choices (A) and (E), "officious" and "meddlesome," mean "interfering, excessively eager to help." Depending on the context, it can also be "overbearing, condescending, and supercilious," choices (B), (C), and (D). However, the context doesn't seem to fit these three words because the assistant was "making suggestions" and sat down when told to. Choice (F), "diligent," means "hardworking, earnest, and busy," but it has no synonym in the list.

Question

18. The young people were not so _____ as their elders when it came to accepting the imposition of martial law including curfews beginning at 5 p.m.

(A) alterable

(B) resilient

(C) amenable

(D) adaptable

(E) tractable

(F) movable

Answer Explanation

The correct answers are (C) and (E). "Amenable," choice (C), and "tractable," choice (E), include the idea of authority that the other choices don't, so they are the best answers. "Amenable" means "willing to comply, willing to listen to authority," and "tractable" means "governable, easily managed." Choice (A), "alterable," means "able to be changed or altered in some way," whereas "adaptable," choice (D), means "capable of changing," so they are synonyms and might fit, except they don't include the idea of authority or governance. Choice (B),"resilient," means "able to recover from adversity" and doesn't fit the sense; nor does choice (F), "movable," meaning "able to be rearranged, impermanent."

Question

19. At the end of the meeting, the participants released a joint statement pledging to continue their dialogue in an effort to improve the _____ relations over trade differences.

(A) taut

(B) stressed

(C) tense

(D) strained

(E) difficult

(F) demanding

Answer Explanation

The correct answers are (C) and (D). Choices (C), "tense," and choice (D), "strained," are synonyms. Although choice (A), "taut," may seem as though it should be a synonym because it means "subject to tension, stretched tight," it is used in reference to people and objects, not to ideas. Choice (B), "stressed," might also seem like a plausible option, but it means "physical, mental, or emotional strain, worry, anxiety." Choice (E), "difficult," meaning "not easy to do, troublesome," might seem to work, but it has no synonym in the list. "Demanding," choice (F), might seem like a synonym, but substitute it in the sentence and it doesn't make sense.

QUESTION 20 IS BASED ON THE FOLLOWING PASSAGE.

Is the Fourth Estate, the theoretical fourth branch of the government that is the press, in jeopardy now that, first, overall news readership is declining even as online readership is increasing, and, second, digital media have gained apparent ascendancy over traditional print journalism? The answer may depend in part on whether the eye of the beholder views jour-
5 nalism, regardless of its form, largely as a disinterested public good, an evanescent medium for democratic comment, or a consumer product. Those holding to the highest ideal of the press as safeguard of our democracy will no doubt lament changes that make Twitter and the like as attractive as any news source. Those holding to the second vision will likely embrace the idea of up-to-the-minute, ever-fresh and evolving ideas and democratized commentary,
10 while those holding to the third conception will bank on the more recent journalistic brands such as Buzzfeed and Politico that "sell" what has always been a product of capitalism. No matter what the perspective, however, it is indisputable that online journalism shifts power away from the publication, which in the era of print functioned as a kind of sentry at the gate of truth, appropriateness, and corporate interest, and transfers that power to the user.

Question

20. Which of the following can be inferred from this passage?
   - (A) In the current age of digital media, the processes and products of journalism are more transitory than ever before.
   - (B) The Fourth Estate has been eroded by new commercial interests that shift motivation from public good to profit.
   - (C) The idea that the Fourth Estate is currently diminished by the ascendancy of digital media depends on a subjective view of the role of the press.
   - (D) Journalism today exists largely beyond the realm of corporate interests and is characterized by a new democratizing impulse.
   - (E) Journalism, regardless of the form it takes, should have a central purpose of serving democratic principles.

Answer Explanation

The correct answer is (C). The main idea of the passage is that people view the purposes of journalism differently, and how you view that purpose dictates how you view the shift away from news readership and print readership. Choices (B) and (E) are incorrect because these ideas are stated directly in the passage as ways of viewing the "press" or media. Choice (D) is incorrect because it is never stated or implied by the passage.

Section 4: Quantitative Reasoning

1. C	11. A	16. C
2. A	12. A	17. B, D
3. D	13. C	18. B, E
4. D	14. C	19. 30
5. B	15. A	20. 57
6. B		
7. C		
8. B		
9. C		
10. B		

Question

1.

Quantity A	Quantity B
$\dfrac{5}{\left(\dfrac{1}{5}\right)^2}$	125

(A) Quantity A is greater.

(B) Quantity B is greater.

(C) The two quantities are equal.

(D) The relationship cannot be determined from the information given.

Answer Explanation

The correct answer is (C).

$$\frac{5}{\left(\frac{1}{5}\right)^2} = \frac{5}{\frac{1}{25}} = 125$$

Question

2.   Quantity A   Quantity B

$\dfrac{1}{2} + \dfrac{1}{3} + \dfrac{1}{4} + \dfrac{1}{5}$ 1

  (A) Quantity A is greater.
  (B) Quantity B is greater.
  (C) The two quantities are equal.
  (D) The relationship cannot be determined from the information given.

Answer Explanation

The correct answer is (A). Convert to decimals and calculate:

$$\frac{1}{2} + \frac{1}{3} + \frac{1}{4} + \frac{1}{5} = 0.5 + 0.33 + 0.25 + 0.20 = 1.28$$

$1.28 > 1$

Question

$$y \neq 0$$

3.   Quantity A   Quantity B

$\dfrac{5}{y}$ $5y$

  (A) Quantity A is greater.
  (B) Quantity B is greater.
  (C) The two quantities are equal.
  (D) The relationship cannot be determined from the information given.

Answer Explanation

The correct answer is (D). Pick numbers:

If $y = 5$, then the result is 1, 25; $1 < 25$

If $y = -5$, then the result is $-1, -25$; $-1 > -25$

Question

$$a > b > 0 > c > d$$

4.

Quantity A	Quantity B
$a + d$	$b + c$

(A) Quantity A is greater.

(B) Quantity B is greater.

(C) The two quantities are equal.

(D) The relationship cannot be determined from the information given.

Answer Explanation

The correct answer is (D). Pick numbers: $a + d$, $b + c$

$-3 + 4 = 1, -1 + 1 = 0$, so not equal and A > B

$-4 + 2 = -2, -1 + 1 = 0$, so not equal and B > A

Question

$$x > 0$$

5.

Quantity A	Quantity B
$x^3 (x - 1)$	$x^4 + x^3$

(A) Quantity A is greater.

(B) Quantity B is greater.

(C) The two quantities are equal.

(D) The relationship cannot be determined from the information given.

Answer Explanation

The correct answer is (B). Simplify:

$x^3 (x - 1) = x^4 - x^3$

$x^4 - x^3 \neq x^4 + x^3$

Since $x \neq 0$, all the numbers will be positives:

So, $x^4 - x^3 < x^4 + x^3$.

So, A < B.

Question

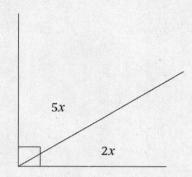

6.

Quantity A	Quantity B
x	15

(A) Quantity A is greater.

(B) Quantity B is greater.

(C) The two quantities are equal.

(D) The relationship cannot be determined from the information given.

Answer Explanation

The correct answer is (B). Set up an equation and solve:

$$5x + 2x = 90$$
$$7x = 90$$
$$x = 12\frac{6}{7}$$

Question

$$x \neq 0$$

7.

Quantity A	Quantity B
$x^{-3}(x^3)$	$\dfrac{1}{x^{-3}(x^3)}$

(A) Quantity A is greater.

(B) Quantity B is greater.

(C) The two quantities are equal.

(D) The relationship cannot be determined from the information given.

Answer Explanation

The correct answer is (C). Simplify:

$$x^{-3}(x^3) = \frac{x^3}{x^{-3}} = 1$$

$$\frac{1}{x^{-3}(x^3)} = \frac{1}{\frac{1}{x^{-3}}(x^3)} = \frac{1}{\frac{x^3}{x^{-3}}} = \frac{1}{1} = 1$$

Question

Sam is 3 times as old as Sue. In 5 years Sam will be 12 years older than twice Sue's age.

8.
	Quantity A	Quantity B
	Sue's age	22

- (A) Quantity A is greater.
- (B) Quantity B is greater.
- (C) The two quantities are equal.
- (D) The relationship cannot be determined from the information given.

Answer Explanation

The correct answer is (B). Turn the problems into equations:

	now	in 5 years
Sue	x	$x + 5$
Sam	$3x$	$3x + 5$

In 5 years Sam $(3x + 5)$ is 12 more than twice Sue's age $(x + 5)$, so that is $2(x + 5) + 12$.

Calculate: $3x + 5 = 2(x + 5) + 12$

$3x + 5 = 2x + 10 + 12$

$x = 17$ Sue now

$3x = 51$ Sam now

22 is greater than 17.

QUESTIONS 9–11 REFER TO THE BAR GRAPH BELOW.

Average Daily Use Per Salesperson
(rounded to the nearest dollar)

Question

9. If there are 33 salespeople in the company, what was the approximate total spent on food and gas for January?

    (A) $24,765

    (B) $25,575

    (C) $29,865

    (D) $35,805

    (E) $36,905

Answer Explanation

The correct answer is (C). Remember there are 31 days in January. Estimate to find a highest and lowest possible number:

Lowest: food > 10, gas > 15
(10 + 15)(31)(33) = 25(31)(33) = 25,575

Highest: food < 15, gas < 20
(15 + 20)(31)(33) = 35(31)(33) = 35,805

25,575 > *answer* > 35,805, so the answer is 29,865

Question

10. In February, the company had an outlay of $21,056 for food. How many salespeople did the company employ for the month?

(A) 28

(B) 47

(C) 56

(D) 73

(E) 75

Answer Explanation

The correct answer is (B). Turn the words into equations—and remember that February has 28 days:

$$16(28)x = 21,056$$
$$448x = 21,056$$
$$x = 47$$

Question

11. The projections for the coming year indicate an increase of 10 percent in the average cost of gas. How much more per day will the company pay out on average for gas for the first 6 months of next year?

(A) $9

(B) $12

(C) $15

(D) $18

(E) $21

Answer Explanation

The correct answer is (A).

$$16 + 10 + 29 + 9 + 16 + 14 = 94$$
$$94 \times 1.10 = 103$$
$$103 - 94 = 9$$

Question

12. The frame shop has a rectangular mat 36" by 22". If a mat is cut from it that is 2" less all the way around, what is the area of the new mat?

(A) 576

(B) 680

(C) 648

(D) 792

(E) 822

Answer Explanation

The correct answer is (A). Drawing a figure will help you solve this problem:

$32 \times 18 = 576$

Question

13. A right circular cylinder's dimensions are changed so that the cylinder's new height equals twice its original height, and the cylinder's new radius equals one-half its original radius. Which of the following describes correctly the resulting change, if any, to the cylinder's volume?

   (A) The cylinder's volume remains the same.
   (B) The cylinder's new volume equals twice the cylinder's original volume.
   (C) The cylinder's new volume equals one-half the cylinder's original volume.
   (D) The cylinder's new volume equals four times the cylinder's original volume.
   (E) The cylinder's new volume equals one-fourth the cylinder's original volume.

Answer Explanation

The correct answer is (C). Let r and h be the original radius and height of the cylinder, and let r_1 and h_1 be its new radius and height. The cylinder's original volume, V, is given by $V = \pi r^2 h$, and its new volume, V_1, is given by $V_1 = \pi \left(r_1\right)^2 h_1$. You know that $r_1 = \dfrac{1}{2} r$ and $h_1 = 2h$, so the new volume equals:

$$V_1 = \pi \left(r_1\right)^2 h_1$$
$$= \pi \left(\frac{1}{2}r\right)^2 2h$$
$$= \pi \frac{1}{4} r^2 2h$$
$$= \pi \frac{1}{2} r^2 h$$
$$= \frac{1}{2} \pi r^2 h$$
$$= \frac{1}{2} V$$

Question

14. Find the perimeter of the figure.

    (A) 7
    (B) 8
    (C) 14
    (D) 16
    (E) 30

Answer Explanation

The correct answer is (C). Using the Pythagorean theorem:

$$a^2 + b^2 = c^2$$
$$3^2 + b^2 = 5^2$$
$$9 + b^2 = 25$$
$$b^2 = 16$$
$$b = 4$$

$$3 + 4 + 3 + 4 = 14$$

Question

15. The original price of a shirt was $40. It was marked down twice before it was sold. First it was marked down 20%, and then it was marked down 15% of its discounted price. What percentage of the original price did it sell for?

    (A) 68%
    (B) 48%
    (C) 32%
    (D) 85%
    (E) 80%

Answer Explanation

The correct answer is (A). Turn the words into equations:

$$40(1 - 0.20) = 40(0.80) = 32$$

$$32(1 - 0.15) = 32(0.85) = 27.20$$

$$\frac{27.2}{40} = 0.68 \text{ or } 68\%$$

Question

16. What is the mean salary of 5 potters when two make $15.50 per hour, one makes $12 per hour, and the other two make $13.50 per hour?

(A) $10
(B) $12
(C) $14
(D) $16
(E) $17

Answer Explanation

The correct answer is (C). Calculate the mean salary:

$$\frac{2(15.50) + 12 + 2(13.50)}{5}$$

$$= \frac{31 + 12 + 27}{5}$$

$$= \frac{70}{5} = 14$$

Question

17. The first term, r_1, of a sequence is 1, and the nth term of the sequence is given by the formula $r_n = r_{n-1} + 7$. Which of the following are terms of the sequence?

(A) 7
(B) 15
(C) 20
(D) 57
(E) 63

Answer Explanation

The correct answers are (B) and (D). According to the given formula, each term of the sequence equals the previous term plus 7. Because the first term is 1, the sequence includes all positive integers that equal a multiple of 7 plus 1. (The first term is 1, the second is 8, the third is 15, and so on.) Only choices (B) and (D) equal a multiple of 7 plus 1 (14 plus 1 and 56 plus 1, respectively), so they are the correct choices.

Question

18. If $x^2 - 11x - 12 = 0$, what are the two possible values for x?

(A) -12
(B) -1
(C) 0
(D) 1
(E) 12

Answer Explanation

The correct answers are (B) and (E). Factor:

$x^2 - 11x - 12 = 0$

$(x - 12)(x + 1) = 0$

$x = 12$ or $x = -1$

Question

19. Lines 1 and 2 are parallel. What is the value of a?

Answer Explanation

The correct answer is 30.

$$3x = 180$$
$$x = 60$$
$$60 + 90 = 150$$
$$180 - 150 = 30$$

Question

20. In the barber shop, a haircut costs $22.50. How many haircuts must be done to cover the monthly rent of $1,276? Round the answer up to the nearest haircut.

Answer Explanation

The correct answer is 57. Calculate:

$1,276 \div 22.50 = 56.71 = 57$

Section 5: Quantitative Reasoning

1. B	11. D	16. C
2. A	12. B	17. A, B, D
3. B	13. A	18. E, F, G
4. D	14. C	19. 4
5. C	15. E	20. 15
6. D		
7. C		
8. C		
9. D		
10. C		

Question

$$w < x < y < z$$

1.　　　　　Quantity A　　　　　　　　　　　Quantity B
　　　　　　　　$w + y$　　　　　　　　　　　　　$x + z$

(A) Quantity A is greater.

(B) Quantity B is greater.

(C) The two quantities are equal.

(D) The relationship cannot be determined from the information given.

Answer Explanation

The correct answer is (B). Compare:

$w < x < y < z$

$w < x, y < z$

$w + y < x + z$

Question

2.　　　　　Quantity A　　　　　　　　　　　Quantity B
　　　　　The number of dimes in \$5.10　　The number of pennies in 2 quarters

(A) Quantity A is greater.

(B) Quantity B is greater.

(C) The two quantities are equal.

(D) The relationship cannot be determined from the information given.

Answer Explanation

The correct answer is (A). Calculate:

$5.10 \div 0.10 = 51$

$0.50 \div 0.01 = 50$

Question

3.

Quantity A	Quantity B
$\frac{4}{3}\left(\frac{1}{2}\right)\left(\frac{11}{9}\right)$	$\frac{3}{4}\left(\frac{15}{16}\right)\left(\frac{15}{12}\right)$

(A) Quantity A is greater.

(B) Quantity B is greater.

(C) The two quantities are equal.

(D) The relationship cannot be determined from the information given.

Answer Explanation

The correct answer is (B). Estimate:

$1 + \left(\frac{1}{2}\right)(1+) \approx \frac{1^+}{2}$

$\frac{3}{4}\left(1^-\right)\left(1^+\right) = \frac{3}{4}$

Question

$$\frac{x}{y} = 12$$

4.

Quantity A	Quantity B
x	y

(A) Quantity A is greater.

(B) Quantity B is greater.

(C) The two quantities are equal.

(D) The relationship cannot be determined from the information given.

Answer Explanation

The correct answer is (D). Pick numbers. Be sure to pick a positive, a negative, and a fraction to test all possibilities.

$\frac{144}{12} = 12$

$\frac{-144}{-12} = 12$

$-144 < -12 < 12 < 144$

Question

Given triangle ABC
Where $AB = BC = CA$

5.

Quantity A	Quantity B
Value of an interior angle	60°

(A) Quantity A is greater.

(B) Quantity B is greater.

(C) The two quantities are equal.

(D) The relationship cannot be determined from the information given.

Answer Explanation

The correct answer is (C). Draw a figure if needed to help you determine the answer. If the three sides are equal, it is an equilateral triangle, and the three angles are equal to:

$$3x = 180$$
$$x = 60$$

Question

6.

Quantity A	Quantity B
$\angle A$	$\angle C$

(A) Quantity A is greater.

(B) Quantity B is greater.

(C) The two quantities are equal.

(D) The relationship cannot be determined from the information given.

Answer Explanation

The correct answer is (D). It is not possible to determine a relationship.

Question

The above shape is made up of 5 congruent squares. The area of the shape is 180.

7.

Quantity A	Quantity B
84	The perimeter of the shape

(A) Quantity A is greater.
(B) Quantity B is greater.
(C) The two quantities are equal.
(D) The relationship cannot be determined from the information given.

Answer Explanation

The correct answer is (C).

$180 \div 5 = 36$

$\sqrt{36} = 6$

$14 \times 6 = 84$

Question

8.

Quantity A	Quantity B
$(11^4)(11^5)$	11^9

(A) Quantity A is greater.
(B) Quantity B is greater.
(C) The two quantities are equal.
(D) The relationship cannot be determined from the information given.

Answer Explanation

The correct answer is (C). Calculate:

$(11^4)(11^5) = 11^9$

Question

9. If the salesperson receives a $5,500 commission on the sale of a yacht, how much did the yacht sell for if the commission rate is 5%?

(A) $110

(B) $1,100

(C) $11,000

(D) $110,000

(E) $1,100,000

Answer Explanation

The correct answer is (D). Calculate:

$$\frac{\$5,500}{0.05} = \$110,000$$

Question

10. Working at their respective rates, Masha can paint a given apartment in x hours, and Olga can paint it in y hours. If Masha and Olga work together, each at her own rate, in how many hours will they paint the apartment?

(A) $x + y$

(B) $\dfrac{x+y}{xy}$

(C) $\dfrac{xy}{x+y}$

(D) $\dfrac{1}{xy}$

(E) $\dfrac{1}{x+y}$

Answer Explanation

The correct answer is (C). If Masha paints the apartment in x hours, then in one hour she paints $\dfrac{1}{x}$ of the apartment. Similarly, Olga paints $\dfrac{1}{y}$ of the apartment in one hour. If they work together, their combined hourly rate, R, will be the sum of their individual hourly rates:

$$R = \frac{1}{x} + \frac{1}{y}$$

$$= \frac{y+x}{xy}$$

This means that when working together, Masha and Olga paint $\dfrac{y+x}{xy}$ of the apartment in one hour. Next, if H is the number of hours it will take them to paint the apartment when working together, then in one hour they will paint $\dfrac{1}{H}$ of the apartment. In other words, $\dfrac{1}{H}$ equals $\dfrac{y+x}{xy}$:

$$\frac{1}{H} = \frac{y+x}{xy}$$

$$H = \frac{xy}{y+x}$$

Question

11. The 20-person staff of a medical center consists of doctors and nurses. Sixty percent of the staff members are doctors, three-quarters of whom are general practitioners, while the rest are pediatricians. If 4 nurses and 4 pediatricians are added, and no other changes are made to the medical center's existing staff, what percentage of the medical center's staff will the pediatricians represent?

(A) 7%

(B) 15%

(C) 20%

(D) 25%

(E) 33%

Answer Explanation

The correct answer is (D). Initially 60% of the 20-person staff are doctors, so there are 12 doctors. Of those, 9 are general practitioners and 3 are pediatricians. If 4 nurses and 4 pediatricians are added, then there are 28 staff members in total, of whom 7 are pediatricians. Thus, the pediatricians will represent $\dfrac{7}{28}$, or 25% of the staff.

Question

12. Evaluate $27^{\frac{2}{3}}$.

(A) 3

(B) 9

(C) 18

(D) 27

(E) 81

Answer Explanation

The correct answer is (B). Simplify and evaluate:
$27^{\frac{2}{3}} = \left(\sqrt[3]{27}\right)^2 = 3^2 = 9$

QUESTIONS 13 AND 14 REFER TO THE FIGURE BELOW.

m is parallel to *n* and *k* is parallel to *l*

Question

13. If m∠3 = 2x, and m∠10 = 63, find the value of x.

(A) 58.5

(B) 63

(C) 72

(D) 117

(E) 119.5

Answer Explanation

The correct answer is (A).

m∠3 = m∠9

$$m∠9 + m∠10 = 180$$
$$2x + 63 = 180$$
$$2x = 117$$
$$x = 58.5$$

Question

14. In the parallelogram formed by the intersection of the lines, what is the sum of the measures of the interior angles?

(A) < 270

(B) < 360

(C)   360

(D) > 360

(E) > 540

Answer Explanation

The correct answer is (C). The sum of the measures of the interior angles of a parallelogram = 360.

QUESTION 15 REFERS TO THE TABLE BELOW.

PURCHASING-POWER PARITY

Rank	Country	PPP Total (billion)	PPP/capita ($)	Population (million)
1.	European Union	10,840	28,600	379
2.	USA	10,400	37,600	290
3.	China	5,700	4,400	1,287
4.	Japan	3,550	28,000	127
5.	India	2,660	2,540	1,049
6.	Germany	2,180	26,600	82
7.	France	1,540	25,700	60
8.	Britain	1,520	25,300	60
9.	Italy	1,440	25,000	57
10.	Russia	1,350	9,300	144
11.	Brazil	1,340	7,600	182

Question

15. Which country in the bottom 5 of population has the highest PPP Total?

    (A) Italy
    (B) Britain
    (C) France
    (D) Germany
    (E) Japan

Answer Explanation

The correct answer is (E). Reading the PPP total for these five nations, Japan at $3,550 billion has the highest PPP total.

Question

16. What is the first month's interest payment on a 1-year loan of $34,000 at 8.28%?

    (A) $2346.00
    (B) $281.52
    (C) $234.60
    (D) $2815.20
    (E) $242.90

Answer Explanation

The correct answer is (C). Calculate:

$$\frac{34,000(0.0828)}{12} = \frac{2815.20}{12} = 234.60$$

Question

17. If m, n, and p are positive integers, and m is a factor of n, and n is a factor of p, which of the following statements are true?

    (A) m is a factor of p

    (B) n is a factor of p^3

    (C) p is the product of $m(n)$

    (D) n is a factor of $m(p)$

Answer Explanation

The correct answers are (A), (B), and (D). Pick numbers:

n	m	p	Statement
8	16	32	8 is a factor of 32
2	4	8	2 is a factor of 512
4	8	16	16 is not the product of (4)(8)
10	20	40	10 is a factor of 80

Question

18. Find the numbers in the sequence from t_5 to t_7, using the formula $t_n = n(n-2)$.

    (A) −1

    (B) 0

    (C) 3

    (D) 8

    (E) 15

    (F) 24

    (G) 35

    (H) 48

Answer Explanation

The correct answers are (E), (F), and (G). Calculate:

$5(5-2) = 15$

$6(6-2) = 24$

$7(7-2) = 35$

Question

19. It takes 3 electricians four 8-hour days to wire a house. If the general contractor wanted the house wired in three 8-hour days, how many electricians should he have hired?

Answer Explanation

The correct answer is 4. Set up an equation:

$(32)(3) = 24x$

$4 = x$

Question

20. David, Eric, and Justin are brothers. David is 6 years younger than Eric, and Justin is 3 years older than Eric. In 3 years, Justin will be twice as old as David. What is the current age of the oldest brother?

Answer Explanation

The correct answer is 15. Let E represent Eric's current age. David's current age is $E - 6$, and Justin's current age is $E + 3$. In 3 years, David's age will be $E - 3$, and Justin's age will be $E + 6$. You are told that in 3 years, Justin will be twice as old as David. Therefore:

$$E + 6 = 2(E - 3)$$
$$E + 6 = 2E - 6$$
$$E = 12$$

Eric's current age is 12, which makes Justin's current age 15. Justin is the oldest brother, so the correct answer is 15.

PRACTICE TEST 4 ANSWER SHEETS

Section 1: Analytical Writing

Analyze an Issue

FOR PLANNING

answer sheet

ANALYZE AN ISSUE RESPONSE

_____
_____
_____
_____
_____
_____
_____
_____
_____
_____
_____
_____
_____
_____
_____
_____
_____
_____
_____
_____
_____
_____
_____
_____
_____
_____
_____
_____
_____
_____
_____
_____
_____
_____
_____
_____

ANALYZE AN ISSUE RESPONSE

_____
_____
_____
_____
_____
_____
_____
_____
_____
_____
_____
_____
_____
_____
_____
_____
_____
_____
_____
_____
_____
_____
_____
_____
_____
_____
_____
_____
_____
_____
_____

answer sheet

ANALYZE AN ISSUE RESPONSE

_____
_____
_____
_____
_____
_____
_____
_____
_____
_____
_____
_____
_____
_____
_____
_____
_____
_____
_____
_____
_____
_____
_____
_____
_____
_____
_____
_____
_____
_____
_____
_____
_____
_____
_____
_____
_____
_____

ANALYZE AN ISSUE RESPONSE

_____
_____
_____
_____
_____
_____
_____
_____
_____
_____
_____
_____
_____
_____
_____
_____
_____
_____
_____
_____
_____
_____
_____
_____
_____
_____
_____
_____
_____
_____
_____
_____
_____
_____
_____
_____
_____
_____

answer sheet

Analyze an Argument

FOR PLANNING

ANALYZE AN ARGUMENT RESPONSE

answer sheet

ANALYZE AN ARGUMENT RESPONSE

_____
_____
_____
_____
_____
_____
_____
_____
_____
_____
_____
_____
_____
_____
_____
_____
_____
_____
_____
_____
_____
_____
_____
_____
_____
_____
_____
_____
_____
_____
_____
_____
_____
_____
_____
_____
_____
_____
_____

ANALYZE AN ARGUMENT RESPONSE

_____

_____

_____

_____

_____

_____

_____

_____

_____

_____

_____

_____

_____

_____

_____

_____

_____

_____

_____

_____

_____

_____

_____

_____

_____

_____

_____

_____

_____

_____

_____

_____

_____

answer sheet

ANALYZE AN ARGUMENT RESPONSE

_____
_____
_____
_____
_____
_____
_____
_____
_____
_____
_____
_____
_____
_____
_____
_____
_____
_____
_____
_____
_____
_____
_____
_____
_____
_____
_____
_____
_____
_____
_____
_____
_____
_____
_____
_____
_____
_____

answer sheet

Section 2: Verbal Reasoning

1. Ⓐ Ⓑ Ⓒ Ⓓ Ⓔ
2. Ⓐ Ⓑ Ⓒ Ⓓ Ⓔ
3. Ⓐ Ⓑ Ⓒ Ⓓ Ⓔ Ⓕ
4. Ⓐ Ⓑ Ⓒ Ⓓ Ⓔ Ⓕ
5. Ⓐ Ⓑ Ⓒ Ⓓ Ⓔ Ⓕ Ⓖ Ⓗ Ⓘ
6. Ⓐ Ⓑ Ⓒ Ⓓ Ⓔ
7. Ⓐ Ⓑ Ⓒ Ⓓ Ⓔ
8. Ⓐ Ⓑ Ⓒ Ⓓ Ⓔ
9. Ⓐ Ⓑ Ⓒ
10. Ⓐ Ⓑ Ⓒ Ⓓ Ⓔ

11. Ⓐ Ⓑ Ⓒ Ⓓ Ⓔ
12. Ⓐ Ⓑ Ⓒ Ⓓ Ⓔ
13. Ⓐ Ⓑ Ⓒ Ⓓ Ⓔ
14. Ⓐ Ⓑ Ⓒ Ⓓ Ⓔ
15. Ⓐ Ⓑ Ⓒ Ⓓ Ⓔ Ⓕ

16. Ⓐ Ⓑ Ⓒ Ⓓ Ⓔ Ⓕ
17. Ⓐ Ⓑ Ⓒ Ⓓ Ⓔ Ⓕ
18. Ⓐ Ⓑ Ⓒ Ⓓ Ⓔ Ⓕ
19. Ⓐ Ⓑ Ⓒ
20. Ⓐ Ⓑ Ⓒ Ⓓ Ⓔ

Section 3: Quantitative Reasoning

1. Ⓐ Ⓑ Ⓒ Ⓓ
2. Ⓐ Ⓑ Ⓒ Ⓓ
3. Ⓐ Ⓑ Ⓒ Ⓓ
4. Ⓐ Ⓑ Ⓒ Ⓓ
5. Ⓐ Ⓑ Ⓒ Ⓓ
6. Ⓐ Ⓑ Ⓒ Ⓓ
7. Ⓐ Ⓑ Ⓒ Ⓓ
8. Ⓐ Ⓑ Ⓒ Ⓓ
9. Ⓐ Ⓑ Ⓒ Ⓓ Ⓔ
10. Ⓐ Ⓑ Ⓒ Ⓓ Ⓔ

11. Ⓐ Ⓑ Ⓒ Ⓓ Ⓔ
12. Ⓐ Ⓑ Ⓒ Ⓓ Ⓔ
13. Ⓐ Ⓑ Ⓒ Ⓓ Ⓔ
14. Ⓐ Ⓑ Ⓒ Ⓓ Ⓔ
15. Ⓐ Ⓑ Ⓒ Ⓓ Ⓔ

16. Ⓐ Ⓑ Ⓒ Ⓓ Ⓔ
17. Ⓐ Ⓑ Ⓒ Ⓓ Ⓔ Ⓕ
18. Ⓐ Ⓑ Ⓒ Ⓓ Ⓔ Ⓕ Ⓖ
19. ▭
20. ▭

Section 4: Quantitative Reasoning

1. Ⓐ Ⓑ Ⓒ Ⓓ
2. Ⓐ Ⓑ Ⓒ Ⓓ
3. Ⓐ Ⓑ Ⓒ Ⓓ
4. Ⓐ Ⓑ Ⓒ Ⓓ
5. Ⓐ Ⓑ Ⓒ Ⓓ
6. Ⓐ Ⓑ Ⓒ Ⓓ
7. Ⓐ Ⓑ Ⓒ Ⓓ
8. Ⓐ Ⓑ Ⓒ Ⓓ
9. Ⓐ Ⓑ Ⓒ Ⓓ
10. Ⓐ Ⓑ Ⓒ Ⓓ Ⓔ

11. Ⓐ Ⓑ Ⓒ Ⓓ Ⓔ
12. Ⓐ Ⓑ Ⓒ Ⓓ Ⓔ
13. Ⓐ Ⓑ Ⓒ Ⓓ Ⓔ
14. Ⓐ Ⓑ Ⓒ Ⓓ Ⓔ
15. Ⓐ Ⓑ Ⓒ Ⓓ Ⓔ

16. Ⓐ Ⓑ Ⓒ Ⓓ Ⓔ Ⓕ
17. Ⓐ Ⓑ Ⓒ Ⓓ Ⓔ
18. ▭
19. ▭
    ▭
20. Ⓐ Ⓑ Ⓒ Ⓓ Ⓔ

Section 5: Verbal Reasoning

1. Ⓐ Ⓑ Ⓒ Ⓓ Ⓔ
2. Ⓐ Ⓑ Ⓒ Ⓓ Ⓔ
3. Ⓐ Ⓑ Ⓒ Ⓓ Ⓔ Ⓕ
4. Ⓐ Ⓑ Ⓒ Ⓓ Ⓔ Ⓕ Ⓖ Ⓗ Ⓘ
5. Ⓐ Ⓑ Ⓒ Ⓓ Ⓔ Ⓕ Ⓖ Ⓗ Ⓘ
6. Ⓐ Ⓑ Ⓒ Ⓓ Ⓔ
7. Ⓐ Ⓑ Ⓒ Ⓓ Ⓔ
8. Ⓐ Ⓑ Ⓒ
9. Ⓐ Ⓑ Ⓒ Ⓓ Ⓔ
10. Ⓐ Ⓑ Ⓒ Ⓓ Ⓔ

11. Ⓐ Ⓑ Ⓒ Ⓓ Ⓔ
12. Ⓐ Ⓑ Ⓒ
13. Ⓐ Ⓑ Ⓒ Ⓓ Ⓔ
14. Ⓐ Ⓑ Ⓒ Ⓓ Ⓔ
15. Ⓐ Ⓑ Ⓒ Ⓓ Ⓔ

16. Ⓐ Ⓑ Ⓒ Ⓓ Ⓔ Ⓕ
17. Ⓐ Ⓑ Ⓒ Ⓓ Ⓔ Ⓕ
18. Ⓐ Ⓑ Ⓒ Ⓓ Ⓔ Ⓕ
19. Ⓐ Ⓑ Ⓒ Ⓓ Ⓔ Ⓕ
20. Ⓐ Ⓑ Ⓒ

Practice Test 4

The test begins with general information about the number of sections on the test (six for the computer version, including the unidentified unscored section or an identified research section, and five for the paper-and-pencil version) and the timing of the test (approximately 3 hours and 45 minutes, including one 10-minute break after Section 3, 1-minute breaks after the other sections for the computer version, and 3 hours and 30 minutes for the paper-and-pencil version with similar breaks). The following practice test contains the five scored sections.

Each section has its own time allocation and, during that time period, you may work on only that section.

Next, you will read ETS's policy on scoring the Analytical Writing responses. Each essay is read by experienced readers, and ETS may cancel any test scores that show evidence of unacknowledged use of sources, unacknowledged collaboration with others, preparation of the response by another person, and language that is "substantially" similar to the language in one or more other test responses.

Each section has specific instructions for that section.

You will be told when to begin.

practice test 4

SECTION 1: ANALYTICAL WRITING

Analyze an Issue
30 minutes

The time for this task is 30 minutes. You must plan and draft a response that evaluates the issue given below. If you do not respond to the specific issue, your score will be zero. Your response must be based on the accompanying instructions, and you must provide evidence for your position. You may use support from reading, experience, observations, and/or course work.

> In an era of increased fiscal responsibility, we must institute a policy of charging entrance fees to all museums and other public buildings in our nation's capital, such as the U.S. Mint, the Library of Congress, and the White House.
>
> Write an essay that takes a position on this proposed policy. As you explain and support your position, also discuss how the likely results or consequences of the policy help to shape your position.

Your response will be read by experienced readers who will assess your ability to do the following:

- Follow the set of task instructions.
- Analyze the complexities involved.
- Organize, develop, and explain ideas.
- Use pertinent reasons and/or illustrations to support ideas.
- Adhere to the conventions of Standard Written English.

You will be advised to take some time to plan your response and to leave time to reread it before the time is over. Those taking the paper-and-pencil version of the GRE® will find a blank page in their answer booklet for making notes and then four ruled pages for writing their actual response. Those taking the computer version will be given scrap paper for making notes.

STOP

> If you finish before the time is up, you may check your work in this section only.

Analyze an Argument
30 minutes

The time for this task is 30 minutes. You must plan and draft a response that evaluates the argument given below. If you do not respond to the given argument, your score will be zero. Your response must be based on the accompanying instructions and you must provide evidence in support of your analysis.

You should not present your views on the subject of the argument but on the strength or weakness of the argument.

The city council's decision to raze four massive residential city blocks in our city center and replace them with new affordable housing is both shortsighted and too costly in both human and economic terms. A more logical and cost-effective solution to the problem of abandoned and ramshackle buildings—and an entire neighborhood in crisis—is to turn the abandoned lots on those blocks into community gardens or urban farms. Once this is accomplished, falling construction, garbage dumps, and sites for nefarious activities will be transformed into beckoning open space. Such a change will help regenerate the entire area by bringing life and beauty to a devastated urban core and by eventually sparking urban pioneering and renewal.

Write an essay that evaluates the logic of these claims and examines the assumptions on which they most likely rest. As you evaluate, raise questions that would have to be answered in order to further evaluate the reasonableness of the recommendation and the argument on which it is based. Be sure to explain how the answers to the questions would help to determine whether the argument and recommendation are reasonable.

Your response will be read by experienced readers who will assess your ability to do the following:

- Follow the set of task instructions.
- Analyze the complexities involved.
- Organize, develop, and explain ideas.
- Use pertinent reasons and/or illustrations to support ideas.
- Adhere to the conventions of Standard Written English.

You will be advised to take some time to plan your response and to leave time to reread it before the time is over. Those taking the paper-and-pencil version of the GRE® will find a blank page in their answer booklet for making notes and then four ruled pages for writing their actual response. Those taking the computer version will be given scrap paper for making notes.

STOP

If you finish before the time is up, you may check your work in this section only.

INSTRUCTIONS FOR THE VERBAL REASONING AND QUANTITATIVE REASONING SECTIONS

You will find information here on the question formats for the Verbal Reasoning and Quantitative Reasoning sections as well as information about how to use the software program, or, if you're taking the paper-and-pencil version, how to mark your answers in the answer booklet.

Perhaps the most important information is a reminder about how these two sections are scored. Every correct answer earns a point, but wrong answers don't subtract any points. The advice from ETS is to guess if you aren't sure of an answer. ETS says that this is better than not answering a question.

All multiple-choice questions in the computer-based test will have answer options preceded by either blank ovals or blank squares, depending on the question type. The paper-and-pencil test will follow the same format of answer choices, but it will use letters instead of ovals or squares for answer choices.

For your convenience in answering questions and checking answers in this book, we use (A), (B), (C), etc. By using letters with parentheses, you will find it easy to check your answers against the answer key and explanation sections.

SECTION 2: VERBAL REASONING

30 minutes • 20 questions

(The paper-and-pencil version will have 25 questions to be completed in 35 minutes.)

For each question, follow the specific directions and choose the best answer.

> **FOR QUESTIONS 1–5, CHOOSE <u>ONE</u> ANSWER FOR EACH BLANK. SELECT FROM THE APPROPRIATE COLUMN FOR EACH BLANK. CHOOSE THE ANSWER THAT BEST COMPLETES THE SENSE OF THE TEXT.**

1. The managing partner of the investment company _____ its yearly earnings in a speech broadcast by satellite to financial analysts around the world. He was ebullient over the results.

(A) announced
(B) boasted about
(C) declared
(D) stated
(E) took satisfaction in

2. Lacking in new or interesting ideas, the conference presentations seemed _____.

(A) unrelenting
(B) continuous
(C) interminable
(D) assiduous
(E) persistent

3. Motivated by the (i) _____ national debt, lawmakers after years of discussion, agreed to eliminate earmarks for local programs from the budget. The consequences touched a (ii) _____ of projects from sewer treatment plants to widening of roadways.

Blank (i)	Blank (ii)
(A) burgeoning	(D) panoply
(B) emerging	(E) plethora
(C) sprouting	(F) diversity

4. In recent recessions economists have noted (i) _____ known as a jobless recovery. A comparison of data shows that the economy begins to grow before the number of jobs increases. This is a(n) (ii) _____ divergence from previous recoveries.

Blank (i)	Blank (ii)
(A) a phenomenon	(D) imperceptible
(B) an episode	(E) precise
(C) an omen	(F) pronounced

5. Recently passed and more (i) _____ regulations related to energy efficiency are putting pressure on vehicle manufacturers to produce more energy-efficient vehicles. This means new designs for cars, trucks, and buses to meet (ii)_____ emission standards. Another (iii) _____ to change is the growing demand for vehicles powered by alternative fuels.

Blank (i)	Blank (ii)	Blank (iii)
(A) stringent	(D) stricter	(G) force
(B) compliant	(E) disciplined	(H) movement
(C) adaptable	(F) sterner	(I) impetus

FOR QUESTIONS 6–20, CHOOSE ONLY <u>ONE</u> ANSWER CHOICE UNLESS OTHERWISE INDICATED.

QUESTIONS 6–8 ARE BASED ON THE FOLLOWING PASSAGE.

Luigi Pirandello's 1921 play *Six Characters in Search of an Author* may be considered the first existentialist drama. The play explores the relationship between imaginary characters and the writer who has created them. The premise of the play is that six characters have taken on a life of their own because their author has failed to complete their story. The characters
5 invade a rehearsal of another play by Pirandello and insist on acting out their lives. Somehow there is an immutable reality for these six characters, despite the fact that they are merely the fabrications of a writer. As the play's structure begins to break down, the characters begin to question how anyone can tell when reality ends and pretense begins. Pirandello leaves his audience wondering the same thing.

6. The passage is primarily concerned with

(A) contrasting the difference between reality and pretense in Pirandello's play.

(B) comparing how Pirandello's play differed from most others of its time.

(C) explaining how the structure of Pirandello's play mirrored real life.

(D) demonstrating how Pirandello challenged his audience's perception of reality.

(E) showing how the characters in Pirandello's play interacted with one another.

7. "Immutable" (line 6) most nearly means

(A) variable.

(B) enclosed.

(C) unsure.

(D) flexible.

(E) enduring.

8. Select the sentence in the passage in which the author provides a succinct description of Pirandello's play.

(A) Luigi Pirandello's 1921 play *Six Characters in Search of an Author* may be considered the first existentialist drama.

(B) The characters invade a rehearsal of another play by Pirandello and insist on acting out their lives.

(C) Somehow there is an immutable reality for these six characters, despite the fact that they are merely the fabrications of a writer.

(D) The premise of the play is that six characters have taken on a life of their own because their author has failed to complete their story.

(E) As the play's structure begins to break down, the characters begin to question how anyone can tell when reality ends and pretense begins.

QUESTIONS 9 AND 10 ARE BASED ON THE FOLLOWING PASSAGE.

"Fifty Years After the Equal Pay Act" is a U.S. government report on the effects of the landmark legislation of the Kennedy Administration. The document details multiple improvements and successes, as women have now integrated most fields of endeavor formerly reserved for men; furthermore, they have risen to the highest levels of achievement in them, attaining
5 formerly unheard of positions such as CEO, Supreme Court Justice, and Secretary of State. Women have also moved in large and ever-increasing numbers into the ranks of the nation's entrepreneurs; moreover, they have dramatically increased their presence among the nation's upper echelons of earners.

Nevertheless, the report also shows that high-profile success stories belie grimmer facts
10 about where women stand in the workplace and economically overall. As the report notes, while overtly discriminatory practices, such as "female worker wanted" ads, have ended, occasional occupational segregation and other barriers to equality persist. Most tellingly, the majority of women currently earns just 77 cents for every dollar earned by men (an 18-cent gain over 1963, made smaller by the fact that many men are now earning less) and
15 disproportionately fills the ranks of low-income jobs, including childcare workers, cashiers, and maids. In fact, a current catchphrase among activists that captures the reality of both low-income jobs and the increasing number of households headed by single women is the "feminization of poverty."

FOR QUESTION 9, CONSIDER EACH ANSWER INDIVIDUALLY AND SELECT <u>ALL</u> CHOICES THAT APPLY.

---

9. Which of the following statements is or are supported by the passage?

(A) Occupational segregation has finally been eliminated.

(B) The 18-cent gain in pay is not as great as the numbers suggest.

(C) Increases in high-profile jobs demonstrate the end of income inequality.

10. The author mentions the "feminization of poverty" in order to

(A) provide a possible explanation for other details in the passage.

(B) provide support for the main findings of the report.

(C) introduce an overarching counterpoint to all claims of progress.

(D) weaken the main point of the government's report.

(E) contrast this detail with earlier information in the paragraph.

QUESTIONS 11 AND 12 ARE BASED ON THE FOLLOWING PASSAGE.

Can the center of the Eurozone hold? Economic crises have undermined the Eurozone since 2007, and while their effects have been less publically visible lately than they were in 2012, when the economic alliance appeared ready to implode, their repercussions are not over. Rising distrust of the Eurozone felt by southern Eurozone countries, including Spain, Italy, Cyprus,
5　Greece, and France, appears to be due to the continuing recessionary trends these nations are experiencing, as well as increases in income disparity and persistent unemployment fostered by the crises. For these reasons, some experts forecast structural change in these governments as economic crisis brews democratic crisis. Meanwhile, a marked divergence in the wealth of northern Eurozone countries, especially Germany, creates an unsustainable binary division.

11.　The passage mentions each of the following EXCEPT the

　　(A) problems of rising mistrust of the Eurozone.

　　(B) recent changes in public perception of Eurozone issues.

　　(C) near destruction of the Eurozone in 2012.

　　(D) relationship between economics and democratic regimes.

　　(E) unsuitability of austerity measures at this time.

12.　The author suggests that divergence in economic prosperity of Eurozone member nations'

　　(A) fosters mistrust of prosperous nations.

　　(B) undermines democracies in southern Eurozone nations.

　　(C) results in the continuation of recessionary trends.

　　(D) creates an opposition that cannot work in the future.

　　(E) causes income disparity in southern Eurozone nations.

QUESTIONS 13 AND 14 ARE BASED ON THE FOLLOWING PASSAGE.

By the end of World War II, European countries were eager to pursue an economic and political amalgamation in order both to increase prosperity in the region and to foster a sense of unity. The European Union, whose origins began in the 1950s, was officially established in 1993. The creation of the Eurozone in 1999 further solidified economic ties between certain
5　European countries. The Eurozone originally consisted of 11 countries, but now includes 17, both in Western and Eastern Europe. Every country that is in the Eurozone must use the euro as its sole legal currency. Monetary rules for the Eurozone are created and maintained by the European Central Bank. Currently, member states have to abide by the rules of the Stability and Growth Pact that was first adopted in 1997. They cannot exceed an annual
10　budget deficit of 3 percent of the gross domestic project or have an inflation rate over 2 percent. Plus all Eurozone countries must maintain a national debt lower than 60 percent of their gross domestic product.

13.　The author's primary purpose in the passage is to

　　(A) present an overview of the Eurozone.

　　(B) analyze the rules of the Stability and Growth Pact of the Eurozone.

　　(C) suggest alternatives to some of the Stability and Growth Pact's rules.

　　(D) emphasize the importance of the Eurozone.

　　(E) show why other countries should join the Eurozone.

14. "Amalgamation" (line 2) most nearly means
    (A) combination.
    (B) severance.
    (C) melting.
    (D) variance.
    (E) anomaly.

FOR QUESTIONS 15–18, CHOOSE THE TWO ANSWERS THAT BEST FIT THE MEANING OF THE SENTENCE AS A WHOLE AND RESULT IN TWO COMPLETED SENTENCES THAT ARE ALIKE IN MEANING.

15. The job applicant was _____ in his interview by not telling the interviewer about his lack of credentials.
    (A) invidious
    (B) disingenuous
    (C) artless
    (D) clandestine
    (E) devious
    (F) indirect

16. Studies of the age-old _____ of nature versus nurture have resulted in some interesting results. Studies of identical and fraternal twins have indicated that a sense of humor is the result of nurture rather than nature.
    (A) paradox
    (B) provocation
    (C) enigma
    (D) challenge
    (E) conundrum
    (F) paradigm

17. Mulling over the various plans for the reorganization of the sales department, the vice president and the HR director finally and _____ chose the plan that laid off the most salespeople but kept the benefits at the same level for those who were left.
    (A) timidly
    (B) diffidently
    (C) reticently
    (D) stingily
    (E) hesitantly
    (F) reluctantly

18. The audience sat in rapt attention as the poet read his poetry with _____ in his deep, rich baritone voice.

- (A) confidence
- (B) grace
- (C) fluency
- (D) panache
- (E) ease
- (F) flair

QUESTIONS 19 AND 20 ARE BASED ON THE FOLLOWING PASSAGE.

Groundwater contamination arises when groundwater becomes polluted by various substances, including chemicals, medications, bacteria, viruses, fertilizer, and fuel. Groundwater contamination can also come from polluted runoff from farms or when factories dump manufacturing wastes in waterways. Once groundwater becomes contaminated, it can be
5 very difficult to remove the contaminants. Sometimes filtration systems can be used, but in other cases, the groundwater may be so polluted as to be rendered undrinkable. Since much of the world's supply of drinking water comes from groundwater, contamination is a serious issue. In communities in some places in the world that cannot afford other sources of water, people may have no other choice than to drink contaminated groundwater with its
10 consequent serious side effects.

FOR QUESTION 19, CONSIDER EACH ANSWER INDIVIDUALLY AND SELECT <u>ALL</u> CHOICES THAT APPLY.

---

19. It can be inferred from the passage that the author would agree with which of the following statements?

- (A) Groundwater contamination should be an important consideration of municipal governments.
- (B) People should consider using alternate sources of water whenever possible.
- (C) Once groundwater contamination is detected, it must be addressed.

20. Select the sentence in the passage that best establishes the author's position.

- (A) Groundwater contamination can also come from polluted runoff from farms or when factories dump manufacturing wastes in waterways.
- (B) Since much of the world's supply of drinking water comes from groundwater, contamination is a serious issue.
- (C) Once groundwater becomes contaminated, it can be very difficult to remove the contaminants.
- (D) Sometimes filtration systems can be used, but in other cases, the groundwater may be so polluted as to be rendered unpotable.
- (E) In communities in some places in the world that cannot afford other sources of water, people may have no other choice than to drink contaminated groundwater with its consequent serious side effects.

STOP

If you finish before the time is up, you may check your work in this section only.

SECTION 3: QUANTITATIVE REASONING

35 minutes • 20 questions

(The paper-and-pencil version will have 25 questions to be completed in 40 minutes.)

For each question, follow the specific directions and choose the best answer.

The test-maker provides the following information that applies to all questions in the Quantitative Reasoning section of the GRE®:

- All numbers used are real numbers.

- All figures are assumed to lie in a plane unless otherwise indicated.

- Geometric figures, such as lines, circles, triangles, and quadrilaterals, *are not necessarily* drawn to scale. That is, you should *not* assume that quantities such as lengths and angle measures are as they appear in a figure. You should assume, however, that lines shown as straight are actually straight, points on a line are in the order shown, and more generally, all geometric objects are in the relative positions shown. For questions with geometric figures, you should base your answers on geometric reasoning, not on estimating or comparing quantities by sight or by measurement.

- Coordinate systems, such as *xy*-planes and number lines, *are* drawn to scale. Therefore, you can read, estimate, or compare quantities in such figures by sight or by measurement.

- Graphical data presentations, such as bar graphs, circle graphs, and line graphs, *are* drawn to scale. Therefore, you can read, estimate, or compare data values by sight or by measurement.

FOR QUESTIONS 1–8, COMPARE QUANTITY A AND QUANTITY B. SOME QUESTIONS WILL HAVE ADDITIONAL INFORMATION ABOVE THE TWO QUANTITIES TO USE IN DETERMINING YOUR ANSWER.

---

1.   <u>Quantity A</u>   <u>Quantity B</u>

       (12)(5)(9)(107)   (8)(104)(5)(12)

(A) Quantity A is greater.

(B) Quantity B is greater.

(C) The two quantities are equal.

(D) The relationship cannot be determined from the information given.

$$a \neq 0$$

a is the reciprocal of B.

2. 　　　　Quantity A　　　　　　　　Quantity B
　　　　　　B　　　　　　　　　　　　a

(A) Quantity A is greater.
(B) Quantity B is greater.
(C) The two quantities are equal.
(D) The relationship cannot be determined from the information given.

3. 　　　　Quantity A　　　　　　　　Quantity B
　　　　$\left(\sqrt[3]{86}\right)^2$　　　　　　　　　　9

(A) Quantity A is greater.
(B) Quantity B is greater.
(C) The two quantities are equal.
(D) The relationship cannot be determined from the information given.

Amelia invests $1,000 at a simple annual interest rate of 3%.
Margot invests $1,200 at a simple annual interest rate of 2%.

4. 　　　　Quantity A　　　　　　　　Quantity B
Amelia's investment after 16 years.　　Margot's investment after 12 years.

(A) Quantity A is greater.
(B) Quantity B is greater.
(C) The two quantities are equal.
(D) The relationship cannot be determined from the information given.

Mary is twice as old as Jay was 5 years ago. Jay is twice as old as Sue.
All together they are 15 years older than Mary is now.

5. 　　　　Quantity A　　　　　　　　Quantity B
　　　　　　Mary　　　　　　　　　　　Jay

(A) Quantity A is greater.
(B) Quantity B is greater.
(C) The two quantities are equal.
(D) The relationship cannot be determined from the information given.

6.   <u>Quantity A</u>   <u>Quantity B</u>

   m∠1 + m∠2 + m∠3 + m∠4   m∠3 + m∠4 + m∠5 + m∠6

(A) Quantity A is greater.

(B) Quantity B is greater.

(C) The two quantities are equal.

(D) The relationship cannot be determined from the information given.

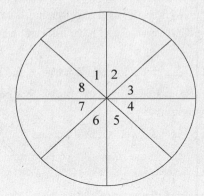

7.   <u>Quantity A</u>   <u>Quantity B</u>

   m∠3 + m∠4 + m∠5   m∠1 + m∠8 + m∠7

(A) Quantity A is greater.

(B) Quantity B is greater.

(C) The two quantities are equal.

(D) The relationship cannot be determined from the information given.

8.   Quantity A   Quantity B
              The mean of x and y 60

(A) Quantity A is greater.

(B) Quantity B is greater.

(C) The two quantities are equal.

(D) The relationship cannot be determined from the information given.

Questions 9–20 have several formats. Unless the directions state otherwise, choose one answer choice. For the Numeric Entry questions, follow the instructions below.

Numeric Entry Questions

The following items are the same for both the computer-based version of the test and the paper-and-pencil version. However, those taking the computer-based version will have additional information about entering answers in decimal and fraction boxes on the computer screen. Those taking the paper-and-pencil version will have information about entering answers on answer grids.

- Your answer may be an integer, a decimal, or a fraction, and it may be negative.

- If a question asks for a fraction, there will be two boxes. One box will be for the numerator and one will be for the denominator.

- Equivalent forms of the correct answer, such as 2.5 and 2.50, are all correct.

- Enter the exact answer unless the question asks you to round your answers.

9. What is the area of a circle with a diameter of 12?

(A) 6π

(B) 12π

(C) 24π

(D) 36π

(E) 144π

10. A bag of cement weighs 94 pounds and a bag of lime weighs 50 pounds. How many pounds does a shipment of 18 bags of cement and 5 bags of lime weigh?

(A) 250

(B) 1,370

(C) 1,442

(D) 1,692

(E) 1,942

11. Given $4f + 4g = 14$ and $15h + 15i = 60$, what is the mean of f, g, h, and i?

   (A) $1\dfrac{7}{8}$

   (B) $2\dfrac{1}{4}$

   (C) $8\dfrac{3}{5}$

   (D) $12\dfrac{3}{4}$

   (E) $18\dfrac{1}{2}$

12. From a well-shuffled deck of cards, what is the probability of drawing a red 8?

   (A) $\dfrac{1}{4}$

   (B) $\dfrac{1}{13}$

   (C) $\dfrac{2}{13}$

   (D) $\dfrac{1}{26}$

   (E) $\dfrac{1}{52}$

13. A right triangle has a base of 12 and a hypotenuse of 13. What is the height of the remaining leg?

   (A) 4

   (B) 5

   (C) 15

   (D) 20

   (E) 25

14. To manufacture soft pretzels, there is a built-in cost of $320 to start the machines and an additional cost for materials of $0.05 per pretzel. If the pretzels sell for 4 for $1.00, how many have to be sold to break even for the day?

   (A) 100

   (B) 160

   (C) 320

   (D) 1,600

   (E) 3,200

QUESTIONS 15–17 REFER TO THE TABLE BELOW.

Tahoe and Suburban Sales
1999–2013

	Tahoe	Suburban
1999	72,000	70,000
2000	127,000	92,000
2001	127,000	101,000
2002	131,000	110,000
2003	126,000	137,000
2004	150,000	132,000
2005	201,000	152,000
2006	209,000	150,000
2007	197,000	132,000
2008	188,000	118,000
2009	151,000	88,000
2010	160,000	76,000
2011	148,000	83,000
2012	90,000	52,000
2013	71,000	42,000

15. What is the range of vehicles sold between 1999 and 2013?

    (A) 42,000

    (B) 194,000

    (C) 167,000

    (D) 280,000

    (E) 290,000

16. If the average price of a Tahoe in 2010 was $35,600 and the average price of a Suburban in 2010 was $57,700, what was the total sales number in dollars for both vehicles that year?

    (A) 1.00812×10^{10}

    (B) 1.65712×10^{10}

    (C) 2.65712×10^{10}

    (D) 2.98112×10^{10}

    (E) 3.12912×10^{10}

FOR QUESTION 17, CHOOSE <u>ALL</u> THAT APPLY.

17. What are the mode and the median of the number of Tahoes sold between 1999 and 2013?

    (A) 71,000

    (B) 127,000

    (C) 131,000

    (D) 148,000

    (E) 151,000

    (F) 180,000

18. Fernanda has 8 books in her reading list, from which she will choose 3 to take with her on vacation. How many different groups of 3 books from these 8 can she make?

    (A) 24
    (B) 56
    (C) 120
    (D) 336
    (E) 6,720

FOR QUESTIONS 19 AND 20, ENTER YOUR ANSWERS IN THE BOXES.

---

19. Jack Rosato pays a flat rate business tax in his township of 0.438% on all invoices. He had invoices totaling $297,849.00 last year. What was his township tax bill? (Round your answer to two decimal places.)

    $ ☐

20. The frequency table shown represents the ages of all the goalkeepers in a soccer league. What is the median age of the league's goalkeepers?

Goalkeeper's Age	Frequency
23	1
25	3
26	2
27	3
29	1
31	3
32	2
34	2
37	1

☐

STOP

If you finish before the time is up, you may check your work in this section only.

SECTION 4: QUANTITATIVE REASONING

35 minutes • 20 questions

(The paper-and-pencil version will have 25 questions to be completed in 40 minutes.)

For each question, follow the specific directions and choose the best answer.

The test-maker provides the following information that applies to all questions in the Quantitative Reasoning section of the GRE®:

- All numbers used are real numbers.

- All figures are assumed to lie in a plane unless otherwise indicated.

- Geometric figures, such as lines, circles, triangles, and quadrilaterals, *are not necessarily* drawn to scale. That is, you should *not* assume that quantities such as lengths and angle measures are as they appear in a figure. You should assume, however, that lines shown as straight are actually straight, points on a line are in the order shown, and more generally, all geometric objects are in the relative positions shown. For questions with geometric figures, you should base your answers on geometric reasoning, not on estimating or comparing quantities by sight or by measurement.

- Coordinate systems, such as *xy*-planes and number lines, *are* drawn to scale. Therefore, you can read, estimate, or compare quantities in such figures by sight or by measurement.

- Graphical data presentations, such as bar graphs, circle graphs, and line graphs, *are* drawn to scale. Therefore, you can read, estimate, or compare data values by sight or by measurement.

FOR QUESTIONS 1–9, COMPARE QUANTITY A AND QUANTITY B. SOME QUESTIONS WILL HAVE ADDITIONAL INFORMATION ABOVE THE TWO QUANTITIES TO USE IN DETERMINING YOUR ANSWER.

$$x > 0$$
$$y > 0$$

1.　　　　　　Quantity A　　　　　　　　Quantity B
　　　　　　　　x　　　　　　　　　　　　y

(A) Quantity A is greater.

(B) Quantity B is greater.

(C) The two quantities are equal.

(D) The relationship cannot be determined from the information given.

2.

Quantity A	Quantity B
$\frac{1}{3}$ of 12	$\frac{1}{4}$ of 16

(A) Quantity A is greater.
(B) Quantity B is greater.
(C) The two quantities are equal.
(D) The relationship cannot be determined from the information given.

3.

Quantity A	Quantity B
$\frac{1}{5} + \frac{1}{5}$	0.04

(A) Quantity A is greater.
(B) Quantity B is greater.
(C) The two quantities are equal.
(D) The relationship cannot be determined from the information given.

$$x^7 = -128$$

4.

Quantity A	Quantity B
x^5	$8x^2$

(A) Quantity A is greater.
(B) Quantity B is greater.
(C) The two quantities are equal.
(D) The relationship cannot be determined from the information given.

$$\frac{5}{16}m = \frac{1}{8}$$

5.

Quantity A	Quantity B
m	$\frac{2}{5}$

(A) Quantity A is greater.
(B) Quantity B is greater.
(C) The two quantities are equal.
(D) The relationship cannot be determined from the information given.

Triangle ABC lies on the xy-plane with A at $(0,0)$, B at $(4,0)$, and C at (x,y).

$$x, y > 0$$
$$area = 24$$

6.   Quantity A   Quantity B
           x 6

(A) Quantity A is greater.

(B) Quantity B is greater.

(C) The two quantities are equal.

(D) The relationship cannot be determined from the information given.

7.   Quantity A   Quantity B
           x 72

(A) Quantity A is greater.

(B) Quantity B is greater.

(C) The two quantities are equal.

(D) The relationship cannot be determined from the information given.

$$x + y = 16$$

8.   Quantity A   Quantity B
    Maximum value of xy 63

(A) Quantity A is greater.

(B) Quantity B is greater.

(C) The two quantities are equal.

(D) The relationship cannot be determined from the information given.

$$8x = 3.2$$
$$y = 4x - 1$$

9.

Quantity A	Quantity B
x	y

(A) Quantity A is greater.

(B) Quantity B is greater.

(C) The two quantities are equal.

(D) The relationship cannot be determined from the information given.

Questions 10–20 have several formats. Unless the directions state otherwise, choose one answer choice. For the Numeric Entry questions, follow the instructions below.

Numeric Entry Questions

The following items are the same for both the computer-based version of the test and the paper-and-pencil version. However, those taking the computer-based version will have additional information about entering answers in decimal and fraction boxes on the computer screen. Those taking the paper-and-pencil version will have information about entering answers on answer grids.

- Your answer may be an integer, a decimal, or a fraction, and it may be negative.

- If a question asks for a fraction, there will be two boxes. One box will be for the numerator and one will be for the denominator.

- Equivalent forms of the correct answer, such as 2.5 and 2.50, are all correct.

- Enter the exact answer unless the question asks you to round your answers.

10. How many miles is it from Kalamazoo to Timbuktu?

(A) 68

(B) 65

(C) 66

(D) 63

(E) 64

11. The local football booster club sells food at all home games. To make the accounting equal, they sell all products for the same price of $1.00. If over the course of the season they sold 4 times as many hot dogs as candy bars, and half as many drinks as hot dogs, and they sold a total of $1,400 worth of food, how many drinks did they sell?

  (A) 200

  (B) 400

  (C) 600

  (D) 800

  (E) 1,400

12. Solve for x: $x^{\frac{3}{2}} = 125$

  (A) −25

  (B) −5

  (C) 5

  (D) 25

  (E) 125

QUESTIONS 13–15 REFER TO THE GRAPH BELOW:

Vegetable Plant Sales in May

13. If in May the sales of tomato plants were $13,482, what were the sales of all the vegetable plants?

  (A) $58,617.39

  (B) $59,871.09

  (C) $60,740.87

  (D) $62,137.83

  (E) $63,820.31

14. Total vegetation sales in May were $124,717.85. What were the total sales of cucumbers and herbs combined?

(A) $34,675.93

(B) $37,897.02

(C) $40,320.04

(D) $42,739.84

(E) $49,887.14

15. What is the ratio of squash sales to eggplant sales?

(A) $\dfrac{2}{9}$

(B) $\dfrac{2}{1}$

(C) $\dfrac{5}{4}$

(D) $\dfrac{4}{7}$

(E) $\dfrac{6}{11}$

FOR QUESTIONS 16 AND 17, CHOOSE <u>ALL</u> THAT APPLY.

---

16. Find the next three numbers in the sequence: 1, –4, 16, –64, …

(A) –4,096

(B) –1,024

(C) –256

(D) 256

(E) 1,024

(F) 4,096

17. For which of the following defined operations does $a \triangle b$ always equal $b \triangle a$, where a and b are integers?

   (A) $a \triangle b = |b - a|$

   (B) $a \triangle b = a^2 - b^2$

   (C) $a \triangle b = (a - b)^3$

   (D) $a \triangle b = a^b$

   (E) $a \triangle b = \left(\dfrac{1}{a} + \dfrac{1}{b}\right)^3$

FOR QUESTIONS 18 AND 19, ENTER YOUR ANSWERS IN THE BOXES.

---

18. Jeff is 3 times as old as Billy, who is 2 times as old as Joe. In 7 years, their combined age will be 3 times Jeff's age now, plus 3. How old is Billy now?

   ☐

19. $\left(\dfrac{1}{3} - 2\right)\left(\dfrac{1}{4} - 2\right) =$

   Give answer as a fraction.

   ☐
   ☐

20. Points $(3, -2)$ and $(-7, 4)$ define a line segment in the coordinate plane. What are the coordinates of the line segment's midpoint?

   (A) $(5, -3)$
   (B) $(2, 1)$
   (C) $(2, -1)$
   (D) $(-2, 1)$
   (E) $(-2, -1)$

STOP

If you finish before the time is up, you may check your work in this section only.

SECTION 5: VERBAL REASONING

30 minutes • 20 questions

(The paper-and-pencil version will have 25 questions to be completed in 35 minutes.)

For each question, follow the specific directions and choose the best answer.

> **FOR QUESTIONS 1–5, CHOOSE <u>ONE</u> ANSWER FOR EACH BLANK. SELECT FROM THE APPROPRIATE COLUMN FOR EACH BLANK. CHOOSE THE ANSWER THAT BEST COMPLETES THE SENSE OF THE TEXT.**

1. Research on school improvement has found that instruction must convey information _____ to be effective. Lessons that don't proceed logically from A to B to C, confuse, rather than inform.

(A) coherently
(B) smoothly
(C) articulately
(D) cogently
(E) eloquently

2. Mechanical weathering, which breaks down rock, includes a number of processes. One is caused by the _____ quality of rock particles. The particles rushing by in water or carried by the wind break down the rocks with which they come in contact.

(A) coarse
(B) rough
(C) rasping
(D) grating
(E) abrasive

3. Critics may consider his style (i)_____ of the worst in advertising art, but he charges (ii)_____ prices for his representational paintings and makes a fortune.

Blank (i)	Blank (ii)
(A) derivative	(D) munificent
(B) a by-product	(E) magnanimous
(C) a complement	(F) exorbitant

4. The (i)_____ view of many Americans for years was that the 1950s were a time of peace and prosperity. However, this (ii)_____ version of the time period is (iii)_____ by the racial unrest that erupted in the latter part of the decade.

Blank (i)	Blank (ii)	Blank (iii)
(A) prevailing	(D) implied	(G) concealed
(B) hypothetical	(E) epic	(H) misrepresented
(C) academic	(F) fictional	(I) belied

5. His grades in school never seemed (i) _____ with his intelligence, and this (ii) _____ assessment was borne out in his later work life. Known for his (iii) _____ ability to penetrate to the core issues, he rose to become CEO of a Fortune 1000 company.

Blank (i)	Blank (ii)	Blank (iii)
(A) congenial	(D) astute	(G) laser-like
(B) commensurate	(E) practiced	(H) discerning
(C) complaisant	(F) adroit	(I) caustic

FOR QUESTIONS 6–20, CHOOSE ONLY <u>ONE</u> ANSWER CHOICE UNLESS OTHERWISE INDICATED.

QUESTIONS 6–8 ARE BASED ON THE FOLLOWING PASSAGE.

American artist Mary Cassatt (1845–1926) is noteworthy for being one of the few women artists to succeed professionally during the late nineteenth century. Because of her friendship with Edgar Degas, she was the only American to take part in the 1879 exhibition of French Impressionist artists in Paris. Though Cassatt's style was influenced by the Impressionists,
5   she developed her own unique style and subject matter. It is easy to see the influence of Degas in her paintings, but her interest in Japanese prints is also reflected in many of her paintings. Much of her earliest work portrays women engaging in home activities, such as reading, sewing, or writing letters. After the French exhibition, Cassatt began to explore what she eventually became famous for: paintings of women caring for children. It is through these
10 paintings that Cassatt highlights the often overlooked role in painting of women as mothers.

6. Select the sentence in the passage in which the author notes influences on Cassatt's style.

   (A) After the French exhibition, Cassatt began to explore what she eventually became famous for: paintings of women caring for children.

   (B) It is easy to see the influence of Degas in her paintings, but her interest in Japanese prints is also reflected in many of her paintings.

   (C) Much of her earliest work portrays women engaging in home activities, such as reading, sewing, or writing letters.

   (D) It is through these paintings that Cassatt highlights the often overlooked role in painting of women as mothers.

   (E) Because of her friendship with Edgar Degas, she was the only American to take part in an 1879 exhibition of French Impressionist artists in Paris.

7. The author's primary purpose in the passage is to

   (A) explain why Mary Cassatt began painting women and children.

   (B) argue that Mary Cassatt was a huge influence on later female painters.

   (C) suggest reasons that Mary Cassatt's art began to change after the Impressionist exhibition.

   (D) analyze the ways that Mary Cassatt was influenced by the Impressionists.

   (E) describe the development of Mary Cassatt's artistic style and themes.

FOR QUESTION 8, CONSIDER EACH ANSWER INDIVIDUALLY AND SELECT <u>ALL</u> CHOICES THAT APPLY.

8. Which of the following statements is supported by the passage?

   (A) Mary Cassatt began to paint women and children as a way to express her frustration with contemporary male artists.

   (B) Mary Cassatt was inspired by several artistic styles from different parts of the world.

   (C) Mary Cassatt expressed a unique perspective through her art.

QUESTIONS 9 AND 10 ARE BASED ON THE FOLLOWING PASSAGE.

Modest Mussorgsky was one of a group of Russian composers known as "The Five" or "The Mighty Handful," whose goal in the late 1800s was to create Russian nationalist music. Mussorgsky's most famous work, the opera *Boris Godunov,* completed in 1873, is the story of the powerful, though flawed Russian tsar who ruled in the early seventeenth century. The
5 opera met with negative criticism from some of Mussorgsky's contemporaries. Another member of "The Five," Nicolai Rimsky-Korsakov, said of *Boris Godunov* that "I adore it for its originality, power, boldness, distinctiveness, and beauty; I abhor it for its lack of polish, the roughness of its harmonies, and, in some places, the sheer awkwardness of the music." Because of this, Rimsky-Korsakov revised the opera after Mussorgsky's death at age forty-
10 one in 1881, correcting what he believed were technical weaknesses in the original score. Rimsky-Korsakov's revised version of *Boris Gudonov* became the preferred edition of the opera. In recent years, however, Mussorgsky's unique style and orchestration have come to be appreciated, even celebrated, and his is the version that opera-goers are more likely to see performed.

9. "Nationalist" (line 2) most nearly means

   (A) loyalty to one's country.

   (B) dedicated to the interests or culture of a nation.

   (C) love of one's country.

   (D) isolationist.

   (E) separatist.

10. The author suggests that Mussorgsky's work

   (A) lacked polish and technique.

   (B) was well-respected by his contemporaries.

   (C) covered complex themes that were far ahead of their time.

   (D) was too technically challenging to perform in the original.

   (E) was not fully appreciated in his own lifetime.

QUESTIONS 11–13 ARE BASED ON THE FOLLOWING PASSAGE.

Despite advances in medicine and technology, the demand for organ transplants remains much greater than the number of organ donors available. Ironically, this is mainly because of the increasing success rate of organ transplant operations over the years. Early transplant operations often failed because patients' immune systems rejected the foreign organ. However, the introduction of the drug cyclosporine in the 1980s helped solve this problem, and organ transplants subsequently became much more routine, which, in turn, resulted in the need for more organ donations.

Researchers looking for a way to solve this problem have begun to work on developing artificial organs, **though this is still in a highly experimental phase.** So far, laboratories around the world have developed artificial hearts, lungs, livers, and other organs, but with only limited success. Other scientists are working on techniques to grow organs from a patient's own cells, **which could ultimately eliminate the need for organ donors.** Yet because this involves cloning and stem cell research, it also raises ethical questions that make this a much more complicated issue than developing artificial organs.

11. What function do the two groups of words in bold type serve in this passage?

   (A) The first presents an argument; the second reinforces the argument.

   (B) The first presents an opinion; the second presents final support for the opinion.

   (C) The first serves as an intermediate conclusion; the second serves as a definitive conclusion.

   (D) The first anticipates the argument's conclusion; the second supports the conclusion.

   (E) The first qualifies a fact; the second states a conclusion.

12. It can be inferred from the passage that the author would agree with which of the following statements?

   (A) The discovery of the drug cyclosporine made it much harder for people who needed organs to get them.

   (B) Scientists should continue to experiment trying to develop organs in order to solve the problem of the organ donor shortage.

   (C) The technique of growing organs from patients' own cells is so potentially divisive that it should be discontinued.

13. If the information in this passage is true, which of the following must also be true?

   (A) Some people who need organ transplants today will not receive them in time.

   (B) Artificial organs will never be a viable option for people needing organ transplants.

   (C) Because of use of the drug cyclosporine, the human body no longer rejects foreign organs.

   (D) Creating organs from patients' own cells will become much easier over time.

   (E) In the future, people will no longer need organ transplants from donor organs.

QUESTIONS 14 AND 15 ARE BASED ON THE FOLLOWING PASSAGE.

In January 2014, the CIA World Factbook listed Nicaragua as Central America's poorest economy and as the Western Hemisphere's second poorest economy. Employment figures alone suggest the nation's economic story: services account for 53% of jobs and agriculture for 28%; the Factbook lists no professional categories of employment. Indeed, the country
5   is primarily known for agricultural products that include coffee, shrimp, tobacco, and sugar, all of which are important exports, along with textiles, which generate most of the remaining jobs in industry. Despite the fact that Nicaragua's economy has recently been growing at a 4% annual rate, debt burdens significantly impair progress. Additionally, the Heritage Foundation notes that Nicaragua's grim economic picture is exacerbated by political factors,
10 including weak rule of law, which discourages both domestic and foreign investment, and anti-free market policies. These include costly regulatory procedures, which have historically led investors down a path of bribery or other corruption, and the prohibitively high cost of long-term financing, which discourages entrepreneurial initiative.

14. "Exacerbated" (line 9) most nearly means
    (A) complicated.
    (B) instigated.
    (C) fermented.
    (D) implicated.
    (E) ameliorated.

15. The passage provides information on each of the following EXCEPT:
    (A) the distribution of employment type in Nicaragua.
    (B) the checks on investment in new enterprise in Nicaragua.
    (C) Nicaragua's ranking among neighboring economies.
    (D) Nicaragua's ranking among world economies.
    (E) the negative effects of the weak rule of law in Nicaragua.

FOR QUESTIONS 16–19, CHOOSE THE <u>TWO</u> ANSWERS THAT BEST FIT THE MEANING OF THE SENTENCE AS A WHOLE AND RESULT IN TWO COMPLETED SENTENCES THAT ARE ALIKE IN MEANING.

---

16. Government economists released a report showing how the _____ housing market was depressing prices across a number of areas in the construction industry.
    (A) obsolescent
    (B) outmoded
    (C) superseded
    (D) moribund
    (E) motionless
    (F) stagnant

17. Many doctors are still _____ digitizing their patients' records. They see the process as expensive and time-consuming and are not convinced of its value.

　　(A) wary of

　　(B) scrupulous about

　　(C) meticulous about

　　(D) skeptical about

　　(E) dubious about

　　(F) critical about

18. Delivered in a defiant tone, the leader's _____ denial of any wrongdoing in his cabinet failed to quell calls for an investigation into the allegations of malfeasance in office.

　　(A) qualified

　　(B) eligible

　　(C) blunt

　　(D) intransigent

　　(E) intractable

　　(F) stark

19. The critic applauded the novel for its wit but decried the one-dimensional nature of its characters. Upon reading the review, the novelist railed against the _____ of critics who can't tell that these characters are supposed to be one-dimensional.

　　(A) perfidy

　　(B) obtuseness

　　(C) treachery

　　(D) ignorance

　　(E) denseness

　　(F) inexorableness

QUESTION 20 IS BASED ON THE FOLLOWING PASSAGE.

Although there are many serious consequences resulting from the destruction of tropical rainforests, perhaps the most significant is that of climate change. Tropical rainforests can absorb about 20 percent of the world's carbon dioxide emissions from the atmosphere, but as rainforests are cut down, less carbon dioxide is absorbed. In addition, by slashing and
5   burning the rainforests, human activities are adding huge amounts of carbon dioxide to the atmosphere, even more than is emitted by factories, planes, and automobiles all over the world. Ultimately, as deforestation continues, the amount of carbon dioxide and other greenhouse gas levels in the atmosphere will rise. This will, in turn, lead to an increase in temperature, eventually resulting in a change in weather patterns and sea levels.

FOR QUESTION 20, CONSIDER EACH ANSWER INDIVIDUALLY AND SELECT <u>ALL</u> CHOICES THAT APPLY.

---

20. The author suggests which of the following will happen in the future if deforestation continues?

(A) There will be no tropical rainforests left in the world.

(B) The Earth's temperature will rise each year.

(C) Less carbon dioxide will be absorbed from the atmosphere.

STOP

If you finish before the time is up, you may check your work in this section only.

ANSWER KEY AND EXPLANATIONS

Section 1: Analytical Writing

Analyze an Issue

Model: 6 points out of 6

Washington, D.C., is the seat of our nation's democracy and a symbol of democratic and egalitarian ideals around the world. Unlike other U.S. cities, it offers visitors a chance to visit, without paying a penny of admission, some of the finest and most important institutions in the world. This is a glorious policy, which should excite our pride, not our parsimony. Certainly, the United States, the richest nation in the world, can afford to extend an open hand to visitors to its own capital.

That open hand must be extended, minimally, to all American visitors. Americans should not have to pay to see the treasures in the Smithsonian museums or to visit the living repositories of their own nation's government and history. Besides the fact that it seems most undignified to ask them to do so, haven't Americans paid for all these things already through their taxes? These museums and their treasures as well as the other free institutions of learning and government in our nation's capital are already the rightful possesions of the American people.

Some possibly unforeseen consequences of a new policy of payment could also prove quite negative. Washington, D.C., earns a substantial amount of money each year through tourism. It seems almost inevitable that tourism and the revenues earned from it would decrease if admission fees were suddenly charged. The school group from Chicago or the senior citizens group from Omaha might still come, but spend fewer days. Other groups and families might decide, given the other costs involved in vacationing in a big city, that it is just as cost effective to go elsewhere. Furthermore, a new policy of payment would mean fewer visitors, and that would probably result in a decrease in the ways in which some of the institutions involved, such as museums that operate restaurants and shops, earn money. Thus, some of the gains in revenue achieved through admission could well be offset by a decrease in revenue at these businesses.

The largest losses, of course, would be to the American public, especially to those who are least able to pay. What resides in their nation's capital is their rightful patrimony, yet they would be disenfranchised from it. Those with the ability to make choices about where and how to spend their money might decide that with the museums and other sites charging a fee, why not take the children to that theme park where they really want to go? In that way, opportunities for enrichment, for learning, and for participating in one's American heritage would all be lost.

This essay scores 6 out of 6 because it

- **answers the task.** With considerable insight, it discusses and explains the writer's views on the policy and considers the consequences of implementing the policy.

- **is well supported.** The writer offers perceptive and persuasive support, beginning with the idea that the United States is the world's richest nation ending with the ideas about rightful patrimony.

- **is well organized.** From the engaging opening to the dramatic placement of the most important ideas last, the essay provides a logical and smooth progression of ideas. Clear, appropriate connections help unify the ideas and ease the reader's passage through the response.

- **is fluid.** Word choices are sophisticated and effective, while sentences demonstrate qualities of directness and variety as well as parallelism.
- **observes the conventions of Standard Written English.**

Model: 1 point out of 6

Its time to face reality and be fiscaly responsable and begin asking visitor's to our nations capitol to pay for going to the many fine places in Washington, D.C. that they don't pay for now. Visitors are use to such fees for almost every other museum they go to and for historical sights across the country. The only place where it would be hard to get use to paying a fee would be for visiting the library.

This essay scores 1 out of 6 because it

- **does not answer the task.** While the writer does state a position, it is not fully explained, and the consequences of implementing the policy are omitted.
- **lacks support and development.** There is only one simple idea that might be categorized as support.
- **has multiple errors in Standard Written English.** While a few errors matter little in a well-organized and well-developed essay, the errors in this piece greatly hinder comprehension.

Analyze an Argument

Model: 6 points out of 6

In this argument, the writer completely dismisses the city council's proposal for a crumbling neighborhood and instead suggests urban renewal by means of community gardens or urban farms. The writer's argument is flawed by a failure to consider all the ramifications of the alternative she suggests, as well as by weak or faulty cause-and-effect reasoning.

A key assumption on which this argument rests is the idea that gardens will eventually regenerate an entire area. In fact, planting, tending, and harvesting gardens will bring activity to an abandoned spot or to a spot used previously only for dumping trash, or possibly for criminal or other unwanted activities. It is also true that reclaiming a lot for a new purpose, and actively involving people in the process of reclaiming it, will discourage others from continuing to dump trash there or otherwise misusing the space. But is it logical to assume that a few lots with gardens are going to change a whole community? How would that happen?

Neighbors will still live in the same broken-down housing next door to or across the street from the gardens. Those without jobs still will not have jobs. Those without hope for the future are surely not going to be inspired to optimism and future plans by the presence of a few gardens. Finally, if people are committing criminal acts in the area, are those people really going to be frightened completely away by gardens, or might they just move farther down the block?

The writer assumes that establishing gardens is the best solution to the problem of a "neighborhood in crisis," but will this plan actually involve current residents of the neighborhood? And if the plan does not involve them, can it work? Those who are going to feel drawn to urban farming are not necessarily the people who occupy the area today. Many of the current occupants, city dwellers in a crumbling neighborhood, may not ever have planted and harvested food before. Having experienced problems in their neighborhood for many years, they may also be the last people who are knowledgeable enough, brave enough, or eager enough to go into a vacant lot and begin getting rid of its "nefarious" occupants and reclaiming the soil. Some may feel as if they are risking their lives or exposing themselves to danger for the sake of beauty—or even a few vegetables.

Of course, what the writer may assume is that outsiders will come into the area, plant and tend gardens, interact with members of the community, and perhaps buy up some lots. Then they will start an urban homestead there, beginning a process of "gentrification." This process could conceivably lead to homes being renovated over time and to a gradual change in the area. But whom would such a change benefit? It would also seem that such a plan is aimed at eventually driving the current occupants out, without providing any affordable housing in place of what could be lost to market forces. It would seem that such a change could be a driver of more homelessness.

Finally, urban gardens may be lovely to look at, but let's not forget about the high lead content of produce typically harvested from these lots because the ground has absorbed lead paint chips for decades. With all the problems that people in the neighborhood already face, should we add food grown in contaminated soil?

This essay scores 6 out of 6 because it

- **answers the task.** The writer clearly and directly uncovers assumptions on which the argument is based. The author also poses clear questions that would have to be answered to decide whether the recommendation and the argument on which it is based are reasonable.

- **is well supported.** Using multiple examples and explanations, the writer fully develops ideas that show how assumptions might be flawed. The writer also asks questions that would need to be answered and explains the importance of such questions.

- **is well organized.** Paragraph 1 clearly introduces the argument and sums up the writer's response to it; paragraphs 2, 3, and 4 state and support different assumptions and the questions they generate; and the final paragraph brings closure to the essay by posing a final question about the possible negative effects of urban farming. Throughout, ideas are connected logically with transitional words and phrases.

- **is fluid and precise.** All the ideas are presented clearly. Words are used accurately; sentences are varied, clear, and direct.

- **observes the conventions of Standard Written English.**

Model: 1 point out of 6

There are ways in which this is a very good argument but also ways in which this argument is not that convincing. Firstly, the argument rests on an important assumption. It being not always the best course of action to completely destroy a neighborhood and then put up affordable housing, which could be worse than, or lead to worse problems than the problems that the neighborhood is clearly already having. The question that has to be asked about this assumption is whether or not destroying a neighborhood is the best course of action. On the other hand, the argument for urban farming is a great one, because urban farming helps to bring people and purposes to urban areas they have abandoned. In many places, urban farms has transformed places that were abandoned or filled up with trash into places of beautiful flowers and delicious fruits and vegetables.

This essay scores 1 out of 6 because it

- **barely answers the task.** Four of the six sentences in this brief response fail to add anything significant to what is stated in the prompt. The writer does not ask a single question about the writer's recommendations.

- **lacks organization and support.** This rambling single paragraph lacks organization by assumption or any other criteria. The only idea that is even barely supported is that urban farming is a good idea; none of the questions raised by the writer's argument are ever even asked, let alone developed.

- **has major problems with the conventions of Standard Written English.** This essay shows no awareness of paragraphing and contains a fragment, an agreement error, and other faults. These problems also scar the essay.

Section 2: Verbal Reasoning

1. B	11. E	16. D, E
2. C	12. D	17. C, F
3. A, F	13. A	18. D, F
4. A, F	14. A	19. A, C
5. A, D, I	15. B, E	20. B
6. D		
7. E		
8. D		
9. B		
10. C		

Question

1. The managing partner of the investment company _____ its yearly earnings in a speech broad-cast by satellite to financial analysts around the world. He was ebullient over the results.

(A) announced
(B) boasted about
(C) declared
(D) stated
(E) took satisfaction in

Answer Explanation

The correct answer is (B). Knowing the meaning of the word "ebullient," which is a clue to the answer, would have helped you, but if you don't know that it means "cheerful, happy, jovial," you can still figure out the answer from the context. Holding a global call with financial analysts indicates that the earnings must have been very good. Choice (B), "boasted about," has this element of intensity more so than choices (A) and (C), "announced" and "declared," which do mean "made known publicly." Choice (D), "stated," also lacks any emotional intensity. Choice (E), "took satisfaction in," might work, but "boasted" fits the mood better with "ebullient."

Question

2. Lacking in new or interesting ideas, the conference presentations seemed _____.

(A) unrelenting
(B) continuous
(C) interminable
(D) assiduous
(E) persistent

Answer Explanation

The correct answer is (C). Choice (C), "interminable," means "very long, seemingly endless" and undoubtedly describes the conference attendees' feelings. Choice (A), "unrelenting," means "unyielding, persistent, not diminishing in intensity," which doesn't fit the sense of the sentence or include the idea of time. Choice (B), "continuous," means "uninterrupted, unceasing," and doesn't fit the sense. The problem wasn't that the presentations weren't interrupted, but that they went on and on. Choice (D), "assiduous," meaning "hardworking, done with care and perseverance" may be true of the presenters making the presentations, but it doesn't fit the context. Choice (E), "persistent," is a synonym for "unrelenting," but it also means "not giving up." The presentations didn't persist, only the presenters, so "persistent" wouldn't be good usage in this sentence.

Question

3. Motivated by the (i) _____ national debt, lawmakers after years of discussion, agreed to eliminate earmarks for local programs from the budget. The consequences touched a (ii) _____ of projects from sewer treatment plants to widening of roadways.

Blank (i)	Blank (ii)
(A) burgeoning	(D) panoply
(B) emerging	(E) plethora
(C) sprouting	(F) diversity

Answer Explanation

The correct answers are (A) and (F). Answer Blank (i): The correct answer is "burgeoning," choice (A), which means "growing or developing rapidly." Choice (C), "sprouting," meaning "emerging and developing rapidly," is a close synonym for "burgeoning," but "sprouting" would sound strange in this sentence. Based on the sentence, you can infer that the budget problem has been around for years, so choice (C) doesn't truly fit the context. For this same reason, choice (B), "emerging," is incorrect.

Answer Blank (ii): Choice (F), "diversity," means "variety" as well as "range" and fits the context. Choice (D), "panoply," means "splendid or magnificent collection" and based on the examples in the sentence, this doesn't fit. Choice (E), "plethora," means "overabundance, excessive in number," and while this may be objectively true, the sentence doesn't indicate this, so choice (E) has to be eliminated.

Question

4. In recent recessions economists have noted (i) _____ known as a jobless recovery. A comparison of data shows that the economy begins to grow before the number of jobs increases. This is a(n) (ii) _____ divergence from previous recoveries.

Blank (i)
(A) a phenomenon
(B) an episode
(C) an omen

Blank (ii)
(D) imperceptible
(E) precise
(F) pronounced

Answer Explanation

The correct answers are (A) and (F). Answer Blank (i): Choice (A), "a phenomenon," best fits the context. It means "an unusual or significant fact or occurrence." Choice (B), "an episode," refers to "a single event in a series or sequence," which doesn't fit the context. Choice (C), "an omen," meaning "an indicator of a future event," doesn't fit the context either.

Answer Blank (ii): Choice (F), "pronounced," meaning "distinct, noticeable," fits with the context of a significant difference. Choice (D), "imperceptible," means "difficult to perceive, subtle" and doesn't fit with the idea that a jobless recovery is a phenomenon, which is a significant difference. Choice (E), "precise," means "sharply exact, designating a certain thing and nothing else" and doesn't make sense in the context.

Question

5. Recently passed and more (i) _____ regulations related to energy efficiency are putting pressure on vehicle manufacturers to produce more energy-efficient vehicles. This means new designs for cars, trucks, and buses to meet (ii)_____ emission standards. Another (iii) _____ to change is the growing demand for vehicles powered by alternative fuels.

Blank (i)
(A) stringent
(B) compliant
(C) adaptable

Blank (ii)
(D) stricter
(E) disciplined
(F) sterner

Blank (iii)
(G) force
(H) movement
(I) impetus

Answer Explanation

The correct answers are (A), (D), and (I). Answer Blank (i): "Stringent," choice (A), means "severe, imposing rigorous standards of performance" and fits the context. Choice (B), "compliant," means "willing to comply, obedient" and doesn't make sense in the sentence. Choice (C), "adaptable," means "able to be adapted, changing easily" and may seem like a possible answer, but reading further in the passage, you'll find that "easily changed regulations" don't fit with the answer for the second blank.

Answer Blank (ii): Choice (D), "stricter," meaning "tougher, enforced rigorously" fits the context (and helps you answer the first blank). Choice (E), "disciplined," meaning "obeying the rules" doesn't make sense; the emission standards are the rules. Choice (F), "sterner," doesn't fit because it means "harsh" as applied to a person or "grim or unyielding or relentless," none of which describe emission standards.

Answer Blank (iii): Choice (I), "impetus," means "a force moving forward, an incentive, a stimulus" and fits the context. Choice (G), "force," might work except that usage dictates the phrasing would need to read "another force for change" and the actual wording is "another force to change," radically altering the meaning of the sentence. Choice (H), "movement," might seem correct, but if you read it in the sentence, it doesn't make sense either.

QUESTIONS 6–8 ARE BASED ON THE FOLLOWING PASSAGE.

Luigi Pirandello's 1921 play *Six Characters in Search of an Author* may be considered the first existentialist drama. The play explores the relationship between imaginary characters and the writer who has created them. The premise of the play is that six characters have taken on a life of their own because their author has failed to complete their story. The characters
5 invade a rehearsal of another play by Pirandello and insist on acting out their lives. Somehow there is an immutable reality for these six characters, despite the fact that they are merely the fabrications of a writer. As the play's structure begins to break down, the characters begin to question how anyone can tell when reality ends and pretense begins. Pirandello leaves his audience wondering the same thing.

Question

6. The passage is primarily concerned with
   (A) contrasting the difference between reality and pretense in Pirandello's play.
   (B) comparing how Pirandello's play differed from most others of its time.
   (C) explaining how the structure of Pirandello's play mirrored real life.
   (D) demonstrating how Pirandello challenged his audience's perception of reality.
   (E) showing how the characters in Pirandello's play interacted with one another.

Answer Explanation

The correct answer is (D). The passage describes the way that Pirandello set up characters to question reality and pretense within the play and used this device to challenge the audience similarly. Choice (A) is incorrect because the passage itself doesn't contrast the difference between reality and pretense in the play but describes how it was done. Choice (B) is incorrect because the passage doesn't discuss other plays of the same time period. Choice (C) is incorrect because the play doesn't mirror real life, but in fact questions the difference between real life and pretense. Choice (E) is incorrect because the passage doesn't describe how the characters in the play interacted.

Question

7. "Immutable" (line 6) most nearly means
   (A) variable.
   (B) enclosed.
   (C) unsure.
   (D) flexible.
   (E) enduring.

Answer Explanation

The correct answer is (E). "Immutable "means "enduring or permanent." Choice (A) is incorrect because "variable" means "changeable," which is the opposite of "enduring." Choice (B) is incorrect because "enclosed" means "surrounded on all sides" and doesn't make sense. Choice (C), "unsure," might seem correct, but the rest of the sentence indicates that a meaning that is somehow the opposite of "fabrications" is needed. Choice (D) is incorrect because "flexible" means "adaptable," and in the context of the passage, the characters have nothing to adapt to because they have no play.

Question

8. Select the sentence in the passage in which the author provides a succinct description of Pirandello's play.

    (A) Luigi Pirandello's 1921 play *Six Characters in Search of an Author* may be considered the first existentialist drama.

    (B) The characters invade a rehearsal of another play by Pirandello and insist on acting out their lives.

    (C) Somehow there is an immutable reality for these six characters, despite the fact that they are merely the fabrications of a writer.

    (D) The premise of the play is that six characters have taken on a life of their own because their author has failed to complete their story.

    (E) As the play's structure begins to break down, the characters begin to question how anyone can tell when reality ends and pretense begins.

Answer Explanation

The correct answer is (D). This sentence offers a short description of the play: six characters take on a life of their own when their author fails to complete their story. Choice (A) is incorrect because this sentence doesn't describe the plot of the play but categorizes it as the first existentialist drama. Choices (B), (C), and (E) are incorrect because these sentences only give details about the play, not a summary.

QUESTIONS 9 AND 10 ARE BASED ON THE FOLLOWING PASSAGE.

"Fifty Years After the Equal Pay Act" is a U.S. government report on the effects of the landmark legislation of the Kennedy Administration. The document details multiple improvements and successes, as women have now integrated most fields of endeavor formerly reserved for men; furthermore, they have risen to the highest levels of achievement in them, attaining

5   formerly unheard of positions such as CEO, Supreme Court Justice, and Secretary of State. Women have also moved in large and ever-increasing numbers into the ranks of the nation's entrepreneurs; moreover, they have dramatically increased their presence among the nation's upper echelons of earners.

   Nevertheless, the report also shows that high-profile success stories belie grimmer facts

10   about where women stand in the workplace and economically overall. As the report notes, while overtly discriminatory practices, such as "female worker wanted" ads, have ended, occasional occupational segregation and other barriers to equality persist. Most tellingly, the majority of women currently earns just 77 cents for every dollar earned by men (an 18-cent gain over 1963, made smaller by the fact that many men are now earning less) and

15   disproportionately fills the ranks of low-income jobs, including childcare workers, cashiers,

and maids. In fact, a current catchphrase among activists that captures the reality of both low-income jobs and the increasing number of households headed by single women is the "feminization of poverty."

Question

9. Which of the following statements is or are supported by the passage?
   (A) Occupational segregation has finally been eliminated.
   (B) The 18-cent gain in pay is not as great as the numbers suggest.
   (C) Increases in high-profile jobs demonstrate the end of income inequality.

Answer Explanation

The correct answer is (B). The passage states that while women have made an 18-cent gain in earnings on every dollar, this number is relative to what men make, and men's earnings have decreased over the same time period. Choice (A) is incorrect because the passage notes that, despite the disappearance of overtly discriminatory practices, some occupational segregation persists. Choice (C) is incorrect because, while the numbers of women with high-profile jobs has increased, the passage specifically states that this progress disguises "grimmer facts" about women's overall progress.

Question

10. The author mentions the "feminization of poverty" in order to
    (A) provide a possible explanation for other details in the passage.
    (B) provide support for the main findings of the report.
    (C) introduce an overarching counterpoint to all claims of progress.
    (D) weaken the main point of the government's report.
    (E) contrast this detail with earlier information in the paragraph.

Answer Explanation

The correct answer is (C). Mentioning the "feminization of poverty" provides an overarching, or dominating, counterpoint to the rosier ideas presented in paragraph 1 as well as an extension of the grimmer claims presented in paragraph 2. Choice (A) is incorrect because the "feminization of poverty" does not explain other ideas; instead, it introduces a more all-encompassing extension of them. Choices (B) and (D) are incorrect because the main findings of the report are mixed and cannot be supported or weakened by a single positive or negative detail or claim. Choice (E) is incorrect because the information in paragraph 2 leads smoothly up to the idea of "feminization of poverty."

QUESTIONS 11 AND 12 ARE BASED ON THE FOLLOWING PASSAGE.

Can the center of the Eurozone hold? Economic crises have undermined the Eurozone since 2007, and while their effects have been less publically visible lately than they were in 2012, when the economic alliance appeared ready to implode, their repercussions are not over. Rising distrust of the Eurozone felt by southern Eurozone countries, including Spain, Italy, Cyprus,

5 Greece, and France, appears to be due to the continuing recessionary trends these nations are experiencing, as well as increases in income disparity and persistent unemployment fostered by the crises. For these reasons, some experts forecast structural change in these governments as economic crisis brews democratic crisis. Meanwhile, a marked divergence in the wealth of northern Eurozone countries, especially Germany, creates an unsustainable binary division.

Question

11. The passage mentions each of the following EXCEPT the
    (A) problems of rising mistrust of the Eurozone.
    (B) recent changes in public perception of Eurozone issues.
    (C) near destruction of the Eurozone in 2012.
    (D) relationship between economics and democratic regimes.
    (E) unsuitability of austerity measures at this time.

Answer Explanation

The correct answer is (E). While the passage clearly points out the unsuitability of the status quo, it does not mention austerity measures. Choices (A), (B), (C), and (D) are mentioned in the passage, so they are not the correct answer to the question. For an EXCEPT or a NOT question, you're looking for the answer that doesn't match the passage.

Question

12. The author suggests that divergence in economic prosperity of Eurozone member nations'
    (A) fosters mistrust of prosperous nations.
    (B) undermines democracies in southern Eurozone nations.
    (C) results in the continuation of recessionary trends.
    (D) creates an opposition that cannot work in the future.
    (E) causes income disparity in southern Eurozone nations.

Answer Explanation

The correct answer is (D). The author asserts in the final sentence that the differences in wealth between Germany and other Eurozone member nations create an unsustainable binary opposition. Choices (A), (B), and (E) are incorrect because the author attributes mistrust and the undermining of democracy to causes such as unemployment and income disparity. Choice (C) is incorrect because the author suggests that these trends are the outgrowth of the economic crises.

QUESTIONS 13 AND 14 ARE BASED ON THE FOLLOWING PASSAGE.

By the end of World War II, European countries were eager to pursue an economic and political amalgamation in order both to increase prosperity in the region and to foster a sense of unity. The European Union, whose origins began in the 1950s, was officially established in 1993. The creation of the Eurozone in 1999 further solidified economic ties between certain
5 European countries. The Eurozone originally consisted of 11 countries, but now includes 17, both in Western and Eastern Europe. Every country that is in the Eurozone must use the euro as its sole legal currency. Monetary rules for the Eurozone are created and maintained by the European Central Bank. Currently, member states have to abide by the rules of the Stability and Growth Pact that was first adopted in 1997. They cannot exceed an annual
10 budget deficit of 3 percent of the gross domestic project or have an inflation rate over 2 percent. Plus all Eurozone countries must maintain a national debt lower than 60 percent of their gross domestic product.

Question

13. The author's primary purpose in the passage is to
    (A) present an overview of the Eurozone.
    (B) analyze the rules of the Stability and Growth Pact of the Eurozone.
    (C) suggest alternatives to some of the Stability and Growth Pact's rules.
    (D) emphasize the importance of the Eurozone.
    (E) show why other countries should join the Eurozone.

Answer Explanation

The correct answer is (A). The passage focuses on the formation of the Eurozone and some of its basic rules—an overview, in other words. Choices (B) and (C) are incorrect because the author doesn't attempt to analyze the rules of the Stability and Growth Pact, but only presents some of them, nor does the author suggest any alternatives. Choice (D) is incorrect because the importance of the Eurozone is never suggested. Choice (E) is incorrect because the author doesn't suggest or even imply that other countries should join the Eurozone.

Question

14. "Amalgamation" (line 2) most nearly means
    (A) combination.
    (B) severance.
    (C) melting.
    (D) variance.
    (E) anomaly.

Answer Explanation

The correct answer is (A). "Amalgamation" means "a combining or uniting." Choice (B) is incorrect because "severance" is a breaking apart, and the second part of the sentence indicates that the nations wanted to foster unity. Choice (C), "melting," means "blending, becoming less visible or distinguishable," which doesn't quite fit the sense of the passage. Choice (D), "variance," means "discord, disagreement, divergence" and is contrary to the facts of the passage. Choice (E), an "anomaly," is something that is different from the usual, and while integration of economic and political interests was an anomaly in Europe at the time, you need to answer the question based solely on the content of the passage, and there is nothing in the passage to indicate this. Therefore, choice (A) is the best choice.

Question

15. The job applicant was _____ in his interview by not telling the interviewer about his lack of credentials.
    - (A) invidious
    - (B) disingenuous
    - (C) artless
    - (D) clandestine
    - (E) devious
    - (F) indirect

Answer Explanation

The correct answers are (B) and (E). "Disingenuous" and "devious," choices (B) and (E), mean "not straightforward, lacking in candor" and fit the context. Choice (A), "invidious," means "unpleasant, offensive, difficult," and there is nothing in the sentence to indicate this. Choice (C), "artless," is the opposite of "disingenuous" and "devious." Choice (D), "clandestine," means "done in secret" and doesn't fit the sense. Choice (F), "indirect" means "roundabout, hinted at," and there is nothing in the sentence to indicate the applicant was hinting at the truth.

Question

16. Studies of the age-old _____ of nature versus nurture have resulted in some interesting results. Studies of identical and fraternal twins have indicated that a sense of humor is the result of nurture rather than nature.
    - (A) paradox
    - (B) provocation
    - (C) enigma
    - (D) challenge
    - (E) conundrum
    - (F) paradigm

Answer Explanation

The correct answers are (D) and (E). Choice (D), "challenge," means "a demanding or stimulating situation or question" and "conundrum," choice (E), is a "puzzling question or problem" and are the better pair of synonyms for the context. Choices (A) and (C), "paradox" and "enigma," are close synonyms, meaning "a seemingly contradictory statement that may be true" and "something seemingly inexplicable, baffling," respectively. Choice (B), "provocation," means "something that provokes or incites, stirring to action" and doesn't fit the context. Choice (F), "paradigm," means "typical example or a relationship of ideas to one another" and doesn't fit, nor does it or choice (B) have synonyms on the list.

Question

17. Mulling over the various plans for the reorganization of the sales department, the vice president and the HR director finally and _____ chose the plan that laid off the most salespeople but kept the benefits at the same level for those who were left.

    (A) timidly
    (B) diffidently
    (C) reticently
    (D) stingily
    (E) hesitantly
    (F) reluctantly

Answer Explanation

The correct answers are (C) and (F). "Reticently" means "reluctantly, unwillingly" and is a synonym for choice (F), "reluctantly." Choices (A) and (B), "timidly" and "diffidently," are synonyms meaning "lacking in self-confidence, shyly." "Timidly" can also mean "hesitantly," choice (E). The fact that there are three similar words should signal that none is correct. There is also nothing to indicate that the two acted timidly. In context, acting reluctantly makes better sense. Choice (D), "stingily," doesn't make sense in the context.

Question

18. The audience sat in rapt attention as the poet read his poetry with _____ in his deep, rich baritone voice.

    (A) confidence
    (B) grace
    (C) fluency
    (D) panache
    (E) ease
    (F) flair

Answer Explanation

The correct answers are (D) and (F). All the choices could fit the sense of the sentence, but there is only one pair of synonyms. Both choice (D), "panache," and choice (F), "flair," mean "distinctive and stylish elegance." Choice (A), "confidence," means "self-assurance." Choice (B), "grace," means "elegance of movement; pleasing, charming." Choice (C), "fluency," means "eloquence." Choice (E), "ease," means "comfortable."

QUESTIONS 19 AND 20 ARE BASED ON THE FOLLOWING PASSAGE.

Groundwater contamination arises when groundwater becomes polluted by various substances, including chemicals, medications, bacteria, viruses, fertilizer, and fuel. Groundwater contamination can also come from polluted runoff from farms or when factories dump manufacturing wastes in waterways. Once groundwater becomes contaminated, it can be
5 very difficult to remove the contaminants. Sometimes filtration systems can be used, but in other cases, the groundwater may be so polluted as to be rendered undrinkable. Since much of the world's supply of drinking water comes from groundwater, contamination is a serious issue. In communities in some places in the world that cannot afford other sources of water, people may have no other choice than to drink contaminated groundwater with its
10 consequent serious side effects.

Question

19. It can be inferred from the passage that the author would agree with which of the following statements?
    (A) Groundwater contamination should be an important consideration of municipal governments.
    (B) People should consider using alternate sources of water whenever possible.
    (C) Once groundwater contamination is detected, it must be addressed.

Answer Explanation

The correct answers are (A) and (C). The author of the passage makes it clear that groundwater contamination is a serious issue and so it would be important for municipal governments to take it seriously and to address the problem once detected. Choice (B) is incorrect because the author doesn't suggest that groundwater shouldn't be used, only that groundwater contamination should be taken care of, and even says that in some areas people have no alternative.

Question

20. Select the sentence in the passage that best establishes the author's position.

(A) Groundwater contamination can also come from polluted runoff from farms or when factories dump manufacturing wastes in waterways.

(B) Since much of the world's supply of drinking water comes from groundwater, contamination is a serious issue.

(C) Once groundwater becomes contaminated, it can be very difficult to remove the contaminants.

(D) Sometimes filtration systems can be used, but in other cases, the groundwater may be so polluted as to be rendered unpotable.

(E) In communities in some places in the world that cannot afford other sources of water, people may have no other choice than to drink contaminated groundwater with its consequent serious side effects.

Answer Explanation

The correct answer is (B). This statement succinctly establishes the author's position: groundwater contamination is a serious issue. Choices (A), (C), (D), and (E) explain details about groundwater contamination that support the author's position, but they don't state the author's position.

Section 3: Quantitative Reasoning

1. A	11. A	16. A
2. D	12. D	17. B, D
3. A	13. B	18. B
4. B	14. D	19. $1304.58
5. C	15. C	20. 28
6. C		
7. C		
8. B		
9. D		
10. E		

Question

1.

Quantity A	Quantity B
(12)(5)(9)(107)	(8)(104)(5)(12)

(A) Quantity A is greater.

(B) Quantity B is greater.

(C) The two quantities are equal.

(D) The relationship cannot be determined from the information given.

Answer Explanation

The correct answer is (A). Calculate:

$(12)(5)(9)(107) = 57,780$

$(8)(104)(5)(12) = 49,920$

Question

$$a \neq 0$$

a is the reciprocal of B.

2.

Quantity A	Quantity B
B	a

(A) Quantity A is greater.

(B) Quantity B is greater.

(C) The two quantities are equal.

(D) The relationship cannot be determined from the information given.

Answer Explanation

The correct answer is (D). Pick numbers:

If a is $\dfrac{1}{1}$, then B is 1.

If a is 2, then B is $\dfrac{1}{2}$.

If a is $-\dfrac{1}{2}$, then B is –2.

Question

3.

Quantity A	Quantity B
$\left(\sqrt[3]{86}\right)^2$	9

    (A) Quantity A is greater.

    (B) Quantity B is greater.

    (C) The two quantities are equal.

    (D) The relationship cannot be determined from the information given.

Answer Explanation

The correct answer is (A). Simplify and evaluate:

$$\left(\sqrt[3]{86}\right)^2 > \left(\sqrt[3]{64}\right)^2$$

$$\left(\sqrt[3]{64}\right)^2 = 4^2 = 16$$

$$\left(\sqrt[3]{86}\right)^2 > 9$$

Question

Amelia invests \$1,000 at a simple annual interest rate of 3%.

Margot invests \$1,200 at a simple annual interest rate of 2%.

4.

Quantity A	Quantity B
Amelia's investment after 16 years.	Margot's investment after 12 years.

    (A) Quantity A is greater.

    (B) Quantity B is greater.

    (C) The two quantities are equal.

    (D) The relationship cannot be determined from the information given.

Answer Explanation

The correct answer is (B). The value, V, of an investment earning simple annual interest of r percent for t years is given by the formula $V = P\left(1 + \dfrac{rt}{100}\right)$, where P is the principal amount invested. The value of Amelia's investment after 16 years will be:

$$V_A = P_A\left(1 + \frac{r_A t_A}{100}\right)$$
$$= \$1,000\left(1 + \frac{3 \times 16}{100}\right)$$
$$= \$1,000(1.48)$$
$$= \$1,480$$

The value of Margot's investment after 12 years will be:

$$V_M = P_M\left(1 + \frac{r_M t_M}{100}\right)$$
$$= \$1,200\left(1 + \frac{2 \times 12}{100}\right)$$
$$= \$1,200(1.24)$$
$$= \$1,488$$

Question

Mary is twice as old as Jay was 5 years ago. Jay is twice as old as Sue.
All together they are 15 years older than Mary is now.

5.

Quantity A	Quantity B
Mary	Jay

(A) Quantity A is greater.

(B) Quantity B is greater.

(C) The two quantities are equal.

(D) The relationship cannot be determined from the information given.

Answer Explanation

The correct answer is (C). Draw a table and turn words into an equation and solve:

		$x = 5$
Mary	$2(2x-5)$	10
Jay	$2x$	10
Sue	x	5
Total	$2(2x-5)+2x+x$	

$$2(2x-5)+2x+x = 2(2x-5)+15$$
$$2x+x = 15$$
$$3x = 15$$
$$x = 5$$

Question

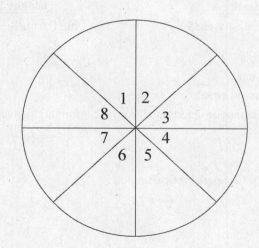

6. | Quantity A | Quantity B |

    $m\angle 1 + m\angle 2 + m\angle 3 + m\angle 4$ $m\angle 3 + m\angle 4 + m\angle 5 + m\angle 6$

    (A) Quantity A is greater.
    (B) Quantity B is greater.
    (C) The two quantities are equal.
    (D) The relationship cannot be determined from the information given.

Answer Explanation

The correct answer is (C). Calculate:
Supplementary angles sum to = 180
$m\angle 1 + m\angle 2 + m\angle 3 + m\angle 4 = 180$
$m\angle 3 + m\angle 4 + m\angle 5 + m\angle 6 = 180$

Question

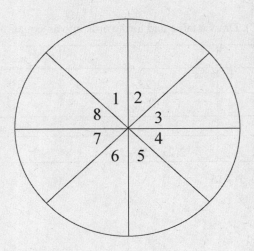

7.   Quantity A   Quantity B
        m∠3 + m∠4 + m∠5   m∠1 + m∠8 + m∠7

- (A) Quantity A is greater.
- (B) Quantity B is greater.
- (C) The two quantities are equal.
- (D) The relationship cannot be determined from the information given.

Answer Explanation

The correct answer is (C). Compare vertical angles:

m∠1 = m∠5
m∠3 = m∠7
m∠4 = m∠8

Question

8.   Quantity A   Quantity B
        The mean of x and y 60

- (A) Quantity A is greater.
- (B) Quantity B is greater.
- (C) The two quantities are equal.
- (D) The relationship cannot be determined from the information given.

Answer Explanation

The correct answer is (B). Calculate:

$$x + y = 90$$

$$\frac{x + y}{2} = 45$$

Question

9. What is the area of a circle with a diameter of 12?

 (A) 6π

 (B) 12π

 (C) 24π

 (D) 36π

 (E) 144π

Answer Explanation

The correct answer is (D). Evaluate:

$$d = 2r$$
$$12 = 2r$$
$$6 = r$$

$$area = \pi r^2$$
$$area = \pi 6^2$$
$$area = 36\pi$$

Question

10. A bag of cement weighs 94 pounds and a bag of lime weighs 50 pounds. How many pounds does a shipment of 18 bags of cement and 5 bags of lime weigh?

 (A) 250

 (B) 1,370

 (C) 1,442

 (D) 1,692

 (E) 1,942

Answer Explanation

The correct answer is (E). Turn the words into equations and solve:

$$total = 18(94) + 5(50)$$
$$total = 1,692 + 250$$
$$total = 1,942$$

Question

11. Given $4f + 4g = 14$ and $15h + 15i = 60$, what is the mean of f, g, h, and i?

- (A) $1\dfrac{7}{8}$
- (B) $2\dfrac{1}{4}$
- (C) $8\dfrac{3}{5}$
- (D) $12\dfrac{3}{4}$
- (E) $18\dfrac{1}{2}$

Answer Explanation

The correct answer is (A). Simplify and evaluate:

$$4f + 4g = 14$$
$$f + g = \frac{7}{2}$$
$$f + g = 3.5$$

$$15h + 15i = 60$$
$$h + i = 4$$

$$f + g + h + i = 4 + 3.5$$
$$f + g + h + i = 7.5$$

$$mean = \frac{f + g + h + i}{4} = \frac{7.5}{4} = 1.875 = 1\frac{7}{8}$$

Question

12. From a well-shuffled deck of cards, what is the probability of drawing a red 8?

- (A) $\dfrac{1}{4}$
- (B) $\dfrac{1}{13}$
- (C) $\dfrac{2}{13}$
- (D) $\dfrac{1}{26}$
- (E) $\dfrac{1}{52}$

Answer Explanation

The correct answer is (D). Evaluate:

2 ways to draw a red 8

52 total outcomes

$$\frac{2}{52} = \frac{1}{26}$$

Question

13. A right triangle has a base of 12 and a hypotenuse of 13. What is the height of the remaining leg?

    (A) 4
    (B) 5
    (C) 15
    (D) 20
    (E) 25

Answer Explanation

The correct answer is (B). Draw a figure:

$$x^2 + 12^2 = 13^2$$
$$x^2 + 144 = 169$$
$$x^2 = 25$$
$$x = 5$$

Question

14. To manufacture soft pretzels, there is a built-in cost of $320 to start the machines and an additional cost for materials of $0.05 per pretzel. If the pretzels sell for 4 for $1.00, how many have to be sold to break even for the day?

    (A) 100
    (B) 160
    (C) 320
    (D) 1,600
    (E) 3,200

Answer Explanation

The correct answer is (D). Turn the words into equations and solve:

$0.25p = 320 + 0.05p$

$0.20p = 320$

$p = 1,600$

QUESTIONS 15–17 REFER TO THE TABLE BELOW.

Tahoe and Suburban Sales
1999–2013

	Tahoe	Suburban
1999	72,000	70,000
2000	127,000	92,000
2001	127,000	101,000
2002	131,000	110,000
2003	126,000	137,000
2004	150,000	132,000
2005	201,000	152,000
2006	209,000	150,000
2007	197,000	132,000
2008	188,000	118,000
2009	151,000	88,000
2010	160,000	76,000
2011	148,000	83,000
2012	90,000	52,000
2013	71,000	42,000

Question

15. What is the range of vehicles sold between 1999 and 2013?

    (A) 42,000

    (B) 194,000

    (C) 167,000

    (D) 280,000

    (E) 290,000

Answer Explanation

The correct answer is (C). Range is the difference from highest to lowest:

$209,000 - 42,000 = 167,000$

Question

16. If the average price of a Tahoe in 2010 was \$35,600 and the average price of a Suburban in 2010 was \$57,700, what was the total sales number (in dollars) for both vehicles that year?

(A) 1.00812×10^{10}

(B) 1.65712×10^{10}

(C) 2.65712×10^{10}

(D) 2.98112×10^{10}

(E) 3.12912×10^{10}

Answer Explanation

The correct answer is (A). Turn the words into equations and solve:

$$total = 160,000(35,600) + 76,000(57,700)$$
$$total = 5,696,000,000 + 4,385,200,000$$
$$total = 1.00812 \times 10^{10}$$

Question

17. What are the mode and the median of the number of Tahoes sold between 1999 and 2013?

(A) 71,000

(B) 127,000

(C) 131,000

(D) 148,000

(E) 151,000

(F) 180,000

Answer Explanation

The correct answers are (B) and (D). Create a table to help you visualize the information:

71
72
90
126
127
127
131
148
150
151
160
188
197
201
209

Mode is the most repeated number: 127,000.

Median is the middle value: 148,000.

Question

18. Fernanda has 8 books in her reading list, from which she will choose 3 to take with her on vacation. How many different groups of 3 books from these 8 can she make?

    (A) 24
    (B) 56
    (C) 120
    (D) 336
    (E) 6,720

Answer Explanation

The correct answer is (B). The number of combinations of n objects in subsets of k is given by the formula $\dfrac{n!}{k!(n-k)!}$. Therefore, the number of groups of 3 books that Fernanda can make from the 8 in her reading list is:

$$\frac{8!}{3!(8-3)!} = \frac{8 \times 7 \times 6 \times 5!}{3! \times 5!}$$

$$= \frac{8 \times 7 \times 6}{3!}$$

$$= 8 \times 7$$

$$= 56$$

Question

19. Jack Rosato pays a flat rate business tax in his township of 0.438% on all invoices. He had invoices totaling $297,849.00 last year. What was his township tax bill? (Round your answer to two decimal places.)

$

Answer Explanation

The correct answer is $1304.58. Turn the words into equations and solve:

$0.00438(\$297,849) = \$1304.58$

Question

20. The frequency table shown represents the ages of all the goalkeepers in a soccer league. What is the median age of the league's goalkeepers?

Goalkeeper's Age	Frequency
23	1
25	3
26	2
27	3
29	1
31	3
32	2
34	2
37	1

Answer Explanation

The correct answer is (28). The total number of goalkeepers in the league is represented by the sum of the numbers in the Frequency column. There are 18 goalkeepers, so their median age is the average (arithmetic mean) of the two middle ages (the ninth and the tenth), when the ages are arranged in ascending or descending order. Nine goalkeepers (one 23-year-old, three 25-year-olds, two 26-year-olds, and three 27-year-olds) are 27 years old or younger, and the remaining nine are 29 years old or older. Thus, the ninth and tenth ages are 27 and 29, and the median age is their average, which equals 28.

Section 4: Quantitative Reasoning

1. D	11. B	16. B, D, F
2. C	12. D	17. A, E
3. A	13. A	18. 4
4. B	14. E	19. $\frac{35}{12}$
5. C	15. B	20. D
6. D		
7. B		
8. A		
9. B		
10. B		

Question

$$x > 0$$
$$y > 0$$

1. | Quantity A | Quantity B |
    |---|---|
    | x | y |

(A) Quantity A is greater.

(B) Quantity B is greater.

(C) The two quantities are equal.

(D) The relationship cannot be determined from the information given.

Answer Explanation

The correct answer is (D). Pick numbers:

x	y
1	2
2	1

Question

2.

Quantity A	Quantity B
$\frac{1}{3}$ of 12	$\frac{1}{4}$ of 16

(A) Quantity A is greater.

(B) Quantity B is greater.

(C) The two quantities are equal.

(D) The relationship cannot be determined from the information given.

Answer Explanation

The correct answer is (C). Evaluate:

$$\frac{1}{3}(12) = 4$$

$$\frac{1}{4}(16) = 4$$

Question

3.

Quantity A	Quantity B
$\frac{1}{5} + \frac{1}{5}$	0.04

(A) Quantity A is greater.

(B) Quantity B is greater.

(C) The two quantities are equal.

(D) The relationship cannot be determined from the information given.

Answer Explanation

The correct answer is (A). Calculate:

$$\frac{1}{5} + \frac{1}{5} = \frac{2}{5} = 0.4$$

Question

$$x^7 = -128$$

	Quantity A	Quantity B
4.	x^5	$8x^2$

(A) Quantity A is greater.

(B) Quantity B is greater.

(C) The two quantities are equal.

(D) The relationship cannot be determined from the information given.

Answer Explanation

The correct answer is (B). Evaluate:

$x^7 = -128$

$x = -2$

$8x^2 = 8(-2)^2 = 8(4) = 32$

$x^5 = -2^5 = -32$

Question

$$\frac{5}{16}m = \frac{1}{8}$$

	Quantity A	Quantity B
5.	m	$\dfrac{2}{5}$

(A) Quantity A is greater.

(B) Quantity B is greater.

(C) The two quantities are equal.

(D) The relationship cannot be determined from the information given.

Answer Explanation

The correct answer is (C). Evaluate:

$\dfrac{5}{16}m = \dfrac{1}{8}$

$m = \dfrac{1}{8}\left(\dfrac{16}{5}\right) = \dfrac{2}{5}$

Question

Triangle *ABC* lies on the *xy*-plane with *A* at (0,0), *B* at (4,0), and *C* at (*x,y*).

$$x, y > 0$$
$$area = 24$$

6. Quantity A   Quantity B
        x   **6**

(A) Quantity A is greater.

(B) Quantity B is greater.

(C) The two quantities are equal.

(D) The relationship cannot be determined from the information given.

Answer Explanation

The correct answer is (D). Draw a figure:

$$area = \frac{1}{2}bh$$
$$24 = \frac{1}{2}4h$$
$$12 = h$$

Therefore, *y* = 12. However, that still does not tell us what *x* equals. *x* could be any positive number, since we don't know anything else about this triangle.

Question

7.   <u>Quantity A</u>   <u>Quantity B</u>
                    x 72

(A) Quantity A is greater.

(B) Quantity B is greater.

(C) The two quantities are equal.

(D) The relationship cannot be determined from the information given.

Answer Explanation

The correct answer is (B). Evaluate:

$$36^2 + 48^2 = x^2$$
$$3,600 = x^2$$
$$60 = x$$

Question

$$x + y = 16$$

8.   <u>Quantity A</u>   <u>Quantity B</u>
        Maximum value of xy 63

(A) Quantity A is greater.

(B) Quantity B is greater.

(C) The two quantities are equal.

(D) The relationship cannot be determined from the information given.

Answer Explanation

The correct answer is (A). Evaluate:

x	y	xy
1	15	15
2	14	28
3	13	39
4	12	48
5	11	55
6	10	60
7	9	63
8	8	64

Question

$$8x = 3.2$$
$$y = 4x - 1$$

9.   Quantity A   Quantity B
                 x y

(A) Quantity A is greater.

(B) Quantity B is greater.

(C) The two quantities are equal.

(D) The relationship cannot be determined from the information given.

Answer Explanation

The correct answer is (B). Evaluate:

$x = \dfrac{3.2}{8} = 0.4$

$y = 4x - 1$

$y = 4(0.4) - 1$

$y = 1.6 - 1 = 0.6$

Question

10. How many miles is it from Kalamazoo to Timbuktu?
    (A) 68
    (B) 65
    (C) 66
    (D) 63
    (E) 64

Answer Explanation

The correct answer is (B). Calculate:

$$25^2 + 60^2 = c^2$$
$$625 + 3,600 = c^2$$
$$4,225 = c^2$$
$$c = 65$$

Question

11. The local football booster club sells food at all home games. To make the accounting equal, they sell all products for the same price of $1.00. If over the course of the season they sold 4 times as many hot dogs as candy bars, and half as many drinks as hot dogs, and they sold a total of $1400 worth of food, how many drinks did they sell?
    (A) 200
    (B) 400
    (C) 600
    (D) 800
    (E) 1400

Answer Explanation

The correct answer is (B). Turn the words into equations and solve:

$$x + 4x + 2x = 1,400$$
$$7x = 1,400$$
$$x = 200$$
$$2x = 400$$

Question

12. Solve for x: $x^{\frac{3}{2}} = 125$

   (A) -25
   (B) -5
   (C) 5
   (D) 25
   (E) 125

Answer Explanation

The correct answer is (D).

$$x^{\frac{3}{2}} = 125$$
$$\left(\sqrt{x}\right)^3 = 125$$
$$x = 25$$

QUESTIONS 13–15 REFER TO THE GRAPH BELOW.

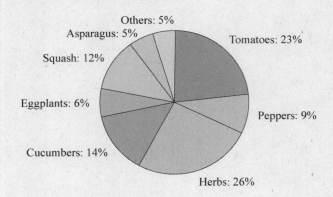

Vegetable Plant Sales in May

Question

13. If in May the sales of tomato plants were $13,482, what were the sales of all the vegetable plants?

(A) $58,617.39
(B) $59,871.09
(C) $60,740.87
(D) $62,137.83
(E) $63,820.31

Answer Explanation

The correct answer is (A). Turn the words into equations and solve:

$$\frac{23}{100} = \frac{13,482}{x}$$

$$23x = 13,482(100)$$

$$23x = 1,348,200$$

$$x = 58,617.39$$

Question

14. Total vegetation sales in May were $124,717.85. What were the total sales of cucumbers and herbs combined?

(A) $34,675.93
(B) $37,897.02
(C) $40,320.04
(D) $42,739.84
(E) $49,887.14

Answer Explanation

The correct answer is (E). Turn the words into equations and solve:

$$\frac{14+26}{100}=\frac{x}{124,717.85}$$
$$40(124,717.85)=100x$$
$$4,988,714=100x$$
$$49,887.14=x$$

Question

15. What is the ratio of squash sales to eggplant sales?

(A) $\frac{2}{9}$

(B) $\frac{2}{1}$

(C) $\frac{5}{4}$

(D) $\frac{4}{7}$

(E) $\frac{6}{11}$

Answer Explanation

The correct answer is (B). Evaluate:

$$\frac{12\%}{6\%}=\frac{2}{1}$$

Question

16. Find the next three numbers in the sequence: 1, –4, 16, –64, …
(A) –4,096
(B) –1,024
(C) –256
(D) 256
(E) 1,024
(F) 4,096

Answer Explanation

The correct answers are (B), (D), and (F). Evaluate:

The sequence is formed by multiplying the previous term by (−4)

$1(-4) = -4$

$-4(-4) = 16$

$16(-4) = -64$

$-64(-4) = 256$

$256(-4) = -1,024$

$-1,024(-4) = 4,096$

Question

17. For which of the following defined operations does $a \triangle b$ always equal $b \triangle a$, where a and b are integers?

    (A) $a \triangle b = |b - a|$

    (B) $a \triangle b = a^2 - b^2$

    (C) $a \triangle b = (a - b)^3$

    (D) $a \triangle b = a^b$

    (E) $a \triangle b = \left(\dfrac{1}{a} + \dfrac{1}{b} \right)^3$

Answer Explanation

The correct answers are (A, E). If $a \triangle b$ always equals $b \triangle a$, then the operation is commutative. Addition and multiplication are examples of commutative operations, whereas subtraction and division are not. Choice (A) features the difference of two numbers, but the absolute value actually renders this operation commutative. (Pick numbers if you need to be certain. For instance, $|3 - 2| = |2 - 3|$. This result holds true no matter what numbers you pick.) Choice (B) features subtraction only—the squares don't matter, since you have the difference between two integers—so the operation is not commutative. (Again, if you're not sure, an example will confirm: $9 - 4 \neq 4 - 9$.) Choice (C) is not commutative: If a is greater than b, then the cube of $a - b$ is positive, while the cube of $b - a$ is negative. Choice (D) is not commutative—for instance, $2^3 \neq 3^2$. Finally, choice (E) is commutative. Simplify the expression to confirm:

$$a_\triangle b = \left(\frac{1}{a} + \frac{1}{b}\right)^3$$

$$= \left(\frac{b+a}{ab}\right)^3$$

$$= \frac{(a+b)^3}{(ab)^3}$$

Because both addition and subtraction are commutative (that is, $a + b = b + a$ and $ab = ba$), this operation is commutative.

Question

18. Jeff is 3 times as old as Billy, who is 2 times as old as Joe. In 7 years, their combined age will be 3 times Jeff's age now, plus 3. How old is Billy now?

Answer Explanation

The correct answer is 4. Turn the words into equations and solve:

	now	+7
Jeff	3(2x)	6x + 7
Billy	2x	2x + 7
Joe	x	x + 7
combined		x + 7 + 2x + 7 + 6x + 7

$$x + 7 + 2x + 7 + 6x + 7 = 3(6x) + 3$$
$$9x + 21 = 18x + 3$$
$$18 = 9x$$
$$2 = x$$
$$2(2) = 4$$

Question

19. $\left(\frac{1}{3} - 2\right)\left(\frac{1}{4} - 2\right) =$

Give answer as a fraction.

Answer Explanation

The correct answer is $\dfrac{35}{12}$. Evaluate:

$$\left(\frac{1}{3}-2\right)\left(\frac{1}{4}-2\right)$$

$$\left(\frac{1}{3}-\frac{6}{3}\right)\left(\frac{1}{4}-\frac{8}{4}\right)$$

$$\left(-\frac{5}{3}\right)\left(-\frac{7}{4}\right)$$

$$\frac{35}{12}$$

Question

20. Points (3,–2) and (–7,4) define a line segment in the coordinate plane. What are the coordinates of the line segment's midpoint?

(A) (5,–3)

(B) (2,1)

(C) (2,–1)

(D) (–2,1)

(E) (–2,–1)

Answer Explanation

The correct answer is (D). The x- and y-coordinates of the midpoint are the averages of the x- and y-coordinates of the end points. Thus, the midpoint's x-coordinate is $\dfrac{3+(-7)}{2}$, which equals –2, and the midpoint's y-coordinate is $\dfrac{-2+4}{2}$, which equals 1.

Section 5: Verbal Reasoning

1. A	11. E	16. D, F
2. E	12. B	17. D, E
3. A, F	13. A	18. C, F
4. A, F, I	14. A	19. B, E
5. B, D, G	15. D	20. C
6. B		
7. E		
8. B, C		
9. B		
10. E		

Question

1. Research on school improvement has found that instruction must convey information _____ to be effective. Lessons that don't proceed logically from A to B to C, confuse, rather than inform.

(A) coherently
(B) smoothly
(C) articulately
(D) cogently
(E) eloquently

Answer Explanation

The correct answer is (A). The context indicates that instruction must be logical, and only choice (A), "coherently," includes the idea of logic; the word means "orderly and logically consistent." Choice (B), "smoothly," means "having no problems or difficulties." Choice (C), "articulately," means "using clear language," which undoubtedly helps instruction, but doesn't fit the context. Choice (D), "cogently," means "appealing to reason, convincing." Choice (E), "eloquently," means "expressing something vividly or movingly."

Question

2. Mechanical weathering, which breaks down rock, includes a number of processes. One is caused by the _____ quality of rock particles. The particles rushing by in water or carried by the wind break down the rocks with which they come in contact.

(A) coarse	
(B) rough	
(C) rasping	
(D) grating	
(E) abrasive	

Answer Explanation

The correct answer is (E). "Abrasive," choice (E), means "wearing something down." Choice (A), "coarse," meaning "rough," and choice (B), "rough," can be eliminated because all rocks are not rough; some are smooth. Choice (C), "rasping," means "filing or scraping with a file" and can also mean "making a grating sound," so it's a synonym for choice (D), "grating," an annoying sound." Neither fits the context.

Question

3. Critics may consider his style (i)_____ of the worst in advertising art, but he charges (ii) _____ prices for his representational paintings and makes a fortune.

Blank (i)	Blank (ii)
(A) derivative	(D) munificent
(B) a by-product	(E) magnanimous
(C) a complement	(F) exorbitant

Answer Explanation

The correct answers are (A) and (F). Answer Blank (i): "Derivative," choice (A), means "based on something else." Choice (B), "a by-product," is something produced in the making of something else and doesn't fit the sense. Choice (C), a "complement," means "something that completes, making a whole" and doesn't make sense (nor would "compliment").

Answer Blank (ii): "Exorbitant," choice (F), means "excessive, overpriced" and matches the context. Choice (D), "munificent," means "generous, philanthropic, benevolent" and makes no sense in the context. Nor does choice (E), "magnanimous," meaning "generous and understanding, noble."

Question

4. The (i) _____ view of many Americans for years was that the 1950s were a time of peace and prosperity. However, this (ii)_____ version of the time period is (iii)_____ by the racial unrest that erupted in the latter part of the decade.

Blank (i)	Blank (ii)	Blank (iii)
(A) prevailing	(D) implied	(G) concealed
(B) hypothetical	(E) epic	(H) misrepresented
(C) academic	(F) fictional	(I) belied

Answer Explanation

The correct answers are (A), (F), and (I). Answer Blank (i): Choice (A), "prevailing," means "current," and for years that was the current view. Choice (B), "hypothetical," means "possible, theoretical," but based on the passage, the view was accepted as true, so it wasn't hypothetical or theoretical. "Academic," choice (C), also means "theoretical" as well as "speculative" and is incorrect for the same reason.

Answer Blank (ii): Choice (F), "fictional," means "creation of the imagination, invented reality" and fits the context. Choice (D), "implied," is incorrect because the passage doesn't indicate that the view was only hinted at or suggested. Choice (E), "epic," is incorrect because it means "very large or heroic" and doesn't fit the context.

Answer Blank (iii): Choice (I), "belied," means "shown to be false" and matches the sense. Choice (G), "concealed," means "hidden" and would make the sentence read that the racial unrest hid the fictional version of the period. Choice (H), "misrepresented," meaning "falsely represented" is incorrect because it, too, would reverse the meaning of the sentence.

Question

5. His grades in school never seemed (i) _____ with his intelligence, and this (ii) _____ assessment was borne out in his later work life. Known for his (iii) _____ ability to penetrate to the core issues, he rose to become CEO of a Fortune 1000 company.

Blank (i)	Blank (ii)	Blank (iii)
(A) congenial	(D) astute	(G) laser-like
(B) commensurate	(E) practiced	(H) discerning
(C) complaisant	(F) adroit	(I) caustic

Answer Explanation

The correct answers are (B), (D), and (G). Answer Blank (i): Choice (B), "commensurate," means "in proportion to." Choice (A), "congenial," means "agreeable, or similar, compatible" and is used in reference to people, so it doesn't make sense. Choice (C), "complaisant," means "obliging, willing to please" and doesn't make sense either.

Answer Blank (ii): Choice (D), "astute," means "perceptive" and fits the context. Choice (E), "practiced," means "expert because of long experience" and doesn't make sense in the context. Choice (F), "adroit," means "quick or skillful in action or thought," but doesn't quite fit the sense, which requires perception, rather than quickness.

Answer Blank (iii): Choice (H), "discerning," might seem like the correct answer because it means "showing good judgment," but choice (G), "laser-like," meaning "highly focused," better fits with "penetrate." Choice (I), "caustic," means "harsh in tone," and nothing suggests this about the person.

QUESTIONS 6–8 ARE BASED ON THE FOLLOWING PASSAGE.

American artist Mary Cassatt (1845–1926) is noteworthy for being one of the few women artists to succeed professionally during the late nineteenth century. Because of her friendship with Edgar Degas, she was the only American to take part in the 1879 exhibition of French Impressionist artists in Paris. Though Cassatt's style was influenced by the Impressionists,
5　she developed her own unique style and subject matter. It is easy to see the influence of Degas in her paintings, but her interest in Japanese prints is also reflected in many of her paintings. Much of her earliest work portrays women engaging in home activities, such as reading, sewing, or writing letters. After the French exhibition, Cassatt began to explore what she eventually became famous for: paintings of women caring for children. It is through these
10　paintings that Cassatt highlights the often overlooked role in painting of women as mothers.

Question

6. Select the sentence in the passage in which the author notes influences on Cassatt's style.
   (A) After the French exhibition, Cassatt began to explore what she eventually became famous for: paintings of women caring for children.
   (B) It is easy to see the influence of Degas in her paintings, but her interest in Japanese prints is also reflected in many of her paintings.
   (C) Much of her earliest work portrays women engaging in home activities, such as reading, sewing, or writing letters.
   (D) It is through these paintings that Cassatt highlights the often overlooked role in painting of women as mothers.
   (E) Because of her friendship with Edgar Degas, she was the only American to take part in an 1879 exhibition of French Impressionist artists in Paris.

Answer Explanation

The correct answer is (B). Cassatt's stylistic inspirations were both Degas's paintings and Japanese prints as this statement clearly points out. Choices (A) and (C) are incorrect because these statements explain the themes of Cassatt's later and early paintings but not influences on her style. Choice (D) is incorrect because this statement describes what Cassatt highlighted in her work but not her influencers. Choice (E) is incorrect because this statement describes Cassatt's participation in the Impressionist exhibition, but it doesn't explain influences on her.

Question

7. The author's primary purpose in the passage is to

   (A) explain why Mary Cassatt began painting women and children.

   (B) argue that Mary Cassatt was a huge influence on later female painters.

   (C) suggest reasons that Mary Cassatt's art began to change after the Impressionist exhibition.

   (D) analyze the ways that Mary Cassatt was influenced by the Impressionists.

   (E) describe the development of Mary Cassatt's artistic style and themes.

Answer Explanation

The correct answer is (E). The passage describes how Mary Cassatt was influenced by Impressionists and Japanese prints but developed her own style and subject matter; in other words, it provides a brief overview. Choice (A) is incorrect because though this information is touched on, the passage doesn't go into any detail about it, so it can't be the primary purpose of the piece. Choice (B) is incorrect because though this might be true, the author neither argues nor mentions this point. Choice (C) is incorrect because although the passage describes how Cassatt's art changed, it doesn't give reasons for the changes. Choice (D) is incorrect because the author never addresses how exactly Cassatt was influenced by the Impressionists.

Question

8. Which of the following statements is supported by the passage?

   (A) Mary Cassatt began to paint women and children as a way to express her frustration with contemporary male artists.

   (B) Mary Cassatt was inspired by several artistic styles from different parts of the world.

   (C) Mary Cassatt expressed a unique perspective through her art.

Answer Explanation

The correct answers are (B) and (C). The passage points out that Cassatt was influenced by the French Impressionists and by Japanese prints. The passage also explores how Cassatt's own style and subject matter were unique. Choice (A) is incorrect because there is nothing in the passage to suggest this.

QUESTIONS 9 AND 10 ARE BASED ON THE FOLLOWING PASSAGE.

Modest Mussorgsky was one of a group of Russian composers known as "The Five" or "The Mighty Handful," whose goal in the late 1800s was to create Russian nationalist music. Mussorgsky's most famous work, the opera *Boris Godunov,* completed in 1873, is the story of the powerful, though flawed Russian tsar who ruled in the early seventeenth century. The
5 opera met with negative criticism from some of Mussorgsky's contemporaries. Another member of "The Five," Nicolai Rimsky-Korsakov, said of *Boris Godunov* that "I adore it for its originality, power, boldness, distinctiveness, and beauty; I abhor it for its lack of polish, the roughness of its harmonies, and, in some places, the sheer awkwardness of the music." Because of this, Rimsky-Korsakov revised the opera after Mussorgsky's death at age forty-
10 one in 1881, correcting what he believed were technical weaknesses in the original score. Rimsky-Korsakov's revised version of *Boris Gudonov* became the preferred edition of the

opera. In recent years, however, Mussorgsky's unique style and orchestration have come to be appreciated, even celebrated, and his is the version that opera-goers are more likely to see performed.

Question

9. "Nationalist" (line 2) most nearly means
    (A) loyalty to one's country.
    (B) dedicated to the interests or culture of a nation.
    (C) love of one's country.
    (D) isolationist.
    (E) separatist.

Answer Explanation

The correct answer is (B). Choice (B), "dedicated to the interests or culture of a nation," is the definition of "nationalist." "Loyalty to one's country," choice (A), may prompt nationalism, but it's not the same. Choice (C), "love of one's country," is the definition of "patriotism." Choice (D), "isolationist," is "one who supports a nation's policy of having no political or economic contacts with other nations." Choice (E), "separatist," is "one who advocates breaking ties with a larger political entity."

Question

10. The author suggests that Mussorgsky's work
    (A) lacked polish and technique.
    (B) was well-respected by his contemporaries.
    (C) covered complex themes that were far ahead of their time.
    (D) was too technically challenging to perform in the original.
    (E) was not fully appreciated in his own lifetime.

Answer Explanation

The correct answer is (E). The author points out that it is only recently that audiences have been able to hear Mussorgsky's opera as he wrote it and not in its revised version. Choice (A) is incorrect because the author implies that Mussorgsky's contemporaries may have felt this, but this was in fact not true. Choice (B) is incorrect because the author points out that Mussorgsky's contemporaries had negative criticisms and even revised his work. Choice (C) is incorrect because although this might be true, the passage doesn't mention this issue. Choice (D) is incorrect because this is never implied; the author states simply that Rimsky-Korsakov felt that Mussorgsky's work needed revision.

QUESTIONS 11–13 ARE BASED ON THE FOLLOWING PASSAGE.

Despite advances in medicine and technology, the demand for organ transplants remains much greater than the number of organ donors available. Ironically, this is mainly because of the increasing success rate of organ transplant operations over the years. Early transplant operations often failed because patients' immune systems rejected the foreign organ. However,
5 the introduction of the drug cyclosporine in the 1980s helped solve this problem, and organ transplants subsequently became much more routine, which, in turn, resulted in the need for more organ donations.

Researchers looking for a way to solve this problem have begun to work on developing artificial organs, **though this is still in a highly experimental phase**. So far, laboratories
10 around the world have developed artificial hearts, lungs, livers, and other organs, but with only limited success. Other scientists are working on techniques to grow organs from a patient's own cells, **which could ultimately eliminate the need for organ donors.** Yet because this involves cloning and stem cell research, it also raises ethical questions that make this a much more complicated issue than developing artificial organs.

Question

11. What function do the two groups of words in bold type serve in this passage?

    (A) The first presents an argument; the second reinforces the argument.

    (B) The first presents an opinion; the second presents final support for the opinion.

    (C) The first serves as an intermediate conclusion; the second serves as a definitive conclusion.

    (D) The first anticipates the argument's conclusion; the second supports the conclusion.

    (E) The first qualifies a fact; the second states a conclusion.

Answer Explanation

The correct answer is (E). The first part sets up the fact that artificial organs are still in the experimental phase, and the second part concludes that organs grown from a patient's own cells could eliminate the need for donors altogether. Choice (A) is incorrect because no argument is presented in the passage. Choice (B) is incorrect because the two statements are not opinions; they can be proven. Choice (C) is incorrect because the first statement is not a conclusion. Choice (D) is incorrect because the passage doesn't set up an argument.

Question

12. It can be inferred from the passage that the author would agree with which of the following statements?

    (A) The discovery of the drug cyclosporine made it much harder for people who needed organs to get them.

    (B) Scientists should continue to experiment trying to develop organs in order to solve the problem of the organ donor shortage.

    (C) The technique of growing organs from patients' own cells is so potentially divisive that it should be discontinued.

Answer Explanation

The correct answer is (B). The point of the passage is to explain that because there is an organ donor shortage, scientists should explore other options for organ transplants. Choice (A) is incorrect because the author points out that the drug cyclosporine made organ transplants easier, not that it made it harder for people to get organs. Choice (C) is incorrect because although the author brings up the ethical questions involved, at no point does the author imply that these experiments should be discontinued because of the issues.

Question

13. If the information in this passage is true, which of the following must also be true?
    (A) Some people who need organ transplants today will not receive them in time.
    (B) Artificial organs will never be a viable option for people needing organ transplants.
    (C) Because of use of the drug cyclosporine, the human body no longer rejects foreign organs.
    (D) Creating organs from patients' own cells will become much easier over time.
    (E) In the future, people will no longer need organ transplants from donor organs.

Answer Explanation

The correct answer is (A). If there is a shortage of organ donations, then it's likely that some people who need organ transplants will not get them. Choice (B) is incorrect because the passage actually implies that artificial organs could be a real option in the future. Choice (C) is incorrect because we can imply that cyclosporine might not work in every case. Choices (D) and (E) are incorrect because although these statements could be true, it is not definite that they must be true.

QUESTIONS 14 AND 15 ARE BASED ON THE FOLLOWING PASSAGE.

In January 2014, the CIA World Factbook listed Nicaragua as Central America's poorest economy and as the Western Hemisphere's second poorest economy. Employment figures alone suggest the nation's economic story: services account for 53% of jobs and agriculture for 28%; the Factbook lists no professional categories of employment. Indeed, the country
5   is primarily known for agricultural products that include coffee, shrimp, tobacco, and sugar, all of which are important exports, along with textiles, which generate most of the remaining jobs in industry. Despite the fact that Nicaragua's economy has recently been growing at a 4% annual rate, debt burdens significantly impair progress. Additionally, the Heritage Foundation notes that Nicaragua's grim economic picture is exacerbated by political factors,
10   including weak rule of law, which discourages both domestic and foreign investment, and anti-free market policies. These include costly regulatory procedures, which have historically led investors down a path of bribery or other corruption, and the prohibitively high cost of long-term financing, which discourages entrepreneurial initiative.

Question

14. "Exacerbated" (line 9) most nearly means
    (A) complicated.
    (B) instigated.
    (C) fermented.
    (D) implicated.
    (E) ameliorated.

Answer Explanation

The correct answer is (A). "Exacerbated" most nearly means "intensified," in the sense of worsened, complicated, or aggravated. Choice (B) is incorrect because "instigated" means "provoked," as does "fermented," choice (C). Choice (D) is incorrect because "implicated" means "suggested an incriminating relationship," which could work in this context, if its connotations did not include ideas of wrongdoing. Choice (E) is incorrect because "ameliorated" means "weakened or lessened," which is the opposite of the meaning expressed by the sentence.

Question

15. The passage provides information on each of the following EXCEPT:
    (A) the distribution of employment type in Nicaragua.
    (B) the checks on investment in new enterprise in Nicaragua.
    (C) Nicaragua's ranking among neighboring economies.
    (D) Nicaragua's ranking among world economies.
    (E) the negative effects of the weak rule of law in Nicaragua.

Answer Explanation

The correct answer is (D). Even though the passage ranks Nicaragua among countries in the Western Hemisphere, there is no mention of its world ranking, so choice (D) is the correct answer. Choices (A), (B), (C), and (E) state information that appears in the passage, so they are incorrect answers to this question.

Question

16. Government economists released a report showing how the _____ housing market was depressing prices across a number of areas in the construction industry.
    (A) obsolescent
    (B) outmoded
    (C) superseded
    (D) moribund
    (E) motionless
    (F) stagnant

Answer Explanation

The correct answers are (D) and (F). "Moribund" means "near death," but it also means "stagnant," choice (F). Choice (A), "obsolescent," means "becoming out of date, obsolete," and is a synonym of "outmoded," choice (B), meaning "unfashionable, no longer useful." The two don't fit the sense of the sentence. Choice (C), "superseded," means "supplanted, set aside" and doesn't fit the sense, nor does choice (E), "motionless," meaning "inactive, not in motion."

Question

17. Many doctors are still _____ digitizing their patients' records. They see the process as expensive and time-consuming and are not convinced of its value.
    - (A) wary of
    - (B) scrupulous about
    - (C) meticulous about
    - (D) skeptical about
    - (E) dubious about
    - (F) critical about

Answer Explanation

The correct answers are (D) and (E). Choices (D) and (E), "skeptical about" and "dubious about," both mean "doubtful." Choice (A), "wary of," meaning "cautious," could fit the sense of the sentence, but there is no synonym for it among the answer choices. Choices (B) and (C), "scrupulous about" and "meticulous about," are near synonyms, but they mean "conscientious, using great care" and "very careful and precise," respectively. While doctors would undoubtedly be careful about entering patient information, that's not the context for the answers. Choice (F), "critical about," means both "being negative about" and "making a careful evaluation" and, whereas the latter definition might work, there is no synonym for the word.

Question

18. Delivered in a defiant tone, the leader's _____ denial of any wrongdoing in his cabinet failed to quell calls for an investigation into the allegations of malfeasance in office.
    - (A) qualified
    - (B) eligible
    - (C) blunt
    - (D) intransigent
    - (E) intractable
    - (F) stark

Answer Explanation

The correct answers are (C) and (F). "Blunt" and "stark," choices (C) and (F), mean "lacking in qualifications or disguise, frank." The opening phrase sets the tone for the sentence, and these are the best choices based on that tone. Choice (A), "qualified," means "limited or modified." Choice (B), "eligible," means "qualified" also, but a "denial" may not be "eligible." Choice (D), "intransigent," might seem like a good choice because it means "uncompromising," but in the sense of "refusing to give in to persuasion," it doesn't fit the context. Choice (E), "intractable," also means "not giving in to persuasion," so it and "intransigent" are synonyms, but they don't fit the sense.

Question

19. The critic applauded the novel for its wit but decried the one-dimensional nature of its characters. Upon reading the review, the novelist railed against the _____ of critics who can't tell that these characters are supposed to be one-dimensional.

    (A) perfidy
    (B) obtuseness
    (C) treachery
    (D) ignorance
    (E) denseness
    (F) inexorableness

Answer Explanation

The correct answers are (B) and (E). The writer is criticizing the critic for his obtuseness and denseness. Choice (B), "obtuseness," means "lacking in perception or intelligence," and choice (E), "denseness," means "the quality or state of lacking intelligence or quickness of mind." Choice (A), "perfidy," means "treachery" and is a synonym of choice (C), "treachery." Although they are a synonym pair, there is no evidence in the passage that the critic betrayed the novelist in any way, so eliminate them. Choice (D), "ignorance," means "lacking in education," and that's unlikely for someone who is a critic by profession. Choice (F), "inexorableness," means "not able to be persuaded," and there is no evidence that the novelist has tried to persuade the critic.

QUESTION 20 IS BASED ON THE FOLLOWING PASSAGE.

Although there are many serious consequences resulting from the destruction of tropical rainforests, perhaps the most significant is that of climate change. Tropical rainforests can absorb about 20 percent of the world's carbon dioxide emissions from the atmosphere, but as rainforests are cut down, less carbon dioxide is absorbed. In addition, by slashing and
5 burning the rainforests, human activities are adding huge amounts of carbon dioxide to the atmosphere, even more than is emitted by factories, planes, and automobiles all over the world. Ultimately, as deforestation continues, the amount of carbon dioxide and other greenhouse gas levels in the atmosphere will rise. This will, in turn, lead to an increase in temperature, eventually resulting in a change in weather patterns and sea levels.

Question

20. The author suggests which of the following will happen in the future if deforestation continues?

    (A) There will be no tropical rainforests left in the world.
    (B) The Earth's temperature will rise each year.
    (C) Less carbon dioxide will be absorbed from the atmosphere.

Answer Explanation

The correct answer is (C). The relationship between carbon dioxide and rainforests is clearly spelled out in the passage, and a reader could accurately infer this idea from the passage. Choice (A) might seem correct, but the author doesn't imply that all the rainforests will be cut down. Choice (B) might also seem correct, but a conclusion this specific is neither stated nor implied.

APPENDIXES

Common Errors in Grammar and Mechanics

The rubrics for both the argument task and the issue task have expectations in regard to both grammar and mechanics. One of the ways a writer can gain a score of 6 is to "demonstrate facility with the conventions of Standard English (i.e., grammar, usage, and mechanics), but [the essay] may have minor errors." The question is: How "minor" are minor errors? The rubric goes on to indicate that errors "in grammar, usage, or mechanics . . . can interfere with meaning." That's the real problem with errors in grammar and mechanics—no matter how minor, they can hinder the reader's understanding of your ideas. Certain errors can stop a reader dead and, thus, interrupt the flow of the ideas that you want to get across. Certain "minor errors" can force the reader to reread the sentence or even a couple of sentences to try to figure out what you mean.

Common Errors in Grammar and Mechanics is neither extensive nor exhaustive, but it focuses on those common problems with sentence construction that trip up many writers, including the best ones occasionally. This information should help you avoid some of the errors that can throw your meaning into question and detract from your analysis. It also highlights some problems with pronouns that, if consistently present, may detract from your score. You won't have much time to edit your response, so concentrate on possible problems in the order that you see here:

- Sentence Faults
- Misplaced Modifiers
- Subject-Verb Agreement
- Pronoun Problems
- A Few Additional Words of Advice

SENTENCE FAULTS

The most important idea to take away from this section on sentence faults is that fixing these problems is not just a matter of cleaning up grammar; it's a matter of making decisions that will make it easier for your reader to understand your ideas. There are three sentence faults, or problems with sentence constructions, that you should be aware of as you write and proofread your responses. You won't have time to do much editing, so concentrate on finding and correcting these three problems first as you review your responses. They can seriously detract from meaning and hinder your reader's understanding of your thesis.

Comma Splice

A comma splice occurs when two or more independent clauses are joined only by a comma.

Sam decided to go back for his umbrella, Jack thought he would get his, too.

641

You can fix a comma fault by separating the two clauses completely with a period, or by separately them less completely with a semicolon. In the example sentence, the ideas are so closely related that a semicolon could be considered the better choice.

> Sam decided to go back for his umbrella; Jack thought he would get his, too.

You can also fix a comma fault by using a coordinating or a subordinating conjunction to join the two clauses.

- With a coordinating conjunction, the two clauses remain equal in importance.
- With a subordinating conjunction, one clause becomes subordinate to the other.

This decision isn't just a matter of grammar; it's a matter of meaning. It's a choice that you, as the writer, need to make. Are the ideas equally important? Or, is there one idea that you want to emphasize over the other? Perhaps you decide that the two ideas are equally important, and you choose to use a coordinating conjunction to connect the two ideas/clauses.

Coordinating Conjunctions

The coordinating conjunctions are:

and	for	so
but	nor	yet
or		

With a coordinating conjunction:

> Sam decided to go back for his umbrella, and Jack thought he would get his, too.

If you decide that one idea is more important than the other, then you need to emphasize that idea. That idea becomes the main clause of the new sentence, and the second idea becomes the dependent, or subordinate, clause. Then you need to use a subordinating conjunction to fix the comma fault.

With subordinating conjunction:

> When Sam decided to go back for his umbrella, Jack thought he would get his, too.

Subordinating Conjunctions

The following are commonly used subordinating conjunctions:

after	if	until
although	in case that	unless
as far as	no matter how	when
as soon as	now that	whenever
as if	once	where
as though	provided that	whereas
because	rather than	wherever
before	since	whether
even if	so that	while
even though	though	why
how		

Run-on Sentence

A run-on sentence has two or more independent clauses that are not connected by either punctuation or a conjunction.

> Sam took his wife's yellow umbrella he couldn't find his when he left for work.

Like comma splices, you can fix a run-on sentence by separating the two clauses with a period if the ideas are equal in importance. If the ideas are equal in importance and closely related, then use a semicolon between the two clauses.

> Sam took his wife's yellow umbrella; he couldn't find his when he left for work.

If the sentences are not equal in importance, the easiest way to correct the problem is with a subordinating conjunction.

> Sam took his wife's yellow umbrella because he couldn't find his when he left for work.

However, there are additional ways to solve the problem with a run-on sentence. You could use a conjunctive adverb or a transitional phrase. Both may require some rewriting of the original sentence.

With a conjunctive adverb:

> Sam couldn't find his umbrella when he left for work; consequently, he had his wife's yellow umbrella.

With a transitional phrase:

> Sam couldn't find his umbrella when he left for work. As a result, he had his wife's yellow umbrella.

TIP

Often in trying to get thoughts down in a timed situation like answering the Analytical Writing tasks, some writers tend to write a series of simple sentences. As you review your responses, if you have a number of simpler sentences in a row, try to combine some of them into a variety of sentences such as compound (using coordinating conjunctions), complex (using subordinating conjunctions, conjunctive adverbs, and transitional phrases), and compound-complex sentences (using both coordinating conjunctions and the other connectors listed in this section).

There are a variety of conjunctive adverbs and transitional phrases you can use to solve run-on sentence problems.

Conjunctive Adverbs

also	incidentally	now
anyhow	indeed	otherwise
anyway	likewise	similarly
besides	meanwhile	still
consequently	moreover	then
finally	nevertheless	therefore
furthermore	next	thus
however	nonetheless	

Transitional Phrases

after all	by the way	in other words
as a consequence	even so	in the first place, in the second
as a result	for example	place, etc.
at any rate	in addition	on the contrary
at the same time	in fact	on the other hand

Like fixing comma splices, fixing run-on sentences is not just a matter of cleaning up a grammar problem. It's a matter of deciding what you want to say—what's important—and choosing the best solution to make your meaning clear.

Sentence Fragment

A sentence fragment is a group of words that has a period at the end, but does not express a complete thought. It may have a verb form, that is, a verbal such as a participle, but that's not the same as a verb.

Sam *carrying* a yellow umbrella to the office.

The following are possible corrections of the problem depending on time:

Sam is carrying a yellow umbrella to the office.

Sam carries a yellow umbrella to the office.

Sam was carrying a yellow umbrella to the office.

Sam carried a yellow umbrella to the office.

There are several types of sentence fragments in addition to the example above and several ways to correct them.

A subordinate clause alone:

Because he thought it would rain. Sam was carrying his umbrella.

Rewritten as a subordinate clause:

> Because he thought it would rain, Sam was carrying his umbrella.

A phrase:

> Sam was ready for rain. *First, his umbrella and then his raincoat.*

Rewritten as a sentence:

> Sam was ready for rain. First, he took out his umbrella and then his raincoat.

A prepositional phrase:

> Sam was impatient for the bus to come. *Kept looking up the street for it.*

Combined and rewritten as a single new sentence:

> Sam, impatient for the bus to come, kept looking up the street for it.

This is an example of a writer's judgment. The writer decided that being impatient was less important to the context of what he or she wanted to say than looking up the street for the bus.

About Using Dashes

Use dashes sparingly. They often mark the work of writers who don't have a command of Standard English, don't know how to develop ideas clearly, or have little to say. Use dashes if you want to show a break in thought, or to emphasize a parenthetical idea, for example, ". . . would be a sufficient reason—unless you are a dog owner."

Misplaced Modifiers

A misplaced modifier is any word, phrase, or clause that does not refer clearly and logically to other words or phrases in the sentence. There are two problems involving misplace modifiers.

The first occurs when a word, phrase, or clause is not close to the part of the sentence that it refers to, thus confusing the reader.

> Sam *wrote* that he was taking her umbrella *in the note he left his wife.*

A clearer version is:

> Sam wrote in the note he left his wife that he was taking her umbrella.

> Sam's *wife* was annoyed because now she didn't have an umbrella *who is usually very easy-going.*

A clearer version is:

> Sam's wife who is usually very easy-going was annoyed because now she didn't have an umbrella.

> At the bus stop, Sam didn't see the *bus trying to stay dry under his umbrella.*

NOTE

It's worth repeating again that the names of the parts of speech are irrelevant. What you need to remember are the different problems you might run into in your writing and how to solve them.

The bus was trying to stay dry under the umbrella? Interesting mental picture, but try:

> At the bus stop, Sam trying to stay dry under his umbrella didn't see the bus.

The second and more major problem with misplaced modifiers occurs when a phrase introduced by a verbal (a word formed from a verb but functioning as a different part of speech) such as a participle doesn't relate clearly to another word or phrase in the sentence. The problem is often the lack of a clear relationship between the subject of the sentence and the phrase.

> *Holding the umbrella sideways, the car* splashed him anyway.

In this sentence, the true subject is missing. It seems that the car was holding the umbrella sideways when the writer meant:

> Holding the umbrella sideways, Sam was splashed by the car anyway.

> *On entering the bus, there* were no seats.

Who entered the bus?

> On entering the bus, Sam saw there were no seats

> *Hot and tired, that* was the perfect end to a perfect day thought Sam ironically.

What? Try instead:

> Hot and tired, Sam thought ironically it was the perfect end to a perfect day.

The above examples are all simple so that you can easily see the problem and the correction. But the following example shows what can happen when a writer writes quickly to get thoughts down. See if you can spot the errors in this excerpt from a response to an issue task and how you think they should be fixed.

> The arts make an important contribution to the economy of communities across the nation this is true. Even when the economy is in trouble. Governments should fund arts programs. When arts programs thrive, tax receipts flow into government coffers. It's not just the artists who make money. But people who work in allied businesses. For example, my small city has a live theater company that produces three plays a year plus has several concerts and dance programs. Having no other theater for a 75-mile radius, it brings in people from the region. These people go to dinner at local restaurants they park in a garage near the theater if they come early, they shop in local stores. All this brings in money to stores and restaurant that have to hire people to serve these theatergoers. Every sale means sales tax for the city and for the state, jobs and income taxes for the state and the federal government.

A revised version might read like this:

> The arts make an important contribution to the economy of communities. Across the nation this is true. Even when the economy is in trouble, governments should fund arts programs. When arts programs thrive, tax receipts flow into government coffers. It's not just the artists who make money, but also people who work in allied businesses. For example, my small city has a live theater company that produces three plays a year plus has several concerts and dance programs. Having no other

theater for a 75-mile radius, people come to my city from across the region. These people go to dinner at local restaurants and park in a garage near the theater. If they come early, they shop in local stores. All this brings in money to stores and restaurants that have to hire people to serve these theatergoers. Every sale means sales tax for the city and the state and jobs and income taxes for the state and the federal government.

As you can see from the examples in this section, it is often necessary to rework sentences to establish the clear relationship between the misplace word, phrase, or clause and the word it modifies. Keep this in mind as you revise your practice drafts so that on test day, you'll be able to spot problems quickly and know a range of options for correcting them.

Subject-Verb Agreement Problems

The following are probably two rules that you've heard a thousand times:

- A singular subject takes a singular verb.
- A plural subject takes a plural verb.

However, the correct subject-verb agreement can still elude a writer when several words, phrases, or even a subordinate clause comes between the subject and the verb. This is especially true when the subject is singular, but a plural noun ends a prepositional phrase just before the verb, or vice versa. Such an error usually doesn't impede understanding and one or two won't hurt your score, but try for as few of these problems as possible.

> Sam's *umbrella* along with his briefcase and gym *shoes were* under his desk.

The correct version may sound odd to your ear, but the verb should be *was*.

> Sam's umbrella along with his briefcase and gym shoes was under his desk.

Here's a plural subject-verb agreement problem:

> The *umbrellas*, which belonged to Sam and Jack and were a riot of color, *was* a welcome sight on the gray day.

In this example, the comma after "color" should clue you that "color" can't be the subject of the verb.

> The umbrellas, which belonged to Sam and Jack and were a riot of color, were a welcome sight on the gray day.

Pronoun Problems

There are a variety of pronouns and a variety of problems you can get into when using them. The most common problems involve using incorrect forms, having unclear antecedents, and confusing pronouns with other words. One or two or even three mistakes with pronouns shouldn't be reflected in your score, but consistent mistakes throughout your response could cause you to lose a point. Unclear antecedents are a meaning issue; if the reader can't tell to whom or to what you're referring, that can affect meaning.

Unclear Antecedents for Pronouns

The antecedent is the word that the pronoun refers to, or stands in for, in the sentence. When you review your essays, check for any problems with clarity so that the reader will have no difficulty in telling to whom or to what pronouns refer.

> Jack and Sam went back to their offices to get their umbrellas because it was starting to rain. They were gone for a few minutes because theirs were across the floor from the elevator.

A clearer version is:

> Jack and Sam went back to their offices to get their umbrellas because it was starting to rain. They were gone for a few minutes because their offices were across the floor from the elevator.

Incorrect Forms

Is it *I* or *me*, *she* or *her*, *he* or *him*, *we* or *them*? Most people don't have trouble figuring out which pronoun to use when the subject of a sentence or clause is singular. The trouble comes when the subject is plural.

> *Her* and I went. *Him* and I went. We and *them* went, or even, *us* and *them* went.

The sentences should read:

> She and I went. He and I went. We and they went.

Objects of verbs and prepositions (*of, for, in, on,* etc.) are another problem area for pronoun forms.

> The umbrellas belong to him and *I*, or even, to *he* and *I*.

> The umbrellas belong to her and *I*, or even, to s*he* and *I*.

> The umbrellas belong to them and *I*, or even, to *they* and *I*.

The correct sentences are:

> The umbrellas belong to him **and** me.

> The umbrellas belong to her **and** me.

> The umbrellas belong to them **and** me.

Confusing Pronoun Forms with Other Words

You've probably heard these rules in every English/language arts class you've ever taken, but they're worth repeating because many writers still make these errors.

- **it's or its**

It's is a contraction that stands for *it is*: ***It's*** raining. (*It is* raining.)

Its is an adjective that modifies a noun: The dog got ***its*** coat wet because ***it's*** raining.

An easy way to test which word you should use is to substitute *it is* in the sentence: The dog g...
is coat wet because *it is* raining. "It is coat" doesn't make sense, so it must be "*its* coat."

- **who's or whose**

This pair of often confused words is similar to the problem—and the solution—with *it's* and *its*. *Who's* is a contraction that stands for *who is*: **Who's** going to take an umbrella? (**Who is** going to take an umbrella?)

Whose is an interrogative pronoun that shows possession: **Whose** umbrella will we take?

Like testing out *it's* and *its*, substitute *who* and *whose* into the sentence: **Who is** going to take **who is** umbrella? "Who is umbrella" doesn't make sense, so it must be "*whose* umbrella."

- **they're, their, or there**

They're is a contraction that stands for *they are*: **They're** going to take umbrellas. (**They are** going to take umbrellas.)

Their is a possessive adjective that shows possession or ownership: Jack and Sam are taking **their** own umbrellas.

There is a pronoun that is used to introduce a clause or a sentence when the subject comes after the verb: **There** were no umbrellas in the closet.

Substitute *they are* in a sentence to see if the substitution makes sense: **They are** looking in **they are** desks for umbrellas. "They are desks" makes no sense, so it must be "*their* desks."

Knowing the difference between **there** and the other two forms is something you must learn; there's no easy solution, which brings up the issue of **there's** and **theirs**.

Theirs is a form of the personal pronoun that shows ownership in the third person (as opposed to the first person [*mine, ours*] or the second person [*yours*]): Those umbrellas are **theirs.** (The umbrellas belong to certain people.)

There's is a contraction that stands for *there is*: **There's** no umbrella in the closet. (**There is** no umbrella in the closet.)

Substitute *there is* in the sentence: **There is** one umbrella, but I doubt that it's either one of **there is.** "There is" at the end of the sentence doesn't make sense, so it must be **theirs,** meaning something belonging to two or more.

A Few Additional Words of Advice

Please keep these ideas in mind as you write and revise your responses:

- **Use Active Voice Whenever Possible.** Passive voice (the parts of the verb *to be*) can weaken your writing. Instead of "Ticket sales were underwritten by a grant," try "a grant underwrote ticket sales."

- **Get Rid of Redundancies.** Avoid wordiness and redundancies just to fill up space. It's the quality of your thoughts that counts toward your score, not the length. Repetition and wordiness can mask a good analysis.

- **Don't Use Jargon, Clichés, and Slang.** Jargon (a strange, outlandish, or barbarous language or dialect) doesn't fit the tone and style required to answer either an issue or an argument task. The use of clichés (trite or overused expressions or ideas) can indicate that the writer is (1) not a very original thinker or (2) trying to fill up space. Slang doesn't fit the tone or style either.

FOUR STEPS TO HELP YOU PRACTICE YOUR GRAMMAR SKILLS

1 To practice what you've learned about correcting common errors that can affect your comprehension, choose four pieces of writing that you've done recently that are about the same length as the Analytical Writing tasks on the GRE®. Review each one to see if you have any of the errors that are described in this section. Revise any errors that you find.

2 Review the two tasks on the Diagnostic Test and any of the Practice Tests (if you have already taken them). Correct any errors that you find.

3 Keep the concepts from this feature in mind as you write any of the remaining writing tasks on the Practice Tests. After you evaluate and score each one, go back and correct any errors. The fewer the errors in Standard English, the better the chance of a score of 5 or 6 on the GRE® and the better presentation you'll make in any written document in your professional life.

4 **Remember:** Errors like the ones described in these pages can make it difficult for the reader to understand your ideas, and that can affect your score.

Often Confused and Confusing Words

The confusion with these words may not come from a misunderstanding of their meaning, but rather from a problem of misspelling. As you review the word pairs in this section, pay special attention to the spelling of each word as well as its meaning.

A

accept: (verb) to receive
except: (preposition) excluding or omitting
       (conjunction) other than, but
He bought all the tulips *except* the white ones.
He would have *accepted* the award in person *except* he was in Hong Kong.

accuse: (verb) to blame
allege: (verb) to state as a fact something that has yet to be proven
He was *accused* of white collar theft and was *alleged* to have stolen $5 million.

adopt: (verb) to take as one's own
adapt: (verb) to change
adept: (adjective) very skilled
Adept at organizational design, she *adopted* the plan and then *adapted* it to her unit's needs.

advice: (noun) opinion
advise: (verb) to express an opinion
He *advised* the accused on his rights, but his *advice* was ignored.

affect: (verb) to influence; to pretend
effect: (noun) result or outcome
      (verb) to bring about (less common usage)
He was able to *affect* her decision, but the *effect* was minimal.
Her downfall was *effected* by her arrogance.

aggregate: (noun) collection of separate parts into a whole
        (verb) to combine into one
total: (noun) a whole without regard to its parts
     (verb) to add up
The *aggregate* budget deficits for the five largest cities *totaled* more than $100 billion; the *total* was staggering.

alternate: (adjective) happening in turns, first one and then the other
        (verb) to take turns
alternative: (noun) choice between two mutually exclusive options
Rather than always meeting on the third Thursday of the month, the *alternative* was to *alternate* between third Thursdays and Tuesdays.

allude: (verb) to refer indirectly to a person, object, or event
elude: (verb) to evade or slip away from
The candidate *alluded* to her opponent by mimicking his answer that "the nuances of the Iran policy *elude*" some who would serve on the foreign affairs committee.

allusion: (noun) reference or mention of something or someone
illusion: (noun) mistaken perception of reality
In an effort to create the *illusion* of erudition in his paper, the student used many *allusions* to Shakespearian characters and themes.

ambivalent: (adjective) holding conflicting wishes, unable to decide, unsure
ambiguous: (adjective) difficult to understand, having more than one interpretation
He was *ambivalent* about the promotion because the new job description was *ambiguous* about to whom he actually reported: the CFO or the COO.

anachronism: (noun) person or object placed in the wrong time
anomaly: (noun) departure from the norm; peculiar, irregular, abnormal
The play had a number of *anachronisms*, but the worst was the presence of a telephone in an 1850s parlor; then there was the greatest *anomaly:* a zombie as the house maid.

arbitrate: (verb) to settle a dispute in a legal sense
mediate: (verb) to act as a go-between, to negotiate between parties
Jack was called in to *arbitrate* between management and the union when the judge ordered an injunction against the strikers.
Will had to *mediate* a dispute between his sons over whose turn it was to have the car.

authoritarian: (adjective) having complete power, expecting complete obedience
authoritative: (adjective) official, very reliable; exercising power
The president was *authoritarian* in his manner because the military backed him up.
The president had a very *authoritative* manner in dealing with his ministers.
This edition of the play is the *authoritative* version; no scholar questions that it represents the author's complete changes.

C

condemn: (verb) to express disapproval
condone: (verb) to excuse, to overlook; to forgive
The dictator *condemned* the protesters as criminals, but he *condoned* the methods his soldiers used to suppress the protesters.

complaisant: (adjective) desirous of pleasing an other
complacent: (adjective) pleased with one's self
The members up for re-election were *complacent,* thinking their record in office was sufficient for re-election. They saw no need to be *complaisant* toward the voters and were soundly defeated as a result.

complement: (noun) completing a whole, satisfying a need
       (verb) to complete a whole, to satisfy a need
compliment: (noun) praise
       (verb) to praise
The full *complement* of engineers who worked on the project was *complimented* on their diligence. The work of the engineers *complemented* the work of the programmers—all of whom received *compliments* on their work.

contention: (noun) point made in an argument; dispute, controversy, quarrel
contentious: (adjective) quarrelsome, always ready to argue
The board meeting turned *contentious* with the *contention* by the new member that the director was out of order.

continual: (adjective) recurring regularly or frequently
continuous: (adjective) occurring without interruption
constantly: (adverb) regularly recurring
The faucet was leaking constantly, and I couldn't stand the *continual* drip-drip; it was worse than the sound of a *continuous* stream of water would have been.

credible: (adjective) believable, plausible
credulous: (adjective) too ready to believe, gullible
The plaintiff's testimony that she had bought drugs on the street thinking they were incense was *credible* only to the *credulous* member of the jury who had recently moved to the city.

D

defective: (adjective) faulty, flawed
deficient: (adjective) lacking some essential part, inadequate
The *defective* part didn't work; it was *deficient*.

deterrent: (noun) something that keeps another from doing something
detriment: (noun) something that causes harm or loss
Star Wars was supposed to be a *deterrent* to war with the Soviet Union, but it was considered by many to be a *detriment* to increased funding for the conventional army.

disinterested: (adjective) impartial
uninterested: (adjective) bored
The mediator was a *disinterested* party to the dispute between the couple, one of whom yawned constantly and seemed *uninterested* in the proceedings.

distinct: (adjective) unmistakable, clear
distinctive: (adjective) something that sets a person or thing apart from everything else, characteristic
I had the *distinct* impression that she wore a red scarf with every outfit so she would be *distinctive* in a roomful of her peers.

discrete: (adjective) separate, distinct, unconnected
discreet: (adjective) prudent, unobtrusive, diplomatic
The scientist was examining *discrete* bits of evidence and finding that they did not support his colleague's theory, but he was *discreet* about his findings until he was sure.

E

elicit: (verb) to draw out, to call forth
illicit: (adjective) unlawful
The lawyer was able to *elicit* from the witness information about the *illicit* bank transactions.

endemic: (adjective) prevalent in a particular area or among a particular group or region
epidemic: (adjective) spreading rapidly
               (noun) outbreak of a contagious disease
With the availability of air travel, an *epidemic* has the potential to spread quickly from being *endemic* to a country to being global.

energize: (verb) to give energy to, to invigorate
enervate: (verb) to weaken
I find that exercise *energizes* me rather than *enervates* me; I find that I am more alert and ready to tackle work after a good run.

expatiate: (verb) to enlarge on, to speak or write at length
expiate: (verb) to make amends for, to make up for
The professor *expatiated* on his favorite poet oblivious to the growing restlessness in his class. In an effort to *expiate* for his digression, the professor dismissed the class early.

expedient: (adjective) suitable, appropriate
           (noun) means to an end
expeditiously: (adjective) acting quickly and efficiently
The *expedient* thing to do was to process the woman's visa request as *expeditiously* as possible so she could visit her ill mother.

F

fortuitous: (adjective) occurring by chance or accident; happening by a lucky chance
fortunate: (adjective) being lucky, having good luck
Jack's winning the lottery was *fortuitous* because it means he'll be *fortunate* enough to begin his career with no debt.

H

humane: (adjective) marked by mercy, kindness, or compassion
humanitarian: (adjective) having the best interests of humankind at heart
                 (noun) philanthropist
Mother Theresa was a great *humanitarian*; she believed that everyone, even the poorest of the poor, deserved *humane* care.

hypercritical: (adjective) excessively critical, overcritical
hypocritical: (adjective) insincere, expressing feelings or virtues that one doesn't have
The review panel's analysis was *hypercritical,* finding fault even with the feeding times used. The chief reviewer expressed sympathy with the lead researcher who thought him *hypocritical* because the two often competed for the same grants.

I

imply: (verb) to suggest indirectly
infer: (verb) to draw a conclusion from
The report *implied* that the deal was fraudulent, and I *inferred* from the details that the executive was the culprit.

incipient: (adjective) beginning to appear, emergent
insipid: (adjective) lacking spirit, dull boring; lacking taste or flavor
The *incipient* revolt was quashed by the army before it could attract many followers.
Lacking in flavor, the tea was as *insipid* as the dull host's conversation was boring.

ingenious: (adjective) inventive, skillful; clever; shrewd
ingenuous: (adjective) candid, frank, straightforward
ingénue: (noun) naïve young woman or girl
Casting the college student as the *ingénue* was *ingenious*; she is perfect for the part of an *ingenuous* newcomer to Broadway.